The Ethics of
Environmental Concern

ROBIN ATTFIELD

The Ethics of Environmental Concern

Second Edition

The University of Georgia Press

Athens and London

First Edition © 1983 by Robin Attfield
Second Edition © 1991 by the University of
Georgia Press, Athens, Georgia 30602

The paper in this book meets the guidelines for
permanence and durability of the Committee on
Production Guidelines for Book Longevity of the
Council on Library Resources.

Printed in the United States of America

95 94 93 92 91   C   5 4 3 2 1
95 94   P   5 4 3 2

Library of Congress Cataloging in Publication Data
Attfield, Robin.
    The ethics of environmental concern / Robin Attfield. — 2nd ed.
        p.   cm.
    Includes bibliographical references and index.
    ISBN 0-8203-1349-1 (alk. paper). — ISBN 0-8203-1344-0 (pbk. :
alk. paper)
        1. Human ecology—Moral and ethical aspects.   I. Title.
GF80.A88   1991
    179'.1—dc20
                                              91-7954
                                                 CIP

British Library Cataloging in Publication Data available

Contents

Preface

In the period since the publication of the first edition, global problems
have made this work increasingly relevant. At the same time local
problems, such as the demise of University College Cardiff, the loss of
many of its staff, and the merger out of which University of Wales
College of Cardiff emerged in 1987–88, have involved pressing difficulties (of overwork and of insecurity) for the college's Philosophy
Section. Resolving to strengthen its work, especially in the areas of
history of philosophy and of applied ethics, the section transformed
adversity into opportunity, expanding its work at all levels (not least in
research), initiating new M.A. degrees in both these areas, receiving
recognition from the Universities Funding Council by way of funding
earmarked for a permanent social ethics post, and setting up the Cardiff Centre for Applied Ethics, of whose work this second edition is
just one of the fruits. Special thanks are in place to the first cohort of
two dozen students of the M.A. in social ethics course, whose interest
in the first edition persuaded me of the need of a second for their successors' sake; to Geoff Boden, a graduate of the section, for unstinted
assistance to the feckless operator of a disobliging word processor; and
more particularly to my full-time philosophy colleagues, Andrew
Belsey, Ruth Chadwick, Michael Durrant and Barry Wilkins, without
whose collaborative initiatives, self-denying perseverance and re-
sourceful teamwork the buoyant and thriving Cardiff philosophy activity would not exist, let alone this second edition.

Acknowledgments

My thanks go to Peter Singer for discussion of a paper related to this book, to Robert Young and Nigel Dower for bibliographical assistance, to Derek Parfit for encouragement, to Tom Regan and Mary Midgley for their comments on chapter 8, and to the Cardiff Philosophical Society, and particularly its student members, for comments on chapter 6. An enormous debt of gratitude is also due to Thomas McPherson for commenting on the first draft of the entire book, to Andrew Belsey for comments on some chapters of that draft and on the entire second draft, and also to the publishers' reader. Their advice and criticisms have proved invaluable; but, like the others here mentioned, they cannot be held responsible for the final text, and would each profoundly disagree with at least some of it.

I am also grateful to the staff of the Library of University College, Cardiff for their tireless help in locating much of the material referred to, to Jean Barber for typing the second draft of chapter 6, and particularly to my wife, Leela Dutt, for encouragement and for reading the entire first draft, as well as enduring the composition of the book at the same time as composing a novel herself.

Introduction

The Ethics of Environmental Concern, though published in 1983, was mostly composed two years earlier, final touches being added in 1982. Since then, public awareness has increasingly been focused on growing problems such as the greenhouse effect, acid rain, holes in the ozone layer and the destruction of rainforests. Awareness has also increased of the impact on the Third World, as well as on nonhuman species, of pollution, deforestation, overfishing and the growth of deserts. Recently there has been a sudden realization of the way that Eastern Europe too is afflicted with 'ecological disaster areas'.[1]

Since those years, there has also been published a considerable number of philosophical essays, collections and monographs in environmental philosophy and ethics, and in cognate subjects such as the philosophy of animal welfare, the environmental bearing of theology and the history of environmental ideas, not to mention countless works on scientific ecology, greener processes of production and consumption, environmental planning and green politics. While it is impossible to take account here of these further fields, mention can be made of leading philosophical monographs and of a more recent work of mine in the area of ethical theory. A chapter has also been added in this edition which reviews some of the more recent work in environmental philosophy and the cognate subjects just mentioned, including some of the reviews of the first edition. It also depicts important recent work on environmental decision making, which some readers may find at least as important as the issues of high theory now to be discussed.[2]

It is sometimes asked what are the credentials and the status of remarks and claims about, for example, the intrinsic value of an animal's flourishing or about our responsibility not to subvert the life-support systems of future generations. While I made no secret in the first edition of my presuppositions about all this, one foreseeable complaint was that (for the most part) I did not argue for them there.[3]

Despite my own cognitivist and naturalist views, acknowledged at page 89 below, I also expressed a willingness there to seek the agreement, in matters of normative ethics and its applications,[8] of people with quite different meta-ethical positions, except where they undermine normative claims in general (as would, for example, instrumentalist accounts of value-language: see page 160). It is another aim of this Introduction to survey some of the meta-ethical positions put forward in recent works of environmental philosophy, though I shall not (for reasons to be explained) be presenting a full-dress defence of my own views here.

The view that no single normative theory is adequate to environmental issues has been put forward by Christopher Stone in *Earth and Other Ethics*,[4] subtitled 'The Case for Moral Pluralism'. Stone favours the application of diverse and unrelated principles to different areas of life and of decision making, for example, environmental issues, family issues and issues of social relations. His version of pluralism is thus quite distinct from the pluralistic respect and toleration appropriate to a multicultural society; each agent is encouraged to harbour a plurality of principles within her own head, and to cope with conflicts between them as best she may. A matching meta-ethic has been propounded by Andrew Brennan in *Thinking About Nature: An Investigation of Nature, Value and Ecology;*[5] Brennan calls his position 'polymorphism' and advocates acceptance of a plurality of conflicting metaphysical and valuational frameworks, and the relativity of value-claims to one or more such frameworks. As Gary Varner has recognised, positions such as Stone's represent a 'fundamental ethical challenge' to environmental ethics,[6] and one with which Varner seems to sympathise; for most work in the field assumes (monistically) that principles and judgements may be found which are (in a nonrelativistic sense) rationally preferable to others, and this the pluralists now dispute. A fourth defence of such pluralism seems to be present in Peter Wenz's *Environmental Justice*. Wenz defines the pluralist position he favours as follows: 'A theory is pluralistic when it contains a variety of principles that cannot be reduced to or derived from a single master-principle'.[7] Wenz, however, urges the modifying and blending of a variety of conflicting principles of justice, and may thus be in favour of reconciling and prioritising principles in such a way as tacitly to endorse after all what he appears to oppose, a monistic normative system.

J. Baird Callicott has well criticised such pluralism,[8] although he may sometimes detect it where it is not to be found.[9] Thus he points out that all such views are liable to generate hopelessly contradictory decisions. They also undermine any serious possibility of consistency on the part of agents who adhere to such a position. It might be added that (at least in the form which accepts the equal validity of diverse perspectives) they are all self-undermining; everyone who accepts such pluralism would have to grant that there could be an equally valid perspective which requires rejecting it. This does not, of course, establish the correctness of monism, let alone of any particular monistic ethic; but it does suggest that anyone who takes any principle seriously is committed thereby to monism and to there being an ethic suited to monistic claims. Further, as Callicott goes on to point out, since pluralism offers no rational basis for resolving ethical conflicts, its adherents are likely, when pressed, to resort to the principle most in line with self-interest.[10]

It becomes all the more important to discover whether any one meta-ethical position is rationally superior to the other candidates (the issue to be considered next); and the same applies to positions in normative ethics (an issue to be addressed thereafter). Now Callicott's own view, what he calls 'the Hume-Darwin-Leopold line of social, humane and environmental ethics', understands our moral sentiments as the products of evolution.[11] Granted that human beings have evolved, this much is hardly controversial. Although it may not settle the content of ethics to the extent that Callicott may suppose (when he selects the views of Hume, Adam Smith, Darwin and Leopold, and prefers them to those of Kant, Bentham, Mill and Regan),[12] it certainly shows that there are limits to the range to viable ethical systems. Callicott seems to have abandoned the emotivism with which he once toyed[13] but does seem to maintain that intrinsic value is projected by human subjects onto objects by which they are suitably excited or otherwise affected.[14] Callicott's meta-ethical views, however, have themselves incurred criticism, not least from the leading environmental ethicist, Holmes Rolston,[15] and also from the nondualist philosopher Michael Zimmerman.[16]

Rolston calls this position 'the theory of anthropogenic intrinsic value'. While he accepts that this theory is not egoistic or anthropocentric, he defends the contrasting view that natural objects (or some of them) are of value in themselves whether or not any human subject ever values them, will value them or even would value them. Only such a theory, he holds, is authentically a theory of *intrinsic* value, as opposed to theories such as Callicott's, in which the value does not exist unless a human being will or would confer it. While Rolston's sense of 'having value' is not entirely clear, what he may well mean is 'supplying interpersonal reasons (whether instrumental or intrinsic) for being fostered, promoted or preserved';[17] if so, his claim that intrinsic value does not wait upon human conferment is surely a cogent one. Rolston goes on to claim that the anthropogenic account of intrinsic value 'is a strained saving of what is really an inadequate paradigm, that of the subjectivity of value conferral'. It is simpler to hold that 'some values are objectively there – discovered, not generated', and that a theory such as his own, of autonomous intrinsic value, can itself value the human appreciation of such independent value, without committing 'a fallacy of the misplaced location of values'.[18] Similar comments, I suggest, are in place about Robert Elliot's theory of value, which makes value relative to one or other human valuational framework.[19]

Zimmerman's criticism of Callicott is also important. For, while the above critique of subjectivist theories of value should stand, Callicott at one stage appeared to move beyond them, claiming that quantum physics requires the distinction between subjects and objects to be discarded, and that a relational account of value, involving reference both to persons and to valued objects, should replace subjectivist theories. To this Zimmerman replies that many interpretations of quantum physics do not require the distinction between subjects and objects to be discarded at all, and that in any case quantum physics alone proves insufficient to commit its practitioners to a rejection of philosophical dualism.[20] Despite Zimmerman's own advocacy of nondualism and his related sympathy for the aims of Callicott's revised account of value, his criticisms suffice to show that talk of subjects and objects remains coherent, quantum physics notwithstanding, and that the above debate about subjectivist and objectivist accounts of value retains its point and its significance accordingly. Nor, I should add, can it be sidestepped by advocacy of an enlarged concept of the self, expanded to include nature in its entirety. Even if this enlarged concept were coherent (but what sense can be made of 'I' where nothing could count as 'you', 'she' or 'he'?), a coherent account would still be needed of the nature of good reasons for action on the part of (old-style) agents or selves.

A number of questions remain unanswered about meta-ethical objectivism (the kind of position upheld by Rolston and, rather differently, by myself). How may the making of truth claims in matters of values be vindicated? How can any such claims amount to knowledge? Do such claims fall foul of the 'naturalistic fallacy', and how, in any case, is it possible to move from facts to values? These are highly important questions, which deserve a much fuller discussion than is appropriate to an introduction. They are also issues which I have tackled, directly or indirectly, in the final three chapters of *A Theory of Value and Obligation,*[21] and my responses to these questions (and to others) are there to be found; objectivity and ethical knowledge are discussed in chapter 10, relativism in chapter 11, and 'the naturalistic fallacy' and naturalism in chapter 12 (by a route rather different from that of Rolston's essays in *Philosophy Gone Wild*[22] and of his discussion of this 'fallacy' in chapter 6 of *Environmental Ethics*). Similarly, chapter 1 there discusses the scope of moral standing (and thus my views about the bearing of meta-ethics on the limits of such standing, asked about by Elliot;[23] also the concept of intrinsic value is defended in chapter 2, and a theory of its application is elaborated in chapters 3–5. My own position is (to put matters technically) cognitivist and naturalist; certain values are necessarily related to certain kinds of fact and can thus be known, while there is also a necessary connection between value and obligations, of which knowledge is also sometimes possible. Intrinsic value (in the sense supplied above) turns out to be the pivotal concept; if nothing has such value, then there are no reasons for action at all, and no obligations either. Knowledge of intrinsic value is what makes it possible to discover which courses of action are desirable and which are obligatory.

Some questions about normative ethics also arise. Here Callicott's most recent work attempts to bring together again animal welfare ethics and the kind of holistic environmental ethics whose warfare he depicted in 'Animal Liberation: A Triangular Affair'.[24] Having been persuaded by Mary Midgley's excellent book *Animals and Why They Matter*[25] that domestic animals have always formed part of (otherwise) human communities, Callicott attempts to reconcile obligations in their regard with obligations to human groups (such as one's family) and with environmental obligations, on the basis of the Leopoldian position that obligations arise within communities, and that communities can now be understood as including the biotic community. Callicott suggests that Leopoldians need not hold that environmental obligations override social obligations arising from communities in the more traditional sense. Indeed, obligations to family (Callicott holds) 'come before obligations to more remotely related human beings'. Peter Singer's view that it might be obligatory to impoverish one's children to prevent starvation in another continent is flatly denied. But preventing human starvation takes precedence over environmental obligations, as also does protecting domestic animals from wild ones.[26]

Compared with Callicott's earlier views, the social ethic here is a strikingly conventional one. But it suffers from failure to explain why conventional beliefs about obligation should be accepted as definitive. (What is so morally special about family ties as to justify letting strangers starve?) In this connection Peter Singer, who has argued cogently for a much more open and egalitarian ethic, is berated for advocating nothing but an egoism amended by abstract principle, and for ignoring sympathy as a fundamental motivation,[27] as if he had never written *The Expanding Circle*.[28] Further problems for such a social ethic are mentioned below at pages 93f and 97, while at pages 157f the limitations of regarding the biosphere as a community are remarked, and in chapter 9 Singer's equal interests principle is interpreted and defended. What is commendable in Callicott's new approach is the attempt to reach a unified theory of obligations relating to humanity, nonhuman animals and the environment. Unfortunately he supplies no rational basis either for identifying the nature and limits of our various obligations or for determining priorities among them.

Some of the alternative proposals for a satisfactory normative ethic are discussed below, not least in the Review of Recent Literature. Unlike Callicott, some of those who advocate an enlarged concept of the self believe that its application will replace the need for an ethic altogether; my grounds for rejecting this position, given above, are supplemented there. So too are the difficulties for the biospherical egalitarianism which used to be favoured by Deep Ecologists (also discussed in chapters 9 and 10 below),[29] and also for the (rather different) biocentric egalitarianism of Paul Taylor.[30]

Others make sturdier attempts at integrating the obligations just mentioned. Some (such as Tom Regan in *The Case for Animal Rights*)[31] rely for the basis of their ethic on rights, a concept argued below not to be capable of settling priorities between rights (167f), and plausibly incapable of coping with obligations with regard either to future generations or to nonhuman species. By locating value and rights in "subjects-of-a-life" only, Regan seems now to have rejected the moral standing of nonconscious living creatures, argued for in chapter 8 below, and in the first chapter of *A Theory of Value and Obligation*. For the reasons given there, I continue to hold that a wider account of the scope of moral standing should be accepted. And parallel remarks are in place, despite the much greater rational resources of Peter Singer's consequentialism, about his restriction of moral standing to sentient creatures.[32] (Such sentientism is further discussed in the Review of Recent Literature.)

By contrast Rolston (in his book *Environmental Ethics*) appeals to a much wider range of values – too wide, perhaps, granted his purported discovery of 'systemic value' as a third kind alongside value of the intrinsic and instrumental sorts.[33] But Rolston appears to adopt more than one overall position. At one stage (chapter 2) he seems to adopt one ethic for social dealings and another for dealings with wild nature; yet the culture/nature distinction cannot be assumed always to warrant differential treatment of otherwise similar creatures. Later in chapter 7 a more integrated axiological model (and a related decision procedure) are presented. The derivative principles elaborated here are mostly admirable, as is the incorporation within the axiological model of the importance of values which cannot be quantified as well as of values which can. The problem, however, lies in the effective absence of justifications for the priorities between the values adopted in the model, for the inclusion of some of these values in the first place, and for deriving these principles from these values. (These matters are further discussed in two hitherto unpublished papers of mine.[34])

More recently, Eugene C. Hargrove's *Foundations of Environmental Ethics* presents an anthropocentric case for the preservation of nature on aesthetic grounds. This work is full of fascinating (if occasionally erratic) insights, about, for example, the impact of the history of philosophy on preservationist attitudes. While I do not accept the intrinsic value of beauty or, again, the beauty of everything natural, I find much of value in Hargrove's aesthetic case (a case which has till now received insufficient attention).[35] Yet the value-theory is too narrow, and insufficiently integrated with any defensible social ethic at that, to meet the requirements of normative ethics. (Hargrove's historical overviews and their current bearing are appraised in two forthcoming essays.[36])

What is needed is a theory which defensibly locates intrinsic value (including relative intrinsic value), and is thus able to underpin the prioritising of principles. This is what is attempted in chapters 3 to 5 of *A Theory of Value and Obligation*. On such a basis, principles of rightness and of obligation then need to be elaborated and defended (something I attempt there in chapters 6 and 7), and to be tested in the areas which traditionally pose the greatest problems for theories of the kind adopted (the consequentialist kind: this I have attempted in chapter 8, which concerns justice, and chapter 9, which concerns population ethics). Intrinsic value is located in the development (up to the level of the ability to exercise them) of the essential capacities (as there defined) of the affected creatures, while relative intrinsic value is expounded in terms of the role of different states, actions and experiences in the life of affected creatures, and of the complexity of the capacities which may be at stake. It is further argued that actions are right which maximise intrinsic value, or which comply with a rule or practice which does this (or would do this); and that such actions are obligatory where a serious difference stands to be made to the value of outcomes. This, however, is as much a caricature as a summary of the case presented; it is included here to show how (and where) the positions of chapters 6 to 9 below have been developed. Beyond this, the interested reader should be referred to that work, not as the definitive solution of all the problems, but as the best attempted solution, as far as its author is able to judge.

Important as ethical theory is, contemporary problems call for more than theory if they are to be solved, and for more than personal reorientation or commitment too. Solutions will need to be coordinated solutions; and thus political and often international action and policies are involved. A little is said about this in the Review of Recent Literature, supplementing what had already been said in chapter 10. Lest, however, anyone should needlessly overlook it, the very great wisdom and positive practicality of *Our Common Future* (the 'Brundtland Report') should at once be drawn to attention.[37] Despite the views of its critics,[38] the recommendations of this report should be commended to all governments and bodies wielding international power with a view to early implementation, as being, in practice, the best hope for a just and sustainable global society. The fact that these proposals are also more or less in harmony with the axiological and ethical theories of this book is, by comparison, but a minor commendation.

NOTES

1   Walter Schwartz, 'Black Death from the East', *Weekend Guardian*, June 16–17, 1990, pp. 4–6.
2   See Robin Attfield and Katharine Dell (eds), *Values, Conflict and the Environment*, Oxford: Ian Ramsey Centre, Oxford and Centre for Applied Ethics, Cardiff, 1989. (Copies of this report of the environmental ethics working party of the Ian Ramsey Centre are available from the Principal's Secretary, Westminster College, North Hinksey, Oxford, OX2 9AT.)
3   Thus Robert Elliot, Critical notice of *The Ethics of Environmental Concern*, *Australasian Journal of Philosophy*, 63, 1985, 499–509, p. 507.
4   Christopher D. Stone, *Earth and Other Ethics: The Case for Moral Pluralism*, New York: Harper & Row, 1988.
5   Andrew Brennan, *Thinking About Nature: An Investigation of Nature, Value and Ecology*, Athens: University of Georgia Press, 1988. My review appears in *Journal of Applied Philosophy*, 6.2, 1989, 237–8.
6   Gary E. Varner, Review of Christopher D. Stone, *Earth and Other Ethics*, in *Environmental Ethics*, 10, 1988, 259–65, p. 264.
7   Peter Wenz, *Environmental Justice*, Albany: State University of New York Press, 1988.

8   J. Baird Callicott, 'The Case Against Moral Pluralism', *Environmental Ethics*, 12.2, 1990, 99–124.

9   For example, in Mary Anne Warren, 'The Rights of the Non-human World', in Robert Elliot and Arran Gare (eds), *Environmental Philosophy: A Collection of Readings*, St. Lucia: University of Queensland Press; Milton Keynes: Open University Press; University Park: Pennsylvania State University Press, 1983, 109–134; and perhaps in Eugene C. Hargrove, 'The Role of Rules in Ethical Decision Making', *Inquiry*, 28, 1985, 3–42. (Hargrove's position there is open to more than one interpretation, like that of Wenz.)

10 Callicott, 'The Case Against Moral Pluralism', pp. 110–12.

11 Ibid., pp. 120–24.

12 Ibid., p. 124.

13 J. Baird Callicott, 'Intrinsic Value, Quantum Theory and Environmental Ethics', *Environmental Ethics*, 7, 1985, 257–75, section I.

14 Holmes Rolston III, at p. 113 of *Environmental Ethics: Duties to and Values in the Natural World*, Philadelphia: Temple University Press, 1988, cites two relevant passages from Callicott: 'Non-Anthropocentric Value Theory and Environmental Ethics', *American Philosophical Quarterly*, 21, 1984, 299–309, p. 305, and 'On the Intrinsic Value of Nonhuman Species', in Bryan Norton (ed.), *The Preservation of Species*, Princeton: Princeton University Press, 1986, 138–72, pp. 142–3 and 156.

15 Rolston, *Environmental Ethics*, pp. 112–17.

16 Michael E. Zimmerman, 'Quantum Theory, Intrinsic Value and Panentheism', *Environmental Ethics*, 10.1, 1988, 3–30.

17 This is the sense of 'intrinsic value' defended in the second chapter of Robin Attfield, *A Theory of Value and Obligation*, London, New York and Sydney: Croom Helm, 1987.

18 Rolston, *Environmental Ethics*, p. 116.

19 Elliot's theory emerges at pp. 502 f of his Critical notice (see note 3 above), and also in 'Meta-Ethics and Environmental Ethics', *Metaphilosophy*, 16, 1985, 103–17. For a further discussion of subjectivism and relativism, see *A Theory of Value and Obligation*, chapter 11.

20 Zimmerman, 'Quantum Theory, Intrinsic Value and Pantheism', pp. 10–15.

21 For details of this book, see note 17 above.

22 Holmes Rolston III, 'Is There an Ecological Ethic?' and 'Are Values in Nature Subjective or Objective', in Holmes Rolston III, *Philosophy Gone Wild: Essays in Environmental Ethics*, Buffalo: Prometheus Books, 1986, pp. 11–29 and 91–117 respectively.

23 Elliot, Critical notice of *The Ethics of Environmental Concern*, p. 507.

24 J. Baird Callicott, 'Animal Liberation: A Triangular Affair', *Environmental Ethics*, 2.1, 1980, 311–38; reprinted in J. Baird Callicott, *In Defense of the Land Ethic: Essays in Environmental Philosophy*, Albany: State University of New York Press, 1989, 15–38.

25 Mary Midgley, *Animals and Why They Matter*, Harmondsworth: Penguin, and Athens: University of Georgia Press, 1983.

26 Callicott, *In Defense of the Land Ethic*, p. 58. Further details of Callicott's position emerge in his essay 'The Conceptual Foundations of the Land Ethic', in that same collection at pp. 101–14, which may also be found in J. Baird Callicott (ed.), *Companion to A Sand County Almanac: Interpretive and Critical Essays*, Madison: University of Wisconsin Press, 1987, at pp. 186–217.

27 Callicott, *In Defense of the Land Ethic*, p. 53.

28 Peter Singer, *The Expanding Circle: Ethics and Sociobiology*, Oxford: Clarendon Press, 1981.

29 The classical expression of this position is to be found in Arne Naess, 'The Shallow and the Deep, Long-range Ecology Movement: A Summary', *Inquiry*, 16, 1973, 95–100; it is further developed in Bill Devall and George Sessions, *Deep Ecology: Living As If Nature Mattered*, Salt Lake City: Gibbs M. Smith, 1985. An appraisal of the different stances of Deep Ecology supporters is presented in my hitherto unpublished paper 'Sylvan, Fox and Deep Ecology: A View from the Continental Shelf'.

30 Paul Taylor, *Respect for Nature: A Theory of Environmental Ethics*, Princeton: Princeton University Press, 1986.

31 Tom Regan, *The Case for Animal Rights*, London: Routledge, 1983.

32 See Peter Singer, *Practical Ethics*, Cambridge: Cambridge University Press, 1979.

33 See my review in *Environmental Ethics*, 11.4, 1989, 363–8.

34 'Reasoning About the Environment'; and 'The Comprehensive Ecology Movement', forthcoming in Edgar Morscher, Otto Neumaier and Peter Simons (eds), *Applied Ethics and Its Foundations*, 1992.

35 See Eugene C. Hargrove, *Foundations of Environmental Ethics*, Englewood Cliffs: Prentice-Hall, 1989; also my unpublished paper 'Preservation, Art and Natural Beauty'.

36 'Has the History of Philosophy Ruined the Environment?', forthcoming in *Environmental Ethics*, 1991, and 'Attitudes to Wildlife in the History of Ideas', forthcoming in *Environmental History Review*, 1991.

37 World Commission on Environment and Development, *Our Common Future*, Oxford, New York: Oxford University Press, 1987.

38 Thus Arne Naess, 'Sustainable Development and the Deep Long-Range Ecology Movement', *The Trumpeter*, 5.4, 1988, 138–42, p. 140, column b.

Introduction to the First Edition

This is an unusual book. It is an exercise neither solely in philosophy nor solely in history, nor certainly in any other single discipline. Part One is predominantly but not exclusively a study in the history of ideas, while Part Two is a philosophical investigation into normative ethics and some of its applications. This sort of structure is dictated by the subject of environmental ethics; indeed a similar structure was employed by John Passmore in his book *Man's Responsibility for Nature*, the one authoritative treatment of environmental ethics so far produced.

In Part One moral traditions are explored, for no satisfactory ethic can be put forward which disregards them. In environmental ethics our moral traditions are often held to be so deficient as to need to be superseded: such views are held, I believe, because our traditions have just as often been misrepresented, and embody ampler resources than they are credited with by Passmore and others.

Attitudes and ideas alone cannot explain or resolve our problems, however. In chapter 1 I review some much more material explanations of our ecological problems (an interdisciplinary undertaking if ever there was one), but conclude that such explanations, though important, are incomplete unless people's underlying beliefs are also studied.

In subsequent chapters attention is focused on traditions of belief common to the areas of the world where ecological problems are most intense, and in particular on Judaeo-Christian beliefs and on the ideas of the Enlightenment. In the ancient and continuous Jewish and Christian tradition of Stewardship I find the makings of an ethic suited to our problems, even though belief in man's dominion has often been misinterpreted to suggest that people may treat nature as they please. But at least as important a source of

current problems as this convenient travesty of our religious tradition
has been the secular belief in perpetual progress of the last two
hundred years. Even so, aspects of this very belief can also contribute
to an environmental ethic, including the heightened awareness of
obligations to posterity and the realization that society can change
its course.

In Part Two moral principles are re-examined. Scientific discoveries have opened up new opportunities and new perils, and
have also disclosed many of the side-effects of our actions on the
complex systems of nature; and our moral horizons have to be
broadened to take this into account. Thus the effects of our deeds
on other species and on future people require us to be more explicit
about our responsibilities in their regard, and to take them more
seriously. If, as I maintain, all worthwhile life is of intrinsic value,
our obligations must be reassessed. No longer can we discount
future people's interests or disregard the interests of fellow-creatures.
It also turns out that some of the central traditions of our culture
have not disregarded them either; and this gives hope that the
principles of a satisfactory environmental ethic can secure acceptance, where proposals for a totally new ethic have no such prospect.

Legitimate ecological concern thus exceeds the limited preoccupation of what has been called 'the shallow ecology movement'
with the problems of pollution and resource-depletion as they affect
the developed world for the next fifty years. It extends to the life-
support systems of the Third World, of the further future, and of
nonhuman species. Yet I do not accept, with the so-called 'deep,
long-range ecology movement', the view that our principal loyalty
should be focused not on fellow-humans or fellow-creatures but on
the biosphere as an organic whole, the constituents of which are
only, supposedly, of value insofar as they contribute to its stability.
Environmental ethics can only proceed by reasoning outwards from
received moral judgements about familiar cases to their implications
and to analogous cases in the future or in the nonhuman realm; it
cannot discard the traditional concern for individuals in favour of
an irreducible concern for biotic systems and expect a hearing.

This is not, of course, to suggest that individual agents should be
free to treat the natural world as they please; nor is it to suggest that
we cannot take into account the countless future people of whose
individual identity we can have no knowledge. Indeed the principles
for which I shall be arguing embody considerable constraints in the
interests of contemporary and future people, as well as of nonhuman
creatures. Nor am I suggesting that ecosystems do not matter: they

are morally as significant as the individual creatures which depend on them.

Many articles and collections of papers have been published on topics in environmental ethics and its historical background. Though it has not been possible to consider all of these, and no claim can be made to any kind of comprehensiveness, I have attempted to present a consistent critique of a good number of the more significant ones, and thereby to introduce their merits as well as their demerits to the reader, in the hope that he or she can take up the subject from there. In doing so I have tried to bear in mind the interests both of philosophers and non-philosophers, but in case some readers find difficulty with some passages in the later chapters I have also attempted to include enough signposts in the text to enable them to follow the main direction of the argument. This said, the argument must in the end, as Passmore remarks at a similar point, speak for itself or not at all.

The Ethics of
Environmental Concern

1

Ecological Problems

Ecological problems have been defined as problems arising 'as a practical consequence of man's dealings with nature',[1] where 'nature' is used of the nonhuman environment of man. Ecology is the science of the complex interplay of natural organisms and natural systems, and brings to light, among other things, the long-term, distant and unexpected consequences of these dealings. Transactions with nature usually have multiple side-effects, and it is wise when considering how to cope with them to keep this fact to the fore: designating the problems as 'ecological' is one way of giving it due recognition. The choice of phrase also reminds us that the problems may be more far-reaching than the frustrated aspirations of one generation of humans to be encompassed by a pleasant environment, important as this can be.

Perceptions of problems

Agreement is less than universal about the identification of ecological problems, but the following would be widely agreed to be examples: pollution; diminishing natural resources; the increasing size of the human population; the destruction of wildlife and wilderness; losses of cultivable land through erosion and the growth of deserts; and the endangering of the life-support systems of the planet. It is not universally realized how human activity causes deserts to spread or life-support systems to be subverted: but such inadvertence would be an unimportant source of disagreement about the problems, were it not an ingredient of the problems itself.

The significant disagreement concerns how to solve the problems, and also, more basically, what makes them problems. Problems are sometimes understood, as by John Passmore,[2] as intolerable costs to humans which human action can eliminate or, at any rate, alleviate.

1

Among those who understand problems in this way, some are concerned principally with costs to humans already alive, while others are prepared to take into account the next fifty or a hundred years, and yet others the distant future. Those who understand problems like this are likely to be satisfied with solutions which effectively safeguard the interests of those humans on whom they focus their attention.

But problems may also be seen where there is actual or possible harm to living organisms in general. Here some extend their purview to the welfare of sentient animals, others to the interests of all living organisms, while yet others concentrate on species, ecosystems or the biosphere as a whole. Occasionally, nonhuman interests are given precedence over human interests in general: the extreme position is that which goes further still and presents humanity as a cancerous growth upon nature, and the human species as constituting the problem itself. Holders of any of these alternative conceptions of the nature of problems will naturally be less satisfied with man-centred solutions, and particularly ones confined to the short-term future. Thus, different views of what makes a problem reflect not only different estimates of possibilities, likelihoods and the limits of tolerance, but also disagreements about moral principles and about what is of value in itself.

Here it is useful to distinguish, with Arne Naess,[3] the shallow ecology movement and its deep, long-range counterpart (though it should be realized that there are many positions between the two). Naess characterizes the shallow ecology movement as being concerned with medium-term human interests, interests for all that often disregarded in traditional economics, and in particular with the interests of people in developed countries.

By contrast the deep movement takes into account distant future generations, the Third World, nonhuman species and, at times, the biosphere as a whole, sometimes regarding them all as having independent moral standing. For example, the term 'conservation' is applied to the concerns and activities of both movements: but, while the shallow movement seeks in the main to conserve mineral and energy resources, and extends the notion of resources to quarriable mountains and cultivable forests, the deep movement is less than happy to regard nonhuman species and their wild habitats as nothing but resources, and is at least equally concerned to preserve wilderness and the fragile equilibrium of natural ecosystems.

Both kinds of conservationist are in conflict with adherents of unstinted growth and of the 'technological fix', people who believe that whatever natural resources are expended can without too much difficulty be replaced through human ingenuity and substitution technology: but even those who allow there to be a problem of conservation clearly differ as to what precisely is bad about the disruptive effects of human action upon the environment, and also therefore as to what attitudes cause the problems and how to solve them.

The deep ecology movement, however, itself incorporates a variety of disparate emphases. Thus those opposed to the use of nuclear energy often argue from the effects of its use on the long-term future, but are sometimes less concerned with the preservation of wildlife, especially when they advocate estuarial barrages as an alternative energy source. Similarly, preservationists concerned for the survival of rare species and for ecological balance are sometimes prepared to countenance culling the members of plentiful species by means such as seal-hunts which inflict a great deal of suffering upon individual animals, while animal welfare and animal rights campaigners can be indifferent to the elimination of plant species except where animals' habitats are destroyed thereby.

There again, the deep movement might be thought to have affinities with those who preach catastrophe resulting from 'over-population'. Themes common to these people and to deep ecologists include the need to safeguard human life in a hundred years' time, and the damaging effects upon nonhuman nature of swelling human numbers. Yet those who favour a reduction in the size of the human population often do so partly from a fear that people in the West will be swamped by multitudes from elsewhere; and to this extent they are scarcely the natural allies of believers in the value of each worthwhile life, whether human or nonhuman, let alone of those who believe in the equality of animals with like capacities whatever their species. Indeed Naess himself makes no mention of concern for the restriction or reduction of population in his depiction of the deep, long-range ecology movement, perhaps regarding such a concern as elitist rather than egalitarian (though he is concerned about levels of crowding among mammals in general). Nevertheless those who are concerned about 'overpopulation' would doubtless lay claim to ecological depth.

Many of the tendencies within the deep ecology movement have been influenced both at the levels of theory and of inspiration by Aldo Leopold's *A Sand County Almanac*, and in particular by his call for a new, environmental ethic. Leopold calls for a recognition of the obligations which are owed to all members of the biotic community (what he calls 'the land'),[4] and to the biosphere as an organic whole: thus he holds that 'a thing is right when it tends to promote the integrity, stability and beauty of the biotic community. It is wrong when it tends otherwise.'[5] The suggestion here is that our traditional ethic lacks resources equal to our problems, and needs a drastic revaluation. This suggestion will be considered through a study of traditional attitudes (in Part One) and by a consideration of principles of obligation and value (in Part Two).

Believing, as I do, that matters of morality admit of truth, I am reluctant to conclude that we can devise or invent a new ethic; and, even if we could invent one, I do not see how it could establish its credibility unless it were not a new departure but an extension, analogical or otherwise, of existing patterns of moral thought. The case for a new ethic should rather consist in exhibiting principles which have not always been recognized but which are nevertheless implicit in our moral traditions, or, perhaps, in morality itself, and which it is important now to acknowledge. If the necessary principles are found to hold a place within our traditions already, then what is required is not so much a replacement of moral traditions (if that were possible), or even their supplementation with new principles, as the more promising endeavour of developing in a more consistent manner themes to which at least lip-service has long been paid.

Despotism, Stewardship and ethical innovation

In the only extended philosophical treatment of ecological problems yet to appear, *Man's Responsibility for Nature*,[6] John Passmore examines Western moral traditions and historical attitudes to nature, and in the course of his subsequent survey of the problems of pollution, resources, population growth and preservation defends the view that no new ethic is needed to cope with the problems, so long as the traditional belief that man has dominion over nature and that people may manipulate their natural environment in their own interests is interpreted in a suitably humble way. What needs to be rejected is the attitude and tradition of Despotism, an interpretation of the Biblical belief in man's dominion according to which everything is made for man, nothing else is of any intrinsic value or moral importance, and people may treat nature in any way that they like without inhibition. Instead we should accept that natural processes are not devised or guaranteed to serve humanity, and that manipulating them requires skill and care. Science, technology and cost/benefit analysis should not be abandoned, but we should not be indifferent to animal suffering, and should bear in mind the consequences of our actions upon our immediate descendants to the limited extent to which Passmore believes they can be foreseen. In the Western tradition of Stewardship Passmore finds a belated interpretation of belief in man's dominion which supplies the seeds of such a chastened position: and because there are such 'seeds' within traditional morality, there is no need to turn to mystical or irrationalist metaphysics or ethics to solve ecological problems.

Passmore's position has been shrewdly criticized by Val Routley,[7] who holds that his triumph over any form of new ethic is too easily won. In part this is because the only alternative ethical positions which he entertains either treat nature as sacred or at least recognize rights throughout the animal and vegetable kingdoms; he neglects to consider the view that there are obligations or responsibilities *concerning* natural objects or people in the distant future, which would not always be obligations owed to them as individuals or involve the recognition that they have *rights*. In part his triumph is too easy because the Stewardship tradition is incompatible with belief in man's dominion if, as Routley believes, that belief holds that nature may be manipulated entirely in the human interest; for this tradition involves obligations to care for the plants and animals of the earth, obligations not deriving from human interests. If there are such obligations, then consistency requires a considerable overhaul of the belief in man's dominion. But the basic unsoundness in Passmore's case lies in his tendency not to count as real any problem which is not a problem for human interests; if so, it is unsurprising that the man-centred ethic which he favours is found to be adequate to their solution. For if nothing could count as a problem which would require a revision of traditional morality for its solution, the discovery that problems recognized as such on this basis can all be solved within the Western moral tradition is an unsurprising hollow victory.

The nature and extent of responsibilities with regard to future people and nonhuman creatures are discussed in later chapters. For the time being it suffices to say that the mere possibility that there are such responsibilities discloses a weakness in Passmore's case. (In chapters 6—9 I shall argue for more extensive obligations than Passmore recognizes, but ones in keeping with the Stewardship tradition.) As to Routley's point about the inconsistency between this tradition and the belief in man's dominion, she is right if her characterization of that belief is granted. But this kind of construal is, as I shall contend in chapters 2—4, a misinterpretation of belief in man's dominion. To some extent, as I argue there, Passmore misinterprets that belief, particularly by underestimating the antiquity and pervasiveness of the Stewardship tradition over the centuries; but when Routley writes as if the Stewardship tradition is out of keeping with belief in man's dominion it is she who misinterprets this belief. If so, then there may be little need for radical departures from the older principles of our moral traditions. Routley's point about the need for an overhaul for the sake of consistency still stands, however (granted the parallel existence of the Despotism tradition). And, as I shall contend, so does the need to reject the wholly man-centred ethic at which she protests, and which she believes to be the dominant assumption of Western moral traditions.

In subsequent writings Passmore has been much more ready to propose revisions of moral (and, to some extent, metaphysical) principles,[8] though in the Preface to the second edition of *Man's Responsibility*[9] he concedes only that these writings are 'more philosophically explicit'. Some of the issues which arise in these more recent papers are discussed in chapters 3 and 4 below. But it is worth observing at this stage how he now understands both the problems and the principles more broadly.[10] Thus he now thinks that pollution can affect nonhuman species in a way that makes it difficult to invoke existing moral principles to condemn the pollutor; that a stronger emphasis than traditional principles seem to permit on obligations to future people is necessary if resources are to be preserved; and that our attitudes to nature and the environment form a major obstacle to the solution of problems such as the preservation of species.

This recent combination of views could, of course, be cited as evidence for Routley's view that theories of what the problems are and of how to solve them are prone to fit together with a noncontingent closeness. Fortunately, however, this need not always be so. For one thing, people can intuitively sense that something is amiss and that there is a problem, without having any clear grasp of the principles which may have been violated and may need to be reaffirmed, and even on reflection they may be in genuine doubt about which these are. A good example is the problem of endangered species, which is certainly a problem in terms of human interests (losses to medical and agriculturai research; foreclosure of a source of aesthetic pleasure and of scientific curiosity), but which seems more of a problem than these grounds alone would warrant.[11]

There can also be a gap between value-theory and moral

principles. Thus it may be agreed that something is an evil (e.g. skin-cancer, whoever the sufferer may be), but not agreed what obligations we may have in its regard (e.g. an obligation to prevent its occurrence in future people unknown to ourselves, as long as it is probable that our acts or omissions in the present will make a significant difference in the matter). So we do not in all cases need to await agreement on principles (much less on social solutions in which they are applied) before particular problems can be recognized as such. Further instances in the area of ecology are the problems of pollution and resource-depletion.

As to Routley's 'hollow victory' criticism, the question of whether Passmore's book falls foul of it need not be settled here. In his second edition he rejects the view that, if Naess' classification of ecological philosophies is adopted, he is a 'shallow ecophilosopher', on the grounds that he has been concerned all along with developing countries as well as developed ones, and also with the destruction of animal species and of wilderness. This being so, he may perhaps be deemed to have changed more over principles and ethical solutions than over the profundity of the problems. At the same time it should be added that he also rejects the attribution of ecological 'depth' to his later writings if depth implies an acceptance of primitivism or mysticism, or the rejection 'of any preference for human interests over the interests of other species';[12] to avoid such attributions he is glad to call himself 'shallow'. Yet his principles have clearly become deeper with time.

What is much more important is the fact that there is considerable scope for reasoning and for persuasion about both problems and principles, even if perceptions of each are often informed by perceptions of the other. Reasoning can be conducted on the basis of acknowledged moral judgements and principles about comparable topics which allow analogies (and disanalogies) to be drawn, or by drawing out the implications of the acceptance of either principles as binding or of problems as problematic. There is also at least the possibility that examining the historical roots of our attitudes to nature and of our problems will allow better-founded judgements to be reached, whether by eliciting the resources of our traditions, by exposing ancient errors which remain influential, or by broadening the perspective within which the issues are tackled.

In any case it is high time for a re-examination of these issues. Like Passmore I begin with a study of Western traditions, partly to set the record straight, and partly to develop an account of the Stewardship tradition, which I find a deeper-rooted seed, and, like

some metaphysical variants within Western traditions, more profound and more fruitful than Passmore does. Next I survey some
more recent roots of contemporary attitudes to nature held in both
Western and Eastern Europe which seem to explain those attitudes
much better than Genesis does. Thereafter, instead of using
Passmore's method of arguing from the problems to the principles
which account for their being problematic and need to be invoked
to solve them, I investigate directly what principles can consistently
and most defensibly be held over our responsibilities with respect to
future generations and nonhuman creatures, and what their bearing
is on current ecological problems.

But before investigating either traditions or principles of value or
of obligation, I shall now turn to the task of setting the more widely
acknowledged problems in their historical context by examining
their causes. Despite the difficulties about conflicts of value, there is
in fact widespread agreement that pollution, the depletion of
resources, population growth and the destruction of wild species
and their habitats constitute problems: medium-term human
interests suffice to make them such. Moreover the fact that they are
problems for long went unrecognized. Taken together, these
circumstances suggest the importance of understanding the causes
of the problems and the factors which perpetuate them. Granted
the conflicts of values which exist over the problems, it should not
be assumed that unearthing their causes is a simple empirical matter,
any more than discovering their solutions is; but it should not be
assumed either that these endeavours are radically flawed by these
disputes, as if they were in principle irresolvable.

In a book about environmental ethics it is worthwhile to make an
attempt to locate the causes of our ecological problems. If we can
arrive at even a tentative grasp of the causes, in the sense of the
factors but for which the problems would not have reached their
current state, we shall understand them better, and we may even be
able to discover how, by reducing or reversing some of the
contributing factors, the problems may be resolved or at least
alleviated. There is a danger here of assuming that all the problems
have one and the same cause, and a counterpart danger of rejecting
as a cause any factor which fails to explain everything. There may
well be no single cause for the various problems, but it is still worth
looking into the theories which purport to disclose one. There is
also the danger that the disclosure of material or efficient causes
may obscure the importance of explanations which turn on beliefs
and attitudes: material and efficient factors may take effect only

where people have mostly failed to see the problems as problems, or have held questionable attitudes and beliefs such as the attitude of Despotism or the belief in the inevitable and providential character of material progress. But a study of the causes of ecological problems can serve to bring out the need to scrutinize just such underlying attitudes, and this is what I believe that it does do in fact.

In the rest of this chapter, therefore, I shall consider the theories that the network of our interrelated ecological problems is caused by population increases, by affluence, by technology, by capitalism and by economic growth. An adequate treatment of these themes would involve a good deal more natural science and social science than I am qualified to deploy, and indeed more than is suited to a study in the fields, mainly, of moral philosophy and the history of ideas. But philosophy is a great deal more susceptible of application to contemporary public issues than used to appear in the heyday of linguistic analysis, as journals such as *Ethics* and *Philosophy and Public Affairs* bear witness; and when it is so applied it needs to draw upon the methods and the understandings of other disciplines. Indeed it is clearly necessary to do so in the course of the present attempt to throw light on the theories and the principles by which problems may be understood and tackled. What follows is obviously open to revision by specialists in the various disciplines concerned; yet if that were enough to deter nonspecialists, no interdisciplinary enquiry could ever begin. But on the issue of the causes of ecological problems just such an enquiry is needed.

The population theory. On this theory the various ecological problems (other than the increase in human population itself) are brought about by the striking upturn in human numbers, or at least would not exist as we know them but for this upturn. World population has been held (prematurely, as it turns out) to be doubling every 35 years,[13] and so, correspondingly, would be the waste products of human economic activity and of humans themselves, and the food, energy and mineral resources which they consume. The increase in pollution and the retreat of wilderness coincide with the increase in population, as does the erosion of overworked tillage and overgrazed pasturage, and the depletion of fossil fuels and minerals. In general, it is held, the nonhuman environment cannot sustain, or be expected to continue to sustain, the increasing rates of population growth; and the problems cannot be resolved unless not only the rate of growth ceases to grow but also population growth itself ceases altogether. Indeed, for preference, there should be some reduction. Each extra person takes an extra toll on the earth's resources, and that is why the burden on those resources has become excessive.

It is difficult to hold that there is *nothing* of merit in this theory. There must, after all, be some level of human population beyond which further increases cannot be sustained by the natural environment: the earth and its several regions have a finite carrying capacity. But the theory too readily assumes that each human being and each human community contribute to the deterioration of the environment. In fact, many communities in many parts of the world have preserved the fertility of the land which they live off over long periods, often enhancing it by techniques such as drainage and terracing; and their own waste products, rather than poisoning the land, have re-entered its natural cycles. Such a harmonious relation to the land could indeed be upset by the pressure of numbers, but this has not happened yet on a global scale (though it could happen if present rates of increase were to persist for long enough). Even the Sahelian region of sub-Saharan Africa, the natural balance of which was upset during the droughts of the 1970s, has reached its present state through colonial policies and a sharp increase in the number of cattle rather than of humans.

Meanwhile the most aesthetically offensive of our ecological problems, pollution, is principally located in the western world, where population growth has been much less striking than it has in the Third World; and the same applies to the depletion of fossil fuels and minerals, at least insofar as their extraction largely reflects the economic activity of the companies and governments of the wealthier countries. Population growth in these countries certainly magnifies the effects of these activities, but, as Barry Commoner has pointed out, pollution and the exhaustion of mineral resources would still take place without it.[14] Thus, though population growth is not irrelevant to their explanation, ecological problems are not greatest where it is most noticeable, and vary with factors quite independent of it.

More will be said (in chapter 7) about the intrinsic value of human lives. But enough has been said already to cast doubt on the belief that each human is an ecological liability, and on theories that bad ecological effects are bound to accrue wherever it is held that extra human lives are welcome. I have not denied that the eventual stabilization of the human population is a necessity if global famine and global war are to be averted, or if our ecological problems are to be resolved. But I do maintain that the theory which sets these problems down to population growth is to be rejected as unduly shallow. To put matters technically, population growth is part of a sufficient condition for some such problems but it is not their necessary condition. At the same time we should reject some of the assumptions about the supposed negative value of people which derive their plausibility solely from the population theory. Pernicious as their activities sometimes are, people are not a cancer.

The affluence theory. This theory does at least concern one of the blatant features of those societies whose activities do seem to underlie most pollution, most of the extraction of minerals and a large amount of the destruction of wildlife and wilderness. It notes that the startling increase in levels of pollution in the post-1945 period has coincided with a marked increase in gross national product per head in Western societies, and in particular in the United States, and concludes that the single most significant factor promoting ecological stress is an increase in individual affluence and consumption.[15] Increased rates of consumer demand and consumer wastefulness would then lead, via increased consumption of fuel and the discarding of products which cannot be re-used, to environmental deterioration. The theory is graphically illustrated by calculations of the large number of slaves which would be equivalent to the power of the gadgetry possessed by the average American.

The affluence theory does not, of course, pretend to explain population growth. Indeed there is evidence from societies such as Japan of a marked fall in the birth-rate coincident with the increase in that society's affluence and the social provisions and sense of security which it has facilitated. There is, moreover, good reason to believe that rapid population growth is actually caused not by affluence but by poverty, lack of development, high rates of infant mortality, and the accompanying sense of insecurity.[16] If so, provision of the basic necessities for development and self-help may well be the best (or indeed the only) way to arrest rapid population increases in poor countries.

But this possible solution of the population problem in no way implies that affluence needs to be spread worldwide. Indeed such a development would probably bring ecological catastrophe long before it was complete. For, though affluence does not explain the population problem, it would appear to exacerbate most of the other developments of ecological concern. In that case those who accept that current Western consumption of fuel and minerals and current Western production of synthetic and non-biodegradable 'goods' is excessive and ecologically burdensome would have reason to aim, like Patrick Rivers,[17] at a simpler style of life: and the spread of such a symbolic life-style could have some impact on the mode of production and consumption in the society where they were adopted.

Commoner, however, rejects the affluence theory. He points out that in the same post-war period as that in which pollution has increased so markedly there has been no matching increase in the average consumption in the United States of shoes, clothing or housing, and that there was actually a slight decrease in the average consumption of carbohydrate and protein. He grants that individuals have had to spend more on these items, but maintains that 'per capita production of goods to meet major human needs' has 'not increased significantly between 1946 and 1968' and has 'even declined in some respects'.[18] Average consumption of household amenities and leisure items, he admits, has indeed increased, as has domestic fuel consumption, but not enough to account for the increase in levels of pollution. This increase is rather to be explained by the use of the new production technologies.[19]

This rejection of the affluence theory leaves lingering doubts. Thus the increased use of cars and of labour saving devices is undeniably a mark of affluence and has quite certainly had an environmental impact. Again, it might be supposed that consumers who purchase the products of advanced technology have some responsibility for its persistence and growth, just as consumers of the products of factory-farms have some responsibility for their perpetuation. Here Commoner would reply that they have little choice, at least over most food, clothing and shelter, and that their connivance cannot be the single most important factor in environmental deterioration. And with this way of articulating a rejection of the affluence theory I should largely agree. Far more important factors are to be found in the new technology, the associated economic forces, and the readiness of those concerned to ignore any costs which do not figure in the balance-sheet of one's own enterprise. If, however, the connivance of consumers makes any difference at all, as surely it does, then consumer revolts and efforts at simpler and less wasteful patterns of life will not be altogether futile.

The technology theory. As Commoner points out,[20] neither the increase in the population of the United States nor the per capita increase in production, nor even their product, suffices to account for the intensification of pollution. He would not deny that if this product were to persist at current rates for any considerable period the environmental effects would be serious, but its impact would largely be due, in his view, to the newer methods of production, involving, for example, detergents, aluminium, plastic and inorganic fertilizers in place of soap powder, wood, steel and manure. Similarly, disposable packaging has replaced returnable bottles, petrol contains more lead, and chlorine production — important in the synthesis of organic chemicals — has involved an enormous increase in the consumption of mercury. Thus the new technology, which has many times the environmental impact of the old, is the crucial missing factor accounting for the difference between the percentage increase in production and the much greater percentage increase in pollution.

To theories such as Commoner's, Sir Fred Catherwood[21] replies that modern technology has sometimes brought environmental benefits. Aluminium, he claims, is less wasteful than steel because of its longer life and its suitability for reuse; and modern methods of sewage treatment and water purification have also brought obvious gains. In general, he adds, modern technology has greatly increased the resources available to mankind and raised the standard of living of the common man. But the benefits of technology are not the present issue. Commoner's claim is that for many cases its costs are intolerable; and over many of the instances which he cites the claim cannot be gainsaid.

The technology theory is not primarily intended to explain such problems as the global increase in population (though even to this the technology of disease control must have made a key contribution), but it does, in Commoner's exposition, explain the recent poisoning of land, air and water, the elimination of much wildlife (through pesticides) and the depletion of many of the earth's mineral resources. It does not, however, explain the considerable ecological damage resulting from human activity prior to 1945,[22] nor does it explain why at this particular time and place these particular processes were adopted. If, however, these developments cannot themselves be explained, efforts to reverse them may well miscarry. We need to know, if possible, the causes of the pollutant processes, or they may survive attempts to make them harmless, or even take on a more serious character, as a result of the very same hidden forces which launched them in the first place. So, until we have explained the rise of the new technology, we have done little more

than move the explanatory problem one stage along without solving it.

Nevertheless Commoner's theory is important. It allows us to
focus more clearly on the immediate explanation of some of our
more recent ecological problems; and it suggests thereby which
societies may need to change, and which methods of production
should be spurned by consumers and planners who believe that
current ways of life are doing unjustified harm either to the present
generation of humans, or to other species, or to people of future
generations.

The capitalism theory. In large measure the new technology was
introduced because it was more profitable: synthetic fibres and
detergents gave better returns on capital than cotton or soap powder.
Similarly, the best (or only) way for farmers in the West to make
profits from arable land has been the heavy and unabating use of
fertilizers and pesticides, despite the effect of the run-off on human
health and the way in which non-biodegradable substances
accumulate as they pass through natural food-chains.

The theory to be considered, then, is that capitalism requires as a
condition of both prosperity and survival the employment of the
most profitable technology available, and that firms competing on
the open market cannot afford to forego the extra profits which
high technology offers. Those which fail to maximize profits will, it
might be held, be out-manoeuvred by competitors who have no
inhibitions. Only if profits are made and maximized will there be
sufficient capital to renew or replace old equipment, and thereby to
maximize future profits, as firms must do on pain of falling behind
or perishing. Thus capitalism is the cause of increased pollution and
the depletion of minerals, as these phenomena are often the
unintended by-products of the business methods required by the
capitalist system.

It is also widely held that capitalism is dependent upon economic
growth, and radically incompatible with the kind of steady-state, no-
growth society which people concerned about ecological problems
often advocate, at least as an eventual desideratum. Capitalism
seems, as Commoner remarks,[23] to depend on the accumulation of
capital, and there would probably be little such accumulation in a
steady-state economy. Again, capitalism seems because of its very
nature to involve a search for new means of making profit, and if
such means were precluded by the rules of a steady-state society, it
might well atrophy and wither, or, more plausibly, resist to the

death the inauguration of such a dispensation. This close dependence of capitalism upon economic growth is, however, disputed, and it is possible to imagine a centrally organized but mixed economy with strict regulations governing reinvestment and also, to prevent disregard of effects on the environment, governing productive techniques. It is even possible to imagine multinational corporations being subjected to similar rules as a result of international agreements. The scenario is very far removed from that of contemporary big business, yet it remains a possibility, however slender.

For present purposes, however, I must leave on one side the extent and nature of the modifications which would be necessary for a society where growth was restricted. The present question is rather whether capitalism as it has been found hitherto has caused pollution and other ecological problems. And part of the answer is that other economic systems have permitted pollution too, including that of the USSR.[24] Hence the overthrow of capitalism would not be guaranteed to resolve our ecological problems: capitalism is not their necessary condition. On the other hand the orientation of capitalism towards the most profitable form of production, however destructive of natural life or natural resources and however costly on any account other than that of company profits and shareholders' dividends, suggests that very considerable modifications to the capitalist system would be required before ecological problems could be overcome. Something similar, no doubt, holds good for centrally controlled economies in which private enterprise has been abolished: economic policy, at any rate, would need a thorough overhaul there too, if natural resources are to be conserved, if wilderness and wildlife are to be left intact, and if the land, the air and the waters are not to be poisoned.

The growth theory. The theories based on population, affluence and capitalism do not seem to explain the problems before us, while the technology theory explains a subset of them, only to pose much the same explanatory problem again at one remove. Indeed ecological problems seem to pervade both Western capitalist societies and Eastern European communist ones; both kinds of society are inclined to seek short-term or medium-term benefits, whether for the whole community or, more often, for circumscribed groups within it, at the cost of considerable damage to the natural environment, to nonhuman species and to their own descendants.

These considerations suggest the need for a broader theory of the cause of our ecological problems. A candidate is the theory that they result from exponential or geometrical growth, growth in particular with respect to five crucial factors — population, food production, industrialization, pollution and consumption of non-renewable resources — and from the interplay of these five kinds of growth. This is the thesis of *The Limits to Growth*,[25] the authors of which hold that the limits to the growth of these factors will automatically be reached within the next hundred years, unless the people of the world alter the current trends and 'establish a condition of ecological and economic stability that is sustainable far into the future'.[26] This comprehensive theory clearly incorporates many of the partial causes so far considered, and supplements them by its greater emphasis on *economic growth*.

Neither population increases nor capitalism explain the problem alone, for the problems sometimes arise independently of them; and neither affluence nor modern technology explain them sufficiently, but seem rather to be symptoms of something more general. Economic growth, however, explains the impact upon nature of the affluent capitalist West and also of the rapidly industrializing communist countries, and together with the growth in human numbers does make global problems such as the current ones all too predictable.[27]

Now it may be granted to this theory that industrialization, pollution and consumption of non-renewable resources are growing exponentially, and that even if food production is not doing so, it is, like population, with which it is keeping pace, still growing steadily. Whether the continuation of current trends would produce the forms of global catastrophe predicted to take place before the end of the next century is disputed,[28] but there is no need to enter into that controversy here. For the case can scarcely be disputed that the continuation of exponential economic growth, allied to a continuation of steady population growth, must prove catastrophic; and from this it follows that economic growth must cease to be exponential, and that preferably the rate of population growth must diminish even more than it has in the 1970s.

It does not follow, however, that either population growth or economic growth is bad, or that the solution to our problems consists in the complete abandonment of both. Nor is it clear that economic growth, any more than population growth (or even in combination with it), constitutes a complete explanation of our problems, without any account being taken of the attitudes or the beliefs which perpetuate it.

Thus Mesarovic and Pestel resist the view that all growth is of an undifferentiated type, and in their Second Report to the Club of Rome[29] urge the need for 'organic' or differentiated growth, the world being viewed as a system of diverse interacting regions, which need to co-operate globally, with growth in some regions and the abandonment of growth in others, if regional (but potentially global) catastrophes are to be avoided. A pattern of economic activity sustainable far into the future is certainly part of their goal, but it is not clear that this need be a pattern of no overall growth whatever. On this view, then, not all growth is bad, though the continuation of exponential growth certainly is. This conclusion is further supported by Thomas Derr,[30] who points out that in economic growth lies the only realistic hope for the poor that global injustices will be remedied.

Just as not all economic growth is bad, so too an explanation of our problems which stops short at economic growth is incomplete and partial. What attitudes give rise to the goal of perpetual growth and perpetuate it as a goal? Unlike the present-day societies of the Western and communist worlds, more traditional societies have often lacked such attitudes. Perhaps, then, a part of the explanation is to be found in the deep-rooted attitudes common to both socialist societies and the West. In the next four chapters I consider theories which claim to find the explanation in their common religious, moral and metaphysical traditions.

NOTES

1   John Passmore, *Man's Responsibility for Nature,* London: Duckworth, 1974 (hereinafter *MRN*), p. 43.
2   *MRN*, pp. 43—5.
3   Arne Naess, 'The Shallow and the Deep, Long-range Ecology Movement. A Summary', *Inquiry,* 16, 1973, 95—100.
4   Aldo Leopold, *A Sand County Almanac and Sketches Here and There,* New York: Oxford University Press, 1949, pp. 203f. The call for such a new ethic has been echoed in Richard Routley, 'Is There a Need for a New, an Environmental Ethic?', *Proceedings of the XVth World Congress of Philosophy,* Varna, 1973, 205—10.
5   Leopold, *A Sand County Almanac,* pp. 224f.
6   See n. 1. A second edition, with a new Preface and Appendix, appeared in 1980.
7   Val Routley, Critical Notice of John Passmore, *Man's Responsibility for Nature, Australasian Journal of Philosophy,* 53, 1975, 171—85.
8   See his 'Attitudes to Nature', in Royal Institute of Philosophy (ed.), *Nature and Conduct,* London and Basingstoke: Macmillan Press, 1975, 251—64; 'The Treatment of Animals', *Journal of the History of*

Ideas, 36, 1975, 195—218; 'Ecological Problems and Persuasion', in Gray Dorsey (ed.), *Equality and Freedom,* Vol. II, New York: Oceana Publications and Leiden: A. W. Sijthoff, 1977, 431—42. The claim that Passmore's metaphysic is revised in 'Attitudes to Nature' is argued in R. and V. Routley, 'Nuclear Energy and Obligations to the Future', *Inquiry,* 21, 1978, 133—79, at n. 12, pp. 175f.

9 *MRN,* 2nd edn, pp. viiif.

10 'Ecological Problems and Persuasion', at pp. 438—41.

11 For a discussion of this issue yielding slightly different conclusions from my own, see Alastair S. Gunn, 'Why Should We Care about Rare Species?', *Environmental Ethics,* 2, 1980, 17—37. See also chapter 8 (below).

12 *MRN,* 2nd edn, p. ix.

13 See Paul R. Ehrlich and Anne H. Ehrlich, *Population, Resources, Environment, Issues in Human Ecology,* San Francisco: W. H. Freeman, (2nd edn) 1972, chapter 2. The structure and overall outlook of this book reflect the theory here depicted (though Paul Ehrlich's more recent work suggests a change of emphasis). Cf. John Breslaw, 'Economics and Ecosystems', in John Barr (ed.), *The Environmental Handbook,* London: Ballantine/Friends of the Earth, 1971, 83—93, p. 92: 'The essential cause of environmental pollution is over-population, combined with an excessive population growth rate'. The current paragraph also reflects broadly the published views of Garrett Hardin and to some extent those of Kenneth Boulding. For a criticism of their prescriptions, see Richard Neuhaus, *In Defense of People, Ecology and the Seduction of Radicalism,* New York: Macmillan and London: Collier-Macmillan, 1971.

14 See further Barry Commoner, *The Closing Circle,* London: Jonathan Cape, 1972, pp. 125—39. For Hardin's view on the Sahel, see Garrett Hardin and John Baden (eds), *Managing the Commons,* San Francisco: W. H. Freeman, 1977, 112—24.

15 This theory is presented and criticized by Commoner in *The Closing Circle,* pp. 136—9.

16 Cf. Susan George, *How the Other Half Dies,* Harmondsworth: Penguin Books, 1976, chapter 2; Peter Donaldson, *Worlds Apart,* London: BBC, 1971, pp. 46—52; Judith Hart, *Aid and Liberation,* London: Gollancz, 1973, *passim.*

17 Patrick Rivers, *Living Better on Less,* London: Turnstone Books, 1977.

18 Commoner, *The Closing Circle,* p. 139.

19 See ibid. p. 144 and generally pp. 140—77.

20 Ibid. p. 140.

21 Sir Frederick Catherwood, *A Better Way, The Case for a Christian Social Order,* Leicester: Inter-Varsity Press, 1975, pp. 104—11.

22 Yet the pre-1945 problems were sufficient to give rise to the first conservationist movement in America. See Pete A. Y. Gunter, 'The Big Thicket: A Case Study in Attitudes toward Environment', in

William T. Blackstone (ed.), *Philosophy and Environmental Crisis,* Athens: University of Georgia Press, 1974, 117—37, p. 124. More strikingly, the theory does not explain the blight caused by the original industrial revolution, or the deforestation of much of the Scottish Highlands in the nineteenth century.

23   Commoner, *The Closing Circle,* p. 274.

24   See ibid. pp. 277—81. For an interesting discussion of the prospects for the limitation of growth in capitalist and communist societies, see chapter 3 of Robert L. Heilbroner, *An Inquiry into the Human Prospect,* London: Calder & Boyars, 1975.

25   Donella H. Meadows *et al., The Limits to Growth,* a report for the Club of Rome's Project on the Predicament of Mankind (1972), London and Sydney: Pan Books, 1974.

26   Ibid. p. 24.

27   See further Edward J. Mishan, *The Costs of Economic Growth,* Harmondsworth: Penguin Books, 1969.

28   See H. Cole *et al., Thinking About the Future: A Critique of The Limits to Growth,* London: Chatto & Windus and Sussex University Press, 1973. The rate of growth of the world population seems to have been decreasing throughout the 1970s: see editorial, *New Internationalist,* 79, September 1979.

29   Mihajlo D. Mesarovic and Eduard Pestel, *Mankind at the Turning Point,* London: Hutchinson, 1975; see pp. 1—5, 55.

30   Thomas Sieger Derr, *Ecology and Human Liberation,* Geneva: WSCF Books, 1973, pp. 89f.

2

Man's Dominion and the Judaeo-Christian Heritage

In this chapter I shall consider the theory that the source of our ecological problems is to be found in the Judaeo-Christian belief that mankind was created to have dominion over nature, a belief which, according to the theory, can be interpreted as implying that humans may treat their natural environment as they like. This theory has to confront the objection that ideas cannot have such a causal efficacy, and also seems to imply that the attitude to nature of the medieval West was improperly exploitative: having considered these difficulties, the second of which I claim to have substance, I proceed to consider whether the theory correctly interprets the Biblical belief in man's dominion, or whether the Old and New Testaments embody, on the contrary, the makings of a much gentler and more enlightened attitude to nature. In the next chapter I consider the evidence for these various attitudes from subsequent Christian history, and in the following chapter I survey the significance for these matters of Judaeo-Christian beliefs about the nature of man. These chapters prepare the way for the presentation of a moral theory in later chapters, as well as throwing light on the resources of Western traditions for coping with ecological problems, which I claim to be much ampler than is usually supposed.

Religion as the source of the problems

What Lynn White calls 'the historical roots of our ecological crisis' are held by him (in an essay with the phrase just quoted as title[1]) to be located in the Judaic and Christian doctrine of creation. More specifically they lie in the belief that man was made in God's image and shares in God's transcendence of nature, and that the whole natural order was created for the sake of humanity. In the more recent past the roots of the crisis may be detected in the alliance of science and technology, only finally cemented in the nineteenth century; but the beliefs implicit in Genesis, or rather in the activist, Western interpretation of Genesis, underlie those distinctive products of the West, science and technology.

Well before the rise of modern science in the sixteenth and seventeenth centuries the medieval West was technologically far ahead of the other cultures of the day, uninhibitedly harnessing natural forces for human ends: moreover this characteristically Western phenomenon was no accident, but embodied the very beliefs newly accepted when paganism was overcome by Christianity. In place of the respect for the guardian spirits of groves, streams and hills afforded by pagan animism, 'Christianity made it possible to exploit nature in a mood of indifference to the feelings of natural objects'. Indeed 'the spirits *in* natural objects, which formerly had protected nature from man, evaporated . . . and the old inhibitions to the exploitation of nature crumbled'.[2] Such being their roots, science and technology are unfit to solve our current problems; rather the remedy must lie in religion, and we should either replace Christianity, the root cause of the problems, with a new religion such as Zen Buddhism, or, failing that, modify it by adopting the pan-psychism of St Francis, according to which all creatures, whether animate or inanimate, have souls and are designed for the glorification of their Creator.

White's paper has, as Passmore observes, exercised widespread influence,[3] partly because of the delayed but increasing impact of Aldo Leopold's call for a new ethic, an ethic still, in his view, lacking in the West, governing man's relation to the land and the whole biotic community associated with it.[4] In particular, White's view that technology, the immediate cause of some of our ecological problems, cannot be expected to solve them alone, commands wide agreement, but there is less agreement about the nature and extent of the other social and moral changes required. More specifically his theory about the religious source of our problems and the corresponding need for a religious remedy has been challenged, not only over his theological interpretations, but also over his historical method.

One possible objection in the area of historical method is that it is fallacious to locate the causes of a phenomenon in its origins, for attitudes, like institutions, may be perpetuated for reasons quite other than those which originated them. Thus it would be a fallacy to represent as the cause of our largely post-1945 ecological problems such ancient Hebrew beliefs as may have originated the Western attitude to nature. This objection, however, has no force, for White can document the persistence of similar beliefs (how similar remains to be seen) among patristic and medieval writers and among more recent scientists, and a concomitant activist attitude to the natural environment. It is certainly odd that the same attitude also pervades a post-Christian age, and also societies such as that of Japan which have never been significantly Christian: but this could be because in the former case there has been no motive for a change of belief about the superiority and the dominance of man, and because in the latter case such was the prestige of Western technology that beliefs such as these could be imported with little or no resistance. White is thus immune from the fallacy of origins.

A more serious charge, however, concerns the extent of his reliance on ideas to explain social phenomena. 'It is difficult,' writes F. B. Welbourn,[5] 'to give so much primacy to the causal efficacy of ideas.' Welbourn's own view is that the function of ideas in history is to legitimize actions and institutions which are to be explained by more material considerations: thus new-found technological power may have been justified after the event by 'suitably selected and interpreted ideas'.[6] Now, it should certainly be granted that religious ideas are often pressed into service as justifications of social and technological developments. Nevertheless I should wish, with White, to question whether either modern science or modern technology can be explained solely by the structure of society or by economic forces and without reference to belief in an orderly creation and in the propriety of using and moulding it for human benefit.

The connection between science and the doctrine of creation is a close one, as I have argued elsewhere:[7] belief in creation implies the possibility of natural science and belief in man's dominion implies that its pursuit is, for some at least, a humanitarian duty. These implications of central Christian doctrines were, admittedly, neglected (but not universally disregarded) for many centuries, but the connection was explicitly argued in the early seventeenth century by Francis Bacon, and later that century the central features of his method were adopted by the Royal Society. Two hundred years later, and against the background of the same beliefs, science began to be applied systematically to technology and medicine, and the Baconian programme began to be fully realised (but without some of the safeguards which Bacon would have favoured); and, although belief in Christianity has waned, belief in the propriety of harnessing natural forces for human benefit has not.

There is also the problem of explaining, on Welbourn's view, why the growth of technology has been so specifically a Western phenomenon, if characteristic Western beliefs and attitudes are not to be invoked. Science and technology elsewhere, as Stanley L. Jaki and White himself have shown, either failed to develop despite promising beginnings, or were directed to devotional and spiritual purposes.[8] Thus, short of some other explanation of the distinctive progress of technology in the West, ideas may play an indispensable role in the explanation of this (and other) social and historical developments, even if they seldom constitute sufficient conditions alone. Accordingly White's theory is not to be rejected on grounds of historical method or of historical materialism: indeed the invocation of traditional ethical and religious attitudes may do much to illuminate ecological problems and the principles required for their solution.

Nevertheless reservations need to be expressed about those passages in which White elicits from his discoveries about medieval technology the attitudes to nature which they bespeak. Remarking on the invention of the eight-oxen plough in Northern Europe in the seventh century and the changes which it brought to agricultural practice, he claims that a crucial change in man's relation and attitude to the soil took place therewith; 'once man had been part of nature; now he became her exploiter'.[9] A similar tone pervades his remarks on the Carolingian calendars of shortly before AD 830, wherein 'passive personifications' of the months were replaced by scenes of 'ploughing, harvesting, wood-chopping, people knocking down acorns for pigs, pig-slaughtering'. Of this change White observes: 'They show a coercive attitude to natural resources . . . Man and nature are now two things, and man is master.'[10]

These comments betray an exaggerated view of the moral and metaphysical significance of new ploughs and new calendars. It is beyond my present scope to question White's conclusions about the social changes which accompanied the introduction of the new plough.[11] But if his comments on their significance are taken seriously it should be inferred that until around AD 800 people in the West regarded themselves as no different from the rest of nature, despite the conflicting account of their Christian beliefs presented by White himself,[12] and that thereafter a grasping, coercive and improper attitude prevailed towards natural organisms, minerals and wilderness. The passages in White's book in which this interpretation is put forward are isolated and untypical ones, and the facts which White presents simply will not bear such an interpretation. Moreover, if an exploitative attitude to nature is fully embodied in heavy ploughing, wood-chopping and acorn gathering, just as much as in the heedless pollution of rivers by mercury compounds and of the atmosphere by strontium 90, it must be asked whether White is concerned about the same attitude to nature as, for example, Barry Commoner, and whether what he is concerned about is really exploitative at all.

White presents no further arguments for the view that these changes embody an improperly exploitative view, yet there seems to be no alternative interpretation of his remarks. (He cannot merely be remarking that man began at that time to exploit nature, in the non-pejorative sense of 'exploit', for on his own account such mere *use* of nature had been current for centuries.) But if the new uses to which nature was put in North-West Europe around AD 800 constitute (improper) exploitation, so, it would seem, must all the other ingenious contrivances of medieval technology which White proceeds to describe with such care and apparent admiration. If so, it is difficult to understand his attitude to his own subject-matter as a historian. The belief that gunpowder might best have been left alone would be understandable, but does White really hold the same about the power of wind and water, the three-field rotation system, and the nutritive powers of broad beans and chickpeas? If not, he may still persuade us that people in North-West Europe in the ninth century were more ready to mould nature for human advantage than those elsewhere, but he cannot persuade us that the changes they made in this direction were for the most part regrettable. Indeed if such developments are what a new religion is required to curtail or prevent, then White seems to have mischaracterized what is needed.

Old Testament attitudes

It is now appropriate to ask whether, as Passmore and Welbourn claim, White has mischaracterized the Old Testament also, and with it at least the roots of the belief which he considers to underly our ecological problems. According to Genesis, God created mankind to have 'dominion over the fish of the sea, and over the fowl of the air, and over the earth and over every creeping thing that creepeth upon the earth',[13] and authorized man to 'Be fruitful and multiply and replenish the earth and subdue it'.[14] White's comment is 'God planned all of this [his creation] explicitly for man's benefit and rule: no item in the physical creation has any purpose save to serve man's purposes.' To what extent will the Old Testament bear this interpretation?

It is generally agreed that on the Old Testament view nature is not sacred. The Creator and his creation are radically distinct, it is idolatrous to worship the latter, and so there is nothing sacrilegious in treating creatures as resources for human benefit. Indeed the passages about man's dominion authorize just that, within certain limits. On the other hand the belief that nature may properly be used by mankind does not, as Passmore points out, justify an irresponsible attitude to nature.[15] At most it removes one possible inhibition to such an attitude: but this inhibition is surely an undesirable one, at least if alternatives can serve instead. For belief in the sacredness of nature makes medical and scientific research not only wrong but actually impious, and this ban would include the science of ecology itself. Against such a view Christian defenders of science such as Boyle have quite properly appealed to the Bible, as Passmore reminds us.[16] The possibility of alternative inhibitions is already implicit in Genesis 1, which authorizes exclusively a vegetarian diet. Only after the Fall and the Flood were human beings authorized to eat flesh,[17] as if the society which transmitted and edited the Genesis narratives was uneasy about meat-eating and sensed that a special justification was needed.

Though the Old Testament eventually allowed flesh to be used for human food, the Laws of Leviticus and Deuteronomy in fact set considerable limits to human dealings with nature, affecting, for example, the treatment of fruit-trees, oxen, mother birds and fallow land.[18] Similarly the Book of Proverbs declares that 'A righteous man regardeth the life of his beast.' Nor, as Welbourn points out, is pagan animism the only form of religion to have imposed restraints on people's treatment of plants and animals; indeed monotheistic religions have a similar capacity, as he ably shows. Thus White's remarks that according to Christianity God intends man to exploit nature 'for his proper ends'[19] and that with the Christian defeat of paganism 'the old inhibitions to the exploitation of nature crumbled'[20] are at best misleading, insofar as Christians have not forgotten the Old Testament. (White cannot be taken as limiting the divine mandate to man's *morally* 'proper ends', as it is supposed to constitute the pernicious root of our ecological problems, rather than merely to authorize behaviour which is morally justified.)

The point can be taken further if White's claim that the Old Testament represents nature as being created solely for man is considered. As soon as this claim is examined, it collapses. In Genesis 1, plants are intended as food for beasts, fowls and reptiles as much as for mankind; and after the Flood all these kinds of creatures are alike instructed to breed and be fruitful. In Job, God is said to send rain for the plants and the uninhabited wilderness (38:25ff), and to have made the wilderness for the wild ass (39:5ff). Still more impressively, Psalm 104 catalogues God's concern for nature and all creatures, among which man figures no more prominently than the birds and the wild beasts. Passmore indeed traces the belief that everything was made for man not to the Old Testament but to Stoic and earlier Greek sources,[21] from which it seems to have been derived by the third century Christian Origen;[22] as we shall see, the influence of Stoicism in this regard did not prevail over that of the Old Testament to anything like the extent which Passmore supposes.

The truth seems to be that the tradition which holds that in God's eyes the nonhuman creation has no value except its instrumental value for mankind has Greek rather than Hebrew sources,[23] and is only one, and not the only (or even, perhaps, the predominant) view of the value of creatures of other kinds to have been held by Christians; not, as White calls it, 'orthodox Christian arrogance'.[24] Indeed even to call it 'Greco-Christian arrogance', as Passmore thinks may be in order,[25] is to go beyond the evidence, as most ancient Greeks and many (perhaps most) Christians have held no such view (see chapter 3). Moreover, since Christians familiar with the Old Testament would assume that in God's eyes various creatures other than humans are of intrinsic value, White must be mistaken in holding that according to Christianity in general man is intended to regard nature as raw material for his own ends alone.

Views such as White's about the supposed Judaeo-Christian origins of belief in the duality of man and nature and in perpetual progress receive some discussion in chapters 4 and 5. Here it remains to consider how far the biblical belief in mankind's dominion is even compatible with the view of man as despot which Passmore regards as the dominant Western tradition, though one only put into practical effect in a thorough-going manner since the time of Bacon and Descartes. For, though he subjects White's theory to considerable qualification, Passmore holds that the Old Testament leaves open the possibility of an attitude of absolute despotism towards nature on the part of mankind: and he believes that this ability has actually occupied the centre of the stage till recently within Christianity.[26] I shall claim in reply that the despotic attitude is a possible interpretation of the Old Testament only by means of selective quotation and disregard for Hebrew thought.

The interpretation of belief in mankind's dominion as involving man as steward or bailiff of creation, charged by God with responsibility for its care, is claimed by Passmore to be largely a recent view, and to have originated (at least among Christians) in the seventeenth century.[27] If he is right, then the predominant Christian belief has been that, except for practices specifically forbidden by God, people are entitled to deal with nature without further limitations and in whatever way they please, like an absolutist prince of the Holy Roman Empire subject only to the largely theoretical constraints of the Emperor.

But the biblical dominion of man is no despotism. If Genesis authorizes mankind to rule nature, it authorizes only the kind of rule compatible with the Hebrew concept of monarchy: and, though the Hebrews were aware of other nations having absolute monarchs, their own kings were never so regarded. Rather they were considered to be answerable to God for the well-being of the realm,[28] and if they failed in their responsibilities, God would send a prophet to anoint another. The attitude ascribed to David at I Chronicles 29:11–14[29] epitomizes that proper to a king; David there attributes all power to God, and acknowledges before God that he and his people cannot even offer up gifts which have not first, like everything else, been bestowed through God's grace. Not surprisingly kings often deviated from the spirit of this humble prayer; but what is at stake is the characteristic Hebrew concept of kingship and dominion, not the practice of all who implicitly accepted the ideals implicit in it. Nor was it only kingship which the Hebrews expected to be exercised responsibly: the same view was taken of the ordinary ownership of property.[30]

John Black derives from Genesis 2:15 a more direct argument for the view that man's dominion was interpreted as the responsible exercise of a circumscribed trust or mandate, and not as despotism. The second or Yahwist account of the creation there relates that 'the Lord God took the man, and put him into the garden to dress it and keep it'.[31] Black interprets 'dress' as meaning to 'till' for both pleasure and profit, and 'keep' as 'protect from harm'. Thus man is put into the world to look after it for God, and, as Black points out, to preserve it as a source of pleasure, and not only as good for food (Genesis 2:9). Passmore[32] considers this authorization to have been superseded by man's expulsion from the garden, which was cursed for his sake; yet the original mandate of dominion, conferred before the Fall, was repeated after it, and the new circumstances then arising can scarcely have been understood to have disburdened humanity of all prior obligations, or to have granted people the privilege of acting as they liked. Living by the sweat of one's brow need not involve the exploitation of nature, as we have seen in connection with heavy ploughing in the seventh century.

Thus, as C. J. Glacken remarks about the belief in man's dominion expressed in Psalm 8, once the background of the Old Testament is understood, the words are much less amenable to being interpreted as arrogant than they may at first glance appear.[33] On the contrary, Glacken, unlike Passmore, is inclined to the conclusion that in the Bible man was 'a steward of God'.[34] In any case the evidence cited above makes it clear that the Old Testament cannot be reconciled with either the anthropocentric view that everything was made for mankind or the despotic view that people are free to treat nature and nonhuman creatures as they please. Moreover for the writers of the New Testament the Old Testament precisely constituted the Scriptures; any Old Testament tenet not explicitly superseded in the new dispensation was for them authoritative. (Admittedly Christians were released in the New Testament from subservience to the details of the Law of Leviticus and Deuteronomy: yet these books themselves continued to be cited as Scriptural.) Thus, short of clear indications to the contrary, the New Testament position will have been identical over the matters under discussion with that of the Old, a position incompatible with the arrogant one ascribed to Christianity by Passmore and others.

New Testament attitudes

In actual fact Jesus, as Passmore grants, stood in the Old Testament tradition when he taught that God cares for sparrows (Matthew 10:29, Luke 12:6). Here, and also when Jesus talked of 'the lilies of the field' (Matthew 7:28−30), the emphasis is on the greater value of people; yet the words chosen about the lilies suggest that God takes delight even in plants, and that their value is an independent one.

Consider the lilies of the field, how they grow; they toil not, neither do they spin: And yet I say unto you, That even Solomon in all his glory was not arrayed like one of these. Wherefore, if God so clothe the grass of the field, which to day is, and to morrow is cast into the oven, shall he not much more clothe you, o ye of little faith?[35]

Earlier (Mark 1:12f), Jesus spent 40 days in the wilderness in the company of wild beasts; and several times he asked his disciples to sail to the other side of the Lake of Galilee to have solitude and escape the multitude (Mark 4:35; 6:45; 8:13). These passages suggest that he regarded nature not only as a resource but also as an asylum and a source of renewal, just as the passage about the lilies suggests that he appreciated natural beauty.

As to the treatment of animals, Passmore believes that his concern was solely for the preservation of human property.

> . . . the other familiar Old Testament prohibitions (against cruelty to animals) . . . sometimes rest on the fact that asses and oxen were a valuable form of property, just as when Luke reports Jesus as asking the Jews 'Which of you shall have an ass or an ox fallen into a pit and will not straightway pull him out on the Sabbath day?'[36]

But this is to beg the question about Jesus' attitude to animals, and, come to that, about the attitude of the Old Testament writers also. The human interest in domestic animals was obviously one reason for protecting them, but it need not have been the only one. Indeed in the Parable of the Lost Sheep (Luke 15:4—7) the marginal benefit of retrieving the hundredth sheep was, all things considered, slight if not negative, but the shepherd still recovered the beast: and, though it is impermissible to argue unrestrictedly from the actors within a parable to the intention of the teller, yet in this case the explicit comparison of the shepherd's care for the sheep to God's loving concern for sinners suggests that we can take it that Jesus was endorsing the shepherd's attitude. Thus Jesus understood and sympathized with disinterested care of animals. Indeed the Johannine Jesus declares (John 10:11) that the good shepherd, by contrast with the hireling, actually lays down his life for the sheep (a passage which, whether historical or not, must have influenced its readers' attitudes to actual flocks as well as to the pastoral care of Christ for his followers).

The only evidence for his holding a despotic view consists in the narratives of his reported treatment of the Gadarene swine (Matthew 8:28—34; Mark 5:1—20; Luke 8:26—39) and of the barren fig-tree (Mark 11:13f, 20—4). Certainly these passages were later used, as by Augustine, as dominical authority for ruthlessness towards animals and plants.

Christ Himself shows that to refrain from the killing of animals and the destroying of plants is the height of superstition for, judging that there are no common rights between us and the beasts and trees, he sent the devils into a herd of swine and with a curse withered the tree on which he found no fruit.[37]

But this passage tells us more about Augustine (whose other views, however, belie his remarks here — see chapter 3) and his polemical powers in castigating his former associates, the Manichaeans, than they do about Jesus. It is peculiarly hard to know how to interpret passages relating nature-miracles; but in these two cases I commend the view of Stephen Clark about the pigs: 'I suspect that there is a parable lurking behind the trivia (who, after all, was keeping *pigs*?)'[38] In the case of the fig-tree, we actually have a version at Luke 13:6—9 of a parable which could easily have been transformed into the Markan narrative. (Similar changes of stories told by Jesus into stories about Jesus seem to be present between the Parable of Dives and Lazarus (Luke 16:19—31) and the raising of Lazarus (John 11:1—44), and between parables about wedding feasts, wedding guests and new wine (Matthew 22:1—14; 25:1—13; Mark 2:19—22) and the miracle performed at Cana in Galilee (John 2:1—11).) Similarly the symbolic significance of swine could well betoken a parable underlying the story about the pigs presented in the three synoptic gospels; which will, if so, have accidentally given the impression of dominical authority for attitudes which, for all that we can tell, Jesus himself would not have shared.

Where attitudes to nature are concerned, the New Testament departed from the Old over its eventual annulment of the distinction between clean and unclean animals (Acts 10, 11), and over its abolition of animal sacrifices in a passage (Hebrews 10:1—18) which speaks with evident distaste of the idea of sins being taken away by 'the blood of bulls and goats'. There is also Paul's stray question implying that God does not care for oxen (I Corinthians 9:10f). Yet when Paul was actually focusing his attention on the subject of nonhuman creatures, rather than delving for the symbolism behind Scriptural proverbs, he held that every creature was in travail awaiting release from decay and participation in the liberty of the sons of God (Romans 8:21f). Passmore indeed allows that Paul intends here that both human and nonhuman creatures are waiting on God,[39] and therefore can hardly ascribe to him nothing but an instrumental attitude to the nonhuman creation. Indeed in another epistle the whole of creation is presented as caught up in the drama of salvation (Colossians 1:15—20). The same broad vision, moreover, is present in Revelation, where the tree of life (22:2) symbolizes the final restoration of the original tree of life of Genesis 2:9, and with it a restoration of the original Garden.

These and other passages altogether preclude a despotic reading of the New Testament; nor is it defensible to hold that the New Testament view of the nonhuman creation was discontinuous (except momentarily) with that of the Old. Even if the stewardship of vineyards and the tending of flocks symbolizes in the New Testament care for the Church rather than for the earth, as Passmore maintains,[40] the benign understanding of nature required by the symbolism must have reinforced the gentle and responsible attitudes to nature which the Old Testament was known to urge.

Passmore for his part sums up the Christian attitude to nature as follows:[41]

What can properly be argued, however, is that Christianity encouraged certain special attitudes to nature: that it exists primarily as a resource rather than as something to be contemplated with enjoyment, that man has the *right* to use it as he will, that it is not sacred, that man's relationships with it are not governed by moral principles.

About the third of these attitudes (that nature is not sacred), and it alone, I should agree with Passmore's ascription, though even here it is appropriate to remark that all terrestrial and celestial bodies are said at I Corinthians 15:40 to have a glory of their own. The remaining attitudes are, as we have seen, foreign to the Christianity of the Bible. Genesis, the Book of Psalms, Job and the gospels bespeak an awareness of nature's beauty; and the awareness, present in both the Old and the New Testament, of the independent value of nonhuman creatures implies constraints upon the treatment of such creatures at least as far-reaching as those which the Old Testament makes explicit. Mankind's dominion is responsible to God, who regards all creation as very good (Genesis 1), and it is entirely mistaken to read into this recognition of the power with which human moral agents are entrusted an absence of moral constraints in its exercise. God is concerned in the Bible with the well-being of other creatures besides mankind (Psalm 104), and people accordingly have obligations to care for nature and not to subvert its integrity by subordinating it ruthlessly to their own purposes. Though the Bible does not set out these obligations in the form of principles, it nevertheless precludes the despotic and anthropocentric attitudes

which White and Passmore alike consider its most natural interpretation; indeed it may well be held to contain, explicitly or
implicitly, many of the ingredients necessary for a responsible
environmental ethic.

NOTES

1 Lynn White Jnr, 'The Historical Roots of our Ecological Crisis', in
   John Barr (ed.) *The Environmental Handbook,* 3—16, reprinted from
   Science, 155 (37), 10 March 1967, 1203—7.
2 Ibid. pp. 11f.
3 *MRN,* p. 5.
4 Aldo Leopold, *A Sand County Almanac with Other Essays on
   Conservation,* New York: Oxford University Press, (2nd edn) 1966,
   p. 238.
5 F. B. Welbourn, 'Man's Dominion', *Theology,* 78, November 1975,
   561—8, p. 561.
6 Ibid. p. 562.
7 Robin Attfield, *God and The Secular: A Philosophical Assessment of
   Secular Reasoning from Bacon to Kant,* Cardiff: University College
   Cardiff Press, 1978, chapter 1.
8 Stanley L. Jaki, *Science and Creation,* Edinburgh: Scottish Academic
   Press, 1974; Lynn White Jnr, *Medieval Technology and Social Change,*
   Oxford: Clarendon Press, 1962. See especially pp. 86, 130f.
9 White, *Medieval Technology,* p. 56. Similar sentences appear at p. 9
   of White's article in *The Environmental Handbook.*
10 At pp. 56f of White's book, replicated closely at p. 9 of his article.
11 But White's methods and findings have been severely criticized by
    R. H. Hilton and P. H. Sawyer in *Past and Present,* 24, April 1963,
    90—100.
12 *The Environmental Handbook,* pp. 10f.
13 Genesis 1:26.
14 Genesis 1:28.
15 *MRN,* p. 9. See further Ian G. Barbour, 'Attitudes Toward Nature and
    Technology', in Ian G. Barbour (ed.), *Earth Might Be Fair,* Englewood
    Cliffs, NJ: Prentice-Hall, 1972, 146—68.
16 *MRN,* p. 11.
17 *MRN,* p. 6.
18 Welbourn, 'Man's Dominion', p. 564.
19 *The Environmental Handbook,* p. 11.
20 Ibid. p. 12.
21 *MRN,* p. 14.
22 *MRN,* p. 16.
23 Thus C. J. Glacken, *Traces on the Rhodian Shore, Nature and Culture
    in Western Thought from Ancient Times to the End of the Eighteenth*

Century, Berkeley, LA and London: University of California Press, 1967, pp. 42—62. In the Preface to his first edition Passmore rightly praises Glacken's work as a 'vast storehouse of learning'.

24 Thus White, *The Environmental Handbook*, p. 16.

25 *MRN*, p. 17. Parallel qualifications are in place over Peter Singer's accounts of Hebrew and Christian views of man and the animals in chapter 5, 'Man's Dominion, a Short History of Speciesism', of his *Animal Liberation, A New Ethic for Our Treatment of Animals,* London: Jonathan Cape, 1976. See Robin Attfield, 'Western Traditions and Environmental Ethics', in Robert Elliot and Arran Gare, *Environmental Philosophy: A Collection of Readings,* St. Lucia: University of Queensland Press; Milton Keynes: Open University Press; University Park: Pennsylvania State University Press, 1983.

27 *MRN*, pp. 29f. At p. 185 he holds that its fullest implications were only first seen by Kant.

28 See Andrew Linzey, *Animal Rights: A Christian Assessment of Man's Treatment of Animals*, London: SCM Press, 1976, p. 15, where he cites the support of Claus Westermann, *Creation*, London: SPCK, 1974, p. 52.

29 Cited by Thomas Sieger Derr, *Ecology and Human Liberation,* p. 73.

30 Ibid. p. 70.

31 Cited by John Black, *Man's Dominion*, Edinburgh: Edinburgh University Press, 1970, p. 48.

32 *MRN*, p. 31. Cf. Westermann, *Creation,* p. 82, whose account I follow.

33 Glacken, *Traces on the Rhodian Shore*, p. 166. See also John Austin Baker, 'Biblical Attitudes to Nature', in Hugh Montefiore (ed.), *Man and Nature*, London: Collins, 1975, 87—109. See also James Barr, 'Man and Nature: The Ecological Controversy in the Old Testament', *Bulletin of the John Rylands Library,* 55, 1972, 9—32; my disagreements with parts of this article will be clear to its readers and mine.

34 Glacken, *Traces on the Rhodian Shore*, p. 168.

35 Matthew 7:28b—30 (Authorized Version). See further J. Donald Hughes, *Ecology in Ancient Civilizations*, Albuquerque: University of New Mexico Press, 1975.

36 Passmore, 'The Treatment of Animals', p. 196.

37 Quoted ibid. p. 197.

38 Stephen R. L. Clark, *The Moral Status of Animals*, Oxford: Clarendon Press, 1977, p. 196.

39 'The Treatment of Animals', p. 198.

40 *MRN*, p. 29.

41 *MRN*, p. 20.

3

The Tradition of Stewardship

It is worthwhile to investigate further whether the central religious and ethical tradition of our culture has been despotic or environmentally responsible. Even if the Bible is not despotic as to its writers' view of nature (as was argued in chapter 2), the teaching of its adherents could still have been so; and if it had been so, then the causes of our ecological problems would be easier to understand, and we should be obliged to depart from this teaching as radically as possible. If, however, as I shall argue in this chapter, the Judaeo-Christian tradition has historically stressed responsibility for nature, and that not only in the interest of human beings, and if its secular critics have often echoed this emphasis, then whatever the causes of the problems may be, our traditions offer resources which may, in refurbished form, allow us to cope with these problems without resorting to the dubious and implausible expedient of introducing a new environmental ethic.

Classical Christian attitudes

Christian attitudes to nature have in fact been much more diverse than their critics suppose. Thus the belief that everything was made for mankind was held by some Christians such as Origen, Peter Lombard, Aquinas and Calvin, but was expressly rejected by others such as Augustine, Descartes, John Ray, Linnaeus and William Paley, and by the Jewish philosopher Maimonides, and was implicitly rejected by many others, such as Alan of Lille, whose high view of nature was anything but an instrumental one.[1]

The Eastern Church, at any rate, seems to have adhered to a compassionate view of nonhuman species. Thus a prayer for animals of Basil the Great accepted, probably on the strength of Romans 8, that God had promised to save both man and beast. There is also the testimony of St Chrysostom, who in the fourth century wrote of the beasts as follows: 'Surely we ought to show them great kindness and gentleness for many reasons, but, above all, because they are of the same origin as ourselves',[2] and apparently regarded this as a requirement of justice.[3] There are many stories of saintly gentleness to animals, and it has been claimed that in Eastern Orthodoxy 'awareness of man's cosmic vision has never been lost to sight, has never ceased to be an integral part of man's redemption'.[4] Thus St Isaac the Syrian in the seventh century urged compassion for all creatures, and 'a heart which could not bear to see or hear any creature suffer hurt, or the slightest pain'.[5] The secular state too accepted (at least in theory) that there is a *jus naturae*, a law which nature has taught all animals, as well as a *jus gentium* which is peculiar to humans, by admitting this distinction of the third century jurist Ulpian into the *Institutes* of Justinian.[6] The recognition of motives such as self-defence and the care of the young as falling under the *jus naturae* suggests that animals were accorded some degree of moral acknowledgement, even if nothing as clear-cut as moral entitlements. Indeed John Rodman has contended that this understanding of the *jus naturae* tradition was widely accepted until it was redefined in a 'hominicentric' way by Hugo Grotius in *De Jure Belli ac Pacis* (1625).[7]

Even in the West, St Bonaventure wrote of St Francis: 'When he considered the origin of all things, he would be filled with overwhelming pity, and he called all creatures, no matter how lowly, by the name of brother or sister, because as far as he knew, they had sprung from the same original principle as himself.'[8] And Nicholas Arseniev has shown how echoes of Francis' cosmic vision persisted, at least among some of his early followers.[9] On the other hand the Stoic view that irrational creatures lack rights heavily influenced Origen, as Passmore has shown,[10] as also did the Stoic belief that nature exists only to serve mankind's interests. Passmore also finds this influence in the anti-Manichaean passage of Augustine already cited in chapter 2, where the view is ascribed to Christ that there are no moral ties between man and animals.[11] But Augustine also rejected the belief that nonhuman creatures have instrumental value only, and that everything was made to satisfy mankind's need or pleasure. Each creature, he held, has value in itself in the scale of creation.[12] Indeed, as I have argued much more fully elsewhere,[13] his position, seen in the round, was far from reflecting 'Greco-Christian arrogance'.

It is instructive, moreover, to trace two traditions depicted by

Passmore, the Stewardship tradition (involving the belief that people are entrusted with a duty to preserve the earth's beauty and fruitfulness) and the tradition of Cooperation with Nature (embodying the view that mankind should endeavour to develop and perfect the natural world in accordance with its potentials) — traditions of which Passmore discovers no trace between pagan antiquity and the seventeenth century. But in fact both views were held widely among Christians in the patristic period in both East and West. Thus, as Glacken points out, Basil's understanding of man as the furnisher and perfecter of creation was further stressed in the West by Ambrose and in the East by Theodoret;[14] and Augustine's praise of improvements to nature and his belief that man participates in God's work through sciences like agriculture as well as in the arts led to the deliberate application of this teaching in the monasteries of the Benedictine rule.[15] As to the belief that man's role is that of God's steward of creation, this view may also be found in the patristic period. Indeed Glacken locates it in *The Christian Topography* of the sixth century traveller, Cosmas Indicopleustes,[16] and implicitly in Basil, Ambrose and Theodoret. Moreover the belief that the land should be improved seems throughout the Middle Ages to have been taken for granted, without this preventing active measures to conserve the forests;[17] while Christian writers such as Albertus Magnus have long since given warnings against damaging the landscape.[18] There is strong evidence, then, against the claim made by Walter H. O'Briant that the Judaeo-Christian tradition regards man as 'apart from nature', and gives people a careless attitude towards the environment, being preoccupied with the salvation of the soul and unconcerned about a world which is not their true home.[19] Some strands of Christian teaching could have fostered such a view, but the underlying metaphysic can scarcely enjoin it, granted the concern to enhance natural beauty and fruitfulness shown by such a representative figure as Bernard of Clairvaux,[20] and the compassion for other creatures evinced by St Isaac the Syrian, one of those desert fathers often associated with the kind of other-worldliness which O'Briant deprecates.

But it is in the matter of the treatment of animals that the accusation that Christianity embodies a despotic view is most insistent. In this area Peter Singer, in *Animal Liberation* and other writings,[21] has supplemented the evidence adduced by Passmore and has drawn even blacker conclusions. I have argued elsewhere[22] that his charges of despotism and anthropocentrism conflict with a good deal of the evidence, though it must be granted that until the

Reformation there was no opposition to practices such as bull-fighting, and that even since then the Christian and other opponents of cruelty to animals have had an uphill struggle.[23] Christianity, however, abolished animal sacrifices,[24] and, though the spectacles of the arena involving contests between animals were not banned when gladiatorial contests were abolished, the continuing ban on attendance by Christians must have contributed to their disappearance in their ancient form.[25] At the same time in both East and West the veneration of the saints, associated in many cases with kindliness to animals, encouraged a gentle attitude,[26] an attitude evidenced also both in the prayers for sick animals in the medieval Roman liturgy[27] and in medieval bestiaries.[28]

Thus though nonhuman creatures were usually omitted in the West from the scheme of salvation, they were not omitted from the moral reckoning of the patristic and medieval period. (Indeed when, as occasionally, they were put on trial, too great a degree of responsibility was imputed.) Domestic animals, of course, continued to be used as beasts of burden, and cattle were still killed for food; but a case has to be made out before these practices are accepted as exploitative, as opposed to the abuses which sometimes accompany them. (Singer himself does not object to killing and replacing animals which lack self-consciousness.[29]) There again, Basil's prayer for 'the humble beasts who bear with us the heat and burden of the day'[30] suggests that beasts of burden were not always treated oppressively.

Thus in the patristic and medieval periods there was a widespread sense of responsibility for the care of the earth and for the completion of God's work of creation, together with an underlying sense that animals should be treated with kindliness and were of more than merely instrumental value. Aquinas, however, held an instrumentalist view of animals,[31] and taught that cruelty to animals is wrong mainly because of the adverse consequences upon the character of the perpetrator and the loss of property to their human owner.[32] Yet he allowed that irrational creatures 'can be loved from charity as good things we wish others to have, in that from charity we cherish them for God's honour and service. Thus does God love them from charity':[33] a sentiment sometimes taken to imply that we should love them, if not for themselves, then because God does. He also contended that Paul's question about whether God cares for oxen implies no more than that God has no regard for them as rational creatures, not that they fall outside the sphere of his providence.[34] Indeed he expects the just man to feel pity at their suffering, lest he should fail to feel compassion for fellow-men.[35]

   Such teaching at any rate allowed Scholastics in the seventeenth
century to maintain the reality of animals suffering against the
Cartesians;[36] it should also be remarked that some of Aquinas'
modern followers, such as Maritain and Journet,[37] have been able to
accept nonderivative duties to animals without abandoning his
overall metaphysical system. Though his doctrines have often
encouraged a despotic attitude to animals, they were not, in fact,
ineradicably despotic.

Early modern attitudes

It was, however, Calvin who explicitly resuscitated the New
Testament metaphor of Stewardship, which he applied both to a
person's possessions[38] and to the care of the earth as a whole,
decrying the 'plundering of the earth of what God has given it for
the nourishment of man' as frustrating God's goodness.[39] Calvin's
version of the Stewardship tradition was anthropocentric, but in the
next century Sir Matthew Hale (who was, according to Passmore,
one of the earliest Christian adherents of this ancient tradition)[40]
gave it an ampler interpretation, somewhat reminiscent of Chrysostom, Basil, Ambrose and Theodoret. Hale, in a notable and much-
quoted passage, concluded that 'the End of Man's Creation was,
that he should be [God's] Viceroy . . . Steward, *Villicus*, Bailiff, or
Farmer of this goodly farm of the lower World', and was endowed
with this 'dominion, trust and care' to restrain the fiercer animals,
defend the tame and useful ones, to conserve and cultivate plant
species, and 'to preserve the face of the Earth in beauty, usefulness
and fruitfulness'.[41] Passmore's comment on Hale's view that there is
such a duty is that it is not a typically Christian view, but embodies a
Pelagian emphasis on what can be accomplished by the human will,
an emphasis which plays down original sin.[42] Certainly Calvin
stressed original sin more than Hale, but he too stood in the
Stewardship tradition and acknowledged that man's dominion is
subject to moral limitations; and as to the claims about Pelagianism,
such a charge would make the patristic adherents of the Stewardship
view and of Cooperation with Nature Pelagians too, including even
Augustine![43] There was, in fact, considerable continuity between
such seventeenth-century advocates of stewardship and the further
adornment of creation as Hale and John Ray on the one hand,[44] and
the fathers and monastic communities of the early centuries of the
Church, as reviewed above, on the other. It should also be stressed
that Hale and Ray, like Basil and Chrysostom (and indeed

Augustine), but unlike Calvin, accepted the intrinsic value of nonhuman creatures.

Now Passmore ascribes the inauguration of a more actively despotic attitude to Francis Bacon and René Descartes, an approach on which, 'since everything on earth is for man's use, he is at liberty to modify it as he will'.[45] Undoubtedly both Bacon and Descartes advocated and pioneered new methods in the investigation of nature. But to what extent did they adhere to the attitude just mentioned, and to what extent did it become accepted as a legitimate Christian view in the period which followed?

Both Bacon and Descartes commended the systematic study of nature so as to improve the human lot.[46] Bacon in particular consciously reinterpreted the doctrine of dominion over nature, which he held to have been twice forfeited, once by Adam's fall and then again by a fall into ignorance. To some degree, he held, it could be recovered through a patient and humble investigation of nature. He opposed those versions of religion which held that natural causes should be treated as sacred and left uninvestigated, holding that God was honoured rather by their study than by wilful ignorance in the face of apparent mystery.[47] Moreover his emphasis was one of technological optimism:[48] 'Now the true and lawful goal of the sciences,' he wrote, 'is none other than this: that human life be endowed with new discoveries and powers.'[49] Indeed in a work of fiction he ascribes to the scientific community of New Atlantis the goal of increasing human power in every possible way.[50]

These passages raise, without answering, the question of whether Bacon simply favoured the alleviation of disease, poverty and famine, or commended uncompromising ruthlessness in the interests of any community equipped with power based on knowledge, at whatever cost to other humans and other creatures. There are certainly times at which he seems to approach the latter view, at any rate when he apparently endorsed the practice of experimenting on live animals in the interests of the progress of surgery.[51] Yet Bacon was also deeply concerned about the misguided uses to which knowledge might be put, and was adamant that neither contemporary nor future people should have to suffer as a result of its pursuit or its applications. Thus in the Dedicatory Epistle of *The Great Instauration* he wrote:

Lastly, I would address one general admonition to all — that they consider what are the true ends of knowledge, and that they seek it not either for pleasure of the mind, or for contention, or for superiority to others, or for profit, or fame, or power, or any of those inferior things, but for the benefit and use of life, and that they perfect and govern it in charity. For it was from lust of power that the angels fell, and from lust of knowledge that man fell; but of charity there can be no excess, neither did angel or man ever come in danger by it.[52]

These are not the words of an advocate of the belief that 'man is at liberty to modify everything on earth as he will'. Rather Bacon was in effect acknowledging constraints on acts which might harm either our fellows or our descendants, and on the kind of motives which have in actual fact prompted exploitation of man and nature.

Ethically, then, Bacon may well have had anthropocentrist leanings, but his opposition to uncharitableness towards people suggests that he could have endorsed Calvin's strictures on 'plundering the earth', though not, perhaps, the duty to preserve the beauty of nature, as well as its usefulness, as recognized and advocated by Hale. Only through the kind of misinterpretation which borders on wilfulness could Bacon be cited in justification of the employment of technology in the heedless pursuit of profit or sectional advantage.

It was, however, the aim of Descartes to 'find a practical philosophy by means of which, knowing the force and the action of fire, water, air, the stars, heavens and all other bodies which environ us, as distinctly as we know the different crafts of our artisans, we can in the same way employ them in all those uses to which they are adapted, and thus render ourselves the masters and possessors of nature.'[53] A despotic attitude is certainly implicit in this interpretation of dominion over nature, an attitude which becomes even more evident over his understanding of animals and other nonhuman species. For Descartes went so far as to maintain that nonhuman creatures lack conscious thought and can be regarded as automata.[54] He does not seem, as Passmore asserts, to have held that animals cannot feel:[55] 'I do not deny sensation, in so far as it depends on a bodily organ', he wrote. But the same passage concludes with a declaration that since animals lack thought, there can be no 'suspicion of crime when [people] eat or kill animals'.[56] Indeed Descartes and several of his followers practised vivisection in the course of their researches.

Yet Descartes held no brief for the unbridled pursuit of power or gain. Defending a decision to delay the publication of his findings, he wrote:

although it is true that each man is obliged to procure, as much as in him lies, the good of others, and that to be useful to nobody is popularly speaking to be worthless, it is at the same time true that our cares should extend further than the present time, and that it is good to set aside those things which may possibly be adapted to bring profit to the living, when we have in view the accomplishment of other ends which will bring much more advantage to our descendants.[57]

The benefits which Descartes hoped to confer on posterity were advances in medicine, which he saw as among the greatest benefits with which human life could be endowed; such pursuits justified the time spent on them much more than 'those which can only be useful to some by being harmful to others'.[58] In theory at least, then, Descartes would have opposed activities aimed at short-term gain which also undermined the life-support systems of our planet; though it may fairly be observed that he foresaw the dangers of science and technology less clearly than either the seventeenth-century critics of his mechanist view of nature were to do, or indeed than had been done by Francis Bacon. There again, Descartes' metaphysic, which will be further discussed in chapter 4, was undoubtedly unsuited to the resolution of ecological problems.

Passmore further contends that Descartes' system in no way depended on revelation, and plays down the traditional emphasis on human limitations and the need for humility: hence it could be inherited unreflectively by a post-Christian Europe and exported readily to non-Christian cultures elsewhere.[59] No doubt elements of his system have been pressed into service in this way; but Descartes himself stressed our dependence on revelation in theology in general and in particular in matters of our inability to discover God's purposes 'by the powers of the mind',[60] and of the requirement of humility to reflect on our faults and the feebleness of our nature.[61] These elements in his system, however, were discarded by some later mechanists who abandoned his theology, such as La Mettrie, D'Holbach and Diderot.[62] Thus Descartes' own remarks suggest that the duty to make the world a better place to live in belongs to a faith involving answerability to God: but it was comparatively easy for some of his followers to omit the traditionally Christian elements in his thought, and to stress his rationalism and his mechanism without the theological and moral constraints with which he tempered them. This is not to imply, however, that the attitude of the French Enlightenment was uniformly more ruthless than Descartes': thus such an advocate of science and a sceptic about revelation as

Voltaire could still reject the view that animals lack feelings and thought, and contend that animals' powers were God-given;[63] while other *philosophes* replaced duties to God with duties to posterity (see chapter 5).

Meanwhile in England the founders of the Royal Society, which received its charter in 1662, set out to employ the methods of Bacon's *Novum Organum* somewhat after the manner of the scientific community in his *New Atlantis.*[64] Their scientific method, like that which he advocated, was secular and autonomous, but they nevertheless perceived their enterprise as a religious duty whereby the Creator was glorified and his workmanship disclosed and published abroad.[65] They rejected the view that nature was 'venerable' and therefore not to be controlled, modified, or understood:[66] but the modifications of the natural environment which they favoured were moderate ones, such as the adornment of the countryside with fruitful fields, orchards and woods, as advocated by John Ray, who was a close associate of the Society's members.[67] Indeed in one of the earliest publications by a member after its foundation, *Silva, or a Discourse on Forest Trees*, John Evelyn warned his readers against excessive deforestation, and exhorted them to take seriously both the theory and the practice of silviculture, so that the nation would be deprived neither of the resources of the woods nor of their beauty. Evelyn, indeed, was concerned about the air of conurbations as well as about the preservation of the forests, and anticipated many later ecological writings in his *Fumifugium*, a study of atmospheric pollution in cities.[68] Accordingly at any rate the first generation of Baconian scientists would have rejected the view that 'man's relations with [nature] are not governed by moral principles'. (It should, however, be acknowledged that Evelyn also participated in experiments on living animals,[69] like several members of the Society.)

The subsequent period

The humanitarian movement, which successfully altered attitudes and practice in matters of slavery, punishment, working conditions and also the treatment of animals gathered strength in the following century, though there had been predecessors of its concern in matters of animal welfare such as Philip Stubbes (1583)[70] and the Massachusetts legislature (1641).[71] In these matters the movement was fostered in its early stages by Christian moralists such as Locke, Wollaston, Balguy and Hutcheson, and in general by Quakers,

Methodists and Evangelicals, as well as by sceptics such as Montaigne, Shaftesbury, Voltaire, Hume and Bentham.[72] Thus Passmore's view that theological doctrines retarded this movement, while sustained by some of the evidence, is in conflict with much of the rest: for the Christian humanitarians were motivated by a profound belief in Christian charity, and by their religious convictions in general, and not in spite of them.[73] Thus Alexander Pope wrote in 1713 about vivisection that 'The more entirely the inferior creation is submitted to our power the more answerable we should seem for our mismanagement of it.'[74] Further examples of Christians concerned to avoid harm to animals are the philosopher Gottfried Wilhelm Leibniz,[75] and the Anglican poet William Cowper,[76] who held that the true appreciation of nature was sullied by the detestable cruelty of blood-sports, from which he rescued a hare. Though the victory of humanitarianism is less than complete in matters of the treatment of animals, it has long been beyond dispute, both among religious believers and others, that it is wrong to treat nonhuman animals as nothing but means to human ends, and it has become a religious and secular commonplace that they should not be treated oppressively.[77]

It is becoming clear that whatever has caused our ecological problems, they cannot be set down to Judaeo-Christian attitudes to nature. This conclusion is further supported by the reasoning of Lewis W. Moncrief.[78] Moncrief holds that Lynn White is mistaken to regard the Judaeo-Christian tradition as causing an exploitative attitude to nature, at any rate directly, and stresses the cultural, technological and social forces which have more directly fostered this outlook. Thus he ascribes our ecological 'crisis' directly to urbanization, increased wealth, increased population and to the rise of the private ownership of resources; and these factors in turn are set down to capitalism (with science and technology in attendance) and the growth of democracy. The connection between all this and the Judaeo-Christian tradition is at most that this tradition may have encouraged capitalism and democracy: but the empirical evidence for this link, Moncrief holds, is slender. (It should be observed that, as Moncrief has in mind democracy in a property-owning form, the link for which he believes the evidence to be wanting would have to be between the Judaeo-Christian tradition and capitalism; even if this tradition fosters democratic self-management, as in some of its forms it undoubtedly does, the link here is irrelevant unless the tradition supports capitalism too.) To this critique of White's position William Coleman has responded by maintaining that the theologian and scientist William Derham, and the apologetic tradition to which he belonged, supply just the empirical evidence which Moncrief believes to be required and missing.[79] Derham, he alleges, gave the blessing of Christianity both to capitalistic enterprise and to science-based technology, and thus White's claims are vindicated, albeit in connection with the period just after 1700, and not with the medieval technology of a millennium earlier.

But, as Coleman admits, other Christians of the period were outspoken in their condemnation of avarice, and Isaac Barrow, Newton's mentor, wrote that, though man could and should use God's terrestrial gifts, he should do so only to meet his daily needs, and under no circumstances so monopolize them as to hinder the satisfaction of the needs of others.[80] Nor do Christian writers of the decades following, such as Swift, retract the traditional strictures on greed and self-aggrandizement. Indeed, as I have argued in 'Christian Attitudes to Nature', Coleman exaggerates both the extent of Derham's blessing on capitalism and its influence. There was no question of 'a divine command to steel ourselves for a ruthless assault upon nature',[81] though there was a somewhat uncritical extension of the legitimate areas of stewardship to all the various callings, trade and war included (and with no qualification about the slave-trade), which contemporary society regarded as respectable. Yet the evidence proffered by Coleman for the link, doubted by Moncrief, between Christianity and untrammelled capitalism, remains too scanty to sustain Coleman's reapplication of White's thesis to the early modern period. Additional evidence, it may be thought, is supplied by Locke's second *Treatise of Civil Government*, with its justification of private property and enclosures; yet even Locke's justification embodied significant constraints, sufficient severely to limit the pursuit of economic growth if they were to be put into effect at the present time. (These constraints are discussed further in chapter 6.)

The actual attitude of the churches, or at least of the Church of England, to the new capitalism may, as R. H. Tawney held,[82] have been one of resignation verging on indifference. Coleman, who maintains, as against this view, that Derham's position was in fact symptomatic of an attitude of actual favour, has not sufficiently made out his case. Indeed the areas to which Christian social teaching was applied at this time seem to have contracted in some quarters to those of individual piety and the prevention of social disorder, though the Evangelicals, Quakers and Methodists upheld the lively concern of their Puritan forebears for social justice (as related above). Undoubtedly there was an insufficient condemnation of the greed and injustice implicit in the excesses of the new capitalism, and an insufficient advocacy of community and fraternity. Yet the awareness of answerability to God was not lost; indeed it was widely appealed to in the nineteenth century by humanitarians and by Christian Socialists. It has also been applied more recently to ecological problems in such works as the 1974 Report of the Doctrine Commission of the Church of England, published in Hugh Montefiore's *Man and Nature*[83] alongside a number of essays in which responsibility for the care of nature is the common theme.

Thus there has been a strong tradition in Europe and lands of European settlement, a tradition of Judaeo-Christian origins but not confined to adherents of Judaism and Christianity, of belief that people are the stewards of the earth, and responsible for its conservation, for its lasting improvement, and also for the care of our fellow-creatures, its nonhuman inhabitants. This tradition, far from being merely modern, has been a continuous one, at any rate among Christians, from the Bible, via Basil, Chrysostom, Ambrose, Theodoret and Bernard of Clairvaux, to Calvin, Hale and Ray and to modern writers like Black and Montefiore. And, though some of its adherents, such as Calvin, have regarded nonhuman creatures as of instrumental value only, or, like the Puritan Philip Stubbes and the Catholic Cardinal Manning, as meriting our care simply because they are loved by God,[84] it has more usually been held that cruelty and injustice in their regard are wrong in themselves, and that these creatures are of intrinsic value, this being, perhaps, the reason for God's love. Variants of this tradition, indeed, have at most times played a leading role in our culture. Accordingly, as Val Routley recognizes,[85] the Stewardship tradition is not confined to human interests, but is concerned with much else besides; indeed the same holds good of the related tradition of Cooperation with Nature (see above), the variant of the Stewardship tradition in which human agents have the role of perfecting the created order by enhancing its beauty and actively conserving and improving its fertility on a sustainable basis.

These traditions, taken together, are at least as representative of Christian history as any despotic view, and may well be considered to offer materials from which an environmental ethic equal to our current problems can be elicited, without the need for the introduction of a new ethic to govern our transactions with nature. Indeed in our existing moral thought and traditions (whether religious or secular) the roots may be found from which, with the help of the findings of ecological science, a tenable environmental ethic can grow.

NOTES

1 On Maimonides, Aquinas, Calvin and Descartes, see *MRN*, pp. 12, 113, 13 and 20; on Peter Lombard, see Passmore, 'Attitudes to Nature', p. 253; on Augustine, Alan of Lille, Linnaeus and Paley, see Glacken, *Traces on the Rhodian Shore*, pp. 198, 216—18 and 424. On Origen see Glacken, pp. 185f, and *MRN*, p. 16; on Ray see Glacken, p. 424 and *MRN*, pp. 21f.

2 C. W. Hume, *The Status of Animals in the Christian Religion,* London: Universities Federation for Animal Welfare, 1957, p. 26, cited by Andrew Linzey, *Animal Rights: A Christian Assessment of Man's Treatment of Animals,* London: SCM Press, 1976, p. 103, n. 22.

3 Thus he declared that 'Even in the case of creatures which lack reason and perception men ought not to deviate from the considerations of what is just and unjust.' This quotation, from Grotius' *De Jure Belli ac Pacis,* I:I:xi, is cited by John Rodman, 'Animal Justice: The Counter-revolution in Natural Right and Law', *Inquiry,* 22, 1979, 3—22, p. 8.

4 A. M. Allchin, *Wholeness and Transfiguration Illustrated in the Lives of St Francis of Assisi and St Seraphim of Sarov,* Oxford: SLG Press, 1974, p. 5; quoted by Linzey, *Animal Rights,* p. 103, n. 22.

5 Nicholas Arseniev, *Mysticism and the Eastern Church* (1925), trans. Arthur Chambers, London and Oxford: Mowbray, 1979, cites this passage at p. 88.

6 Rodman, 'Animal Justice', p. 3.

7 Ibid. pp. 3, 10 and 20, n. 2.

8 Otto Karrer (ed.), *St Francis of Assisi, The Legends and the Lauds,* trans. N. Wydenbruck, London: Sheed & Ward, 1977, at p. 161; a passage cited by Linzey, *Animal Rights,* p. 103, n. 22.

9 Arseniev, *Mysticism and the Eastern Church,* p. 102.

10 *MRN*, p. 16.

11 *MRN*, pp. 111f; 'The Treatment of Animals', p. 197.

12 Glacken, *Traces on the Rhodian Shore,* p. 198.

13 Robin Attfield, 'Christian Attitudes to Nature', *Journal of the History of Ideas,* 44, 1983.

14 Glacken, *Traces on the Rhodian Shore,* pp. 192, 299, 300.

15 Glacken, *Traces on the Rhodian Shore,* pp. 200, 299f., 304—6. On the Benedictine attitude to nature, see ibid., pp. 302—4, and Robert Nisbet, *The Social Philosophers,* London: Heinemann, 1974, pp. 326—8, esp. 327, and 334. See also René Dubos, 'Franciscan Conservation and Benedictine Stewardship', in David and Eileen Spring

(eds), *Ecology and Religion in History,* New York, Evanston, San Francisco and London: Harper & Row, 1974, 114—36.

16 Glacken, *Traces on the Rhodian Shore,* pp. 300f.

17 Ibid. pp. 313—46.

18 Ibid. p. 315.

19 Walter H. O'Briant, 'Man, Nature and the History of Philosophy', in William T. Blackstone (ed.) *Philosophy and Environmental Crisis,* Athens: University of Georgia Press, 1974, 79—89.

20 Glacken, *Traces on the Rhodian Shore,* pp. 213f; Dubos, 'Franciscan Conservation and Benedictine Stewardship', p. 133.

21 Peter Singer, *Animal Liberation, A New Ethic for Our Treatment of Animals,* London: Jonathan Cape, 1976, chapter 5, 'Man's Dominion, a Short History of Speciesism', pp. 202—34; see also his *Practical Ethics,* Cambridge: Cambridge University Press, 1979, p. 77, and his 'Not for Humans Only: The Place of Nonhumans in Environmental Issues', in K. E. Goodpaster and K. M. Sayre (eds), *Ethics and Problems of the 21st Century,* Notre Dame and London: Notre Dame University Press, 1979, 191—206, pp. 192f.

22 Robin Attfield, 'Western Traditions and Environmental Ethics'; in Robert Elliot and Arran Gare (eds), *Environmental Philosophy: A Collection of Readings,* St. Lucia: University of Queensland Press; Milton Keynes: Open University Press; University Park: Pennsylvania State University Press, 1983.

23 The story is told in E. S. Turner, *All Heaven in a Rage,* London: Michael Joseph, 1964.

24 Eusebius, 'Oration in Honour of Constantine on the Thirtieth Anniversary of his Reign', 2, in Maurice Wiles and Mark Santer (eds), *Documents in Early Christian Thought,* Cambridge: Cambridge University Press, 1975, p. 232.

25 H. H. Milman, *The History of Christianity from the Birth of Christ to the Abolition of Paganism in the Roman Empire* (3 Vols.), London: John Murray, 1840, Vol. 3, p. 460.

26 Glacken, *Traces on the Rhodian Shore,* pp. 309—11; also W. E. H. Lecky, *History of European Morals from Augustus to Charlemagne* (1869), London: Longmans, Green, 1913, Vol. II, p. 171.

27 C. W. Hume, *The Status of Animals in the Christian Religion,* pp. 94—8.

28 T. H. White (trans. and ed.), *The Book of Beasts,* London: Jonathan Cape, 1954, especially the Appendix, p. 247; cited by A. R. Peacocke, *Creation and the World of Science,* Oxford: Oxford University Press, 1979, p. 278.

29 'Killing Humans and Killing Animals', *Inquiry,* 22, 1979, 145—56, pp. 152f; *Practical Ethics,* p. 104.

30 John Passmore, 'The Treatment of Animals', *Journal of the History of Ideas,* 36, 1975, 195—218, p. 198.

31 Thomas Aquinas, *Summa Contra Gentiles,* trans. Anton Pegis *et al.,* (5

Vols.), Garden City, NY: Image Books, 1955—57, III:II:112(1).

32 Ibid., III:II:113. In 'Western Traditions and Environmental Ethics', I have argued that this summary of Aquinas' position may be an incomplete one (see n. 47 there).

33 *Summa Theologiae,* (60 Vols.), London: Eyre and Spottiswoode, and New York: McGraw-Hill, 1964, 2:2, q. 25, a3.

34 *Summa Theologiae,* 1, q. 103, a5, ad2. See further 'Western Traditions and Environmental Ethics', section I.

35 *Summa Theologiae,* 2:1:102, a6, ad8.

36 Pierre Bayle, 'Rorarius', in *Historical and Critical Dictionary* (1697), trans. and ed. Richard H. Popkin, Indianapolis and New York: Bobbs-Merrill, 1965, 213—54, pp. 221—31.

37 Passmore, 'The Treatment of Animals', p. 206, and n. 43 there.

38 'Let every one regard himself as the steward of God in all things which he possesses': John Calvin, *Commentary* on Genesis 2:15; quoted, from a translation of 1847, by F. B. Welbourn at 'Man's Dominion', *Theology,* 78, 1975, 561—8, p. 563.

39 A passage cited by André Bieler, *La Pensée economique et sociale de Calvin,* Geneva: Georg, 1959, at pp. 432—35, and translated by Thomas Sieger Derr in *Ecology and Human Liberation,* Geneva: WSCF Books, 1973, p. 20.

40 *MRN,* pp. 29—31, 185.

41 Sir Matthew Hale, *The Primitive Origination of Mankind,* London, 1677, cited by Glacken, *Traces on the Rhodian Shore,* p. 481, by Black, *Man's Dominion,* pp. 56f, and by Passmore at *MRN,* p. 30.

42 *MRN,* pp. 30f.

43 See sections III and IV of 'Christian Attitudes to Nature'.

44 See John Ray, *The Wisdom of God Manifested in the Works of Creation,* London, 11th edn, 1743, 164f; a passage cited by Glacken *Traces on the Rhodian Shore,* p. 484, by Coleman 'Providence, Capitalism and Environmental Degradation', p. 31, and in section IV of 'Christian Attitudes to Nature'.

45 *MRN,* p. 17.

46 Both philosophers are discussed in much greater detail in chapter 1 of Robin Attfield, *God and The Secular,* Cardiff: University College Cardiff Press, 1978. Passmore discusses them in *MRN,* pp. 18—21.

47 Thus *Novum Organum* I:89. See *The New Organon,* ed. Fulton H. Anderson, Indianapolis and New York: Bobbs-Merrill, 1960, pp. 87—9.

48 *MRN,* p. 19.

49 *Novum Organum,* I:81.

50 *The New Atlantis,* in Francis Bacon, *The Advancement of Learning and the New Atlantis,* ed. Arthur Johnston, Oxford: Clarendon Press, 1974, p. 239.

51 Ibid. p. 241 (from *The New Atlantis*).

52 In *The New Organon,* pp. 15f.

53 René Descartes, *Discourse on Method*, Part VI, from Elizabeth S. Haldane and G. R. T. Ross (trans.), *The Philosophical Works of Descartes*, Cambridge: Cambridge University Press, 1967, Vol. I, p. 119.
54 The passages of Descartes on these topics are conveniently gathered together in Tom Regan and Peter Singer (eds), *Animal Rights and Human Obligations*, Englewood Cliffs, NJ: Prentice-Hall, 1976, pp. 60—6.
55 'The Treatment of Animals', p. 204.
56 Regan and Singer, *Animal Rights and Human Obligations*, p. 66.
57 Haldane and Ross, *The Philosophical Works of Descartes*, Vol. I, p. 122; from *Discourse on Method*, Part VI.
58 Ibid. p. 130; from *Discourse on Method*, Part VI.
59 *MRN*, p. 21.
60 Haldane and Ross, *The Philosophical Works of Descartes*, Vol. I, p. 271; *Principles of Philosophy*, Third Part, Principles I—III. On Descartes on revelation, see 'God and Nature in the Philosophy of Descartes' by David C. Goodman, in *Towards a Mechanistic Philosophy*, Milton Keynes: Open University Press, 1974, 5—43, pp. 13f.
61 Haldane and Ross, *The Philosophical Works of Descartes*, Vol. I, p. 402: *The Passions of the Soul*, Article CLV.
62 See 'The Enlightenment: Deists and 'Rationalists'', by David C. Goodman, in *Scientific Progress and Religious Dissent*, Milton Keynes: Open University Press, 1974, 33—68, pp. 49—52, 60—6. Rodman ('Animal Justice', p. 9) represents La Mettrie as standing in the *jus naturae* tradition against those like Grotius and Püfendorf who played down the similarities between the behaviour of humans and animals. But La Mettrie in fact contended that humans, animals and indeed plants are all alike because they are all machines. Even his book *Les Animaux plus que machines* (La Haye, 1751) was intended to show that humans have souls, and are non-mechanical, *no more than animals*.
63 From his entry 'Animals' in *Philosophical Dictionary*; presented in translation by Regan and Singer, *Animal Rights and Human Obligations*, pp. 67f.
64 See Margery Purver, *The Royal Society: Concept and Creation*, London: Routledge & Kegan Paul, 1967.
65 Thus Robert Boyle entitled one of his works *The Christian Virtuoso* (London, 1690).
66 *MRN*, p. 11; see also Attfield, *God and The Secular*, chapter 1.
67 See the passage cited in n. 44 (above), which echoes some of the words of Basil's *Hexaemeron*. On William Coleman's treatment of Ray, see 'Christian Attitudes to Nature', section IV.
68 Glacken, *Traces on the Rhodian Shore*, pp. 485—94.

69   Turner, *All Heaven in a Rage,* p. 46.
70   Ibid. p. 35.
71   Lawrence Stone, *The Family, Sex and Marriage in England, 1500–1800,* London: Weidenfeld & Nicolson, 1977, p. 237.
72   On Locke, see Robert S. Brumbaugh, 'Of Man, Animals and Morals: A Brief History', in Richard Knowles Morris and Michael W. Fox (eds), *On the Fifth Day, Animal Rights and Human Ethics,* Washington DC: Acropolis Books, 1978, 6–25, pp. 17 and 25, n. 4. On Wollaston, Balguy and Hutcheson (Christians all) see 'The Treatment of Animals', p. 209, which mentions efforts by Evangelicals at pp. 209–11. For Quakers cf. John Woolman's statement of 1772 in *Christian Faith and Practice in the Experience of the Society of Friends,* London: London Yearly Meeting of the Society of Friends, 1960, para. 478. On Methodists, see Turner, *All Heaven in a Rage,* p. 50. On Montaigne, Hume and Bentham, see 'The Treatment of Animals', pp. 208ff and 211. Shaftesbury is mentioned by Norman S. Fiering, 'Irresistible Compassion: An Aspect of Eighteenth Century Humanitarianism', *Journal of the History of Ideas,* 37, 1976, 195–218, p. 202, and Voltaire in *Animal Liberation,* p. 220.
73   Cf. the couplet from a hymn of Isaac Watts (1674–1748), an Independent, 'Creatures as numerous as they be/Are subject to Thy care;' in *The Baptist Hymn Book,* London: Psalms and Hymns Trust, 1962, hymn 58. (Parts of the present paragraph appear also in 'Western Traditions and Environmental Ethics'.)
74   Turner, *All Heaven in a Rage,* p. 48.
75   See the story of Leibniz's concern for a tiny worm which he had been observing, as related by Immanuel Kant, *Lectures on Ethics,* trans. Louis Infield, New York: Harper & Row, 1963, pp. 239–41.
76   William Cowper, *The Task,* Ilkley and London: Scolar Press, 1973, Book III, pp. 106–9.
77   Turner, *All Heaven in a Rage,* pp. 114, 120, 151, 161.
78   Lewis W. Moncrief, 'The Cultural Basis for our Environmental Crisis', *Science,* 170, 508–12; reprinted in *Ecology and Religion in History,* 76–90.
79   William Coleman, 'Providence, Capitalism and Environmental Degradation', *Journal of the History of Ideas,* 37, 1976, 27–44, p. 37.
80   Ibid. p. 38.
81   Ibid. p. 35.
82   Ibid. p. 28.
83   Hugh Montefiore (ed.), *Man and Nature,* London: Collins, 1975.
84   Turner, *All Heaven in a Rage,* pp. 35, 165.
85   Val Routley, Critical Notice of *Man's Responsibility for Nature, Australasian Journal of Philosophy,* 53, 1975, 171–85, p. 174.

4

Nature and the Place of Man

From what we have seen so far, our moral traditions already embody an ethic on which humans are the stewards and guardians of nature, an ethic which derives from the Judaeo-Christian tradition and is apparently well-suited to our current ecological problems. But it remains appropriate to enquire whether our underlying view of reality and our traditional interpretations of the scheme of things are sufficiently suited to our problems, or whether, as a number of writers have maintained, we need a new way of regarding mankind and the world, or, in other words, a new metaphysics. Latterly John Passmore has claimed that the elaboration of a new metaphysics suited to environmental problems is 'the most important task which lies ahead of philosophy';[1] John Rodman has urged a holistic ethic based on 'the nature of things';[2] Henryk Skolimowski has advocated, as the counterpart of the ecological humanism which he commends, an evolutionary cosmology which gives rise to an ethic of reverence for life;[3] and, as we have seen in chapter 3, Walter H. O'Briant has criticized the 'religious' view of 'man apart from nature' in favour of a more organic view of the universe, mankind included. To what extent, it should be asked, should our traditional metaphysics be rejected or revised, and what range of metaphysical positions can prove equal to current insights and problems?

No comprehensive treatment of these issues can be attempted here; yet it is worthwhile to stand back so as to make sure, if possible, that the principles of value and obligation presented in other chapters are not vitiated by adherence to a fundamentally inappropriate metaphysics. I shall first investigate O'Briant's critique; this will involve a brief historical survey of Judaeo-Christian metaphysical positions. I shall then consider which metaphysical views satisfy the requirements of evolutionary theory, ecological science and belief in the intrinsic value of forms of nonhuman as well as human life.

Theistic anthropology

In his essay 'Man, Nature and the History of Philosophy',[4] O'Briant depicts two views of man and nature in our culture, the religious view of 'man *apart from* nature' and the scientific view of 'man *a part of* nature'. In the Judaeo-Christian tradition man alone is made in the image of God and alone has a rational soul, something which sets him apart from all other creatures. Man has dominion over the other creatures, according to O'Briant's interpretation, in the sense that they 'were put here by the Creator for man's use and enjoyment'.[5] Though his body is material his soul is immaterial and incorruptible: in this tradition man is sometimes regarded as comprising a union of body and soul, and sometimes as consisting in the soul alone, a supernatural being temporarily imprisoned in a natural body.

On the scientific view, by contrast, man differs from the other animals not in kind but in degree. He is an animal among his fellow animals, and has no dominion over them except insofar as his intelligence makes him their effective superior. As an animal he is mortal, and made of matter like everything else, for there is no soul and no Creator, nor anything else which cannot be investigated empirically. Indeed there may be nothing more distinctive about man than the relative absence of body hair.

The religious view, O'Briant believes, is in need of radical reform. As we have seen, he believes that its preoccupation with the salvation of the immortal soul has issued in the view that the natural world is not our home, and indeed that 'our animal nature is vile and contemptible':[6] also it involves a 'careless attitude' toward the environment. The connection is that religious beliefs about salvation make people see themselves as exempt from the consequences of past misbehaviour, and not ultimately a part of the world at all. So people have felt 'comfortable in raping and pillaging this earthly abode'.[7] Not that O'Briant commends the 'scientific view' which he describes, with its empiricism, its mechanism and its scepticism about values; rather he favours the ontology of philosophers such as Leibniz who refuse to admit a radical distinction between the living and the nonliving. But he is clear that our religion and our metaphysics need revision, as well as our ethics, if we are to solve the problems affecting ourselves and our environment.[8]

O'Briant's characterization of the scientific view will not be discussed here. Many different metaphysical and ethical views have, in fact, been held by scientists; for my own part I have attempted elsewhere[9] to set out the logic of the relations between theism and empirical science, and in chapter 5 I shall return to the bearing upon ecological matters of belief in technological progress. As to our religious tradition, I shall here assume, on the strength of the preceding chapters, that the Bible does not take the dominion of man to imply that all other creatures were made solely for man's use and enjoyment, and that Jews and Christians have not standardly construed it in this sense. I shall also assume that as Leibniz, whose metaphysics O'Briant favours, believed both in God as creator and in the immortality of the soul, not all those holding such beliefs are thought to hold exploitative attitudes or to suffer from metaphysical arrogance.

In connection with O'Briant's account of the 'religious view' it should next be remarked that belief in the immortality of the soul is not, in general,[10] a biblical belief — nor a centrally Christian one, Leibniz notwithstanding. Prior to the latest stages of its composition (e.g. Job 19:25−27, 2 Maccabees 7:23, 28f), the writers of the Old Testament did not believe in personal survival of death, and the passages about man's creation in God's image must be interpreted otherwise. The author of Ecclesiastes could even claim that 'a man hath no pre-eminence above a beast' as man and beast die alike, and alike return to their native dust.[11] (On this passage Black[12] comments that the very biblical elements which it has been most difficult to assimilate into orthodox Christianity may have a peculiar appeal in the twentieth century: be this as it may, the passage is a striking affirmation of human kinship with the beasts.) The New Testament writers, for their part, affirm a belief in eternal life and in the resurrection of the body, rather than in a soul possessed of natural immortality: and so does the 'Apostles' Creed'. Even Paul's distinction between flesh and spirit concerns not, as has often been supposed, different elements of a person or even different sets of desires, but rather two opposed ways of life, one in accordance with God's will and the other heedless of it.[13] In general the Bible does not take a radical dualist view of man as composed of a separable body and soul; rather the soul is what gives life to a body, though 'soul' is sometimes metaphorically used of the quality of a person's moral or spiritual life.[14]

Belief in a separable and naturally immortal soul entered Christianity rather from Platonism, but the ideas of Platonizing

Christians such as Origen had to compete not only with the Hebraic view but also with that of Aristotle on which the soul is the form of the body.[15] Indeed the Christological controversies of the fourth and fifth centuries can be regarded as a struggle between the Platonizing tradition of Alexandria, in which the Word constituted the soul of Christ, and the more Aristotelian view of the Antiochenes, on which Christ's body was informed by a human soul, without which he could not have been a man. On this view it was with a complete human, and not just a body, that the Word was united.[16] At this stage, though all Christians believed in life after death, not all took this qualitatively to differentiate mankind from the beasts, as we have seen over Basil the Great, Chrysostom and Francis in chapter 3.[17]

In more recent centuries the single most influential view has been that of Aquinas.[18] As an Aristotelian, Aquinas held that plants have vegetative souls and animals sensitive souls, but contrasted with these the rational soul of man which, as it can operate without reliance on bodily organs, can exist independently of the body. But a disembodied soul is not a person, and is confined to the powers of intellect, will and memory. A soul is properly the form of a body, and there can be no human life without either body or soul. A man is not, as Plato held, a soul using a body, nor is a body a substance in its own right, for without a soul it perishes. Rather a man is an ensouled body; and human life can only be restored after death if God resurrects a body for the disembodied soul to inform.

These views allowed Aquinas to acknowledge that man is generically akin to the animals, even though specifically different. His actual attitudes to animals have been explored already in chapter 3: it remains only to observe that his instrumentalist view was not required by his beliefs either about the human soul or about the bodily and sensitive nature which men and animals share. Indeed O'Briant seems right to exempt versions of Christianity on which people are, like other animals, essentially composed of the union of a body and a soul from the charge of contempt for animals and for our animal nature. The Thomist metaphysic, indeed, does not require the despotic attitude to animals held by Aquinas himself; and as to human nature (and the nature of creatures in general) Aquinas believed that God's providential activity does not overthrow or destroy it, but preserves it with a view to its perfection.[19]

Nevertheless Christians have at times thought of man as nothing but a soul. Such seems to have been the view of the heretical Christian, Origen, who believed that souls were fallen angels, punished by being made to inhabit mortal bodies;[20] these beliefs, however, were not readily accepted in face of the common belief of Christians that God had taken on flesh for the sake of man's salvation without being defiled thereby. Nor, as we have seen in chapter 3, did the efforts of Eastern monasticism to mortify the flesh issue invariably in contempt for nature.

The belief that man survives death as a soul, albeit as a soul which in life is closely attached to the body, exercised a widespread impact, not least among Christians, through the advocacy of Descartes, in whom O'Briant finds an alternation between the 'religious' and the 'scientific' view.[21] Descartes regarded bodies, both human and animal, as mechanisms; but construed the subject of reason and will as an immaterial substance, which was not subject to dissolution at death, and in which human immortality was located. Unlike Aquinas, Descartes derived the soul's immortality from its immaterial nature; and in this he was followed by many writers such as Samuel Clarke and Richard Price[22] who saw no other way of reconciling Christian beliefs about life after death with science.

Descartes' dualism and his view of animals as automata lead, as we have seen, to an insensitivity towards beasts. But it did not in his own case engender otherworldliness or irresponsibility in moral matters. Nevertheless it was prone to produce in some of his philosophical heirs a disparagement of the body and of the joys of this life, as sometimes in that in many ways enlightened figure, Richard Price.[23] In a period when the doctrine of the natural goodness of creation often went understressed, the Cartesian distinction between mind and matter must at times, as O'Briant implies, have led to a sense that man was not truly at home on earth, and that as far as his true interests were concerned the natural order was as dispensable as his natural body. Indeed, as William Blackstone has written, 'There is no room for an ecological ethic within the Cartesian metaphysic.'[24]

Doubts should be expressed, though, about whether these attitudes have actually led to improper exploitation of the environment (if this can be considered separately from the matter of the treatment of animals). The link suspected by O'Briant is that if salvation is in another world and God's forgiveness exempts people from the consequences of their sins, then these consequences can be disregarded. This criticism of Christianity as 'antinomian' is an age-old one, and has at other times been focused on sayings such as Augustine's 'Love and do as you like'. Yet with negligible exceptions Christianity has always stressed the need for sanctification or moral development, whether this was seen as desirable for the sake of fellow-creatures or as evidence of the repentance which God required as a condition of salvation. As I have allowed in chapter 3, other-worldliness has sometimes led to a narrowing of Christian social teaching; but it is doubtful if, beyond that, a careless attitude to nature has been engendered.

Further metaphysical options

Yet O'Briant is right in stressing the problems for humans about their own identity which arise from Cartesian dualism, and in holding that beliefs such as the denial of our kinship with creatures of other species are prone to vitiate our practice. In the last century it has been the Darwinian theory of evolution by natural selection which has undermined this denial; but it is important to realize that not all Christians have endorsed Descartes' radical dualism, and that its rejection is not the rejection of our religious tradition as a whole. Thus John Locke held that, for all we know, that which thinks in us may be material, and that God may add to matter the power of thought, just as he adds that of vegetation to peach-trees, and of sense and spontaneous motion to elephants.[25] Indeed Locke employed the status of animals as an argument against dualism. For it seems arbitrary either to hold that animals are bare machines without sensation or to hold that, despite their lack of intellectual and moral capacities, they have immaterial substantial souls, the solution preferred by Cudworth.[26] But if the remaining alternative, that matter can feel, is adopted, then it is arbitrary to deny that matter can think.[27]

A few years later, the scientist, philosopher and theologian, Joseph Priestley put forward the view that humans are systems of matter. Like Locke, Priestley was aware that the Bible teaches the resurrection of the body rather than the immortality of the soul, and Priestley added the claim that belief in an immaterial soul was a perversion of Christianity introduced from Greek philosophy.[28] Price replied that belief in an immaterial soul was indispensable for Christianity and for any account of consciousness; and he subjected Priestley's theory to searching objections, as had Clarke the somewhat cruder theory of Locke's materialist follower, Anthony Collins.[29] Nevertheless it does not seem impossible to reconcile Priestley's position with ordinary understandings of personal identity, or with the belief in the resurrection of a former person with identity intact. Thus the Christian tradition itself includes at least two alternatives to the dualism of mind and matter which O'Briant and Blackstone see as harmful, Priestleian materialism, and also the older view of Aquinas.

Blackstone, indeed, suggests that 'a metaphysic suitable as a companion to a genuine environmental ethic' may be found in Aristotle, Spinoza or Aquinas;[30] while the alternatives considered by O'Briant are the metaphysical systems of Spinoza and Leibniz. But Spinoza's necessitarianism and belief that there is only one substance, all truths about which follow from its nature, seem to underrate the activity and spontaneity both of people and of animals; and in fact, as Passmore points out in 'The Treatment of Animals', Spinoza held attitudes to nonhuman creatures which were exploitative in no small measure. 'I do not deny that beasts feel,' he wrote, 'but I deny that on that account we should not consult our necessity and use them as much as we wish and treat them as we will, since they do not agree with us in nature, and their emotions are in nature different from human emotions.'[31] Even if Spinoza's system were purged of these attitudes, its necessities are too rigid for the metaphysical counterpart of an environmental ethic, and, as we shall see, its treatment of individuals as mere modes of one substance is ethically hazardous, even if the problems about its intelligibility are waived.

O'Briant's preferred alternative is the system of Leibniz, who held that no metaphysics based on inert matter can explain activity or consciousness, and maintained instead that the fundamental units of reality (the monads) are themselves active and possessed of (unconscious) perception. Leibniz's monadology enabled him to stress the similarities as well as the differences between humans and other animals, and to admire their diverse perfections. Though his system has seldom been accepted as a whole, his belief that the organic underlies the mechanical has been revived this century in A. N. Whitehead's doctrine of 'organic mechanism'.[32] Indeed L. Charles Birch has summarized this position in a form O'Briant would be likely to applaud: 'Man is not separate from nature, but a part of nature.'[33] There are in fact considerable difficulties in the way of the acceptance of Leibniz's unextended monads as the basis of everyday physical objects, though there may be less in the way of accepting the view that the capacity for life and consciousness is proper to the elementary particles of matter (a view which Leibniz himself rejected).[34]

While radical Cartesian dualism can be rejected on grounds such as its failure to make action or perception possible, whether in humans or in other animals, and also on evolutionary grounds yet to be presented, it is perhaps unnecessary for present purposes to adjudicate between the remaining metaphysical possibilities. For it is possible to recognize both the kinship of mankind and the other animals and the characteristic rational, cultural and moral capacities of humans on a variety of theories, including Priestleian materialism, Leibnitian monadology, Whitehead's organic mechanism and the Thomist view of man and other animals as ensouled bodies. None of these theories, I suggest, requires the undervaluation of nonhuman creatures (even though Thomism has at times been so interpreted);[35] and, though not all can be equal to reality, it would be superfluous here to attempt to decide between their relative merits. For present purposes, at any rate, a Lockean agnosticism about the nature of that in us (and in the other animals) which feels and thinks will suffice.

Requirements for a satisfactory metaphysics

It is nevertheless worth asking what are the requirements for a metaphysics which encourages sensitiveness towards the natural environment as well as towards human nature. In this connection Mary Midgley makes the point that if human nature is to be understood against the background of the kindred nature of other animals (and it is certainly unlikely to be well understood otherwise), then theories on which human nature as it is could never 'have evolved without celestial interference'[36] are to be rejected. But the theories of Plato and of Descartes can only be squared with belief in evolution if at some stage a wholly alien element was supernaturally added to existing organisms. On their theories, after all, the loss of the body makes little difference to the real person, who continues to exist as a soul. Such a soul is therefore discontinuous with all other characteristics of living organisms, and could not evolve from them. But, as Midgley remarks, such 'celestial interference . . . does not make sense in a nonreligious context . . . [or] in a Christian one either. Christianity is not Platonism. If God created through evolution, he surely designed it and used it properly.' And in fact she goes on to suggest that 'a far more coherent view of human wholeness' is supplied by Bishop Butler, with his contrasting accounts of behaviour which fits the balance of our natural desires, and behaviour disproportionate to their integration.[37] Indeed Midgley's evolutionary requirement is plausibly satisfied by the metaphysical views, presented above, of Aquinas, Leibniz, Priestley and Whitehead alike.

Midgley has another requirement for a satisfactory metaphysics, namely that we must not only refrain from holding, with Kant, that animals and the rest of creation exist for man and that man is nature's ultimate end,[38] but that we need to hold that other creatures either have no point or value or have a point which is quite alien to human purposes. Only thus can we escape from the narrowness of human concerns, and take pleasure in what exists independently of ourselves, and only thus can we benefit from the study of the adaptedness of different creatures each to its peculiar niche and role.[39]

A parallel requirement for a satisfactory metaphysics is suggested in Passmore's contention that 'the philosopher has to learn to live with the "strangeness" of nature, with the fact that natural processes are entirely indifferent to our existence and welfare — not *positively* indifferent, of course, but *incapable* of caring about us — and are complex in a way that rules out the possibility of our wholly mastering and transforming them'.[40] Passmore is partly rejecting here two forms of anthropocentric metaphysics. Cartesianism, he holds, encourages the exploitation of nature as 'the rightful manipulation of a nature which is wax in man's hands'.[41] He grants that Descartes rejected the view that everything else in creation exists for man, but ascribes to him the attitude that everything that man finds on earth may and should be transformed for his use,[42] like the wax which was Descartes' favourite example of variability. (This kind of account may not be altogether fair to Descartes.) Passmore is also rejecting the Hegelian metaphysics of nature on which its exploitation is held to constitute 'the humanising of it in a manner which somehow accords with nature's real interests',[43] and on which nature becomes of value only through the taming of its initial state by man.

That some of Descartes' followers adopted the views attributed to Descartes, or that Marx and others (see chapter 5) in large measure took over those attributed to Hegel can scarcely be doubted. Passmore finds them defective not in rejecting the pre-Christian view that natural objects are sacred; for natural objects cannot be swayed by arguments, can be scientifically understood, and may rightly be in some measure transformed for the sake of 'civilization' and human interests. Rather he finds them defective in neglecting facts such as that 'natural processes go on in their own way, in a manner indifferent to human interests and by no means incompatible with man's total disappearance from the face of the earth', and that human interventions in these processes set off a chain of interactions, some of them unforseeable. If these facts are granted, then we neglect the autonomous nature of natural objects and processes at our peril, and should not construe them either as wax in our hands or as requiring our efforts to realize themselves. I suspect that Passmore is additionally holding that such attitudes to the exploitation of nature are morally wrong, as well as misconceived: certainly this is suggested by his beliefs that the wilful destruction of natural objects is blameable even when human interests are unaffected,[44] and that a more realistic philosophy of nature can promote respect for natural processes.[45] If so he needs to hold some such premise as that some of these objects and processes have an intrinsic value of their own (though, as I shall contend in chapter 8, the importance of understanding natural systems does not require locating intrinsic value in such systems, as holists sometimes require).

Now this rejection of anthropocentrism and the related refusal to undervalue nature are, as we have seen, required by the Old and New Testaments alike. We have also seen how these attitudes clash with Stoic (and, as Passmore points out, with Aristotelian[46]) tenets adopted by Origen, Aquinas and in some places by Kant, and accordingly how some elements in these thinkers' ideas need to be discarded. In chapter 3, moreover, it was argued that the Judaeo-Christian tradition can consistently accommodate the kind of nonanthropocentric metaphysics which is now commended by Passmore. Can it also accommodate the acceptance of nature's 'strangeness' required by Midgley and Passmore?

Satisfying the requirements

It is clearly essential at the very least that nonhuman living creatures should not be regarded as nothing but chattels, property or resources. Val and Richard Routley now hold that the Stewardship tradition involves regarding the world as either human or super-human property,[47] the tenants of which should treat it as resources belonging to the owner. Peter Singer seems to adopt a similar interpretation;[48] and Henryk Skolimowski likewise holds that in the Christian cosmology 'everything is God's personal property' and that for this metaphysics an ethic of reverence for life is an 'anomaly'.[49] But this theory makes the Stewardship tradition adopt an instrumentalist view of nonhuman creatures, which in actual fact its adherents have usually rejected. The suggestion may be that stewards are essentially managers who act on behalf of owners; if so, it should be replied that stewards can be curators, trustees, guardians and wardens, and that in any case the point of the metaphor is the steward's responsibility and answerability, not the devaluation of the world which is their trust, and which is regarded as a reflection of the divine glory, and judged by its creator to be 'very good'. Even if the tradition is secularized and adopts a nontheistic form, people do not forfeit their responsibilities, but remain answerable to the community of moral agents for the fostering and the preservation of all that is intrinsically valuable.

Nevertheless Passmore expresses strong reservations about people's ability to 'face their ecological problems in their full implications' unless they see themselves as left to their own devices, without metaphysical guarantees of survival.[50] Natural processes must not be seen as 'so constructed as to guarantee the continued survival of human beings and their civilisation'.[51] Hence a sufficiently naturalistic understanding of man is needed to guarantee that people are dependent on natural processes. This much, I should contend, can be accepted by anyone, whether a theistic believer or not, who accepts a sufficient kinship between humans and other species to recognize the essentially physical nature of both. Certainly theism does not entail that the earthly survival of our species is supernaturally guaranteed; and, as we have seen, belief in the survival of death need not impair conscientiousness about this-worldly obligations. Further, to affirm the naturalness of humanity commits us neither to the devaluation of nature feared by Skolimowski as a concomitant of some forms of the scientific world-view,[52] nor on the other hand to 'radical biotic egalitarianism',[53] the theory which makes all living creatures have the same intrinsic value, and which Blackstone shows good reason to reject on the count of its unacceptable implications.

Yet for Passmore nature's strangeness consists not only in its less-than-total conformity to human purposes, but also in the gulf between the human and the nonhuman.[54] In part Passmore is here reminding us of nature's otherness, rather as Rodman insists on the inappropriateness of applying to alien creatures, with distinctive ways of life of their own, standards which relate solely to humans.[55] But he is also stressing, to an unusual degree among writers on ecological subjects, the peculiar value of humans and what they create. This far, I suggest, we can follow him: our metaphysics should not so 'naturalize' man as to obscure the difference between characteristic human capacities and relations and the capacities (and in some cases relations) characteristic of other species. To do so is to disown the very responsibilities for future people and for the natural environment which it is essential for normative ethics to stress (see chapters 6—9). Indeed much more is distinctive about mankind than the relative absence of body hair: in fact the importance of stressing the powers of commission and omission which these responsibilities presuppose is a central reason for upholding the belief (so easily misinterpreted) in man's dominion. Yet the peculiar value of the fulfilment of characteristic human capacities can be granted without denying the possibility of rights on the part of nonhuman animals, as Passmore frequently does. Nor can it be necessary for an environmental ethic to be committed to treating species-boundaries *in themselves* as a proper basis for discrimination and differential treatment.

Awareness of our dependence on natural processes and cycles is sometimes thought, particularly by adherents of what Naess calls the 'deep' ecology movement, to require a shift at the level of metaphysics away from an atomistic view of society and the world to an acceptance of systems and wholes as the fundamental units of reality and the ultimate focuses of loyalty. Such seems to be the view of a number of ecological writers, including Leopold, Clark and Rodman.[56] A virtue of this view is its resistance to attempts to construe all morality as concerned with individual rights and interests and to project Western property systems onto the universe as a whole. But the egoistic pitfalls of moral individualism can be avoided without denying the reality of individuals, and the scientific discovery of our interdependence with the other constituents of natural ecosystems does not show these systems to have value in themselves.[57] Though Passmore is mistaken in objecting to Leopold's 'land ethic' that obligations arise only within those communities where they are recognized,[58] he is right to hold that interdependence need not imply a moral relationship. As the Routleys remind us, we need to be able to see ourselves as belonging to societies and systems, and can take pride in communal as well as in individual fortunes;[59] yet there are manifest dangers in any such metaphysical monism as that presented by John King-Farlow,[60] on which the perfection of the one Substance is vastly more important than the well-being of the persons who are among its constituents. Real as social systems and ecosystems are, we should not forget that their value turns on the flourishing of the no less real individual organisms which make them up.

A metaphysics, then, which is suited to our ecological problems needs to treat humans alongside the rest of the natural order in a naturalistic way, without being reductionist about their irreducible characteristics. It must not deny the reality of the natural systems on which we depend, yet must allow the reality of their individual members, and uphold the responsibilities which as individuals and groups people have for the care of the natural environment. For man is neither 'apart from nature' nor simply 'a part of nature', whether nature is regarded as a collection of atoms or organisms or as a single organic system. It must further renounce anthropocentrism, recognize nature's autonomy and otherness and the value of nonhuman creatures, and take full account of evolution. Thus, as Skolimowski points out, since mankind is the outcome of evolution, 'the universe is to be conceived of as the home for man';[61] and, though Skolimowski may be too ready to ascribe value to whatever emerges from the evolutionary process, he is nevertheless right to point out that 'we are the custodians of the whole of evolution'.[62]

Platonism and Cartesianism do not, as we have seen, satisfy these criteria; nor do the anthropocentric aspects of Aristotelianism and of Thomism. But the systems of Aquinas, Leibniz, Priestley and Whitehead are, I should claim, equal to these requirements, or can be reconciled with them. Indeed a new metaphysics is needed only insofar as these longstanding systems need to be made more explicitly consistent with the criteria which have been supplied. Thus the Judaeo-Christian tradition, of which at least the first three of these systems are recognizably variants, is not essentially productive of metaphysical arrogance, despite the fact that such arrogance has often besmirched it. Nor is it committed to regarding man as 'apart from nature'. Indeed it embodies indispensable insights about human capacities and obligations, such as that people are the custodians and stewards of a precious natural order, and have a creative role in actively enhancing it, as well as being among its participants — insights which we cannot afford to disregard.

NOTES

1 John Passmore, 'Attitudes to Nature', in Royal Institute of Philosophy (ed.) *Nature and Conduct*, London and Basingstoke: Macmillan Press, 1975, 251—64, p. 261; *MRN,* (2nd edn) p. 215.
2 John Rodman, 'The Liberation of Nature', *Inquiry,* 20, 1977, 83—145, p. 95.
3 Henryk Skolimowski, 'Ecological Humanism', in *Eco-Philosophy,* Boston and London, Marion Boyars, 1981, pp. 53—89.

4   Walter H. O'Briant, 'Man, Nature and the History of Philosophy', in William T. Blackstone (ed.), *Philosophy and Environmental Crisis,* Athens: University of Georgia Press, 1974, 79—89.
5   Ibid. p. 80.
6   Ibid. pp. 82f.
7   Ibid. pp. 85f.
8   Ibid. pp. 86—8.
9   See Robin Attfield, *God and The Secular,* Cardiff, University College Cardiff Press, 1978, chapter 1.
10 Wisdom 3:4 and 5:15 are apparent exceptions, but even there immortality is not natural to man's soul, but a supernatural gift.
11 Ecclesiastes 3:19f.
12 John Black, *Man's Dominion,* Edinburgh: Edinburgh University Press, 1970, pp. 39f.
13 Cf. J. A. T. Robinson, *The Body,* London: SCM Press, 1952, chapters 1 and 3.
14 Cf. Alan Richardson (ed.), *A Theological Wordbook of the Bible,* London: SCM Press, 1957, under 'Spirit', I(c), p. 234.
15 Aristotle, *De Anima* II, 412a, 20f.
16 Cf. J. N. D. Kelly, *Early Christian Doctrines,* London: Adam & Charles Black, (4th edn) 1968, pp. 280f.
17 See chapter 3 (above), nn. 30, 2 and 8.
18 *Summa Theologiae* 1, q75, articles 2—6. See also Herbert McCabe, 'The Immortality of the Soul', in Anthony Kenny (ed.), *Aquinas: A Collection of Critical Essays,* London: Macmillan Press, 1969, pp. 297—306.
19 *Summa Theologiae* 2:1, q10, a4.
20 Kelly, *Early Christian Doctrines,* pp. 180—8.
21 O'Briant, 'Man, Nature and the History of Philosophy', pp. 83f.
22 Samuel Clarke, *Letter to Dodwell, Etc.,* (1706), (6th edn) London, 1731; Richard Price, *A Free Discussion of Materialism and Philosophical Necessity, in a Correspondence between Dr Price and Dr Priestley, Etc.,* London, 1778.
23 Price, 'The Nature and Dignity of the Human Soul', *Sermons,* London, c. 1790.
24 William T. Blackstone, 'The Search for an Environmental Ethic', in Tom Regan (ed.), *Matters of Life and Death,* Philadelphia: Temple University Press, 1980, 299—335, p. 312.
25 John Locke, *Second Reply* to the Bishop of Worcester, *Works,* London, 1823, Vol. IV, pp. 460f. The reference is derived from Michael Ayers, 'Mechanism, Superaddition and the Proof of God's Existence in Locke's *Essay*', *Philosophical Review,* 90, 1981, 210—51, p. 238. Ayers there contests the view of Margaret Wilson that the possible addition of these powers was regarded by Locke as an exercise of the divine *fiat* and contrary to the nature of the things affected. Ayers maintains that

Locke's main position was agnosticism about the nature both of matter and of that which thinks.

26   Ralph Cudworth, *The True Intellectual System of the Universe,* (2nd edn) London: 1743, p. 745; cited by Ayers (see above) at n. 64, p. 239.
27   This account of Locke's position is derived from Ayers (see above), pp. 237—9.
28   In *A Free Discussion*; see n. 22. His materialism is expounded there at pp. 112f.
29   The correspondence of Clarke and Collins is published in Clarke, *Letter to Dodwell, Etc.*
30   Blackstone, 'The Search for an Environmental Ethic', p. 312.
31   Spinoza, *Ethics,* Part IV, Prop. XXXVII, Note 1. From *Spinoza's Ethics,* trans. Andrew Boyle, London: Dent, Everyman's Library, 1910.
32   A. N. Whitehead, *Science and the Modern World,* Cambridge: Cambridge University Press, 1926; see also his later works.
33   L. Charles Birch, *Nature and God,* London: SCM Press, 1965, p. 69.
34   See H. G. Alexander (ed.), *The Clarke—Leibniz Correspondence,* Manchester: Manchester University Press, 1956.
35   See Turner, *All Heaven in a Rage,* pp. 162—6.
36   Mary Midgley, *Beast and Man: The Roots of Human Nature,* Hassocks: Harvester Press, 1979, p. 254.
37   Ibid. pp. 266—77.
38   Kant, however, seems later to have abandoned this view: see Glacken, *Traces on the Rhodian Shore,* pp. 540f.
39   Midgley, *Beast and Man,* pp. 357—9.
40   'Attitudes to Nature', p. 260; *MRN,* (2nd edn) p. 214.
41   'Attitudes to Nature', p. 259; *MRN,* (2nd edn) p. 213.
42   'Attitudes to Nature', p. 256; *MRN,* (2nd edn) p. 210.
43   'Attitudes to Nature', p. 259; *MRN,* (2nd edn) P. 213. Cf. *MRN,* pp. 32—5.
44   'Attitudes to Nature', p. 263; *MRN,* (2nd edn) p. 217.
45   'Attitudes to Nature', pp. 263f; *MRN,* (2nd edn) pp. 217f.
46   *MRN,* p. 14.
47   Val and Richard Routley, 'Social Theories, Self Management and Environmental Problems', in Don Mannison, Michael McRobbie and Richard Routley (eds), *Environmental Philosophy,* Canberra: Australian National University, 1980, 217—332, p. 324.
48   Peter Singer, 'Animals and the Value of Life', in Tom Regan (ed.), *Matters of Life and Death,* 218—59, p. 231.
49   Skolimowski, *Eco-Philosophy,* p. 83.
50   *MRN,* p. 184.
51   'Attitudes to Nature', p. 260; *MRN,* (2nd edn) p. 214.
52   Skolimowski, *Eco-Philosophy,* pp. 8—13.
53   Blackstone, *Philosophy and Environmental Crisis,* p. 303.

54 'Attitudes to Nature', p. 261; *MRN,* (2nd edn) p. 215.
55 'The Liberation of Nature', pp. 94, 118.
56 Leopold, *A Sand County Almanac and Sketches Here and There,* New York: Oxford University Press, 1949, pp. 224f; Clark, *The Moral Status of Animals,* Oxford: Clarendon Press, 1977, pp. 114 and 171; see also his review of Goodpaster and Sayre, *Philosophical Books,* 21, 1980, 237—40; Rodman, 'The Liberation of Nature', p. 89. See also Holmes Rolston III, 'Is There an Ecological Ethic?' *Ethics,* 85, 1975, 93—109, p. 106; Kenneth Goodpaster, 'From Egoism to Environmentalism', in K. E. Goodpaster and K. M. Sayre (eds), *Ethics and Problems of the 21st Century,* 21—35, pp. 29f; and J. Baird Callicott, 'Animal Liberation: A Triangular Affair', *Environmental Ethics,* 2, 1980, 311—38, pp. 327ff.
57 See chapter 8 (below); also Robin Attfield, 'Methods of Ecological Ethics', *Metaphilosophy,* 14, 1983, 195—208.
58 *MRN,* p. 116.
59 See 'Social Theories, Self Management and Environmental Problems', *passim.*
60 John King-Farlow, *Self-Knowledge and Social Relations,* New York: Science History Publications, 1978, pp. 216—19.
61 Skolimowski, *Eco-Philosophy,* p. 74.
62 Ibid.

5

Belief in Progress

Why are the societies of both Western and Eastern Europe, and those which descend from them, so expectant of perpetual growth and perpetual increases in human power and happiness? The Judaeo-Christian tradition does not seem to explain these deep-rooted attitudes, despite the views of White to the contrary;[1] yet they do appear to prevail wherever Western (or Soviet) science, technology and institutions are to be found.

This suggests the importance of discussing a more recent idea from the common background of these societies, the idea of progress, a widespread presupposition in one version or another, in both capitalist and Marxist social systems. I shall not argue that this idea as such is at the root of our problems or that it should be rejected; indeed I believe it to be of great value in some of its forms. Yet in other forms it does, I shall argue, underlie our problems. I shall therefore be considering its nature and origins, the extent to which it is tenable, and whether it is compatible with attitudes appropriate to our current dilemmas.

The modern belief in progress

The hope that the passage of time would convey benefits to human well-being, material benefits included, through the application of knowledge about nature originated significantly in the seventeenth century with Francis Bacon and René Descartes. The view which I am here adopting of the idea of progress as a distinctively modern one was put forward by the rationalist historian J. B. Bury,[2] and was not challenged by a writer with a very different standpoint, the theologian John Baillie, for all that he regarded belief in progress as a Christian heresy.[3] John Passmore, certainly, has shown that the

belief that progress comes about by a process of natural development, inherent in human history, can be traced back to Joachim of
Flora in the twelfth century, and that for Joachim the guarantee of
progress was divine providence;[4] but he also holds that belief in the
inevitability of progress, providence or no providence, did not
become part of a systematic social doctrine till the time of
philosophes such as Turgot in France and of Leibniz's eighteenth-
century followers in Germany.[5]

As against all this Robert Nisbet has recently contended that the
belief in progress is not a distinctively modern belief, but originated
with the Greeks, was fostered by Christian millennarianism and is
characteristically sustained by religious faith.[6] Nisbet succeeds in
showing that some of the Greeks believed in periods of improvement, that Augustine prepared the way for millennarian and secular
concepts of progress, and that there is more continuity between
ancient, medieval and modern attitudes to progress than Auguste
Comte and his followers have allowed. Yet he does not succeed in
overthrowing the distinctiveness of the modern idea of progress. As
Passmore had already pointed out:

it is one thing to assert that over a limited period of time the human
situation has improved, or will improve, whether in knowledge or in artistic
achievement, quite another thing to assert that mankind as a whole is
gradually perfecting itself — not only in some particular respect but
universally — and that it will continue to do so throughout the course of
human history.[7]

Indeed for all the encouragement that Judaeo-Christian beliefs give
to scientific enquiry and to the related hope of the amelioration of
the human condition, belief in perpetual progress is no part of
orthodox Judaism or Christianity, nor, as we shall see, have the
various bases, sought over three hundred years to guarantee the
perpetuation of progress, usually been religious ones.

The hope which Bacon and Descartes cherished for earthly
advancement and the alleviation of the human lot was grounded, as
John Baillie says,[8] in the prospect of the growth of scientific
knowledge. Contrary to the impression which Joseph Priestley gave
and which Carl Becker reinforces,[9] Bacon did not quite identify
knowledge with power, but he did hold that the former is necessary
for the latter: 'Human knowledge and human power meet in one;
for where the cause is not known the effect cannot be produced.'[10]
So long as unintended achievements are left out of account, we can

agree; indeed Morris Ginsberg has given Bacon's claim a wider, yet still plausible application: 'It remains that if knowledge is not a sufficient, it is a necessary condition of progress.'[11] Since, further, both Bacon and Descartes supplied grounds for hope of scientific advance, they both prepared the way for the belief in the inevitability of progress: yet neither of them shared this belief. As Baillie relates, they were each content to demonstrate that the kind of progress in which they were interested was possible and to 'argue against the assumption of its impossibility'.[12] Indeed there was no inconsistency between this position and the Christianity which both professed.

With Baillie I accept Bury's view that 'Fontenelle was the first to formulate the idea of the progress of knowledge as a complete doctrine.'[13] In this doctrine, the progress of knowledge was presented as certain and as continuing indefinitely. Fontenelle based his claim on the constancy of nature and of human nature: each generation is therefore able to benefit from the discoveries of the previous one, and to avoid their mistakes. As against Fontenelle, we might fear that in some disciplines errors, ancient and modern, would be perpetuated and discoveries disregarded: but the reply is a cogent one that the critical methods of empirical science make this likely in only a minority of cases within its domain. Nor is the proneness of humans to mould their ideas and institutions an insuperable objection to Fontenelle's conclusion. The real problem lies in the possibility that technological discoveries, supposed to be progressive, will undermine the conditions in which science or other forms of civilized life can be practised at all: to this extent the doctrine that technological progress will continue indefinitely is capable of proving self-destructive.

Accordingly assertions of indefinite progress of any kind are insecure; yet if human nature allows of social improvements, their possibility should not be underestimated. John Passmore has recounted how a succession of social theorists in the eighteenth and nineteenth centuries explored this possibility.[14] This is not the place to enter into the detail of their theories; but it is important to note that they all depend on the rejection, made explicit by John Locke, of the Augustinian doctrine of original sin. In *The Reasonableness of Christianity* Locke denied that people are born with an innate inclination towards depravity.[15] Any innate bias to evil with which a man is born can, he held, be removed, or at least counter-balanced, by education. Locke did not accept, as many contemporary Latitudinarian theologians did, that people are born with benevolent propensities: but he did reject the doctrine that everyone is beset with an innate maleficent bias which supernatural grace alone can remedy.

Locke's claims for education concern in effect the possibility of individual moral improvement, and underlie most secular theories of social or moral reform. Doubtless Locke was prone to exaggerate, as he at one point admitted,[16] the extent to which people are born without instincts or natural inclinations, and may 'be moulded or fashioned as one pleases'; but the orthodox Augustinian doctrine, if consistently applied, could suggest the futility of all efforts at social reform which in any way depended on, or were designed to promote, increased cooperation or wisdom, including even the efforts of Benedictine and Cistercian communities to improve the land (efforts which owed much to Augustine's other teaching). The theology of Augustine, indeed, allows so low a place to human self-determination that numerous Christians down the ages have had to qualify it to acknowledge the role of human effort in any consistent scheme of Christian ethics. Thus even if Locke's positive views misconstrue human instincts and inherited capacities, his claim that there is for each generation of new-born humans the possibility of moral development, and that it can be fostered by entirely secular means, was both an influential and a salutary one. It was, indeed, a modification of the Judaeo-Christian tradition vital for all branches of ethics, environmental ethics included. Even if, morally speaking, no generation starts off in a better position than its predecessor, yet later generations can inherit the advantages of an enhanced social and natural environment.

The modern belief in progress, however, as Passmore, Baillie and Bury agree, originates with the Abbé de Saint-Pierre, who moved in some of the same circles as Fontenelle towards the end of the latter's long life. According to Baillie 'what Saint-Pierre did was to combine Bacon's and Descartes' belief that increase in knowledge was the secret of social and moral progress with Fontenelle's belief in the inevitability of the former; so reaching as a conclusion the belief in the inevitability of the latter'.[17] Saint-Pierre, however, contributed more than a simple application of an elementary argument-form; for, as Baillie himself accepts, Bacon and Descartes did not believe that advances in knowledge would guarantee any sort of progress; nor were they concerned, for the most part, with moral progress at all.[18] At most they harboured hopes of more commodious living (Bacon) or improvements in medicine of benefit to future generations (Descartes). But Saint-Pierre maintained that advances in knowledge were as feasible in the social and political spheres as in the physical, and that in each case corresponding and continuous progress would inevitably follow. Here for the first time is a prediction of ever-increasing happiness and steady moral progress, based on gains to knowledge (such as those made by Descartes, Newton and Locke) and on legislation for social reform. Indeed the recent contributions to knowledge were held, by Saint-Pierre and soon by many others, to suggest that just as the present was an improvement on the past, so the future was bound to bring unlimited further progress.

As Becker and Baillie both relate, views such as these fostered a discontent with existing social arrangements and an ardent desire for social reform, which in the France of Louis XV was certainly overdue. More generally, there is no reason to doubt that understanding of human society is possible and can contribute to the introduction of more beneficent arrangements. What is more doubtful is either that the application of such knowledge is bound to succeed in its aims, or that knowledge of man and society is to be expected to be as well-attested, secure or cumulative as knowledge of mathematics or physics, granted the difference in subject-matter. Besides, as Passmore points out, 'there were great difficulties in the purely inductive argument for progress'. On no criterion did the past bear out the theory of steady improvement, even if the extrapolation from the past to the future had been a permissible one. Yet the belief in the irresistibility of progress, which set in at this stage, has nevertheless been an immensely influential one in fostering confidence in deliberate changes intended to assist that process along.

With qualifications, similar views about the past, the present and the future were put forward by Voltaire (though, as Bury remarks, his optimism was always tempered with cynicism),[19] Turgot (who accepted that progress might be accidental, and who took a more favourable view of the Christian Middle Ages than the other *philosophes*),[20] Chastellux (who concluded that progress began with the Renaissance, before which all ages were ages of misery)[21] and Condorcet (who believed in uninterrupted progress through nine ages, each superior in knowledge and enlightenment, about to culminate in a tenth age of equality and still greater knowledge, health and virtue).[22] These writers argued on the basis of actual historical progress. But unless the argument that greater knowledge promotes wiser actions is successful, it is hard to see how the discovery of progressive historical tendencies could constitute grounds for optimism: unless these tendencies operate through a credible and continuing mechanism, there is no reason to expect the lessons of history to apply to the future. One mechanism, proposed by Turgot and by Adam Smith,[23] was the production of economic growth by private enterprise operating in a framework of laissez-faire liberalism; Nisbet indeed regards belief in economic growth, which was also harboured by Voltaire and Condorcet, as the natural background to belief in progress.[24] To the extent that these beliefs really belong together, the belief in progress must share some of the blame for our ecological problems; certainly far from all the fruits of economic growth can be regarded as social improvements. (Yet, as Mill was later to point out, there can be social progress even if economic growth is curtailed.)

Nevertheless the new emphasis of the *philosophes* on the human future was morally an important one (see chapter 6). People who expect either a continuing decline of man and nature, or the persistence of the social and natural order of their day, can readily believe that there is little they can do for posterity. Such views do not preclude all sense of obligation: but that sense can be heightened when people become aware that the lot of their descendants depends in large measure on themselves. A different perspective on the attitude of the *philosophes* to posterity is supplied in Becker's chapter 'The Uses of Posterity',[25] in which he exhibits the way in which, for many of the *philosophes*, posterity became the focus of religious feelings previously associated with life after death. (Diderot, to cite one among Becker's many examples, declared that 'La postérité pour le philosophe, c'est l'autre monde de l'homme religieux.') But we should beware of applying to them a theory of psychological projection or irrational wish-fulfilment: some of them, indeed, such as the Abbé de Saint-Pierre, Richard Price and Joseph Priestley, continued to believe in the next world as well as looking forward to a better future in this one. Certainly in the case of Robespierre concern for posterity observably diminished concern for the generation of his contemporaries; yet, once there are grounds for holding that our descendants can be benefited by our actions or harmed by our omissions, it is irresponsible to disregard them, and it is to the credit of the *philosophes* that they realized this.

Metaphysical guarantees

Besides arguments for progress taken from science, education and history, there were also metaphysical arguments. Thus the view of Leibniz that every potentiality must at some time be actualized was capable either of being restricted, as at first it was, to individual lifetimes as opposed to the career of humanity as a whole (thus Moses Mendelssohn), or instead, of being applied to the development of the species through time (as in Immanuel Kant's *Idea of a Universal History*[26]). With Kant the fulfilment of human potentialities is located in a perfect universal state which will guarantee perpetual peace, and which will come about precisely through the evil inclinations, and the consequent struggles, to which humanity is prone. The evidence of history was, as Kant saw, insufficient to warrant his conclusion: the basis of his assurance was rather that the human sense of duty requires us to believe that there can be conditions in which it is universally enthroned.

Though Kant explicitly rejected the doctrine of original sin, he eventually relied on divine grace, as Joachim had before him, to provide for the consummation of his ideal commonwealth.[27] But appeal to divine interventions is just as unsupportable in theories about the human future as in explanations in physics:[28] it is one thing to set up an ethical commonwealth as an ideal, and hope for its fulfilment, and quite another to assert its inevitability, particularly where there is no earthly means of enacting it within the envisageable future. Indeed believers in its inevitability may easily subordinate all else to its attainment, and cut corners in bringing it in.

Conscious of this very possibility, Kant's former pupil Herder held that it is rather by performing their duty to the present generation that people best further the arrival of an ideal society. Unlike those *philosophes* who had stressed the misery of the past (or of the present) he held that every age is capable of relative perfection, and the fulfilment appropriate to its own circumstances. Impressed as he was by the variety of empirical conditions in which societies are set, he had no place for those 'final causes' which Kant had reintroduced into the philosophy of history. But he was enough of a believer in the progress and the progressive education of humanity, to which every society can contribute, both to deplore some episodes in the past (the barbarities of the Roman Empire, and the persistence of the Roman Church after the Reformation), and to avoid that historical relativism which precludes the judgement that one society can constitute an improvement on another. With Passmore I agree that he needed such a view if he was to retain belief in the possibility of progress: it is indeed needed for all inter-societal appraisals, whether concerned with chronological development or not.[29]

As well as being interested in empirical particularities, Herder was a speculative thinker, who laid down laws of history. His principal law was that 'all the destructive Powers in Nature must not only yield in the Course of Time to the maintaining Powers, but must ultimately be subservient to the Consummation of the Whole'.[30] Evils, Herder believed, serve as a stimulant to progress; his law guarantees that after the stimulated changes have occurred, their stimulants wither away. His laws were supposed to be laws of nature, but turn out to be just as metaphysical as the factors taken to guarantee progress by Kant.

Among Herder's successors in Germany as philosophers of history, Fichte, Schelling and Hegel, his empirical emphasis was disparaged and suppressed, and attention was further concentrated on the discovery of laws of development. With Fichte, all history tends unendingly yet necessarily towards the realization of freedom.[31] Nature too is involved in the process: earthquakes, volcanoes and hurricanes are nothing more than 'the last struggles of the rude mass against the law of regular, progressive, living and systematic activity to which it is compelled to submit'.[32] Thus nature has not yet become subject to regular laws or to human efforts, but it is destined eventually to become controlled, regularized and humanized. (Indeed progress has often been defined in terms of the increasing power of man over nature.[33]) Schelling regarded society as an organism, the growth of which is deducible from biological laws;[34] for his part Hegel regarded history as a developing revelation of divine reason, the emergence of 'consciousness of its own freedom on the part of Spirit',[35] but a process which was already complete in his own day. For these idealists, empirical history at best served to illustrate processes which are deducible by *a priori* reasoning. Their stress was on the inevitability of development rather than of scientific or moral progress; but their influence was considerable on later French as well as German thought, so much so that the idea of historical development became a commonplace even among people who execrated the memory of the pre-revolutionary *philosophes*.[36]

In post-revolutionary France a new generation of thinkers attempted to explain how to organize for progress and to delineate its sociological laws — first Saint-Simon and then Comte. With Saint-Simon the close cohesion of religious, political and social systems was stressed, and a law supplied of the alternation of epochs of organization or construction and of criticism or revolution.[37] Saint-Simon's emphasis on the role of religion in historical development supplemented that accorded to knowledge by Condorcet (and would doubtless have been approved by White). He accordingly predicted that on the road to social happiness a new physicist religion would replace Christianity and Deism. His theories also allowed him to advocate a more immediate and practical condition of social progress, the amelioration of the lot of the working classes. With Comte the fundamental law of history consisted 'in the growing power of altruism over egoism brought about by a fusion of intelligence and sympathy'.[38] Like Condorcet and Fichte, Comte divided history into stages: every branch of knowledge passes in his account through first a theological state, next a metaphysical and finally a positive or scientific one. The dynamic of history is largely supplied by ideas, which in all disciplines need to be raised to the third stage. Political, moral and intellectual progress are so closely related that material and social development proceed in step with that of the intellect. In the third stage, society will be organized along the principles of scientific sociology.[39] Comte did not believe that progress would be indefinite, but he was convinced that it would be continuous. It is entirely predictable that mankind will arrive at a science-based harmony with its environment, and equally clear what people in the interim should do and may rightly be coerced into doing.[40] It is unlikely that the adherents of such an ethic would be willing to adjust their practice in the light of new ecological or other insights, or would be allowed to do so.

Progress popularized

The French thinkers of the early nineteenth century put the idea of progress firmly on the map, not least by blending the German belief in inevitable temporal development with the historically based confidence of the French enlightenment that intellectual and moral improvements would continue in the future. A sign of the times was the definition of civilization advanced by François Guizot in terms of both progress and development. The very word 'civilisation', he claimed, 'awakens, when it is pronounced, the idea of a people which is in motion, not to change its place but to change its state, a people whose condition is expanding and improving. The idea of progress, development, seems to me the fundamental idea contained in the word *civilisation*.'[41] (Guizot's notion of civilization included not only social movement towards prosperity and justice but also intellectual development in individuals of cultivated ideas and sentiments.)

Strictly, as Bury remarks, Guizot's definition implies that there is no such thing as a civilization in a state of equilibrium; such an assumption would, of course, have to be revised before a sustainable society, able to live in harmony with its natural environment, could come about. But significantly, and without further demur, Bury in 1920 wrote of Guizot that 'his view of history was effective in helping to establish the association of the two ideas of civilisation and progress, *which today is taken for granted as evidently true*' (my italics).[42] In this form the idea of progress was soon popularized both in Britain and America:[43] it is accordingly unsurprising that many in the twentieth century have regarded a society which lacks growth as retrogressive and intolerable.

It should also be acknowledged that in this period the idea of progress became associated with that of equality, both by Robert Owen in Britain and by Pierre Leroux in France, and that belief in the possibility of each strengthened belief in that of the other. Also in the writings of William Godwin and, now, of Proudhon, it was seen to be possible to give progress an anti-authoritarian interpretation, far removed from that of Comte. Much more influential than the ideas of either the first socialists or the first anarchists were the distinctive doctrines of Marx and Engels (indeed any assessment of the idea of progress of this or succeeding periods must depend on which of the various conceptions of social advance is in question). A much more immediate influence, however, in the widespread adoption in Western Europe and America of belief in progress was exercised by the writings of Herbert Spencer, whose understanding of progress was of a very different complexion again.

Spencer had already adopted a theory of the evolution of society in his *Social Statics* of 1851,[44] well before the publication of Charles Darwin's *The Origin of Species* in 1859; but Darwin's theories served to give a widespread credibility to his claim, publicized in a sequence of further works, that the whole universe, organic and inorganic, is in process of evolution. As has been seen in chapter 4, acceptance of Darwinism can also give rise to an enhanced sense of kinship to the natural order: and, as T. H. Huxley pointed out, it certainly need not lead to an ethical belief in the survival of the fittest. But Huxley, in order to arrive at this conclusion, had to stress the discontinuity between biological evolution and social progress;[45] whereas Spencer, in asserting their continuity, had an easier task. How, he could ask, can man reverse the law of life?

Spencer's own law of evolution was no improvement on the proposed laws of history of Condorcet, Herder, Fichte or Comte.[46] But if life-forms survive by adaptation, then there is a superficial cogency to his belief that evils, being manifestations of maladaptedness, will wither away as better adapted forms emerge and thrive. Spencer believed that adaptive characteristics can be transmitted down the generations, and therefore expected continuing, and eventually perfect, adaptation to come about.

Spencer's derivation of an ethic from the theory of evolution becomes all the more suspect when he argues from a final cause, and claims that 'the ultimate purpose of creation is to produce the greatest amount of happiness, and to fulfil this aim it is necessary that each member of the race should possess faculties enabling him to experience the highest enjoyment of life, yet in such a way as not to diminish the power of others to receive like satisfaction.'[47] To follow Bury's expression of the implications, 'Beings thus constituted cannot multiply in a world tenanted by inferior creatures; these, therefore, must be dispossessed to make room; and to dispossess them aboriginal man must have an inferior constitution to begin with; he must be predatory, he must have the desire to kill. In general, given an unsubdued earth, and the human being "appointed" to overspread and occupy it, then, the laws of life being what they are, no other series of changes than that which has actually occurred could have occurred.'[48]

Admittedly Spencer holds that to retain these predatory characteristics is to be unfit for man's present social state.[49] Nevertheless Spencer here endorses all depredations past, and might easily be construed as authorizing, in the name of the ultimate purpose of creation, ruthlessness on the part of anyone finding himself confronted by wild nature or by primitive peoples. Moreover even in future ages, to which more altruistic codes will, on his views, be appropriate, the idea of preserving or protecting vulnerable species, habitats or human cultures would be futile and misguided. Spencer may have considered that he was expounding Genesis, but, as Bury points out, the role of Providence in his earlier writings is just to set in motion immutable forces, a role which in later writings was occupied by 'the Unknowable, existing behind all phenomena'.[50] Indeed this transition was a tacit acknowledgement that Spencer's views were entirely alien to those of the Old Testament about God, man and nature.

Spencer's conflation of the notions of evolution by natural selection and of progress was widely accepted, so that evolution in society came to be regarded as desirable, and progress as a natural necessity. Not everyone would have allowed that the survival of the fittest was the criterion of such progress; but it was all too often assumed to be so in the ethics of business, while in society in general 'social Darwinism' made it all the harder for critics of exploitative attitudes, whether towards mankind or nature, to carry conviction. Similarly Spencer's laissez-faire liberalism has been so widely adopted as often to rule out the prevention of exploitation by law. The climate of opinion could in theory have been tempered by the extension of Mill's criterion of right action, the promotion of the greatest happiness of the greatest number, to include the members of future generations, as commended by Kidd;[51] but at a time of technological, commercial and imperial expansion, the very belief in progress seemed to guarantee that fresh ideas or resources would always turn up to meet future contingencies, which could therefore be left to themselves.

Marxist ambivalence

Hegel's belief in the inevitability of historical development was inherited not only by the French founders of sociology but also by Karl Marx and Friedrich Engels. Marx and Engels accepted Feuerbach's view that Hegel's critique of Christianity needed to be inverted, so that talk about God is seen as a confused way of talking about humans and their relationships. They also rejected Hegel's view that the theses, antitheses and syntheses of history were stages in the self-realization of Spirit, in favour of the doctrine that they were 'historical phases in the development of production'[52] and of the corresponding relations to the means of production of different economic classes, and that they would inevitably culminate by means of revolution in a society where all class-divisions had been abolished.

According to Marx, man is alienated under the conditions of capitalism from his own essence, and his alienation can only be overcome when capitalism is overthrown: only then will a truly free and human society emerge. I have elsewhere endeavoured to elucidate the sense of 'alienation';[53] here it should be remarked that their Soviet followers credit the founders of Marxism with having discovered the laws of history, and with them grounds for confidence in irresistible future progress. Thus Academician Innokenty Gerasimov writes, 'Only Marxist-Leninist theory and methodology of scientific analysis were able to reveal the objective laws of the multifarious processes of interaction between nature and society in the general evolution of mankind and the change of the basic social formations.'[54]

Two strands are to be discerned in the attitudes of Marx and

Engels to nature. One is the belief derived from Fichte, that nature must be humanized, and will only then itself be fulfilled. Though the language used often concerns, in Engel's phrase, 'the reconciliation of mankind with nature', the idea is explicated in terms of rational control. Thus Gerasimov writes:

In *Anti-Dühring* Engels points out that until the scientific control of the forces of nature is subordinated to the rational control of productive relations between people, these forces '. . . are at work in spite of us, in opposition to us, so long they master us . . .' The position changes fundamentally in planned socialist and communist societies.[55]

Similarly another contribution to the same collection of essays, by Academician Yevgeny Fyodorov and Ilya Novik, ascribes parallel views to Marx, who 'wrote that socialised man . . . rationally regulated their [*sic*] interchange with Nature, "bringing it under their common control, instead of being ruled by the blind forces of Nature . . ."'.[56] And in the same spirit these writers object to the posture of some Western ecological writers opposed to economic growth as 'a rejection of the humane ideal of social progress'. They prefer 'the rationally understood program of the optimisation of the biosphere'.[57] In this they are true to Marx; 'whenever Marx writes of the "slumbering potentialities" of nature, he is always referring to the objective possibility, inherent in nature, of its transfer into definite use-values,'[58] i.e. use-values for man. Howard L. Parsons, indeed, rejects the accusation that Marx denied the value of the external, non-human world of nature, but unconvincingly.[59] Indeed, as Parsons allows,[60]

Marx and Engels shared the attitude toward nature held by contemporary men of industry and commerce and by the millions of settlers migrating to new lands to struggle with the hardships of the frontier. Whereas eighteenth-century Europeans, for example, viewed America as a utopian garden of abundance, freedom and harmony, the nineteenth-century immigrants saw the wilderness as an obstacle to be conquered[61] and as a reservoir of potential wealth to be subdued and transformed by the labours of man.[62]

The other relevant strand in Marx and (much more emphatically) in Engels is a rejection of the kind of predatory exploitation of nature characteristic of capitalism and of much science-based technology, an advocacy of the recycling of the waste products of industry, and a surprisingly modern stress on the need to take account of side-effects and long-term consequences. Thus Marx holds that 'all progress in capitalistic agriculture is a progress in the art, not only of robbing the labourer, but of robbing the soil; all progress in increasing the fertility of the soil for a given time, is a progress towards ruining the lasting sources of that fertility.'[63] Capitalism, by concentrating people in large towns, prevents the return to the soil of human waste products, and thus further 'violates the conditions necessary to lasting fertility of the soil' and 'disturbs the circulation of matter between man and soil'. The wool and silk industries are commended for utilizing their own worn or defective products, and the chemical industry for utilizing not only its own waste but also that of many other industries.[64] In the same spirit Fyodorov and Novik advocate 'new wasteless production based on closed-cycle technology' as one of the long-term methods of production without pollution.[65]

There again, a fellow essayist is able to cite Engels, who was undoubtedly a pioneer of ecological consciousness, as a critic of technological optimism. 'Let us not, however,' wrote Engels, 'flatter ourselves on account of our human victories over nature. For each such victory takes its revenge on us. Each victory, it is true, in the first place brings about the results we expected, but in the second and third places it has quite different unforeseen effects which only too often cancel the first.'[66] Engels' examples include the devastation resulting from the deforestation of Southern Europe by primitive peoples, the introduction into Europe of the disease of scrofula together with the potato, and the loss of the soil of the Cuban uplands when Spanish planters burned the forests for the sake of fertilizer for *one* generation of coffee bushes and quick profits. Much the same happens, he holds, when manufacturers aim at immediate profit and disregard results which are other than immediate: bourgeois economics is, he holds, predominantly beset with the same flaws (a claim which, as was pointed out in chapter 1, it is hard to gainsay).[67] Engels' sentiments, indeed, assist Oldak in arguing in his turn for closed-cycle technology, as also for a reformed system of economics, and for planning which takes account of the needs of both present and future generations.

The representatives, then, of modern Soviet orthodoxy are enabled by Marx and Engels, as well as by the revelations of recent scientific research, both to criticize careless technology (and not only in capitalist societies[68]) and to encourage the recycling of waste products and pollution-free production. At the same time they reject the ideal of the cessation of growth,[69] insisting that 'Mankind is capable of developing progressively, provided that it takes account in its activity of the tasks of *optimising the biosphere*' (my italics).[70] For 'Mankind can not only predict and avert a future degradation of the environment, but even ensure its purposeful improvement,'[71] (One of the means suggested by another contributor, Academician Nicolai Semenov, is to discover how to replicate the natural process of photosynthesis artificially, and then to occupy the greater part of the deserts of the entire planet with industrial plant to reap the proceeds.[72]) It is difficult to avoid the conclusion that the confidence of Soviet scientists that improved technology can and will solve all ecological problems is also derived from the predictions of Marx and Engels that the eventual overcoming of the tensions between man and nature, and the development of a fully humanized nature and society, are each inevitable.

Belief in progress assessed

Nevertheless much can be granted to the prophets of progress. Bacon and Descartes were correct to hold that scientific progress is not impossible, Locke to hold that individuals can develop morally without supernatural assistance, and Fontenelle in holding that scientific and technological knowledge are (at least normally) cumulative. For, despite disavowals by some philosophers of science,[73] natural science has progressed wherever extra phenomena can be explained alongside familiar ones, and new ones predicted,[74] and technology has advanced wherever new techniques, and hence new human powers, for the control of natural processes or the production of goods have become available. Indeed there has even been some advance in the understanding of human society (e.g. in the matter of trends in population growth); and there has been a widespread increase, partially due to the *philosophes*, to Kant and to the founders of Marxism, in awareness of our obligations to future generations and of the possibility of equipping them with an improved natural and social environment. There is no need to concede to the intellectual or the moral relativist that such talk is incoherent, nor to the pessimist that all effort is doomed to futility.

But this is not to accept, with Saint-Pierre, that knowledge of society must advance in step with knowledge of nature, or that intellectual progress guarantees progress in happiness or in virtue; nor with the *philosophes* that the evidence of history entitles us to expect perpetual progress, however well theorists such as Herder, Saint-Simon and Spencer have attempted to deal with the counter-evidence. Nor is it to accept, with the German idealists, that in the course of history the full potential of either man or nature is certain to be realized, nor with Condorcet, Herder, Saint-Simon, Comte, Marx or Spencer that there are laws of history at all, let alone ones ensuring progress. Indeed it is surely a misconception to hold that any natural law, such as that of evolution by adaptation and selection, governs human history: for (as Soviet Academicians frequently assert) mankind moulds its own future, not least by deliberate action and other choices formed under the influence of ideas, and is free, as T. H. Huxley pointed out, to protect the weak and vulnerable, who might in the ordinary course of nature have perished, and, we might add, to falsify laws of history and make the unimaginable come true.

Understanding human society involves, as Saint-Simon says, an understanding of the interconnectedness of many aspects of life, the political, moral and religious among them: even if economic forces were unduly neglected before the time of Marx, the significance of ideas, though doubtless exaggerated by Comte, should not be underplayed. For this very reason it is important to see that some ideas are dangerous. Such, as we have seen, is the idea of perpetual progress in both East and West; such was the evolutionary ethic of Spencer, which forewent for at least some times and places the inhibitions inherent in received morality against predatory attitudes; such was Guizot's notion that civilization must be progressive, both culturally and materially, and that without these tendencies any society is uncivilized; and such, I suggest, are the Marxist ideas that 'nature must be humanised' and that 'the biosphere must be optimised' for human benefit.

Engels too readily assumed a conflict between man and nature, and that where man does not control nature, its unsubdued forces control him. Despite his understanding of the way that human 'conquests' of nature can recoil on the conqueror's head, he continued to insist on conquest, even though he used, to describe it, the language of unity with nature and of overcoming the 'contra-diction' between man and nature which he found in Christianity.[75] But, even if human needs often have moral precedence over those of other species (see chapter 9), it is mistaken to regard nature as *either* hostile *or* subdued. For this is nearly as anthropocentric as holding that everything exists for mankind, or that nothing is indifferent to the interests of humanity. Yet life in an optimized biosphere, where nothing on the earth's surface was wild, might easily not be worth living.

Thus Engels' valuable ecological insights fall short of their promise when conjoined with belief in the inevitability of material and technological progress. But much more harmful still has been the prevalent belief in progress in Western society, which has been (until recently) too little influenced by any such insights. Certainly the moralizing of the idea of progress, under the influence of advocates of equality and of freedom, has allowed it to be used as a valuable weapon of social criticism; and advances in the understanding of nature and society have facilitated and enhanced this effect.[76] But the uncritical notion which the same idea has often sponsored, that whatever can be done must be done, that modernization is improvement, and that to oppose the exploitation of opportunities for profit is to fight against the tide of history has served as a rationale for graspingness and has underlain many of the disruptions of nature, both home-grown in the West and exported by the West worldwide. Rather than the beliefs of Judaism and Christianity, the attitude in large measure responsible for environmental degradation in East and West has been the belief in perennial material progress inherited from the Enlightenment and the German metaphysicians, as modified in the West by the classical economists and sociologists, by liberal individualism[77] and by social Darwinism, and in Eastern Europe by the unquestioned deference accorded to Marx and to Engels.

Accordingly there is reason to reject belief that progress is irresistible, that nature should without limit be humanized, or that technological and social planning is bound to solve all our problems. Yet there is no reason to reject belief in the desirability or the possibility of many of the strands in the notion of progress. We can in some measure mould our own future, and to do so we need whatever understanding of nature and society we can come by, combined with a moral vision of states of society and of the world which would count as better than the present ones, and such grounds as there are for hope that we can move towards them. These indeed are prerequisites for the conservation of resources and the preservation of endangered species and vulnerable habitats, as well as for human well-being and social and international justice. But to accept this is to adopt a form of belief in progress; thus, far from all of the humane, secular tradition of the Enlightenment philosophers, of Kant, Marx, Engels and the others needs to be rejected. Indeed the combined resources of this and the older Judaeo-Christian tradition, suitably refined, are capable of allowing us to cope with our ecological problems without devising a new metaphysics or a new ethic. In Part Two an attempt will be made to reason from accepted judgements to a satisfactory environmental ethic, and to observe a few of its social implications.

NOTES

1 John Barr (ed.), *The Environmental Handbook*, London: Ballantine and Friends of the Earth, 1971, p. 10.
2 J. B. Bury, *The Idea of Progress*, London: Macmillan Press, 1920.
3 John Baillie, *The Belief in Progress*, London, Glasgow and Toronto: Oxford University Press, 1950.
4 John Passmore, *The Perfectibility of Man,* London: Duckworth, 1970 (hereinafter *PM*), 212–15.
5 *PM*, pp. 195, 216.
6 Robert Nisbet, *History of the Idea of Progress,* London: Heinemann, 1980.
7 *PM*, p. 196.
8 Baillie, *The Belief in Progress,* p. 103.
9 Joseph Priestley, *An Essay on the First Principles of Government and on Political, Civil and Religious Liberty*, London: (2nd edn) 1771, pp. 4f, cited by Carl Becker, *The Heavenly City of the Eighteenth-Century Philosophers,* New Haven and London: Yale University Press, 1932, pp. 144f.
10 *Aphorisms*, Book One, III: *The New Organon,* ed. Fulton H. Anderson, Indianapolis and New York: Bobbs-Merrill, 1960, p. 39.
11 Morris Ginsberg, *The Idea of Progress: A Revaluation,* Westport, Conn.: Greenwood Press, 1953, p. 77.
12 *The Belief in Progress,* p. 104.
13 Bury, *The Idea of Progress*, p. 110.
14 *PM*, chapter 8, 'Perfecting by Social Action: The Presuppositions'.
15 *PM*, p. 159.
16 At the end of his *Concerning Education*, cited at *PM*, p. 159. For a sustained critique of the Lockean view that the new-born infant is a *tabula rasa,* see Mary Midgley, *Beast and Man: The Roots of Human Nature,* Hassocks: Harvester Press, 1979.
17 *The Belief in Progress*, p. 108.
18 Ibid. pp. 102–4; see also chapter 4 (above).
19 Bury, *The Idea of Progress*, p. 150.
20 Ibid. pp. 156f.
21 Ibid. pp. 186–8.
22 Ibid. pp. 208–10; Baillie, *The Belief in Progress*, pp. 115f.
23 Nisbet, *History of the Idea of Progress,* pp. 185, 189.
24 Ibid. pp. 334f.
25 Becker, *The Heavenly City of the Eighteenth-Century Philosophers,* pp. 119–68.
26 *PM*, pp. 215–19.

27 *PM*, p. 220.
28 Cf. chapter 2, 'Physical Theology', of Robin Attfield, *God and The Secular,* Cardiff: University College Cardiff Press, 1978.
29 I have discussed these matters further in 'Against Incomparabilism', *Philosophy,* 50, 1975, 230—4, and in 'How Not to be a Moral Relativist', *The Monist,* 62, 1979, 510—21.
30 Cited at *PM*, p. 226.
31 Bury, *The Idea of Progress,* p. 251.
32 Cited at *PM*, p. 233.
33 Black, *Man's Dominion,* Edinburgh: Edinburgh University Press, 1970, p. 105.
34 Bury, *The Idea of Progress*, p. 251.
35 Cited at *PM*, p. 233.
36 Bury, *The Idea of Progress,* pp. 260—77.
37 Ibid. pp. 282—5.
38 Ginsberg, *The Idea of Progress: A Revaluation,* p. 24.
39 Bury, *The Idea of Progress*, pp. 291—4, 299—301.
40 Ibid. pp. 304—6.
41 Cited ibid. p. 274.
42 Ibid. p. 276.
43 Ibid. pp. 309—12.
44 Ibid. pp. 336f, *PM*, p. 241.
45 Ibid. pp. 344f; *PM*, pp. 244f.
46 'Evolution is an integration of matter and concomitant dissipation of motion; during which the matter passes from a relatively indefinite, incoherent homogeneity to a relatively definite coherent heterogeneity; and during which the retained motion undergoes a parallel trans-formation.' Presented at p. 47 of F. Howard Collins, *Epitome of the Synthetic Philosophy of Herbert Spencer*, London: Williams & Northgate, 1889. (Collins' *Epitome* ran to multiple editions in Britain, America, France, Germany and Russia.)
47 Bury's paraphrase, *The Idea of Progress*, pp. 338f.
48 Ibid. p. 339.
49 *PM*, p. 241.
50 Bury, *The Idea of Progress,* p. 339.
51 Ibid. p. 347.
52 Karl Marx, *Selected Works*, 2 Vols., Moscow, 1949 and London, 1950, Vol. II, p. 410, cited in *PM*, p. 236.
53 In 'On Being Human', *Inquiry*, 17, 1974, 175—92.
54 Innokenty Gerasimov, 'Man, Society and the Geographical Environ-ment', in *Society and the Environment: a Soviet View* (ed. anon.), Moscow: Progress Publishers, 1977, 25—36, p. 25.
55 Ibid. p. 26. His quotation is from F. Engels, *Anti-Dühring,* Moscow, 1975, p. 320.
56 Yevgeny Fyodorov and Ilya Novik, 'Ecological Aspects of Social

Progress', in *Society and the Environment*, 37—55, p. 43. Their quotation is from K. Marx, *Capital*, Vol. III, Moscow, 1974, p. 820. See also Richard and Val Routley, 'Social Theories, Self Management, and Environmental Problems', in Don Mannison, Michael McRobbie and Richard Routley (eds), *Environmental Philosophy*, Canberra: Australian National University, 1980, 217—332, p. 318.

57   Fyodorov and Novik, 'Ecological Aspects of Social Progress', p. 47.

58   Alfred Schmidt, *The Concept of Nature in Marx*, New York: Humanities Press, 1972, p. 162, cited by Howard L. Parsons, *Marx and Engels on Ecology*, Westport, Conn. and London: Greenwood Press, 1977, p. 49.

59   Parsons, *Marx and Engels on Ecology*, pp. 43f, 49—51.

60   Ibid. p. 37.

61   At this point Parsons refers, as his source, to Leo Marx, *The Machine in the Garden: Technology and the Pastoral Ideal*, New York: Oxford University Press, 1964.

62   Here Parsons cites Roderick Nash, *Wilderness and the American Mind*, New Haven: Yale University Press, 1967, chapter 2.

63   Karl Marx, *Capital*, Vol. I, trans. Samuel Moore and Edward Aveling, ed. F. Engels, New York: International Publishers, 1967, pp. 505—7; cited by Parsons, *Marx and Engels on Ecology*, p. 174. Cf. his pp. 183f.

64   Karl Marx, *Capital*, Vol. III, trans. Ernest Unterman, ed. F. Engels, New York: International Publishers, 1967, pp. 101—3; cited by Parsons, *Marx and Engels on Ecology*, pp. 177f.

65   Fyodorov and Novik, 'Ecological Aspects of Social Progress', p. 53.

66   F. Engels, *Dialectics of Nature*, Moscow, 1974, p. 180, cited by Pavel Oldak, 'The Environment and Social Production', *Society and the Environment*, 56—68, p. 56.

67   F. Engels, *Dialectics of Nature*, New York: International Publishers, 1954, p. 246; Parsons, *Marx and Engels on Ecology*, p. 182.

68   Fyodorov and Novik, 'Ecological Aspects of Social Progress', pp. 43f; Oldak, 'The Environment and Social Production', p. 61.

69   Fyodorov and Novik, 'Ecological Aspects of Social Progress', pp. 37—41; Oldak, 'The Environment and Social Production', p. 64.

70   Fyodorov and Novik, 'Ecological Aspects of Social Progress', p. 48.

71   Gerasimov, 'Man, Society and the Geographical Environment', p. 34.

72   Nicolai Semenov, 'Energetics for the Future', *Society and the Environment*, 69—98, pp. 93f.

73   Thus Mary Hesse, 'On the Alleged Incompatibility between Christianity and Science', in Hugh Montefiore (ed.), *Man and Nature*, London: Collins, 1975, pp. 121—31.

74   Cf. Ginsberg, p. 51.

75   In *Dialectics of Nature*; Parsons, *Marx and Engels on Ecology*, p. 180.

76   Thus Ginsberg, *The Idea of Progress: A Revaluation*, p. 71.

77   See Mary Midgley's strictures on individualism in 'The Limits of

Individualism', chap. 17 of her book *Evolution as a Religion,* London: Methuen, 1985, pp. 139—48, and those of Val and Richard Routley on conventional liberalism in 'Human Chauvinism and Environmental Ethics' in *Environmental Philosophy,* 96—189, pp. 97—120.

PART TWO   APPLIED ETHICS

6

Future Generations

I now turn to ethical considerations, and in this chapter in particular to the nature and grounding of our obligations towards future people. This will require a change of method, away from a historical approach to a more traditionally philosophical one. Thus in order to consider the basis of our obligations, I shall be reviewing various theories of normative ethics, theories about the criteria of right action and of obligation. But I shall also be concerned with particular obligations, ones attested by widespread intuitive judgements or by moral reflection on them, even where they do not tally with the predictions or the yield of the theories.

The issue of obligations to future generations proves to bring out the inadequacy of several such theories, and a method is accordingly in place which allows theories to be revised or even rejected where they fail to account for deeply held reflective moral intuitions, rather than one which requires judgements to be uniformly tailored to fit one or another theory. Reflective judgements are, after all, the principal data from which theories in normative ethics are constructed, with the manifest proviso that judgements which are inconsistent must be revised with the help of theory, rather than being sustained at the expense of inconsistency. One of my aims, then, is to arrive at a 'reflective equilibrium' between judgements and theory, and between normative principles and their application.

In my own view, in fact, there are recognizable limits and a recognizable scope to moral reasoning, discernible from *a priori* considerations such as the meaning of the very concept of morality, as well as from the *a posteriori* study of particular judgements; but I shall not be arguing the matter here, and mention it mainly to avoid giving the misleading impression that the methodology of reasoning in ethics is limited to a consideration of the interplay of intuitions and normative theories, the kind of interplay presented just now.

Nevertheless the present chapter is a study of just such an interplay.

Readers, however, may well feel entitled to know what view is here assumed of the status of moral talk and moral claims. My view, argued elsewhere,[1] is that moral discourse is not concerned merely with prescriptions or expressions of attitude or commitment; it aspires to truth and actually admits of knowledge. This view has recently been ably defended by Renford Bambrough,[2] though I should add that I am more sympathetic than he is to naturalism, the view that moral judgements can be validly derived exclusively from facts (e.g. facts about harms or benefits) and conceptual truths. But my naturalism does not prevent me from finding common ground with anti-naturalist writers such as K. S. Shrader-Frechette,[3] at any rate in the area of applied ethics. The current enterprise, then, is aimed at discovering the truth about some of our obligations: and to this enterprise writers of various meta-ethical persuasions seem to have contributed, even if they do not acknowledge that there is such a truth.[4] But as I am not defending moral objectivism here, I cannot complain if some readers treat the chapters which follow as simply a search for the best available consistent and defensible ethical position.

The issue of obligations to future generations is a good starting-point for a discussion of ecological ethics. There are other distinct issues, important examples of which (the status of animals; the value of life) will be discussed in subsequent chapters. The current issue has been chosen because it allows (and indeed requires) normative theories to be assessed, because of its key role in ecological issues, and because it can be tackled without a comprehensive value-theory being elaborated. To keep the present chapter within reasonable limits, I have as far as possible postponed the issues of the obligation to perpetuate the human population and of the intrinsic value of future people, though it has not been possible at all points to avoid related matters, particularly where the question arises of the representation of the interests of possible people who on some plans will exist and on others will not. For the most part, however, I shall be concerned with obligations to people who, for one reason or another, *will* exist, irrespective of whether there should have been less (or more) of them, and whether earlier generations should have acted earlier to modify their numbers.

The importance of posterity in the beliefs of Enlightenment thinkers has already been discussed in chapter 5; indeed their recognition that it is increasingly within the power of those alive to affect the interests of those who are to follow belies the frequent claim in recent literature that there is nothing about the current issue to learn from the philosophical tradition. Yet the extent and the basis of our obligations in the matter are yet to seek. There again the ethic of stewardship, presented in chapters 2 and 3 as immune to the objections of which some other interpretations of the Judaeo-Christian tradition fall foul, might be thought equal to the need to cater for the interests of our successors. Indeed Brian Barry at one point seems, however inadvertently, to regard a recognizable version of it as suiting this need, in preference to all the traditional theories of normative ethics.[5] But to discover whether it really has implications which transcend concern for the interests of humans and other organisms, as he seems to think, it is most convenient to work out first the bearing of some of these theories, and then see whether, as Barry seems to suggest, it is in conflict with them.

Genuine obligations

On the assumption, then, that there will be people in the future, what obligations do we have in their regard? Here there is, as Gregory Kavka has pointed out,[6] an analogy with the case of the obligations of rich individuals and groups to offer aid to strangers in desperate need. If there are such obligations, then where the needs of future people compare with those of contemporary strangers, the same obligations would seem to exist to make sacrifices to alleviate needs which would otherwise be desperate. But future people will need clean air and water, fertile land, and the same natural ecosystems as those on which we ourselves depend, and we can sustain or mar all these things, and conserve or exhaust resources (some renewable, some non-renewable) which they will also require. Since they are in no way relevantly different from contemporary strangers, we have corresponding obligations in the two cases.

That rich societies do have obligations to contemporary strangers in desperate need is a proposition answering to a widespread intuitive judgement, and also a proposition which has been well argued for elsewhere.[7] Once it is accepted that we, the affluent, are morally responsible, in cases where we could prevent it, for the avoidable suffering or misery of a stranger, it is implausible to hold that distance in space makes any difference. (The ability to prevent suffering is certainly a matter of degree, but the degree does not vary with spatial distance.) And the same reasoning which suggests that we have obligations wherever we can prevent suffering or misery to contemporary strangers, however distant in space, suggests that we have similar obligations to future strangers, however distant in time: for distance in time is just as irrelevant as distance in space. Since a whole variety of plausible principles give rise to the same conclusion, it is not necessary to explore its grounds in more detail at this stage.

Richard and Val Routley reach a conclusion about the wrongness of exposing future people to one particular danger, the danger of radiation from nuclear wastes, by means of a graphic analogy. If someone consigns a container full of highly toxic and explosive gas to an overcrowded bus belonging to a poorly managed Third World bus-line, a bus with a long journey to make over hazardous roads, we should regard their action as morally appalling, even if they themselves stand to lose a great deal if they do not thus despatch it. Excuses such as that the worst *may* not happen, or that the passengers *may* be killed by a road accident first, would not be tolerated. 'To create serious risks and costs, especially risks to life and health for . . . others, simply to avoid having to make some changes to a comfortable life-style, or even for a somewhat better reason, is usually thought deserving of moral condemnation, and sometimes considered a crime.'[8] Yet in many respects, the Routleys claim, such an act is analogous to acts with effects on future people like producing and storing toxic nuclear wastes which will be radioactive for over a million years, initiated when no safe way of packaging them is known.

Whether or not they are right (and some reasons for endorsing their view emerge in the course of the current chapter), the bus analogy certainly does mirror any case where we inflict risks and dangers on future people without a good reason, such as the need to overcome a comparable evil threatening millions of people in the present. And even where present costs are at stake, there is no excuse for ignoring costs and risks to future people; present costs may be included in our moral deliberations, but we must not disregard all considerations besides. If so, then it must be acknowledged that we have obligations with regard to future people.

Discounting

But do the needs of future people merit *equal* consideration to that due to present people's needs? Kavka considers three reasons for giving less consideration to the future than to the present, and rejects them all, and others including the Routleys go through some parallel reasoning.

Kavka first considers the view that the very temporal location of future people entitles us to downgrade their interests. The fact that they do not even exist at present has certainly raised problems about whether we can speak of them as having rights; yet, granted that 'in the normal course of events' they will exist, and will be in no relevant way unlike current holders of rights, and that we have it in our power seriously to undermine their interests, there is little reason to cavil at Feinberg's conclusion that they have rights now which can be claimed on their behalf, unless 'right' is so narrowly defined as to make this conclusion false.[9] (We can either construe Feinberg's conclusion as meaning that there are rights which, when they are alive, they will have against our generation, or allow, with the Routleys, that nonexistent entities may even so have properties — bearing rights in the present included.) Kavka's reply to those who discount the needs of future people just on grounds of their temporal location is that as it is recognized that rational prudence treats an individual's future desires as being on a par with present ones, it should also be recognized that a rational morality would attach no intrinsic importance to the temporal location of people's welfare. (Kavka is here setting on one side for the moment *uncertain* future desires, and in this I follow him.)

There is, however, an apparently more plausible ground for discriminating purely on the basis of time, a ground which is seldom remarked. The present generation is the last one which can help those now alive, whereas people in the distant future can be assisted by a number of succeeding generations as well as by the present one. Thus the responsibility of saving for future generations can be shared between the various earlier ones. So in matters where there is reason to think that other generations will be able and willing to play a part, the current generation does not bear the entire burden, and its obligation to provide for some future needs is therefore lesser than its obligation in cases of some contemporary needs, which will be catered for now or never.

The immediate rejoinder to this is the observation that some present actions engender risks or harms to future generations whatever anyone else does henceforth, and that in those cases the opportunities open to our immediate successors to help their own successors are irrelevant. The more general point is perhaps as follows. Where action is needed, but others are likely to do what is necessary (in whole or in part), the difference that we make, and at the same time the extent of our obligation, is less than when, by action or inaction, we make a crucial difference to the future course of events. But in fact we have it in our power irreversibly to mar the distant future; so the general point just made has no bearing on a great many possible present actions with distant effects, and thus does not show the temporal location of the effects of our actions to be of any moral significance in itself. Indeed the general point applies indifferently whether the effects are close or distant, while at the same time explaining the fact that our responsibility to distant generations is in many cases a shared one.

Kavka next considers ignorance and uncertainty. It may be alleged, he remarks, that we cannot know what future people will want, so we cannot rate their interests on a par with those of contemporaries. But, as he says in reply, we can be confident about much that they will need whatever they want — good health, food, shelter and security; and there is much that we can do to facilitate these needs. The same reply is offered by Robert E. Goodin to another form of uncertainty argument, the argument that the costs to future people of present deeds are uncertain, as they are risks, not certainties, as future technology may dispel them, and as everyone may be dead before they have any effect; so we can discount future interests.[10] But the possibility that everyone will be dead before our deeds can harm anyone is, as the Routleys point out, an unacceptable excuse, as is also putting on others the burden of finding means to avert dangers devised by ourselves; and though, as Goodin allows, merely probable risks are less bad than certain ones, much current action is subversive of interests and desires which future people are certain to have. (And if so, Shrader-Frechette is all the more clearly right to point out that the uncertainty of costs does not entitle us to disregard them altogether.[11])

Kavka finds a variant of the argument from ignorance in the claim of Martin Golding that we should regard future people as members of our moral community only if we know what to desire for them, but that we cannot know this for distant generations, as we cannot know what their conception of the good life for man will be.[12] In reply, Kavka denies that holding any particular substantive conception of the good life is necessary for membership of the human moral community. So long as there are people with our vulnerabilities and our general capacities, they will be entitled to our moral concern whatever their beliefs and desires; though doubtless, for one reason or another — their genetic endowment and the general circumstances of social life may be suggested — their conception of the good life will be importantly similar, at least in form, to our own. Thus our ignorance as to their substantive conceptions is no reason for limiting our obligations, as Golding would do, to at most the immediate generations of our successors. Indeed, as the Routleys point out, if we can affect future people by storing nuclear wastes for a million years, we have obligations to at least some 30,000 generations.[13]

Kavka considers, thirdly, the relevance of the contingency of future people, the fact that they may not exist at all, and that how many there are depends in large measure upon ourselves. Feinberg presents a related problem: we do not know who these future people will be, and so, it could be held, we can scarcely owe them obligations.[14] But as he remarks, our nearly certain knowledge that there will be a human future is what matters: we do not need to know people's identity before we can have obligations in their regard. The Routleys present another version of this problem: our ignorance of the numbers of future people, and of most other statistics about them, might be thought to suggest that we cannot weigh their claims alongside those of present people. But as they observe, our ignorance of numbers does not permit us to ignore these claims, even if in some cases the resulting conflicts would be difficult to resolve: for determinacy of numbers is not a pre-condition of moral relevance, and any theory which makes it so is not to be taken seriously in this respect.[15]

But if we can affect the number of future consumers, do we not have a prior obligation to current ones, who exist anyway? As to future ones, perhaps what we ought to do is to curtail their numbers, and thus resolve the possible conflict of interests. This is the version of the contingency problem raised by Kavka himself. I cannot pursue all the implications here, since it raises the complex issues of whether we ought to limit the human population, and whether we should do anything wrong if we allowed it to die out. (To these issues I shall return in the next chapter.) For the present, suffice it to say that the problem concerns possible people only in the sense of 'ones whom we and the groups to which we belong could bring into existence if we chose' (ones called by Trudy Govier 'volitionally possible people'[16]), but not ones who will probably exist anyway, and over whose existence we have no control. In actual fact we can be very nearly certain that there will be a very great many future people, and, once we accept their future existence as given, the present problem ceases to supply a ground for subordinating their interests to those of existing contemporaries.

Goodin mentions two other possible grounds for discounting future interests: the prospect that future people will be better off than ourselves, and the supposed diminished value of benefits which are enjoyed later rather than earlier. His reply on the first count is that future people may for all we know be worse off, and that we should need to know that they will be a good deal richer than ourselves before we could justifiably burden them with the risks of leaking radioactive waste storage dumps. He might have added, had he not been restricting himself to energy policies, that actions of ours which imperil life-support systems could undermine the vital interests of our successors, however rich, and so the effect of discounting could be one of irretrievable disaster for them in exchange for much lesser welfare gains to our contemporaries.

The second count depends on an analogy between costs, benefits and monetary values. The value of money depreciates over time with inflation, so a dollar now is worth much more now than it will be in ten years' time. Something similar is also often true of both benefits and costs: delaying either often involves some of the other. But as Goodin points out, this is no argument for a social discount rate. Interest rates are unstable and unpredictable, and many damages which may be suffered in future as a result of present actions cannot be compensated for in money, even if funds are now invested with a view to the interest providing for predicted costs. Besides, as Derek Parfit points out, benefits are often not reinvested but consumed, and are thus of no greater benefit to anyone than similar benefits received later; while in other cases there is no gain involved in delayed costs, as for example if a genetic defect is suffered by one person in 20 years rather than by another next year. Hence the costs and benefits of deferment should be reckoned only where they will exist; they do not justify a diminished weighting of future interests in general.[17] It should be added that even quite low rates of discounting the future have the effect of attaching a quite negligible value to any at all distant future interests, and are thus, as the Routleys point out, open to the same moral objections as policies which write off future people entirely.[18]

Indeed I can best summarize the conclusion so far reached by endorsing theirs: *there is the same obligation to future people as to the present.*[19] Future people count, to speak morally, as much as present ones. Our obligations in their regard are only lessened where special known factors supervene, for example, cases where efforts on their behalf are likely to miscarry. Our obligations to people are not lessened at all by the mere fact of their futurity.

Superseded theories

This conclusion, however, based as it is on reflection on widespread moral intuitions, is, as Brian Barry has pointed out,[20] in conflict with several classical theories of the circumstances which give rise to obligations, and of the scope and limits of our duties. Barry stresses the asymmetry of power between generations which do not overlap; earlier ones can help or hurt later ones, but later ones cannot affect earlier ones (except over their members' reputations). On no less than three classical theories this asymmetry disqualifies the later generations from being the beneficiaries of obligations owed by the earlier ones. The discussion of these theories, which now follows, prepares the way for a search for a more adequate normative theory, one which as well as coping with other departments of morality can also account for our very real obligations towards future people.

According to one theory, that of David Hume, justice and moral obligations have their point because they are in the general interest of partially self-interested persons, persons of approximately equal strength and vulnerable to each other. As Barry points out elsewhere,[21] Hume held that justice arises and has a point in conditions of moderate scarcity, but that there are no obligations where scarcity is extreme; and that it has force among parties who are vulnerable to one another, but would have none in relations between humans and a weaker species, however rational and intelligent its members. Now granted the asymmetry of power between present and future generations, the latter must be regarded by a Humean as in the same position as such a weaker species, and so obligations to them (or even in their regard) would have to be denied. Nor is this surprising, if morality is construed as an artifice of self-defence which at normal times benefits all participants.

Should we then hold to Hume's theory, despite its failure to uphold obligations towards future people? Barry is, I suggest, right to reject it. Hume succeeds in portraying circumstances in which justice might arise and be accepted as advantageous, and then confuses and conflates these circumstances and the limits of justice. In fact his theory is in several ways in violation of our moral intuitions. Thus we do not hold that the right to life holds only in conditions of moderate scarcity, but lapses in circumstances of famine. Nor do we hold that there can be no obligations owed to the defenceless. Indeed, as Barry observes, even Hume does not manage consistently to maintain otherwise.[22]

The second longstanding view discussed by Barry is that obligations arise through people living beside others in a community with its reciprocal relationships. Such a view clearly has no place for obligations to those of our successors who are born after we die. Barry finds such a view in Golding,[23] though Golding does allow there to be possible obligations to those future people with whose conception of the good life ours has enough in common. But, as we have seen, this is too restrictive: and if Golding's community theory is to be rejected on this count, so *a fortiori* must any theory be which does not make provision for non-members of the community to which the agent happens to belong.

Thirdly Barry considers the view on which obligations are grounded in entitlements to property, a view which he ascribes to John Locke and to Robert Nozick's book *Anarchy, State and Utopia*.[24] On this view those who come by a good justly may do what they like with it, and owe no obligations with respect of it to anyone. (Locke in fact accepted such property rights only if there were comparable gifts of nature left over and to spare for others,[25] but seems too readily to have assumed that the condition would always be satisfied.[26]) But if no obligations are owed to contemporaries (except over property rights of theirs), no more, to say the least, will be owed to the people of the future, who never hold property rights at the same time as any of their predecessors.

But once again the theory under consideration conflicts with widely held moral intuitions besides the ones about future people. Thus we do not hold that there is no obligation to give material assistance to a person in desperate need whom we can help, whether a member of our community or a stranger; and, there again, justice may require a redistribution of property (as, plausibly, in several Latin American countries), however justly it was arrived at.

Accordingly I accept Barry's rejection of all these theories of normative ethics. Barry next discusses the theory of John Passmore, which yields the conclusion that our obligations are to immediate posterity only.[27] Passmore draws on the presumed support of the diverse normative theories of Jeremy Bentham, Henry Sidgwick, John Rawls and Martin Golding; but the Routleys cast serious doubt on whether any of them afford it.[28] Passmore's own basic theory is that our obligations depend on what we love. Accordingly, as our loves do not stretch into the distant future, neither do our obligations. To this theory it may be replied that obligations can exist irrespective of feelings; that we have obligations to many distant people about whom we have no feelings; and that the claim

that an obligation lapses just because a love has lapsed would be too
easy a way of disowning an obligation. Passmore also appeals
sometimes to the view that obligations depend on membership of a
community, a view which has already been rejected. He also makes
great play with the uncertainty of future people's interests. But, as
Barry retorts, 'Of course, we don't know what the precise tastes of
our remote descendants will be, but they are unlikely to include a
desire for skin cancer, soil erosion, or the inundation of low-lying
areas as a result of the melting of the ice-caps.'[29]

Towards a better theory

What theory of normative ethics, then, is equal to giving a coherent
treatment of obligations to future generations? This question is now
pursued with the help of Jere Paul Surber's survey.[30] Surber, like
Barry, concludes that no existing type of theory is satisfactory.
Surber considers in turn deontic theories, utilitarian theories and
the position of Golding. He does not find anyone in the literature
even attempting to apply a deontic theory to the issue of obligations
to the future, though strictly John Rawls' theory (to which I shall
return) is such, for Rawls holds that it is not exclusively their
consequences that justify actions or rules,[31] and he certainly discusses
what he himself calls 'The Problem of Justice between Generations'.[32]
But Surber seems to mean by 'deontic theories' rather theories on
which agents possess rights which cannot be abridged, whatever the
circumstances, or on which some actions are wrong, whatever the
consequences. Some of his criticisms of such theories are less than
convincing, but I accept his central criticism that if such a theory
accepted obligations to the future alongside ones to the present, it
would lack the resources to decide the priorities between these
various obligations, just as in general such theories characteristically
offer no solution when obligations conflict; and we should lack just
the sort of guidance which we might reasonably expect from a
theory whose role is to disclose which act is morally right. (I shall
later consider whether Rawls surmounts this objection by supplying
acceptable principles and rules of priority.)

But Surber does not, in the end, find the position of Golding a
satisfactory one, and is quite unimpressed with utilitarianism. He
grants that, being a future-orientated, consequentialist type of
theory, utilitarianism is apparently well-suited to dealing with
obligations towards future people. But he holds that the 'classical
formula' on which 'that action (or rule) is the most desirable which

will maximize the average utility' is inapplicable when applied to any generation of future people, as we cannot deal in averages when the number of the population is not fixed.

Though I shall be criticizing in chapter 7 some of the deliverances of this, the Average theory version of utilitarianism, the theory is often regarded as being better able to cope with examples where populations are not fixed than its counterpart, the Total theory. And I do not think that Surber's objection suffices to overthrow this assessment. According to the Total theory, it is desirable (or, on other interpretations, obligatory) to maximize total utility. As Surber points out, where populations are fixed, the two theories commend exactly the same acts (or rules), for total and average vary together. They diverge only where the average and the total part company, i.e. in cases where the denominator (the number of people involved) is itself at issue. And here it is often supposed that the Total theory requires the population to be maximized, and that it is an advantage of the Average theory that it does not.

Surber derives his criticism of the Average theory from J. Brenton Stearns,[33] who persuades himself that the indeterminacy of the number of future people makes the Average theory collapse. But upholders of this theory need only maintain instead that the average utility is the average of that of however many people there will be. On their view if an increase in numbers raises this average it should be preferred, but if it lowers the average it should be rejected. The only issue on which it is not equipped to deliver a judgement one way or the other is that of which to prefer of two different populations with the same average utility. But, this issue aside, the theory is not open to Surber's and Stearns' objection, nor therefore to that of the Routleys to theories which require determinacy as a condition of supplying a moral judgement. (Indeed we could in many cases know that total or average welfare would rise or fall without having any particular quantitative level in mind: so utilitarianism in general is immune to this objection.)

Much more than Surber, Stearns is impressed with the fact that the arguments used by conservationists are almost always utilitarian, and naturally so. Concern to conserve resources, ecosystems and gene-pools, or to prevent pollution and ugliness, is most readily grounded in benevolence towards the interests of our contemporaries and successors. (Some conservationists hold that arguments from human interests are insufficient, but I shall postpone arguments concerning other interests to later chapters.) So despite some misgivings, Stearns operates within the utilitarian tradition, and adopts a variant of the Total theory. We have an obligation, he holds, to maximize intrinsic goods and to minimize intrinsic evils, irrespective of which people they befall. Our obligation then is not to definite people, but 'to see to it that human existence continues at a fairly high level of intrinsic value'.

These distinctions, and the rival merits of the Total theory and the Average theory, will be more fully discussed in the next chapter, where their relations with the population issue and with the value of life will be explored. For present purposes it is worth noticing that either of these two versions of utilitarianism could defensibly be held to underpin obligations to future generations, at least as far as we have seen. The only unanswered objection to either so far is the standard criticism of the Total theory that it requires too high a level of population. But as it does not require us to bring into existence people who will not lead lives worth living, or people whose addition to the population diminishes the total happiness, this objection is by no means obviously fatal. This is far from the end of the matter, but the Total theory is obviously not indefensible.

Surber in fact rejects Stearns' own version of the Total theory because Stearns combines it with belief in duties to definite (existent or 'contracted for') people, and believes that this duality of principles gives rise to incommensurable obligations within utilitarianism; and this, it will be recalled, is the weakness over which Surber rejected deontic theories earlier. But it is not clear that benevolence to known persons is incommensurable with benevolence to future persons of indefinite identity: there seems nothing incoherent in asking whether cheap energy for some of the former outweighs the risks of radiation leaks for rather more of the latter. Stearns gets into the position of accepting irreducible duties to assignable persons as well as the duty of benevolence through his less-than-total rejection of Jan Narveson's form of utilitarianism, on which our duties are limited to assignable persons (plus duties of non-maleficence),[34] a theory also to be discussed in the next chapter. Believing that our duties extend beyond this, he takes our duties in the connection of indefinite future people to be incommensurable with some of the duties which Narveson acknowledges: but this concession is, as far as I can see, unnecessary.

Surber, however, has another objection to utilitarian theories in general. Some of the benefits which obligations to future generations secure are, he holds, incalculable. His examples are the *possibility* of encountering a natural environment, and the *experience* of deciding for themselves how to manage it. But utilitarianism, he holds, can only treat with calculable goods.

I, too, doubt whether these goods derive their value solely from the amounts of happiness which they facilitate, and therefore reject any purely hedonistic form of utilitarianism. But I believe that other forms of consequentialism (to which the term 'utilitarianism' is sometimes applied by extension), which count the ability to exercise essential human powers as an intrinsic good alongside happiness, can cope with the examples just mentioned. For, as long as terms like 'more' and 'less' can intelligibly be applied, consequentialists do not need to calculate the value of, say, experiences in terms of units of intrinsic value of their own devising. The use of numerical examples in discussions of utilitarian theory misleads us if we assume that it can only deal with given quantities. The same point applies, so far as their effect on humans is concerned, to Surber's other examples — the loss of an animal species or of the beauty of an unspoiled forest. And even though other interests or considerations plausibly enter into these examples (e.g. animal interests), that is no reason for taking them to involve evils with which utilitarianism cannot deal.

Barry too has an objection to utilitarianism, or at least to the Total theory, an objection which it is important to consider. Having rejected as spurious the claim that ignorance of the future exonerates us of obligations concerning its more distant generations, Barry nevertheless expresses sympathy for the conclusion of John Passmore that what utilitarianism requires of us is too rigorous.[35] I propose to take this view not as a refusal to undertake acknowledged obligations, but as a rejection of the belief that they exist. What, then, is implausible or extreme about the obligations involved in the Total theory? At times Barry implies that consequentialism might conflict with justice, a claim which I have contested elsewhere.[36] But the present context suggests that Barry's objection is rather along the following lines: the Total theory requires us to give equal consideration, as far as we can make any difference, to all generations, present and future; but this extends the duties of the present generation up to, and possibly beyond, the limits of our capacities.

It is not at all clear, however, that this conclusion follows. I do not just have in mind the fact that we cannot have duties beyond our capacities. The main way in which we can serve the people of the distant future is by *refraining* from various actions which would imperil their environment or their health, and these omissions are well within our powers. Besides this, the renewable resources which they will need can be provided for, as far as it is up to us, by conserving them in a self-renewing (or at least renewable) condition:

and the same applies to those institutions the bequeathing of which to our successors constitutes our main obligation to them in Passmore's view.

As to savings, two points are significant. As we may learn from Kenneth Boulding,[37] future people will have most call for a stock of unexhausted natural resources (and of knowledge in the arts and the sciences), rather than for the means to a high level of consumption. Again the likelihood that some of our more immediate successors will provide for some of the needs in question diminishes the difference which can be made by ourselves. Problems certainly remain over the use of some non-renewable resources (e.g. ores and fossil fuels), but, all things considered, the obligations which the Total theory generates do not seem to be unrealistically exacting, extensive though they are. (It is interesting to note that Barry's objection here presupposes the falsity of Surber's objection about calculating benefits.)

The contractarian approach

Barry, however, prefers to investigate the possibility of grounding obligations to future people in a contractarian approach, such as that of John Rawls' *A Theory of Justice*, even though he is not eventually satisfied with this approach. The Total theory, Barry holds, requires too many sacrifices for the sake of actualizing extra people, the Average theory too few; while the Total theory is also accused (but surely mistakenly) of allowing a policy of producing a massive population for the next two centuries, leading to the extinction of the species.[38] (But it is surely implausible that this would even be the best way of maximizing the number of future humans, let alone their happiness.) The Routleys, also, are hostile to utilitarianism, and attempt to reconstruct a Rawlsian basis for our obligations to future people,[39] while Shrader-Frechette, who is so hostile to utilitarianism as to conclude that policies which are inegalitarian are *therefore* utilitarian(!), clearly also favours a Rawlsian approach.[40] So I shall now investigate the adequacy of the Rawlsian theory as the basis of our obligations.

Rawls' basic assumption is that those rules are just which would be chosen by rational contractors, parties about to embark on life with a good understanding of human affairs in general but no knowledge of their own future setting or distinctive beliefs. Their ignorance guarantees that they do not devise rules so as to benefit themselves; and it also has to be assumed that they are rationally self-interested and never sacrifice self-interest either for the sake of others' good or for their harm. But Rawls has a problem about future generations. He considers it too far-fetched to imagine the contracting parties being members of the different generations which will be spread out through history; and, adopting as he does the interpretation of his 'original position' in which the parties know that they are of the same generation as each other, he has to change his assumptions about motivation in order to generate a just savings principle from their choices. Each party is therefore assumed to care for his own immediate descendants, and sees to it that rules are chosen which provide for them.[41]

Rawls' modification of the motivations of the parties in the original position is properly attacked by Barry on grounds of method: it is an *ad hoc* device, guaranteed to derive obligations which correspond with the author's intuitions. It is also arbitrary and implausible: if the parties care for their descendants, why should they not also care for their families and their friends? Besides, the derived principle of just savings has no bearing on the question of obligations to *distant* future generations.[42]

Barry accordingly concludes that instead of this motivational device, Rawls should have dropped the postulate that the parties in the original position are contemporaries. This view is considered (but not endorsed) by D. Clayton Hubin,[43] and accepted by the Routleys.[44] Instead Rawls should have assumed that all generations are represented (Barry), or better, that some are (the Routleys). Hubin in fact raises the difficulty for such a move that the circumstances of justice, as depicted by Hume and largely echoed by Rawls,[45] do not exist between generations. But, as we have seen, Barry has well criticized the view that where Hume's circumstances of justice are absent, no obligations of justice exist between the parties. (Hubin's own view is that injustice towards future generations is possible, but only where it issues from injustice to an agent's contemporaries, with their natural concern for their children and grandchildren.[46] This, however, is to assume that we only have obligations to people as a result of voluntary agreements, communal ties, or the like: it has been argued above that in fact the basis of obligation is much broader than this.)

The original position as revised by Barry and the Routleys will clearly yield unsuitable results if the parties are required to believe that justice only arises in the kind of circumstances portrayed by Hume: so this belief must be discarded. So also should be the belief that all generations are represented, for the parties could deduce from this belief and some simple arithmetic how many generations there will be; but this is one of the issues which in some measure is supposed to depend on their deliberations.[47] The scenario provided by the Routleys, however, goes some way towards resolving this problem, as the parties know only that some (not all) generations are represented, and do not know which ones.

From this interpretation of Rawls' original position the Routleys are able to show that there would be chosen not only, as Rawls allows, a just savings principle but also a principle governing the just distribution and rate of usage of material resources over the generations. This principle would severely restrict the consumption of non-renewable resources, since their depletion threatens the interests of later generations, except where substitutes can be found. At the same time, as the Routleys plausibly claim, these interests would preclude the development of energy from nuclear fission at any time before safe storage methods for waste products had been discovered. F. Patrick Hubbard, working with approximately the same interpretation,[48] similarly derives both a principle guaranteeing a minimum of resources to all generations and also one setting a ceiling or maximum on consumption, which would prevent exponential increases in production and pollution and facilitate a sustainable form of society. As he recognizes, the minimum and the maximum would in some circumstances be far apart, and in others coincide. He also considers the possibility that liberty might need to be restricted to ensure compliance with the ceiling principle.

Similarly Victor D. Lippit and Koichi Hamada 'extend' Rawls' original position to supply principles of intergenerational distribution: their requirement that 'people do not know into which generation they will be born,'[49] taken in the context of their claim that no one can effectively represent future generations, suggests that the parties are not drawn from the same generation as each other. They point out that later generations, though advantaged in respect of technology and capital stock, are not advantaged as to the state of the natural environment: 'if current trends are not reversed future generations will live by making grotesque adaptations to a polluted environment or not live at all.'[50]

Accordingly the principles which would be chosen in their extended original position include one enjoining absolute limitations on polluting activities (the 'polluters-stop principle') — but this is surely too drastic — and one requiring 'each generation to leave the earth's environment no more polluted than it was at the time of that generation's arrival on the scene'.[51] The only permitted exceptions would be granted to prevent the current generation becoming the most disadvantaged; for the sake of its food supplies, some environmental disruption could be allowed, but not, for example, for the sake of every family having a car. Altogether the effect of the application of these principles would be the curtailment, though not a total prohibition, of further economic growth.

Such principles could readily be supplemented, for example, by ones governing the preservation of species and of wilderness. Indeed many of them could readily be derived from other normative theories, such as either the Average or the Total theories within the utilitarian tradition. The Rawlsian framework is proving to be a valuable one in allowing economists as well as philosophers to review long-cherished assumptions about efficiency and discounting. But it also has serious defects, not all of which can be remedied by modifications of the original position.

Not by contract alone

One problem, raised by both Leon H. Craig and by Barry,[52] is that as the number of generations or of future people who will eventually live is not settled prior to the decisions made in the original position, anything there agreed will be prejudicial to the interests of generations which *might* exist, unless they are somehow represented. Otherwise many possible generations may be prevented from existing. Whether possible people have interests is, of course, disputed: but it is clear that if there is no representation of possible people the outcome could easily be the extinction of humanity in a few centuries' time — a very great evil on most views.

The solution to this difficulty seems to be the inclusion of representatives of possible people in the original position. But this solution (which Barry seems to envisage in a parenthesis probably intended as whimsical) is surely an illusory one: for as they are infinite in number, their total presence is out of the question; and, for the same reason, no delegation representing them could fairly be assigned any particular number of votes to counterbalance the votes of the representatives of actual people. Perhaps their representatives could be assigned a veto (likely to be applied to *any* proposal involving the consumption of resources in our period of history). Or perhaps no one should be allowed to know that they themselves are going to be actual. But it then becomes difficult to tell what principles would be arrived at in such an assembly, and even harder to see why we should accept them as just ones.

It will be readily allowed, of course, that possible persons are a problem for any normative theory. But the present point is that for Rawls' theory the problem seems to be insuperable. Possible people will appear again in the next chapter. For the present I turn to a different problem for Rawls and his followers.

The problem is that there is reason to doubt Rawls' most basic assumption, that all and only those rules chosen in some suitably depicted original position would be just. The reason consists in the fact that the contracting parties are self-interested humans: there is nothing to ensure that they see justice done to all the other candidate holders of rights. Certainly they will provide for all the kinds and conditions of human life of their own generation, as they each know that such might be their own kind and condition. But they will not devise rules which accord rights to members of nonhuman species, which thus must fall outside the domain of justice. Now certainly Rawls holds that duties to animals fall under a quite separate province of morality, that of compassion; but if, as Feinberg holds, animals can have moral rights,[53] or if obligations are in some other way due to them, and if the same holds good of the rational denizens of other planets whom we may some day encounter, then this is not enough. Besides, if Barry is right about Hume, then Rawls is mistaken in following Hume's account of the circumstances of justice, and accordingly the rules of justice will not be confined to those which Rawls' more or less equal contracting parties, selected to satisfy these conditions, would choose. The present point is not just that the beliefs of the contracting parties should be varied (as above): it is rather that they are unsuitable as parties fit to decide what shall be just.

Accordingly in order to discover principles of obligation and of justice, there is reason to doubt whether our method should be to ask what rational people would choose or bargain for, and all the more reason to doubt whether Rawls' principles, either of substance or of priority, are the correct ones, since (apart from whatever intuitive appeal they may happen to have) they rest upon his dubious basic assumption. It is open to us to reason direct from the needs of people (including, perhaps, possible people) and of members of species with similar capacities and vulnerabilities; indeed this is what is done by those variants of consequentialism which allow prominence to needs (and not just to happiness).[54] Such a position, unlike its rivals, is so far unscathed, and will be explored further in the chapters following.

But it by no means follows that the principles governing

obligations to future generations which have been arrived at on a Rawlsian basis must be abandoned. Certainly they need to be supplemented, but in most cases it turns out that a plausible consequentialist theory will supply suitable foundations for the principles put forward on a Rawlsian basis by the Routleys, Hubbard, and Lippit and Hamada. So it is worth discovering what principles such a form of consequentialism sustains.

Implications of consequentialism

Now the form of consequentialism which I shall further expound and defend in chapter 7 is a version of the Total theory. On this version the maximization of intrinsic value is always morally desirable and, where a significant difference can be made, it is also morally obligatory. Intrinsic value is best maximized, I shall further be claiming, by provision for everyone's basic needs; and this clearly involves equal provision for the needs of each generation, once population has stabilized.

It has been suggested by Kavka that just this kind of equal provision could be implemented by applying across the generations a form of the condition which John Locke laid down for (as it so happens) the acceptability of private property, namely that each should leave enough and as good for others. Thus each generation may 'use the earth's physical resources only to the extent that technology allows for the recycling or depletion of such resources without net loss in their output capacity'.[55] Non-renewable resources may be used, so long as they are not wasted, but only on condition that renewable resources are conserved and technology so applied that the remaining resources (non-renewable ones included) can sustain the same levels of population as earlier. A generation which more than replaces its own numbers would be required to leave proportionately more total resources, so that equal provision could be made for each member of the next generation. Increases in resources would take the form of improved technology; as we have seen, even though it cannot be assumed that every problem has a technological solution, there is reason to believe that technology can continue to solve problems in its own proper sphere by building on achievements and knowledge attained in the past. Kavka's 'Lockean standard' thus involves the conservation of renewable resources, and technological improvements which match depletions in non-renewable ones. As he says, 'If all succeeding generations abided by it, mankind could go on living on earth indefinitely' (or could if the environment too were suitably conserved).

It may be objected to what I am suggesting that consequentialist theories need not be committed to equal provision for the needs of different people, whether in one generation or in more; and doubtless some variants of consequentialism are vulnerable to this objection. But, as proponents of the law of diminishing marginal utility have long since been claiming, provision for basic needs does much more good than provision for what is less needed or not needed at all: and so the best way to bring about states of the world with the greatest intrinsic value is to provide equally for the needs of all, with priority being accorded to needs which are basic. If so, consequentialist theory can furnish a grounding for a good number of our intuitive beliefs about obligations of justice (e.g. obligations towards future people), and about such rights as they either will have or do have already. Thus Kavka's 'Lockean standard' exactly fits the requirements of a plausible consequentialist theory.

Kavka is also concerned, in fact, about the distribution of burdens between the generations, and solves it in the first instance by holding that each generation is obliged to provide for the availability to each future generation of benefits equal to those enjoyed by itself. But when he confronts the problem of inaugurating this overall intergenerational arrangement, he remarks that the current generation would be overburdened, granted the investments needed to bring about the sort of development in poor countries which alone is likely to stabilize world population at a level at which it can be sustained.[56] From this he concludes that our generation would be justified in using up more than would otherwise be its fair share of resources, if by doing so it could create the conditions in which the Lockean standard would become possible for future generations without excessive sacrifice. This is a salutary way of relating solutions of developmental and ecological problems, and serves to draw attention to the fact that world society can only be sustainable if it is also just. If, then, the claim about the need for investment for development and the stabilization of the human population is accepted, this distribution of burdens and exemptions is also supportable in the name of maximizing the satisfaction of needs.

Kavka's 'Lockean standard' is all of a piece with Surber's concern that the current generation should provide for equivalent possibilities and opportunities for experience and choice for future people to those enjoyed by itself.[57] As argued above, this concern will readily fit into a consequentialist framework; it seems also to call for the kind of equal provision principle which Kavka favours. So too does

Boulding's stress on the importance of conserving the stock of natural resources and on minimizing pollution.[58] (Kavka's programme does not seem to outlaw pollution, as Lippit and Hamada would, but requires its containment and the prevention of its escalation. Thus waste heat would be minimized to avert the eventual overheating of the atmosphere or of the more industrialized zones.) Similarly Barry maintains that the overall range of opportunities available to successor generations should not be narrowed: if some are closed off — for example, by the depletion of resources — others should be opened up, even at the cost of some sacrifice.[59] And Mary Williams argues that instead of the discounting of the interests of future people, utilitarianism enjoins a policy of 'maximum sustainable yield', on which renewable resources are harvested at a level which can be maintained indefinitely.[60] (This conclusion, however, needs to be modified when the interests of nonhumans are taken into account.[61])

The 'Lockean standard' also accommodates several proposals put forward by followers of Rawls. This applies to the restriction advocated by the Routleys on any one generation's use of material resources, and similarly to Hubbard's principle of a consumption maximum, though as we have seen, the maximum might in fact need to be varied, and the principle of equal provision for each generation is best expressed in a positive way, rather than in the form of an absolute restriction on growth, which might too greatly narrow future opportunities, especially for the poor. The Routleys' conclusion that nuclear power programmes ought to be avoided, at least until safe storage techniques exist, is also upheld, as otherwise the risks to future people are too great. Indeed, as Goodin points out, almost any serious decision procedure for the assessment of risks supports the anti-nuclear case.[62] Finally Lippit and Hamada's principle requiring each generation to leave the earth no more polluted than it received it is for all practical purposes congruous with Kavka's programme.

That programme, it must be allowed, could well be chosen as an intergenerational rule by a gathering of representatives randomly selected from the different generations. But, granted the defects mentioned above in contract theories of justice (and indeed in the other nonconsequentialist theories considered), it is important that it can also be supported from within the consequentialist tradition. This, I should claim, is its true basis: the 'Lockean standard' is right because it maximizes the satisfaction of human need throughout the generations without undue harm to nonhuman species. This claim is further vindicated in chapter 7 and in the chapters following.

But what is this claim if not an interpretation and a defence of the ideology of stewardship? Stewardship can after all be described and defended in terms of human interests (alongside the interests of other creatures),[63] even though, for the religious believer, it continues to constitute an expression of responsibility before God, and before the moral community of which God is the principal member. No new ethic is needed to cater for our treatment of our successors: what is needed is the detailed application of some very ancient traditions.

NOTES

1	Robin Attfield, 'The Logical Status of Moral Utterances', *Journal of Critical Analysis,* 4 (2), 1972, 70—84.
2	Renford Bambrough, *Moral Scepticism and Moral Knowledge,* London and Henley: Routledge & Kegan Paul, 1979. See especially chapters 2—3. My reservations are expressed in a review in *The Philosophical Quarterly*, 31, 1981, 177—8.
3	K. S. Shrader-Frechette, *Nuclear Power and Public Policy,* Dordrecht, Boston and London: Reidel, 1980. My disagreement over meta-ethics concerns her remarks on the so-called 'naturalistic fallacy' in chapter 6.
4	An example is Jonathan Glover's book, *Causing Death and Saving Lives,* Harmondsworth: Penguin Books, 1977. Glover waives all claims to moral objectivity at p. 35, but supplies an admirable example of the search for it throughout his book.
5	Brian Barry, 'Justice Between Generations', in P. M. S. Hacker and J. Raz (eds), *Law, Morality and Society,* Oxford: Clarendon Press, 1977, 268—84. See in particular p. 284.
6	Gregory Kavka, 'The Futurity Problem', in R. I. Sikora and Brian Barry (eds), *Obligations to Future Generations,* Philadelphia: Temple University Press, 1978, 186—203, p. 187. (Kavka's article is reprinted in Ernest Partridge, *Responsibilities to Future Generations,* New York: Prometheus Books, 1981, 109—22.)
7	See Peter Singer: 'Famine, Affluence and Morality', *Philosophy and Public Affairs,* 1, 1971—72, 229—43; 'Reconsidering the Famine Relief Argument', in P. G. Brown and H. Shue (eds), *Food Policy,* New York: Free Press, 1977, 36—53. Several of Singer's fellow-contributors argue to this effect in William Aiken and Hugh La Follette (eds), *World Hunger and Moral Obligation,* Englewood Cliffs, NJ: Prentice-Hall, 1977, in which 'Famine, Affluence and Morality' is reprinted. Onora Nell argues to the same conclusion from a different premise in 'Lifeboat Earth', *Philosophy and Public Affairs,* 4, 1974—75, 273—92. I have

presented some considerations in support of Singer's stance in 'Supererogation and Double Standards', *Mind*, 88, 1979, 481—99.

8   R. and V. Routley, 'Nuclear Energy and Obligations to the Future', *Inquiry*, 21, 1978, 133—79, p. 135.

9   See Joel Feinberg, 'The Rights of Animals and Unborn Generations', in William T. Blackstone (ed.), *Philosophy and Environmental Crisis*, Athens: University of Georgia Press, 1974, 43—68; also in Richard A. Wasserstrom (ed.), *Today's Moral Problems* (2nd edn), New York: Macmillan Co. and London: Collier-Macmillan, 1979, 581—601; and in Ernest Partridge (ed.), *Responsibilities to Future Generations*, 139—50. See also the papers there by Ruth Macklin, Richard T. de George, Galen K. Pletcher and Annette Baier. All these writers accept obligations to future generations. Whether we speak of future people's rights depends on the sense of 'right', and as Baier says, is a subordinate issue. As is argued in chapter 7, not all morality turns on rights.

10 Robert E. Goodin, 'No Moral Nukes', *Ethics*, 90, 1980, 417—49, at p. 429.

11 Shrader-Frechette, *Nuclear Power and Public Policy*, chapter 3. Though there is insufficient space to launch into a full assessment of the risks of nuclear energy, the conclusions reached in this paragraph will stand independently of such a study.

12 Martin Golding, 'Obligations to Future Generations', *The Monist*, 56, 1972, 85—99, p. 97f., reprinted in Partridge (ed.) *Responsibilities to Future Generations*, 61—72. Daniel Callahan's reply to Golding embodies points parallel to Kavka's; thus he insists that 'our moral community' be construed as the human community and not some subsection of it. See Callahan's paper 'What Obligations do we have to Future Generations?' in *American Ecclesiastical Review*, 164, 1971, 265—80, reprinted in *Responsibilities to Future Generations*, 73—85.

13 R. and V. Routley, 'Nuclear Energy and Obligations to the Future', p. 137. I have argued in 'On Being Human', *Inquiry*, 17, 1974, 175—92, that human nature and needs set limits to defensible substantive conceptions of the good life for a human.

14 Feinberg, 'The Rights of Animals and Unborn Generations', p. 65.

15 R. and V. Routley, 'Nuclear Energy and Obligations to the Future', pp. 158—60.

16 Trudy Govier, 'What Should We Do About Future People?' *American Philosophical Quarterly*, 16, 1979, 105—13.

17 Derek Parfit, 'Energy Policy and the Further Future', forthcoming in Peter Brown and Douglas MacLean (eds), *Energy Policy and Future Generations*, Tottowa, NJ: Rowman & Littlefield.

18 R. and V. Routley, 'Nuclear Energy and Obligations to the Future', p. 150. A similar point is made by Kenneth Boulding in 'The Economics of the Coming Spaceship Earth', in John Barr (ed.), *The Environmental Handbook*, 77—82, p. 81.

19 'Nuclear Energy and Obligations to the Future', p. 161.

20   Barry, 'Justice Between Generations', at pp. 270—6.
21   Barry, 'Circumstances of Justice and Future Generations', in R. I. Sikora and Brian Barry (eds) *Obligations to Future Generations,* 204—48: also David Hume, *A Treatise of Human Nature* and *An Enquiry Concerning the Principles of Morals,* in T. H. Green and T. H. Grose (eds), *The Philosophical Works* (4 Vols.), London: Longmans, Green, 1874—75.
22   'Circumstances of Justice and Future Generations', p. 221. See further Mary Midgley, 'Duties Concerning Islands', in Robert Elliot and Arran Gare (eds), *Environmental Philosophy: A Collection of Readings,* St. Lucia: University of Queensland Press, 1983.
23   'Justice Between Generations', p. 272.
24   Robert Nozick, *Anarchy, State and Utopia,* Oxford: Blackwell and New York: Basic Books, 1974.
25   See Kavka, 'The Futurity Problem', p. 200.
26   See F. Patrick Hubbard, 'Justice, Limits to Growth, and an Equilibrium State', *Philosophy and Public Affairs,* 7, 1977—78, 326—45, p. 345, n. 12.
27   John Passmore, *MRN,* p. 91. A similar view is held by Peter Laslett in 'The Conversation Between the Generations', in Royal Institute of Philosophy (ed.), *The Proper Study,* London and Basingstoke: Macmillan Press, 1971, 172—89, and is open to parallel objections.
28   R. and V. Routley, 'Nuclear Energy and Obligations to the Future', pp. 144—9, 166—73, and 176, n. 14.
29   'Justice Between Generations', p. 274.
30   Jere Paul Surber, 'Obligations to Future Generations: Explorations and Problemata', *Journal of Value Inquiry,* 11, 1977, 104—16.
31   See Robin Attfield, 'Toward a Defence of Teleology', *Ethics,* 85, 1975, 123—35, pp. 128—31.
32   John Rawls, *A Theory of Justice,* London, Oxford, New York: Oxford University Press, 1972, Section 44, pp. 284—93.
33   J. Brenton Stearns, 'Ecology and the Indefinite Unborn', *The Monist,* 56, 1972, 612—25. Reprinted in Richard A. Wasserstrom (ed.), *Today's Moral Problems,* 602—13.
34   Jan Narveson, 'Utilitarianism and New Generations', *Mind,* 76, 1967, 62—72.
35   Barry, 'Justice Between Generations', p. 275.
36   See 'Circumstances of Justice and Future Generations', p. 219: Robin Attfield, 'Toward a Defence of Teleology'; also 'Racialism, Justice and Teleology', *Ethics,* 87, 1977, 186—8.
37   Boulding, 'The Economics of the Coming Spaceship Earth', p. 78.
38   These objections are to be found in 'Justice Between Generations', pp. 283f.
39   See R. and V. Routley, 'Nuclear Energy and Obligations to the Future', pp. 151f, and 167—73, respectively.

40   See Shrader-Frechette, *Nuclear Power and Public Policy,* pp. 94 and
     149, and 122f, respectively.
41   Rawls, *A Theory of Justice,* Sections 4, 24, 25, 44 and 45.
42   'Justice Between Generations', pp. 279f. Also D. Clayton Hubin, 'Justice
     and Future Generations', *Philosophy and Public Affairs,* 6, 1976—77,
     70—83 (see p. 75, n. 4).
43   Hubin, 'Justice and Future Generations', pp. 72—81.
44   R. and V. Routley, 'Nuclear Energy and Obligation to the Future',
     pp. 167f.
45   *A Theory of Justice,* p. 127.
46   Hubin agrees with Edwin Delattre that obligations regarding future
     persons should not be analysed as obligations owed to those persons.
     See Delattre, 'Rights, Responsibilities and Future Persons', *Ethics,* 82,
     1972, 254—8.
47   Thus Barry, 'Justice Between Generations', p. 281.
48   F. Patrick Hubbard, 'Justice, Limits to Growth, and an Equilibrium
     State'. For his interpretation of the original position, see p. 330, n. 4.
     Cf. the principles of maximal and minimal provision for future
     generations derived by Michael Bayles in 'Famine or Food: Sacrificing
     for Future or Present Generations' in Partridge (ed.) *Responsibilities
     to Future Generations,* 239—45.
49   Victor D. Lippit and Koichi Hamada, 'Efficiency and Equity in
     Intergenerational Distribution', in Dennis Clark Pirages (ed.), *The
     Sustainable Society,* New York and London: Praeger Publishers, 1977,
     285—99. The requirement here quoted is from p. 293.
50   Ibid. p. 295.
51   Ibid. p. 297.
52   Leon H. Craig, 'Contra Contract: A Brief Against Rawls' Theory of
     Justice', *Canadian Journal of Political Science,* 8, 1975, 63—81; Barry,
     'Justice Between Generations', pp. 280—3.
53   Feinberg, 'The Rights of Animals and Unborn Generations'. This
     criticism of Rawls has been made by Michael S. Pritchard and Wade
     L. Robison, 'Justice and the Treatment of Animals: A Critique of
     Rawls', *Environmental Ethics,* 3, 1981, 55—61, and by Mary Midgley
     in 'Duties Concerning Islands'.
54   Stephen Bickham, in 'Future Generations and Contemporary Ethical
     Theory', *Journal of Value Inquiry,* 15, 1981, 169—77, holds that no
     current normative theory can cope with the objections to it until our
     metaphysical presuppositions are revised. This I believe to be too
     pessimistic a view.
55   Kavka, 'The Futurity Problem', p. 201.
56   Like Kavka, I reject the view of Garrett Hardin in *The Limits of
     Altruism,* Bloomington: Indiana University Press, 1977, that famine
     relief and improved nutrition in poor countries in the present diminish
     the quality of life there in the future. But space is lacking for any

ampler discussion of international politics, or of the nature or levels of whatever authorities would be called for to implement the policies here advocated. Indeed the conclusions arrived at in the present book preclude neither world government, nor anarchism, nor intermediate arrangements.

57 Surber, 'Obligations to Future Generations', p. 115.
58 Boulding, 'The Economics of the Coming Spaceship Earth', pp. 78 and 81f. I take the conservation of renewable resources such as trees to be compatible with the planned use of non-renewable resources such as coal.
59 'Circumstances of Justice and Future Generations', p. 243.
60 Mary B. Williams, 'Discounting Versus Maximum Sustainable Yield', in Sikora and Barry, *Obligations to Future Generations,* 169—85.
61 The need for an ampler utilitarian position is well argued by Peter Singer in 'Not for Humans Only: The Place of Nonhumans in Environmental Issues', in K. E. Goodpaster and K. M. Sayre (eds), *Ethics and Problems of the 21st Century*, Notre Dame and London: University of Notre Dame Press, 1979, 191—206.
62 Goodin, 'No Moral Nukes', pp. 435—43.
63 *Pace* Barry, 'Justice Between Generations', p. 284.

7

Multiplication and the Value of Life

The increasing size of the human population is widely regarded as an ecological problem. A social problem it certainly is, at least in some places; and it results in some measure from people's transactions with other species, since advances in the control of disease must be part of its explanation. Indeed this is already enough to make it an ecological problem. But it also results, plausibly, from poverty in places where life-expectancy is short, and to this extent is to be seen as one facet of the many-sided problem of development and underdevelopment, rather than as primarily an ecological issue. There is another ground, however, for regarding it as an ecological problem: its role in causing squalor, pollution, erosion, the loss of forests and the growth of deserts. As remarked in chapter 1, it is probably not the main cause of these problems; but if it even exacerbates them, as it surely does, then its ecological significance is considerable. The growth in human numbers also seems to endanger numerous nonhuman species, and thus contributes to yet another ecological problem.

But before anyone can designate the problem one of 'overpopulation' (manifestly a normative expression), let alone talk of 'the population bomb',[1] some idea is needed of what an optimum human population would be like, or at any rate of what population changes would count as improvements, and thus of what level of population we ought to aim at. This, as Michael Bayles points out,[2] is an issue prior to such other population issues as the rate at which change is due and the methods of control to be employed; and it is also an issue which at once takes us to basic principles of normative ethics. It also takes us to basic questions about value, such as whether all life is valuable, or only certain kinds and qualities of life, and, if only certain kinds, then which. To dwell on these issues may seem to risk losing sight of the practical problems; yet to leave them unexamined, or to take for granted the answers to them, involves lacking a clear view about what the problems are and what makes them problems. On such a basis as this, even if satisfactory solutions are found, their discovery can at best be an accident, and we stand to overlook ways in which, through provision for a quite different population, we might have made the world a much better place.

Principles of obligation and of value in population matters are also required to supplement the discussion of obligations to future generations in chapter 6. It was there claimed that we have far-reaching obligations to whatever people there will be. But it was necessary to postpone the question of how many people we should cause to exist or allow there to be; and without some answer to that question the answers so far arrived at are plainly deficient.

The points so far made may supply some kind of explanation of the fact that most of the writings of philosophers on population issues concern the bearing of basic principles on human numbers rather than issues such as which forms of population control are allowable, and which forms, if any, of political pressure may be employed to foster it. Most of the writers concerned have a vivid awareness of the urgency of population issues, yet their concern to be right over matters of principle must surely be applauded. By contrast, where a philosopher deals only with the more immediate problems, the resulting discussion is prone to appear somewhat superficial,[3] and this even though the problems are on a worldwide scale.

Yet the layman who turns to philosophers for help over matters of principle may here be beset with perplexity. Thus only some theories of normative ethics, those which make obligations and justifications turn on an action's consequences, seem to have anything relevant to say on the level of the human population at future times. As we have already seen in chapter 6, other theories either have nothing to offer, or fail to give a satisfactory account of the extent to which principles relating to anything other than consequences override principles of a consequentialist character. Among consequentialist theories, however, negative theories, enjoining the diminution of suffering and misery, would best be satisfied by the painless elimination of humanity altogether, an ideal which clashes with most people's most deeply felt intuitions; while positive theories at least seem to run the risk, by enjoining the maximization of happiness or of years of worthwhile life, of encouraging yet further increase in the growth of population.

In due course I shall argue that this perplexity would be premature. But first I shall present the main positive consequentialist theories, and also the various difficulties with which they are confronted. The examination may also serve to bring to light widespread values which people are prone to forget that they hold once they are confronted with the quite genuine problems associated with population growth.

The Total theory and the Average theory

As was mentioned in chapter 6, both the Total theory (which, despite Surber, must be regarded as the classical form of utilitarianism) and the Average theory commend or enjoin the maximization of utility. Utility is most usually construed as happiness or the means to happiness, and the two Theories require respectively the maximization of the total happiness level of a population and of the average happiness level. Alternatively these theories can require the maximization not of the level of happiness but of some other (or some more inclusive) state of people which may be regarded as intrinsically valuable, such as well-being or periods of worthwhile life. As I have rejected in chapter 6 the belief that nothing but happiness is of intrinsic value, and accepted the view that the satisfaction of people's basic needs does much more good than the provision of other goods, my own commitment is clearly to one of the alternatives. But this said, it is simpler to follow for the present the practice of most writers in treating the Total and the Average theories as concerned with levels of happiness.

The main objections to the Total theory were prefigured in chapter 6. It seems to require population to be maximized; and (though this has not till now been treated as an objection) it seems to require us to make happy people rather than to make people happy, and thus to be more concerned with happiness than with people. More precisely, it implies that it would be better, with respect to a population of any given size enjoying distinctly worthwhile lives, for there to be a larger population so long as life remained a little more than barely worth living. For each extra just-about-happy person would, up to this point, add to the total of happiness. This conclusion is widely regarded with horror, and it has become customary for philosophers to refer to it as the

'Repugnant conclusion'. There again the other objection arises because the Total theory seems to be impersonal, and seems to advocate the procreation of extra people simply as bearers of happiness, as if happiness were a product like milk.

The Average theory is often supposed to overcome these difficulties, and to provide for the maintenance of a high level of happiness rather than for the enjoyment of a relatively low level on the part of large numbers. But the Average theory has implications of its own which are altogether counter-intuitive.[4] Thus where there is a high average level of happiness the theory prohibits the addition of any children whose happiness level would be even a little lower than the previous average (unless the addition further increases the already high happiness level of existing people). Indeed in this connection the Average theory appears to discriminate in favour of present people against future ones. But this would not always be the case: for where a population lives in extreme misery, the theory requires the conception of any number of people whatever, as long as the average happiness can be raised thereby, even if the extra people are miserable themselves and wish they had never been born. There is no discrimination here, but the upshot is a most dubious social policy. Again, if a happy population can only reproduce itself at the expense of a slight but continuous deterioration in resources and happiness-levels, then the theory forbids any reproduction and requires the extinction of humanity.

It has also been suggested that the Average theory requires the elimination of the miserable from among an otherwise happy population. But it need not require this, as the miserable could instead be provided with the means to happiness; and as the provision of basic needs makes a great deal of difference to people's happiness and brings about a great deal of good (on all accounts), it is likely that the average would be better raised in this way. For similar reasons the Total theory, which is sometimes subjected to a parallel objection, also survives it.

Nevertheless the Average theory is vulnerable to the other objections just given: most strikingly it could require the production of extra people so as to maximize happiness (rather as the Total theory is accused of doing), and it could involve the extinction of the species. Also, as it can require the calling of extra people into existence for the sake of levels of happiness, it is open to the charge of impersonality; and so (as Anglin points out), if it is ever an objection that a theory is more concerned with happiness than with people, then the objection applies to the Average theory as much as to any other.

The Person-affecting principle

Now in the view of a number of philosophers, what is wrong with both the Total and the Average theories is that they involve concern for possible people. The true appeal of consequentialist theories such as utilitarianism, on these philosophers' view, is that they call upon us to make actual people happy, leaving possible people out of account. Accordingly they urge that utilitarianism be understood to concern promoting the happiness either of existing people only or, more cogently, of existing people plus people who are likely to exist whatever any particular agent may do. In the course of attempts to state this interpretation of utilitarianism in a form immune to objections, various forms of it have been put forward.[5] They have in common what Derek Parfit has called the Person-affecting principle: the better of two outcomes is the one which affects people for the better, and the worse is the one which affects them for the worse. Merely possible people are not in this connection regarded as people.

But, despite its intuitive plausibility, the Person-affecting principle has been subjected to searching criticisms, in particular from R. I. Sikora and Derek Parfit.[6] Thus Sikora remarks that it can yield a conclusion similar to the Repugnant conclusion mentioned above. Imagine a population of fairly unhappy people (e.g. the survivors of a nuclear war), able, at some sacrifice to themselves, to raise both the average and the total happiness and repopulate the world by producing and rearing some test-tube babies who would predictably be very happy. The principle forbids them to enter upon this policy of making happier people; and thus, by giving priority to actual people, ensures in at least these circumstances a low level of happiness, even though humanity might have had a brighter future. Yet it is the contrivance of avoidably low levels of happiness which is supposed (in part) to give the Repugnant conclusion its repugnant character. Sikora's argument occurs in the course of a survey of all the possible kinds of 'ontological preference theories' — theories which prefer the interests of actual persons, and take it to be wrong to require them to make sacrifices to bring about the existence of possible persons — a survey which shows that they all embrace a form of 'Repugnant conclusion'.

There again, the Person-affecting principle cannot be taken to construe the likely people, whose interests are to be heeded, as people likely to exist whatever anyone does; for of these there are very few, and all other future people could be disregarded. It must concern people likely to exist whatever a particular agent or other subgroup of humanity may do; but the people likely to exist whatever any *one* group does will be different in identity and number from the people likely to exist whatever any second or third group may do. This being so, the principle exhorts different population policies for each different group of agents. Besides, there would be no co-ordination between these policies: for each group would have to take account of the likely offspring of other groups, but not the potential offspring of their own group, which it is within their power to prevent from coming into existence at all.

Another group of difficulties for the Person-affecting principle cluster around the issue of the identity of future people, and have been raised by Derek Parfit. Thus the adoption of different social policies very considerably affects which people are born, granted that even the postponement of conception issues in the birth of a different child. Consider a policy of consumption, which yields a higher standard of living for a hundred years than a policy of conservation would, but a lower standard of living thereafter. Such a policy does not harm any actual or likely people, nor, if it is carried out, is anyone worse off in a hundred years' time than they would have been on the other policy: for on the other policy they would not have existed, and different people would have existed in their place. Thus the Person-affecting principle cannot criticize this objectionable, consumption-orientated policy, as it affects no one, likely or otherwise, for the worse.

A parallel point can be made about individual mothers. A mother who bears a handicapped child, but had the opportunity to bear a healthy and happy one by postponing becoming pregnant, might well, in fact, be subject to moral criticism; yet no child has been affected for the worse. But on the Person-affecting principle she is above criticism. Moreover social planners who could advise such mothers to postpone conception but fail to do so can only be blamed to the extent that the mother and other actual persons are made miserable as a result of their omission.

Thus the Person-affecting principle is satisfactory until it is applied to the issues for the sake of which it was introduced — cases of decisions about the existence of future people. Where populations are constant it fares well enough, but yields exactly the same results as the Total and Average theories, and thus has no advantage over either of them. But in the area of morality with which I am at present concerned, its failure is a disastrous one. Indeed, since as time goes on the proportion of people alive whose individual existence is at present actually likely is a proportion which decreases progressively, the principle authorizes us to disregard most (at least) of the people of a century from now, and almost all their successors. But the wrongness of such disregard has been amply exhibited in chapter 6.

Narveson in fact holds the view which most people could endorse, that there is an obligation not to bring into existence people whose lives would be miserable. He attempts to reconcile this view with the Person-affecting principle on the basis that such people would otherwise be actual, and would experience misery which can actually be prevented. But this is to allow the moral significance of at least some possible lives. Proponents, for example, of the Total theory are concerned about possible lives on just the same basis, i.e. that they could be made actual, and that the quality of these lives thus forms an element in one or more of the options open to actual agents. At the same time Narveson denies any obligation to bring into existence people whose lives would be worthwhile, and adds that new additions to the population 'ought to be made if the benefit to all, *excluding* the newcomer, would exceed the cost to all, *including* him or her, as compared with the net benefit of any alternatives which don't add to population'.[7]

But this position is no more plausible than the basic Person-affecting principle. Thus it fails to explain why the mother of the handicapped child was wrong not to delay and conceive the happy child instead. Further, it takes into account the misery which unhappy people would complain of if they became actual, but disregards the blessings which people enjoying a worthwhile life would prize if they became actual, as Timothy Sprigge has pointed out,[8] and this without any defensible rationale. (Thus it will not do to say that our only obligations are to prevent bad future states of affairs, for reasons already pointed out.) Again, granted that we have obligations to promote the welfare of actual people, and are willing to produce extra people to do so, it is hard to justify ignoring their welfare, and thus treating them, as Narveson effectively does, as second-class citizens. Finally, the asymmetrical position would in some circumstances actually require the extinction of the human species.[9]

One of Narveson's more emphatic claims is that 'duties which are not owed to anybody stick in the conceptual throat.'[10] But despite his belief that all duties are owed to someone (surely a generalization which does not hold once duties are construed as whatever it is wrong not to do), and to actual persons at that, he himself deviates from the Person-affecting principle by allowing (negative) duties with regard to possible (unhappy) people. Thus possible people sometimes count, and further reflection is required to discover when they count and in what ways.

Efforts at salvage

Trudy Govier has attempted to defend Narveson's basic position by holding that we should pay some heed to the interests of 'epistemically possible people' (those who are likely to exist for reasons independent of our choices) but less to those of 'volitionally possible people' (those whose existence would depend on our choices). Govier attempts to meet Parfit's objections over identity by acknowledging that different people will exist on different social policies but maintaining that we ought to consider *'those people who will likely exist at a future time'*.[11] These I take to be any members of the variable class of likely future people: if on any policy there will be *n* people, then even though their identity would differ as between policies, the *n* people who there will be are the ones we should care about.

But this revision merely diminishes the size of the population of second-class citizens. For Govier remains committed to Narveson's asymmetry with respect to volitionally possible people. Yet wherever families are planned, all the future offspring are, seen from the present, volitionally possible. Indeed despite Govier's attempts to justify the asymmetry, most of the objections to Narveson's position are objections to hers also. Nevertheless as she accepts positive obligations with regard to epistemically possible people, whatever their identity, her position marks an advance on that of Narveson.

Another philosopher who has attempted a consistent position which implies the kind of asymmetry favoured by Narveson is Peter Singer. Singer has contended that the appealing ingredient in utilitarianism is the following axiom: 'Given that people exist, or will exist independently of our actions, it is better that they be happy than that they be miserable, and the happier they are, the better it is.'[12] Like Narveson and Govier, Singer was unwilling to recognize value in any additional lives. But to cope with Parfit's identity objections, he devised a population policy which did not require the interests of any fixed group to be given priority, but did require that there be always a group of the population of the size of the least population possible, enjoying at least the average (and thus also the total) happiness which the least population would have.

Now as Parfit and Sikora have pointed out,[13] the spirit of Singer's remarks involves also an obligation to maximize the happiness of such a group (hereinafter the 'core'), even if this requires procreating extra people. But this would be done for the sake of the core, not of the extra people, unless some of them happened to belong to it. Singer, however, believed that wherever extra people would be miserable his principle implied an obligation not to produce them, because of the side-effects arising for others from the fact that the extra people in question would be better off dead. No corresponding positive obligation existed, in Singer's belief, where extra people would be happy.

But Singer's principle does not even guarantee the asymmetrical view which he favoured, for, as Parfit points out, the side-effects of the existence of miserable people could be beneficial to the core group. Besides this, it labours under serious difficulties itself. Thus it can require a succession of additions to the initial population, so long as a subset of the new total is on average as happy at each stage as the population at the previous stage had on average been, until a large, barely happy population is attained, as in the 'Repugnant conclusion'. Thus Singer's principle fails to fare any better than the Total theory. Further, as Sikora remarks, it can prefer a smaller addition of barely happy people to a larger addition of moderately happy people, so long as the core is better off. Again, if the minimum number (the core) is small, but happiest in a very large population of otherwise barely happy people, this population is preferred to one where the core is only slightly less happy, and everyone else is as happy as the core. Again, it could require parents not to make sacrifices in the timing of conception so as to increase the happiness of a resulting child. Moreover it could require the present generation to use up and benefit by a scarce resource of which, as they might be aware, future people would have more need to cure an inherited disease. But each of these preferences of the theory is, at least apparently, wrong; and in some cases there is no need of the qualification.

There is also a technical difficulty inherent in Singer's principle. As previously mentioned, it can require successive increases in population with a diminishing overall average happiness, so long as after each increase there is a core at least as happy as the population had been on average up to that stage. Accordingly the principle can require in two moves a development which it would initially have forbidden, and can thus represent such a development as both forbidden and obligatory. (For the average happiness of the larger population at each stage is allowed to be lower than beforehand, and this lower level is all that the core at the next stage has to be allowed to sustain; so after two transitions there may be no group of the same size and happiness level as the initial population.) Singer's solution to this problem of 'intransitive preferences' (where B is better than A, C better than B, but C is worse than A) consists in holding that as the forbidden outcome can be foreseen, the first application of the principle must be regarded as forbidden. But, as Parfit remarks, this is unacceptable unless some independent ground is supplied for not doing what the principle requires.

The interests of potential people

Now Singer, like Govier, advanced beyond Narveson by accepting the moral relevance of at any rate a minimum predictable number of future people, whatever their identity, but his principle fails where the interests of others who might become actual are disregarded. How can these interests be accommodated? One way might be that of philosophers who defend a principle on which all possible people have interests and rights as such. Thus R. M. Hare holds that it is morally wrong, other things being equal, to prevent potential people from becoming actual.[14] (Among potential people Hare includes foetuses and also pairs of gametes, even ones which are not currently united: indeed in his article 'Survival of the Weakest' he includes people who could be born within the next two years.[15]) Hare defends his position by appealing to the widely accepted basic principle that we ought to treat others as we would wish to be treated, and this Hare applies to the bestowal of life. The obvious difficulty, however, arises over holding that all potential people, whether foetuses or hitherto unconceived potentialities, count as people: for if they do not, then no question of the interests or rights of potential people can arise.

Can conception constitute harm or benefit? The issue is far from clearcut, but has been illuminatingly discussed by Parfit and by T. G. Roupas.[16] In the light of their discussions, perhaps the most cogent view is that for an actual person leading a worthwhile life, to have been conceived was indeed a benefit, but that conception is no benefit to merely potential people, as they are then nonexistent.

There is a sense in which potential people can have rights and interests: the sense in which actual people have interests and rights which can count as reasons for action on the part of others at times prior to their lives, and when they are merely potential. But potential people do not, *as such*, have interests or rights. We do not let them down by allowing them to remain nonexistent. (If I am right, conception cannot constitute harm, as nothing exists beforehand to be harmed,[17] yet to a person leading a wretched life conception will have been a crucial liability, without which none of life's miseries would have arisen.) But if potential people do not, *as such*, have interests, then Hare's principle has already been rejected.

Now if potential people were people who stood to be affected by conception, then, as Parfit has pointed out,[18] the Person-affecting principle could be reinstated in a form which would be free of the deficiencies highlighted above. For its deficiencies lie in its failure to provide for the interests which potential people have, or rather would have if they became actual. But if potential people are themselves people liable to be affected by the course of events, then their interests would be covered already by the principle. If this were so, however, the principle would have lost the reason for which it was introduced, which was precisely to exclude these supposed interests from consideration.

It is surely preferable to allow the Person-affecting principle to have the application intended by its sponsors, who would of course deny that potential people in general have interests. I have already supplied reasons for doubting the view that morality fundamentally consists in duties owed to individuals (or, therefore, in individual rights): accordingly the Person-affecting principle, which presupposes otherwise, may be rejected (as I have claimed it must be in any case), and does not need to be modified so as somehow to include possible people, even if such a modification were plausible. If extra happy or worthwhile lives are valuable and should be provided for, this can be expressed in some more impersonal principle, such as the Total theory or a variant of it. I now present the case for just such a position, step by step.

The value of worthwhile life

That in fact each worthwhile life is intrinsically valuable has been impressively argued by Roupas; by 'worthwhile' Roupas means a life the liver of which is or would be glad to be alive. If his conclusion is right, this may account for the cogency of Hare's claim that there is at any rate something regrettable about abortions (or most abortions), in that the further development of something potentially valuable is forestalled. (Many abortions may still be right, but that is not the present point.) Each agent who is glad to be alive, Roupas observes, must prefer a world in which he exists and is glad to be alive, to one in which he does not exist at all. This granted, it can further be maintained that the former state of affairs is of greater value than the latter. For, an observer who is asked to consider the two states of affairs from the point of view of each individual present in either will discover this preference, and, so long as the other individuals concerned are all present in both states of affairs, will discover no countervailing preference; and if then asked which state is preferable if he has an equal likelihood of being any of these individuals, he will still prefer the first, and would actualize it on this basis if he could. This impersonal and 'objective' procedure for determining judgements of value is elaborated by Roupas on the basis of work by J. C. Harsanyi,[19] and is also employed to support the conclusion that, provided someone continues to be glad that they are alive as long as they are alive, a longer life is in their case more valuable than a shorter one, and the further conclusion that a life's value is unchanged by *whose* life it is.

Not everyone, perhaps, will endorse Roupas' method for arriving at judgements of value. It might, for example, be held to be weighted in favour of entities capable of preferences; or it might be contended that such judgements need not be functions of preferences at all. Yet there is a striking agreement between Roupas' conclusions and those of Jonathan Glover, arrived at by the quite distinct method of examining the presuppositions of widespread reflective moral beliefs.[20] Glover, indeed, points out that the mere desire to live does not show that the continuation of life would be either in the interests of the person concerned or worthwhile; and this is a modification which Roupas could, perhaps, allow, as long as his impartial observer could be equipped with the requisite information about which lives were in the interests of the people (or animals) living them. (Glover, in fact, does not tell us what a worthwhile life consists in; nor is there space to discuss the matter further here — though I have elsewhere discussed some of its key aspects.[21]) But if the notion of a worthwhile life can for the moment be taken for granted, and it can be allowed that gladness to be alive is a good indicator, but not an invariable concomitant of a worthwhile life, then Roupas' conclusions about what is valuable may for present purposes be accepted as expressing an important part of the truth, whether on the basis of his own method or on that of reflection on our intuitive judgements. (It should be noted that Roupas' conclusions do not cover the same range of cases as Hare's view, even though both concern possible as well as actual people, for Roupas' position concerns only those lives which would, if made actual, be worthwhile, whereas Hare's position lacks any such restriction.)

Objections to the Total theory assessed

Now as Roupas remarks, his position is congruous with the Total theory of utilitarianism, without entailing it. If further we ought to maximize whatever is of intrinsic value, and we accept Roupas' view, we do seem to be thrust back into accepting a form of the Total theory, complete with the 'Repugnant conclusion'. To many readers this may seem a disastrous idea: I will attempt now to explain why it is not.

To begin with, the Total theory, as Hare, Singer and Sikora have all pointed out,[22] does not require an increase in the human population of our planet. This point needs to be amplified. With 800 million people already living in absolute poverty, additions to the population are very unlikely in most cases to increase the total of happiness, or, to follow Roupas' and Glover's account of value, of years of worthwhile life. If the additional people are not mal-nourished or miserable themselves, their arrival would in any case be likely to lengthen the worldwide food queue; and if they have more purchasing power than those least able to procure food, they will prevent yet more people in poor countries from being able to afford what they need. Just on this count alone, then, the Total theory probably commends a standstill rather than an increase in world population. (For current circumstances, the Average theory may even counsel a drastic reduction: something which is unlikely to commend it, granted the theory of value just accepted. But we have already encountered conclusive objections to the Average theory.)

The next point to note is that it is mistaken to isolate a population policy from among the deliverances of a general theory of normative ethics. Thus, as the current world population could be fed, and a vast amount of difference would be made to the worthwhileness of lives if it were, the Total theory must advocate that it should be. But if suitable measures were to be set afoot, including a development policy enabling people to be properly fed in perpetuity without needing to rely on donations from others, then the Total theory would not advocate for these conditions an overall decrease in population (though it might well prefer a decrease as against maintaining current population levels without such a development policy). Yet it would still probably not advocate an overall increase, for the following reason.

The Total theory, even if it enjoins a larger number of lives than some of its rivals, does not require them to be simultaneous. Much the likeliest way to maximize the number of worthwhile lives is to guarantee a population level sustainable into the indefinite future; and to maximize population in the short term might precisely exclude this outcome, through the exhaustion of resources, the ruination of fertile land, pollution, losses to the natural gene-pool or the breakdown of whole ecosystems on which humans ultimately depend. Thus the theory commends no higher a population than the maximum sustainable, and, for the reasons given above, a somewhat lower one in current conditions.

Further, the requirement of the theory to add worthwhile lives cannot be applied to the planetary population as if there were infinite space to accommodate extra people in the manner to which the more fortunate of existing people have become accustomed. Space and resources are limited, and to ignore these limitations is likely to involve multiplying misery; indeed this would be likely even if there were no problem about the supply of food.

The general moral of these various points is that the horror with which the Repugnant conclusion is received may well be caused by applying it to conditions for which no such conclusion of the theory could imaginably be yielded.

At the more theoretical level, Anglin has isolated three reasons why people find the Repugnant conclusion repugnant.[23] It ignores the quality of individual lives, it allows sheer numbers to make a morally relevant difference, and it advocates the production of people for the sake of utility. In each case Anglin replies that the complaint applies to *any* utilitarian theory, for all such theories allow trade-offs between individuals' happiness for the common good, welcome extra happy lives, and, unlike the theory of Narveson, advocate levels of population solely on the basis of their theory of value, and without importing independent principles.

To some, this may appear a catalogue of reasons for rejecting utilitarianism, or, come to that, any other consequentialist theory. Yet *on any theory* conflicting interests or values must be weighed up against each other. There again, the objection about numbers basically turns on whether each worthwhile life is valuable, and whether, as Parfit has argued, 'more count for more'.[24] Finally the Total theory does not strictly enjoin the production of people so as to be the bearers or locations of the abstraction, utility. It seeks, among other things, to maximize lives of intrinsic value (either happy ones or worthwhile ones) — and to maximize their length — and any such life would necessarily be enjoyed by a person (or other animal), even if not all the persons concerned are currently actual ones. It has already been concluded that duties need not be owed to actual (or even to likely) people, and by expressing this truth the Total theory is in one way impersonal. But it is not impersonal in the way in which a theory might be which required people to be produced not for the sake of the intrinsic value of their own lives but for the sake of some ulterior abstraction like the glory of the nation or the race.

Thus the Total theory does not yield the Repugnant conclusion in the actual world; and even though the Conclusion might be yielded in some possible (ampler) world, that does not seem to be a conclusive reason for rejecting the Total theory. For the alternative theories fare far worse. (In case this is still not clear, see Sikora's *tour de force* in which all the alternative possibilities are reviewed and found wanting.[25]) The Total theory is immune to the main objections and has much to commend it (including considerations in defence of consequentialism which I have put forward elsewhere[26]), and the theory of value which was presented above lends the Total theory further support. Besides all this, arguments have been put forward by Parfit in favour of the Repugnant conclusion, by Anglin in favour of an obligation to bring extra people into existence, and by Sikora in support of the Total theory itself.[27]

Accepting the Repugnant conclusion

Parfit's argument runs as follows. By comparison with there being just a given population with lives very well worth living, it would be at least no worse if there also existed, perhaps somewhere else, a like number of people with a lower quality of life, but with lives still worth living. (There might be no injustice here, if perhaps the two groups did not know of each others' existence.) If we call the state of affairs with the given population 'A', and the second situation 'A Plus', then A Plus is better than A, or at any rate, no worse. We now envisage a state of affairs, B, with the same numbers as A Plus, all parties equally well off (i.e. leading equally worthwhile lives), and an average quality of life slightly higher than the average in A Plus, but

markedly lower than in A. It is now hard to deny that state of affairs
B is better than state A Plus, and thus that, as A Plus is no worse
than A, B is better than A. We thus arrive by two natural stages at a
conclusion favoured by the Total theory and incompatible with the
Average theory: it is better for the average level to drop from a very
high one if the population at the same time doubles. But by parity of
reasoning, further reductions of level and doublings of numbers are
also desirable, until we reach a very large population with a uniform
level of quality of life just above that at which life is barely worth
living.

Now Parfit in fact wrestles with this Repugnant conclusion with a
view to rejecting it if possible. But the move from A Plus to B
cannot be rejected either by Average theorists or by anyone else
who accepts the law of diminishing marginal utility. As to the move
from A to A Plus, the Average theory was criticized above for
rejecting this transition, which is clearly in place on any theory of
value remotely similar to that of Roupas and Glover.

The problem, then, is to explain people's reluctance to accept the
conclusion. This reluctance, I suggest, stems partly from the
presumption that a succession of such doublings of population and
lowerings of levels of quality (or worthwhileness) of life could take
place on our planet without grave side-effects, and is thus being
proposed as an improvement. In fact any additional numbers would
issue certainly in famine and probably in epidemics and war, making
life worse for all. There again, people reflecting on the two
transitions may too readily assume that they themselves are to be
included in the population in state of affairs A, and stand to lose
much that they enjoy. But to adopt an impartial view, as Roupas
points out, they must imagine (instead) that they have an equal
likelihood of being one of the extra people in A Plus. The experience
of these people would not be of falling standards but, in most cases,
the discovery that life is sweet.

One further remark is in place. For some populations, a doubling
is readily possible without anyone's life being miserable or not
worth living. But actual doublings often fall short of this. Where this
would be the case for a significant number of people, the overall
balance of good over evil (at any rate on the account of value
shortly to be introduced) would cease to rise, and the Total theory
would authorize a halt to be called.

The Extra Person Obligation

I now turn to Anglin's Extra Person Obligation argument. Trimmed of its detail Anglin's argument is based on the premise that it is obligatory to bring into existence a happy person at slight cost to oneself rather than to bring into existence at no cost to oneself someone whose happiness would be exactly matched by their unhappiness. But to do the latter is no better or worse than bringing no one into existence. Therefore, in a choice between the first course of action and doing nothing, the former is obligatory. The more problematic premise is the first one, but, as Anglin says, an Average theorist must accept it. But if this premise is accepted, there is an Extra Person Obligation, which could, if conditions allowed it to apply many times over, yield a Repugnant conclusion. But no conclusion can be repugnant which issues from a genuine obligation. More significantly there is sometimes an obligation to bring extra people into existence even at some cost to existing people.

Anglin's argument is an attempt to replace an argument of Sikora which Anglin finds inconclusive. Sikora's argument begins with the premise that it would be permissible to allow the coming into existence of a 'package' of extra people of whom the vast majority would be happy but of whom at least one would be very unhappy (and accordingly there is no obligation not to do so). But there is an obligation not to bring into existence a person who will be very unhappy. Therefore there must be an obligation to bring into existence the happy people, an obligation which overrides the obligation not to bring into existence the very unhappy person.[28] Anglin's reaction is that the obligation might be overridden by the prospect of happy people, even if bringing them about was not obligatory: for it could be an act of supererogation. But it takes an obligation to override an obligation: so Sikora's argument succeeds after all, or so I should contend.

Jonathan Bennett further objects to Sikora's conclusion as follows. The case for continuing the human species (for no less is at stake) could turn on the utilities of actual people, because of the suffering which the phasing out of the species would cause. But this consideration scarcely justifies humanity being continued for millennia, and in any case fails to account for the Extra Person Obligation which Anglin so cogently argues to exist even where there is some cost to existing people. Alternatively the case might lie, according to Bennett, in the importance of projects which matter to us — the living — being continued, on the axiom that unfinished business must be completed. This is only plausible if projects can be given the kind of significance accorded them by Bernard Williams, against which I have argued elsewhere.[29] Bennett's third point boils down to the claim that the factors which outweigh the obligation need not generate another obligation: here I believe that Sikora is right to reply that if they do not generate an obligation, they are too slight to count. Sikora's argument thus stands. It follows that there is a fairly extensive obligation upon existing people to bring into existence people who, as far as can be foreseen, will lead happy or worthwhile lives.

The Total theory defended and modified

Sikora proceeds to develop his argument further so as to produce a new defence of the Total theory.[30] His earlier argument may be taken to suggest that there is at least as much value in increasing happiness by adding extra people as there is negative value in adding unhappy people. But, as he now adds, where equal amounts of unhappiness are in question, adding unhappy people is just as bad as making actual people unhappy. Therefore there is at least as much positive value in increasing the happiness total of the world by adding happy people as there is in preventing an equal amount of suffering (or adding an equal amount of happiness) for those alive.

But the earlier argument, as Sikora acknowledges, may not show that the value of extra happy lives balances the negative value of the same number of unhappy lives. What is really at stake here is whether the misery of either an existing or an extra life is no more important than an extra happy life, and accordingly whether, other things being equal, it is indifferent whether resources are spent on rearing an additional happy person or on preventing someone's misery. It is not in question that many agents should do both (indeed perhaps most should). Nor am I suggesting that the race should not be continued until all existing misery has been relieved, a view which would in any case be ruled out by the earlier argument, an argument which I have accepted. The point is rather that the earlier argument is compatible with the prevention of misery being much more important than the production of happiness.

As Sikora points out, to accept this is to forfeit the simplicity of classical utilitarianism. It certainly involves a modification of that position. But, as I have pointed out earlier, I cannot accept that happiness is the only good; and I further maintain that the satisfaction of people's basic needs does much more good than does increasing the happiness of those whose basic needs are satisfied already. But I can go along with Sikora when he argues that in any case what we ought to do is to maximize the balance of whatever is intrinsically valuable over what is intrinsically bad, and that the obligation to bring into existence people with worthwhile lives is still derivable on this basis.[31]

But the modification of the Total theory just introduced allows me also to agree with James P. Sterba's case for a policy involving a severe restriction on any increase on the current world population.[32] Sterba argues as follows:

Given that the welfare rights of future generations require existing generations to make provision for the basic needs of future generations, existing generations would have to evaluate their ability to provide both for their own basic needs and for the basic needs of future generations. Since existing generations by bringing persons into existence would be determining the membership of future generations, they would have to evaluate whether they are able to provide for that membership. And if existing generations discover that, were the population to increase beyond a certain point, they would lack sufficient resources to make the necessary provision for each person's basic needs, then it would be incumbent upon them to restrict the membership of future generations so as not to exceed their ability to provide for each person's basic needs.

Accordingly, Sterba holds, the welfare rights of future generations justify a compromise position between the policies of the Average and the Total theories. But in fact the position reached (which, incidentally, turns on needs rather than on rights) may be regarded as a modification of the Total theory, on which intrinsic value is most readily maximized by provision for basic needs and prevention of the existence of people whose basic needs would not be satisfied, and these contributions to the worthwhileness of present and future lives, for that very reason, take priority over the fostering of happiness.

Implications of the modified theory

What policy, then, does the modified Total theory sustain? Does it, for example, imply the Repugnant conclusion? It does not imply this conclusion in our actual world, and for the same reasons as those given above about the implications of the unmodified theory. In a possible world with enough space and resources, and with mechanisms to ensure the even distribution of these resources, it would imply something like the Repugnant conclusion (though only if the interests of nonhumans were not undermined thereby). But as basic needs should be taken to include the need to develop essential human capacities, including the capacity for practical reason, at least some provision for education (formal or informal) would be included, and thus a quality of life rather above that of the barely tolerable would be involved. In such a world there might be privations, but life would be distinctly worthwhile for nearly everyone except, perhaps, the incapacitated. But all this is a depiction of the most that the modified theory could imply for a world very different from our own.

Does the modified theory, on the other hand, provide for the continuation of human life at all? The obligation to do so, successfully defended by Sikora, concerns cases where even if some miserable people are produced, many more people are also born who are expected to lead worthwhile lives. Thus, even on Sikora's view, if all or most of our possible successors would be expected to lead miserable lives, we should have no obligation to bring them into existence; indeed we should have an obligation, other things being equal, to refrain from doing so. The area of apparent conflict, however, concerns cases where worthwhile lives cannot be produced without some other people being born who are expected to lead lives of misery. But such cases, it might plausibly be held, are not too dissimilar to the state of the actual world, and do also genuinely raise the question of whether, on the modified theory, it is right to continue the human race under current conditions. Sterba himself seems not to doubt this, but a critic might question his consistency.

The following considerations, however, suggest that the conflict is more apparent than real between the policies yielded by the modified and unmodified theories. Firstly, any population, even one where everyone's basic needs are supplied, is likely to include some miserable people, including some whose lives are not worthwhile. But this is no criticism of that generation's predecessors; nor does Sterba's position imply that such a population should not be brought into existence. Secondly, as the current world population could be fed, and resources exist to satisfy everyone's other basic needs, there is a sense of 'provide for' in which the basic needs of successive generations are provided for, so long as succeeding generations are of the same size as the present one. Thus, as long as Sterba's remarks are taken in this sense (as I suggest that they should be), he can consistently advocate a policy of zero population growth (in which the world population gradually replaces itself), and is not committed to a policy of zero birth rate (in which it is not allowed to do so). Thirdly, though there is another sense of 'provide for' in which basic needs are not provided for unless what is needed is accessible to the person concerned, Sterba cannot be interpreted as advocating provision for basic needs in this sense. For such provision depends on just institutions, and each generation has at least the final say over what its own institutions shall be. The current generation may well have an obligation to provide in the stronger sense for the basic needs of all its members, as Sterba would doubtless agree; but it cannot be obliged in this sense to provide for its successors. It can, of course, facilitate this sort of provision by inaugurating fair institutions, encouraging equitable forms of development in the Third World and by shouldering the obligations mentioned in the last chapter, but it cannot guarantee the provision of future people's needs, whatever their number.

Thus Sterba's position is in keeping with the Extra Person Obligation which (in different forms) both Anglin and Sikora defend. What it adds is a limit to the range of circumstances in which that obligation holds good. Thus if the basic needs of all members of a population could not be provided for, however just its distributive system, then it would be wrong to produce a population of that size rather than to bring into existence a smaller population the needs of which could be provided for. (Since the larger population would be likely to be beset with widespread misery, this is a conclusion which Sikora might accept, but he could not accept it for cases where there was more happiness than unhappiness.)

It follows that increases in the world population should be severely restricted, but that within this restriction as many people as possible who are likely to lead worthwhile lives should be brought into existence, except where their arrival would mean that other people's basic needs could not be met (whether those other people were contemporaries or successors). It does not follow, in theory, that population should be restricted to its current level, as a greater total could be fed and provided for. On the other hand the prospects that social and international arrangements will be so improved that everyone, or even nearly everyone, in an increased population could lead a worthwhile life are minimal; and besides this any increase is likely to lead to severe strain on vital ecosystems and on nonhuman species, at least if the increased population is to be sustained indefinitely. Another consideration militating against a policy of increase is the obligation argued for by Kavka (and implicit, as was remarked in chapter 6, in the obligation to provide for basic needs equally) that each generation should leave the planet in as good a state for its successors as that in which it was received, except in the case of an initial generation which needs to invest resources to make this obligation capable of fulfilment by its successors. For we could well make this obligation impossible to fulfil by increasing the population beyond the minimum by which, as demographers tell us, it is certain to increase whatever we do.

A general population policy is also affected by the consideration that rapid change in population size usually produces undesirable side-effects and suffering. Thus if it is agreed that a sustainable population is to be aimed at, its level depends in part on rates of change of a non-disastrous character as well as on the current population size. In the actual world, population increase itself is proceeding at a rapid rate, with undeniable strains on the social service provisions of many Third World countries, and this con-stitutes an independent argument for less rapid increases. But any rapid reversal of population trends would also involve acute social strains. Accordingly we need a policy in which sustainability and zero population growth is an eventual aim, and in which these aims are attained by a gradual and progressive diminution of the present rate of increase. It will doubtless follow that each country should have a population policy of its own, and also that a more equitable system of international arrangements should be introduced. But these matters cannot be taken further within the present book.

On not disparaging life

What should here be remarked is that the existence of each extra person is not the curse which some ecological writers purport to believe. Certainly if there are too many simultaneously, the planetary life-support systems may be irreparably damaged, imperilled species may be lost, and even in the short term there may be war, famine and pestilence. Yet all this is tenable only if some lives are of value; and in fact, as we have seen, there is good reason to accept the value of each and every worthwhile human life, and of each person concerned having what they need to live such a life. This theory of value will need to be supplemented when members of other species are taken into account (see chapter 8); but that would not detract from its truth.

Thus the traditional belief of most communities, Judaeo-Christian and otherwise, that children are a blessing and that life (except where special factors make it not worth living) is a gift, is not merely the product of adverse evolutionary conditions and the vagaries of human history, as some philosophers speculatively maintain. It is all of a piece with the theory of value advocated above; and but for some such theory of value little sense could be made of our various obligations in matters of population. I do not wish to enter here into issues such as the morality of abortion, beyond remarks made above over Roupas' theory; but make these concluding remarks rather to point out that, though multiplication has its limits (ecological limits among them), there is nothing intrinsically wrong with it.

NOTES

1   Cf. the title of Paul R. Ehrlich's *The Population Bomb*, London: Pan Books/Ballantine, 1971.
2   In the editor's Introduction to Michael D. Bayles (ed.), *Ethics and Population*, Cambridge, Mass.: Schenkman, 1976.
3   Cf. Robert G. Burton, 'A Philosopher Looks at the Population Bomb', in William T. Blackstone (ed.), *Philosophy and Environmental Crisis*, 105—16.
4   In the passage which follows, I draw on two papers in R. I. Sikora and Brian Barry (eds), *Obligations to Future Generations*, Robert Scott, Jnr, 'Environmental Ethics and Obligations to Future Generations', 74—90, and L. W. Sumner, 'Classical Utilitarianism and the Population Optimum', 91 — 111; and also on Bill Anglin's paper 'The Repugnant Conclusion', *Canadian Journal of Philosophy*, 7, 1977, 745—54.
5   Cf. Jan Narveson, *Morality and Utility*, Baltimore: John Hopkins Press, 1967, pp. 46—50; 'Utilitarianism and New Generations', *Mind*, 76, 1967, 62—72; 'Moral Problems of Population', in Michael D. Bayles (ed.) *Ethics and Population*, 59—80; 'Future People and Us', in Sikora and Barry (eds), *Obligations to Future Generations*, 38—60; Thomas Schwartz, 'Obligations to Posterity', in ibid. 3—13; Mary Warren, 'Do Potential People Have Moral Rights?' in ibid. 14—30; Trudy Govier, 'What Should We Do About Future People?', *American Philosophical Quarterly*, 16, 1979, 105—13. A partially similar position was adopted by Peter Singer in 'A Utilitarian Population Principle', in *Ethics and Population*, 81—99.
6   R. I. Sikora, 'Utilitarianism: The Classical Principle and the Average Principle', *Canadian Journal of Philosophy*, 1975, 409—19; 'Is it Wrong to Prevent the Existence of Future Generations?', in Sikora and Barry (eds), *Obligations to Future Generations*, 112—66; 'Utilitarianism and Future Generations', *Canadian Journal of Philosophy*, 9, 1979, pp. 461—6. (Sikora's argument has been criticized by Jefferson McMahan

in 'Problems of Population Theory', *Ethics*, 92, 1981—82, 96—127;
Sikora shows that his case remains substantially intact in 'Classical
Utilitarianism and Parfit's Repugnant Conclusion: A Reply to
McMahan', ibid. 128—33.) For Derek Parfit's contribution, see 'Rights,
Interests and Possible People', in Samuel Gorovitz *et al.* (eds), *Moral
Problems in Medicine,* Englewood Cliffs, NJ: Prentice-Hall, 1976,
369 — 75; 'Energy Policy and the Further Future', in Douglas
MacLean and Peter Brown (eds), *Energy and the Future*, Totowa, NJ:
Rowman & Littlefield, 1983; and 'Overpopulation, Part One' (unpub-
lished paper), revised as 'Future Generations: Further Problems',
Philosophy and Public Affairs, 11, 1981 — 82, 113 — 72.

7 'Future People and Us', p. 55.

8 Timothy L. S. Sprigge, 'Professor Narveson's Utilitarianism', *Inquiry,*
11, 1968, 337—41, cited by William Anglin, 'In Defense of the
Potentiality Principle', in Sikora and Barry (eds), *Obligations to Future
Generations*, 31—7, p. 35.

9 Further trenchant criticisms of such an asymmetrical position are to
be found in James P. Sterba, 'Abortion, Distant Peoples and Future
Generations', *Journal of Philosophy,* 77, July 1980, 424—40.

10 'Future People and Us', p. 45.

11 Trudy Govier, 'What Should We Do About Future People?' The
passage quoted is from p. 111 (Govier's italics). (On page 113a there is
a misprint at line 13. If her summary is to fit her text, 'dependent' must
be read as 'independent'.)

12 Peter Singer, 'A Utilitarian Population Principle', p. 86. See also his
Practical Ethics, pp. 87f.

13 Parfit in 'On Doing the Best for Our Children' in Bayles (ed.), *Ethics and
Population*; Sikora in 'Is it Wrong to Prevent the Existence of Future
Generations?' (see especially pp. 127—32). Singer has acknowledged
in the light of Parfit's criticisms that his attempt to defend an
asymmetrical theory of obligations failed: see his 'Killing Humans and
Killing Animals', *Inquiry*, 22, 1979, 145—56, p. 155, n. 5. But the
revised position which he there adopts, a combination of Govier's
position where self-conscious beings are concerned and the Total
theory where merely conscious ones are in question, is still open to the
objection of disregarding the interests of people who will exist if the
agent makes them actual.

14 R. M. Hare, 'Abortion and the Golden Rule', *Philosophy and Public
Affairs,* 4, 1974—75, 201—22, p. 212.

15 R. M. Hare, 'Survival of the Weakest', in Samuel Gorovitz *et al.* (eds),
Moral Problems in Medicine, 364—9, p. 366.

16 See Derek Parfit, 'Rights, Interests and Possible People', 'Overpopulation, Part One' and 'Future Generations: Further Problems';
T. G. Roupas, 'The Value of Life', *Philosophy and Public Affairs,* 7,
1977—78, 154—83. See also Jefferson McMahan, 'Problems of
Population Theory', pp. 104—7.

17 A somewhat similar view is taken by Michael Bayles in 'Harm to the

Unconceived', *Philosophy and Public Affairs,* 5, 1975—76, 292—304, and by George Sher in 'Hare, Abortion and the Golden Rule', in that same journal, 6, 1976—77, 185—90.

18 In 'Overpopulation, Part One'; an echo of the point remains in 'Future Generations: Further Problems'. See also Jefferson McMahan, 'Problems of Population Theory', pp. 101f.

19 Roupas explains his sources and how he modifies them in n. 12 on p. 127.

20 Glover, *Causing Death and Saving Lives,* pp. 45—57.

21 In 'On Being Human', *Inquiry,* 17, 1974, 175—92.

22 Hare in 'Abortion and the Golden Rule', p. 218; Singer in 'A Utilitarian Population Principle', p. 82; Sikora in 'Is it Wrong to Prevent the Existence of Future Generations?', pp. 118f and p. 158, n. 4.

23 'The Repugnant Conclusion', pp. 748ff. (I add extra reasons below. Taken together, Anglin's reasons and mine supplement Sikora's account of why the conclusion is thought to be a Repugnant one, and our assessments of them suffice to show that, even if, as McMahan holds, the conclusion seems Repugnant for reasons beyond those which Sikora allows, the appearance of repugnancy can be allayed.)

24 Derek Parfit, 'Innumerate Ethics', *Philosophy and Public Affairs,* 7, 1977—78, 285—301, p. 301.

25 Sikora, 'Is it Wrong . . .', pp. 114—16, 119—32, 133—6.

26 In 'Toward a Defence of Teleology', *Ethics,* 85, 1975, 123—35.

27 For Anglin, see 'The Repugnant Conclusion', pp. 752—4; Parfit's argument is presented in the 1973 draft of 'Overpopulation, Part One', in 'Future Generations: Further Problems', by McMahan; 'Problems of Population Theory', pp. 122f; and by Singer in 'A Utilitarian Population Principle', p. 94; for Sikora, see 'Is it Wrong . . .', pp. 140—5. It should be remarked that the Extra Person Obligation is obligatory only where the alternatives are to do nothing or to do something of less value than producing a worthwhile life. For many couples there are alternatives of equal or greater value, and so the obligation does not apply.

28 Sikora, 'Utilitarianism: The Classical Principle . . .', pp. 412—16, summarized by Anglin in 'The Repugnant Conclusion', p. 752, and presented afresh by Sikora in 'Is it Wrong . . .', pp. 136—40.

29 Jonathan Bennett, 'On Maximizing Happiness', in Sikora and Barry (eds), *Obligations to Future Generations,* 61—73; Bernard Williams and J. J. C. Smart, *Utilitarianism, For and Against,* London and New York: Cambridge University Press, 1973, pp. 113—17; Robin Attfield, 'Supererogation and Double Standards', *Mind,* 88, 1979, 481—99, pp. 492—4.

30 'Is it Wrong . . .', pp. 140—5. (I have here presented his argument in simplified form. I have also omitted his mention of timeless utilitarianism, as its role in the argument is not clear.)

31 Ibid. pp. 144f.

32 'Abortion, Distant Peoples and Future Generations', pp. 433f.

8

The Moral Standing of Nonhumans

So far I have confined the basis of the argument to human interests. If the interests of future humans, including those whom we could bring into existence, are taken into account, there is already a formidable case for the conservation of natural resources, wildlife, wilderness and ecosystems, as also for population policies allowing people to have what they need if their lives are to be worthwhile. But perhaps not only humans are entitled to moral consideration. Perhaps some nonhumans, or even nonhuman nature in general, are of moral relevance. There again, perhaps some nonhumans, or some states of nonhumans, are of value in their own right. These are the questions to be tackled in the present chapter.

As Kenneth Goodpaster has observed,[1] the question of the scope and limits of moral consideration is not to be confused with that of moral significance. An answer to the first question commits nobody to any particular view about the relative importance of one set of claims or interests over another. The question of moral significance is a subsequent question, and though it surfaces from time to time in the current chapter, a fuller treatment is postponed to the chapter following. Yet the answers to the first question can throw light on the second, particularly if they include a theory of intrinsic value. For, once we know the basis of a thing's value, we can begin to compare that value with the value of other states or beings, and to consider priorities.

The present investigation has a bearing at once on applied ethics, normative ethics and meta-ethics. Thus if some animals' interests are to be taken into account, there is an extra ground for preserving their habitats. Normative theory is also affected, for we should be maximizing the satisfaction not just of human needs but, perhaps, some animals' needs too. But this is only possible if, at the level of meta-ethics, the concept of moral consideration is taken to allow the interests of nonhumans to count. In theory the meta-ethical question, 'Can x be morally considered?' is distinct from the normative question, 'Should x be morally considered?' In a similar spirit Feinberg tries to keep separate the questions, 'Can animals have rights?' and 'Do animals have rights?'[2] But, as Goodpaster points out,[3] they are closely related; and, although he accepts too readily that meta-ethical beliefs may be tailored to normative ones, it is certainly not easy to see how, once it is acknowledged that x is a possible object of beneficence, the claim that x should be taken into account beneficently should be resisted, unless the analogies between it and accepted cases of items having moral standing are very weak.

Though rights have just been mentioned, the current investigation (and, in general, the current volume) does not concern the location of rights. For even if only some humans bore rights, or even if nothing at all bore rights, it would still be possible that humans or other animals or plants deserved moral consideration. Rights are not the only basis of moral concern: something can lack rights, yet still have moral standing. Besides, no consequentialist can treat rights as morally basic; such claims as I make from time to time about rights should be construed as being grounded in the good which accrues, or the evil avoided, when rights are recognized and respected. It is in any case in order to search beyond rights to their moral grounds. Moreover rights-talk is used in a wide range of senses, depending on whether rights are regarded merely as liberties, or are taken always to be matched by corresponding obligations,[4] or are strong grounds against interference,[5] or can only be overridden when very great harm would otherwise result,[6] or are 'side-constraints' not to be overridden at all (except perhaps when they clash with each other).[7] Accordingly rights-talk needs its sense to be elucidated before it can be appraised; the range of application varies with the sense employed, and things could well have value without most (or perhaps any) of the senses of 'rights' applying to them.

Sentience and other capacities

Do only humans, then, deserve moral consideration? Indeed do all humans deserve it? As Richard Routley points out,[8] a social contract theory would lead us to limit consideration to the contracting individuals: but such theories, as was observed in chapter 6, improperly omit even those humans who are not in a position to enter into contracts. Similarly, as Geoffrey Warnock remarks,[9] the Kantian position on which only rational agents can be respected is intolerably narrow: this position, after all, omits infants and imbeciles. But if infants and imbeciles are instead included, as they ordinarily are, then it is extremely hard to justify excluding those animals which can, like them, suffer pain and frustration.

Most infants and many mentally defective people, certainly, share capacities (in the sense of potentials) for rationality, rule-following and self-determination lacked by most, if not all, nonhuman animals; and these are capacities essential to humanity in the sense that the lack of them from most members of a species shows it not to be human, and at the same time inessential to other species. This fact may not be without its significance, as an organism's inherited capacities (essential ones included) are, it is reasonable to maintain, determinative of its good as a member of its kind; and the potentials of a chimpanzee or a dolphin are different from those of humans. Indeed it seems reasonable to hold that a worthwhile life involves the ability to exercise the essential capacities of one's species. If so, then human individuals with the capacities mentioned need to be allowed to develop them or they will be deprived of their good. Yet all this, though important for value-theory, is beside the present point. For some imbeciles, infant ones included, lack these potentials, yet do not for that reason forfeit moral consideration. And if they do not, then those animals which can likewise suffer pain and frustration must also have moral standing, quite apart from the case for it which might be based on their having some capacities in common with most humans and some distinctive ones of their own.

Sentience, then, seems sufficient to qualify an organism for moral consideration. This could be because, as hedonists claim, pleasure is the sole good and pain the sole evil; if the balance of pleasure over pain is to be maximized, all creatures susceptible to either must be taken into account. But it is reasonable to hold that there are other goods, among them the ability to exercise self-determination, and other essential (but not in all cases distinctive) human capacities: for these, sentience is doubtless in most cases necessary, but the value of autonomy, etc., does not seem to depend on the pleasure which it may give rise to. Nevertheless pleasure and pain remain of positive and negative value in themselves, even if they are not the sole good and evil, and accordingly the (current) susceptibility to them is indeed sufficient for being morally considered. Thus most nonhuman animals have moral standing alongside humans, even if, perhaps, there are differences of value in the goods and evils to which they are liable.

Tom Regan's view of the importance of sentience[10] is that it is a logically necessary condition of a being having or leading one form of life that is better or worse for the being in question, one involving pleasure and pain. The mere value of pleasure and pain, he holds, does not explain why it is wrong to treat beings susceptible to them only as a means: intrinsic value really attaches to beings which are the subjects of a life which can be more or less valuable from their point of view. Regan's position presupposes that only individual organisms have intrinsic value, not their experiences or dispositions; and he considers that only the possession of intrinsic value makes it wrong for a being to be treated as a means. (Having intrinsic value is itself suggested as a necessary and sufficient condition of having irreducible moral rights; but, as I have indicated, the question of rights is not one which I shall here be considering.)

But if pleasure is of intrinsic value and pain of intrinsic negative value, the susceptibility to each of them *does* explain the wrongness of being treated solely as a means: or rather does explain it if it is allowed that we are obliged, in nonmarginal cases, to maximize intrinsic value. For if the organism in question were treated solely as a means, its liability to pain or pleasure would be totally disregarded: whereas if it is taken into account, the organism will not be treated as if it were of no moral relevance at all — indeed it will sometimes make a crucial difference — even if its importance is sometimes outweighed by that of other beings. Accordingly there is no need to regard only individual organisms as possessed of intrinsic value, rather than their states and experiences: the moral relevance of these beings can readily be maintained in the absence of this stipulation.

As to the suggestion that the necessary and sufficient condition of being an organism not to be treated only as a means (and thus of being of moral relevance in one's own right) lies in being the subject of a life which can be better or worse from one's point of view, I believe that there is here a sufficient condition of moral relevance but perhaps not a necessary condition. This is certainly so if the proposed criterion is taken in a strong sense and requires the organism to have a concept of its own identity and future. Peter Singer sometimes[11] uses this form of the criterion to mark off most humans and a few animals (beings whose deaths he believes to be intrinsically evil) from infants, some imbeciles and most nonhuman animals (to kill which is wrong, if at all, because of effects on other beings). But he is rightly concerned about the pains and pleasures of many creatures which do not satisfy the criterion in this form as well as about those which do.

The criterion also admits of a weaker sense which requires neither a concept of the self nor a sense of the future: something could be a subject of a life which can be better or worse from its point of view so long as it is conscious and has attitudes of gladness or frustration to what befalls it. All such organisms have a good of their own (to be glad or frustrated about), even perhaps some which do not have pleasant or painful sensations. (This could be true of some insects, fish or molluscs.) Now if whatever is susceptible to satisfaction and frustration merits moral consideration, then the Regan criterion, even in this weaker sense, marks a sufficient condition of moral relevance. But it is far from self-evident that it marks a necessary condition. For it is plausible that many creatures which do not satisfy it have interests and are capable of being benefited, and it is not obviously absurd to hold that whatever has interests falls within the class of 'moral patients'. Accordingly the interests criterion now falls due for consideration.

Regan's view about the scope of interests in one recent paper was that only conscious or potentially conscious beings have interests: thus human foetuses may qualify, but trees are explicitly excluded.[12] But Regan may here be using 'interests' in a special sense — he glosses 'having interests' as 'having desires, needs, etc.' — a sense other than that of 'having a good of one's own': for in subsequent and previous writings he has held that nonconscious beings can have a good of their own, and has criticized Feinberg for claiming to show that they cannot.[13]

At all events this restrictive view of the scope of interests is adopted without qualification by Feinberg,[14] who thus excludes 'mindless creatures' from the class of things with interests, though he is not altogether consistent about this. Feinberg is of the clear view that interests require desires or aims on the one hand, and cognition on the other. He also holds that when we speak of the good or the needs of plants, the functions which they need to discharge 'are assigned by human interests, not their own'. On the other hand, in an earlier passage concerning the conditions for a thing to have a good of its own, he lists as one of the alternative requirements for having a conative life, which may in turn qualify a thing for having a good of its own, 'latent tendencies, direction of growth and natural fulfillments' (sic).[15] But plants manifestly satisfy all the elements of this requirement. Moreover, as Goodpaster observes, it is absurd to hold that humans have assigned to trees the functions of growth and maintenance (or, we might add, many others). Indeed the needs of trees have not altered since long before humans existed on the planet.

I have assessed Feinberg's views elsewhere,[16] and here wish only to reaffirm the obvious truth that trees and other plants have a good of their own (a good which often conflicts with the interests of people). Accordingly neither sentience, consciousness or cognition are necessary for needs and interests. Having a good of their own, trees can be beneficiaries of human action, and are thus at least serious candidates for moral standing. As Goodpaster realizes, their lack of enjoyments, etc., may well make them of less moral significance than are sentient creatures, and we may take it that this is because less that is of value can befall them. But he concludes at this stage that, however slight their moral significance may be, all living things are 'morally considerable'.

But is being a possible beneficiary or having interests a sufficient condition of being deserving of moral consideration? Goodpaster's main argument for holding that it is so, apart from his replies to objections, lies in the necessary connection between beneficence and morality. This connection granted, the range of application of each is likely to be the same. This argument is reaffirmed in stronger form in a reply to W. Murray Hunt.[17] Beneficence and non-maleficence, he there points out, are central in morality. Accordingly as inanimate objects have no interests and cannot be benefited or harmed, they cannot be given moral consideration: but as living creatures do fall within the scope of beneficence, so they do within that of morality. This argument does indeed show this in the weak sense that moral consideration for the good of plants is not a conceptual impossibility, but does not show that the interests of plants ought to be taken into account. If so, an obstacle for the belief that plants merit moral consideration has been removed, but the belief itself, despite beginning to look less eccentric, has not been established.

Goodpaster also has a subsidiary argument, designed to explain reluctance to accept his conclusion. There is probably a noncontingent connection between theories of value and conceptions of 'moral considerability'. In particular the sentience criterion of the latter ties in with a hedonist theory of value. Thus anyone who accepts, as many people do, that only enjoyment is of positive intrinsic value and only pain is of negative intrinsic value is unlikely to accept that items not susceptible to either are morally to be considered. This is, I think, true; but to support his own conclusion further from this angle Goodpaster would need to put forward a cogent view of the value which attaches to nonsentient life or its states. For even if hedonism is rejected, what replaces it need not repose value in plants, or be echoed by a theory which accords them moral consideration. (In fact Goodpaster has more recently located value in the biosphere as a whole;[18] attention will be given later to such holistic theories.)

Environmental concern

Nevertheless the dealings of humans with nonconscious items in their environment do, as Regan points out, have their 'moral dimensions'.[19] (Thus it is widely believed to be wrong to eliminate a species, whether its members are conscious or not, or to destroy trees or forests without good cause; and there are also objections to tampering with some inanimate natural objects, as when mountains are quarried or rivers dammed.) Regan accordingly depicts an 'environmental ethic', and urges in its defence that the most common alternative ways of accounting for moral concern in these matters do not suffice to do so. In the environmental ethic which Regan presents it is acknowledged not only that some nonhumans have moral standing[20] but also that all conscious and some nonconscious beings have too. The same beings would be held to have value independently of any awareness or appreciation of them or interest in them on the part of any conscious being.[21] (Though Regan here employs the phrase 'inherent value', I shall continue to use 'intrinsic value', as 'inherent value' is also used in a contrasting sense, as will be seen below.) This value would be consequential on their other natural properties.

Regan is right to hold that the alternatives which he considers cannot account for environmental concern. Thus the argument that despoliation of nonconscious nature (e.g. unchecked strip-mining) is wrong because it makes its agents ruthless towards humans (or other animals) is as vulnerable as its empirical premise — that these effects do actually ensue. Besides, the objections to such practices would remain even if there were no such effects.

Another argument which Regan considers turns on the ideal of not destroying anything unthinkingly or gratuitously. Plundering the environment, so goes the argument, is wrong because it violates this ideal. Another form of this argument is put forward by Passmore,[22] who holds that our reactions to such deeds are explained by our disapproval of vandalism and wanton destruction, and that accordingly no such environmental ethic as Regan here proposes is required. The answer to this argument is that if vandalism is wrong then either, as I have claimed elsewhere,[23] some evil effect is perpetrated and there is a loss of value to the world, or, as Regan holds, the object which is destroyed must itself have value. Thus the vandalism theory is parasitic on an account of value which it does not supply. It does not follow, as Regan seems to think, that objects which can be vandalized must have intrinsic value,[24] for their value could depend on states of conscious perceivers. But the possibility that some of them or their states have intrinsic value remains an open one.

The next argument is that what makes it wrong to extirpate whole species or destroy forests is the adverse effect of doing so on the balance of pleasure over pain. As Regan acknowledges, this theory is not human-centred, as it can take into account animal pains and pleasures: and if it is sufficiently broadened as to include human interests and the interests of sentient beings in general, it accounts for more of our judgements in environmental matters than Regan allows. Thus it is important to preserve many plants and animals for reasons of scientific research, for recreation, retreat and the enjoyment of natural beauty in their habitats, and to retain as wide a gene-pool as possible for the sake of medicine and agriculture. These reasons are well presented by Passmore[25] and drawn just from human interests. If the interests of nonhuman animals are also taken into account, there are also reasons against practices such as clear-cutting forests, as the Routleys and Singer have contended.[26]

But any such theory is open to a difficulty noticed by Laurence H. Tribe: if these interests only are taken into account, it would often be justified to replace natural trees with plastic ones.[27] Many of the functions of trees can be carried out by alternative plants with greater practical benefits to humans; and though the reasons just given require the preservation of some trees, they may well not be conclusive in all cases. Indeed if we reason from pleasures rather than interests, fashion could lead to plastic trees being preferred and thus dictate their universal installation. The appalling implication that natural environments should be replaced by plastic ones justifies, in Regan's view, rejecting the theory.

A way forward consists in rejecting the hedonism which is the focus of Regan's protests, and adopting a theory in which the development of humans' aesthetic capacities counts among intrinsic goods, and also the development of individual wild animals after their kinds in their natural surroundings. But even such a broadened consequentialist theory seems at risk of allowing too much replacement of the natural by the plastic, and to be in danger of yielding this implication for as long as trees are only considered instrumentally and accorded no value of their own.

The fourth argument considered by Regan is based on the premise that parts of the natural environment symbolize cultural values which cannot satisfactorily be expressed without them, and that the loss of significant scenes and places diminishes ourselves. This consideration is held by Mark Sagoff to override utilitarian considerations.[28] A similar argument has also been presented about historical landmarks by M. P. and N. H. Golding.[29] The symbolic value of natural objects probably does explain a good deal of our concern to preserve them: but the argument is, as the Goldings acknowledge about theirs, grounded in human interests — interests which cannot claim immunity from comparison with other such interests. This, indeed, makes the argument a salutary one, as far as it goes: for it reminds anyone who assesses actions by their consequences that they must not neglect the effects which an action has, both upon the agent and upon others, through its psychological or cultural significance as a symbol.

But the argument is defective for reasons which include those given by Regan. Firstly there are difficulties in identifying which values should be expressed: manifestly our culture embodies diverse valuations of wilderness itself (to cite the conflict of values most immediately relevant to the matter in question), and it is not clear that we should prefer the values of the cultural elite who value it highly to those of the rest. Secondly the argument is powerless where the local culture (or the culture of the time) does not call for the preservation of nature. Indeed the argument could actually in some circumstances enjoin the manufacture and preservation of plastic forests. Besides this, the argument is no stronger than the potency of the symbolism of wild nature: even if for some people a river symbolizes freedom or the hills integrity, it is difficult to believe, except in cases of historical landmarks, that the symbolism will be perennial or persistent. There again, many of the species liable to be extinguished through the unintended side-effects of human activity have not sufficiently obtruded themselves upon human consciousness as to enter into our systems of self-expression at all; but their members can scarcely lack all standing simply because we have failed to notice them.

The four arguments which Regan considers, then, do not seem to account for certain widespread moral judgements, and do further suggest that trees have a value which in some cases is not purely instrumental. But this does not show that they (or their flourishing) have intrinsic value, and thus constitute a wholly independent object of moral concern. Much less does it show that inanimate natural objects have such a value: indeed about objects such as rocks and rivers I follow Goodpaster in holding that things which lack a good of their own cannot be the objects of moral consideration (as opposed to the creatures which live in or around them), or have intrinsic value. Some theory, certainly, is needed to explain the non-instrumental value which we attach to a variety of natural objects. But it is still an open question whether this value lies in the desirability of diversity, or in the value of species, rather than in the value of their individual members, or indeed in the value of the experience of wild things not made or controlled by people. There is also the alternative theory to consider that what is of intrinsic value is not individual organisms but entire ecosystems, each regarded as a community, or the biosphere, or the planet, and that the value of individual natural objects consists in their participation in the value of a greater whole.

The value of diversity

The value of diversity is a longstanding theme in our culture, a theme the history of which has been traced in A. O. Lovejoy's *The Great Chain of Being*.[30] The more diverse a world is, it has often been held, the better. In ecological connections this is an attractive principle: thus it accords a measure of value to those unimposing species which often turn out to play an indispensable role in an ecosystem, and still more to ecosystems which are internally diverse and which often turn out to be more stable for that reason than simpler ones. But this could all be accounted for by the importance of the preservation of a system of interdependent creatures, rather than by the value of diversity itself; and the reason for the importance of such systems being preserved could be the benefit of the sentient beings involved in it (sometimes including humans), or the external benefits to humans of the system remaining intact (e.g. a large gene-pool, recreation, scope for scientific research). Moreover where diversity is valued independently of these grounds, it is plausibly of value because of the enjoyment it affords to those able to experience it. Once it is granted that the enjoyment of sentient creatures is desirable for its own sake, and that it is in general increased by the experience of diversity both in the worlds of nature and of human culture, it may readily be acknowledged also that this, together with the range of worthwhile activities which it facilitates, is why value is attached to diversity.

This account of the value of diversity cannot be accused of being human-centred, as it includes the value of some of the experiences and activities of nonhumans. Moreover it does not follow from it that there is nothing inherently bad about the loss of a species; for there may well be other reasons to think that there is something bad about this, lying either in living species, or in their members, or in states of their members. But diversity extends indifferently to the inanimate as well as to the animate, and I cannot see that there is any reason to accept that the more kinds there are, of whatever nature, the better. I have explored the question of the value of diversity further elsewhere;[31] as to the effects of diversity, Passmore has argued persuasively that they are a mixture of good and bad.[32] So we may accept that diversity is valuable by making our lives, and those of our fellow-creatures, fuller and richer, without being of value in itself; and proceed to the question of the value of living species.

The value of species

Ample reasons why the elimination of a species is usually contrary to human interests have been given above: to these Peter Singer adds that there would often also be consequential harm to members of other nonhuman species.[33] But, as he points out, species are not, as such, conscious entities. Can species be said to have interests? According to Singer it follows that they cannot. Though I reject his reasoning, I believe that the conclusion that species lack interests is correct, at least if it means that a species has no interests over and above those of its members. Viewed abstractly, a species has interests no more than abstract classes have in general; and, though species are often viewed concretely, as the current population of the species, the interests which may then be spoken of reduce to those of the current members without remainder. Where the interests of further species are at stake, it is of course often desirable that there should be, for example, grass or legumes, without it mattering which individual organisms stay alive; but in questions of intrinsic value, the value would have to turn on that of particular individuals, or at least on particular flourishing states being attained by some individuals or other.[34]

But it is important not to forget the future members of a species. In some small measure this consideration is already implicit in the mention of the interests of the current members. For, among sentient organisms, it is often in the interests of those currently alive that their immediate successors should thrive. Yet, as was remarked in chapter 7 about humans, this point on its own hardly justifies preserving a species in perpetuity. The real question concerns whether the future members of nonhuman species will have value and should be considered in the present, in any way analogous to that which was claimed in that chapter for future people. The answer here must be that where the existence or the flourishing of future beings would have value, and we can facilitate or prevent it, we must take it into account. But the elimination of a species guarantees that it will have no future members; and many species are precisely threatened with extinction, either through the direct effects of human action or through reluctance to forestall the effects of pollution, the loss of natural habitats or other harmful trends. Therefore we must take into account the value of the future members of these species.

This is to say nothing about the extent of their moral significance, which might well easily be overridden in many cases. (Nor is it to declare that future nonconscious organisms are of intrinsic value, as the issue of the value of present ones remains unresolved.) But where members of these species (or their states) have value, it is to say that their future members have moral standing, including those possible future members the existence of which we can veto altogether. And in this area, as in that of future people, we could have duties regarding future creatures without owing the duties to particular ones or even knowing their identity. Thus for practical purposes we can speak of the value of the continued life of a species, although this value in fact hangs on that of the several present and future members.

Conscious and nonconscious life

Now to see how far such commitments would extend, we need to resolve the issue of the intrinsic value of nonconscious living organisms. But before that can be done it is necessary to assess a rival theory of Frankena and Singer. William Frankena follows C. I. Lewis in calling 'inherent value' the value which an object has through its ability to contribute to human life by its presence, and contends that this is the kind of value which attaches to things whether alive or not which are interesting to watch or study, or beautiful to contemplate, or which heal us when we are with them. C. I. Lewis' example is a painting. Frankena contrasts such inherent value with instrumental value, and applies the notion to natural as well as cultural items which benefit those who observe or contemplate them.[35] His example is the value which birds have for bird-watchers. (As birds are sentient, he would doubtless allow them intrinsic value too, but he would not say the same for plants or rocks.)

Peter Singer holds a similar view, expressed in different terms. Singer considers the suggestion of Val Routley that the destruction of a species is analogous to that of a great work of art, and that some of the 'immensely complex and inimitable items produced in nature' (Singer's quotation) have a non-instrumental value, just as a great painting has value 'apart from the pleasure and inspiration it brings to human beings'.[36] He replies by asking how it can be shown that a work of art such as Michelangelo's *Pieta* has value 'independently of the appreciation of those who have seen it or will see it'. It is unfortunate that Singer appears to imply that, not being non-instrumental, the value of the *Pieta* is merely instrumental, for his views suggest that he could agree with Frankena in holding its value not to be instrumental either, but inherent. But in any case his view is that its value depends on the possibility of its being perceived and enjoyed, and he sustains this view with a thought experiment not unlike that of Richard Routley, and a variant recently put forward by myself.[37] We imagine the last sentient being on earth making a bonfire of all the paintings in the Louvre. As long as the possibility of a visit from interstellar tourists is excluded, Singer does not hold that anything wrong is done. (He should perhaps exclude the likelier possibility also that the agent would have enjoyed the paintings later, by stipulating that the last sentient being knows that he or she is shortly to die.) If so, the value of works of art is inherent rather than intrinsic. Now if we also rule out the possibility that the interests of the dead, or of God, make a difference, it is hard to conclude that the act is wrong; and this conclusion is fortified by the reflection that inanimate objects have no good of their own. Works of art thus have inherent rather than intrinsic value, and if there really is an analogy between them and species (or their members), as has also been suggested by Stanley Benn,[38] then the analogy, *pace* both Benn and Val Routley, supports no stronger conclusion than this about any of the items concerned.

My agreement with Frankena and Singer applies not only to works of art but also to natural objects like rivers and rocks. Thus both the symbolic significance which they sometimes have and their curious diversity turn out to be facets of their inherent value. Nor should I dispute that very many living species, whether sentient or nonsentient, are possessed of inherent value also: an example is supplied by what Regan pleasantly calls 'pleasures rooted in real redwoods'. This may seem to clash with Mary Midgley's point, mentioned in chapter 4, that wild nonhuman creatures must be held either to have no point or value or to have a point which is quite alien to human purposes.[39] But the conflict is only apparent. As far as any intrinsic value which they may have is concerned, Midgley's view may be accepted; but granted her observation that we can derive pleasure and renewal from that which is wild and alien to our purposes, it follows that in any case the wild and alien creatures concerned have inherent value. What is clear, however, is that it does not follow from their having inherent value that this is the only value which they have. Singer is easily able to arrive at his view that this is the extent of their value, holding as he does that trees only have interests and needs in much the same sense as that in which cars do.[40] But cars lack natural fulfilments and, except in an artificial sense, direction of growth; trees, by contrast, have a good of their own, quite independent of that of people or other purposers.

Accordingly, although Goodpaster's reminder that plants have a good of their own does not establish that they have moral standing, there is some analogy between them and items which are widely agreed to have such standing, consisting precisely in their having interests and in the qualities and capacities which make this true. Thus the capacities for growth, respiration, self-preservation and reproduction are common to plants and sentient organisms (as also to many unicellular organisms). So there is an analogical argument for holding that all the organisms concerned not only can but also do have moral standing. There is, in fact, a qualification to make, as the analogical argument applies only to organisms with interests; and though sentient organisms whose flourishing was in the past clearly still have interests as long as they have any prospect of consciousness, the same cannot be said, in general, of nonsentient beings. For the interests of these beings lie in the fulfilment of their capacities, and once this fulfilment is in the past and decay sets in (often through the flourishing of other organisms) their interests decline and vanish. Only what retains a potential for realizing the generic good of its kind has interests and is valuable, even if the above argument is accepted; and accordingly it may well be that living organisms are not valuable as such, but that what is valuable is their flourishing or their capacity for flourishing after the manner of their kind, for as long as such a capacity can to any extent be sustained.

But can the argument be allowed to proceed even this far? For its implications seem devastating, and there are in any case disanalogies to consider. The implication which Goodpaster considers of respecting all life is that one cannot *live* on these terms, and Passmore actually accepts a corresponding objection to Schweitzer's view that all life merits reverence.[41] This implication is not greatly weakened by the qualification about organisms which are past their prime, as millions of others remain to be considered. The objection may thus be expressed as follows. If plants (or bacteria) have any more-than-negligible moral significance, then in their millions their interests must sometimes outweigh those of individual humans or other sentient beings; but this flies in the face of our reflective moral judgements, and should thus, short of compelling reasons, be rejected.

To this, however, there is a reply. Moral standing should not, as we have seen, be confused with moral significance; and the unacceptable conclusion is implied only by claims about the moral significance of plants and bacteria, not by claims about their moral standing. For they could have a moral standing and yet have an almost infinitesimal moral significance, so that even large aggregations of them did not outweigh the significance of sentient beings in cases of conflict. It could be that their moral significance only makes a difference when all other claims and considerations are equal (or nonexistent). Yet, as Goodpaster says, as long as plants have moral standing, it is worth bearing this standing in mind as a 'regulative consideration' which should at least ideally be taken into account. (In the actual world, the inherent and instrumental value of plants and generally of nonconscious organisms will quite often outweigh other moral considerations, and will constitute the main reasons against, for example, eliminating a species. But the intrinsic value of healthy plants could still add slightly to those considerations.)

The argument thus survives this objection, but it is no stronger than its analogical basis allows, and at this point the disanalogies between conscious and nonconscious organisms become important. The limited nature of the interests of the latter has already been noted. Moreover they cannot be pained or gladdened, satisfied or frustrated; and, except for the most primitive, they have no prospect of ever evolving into anything which could bear characteristics of this kind. There again they are not the subjects of a conscious point of view, and theories which base value on choices or preferences between living the life of one creature and the life of another are apt to accord them no value whatsoever.[42] Besides this, they are not in any morally interesting sense agents, even though causally their activity is vital for those beings which are so.

But how much do the disanalogies count for? Doubts were expressed in chapter 7 about theories which rest values on preferences; and the disanalogies do not annul the interests which seem to qualify plants (and the rest) for intrinsic value. The importance of the disanalogies seems rather to concern moral significance. Thus if pain and frustration constitute what is centrally of negative value, but plants and bacteria are susceptible to neither, then relatively little of negative value can befall them: and this suggests that relatively little of positive value can befall them either. If so, their moral significance will indeed be very slight, but this does not begin to show that they lack moral standing.

Even if plants have only slight moral significance, their moral standing would account for Benn's remark that 'if the well-being of persons could not be protected anyway, it would certainly be better to leave behind a world of living things than a dead world', and also for what Stephen Clark calls 'our distress at the destruction of a living tree',[43] a distress which, Clark holds, 'is not merely at our loss of pleasure in its beauty'. To test whether this is so, we need to imagine a state of affairs in which there are no sentient organisms, so that no one is impoverished by the tree's destruction. We thus imagine that all sentient beings, human and nonhuman, are doomed to imminent nuclear poisoning, and that this is known to the last surviving human. In 'The Good of Trees' I asked whether the survivor does wrong if he chops down with an axe 'the last tree of its kind, a hitherto healthy elm, which has survived the nuclear explosions and which could propagate its kind if left unassaulted'. Most people who consider this question conclude that his act would be wrong. I still believe that this is a valid test, which survives the objections about method which I there considered; and, though I grant that stray intuitions may need to be reined in by a consistent moral theory, in this case intuitions confirm a theory which already has some independent support. But it should be acknowledged that the destruction of the elm is seen in a worse light than might otherwise prevail because it involves the elimination of a species and guarantees that there will be no future elms. Destroying without good reason a tree of a plentiful species might be regarded as somewhat less serious, though still, doubtless, as wrong.

Yet even so, the case of the destruction of the last elm, where the existence of future elms is at stake, is still a fair test of whether elms are of intrinsic value: and the judgement that they are helps to explain our objections to the elimination of species (and to letting them die out) as well as our regrets at individual uprootings, as expressed by Clark. Further, though a species does not constitute a moral individual, the case of the last elm shows how the extinction of a species is worse than the killing of individual members. (I am not suggesting that eliminating a species is always wrong, but rather that, whatever the inherent or the instrumental value of the members, it always constitutes a significant intrinsic evil which needs to be weighed up against the benefits which may derive from it. Nor *a fortiori* am I suggesting that it is always wrong to tear a leaf from a tree, but I do consider Frankena to be mistaken when he implies that there is no harm in doing so whatever.[44])

Holism

On the theory which has been advanced, then, the class of things with moral standing does not extend beyond that of individual beings with a good of their own. Thus when species count it is because of their individual members, whether actual present ones or future ones which could live and flourish unless deprived in the present of the necessary ancestors. This type of theory, however, is likely to be criticized by those who see such positions as unduly atomistic, a mere extension of moral standing from moral agents *via* other humans to nonhuman animals and individual plants, rather than to the biotic community, or to nature as a whole. As Frankena remarks, phrases such as 'everything' and 'all life' may be taken either distributively or collectively; and he observes that Holmes Rolston[45] both pleads the intrinsic value of 'every ecobiotic component' and commends the enlargement of the moral focus 'not only from man to other ecosystemic members, but from individuals of whatever kind to the system, . . . (a) community (which) holds values'. Also Goodpaster himself in 'On Being Morally Considerable' takes seriously the possibility of the biosphere having moral standing,[46] and in his later 'From Egoism to Environmentalism' contends that the enlargement of the class of morally considerable beings cannot without arbitrariness be tied to individuals but must extend to systems as well:[47] only thus can we escape an 'individual-istic' model of thought and the 'concentric reasoning' of humanism enlarged. Sympathy for such a move has been expressed too by Clark,[48] and has been encouraged by the claim, made in a scientific journal, that the biosphere may be regarded as an organism.[49]

There are two strands in this accumulating holistic view, one which conceives of the biosphere as a community and the other which conceives of it as an organic whole. Both may be traced to the writings of Aldo Leopold. Leopold advocates a 'land ethic' in which the scope of ethics is enlarged; and sometimes he interprets this as the enlargement of the moral community. 'All ethics so far evolved rest on a single premise: that the individual is a member of a community of interdependent parts . . . The land ethic simply enlarges the boundaries of the community to include soils, waters, plants, and animals, or collectively: the land.'[50] The suggestion here is that whenever two or more natural things are interdependent, they bear mutual obligations, and that this is the case within the community which Leopold calls 'the land'.

This suggestion has been severely criticized by Passmore,[51] even though he accepts that all the elements listed by Leopold form part of an ecological 'life-cycle'. But this sense of 'community', he holds, fails to generate ethical obligation. For obligations to be generated there must be two conditions which are not satisfied in the ecological case: common interests among the members, and the recognition of mutual obligations. But the second requirement begs the question against Leopold, and is in any case too strong; thus people in a community can have obligations without there being recognition of these obligations on all sides, and indeed it cannot be necessary that obligations should be recognized for them to exist. As to the first requirement, the suggestion that common interests are shared, for example, by humans and bacteria cannot be denied unequivocally, and is in some ways quite cogent.

Leopold's suggestion has been elaborated by J. Baird Callicott, who stresses that it is absurd if taken to imply that trees, rocks and rain have duties and are subject to ethical limitations. These limitations apply only to moral agents, but these agents, who are aware of mutual obligations in the human community, should recognize that they are also members of the interdependent biotic community, and accept parallel obligations to its other members.[52] Similarly Clark urges us to recognize the claims of other creatures in 'earth's household', the land community.[53]

But, as Benson has written in reply, 'not every relationship of

mutual dependence automatically carries with it a moral relationship.'[54] This is clearly true where that on which we depend is
inanimate and lacks a good of its own. Clean air should be preserved
not for its own sake but for that of living creatures. Where living
creatures with a good of their own are concerned, there is, as we
have seen, the possibility of a moral relationship (of human to
fellow-creature), but even this need not amount to a matter of
obligations *to* particular plants or animals. We are obligated, I
should grant, to take their interests into account, but this holds
good of creatures whether they and we are interdependent or not.
Conversely interdependence does not proportionately strengthen
our obligations in this regard, but rather strengthens the argument
from human interest to preserve the systems of which they form
part. Thus to represent the biosphere as a moral community serves
as an evocative metaphor of the consilience of self-interest and
morality, but does not add extra grounds for respect to the 'ecobiotic
components'.

Leopold has also written that 'a thing is right when it tends to
preserve the integrity, stability, and beauty of the biotic community.
It is wrong when it tends otherwise'.[55] This passage could be
construed as expressing a concern for all the members of the
biosphere, considered distributively, in accordance with the obligations internal to a community. But it seems to go further and make
the criterion of right conduct the preservation of the biosphere as a
whole. This is unlikely to mean the maximizing of intrinsic value
within it, for talk of its 'integrity, stability and beauty' suggests
otherwise. More probably it concerns upholding its systems and its
diversity. A similar view is taken by Thomas Auxter,[56] who assesses
the rights of individuals and species by their contribution to the
richness of the biosphere, to the greater development of systems,
and to their members' mutual co-adaptation.

Now the stability of ecosystems is clearly crucial for the
maintenance of all life; no new ethical basis is required to support it.
Co-adaptation is desirable for the same reasons. Diversity is, as we
have seen, of inherent value, and this accounts for our preference
for rich natural systems. Neither the preservation of ecosystems,
however, nor diversity are of intrinsic value, and their conjunction
is not guaranteed to foster what is such, or even to cohere with it.
Thus the death of a quarter of the human population would not
prejudice ecosystems or the diversity of species; and though the loss
of individual diversity would be inestimable (and Auxter could
perhaps deplore it as such) I doubt if this would infringe Leopold's

criterion. To put matters in a different way, if the whole biosphere is regarded as having moral standing, then there can be a conflict between maximizing its excellences and maximizing the intrinsic value of its components.

But the biosphere will only have intrinsic value or moral standing if, as Frankena puts it, it has 'a value that is not reducible to the value in or of the lives or beings of the entities which make it up'.[57] Like Frankena, I can see no reason to accept this view. Certainly everything which is of value (and located anywhere near our planet) is located in the biosphere, and the systems of the biosphere are necessary for the preservation of all these creatures. But that does not give the biosphere or its systems intrinsic value. Rather it shows them to have instrumental value, since what is of value in its own right is causally dependent on them. As to the biosphere as a whole, with all its richness and beauty, those features which it has but which its components lack suggest that its value is inherent. Admittedly if all its conscious members expired, it would retain its beauty, but there would be value in this beauty only as an object of contemplation either by further conscious beings or by ourselves as we envisage its lonely grandeur.

I cannot therefore accept the full claims about intrinsic value of the 'deep, long-range' environmental movement;[58] more particularly I do not find intrinsic value in inanimate beings (or in each and every animate one), or again in ecosystems, the biotic community or the biosphere. Nor can I accept the mystical metaphysics which sometimes accompanies these judgements of value, a metaphysics on which the distinctions between individual organisms pale before the unity of the whole, of which moral agents and other apparent individuals are mere manifestations. Such talk is parasitic on belief in the substantiality of the 'ecobiotic components', and neither their reality nor their value can be disregarded at the stage when thought has reached the level of the biosphere as a whole, not at any rate with consistency intact.

Similarly there seem no grounds to accept what Henry Byerly has characterized as the 'Holist Design Principle', which 'tells us not to interfere with natural systems because this would be to act contrary to the general design of nature'.[59] Seriously to hold that 'Nature knows best' (Barry Commoner's Third Law of Ecology[60]) is to abandon the attempt to do what is best in the light of the best evidence about the consequences: and there is no reason to suppose either that nature intends otherwise (or indeed intends anything), or that God prefers the nonrational zones of creation to proceed unaffected by rational creatures. Nor could it be so, since rational creatures are part of nature, and survive by employing their naturally endowed capacities for the purposive modification of their natural surroundings. Nor, *a fortiori*, should we with Leopold make the stability, integrity and beauty of the biosphere the sole criterion of morality. With Byerly I recognize the need for an alternative principle which exhorts caution over random changes to crucial natural systems without prohibiting action to make the world a better, or a tolerable, place.

Values and valuers

Nevertheless by accepting the intrinsic value of some nonconscious entities I am clearly rejecting most forms of the plausible view that what is of value is necessarily valued by some conscious subject. (Not all forms need to be rejected, as this doctrine could concern just those subjects who value what there is good reason to value: but I need to reject any form of it in which what conscious subjects prefer determines what is valuable, rather than *vice versa*.) This doctrine has been termed the 'no detachable values assumption' by Richard and Val Routley,[61] who have effectively criticized the argument that only the interests of valuers, and what promotes those interests, are of value. As they point out, even such an instrumentalist theory of value carries an assumption of its own about what is intrinsically of value: and if such an assumption concerns the interests of a privileged class only and omits other interests, the assumption cannot easily be defended. Doubtless, it may be acknowledged, lines have to be drawn somewhere between what is of value and what is not, and not all delimitations can be 'chauvinist'; but the line which is actually drawn must nevertheless be a defensible one. The Routleys' critique of the 'no detachable values' assumption also serves to show that any theory of value, however instrumentalist in tenor, must recognize intrinsic value somewhere, or there is nothing which gives anything of value its point. Accordingly there is nothing mystical or irrational in talk of intrinsic value, or attempts to locate it. Such attempts must, as we have seen, begin with agreed cases and then proceed outwards through a consideration of analogies and disanalogies, as has been attempted above.

By this method I have arrived at a position at once deeper than the shallow environmental movement and shallower than the mystical depths of the deeper movement of Naess' characterization.

In brief, I have arrived at a position on which whatever has interests of its own has moral standing and on which the realization of those interests has intrinsic value. This view may be accused alike of chauvinism by holists and of irrationality by adherents of the growing consensus view that all and only the sentient have moral standing. It may also be resisted by those who hold that value is too far detached from valuers. But to these positions I have given my responses already.

Finally the position adopted should be related to the Judaeo-Christian theistic tradition. What is asserted coheres well with the Old and New Testaments, and conflicts only with such later adherents of the tradition as Aquinas, Descartes and Kant. Frankena, in fact, gives several positions which a theist might hold in matters of moral standing, some of which would not cohere with the position presented above.[62] On his first alternative all that matters morally is whether we are benefiting or harming God. On this view, strictly interpreted, only states of God are of intrinsic value, whereas states of creatures are only of derivative value, the extent of which depends on their effects on God. This alternative, as Frankena sees, may well be rejected by those who hold that God cannot be harmed or benefited: but his second alternative, on which what matters is obeying God's commands or loving what he loves, has a parallel upshot. For once again only the fulfilment of God's will is of intrinsic value, and the states of creatures have value only insofar as they contribute to it. Frankena's third alternative is that what matters in morality is promoting 'the glory of God' in a sense irreducible to that of the preceding alternatives, a sense which Frankena does not supply. His final alternative splits into two: either the wholehearted love of God is morally basic, and love of one's neighbour is subordinate to it; or the love of God and of neighbour are co-ordinate and each basic in their own right.

Now according to Frankena, only if the second variant of the final alternative is adopted is anything but God or his states or will of intrinsic value. Yet the third alternative, as he describes it, need not be interpreted as excluding this. Thus the glory of God could consist in the flourishing of his creatures, and this could be what counts primarily in morality. At any rate a theist is free to adopt such a view, which coheres with the position of this chapter. It may, of course, be asked why the fulfilment of creatures' interests redounds to God's glory: but if *ex hypothesi* this happens to be his creative purpose, the answer is to hand. Love of God could still supply an extra motive for love of fellow creatures, but it would not be the only route to such a love. The remaining question is whether creatures have an additional, inherent value through the creator's enjoyment of them. This could be so, as long as God's enjoyment is not treated as an episode. But it would not affect the grounds of human action. For whatever has inherent value of this sort also has it because of the possible enjoyment of creatures; and though it could persist when all conscious creatures have perished, no extra reason is provided in the form of preserving things for God to enjoy, as his enjoyment is timeless, and unaffected by change, decay or death. I conclude that the above discussion is fully in line with biblical talk of God's love for his creatures and injunctions to do his will.

NOTES

1   'On Being Morally Considerable', *Journal of Philosophy*, 75, 1978, 308—25.
2   Joel Feinberg, 'The Rights of Animals and Unborn Generations', in William T. Blackstone (ed.), *Philosophy and Environmental Crisis*, 43—68.
3   'On Being Morally Considerable', p. 312.
4   Senses distinguished by Lawrence Haworth in 'Rights, Wrongs and Animals', *Ethics*, 88, 1977—78, 95—105, p. 95.
5   Ibid. p. 102.
6   Thus Tom Regan, 'Animal Rights, Human Wrongs', *Environmental Ethics*, 2, 1980, 99—120, p. 113.
7   Thus Robert Nozick, *Anarchy, State and Utopia*, Oxford: Blackwell, 1974. Nozick applies the notion to animals at pp. 28—42.
8   'Is There a Need for a New, an Environmental Ethic?', *Proceedings of the XVth World Congress of Philosophy*, Varna, 1973, Vol. I, 205—10, p. 210.
9   *The Object of Morality*, New York: Methuen, 1971, pp. 150f. Much the same applies to the egoistic position, with which Narveson has recently found himself in sympathy; for on that position, as Regan has observed, there are no grounds whatever to give consideration to those infants and imbeciles who have no friends or family to care about their fate. See Jan Narveson, 'Animal Rights', *Canadian Journal of Philosophy*, 7, 1977, 161—78, and Tom Regan, 'Narveson on Egoism and the Rights of Animals', ibid. 179—86.
10 'An Examination and Defense of One Argument Concerning Animal Rights', *Inquiry*, 22, 1979, 189—219, section IV, 204—12.
11 In 'Killing Humans and Killing Animals', *Inquiry*, 22, 1979, 145—56, and in 'Not for Humans Only: The Place of Nonhumans in Environmental Issues', in K. E. Goodpaster and K. M. Sayre (eds),

Ethics and Problems of the 21st Century, Notre Dame and London: University of Notre Dame Press, 1979, 191—206.

12   Ibid. p. 205.
13   Regan contends, against Feinberg, that in one ordinary sense of 'interests' it is not impossible for nonconscious beings to have interests, in 'The Nature and Possibility of an Environmental Ethic', *Environmental Ethics*, 3, 1981, 16—31, p. 19, and also in 'Feinberg on What Sorts of Beings Can Have Rights', in *Southern Journal of Philosophy*, 14, 1976, 485—98, pp. 494—7.
14   'The Rights of Animals and Unborn Generations', pp. 51—7.
15   Ibid. p. 49.
16   Robin Attfield, 'The Good of Trees', *Journal of Value Inquiry*, 15, 1981, 35—54. (This paper was in fact accepted for publication some time before Goodpaster's paper was drawn to my attention.)
17   W. Murray Hunt, 'Are *Mere Things* Morally Considerable?', *Environmental Ethics*, 2, 1980, 59—65: Kenneth Goodpaster, 'On Stopping at Everything: A Reply to W. M. Hunt', *Environmental Ethics*, 2, 1980, 281—4.
18   In 'From Egoism to Environmentalism', in Goodpaster and Sayre (eds), *Ethics and Problems of the 21st Century*, 21—35, pp. 28—33; also in 'On Being Morally Considerable', p. 323.
19   'The Nature and Possibility of an Environmental Ethic', p. 21.
20   The phrase 'moral standing' is modelled on the title of Christopher Stone's book *Should Trees Have Standing?*, (Los Altos, Cal.: William Kaufman, 1974), in which Stone argues that some natural objects should be accorded legal rights.
21   Regan, 'The Nature and Possibility of an Environmental Ethic', p. 27.
22   *MRN* p. 124 and p. 217 (in 2nd edn, 1980).
23   'The Good of Trees', section II.
24   Regan, 'The Nature and Possibility of an Environmental Ethic', pp. 22f.
25   *MRN*, pp. 101—10.
26   R. and V. Routley, *The Fight for the Forests*, Canberra: Australian National University Press, 1974; Singer, 'Not for Humans Only', p. 198.
27   Laurence H. Tribe, 'Ways not to Think about Plastic Trees', *Yale Law Journal*, 83, 1974, 1315—48.
28   'On Preserving the Natural Environment', *Yale Law Journal*, 84, 1974, 205—67.
29   'Why Preserve Landmarks? A Preliminary Inquiry', in Goodpaster and Sayre, *Ethics and Problems of the 21st Century*, 175—90.
30   *The Great Chain of Being*, Harvard, Mass., Harvard University Press, 1936.
31   In 'The Good of Trees', section II.
32   *MRN*, 119—21.
33   'Not for Humans Only', p. 203.
34   For another view see Stephen Clark, *The Moral Status of Animals*, Oxford: Clarendon Press, 1977, p. 171.

35   See W. K. Frankena, 'Ethics and the Environment', in Goodpaster and
     Sayre (eds), *Ethics and Problems of the 21st Century,* 3—20, p. 13.
     C. I. Lewis' position is cited at p. 20, n. 23.
36   'Not for Humans Only', p. 203. Cf. Val Routley, Critical Notice of John
     Passmore, *Man's Responsibility for Nature, Australasian Journal of
     Philosophy,* 53, 1975, 171—85, p. 175.
37   Richard Routley, 'Is There a Need for a New, an Environmental
     Ethic', p. 107; Robin Attfield, 'The Good of Trees', sections II and III.
38   'Personal Freedom and Environmental Ethics: the Moral Inequality of
     Species', in Gray Dorsey (ed.), *Equality and Freedom,* New York:
     Oceana Publications, 1977, Vol. II, 401—24, p. 415.
39   Mary Midgley, *Beast and Man,* pp. 357—9.
40   Singer, 'Not for Humans Only', p. 195.
41   Goodpaster, 'On Being Morally Considerable', p. 322; Passmore, *MRN,*
     pp. 121—4. Cf. Albert Schweitzer, *Civilisation and Ethics,* 1923; trans.
     C. T. Campion, 3rd edn, London: Adam and Charles Black, 1946,
     p. 244.
42   Cf. the theory of Singer, 'Not for Humans Only', p. 199f; also that of
     Roupas, discussed in chapter 7 (above).
43   Benn, 'Personal Freedom and Environmental Ethics', p. 421; Clark,
     The Moral Status of Animals, p. 172.
44   Frankena, 'Ethics and the Environment', p. 11.
45   Ibid. pp. 11f; and p. 20, nn. 19, 20; Holmes Rolston III, 'Is There an
     Ecological Ethic?', *Ethics,* 85, 1975, 93—109, pp. 101, 106. My own
     criticisms of holistic ethics are further developed in 'Methods of
     Ecological Ethics'.
46   'On Being Morally Considerable', p. 323.
47   'From Egoism to Environmentalism', Goodpaster and Sayre (eds),
     Ethics and Problems of the 21st Century, 21—35, pp. 29f.
48   *The Moral Status of Animals,* p. 170.
49   J. Lovelock and S. Epton, 'The Quest for Gaia', *The New Scientist,* 65,
     1975, 304—9, cited by Goodpaster (see above), p. 35, n. 25. See also
     J. E. Lovelock, *Gaia: A New Look at Life on Earth,* Oxford: Oxford
     University Press, 1979.
50   *A Sand County Almanac,* New York: Oxford University Press, 1949,
     pp. 203f, cited by Clark (see above), p. 164.
51   *MRN,* p. 116.
52   J. Baird Callicott, 'Elements of an Environmental Ethic: Moral
     Considerability and the Biotic Community', *Environmental Ethics,* I,
     1979, 71—81, p. 76. Callicott takes matters further in 'Animal
     Liberation: A Triangular Affair', (see chapter 4, n. 56, above), to
     which I have replied in 'Methods of Ecological Ethics'.
53   *The Moral Status of Animals,* p. 164.
54   John Benson, 'Duty and the Beast', *Philosophy,* 53, 1978, 529—49,
     p. 542.

55 *A Sand County Almanac,* pp. 224f; cited by Frankena, 'Ethics and the Environment', p. 12 and p. 20, n. 21; and by Goodpaster, 'From Egoism to Environmentalism', p. 21.

56 'The Right not to be Eaten', *Inquiry,* 22, 1979, 221—30, pp. 222f, and p. 228f, n. 2.

57 'Ethics and the Environment', p. 17.

58 Arne Naess, 'The Shallow and the Deep, Long-Range Ecology Movement', *Inquiry,* 16, 1973, 95—100.

59 Henry Byerly, 'Principles of Noninterference with Nature in Ecological Ethics', in *Ethics, Foundations, Problems and Applications, Proceedings of the Fifth International Wittgenstein Symposium,* Vienna: Verlag Hölder-Pichler-Tempsky, 1981, 318—20.

60 *The Closing Circle,* London: Jonathan Cape, 1972, p. 41.

61 'Against the Inevitability of Human Chauvinism', in Goodpaster and Sayre (eds), *Ethics and Problems of the 21st Century,* 36—59; see p. 42, and the discussion at pp. 42—52, and p. 58f, n. 13. For a contrary view, see Robert Elliot, 'Why Preserve Species?', in *Environmental Philosophy,* (see chapter 4, n. 47, above), 8—29, pp. 18—21. I favour a more objectivist view than the Routleys or Elliot.

62 Frankena, 'Ethics and the Environment', p. 8. See also my criticism in chapter 4 (above) of the Routleys' understanding of theistic ethics.

9

Inter-species Morality: Principles and Priorities

Granted that nonhuman animals and most plants have moral standing, what principles of inter-species morality should we recognize? What, indeed, is the relative moral significance of the various species and their members, and what bearing does their moral significance have on our practice? These are the questions to be addressed in the course of the present chapter.

I have argued that each of a wide range of organisms has moral standing. But no particular conclusion follows about their relative moral significance. Some, such as Arne Naess, favour, insofar as it is possible, the equality of species,[1] while others, such as Philip Devine, hold that humans may be preferred to nonhumans simply as such.[2] The latter view is stigmatized by Peter Singer (following Richard Ryder) as speciesism,[3] and in its stead Singer has proposed the principle that 'the interests of every being affected by an action are to be taken into account and given the same weight as the like interests of any other being.'[4] I shall begin by examining this Equality of Interests principle, but shall bear in mind at the same time the views of those who, for various reasons, reject discussions of interests and rights as irrelevant in ecological matters, whether because they are based on an unduly individualist, atomistic and man-centred method[5] or because they hold that nonhumans lack interests and rights altogether.[6]

Equal consideration

Singer's principle is clearly less radical than that of Naess, for some

166

organisms lack interests possessed by others, and will thus not receive as much consideration if this principle is accepted. It is indeed intended as a merely formal principle, which through settling which creatures' pains and pleasures count and how much they count allows the calculation of costs and benefits to begin. As such it might be regarded as entirely nonarbitrary, since entities lacking interests are discounted solely on the grounds that they cannot be benefited. Singer, a utilitarian, favours maximizing the balance of intrinsic good over evil, and this will be accomplished only if like interests are given nothing but the same weighting as each other. Accordingly the principle is devised so as to debar either nonsentient organisms being treated on a par with sentient ones (as deep ecological radicals sometimes urge) or the suffering of nonhumans not being considered equally with the like suffering of humans (in the manner of speciesism).

Now if the argument of chapter 7 is accepted — that there are obligations with respect to possible people (an argument extended in chapter 8 to apply to some possible nonhumans), then this Equality of Interests principle cannot supply the sole basis for deciding which of an action's effects to take into account. But insofar as items already in existence are concerned, the principle must be a sound one, once it is duly interpreted. For what has interests, it has been concluded, has moral standing, and the principle ensures that nothing with moral standing is disregarded. Moreover as long as intrinsic good is done when interests are satisfied, then the principle exactly captures these vital tenets of value theory and applies them appropriately to action. Certainly an appropriate account of 'like interests' is required, and depends for its application on a suitable account of what interests consist in. But unless some rival account of intrinsic good (perhaps a holistic one) is preferred, Singer's principle surely reflects a large part of the truth.

Many writers, of course, harness the issue of which items to take into consideration and the issue of which have rights (an approach at which holists protest just as they do at giving pride of place to interests). Thus Leonard Nelson holds that having interests is necessary and sufficient for a being to have rights,[7] and H. J. McCloskey, who used to take this view and who has all along rejected belief in animal rights, used also to claim that nonhuman animals lacked interests;[8] but more recently, having dropped this claim, he has also laid down much stronger requirements for the possession of rights than Nelson or than the slightly more cautious position adopted by Joel Feinberg.[9] R. G. Frey, despite a general scepticism about natural rights, has taken great pains to argue that animals lack interests in any relevant sense, lest this should be thought to give them rights;[10] and Tom Regan has contended that unless we ascribe to most humans and some animals rights which can only be overridden with very good reason, our reflective moral judgements cannot stand up.[11] (Regan seeks to avoid any consequentialist aggregation of good and evil and the resulting trade-offs, but seems to incur similar, if not worse, problems by according potentially conflicting rights to multitudes of creatures, especially as none of these rights is at all easily to be overridden.) Without endorsing the position of the holists, I do not regard it as necessary to locate rights where they belong before settling issues of priority of consideration: for, granted the value of benefits and the negative value of their counterpart evils wherever a beneficiary can be found, we can proceed direct to the requirement to take good and bad consequences into account if our actions are to be morally justifiable.

Now the issue of interspecific priorities between conflicting interests could be much simplified if it could either be accepted, with Frey, that nonhuman animals lack beliefs and desires and therefore lack interests, or with Ruth Cigman that for them death is no misfortune,[12] or, with Singer, that those beings lack interests which lack the capacity or potential for feeling pleasure or pain.[13] For in each case the possible area of conflict would be much diminished. But I am satisfied by the arguments of Joseph Margolis[14] that many nonhuman animals have both beliefs and desires, and thus the kinds of interests which go with them; the fact that death deprives many animals of the fulfilment of their specific potentials satisfies me that death can be an evil even where no concept of death is held; and I have argued above, especially in chapter 8, for the rejection of hedonism and for the belief that many nonsentient organisms have a good of their own, and therefore I cannot accept the view that interests stop where sentience does.

This being so, the Equality of Interests principle must be applied to a wider range of creatures than Singer intends, and to a greater variety of interests which one and the same creature may have. Thus humans have an interest in being able to make autonomous choices and to form friendships, and in preserving their self-respect, as well as in being free from pain; while nonhuman creatures, whether sentient or nonsentient, also have an interest in flourishing after their kind by developing their own specific capacities. Granted this plethora of interests, it is important to decide under what descriptions the interests of members of different species are to be identified and compared.

Classification of interests

One of the alternative classifications suggested by Devine[15] would turn on the intensity of the feelings which an organism stands to enjoy or suffer. This interpretation of Singer's principle is rejected by Devine because it omits interests, such as those of sleepers, which need not turn on feelings at all. But this objection does not make it inappropriate for an adherent of the principle to consider the interest of creatures in not being severely hurt. The real objection to classifying interests in that manner is that the role of the interest in the life of the creature concerned is ignored. The interest in not suffering acute pain is for some creatures just that; for others it also involves an interest in forgoing the fear and confusion which would accompany the pain; and for some humans it further involves an interest in being able to have unsullied memories and to form and implement future plans with confidence, and in being spared a sense of humiliation and rejection. Despite this objection, the interest in not being severely hurt remains an interest, but two creatures share it as a 'like interest' only where no other interests are at stake.

Another classification considered by Devine is by 'the general kind' of the interests: his example is the need for water, shared by plants and human beings. Devine's point here is that if this interest of a plant and a human is considered equally, the outcome (equal shares of water) is morally absurd. Singer, of course, would not acknowledge the example as a problem, as he holds sentience to be necessary for the possession of interests; but in this, as has been argued in chapter 8, he seems to be wrong. Accordingly interests must not be classified in a way which generates such acutely counter-intuitive judgements. But the problem does not lie in classifying interests by their general kind (such as the interest in exercising autonomous choice). Rather it lies in isolating an interest under a description such as 'the need for x' without mention of the other needs which depend on the fulfilment of the given need. For if the full range of interests which are at stake are taken into account, the Equality of Interests principle is not as obviously misguided as Devine supposes.

Nevertheless the difficulties just mentioned suggest that interests be somehow classified by their level of complexity or sophistication. Thus Aubrey Townsend, in the course of a critical notice of Clark's and Singer's books about the proper treatment of animals,[16] contends that morality is concerned with diverse kinds of interests, an interest in welfare (which he takes to concern the living of a pain-free happy life) and an interest in autonomy, and that autonomy normally trumps welfare. I have argued elsewhere against just such a claim,[17] but without accepting Townsend's priorities I can acknowledge that some moral responses are only possible towards an autonomous agent, and that in the sense of 'autonomy' which he derives from Stanley Benn[18] only humans (and only some of *them*) are autonomous. This sense involves the ability to make and execute decisions and plans in the light of more-or-less rational beliefs and preferences. Now on many occasions when there is an opportunity to recognize and foster such autonomy, this interest may well be accorded priority over any conflicting interests: but, as I shall argue, such a priority cannot be taken for granted, particularly where the basic interests of a beast clash with a peripheral interest of a human, like the broadening of the scope for autonomous action.

Benn himself, as I have pointed out in chapter 8, accepts the moral standing of 'works of nature', including even ecosystems: they are *'axiotima'*, things which it is appropriate to value or esteem. But he holds that the needs of humans, or at any rate persons, generally takes precedence over those of other *axiotima* because of their distinctive capacities; and that even if humans can only be saved from biological extinction by conserving the biosphere, nevertheless if this were to involve the 'institutional bridling of human creative intelligence', which is precisely 'the capacity which constitutes the human species a threat to the biosphere', these measures would not be justified.[19] Benn is here expressing moral opposition to totalitarianism at all costs; yet his determination to preserve creative intelligence from any measures of coercion necessary to prevent the extinction of humanity and the endangering of most *axiotima* too seems disproportionate and potentially self-frustrating. Creative intelligence, for one thing, would not need to be institutionally bridled in all respects, or all politically significant respects, in order to avert disastrous manipulation of the environment; for another thing, the only prospect for the survival of creative intelligence is probably some curtailment, voluntary or otherwise, of its exercise. Thus the choice with which Benn presents his readers between man and the biosphere is a misleading one. But in any case Benn does not make out his case for holding that urgent anthropocentric agendum-grounds (or reasons for action) should generally take precedence over urgent nonhuman needs. Even if it is granted that we have reason to cherish distinctive human capacities, this does not entitle us to prefer the interest in their realization in general over the nondistinctive interests of humans or the interests of nonhumans. Such a two-level theory of types of interest is excessively rigid, and obscures the genuine moral conflicts which exist over, for example, the eating of meat, over animal experiments, and over agricultural developments which contribute to the eclipse of wild species.

Self-consciousness

Another two-level theory of interests has, however, been put forward by Peter Singer himself. In his paper 'Killing Humans and Killing Animals' he argues that, while the suffering of nonhuman animals and of humans should be taken into consideration equally, where killing is concerned the possession of the capacity to see oneself as a distinct entity with a future marks a relevant difference between most humans (plus any other animals which have it) and all other animals, including some humans, which do not.[20] For those with this capacity, death involves the frustration of autonomous plans and projects, whereas the painless death of those who lack it spells at worst a loss of pleasure, and this can be made good by producing another animal which leads a pleasant life instead of the one which is killed. Thus entities lacking the concept of a self are replaceable, and where they are concerned we should simply seek to maximize the balance of pleasure over pain, as the Total theory of classical utilitarianism maintains; but entities which have this concept are in an important sense irreplaceable, and among such entities we should give precedence to existing ones, or ones which will exist in future independently of our decisions, rather as the Person-affecting principle enjoins.

I have already criticized this partial adoption of the Person-affecting principle (see chapter 6) over the discounting of possible people whose existence would depend on us. Here I have a different point to make, a point about capacities. Singer's recognition of the capacity of self-consciousness constitutes an enrichment of his hedonism, but he does not take enough capacities into account. This may be brought out in connection both with human infants and with nonhuman animals. Thus the killing of a human infant deprives it of much more than pleasure (and of the capacity for future enjoyment, remarked by Singer in 'Not for Humans Only'[21]). Unless it is very severely subnormal, it will have the potential for developing all the capacities characteristic of humans (including those for practical and theoretical reasoning, for autonomy, for forming friendships, for meaningful work and for self-respect), and its death deprives it of all prospect of the goods which consist in developing these potentials. As to nonhuman animals, Michael Lockwood adapts an example of Christina Hoff to give his readers pause over the replaceability thesis.[22] To suit the convenience of pet-owners who cannot take pets on holiday with them and prefer a new pet when they return, the company 'Disposapup Ltd' rears and supplies puppies, takes them back and kills them at holiday-time, and supplies replacements on demand. Though the activities of Disposapup are much less horrific than factory farming, we may well condemn them as immoral, even if we detach ourselves from the propensity to treat pets as humans. If so, I suggest, we should need to appeal to more than the puppies' loss of pleasure, and to point to the natural fulfilments of canine potentials of which all of the firm's puppies are deprived. (Others might express this protest as one directed at the manipulation of nature: but this protest would be ungrounded unless the development of natural potentials matters.)

So Singer's two-level theory of interests (those based on sentience and those based on self-consciousness) seems, like those of Townsend and Benn, to be unduly insensitive to the great variety of potentials among both humans and nonhumans, and the related goods constituted by developing them and flourishing after one's kind. As John Benson comments, even if animals in factory-farms were anaesthetized, and thus could not suffer, there would still be reason to protest at depriving them of natural fulfilments.[23] But Singer seems to lack the resources for sharing in the protest.

Two-factor Egalitarianism

A theory which supplies a more elaborate classification of interests, and thus takes account of a greater variety of types, has been put forward by Donald VanDeVeer.[24] In his theory of Two-factor Egalitarianism, two kinds of variable which have already been noted are brought to the fore, the role of an interest in a creature's life and the psychological capacities of the creature. Within any one creature's life, some interests are basic and some are peripheral, while others are serious interests, in that their neglect or frustration is costly to the creature's well-being without threatening its survival.

Thus because of their different importance, basic interests should in general be preferred to serious and peripheral interests, and serious interests, while not outweighing basic ones, take precedence over those which are peripheral. But this principle would require us to give equal weight to the basic interests of creatures with very different psychological capacities, (as in Devine's objection to Singer). To avoid such an outcome VanDeVeer adopts the 'Weighting principle',[25] on which, with some qualifications, 'the interests of beings with more complex psychological capacities deserve greater weight than those with lesser capacities'. As the former are preferred to the latter because of their capacities rather than their species, the charge of discrimination on the mere basis of species-membership is averted (or so VanDeVeer hopes).

The fully-fledged version of Two-factor Egalitarianism runs as follows:

Where there is an interspecies conflict of interests between two beings, A and B, it is morally permissible, *ceteris paribus*:
(1) to sacrifice the interest of A to promote a like interest of B if A lacks significant psychological capacities possessed by B;
(2) to sacrifice a basic interest of A to promote a serious interest of B if A substantially lacks significant psychological capacities possessed by B, [and]
(3) to sacrifice the peripheral interest to promote the more basic interest if the beings are similar with respect to psychological capacity (regardless of who possesses the interests).[26]

Now clearly this position relies heavily on the Weighting principle, and requires a very heavy weighting for significant psychological capacities. Accordingly it also rests on the assumption that some capacities (or their development or exercise) are more valuable than others. Can these principles be upheld?

VanDeVeer has three defences of the Weighting principle. Firstly humans are typically subject to certain kinds of suffering to which other animals are not subject, so the same treatment may harm a human more than a nonhuman because of the greater human ability to foresee the future. Preferring the human in such a case, we may remark, is in keeping with most interpretations of the Equality of Interests principle, as the interests at stake are unequal. Secondly some creatures are more prone than others to deferred suffering, and the difference is a function of the psychological capacities involved. This is again a utilitarian consideration which Singer could endorse. Thirdly the cost in opportunities foregone will be heavier in the case of, for example, human death than with nonhuman deaths, again because of the much greater human capabilities. To the extent that these capabilities are not confined to suffering and enjoyment, a hedonist cannot grant the relevance of this point; but adherents of the Equality of Interests principle clearly can. So also, in a way, does Bonnie Steinbock,[27] when she writes that freedom from suffering is a minimal condition for exercising capacities which humans have and animals do not, capacities for responsibility, altruistic reasons for action and self-respect; and that as we value these capacities human suffering is regarded as more deplorable than animal suffering. Since, however, not all humans in fact have these capacities and it is possible that not all nonhuman animals lack them, Steinbock could only maintain her position of valuing every human life more than any animal life on the basis of preference for humans as such.

Do those who accept VanDeVeer's reasons need to accept his Weighting principle and his Two-factor Egalitarianism? Only, I suggest, with some qualifications. Thus the more complex activities would be relevant only where their development or exercise is at stake; and though, in cases of conflict, this is usually so, particularly when the needs of the more sophisticated creature for survival are in question, it would not always be so. Thus in the case of a human who is deprived of meat from a factory-farm, though serious interests (the exercise of autonomy and the symbolic significance of a feast) may be at stake, it is unlikely that the prospects for a worthwhile life in the long-term are at risk, whereas the basic interests of the animals concerned (in avoiding suffering and premature death) are certainly at stake. Yet VanDeVeer's second principle would probably (and perhaps contrary to his intentions) allow most current forms of factory-farming to continue; and to this extent he is vulnerable to a charge of speciesism. His principles accordingly need modifying to ensure that one or other of his reasons for accepting the Weighting principle actually applies to each case of 'sacrifice' of basic or serious interests. This granted, however, the Equality of Interests principle is satisfied. (His principles are still not comprehensive, as they do not tell us the weight to be attached to the interests not related to psychological capacities at all, such as those of plants, apart from implying that interests which are related to such psychological capacities take precedence over those which are not, a principle which could be questioned.)

VanDeVeer's third reason, however, (the cost of the loss of valuable opportunities) turns, as Steinbock's views do, on the view that the exercise of some capacities is more valuable than that of others. A similar point seems to be envisaged when Devine talks of animal pain being deficient in 'conceptual richness';[28] while Singer, who would resist Devine's application of the idea, himself holds that 'it is not arbitrary to hold that the life of a self-aware being, capable of abstract thought, of planning for the future, of complex acts of communication, and so on, is more valuable than the life of a being without these capacities'.[29]

Benson, however, rejects any such claims about relative intrinsic value, holding that 'to make those characteristics which make human life valuable to a man into the standard to judge of the value of life seems to be a good example of speciesism'.[30] Such hierarchies are also opposed by Clark[31] and by John Rodman,[32] and these writers are certainly right in stressing the different forms of active life to which different nonhuman species are adapted, and how their interests plausibly depend on the capacity to achieve the relevant form of life.

Having rejected belief in the intrinsic value of lives of differing capacities, Benson develops a different account of the value of life in terms of its value *to the creature concerned*. A creature's life has value for the creature if it has self-awareness and the capacity to plan ahead, and it is wrong, for that reason, to kill that creature. Yet even creatures which lack these capacities may still have a point of view and lives of value for themselves, as long as they have the capacity to enjoy and go on enjoying the life proper to their kind; and it is at any rate possible to hold that killing such a creature is also wrong. What is apparent here is that Benson holds, where action is concerned, that some creatures' continued life constitutes an independent moral consideration (the continued life of those with self-awareness and the capacity to plan ahead), and that the continued life of other creatures may constitute such a ground, but not so clearly.

I submit that this position is no different from one on which the life proper to the kind of each of them is held to be of intrinsic value, but in different degrees. For something is of intrinsic value if there are nonderivative moral reasons for fostering, desiring or cherishing it, and this is just what Benson accepts about the continued lives of nonhuman animals: and he also accepts, in effect, that it is true of lives with different capacities to different degrees. Nor is this just an *ad hominem* reply to Benson. For anyone who counts as morally relevant the different degrees to which the continuation of the form of life to which it is adapted is of value to a creature, and/or the differences in opportunities for self-realization foregone by the deaths of different creatures, is thereby acknowledging that varying degrees of *intrinsic* value attach to lives in which different capacities are realized. This position is compatible with recognizing that, other things being equal, nonhuman animals should be allowed to develop the full range of capacities natural to themselves, and that wild (and domesticated) creatures are not substandard humans, of value only through embodying a pale reflection of human traits, but have fulfilments of their own which are other than ours.

The proposition that lives in which some capacities are available and realized are of more value than lives in which they are not can be criticized in other ways. Thus Cora Diamond holds that capacities such as that for suffering are not morally fundamental, but rather various relationships and the forms of (social) life of which they form part.[33] But if these relationships happen to exclude a creature the capacities of which are as a result disregarded, then the resulting practice is open to moral criticism; and the same applies if relationships bring it about that creatures with capacities of radically different types are treated as if they were of equal value. The same reply may serve for anyone who goes beyond Benson and refuses to count, say, the deaths of those creatures with self-awareness and the ability to plan ahead and of those without these capacities as of different moral significance; normal humans should not be treated like ants, nor, come to that, should intelligent chimpanzees, and this even though they all, ants included, have moral standing.[34]

There is also the possible criticism that the moral recognition of different capacities commits us to meritocracy and to favouring the intelligent within human society: but this objection has been effectively countered both by VanDeVeer and by Steinbock,[35] who point out that there may well be thresholds below which differences in capacity do not count, and that for most (though not all) purposes a certain minimum intelligence qualifies all humans for equal treatment. Accordingly I conclude that because of the good which the creatures concerned stand to gain or lose, lives in which some capacities are realized are more valuable than those in which they are not or cannot be, and that the Equality of Interests principle must be interpreted accordingly. Thus when the realization of these capacities is at stake, the basic and serious interest of beings which have them outweigh the basic and serious interests of those which lack them. To this (limited) extent VanDeVeer's Weighting principle may be accepted, but it should not be accepted in the less qualified way in which it was originally presented.

Acceptance of the Equality of Interests principle and of this form of the Weighting principle commits me to a version of VanDeVeer's Two-factor Egalitarianism. But it has to be understood that creatures with capacities for more valuable forms of life receive priority over others only where the ability to exercise those capacities is genuinely at stake; a clause to this effect needs to be inserted in (1) and (2) of VanDeVeer's formulation, so that B's interests can be preferred only where B's ability to exercise significant psychological capacities which are lacked by A would otherwise be forfeited or imperilled. It should be added that, as creatures incapable of consciousness lack a point of view and thus forfeit nothing of which they could have been aware even when they are killed, the interests of conscious creatures normally take precedence over theirs; but that, as they have moral standing (see chapter 8), when at any rate a large number of them are at stake (as when a forest is threatened), or when the possible existence of multitudes of future ones could be foreclosed (by the elimination of a species) their otherwise almost negligible intrinsic value as individuals amounts to a serious moral ground, quite apart from their inherent and instrumental value. At times, too, it will be wrong to damage or destroy a tree or plant because the mere pleasure which the act of destruction would give is of even slighter moral significance than the continuing life of a healthy plant. What all this amounts to is the basis for an expanded version of the Total theory; but this is not the place to attempt to expound such a theory further, for there are objections yet to be answered.

Discrimination

Any theory on which like interests merit like consideration has to face the objection that humans with like capacities and thus like interests to those of nonhumans may rightly be accorded priority, or so it may be claimed. This claim is sometimes based on consequentialist grounds, which consequentialist adherents of the Equality of Interests principle could accept. Thus, to Singer's contention that one should only be willing to inflict suffering on a nonhuman animal if one would also be willing to inflict it on a human of like intelligence, it may be replied that suffering will be caused in other humans who care about the human of severely subnormal intelligence,[36] and also that any experimentation on such humans would have the bad consequence of weakening people's inhibitions against the infliction of suffering on humans in normal cases. These effects upon third parties of the like treatment of like interests are on any account morally relevant, and do justify some differential treatment, without the principle (on which like interests merit like *consideration*) being overthrown. Indeed the importance of the preservation of inhibitions seems to be the most that can be said for the Overflow principle advanced by Devine:

Act towards that which, while not itself a person, is closely associated with personhood in a way coherent with an attitude of respect for persons.[37]

Common acceptance of this principle, or something like it, may indeed explain our respect for dead bodies; but, beyond the argument from inhibitions, it is hard to see how to justify the principle (except insofar as the interests of nonpersons are morally significant in their own right), and harder still to see why the Equality of Interests principle should be discarded in its favour.

A different kind of objection is propounded by those who hold that humans may be given preferential treatment because of the relationships in which they stand, a point employed by Benson[38] as well as by Diamond, and elaborated by Leslie Pickering Francis and Richard Norman.[39] I have already pointed out, though, that this principle discriminates against those who stand in few relationships or in none. It is further weakened by a salient observation of Francis and Norman themselves. Thus some so-called imbeciles, including some sufferers from Down's syndrome, have a much greater intelligence and capacity for communication than any nonhuman animals, and in such cases the value of their lives is generally recognized; but in other cases of severe subnormality, such as cases of anencephaly, the possibility that passive or even active euthanasia is justified is being seriously debated. Their point is that the only humans with whom the capacities of some animals will stand comparison are ones the value of whose lives is in doubt. But if it is in doubt despite the relationships in which they stand, then the existence of such relationships does not seem to make a crucial difference to the treatment which they should have, or indeed to be the crucial moral factor in their regard.

In any case the criterion of standing in particular relationships cannot in itself be other than arbitrary. Yet the point made by Francis and Norman that for most nonhuman animals various forms of relationship (linguistic, economic and political) are impossible is significant, and for the reason that it turns on the capacities of the various creatures concerned. Certainly what is good about capacities is their development or their exercise, but their mere possession is what makes it possible for others to deprive or facilitate such development, and thus to qualify them for differential treatment. But such points about capacities can be accepted by adherents of the Equality of Interests principle. It should be emphasized here that capacities here include potentials, and thus explain the priority which can rightly be given to normal newborn human infants over nonhuman animals with comparable current powers.

The other basis on which discriminating in favour of humans when nonhumans have like interests is sometimes defended is the need to draw a clear line. Even if, it is argued, severely retarded humans do not merit preferential treatment in their own right, it is still better to treat them as if they did, so as to have an easily applicable line to draw between beings to be treated as persons and others. Devine, who propounds this case, also holds that once the line has been drawn there is no injustice in giving priority to those who would not individually have qualified to be on the favourable side of it but happen to fall so nonetheless.[40] Now it is undoubtable that in some cases such drawing of lines prevents the undermining of morally important inhibitions, and this may partially justify our unwillingness to experiment on severely retarded humans who happen also to have no friends, guardians or relations who might suffer or object in consequence. On the other hand where a better line can be drawn, we may well be responsible for unnecessary suffering if we fail to draw it and opt for the criterion of being human instead. Thus VanDeVeer is surely right to deny that we should save the life of an infant human with Tay-Sachs disease by means of a kidney transplant from a healthy chimpanzee of greater capacities;[41] and if we strive to preserve all human life we might also inflict extra years of life on someone who would be better off dead. Thus the principle of giving priority to humans is not to be preferred to one on which all the interests concerned are duly considered, weighed up and served as best may be. (Far less should we prefer the interests of humans where, as over eating meat from factory-farms and over painful experiments on laboratory animals to test the safety of luxuries, far greater interests are at stake for the nonhuman than for the human.)

Holist priorities

Before closing this chapter I should remark the very different emphasis of ethical holists, and in particular of John Rodman and of J. Baird Callicott.[42] These writers find in the humanitarian ethic of

Singer little more than an extension of the privileged class with moral standing which is permitted to exploit all else besides; they are much more concerned with species and with the biosphere than with individual beings, and they regard domestic animals as so degenerate a form of life, and as so symbolically harmful as to discount their interests (as opposed to those of wild animals) and to favour phasing them out. They would probably welcome my acceptance of the moral standing of virtually all living creatures, but would still object to what they would regard as a homocentric hierarchy of values (this objection I have already considered) and to yet a further deployment of the 'Method of Argument from Human Analogy and Anomaly'.[43]

Now certainly if the sole moral criterion is the preservation of the integrity, stability and beauty of the biotic community then very different principles will be arrived at from the above and also from those of Singer. Thus suffering will only count as an evil where its effects are ecologically bad; and where they are held to be good (as over culling the white-tailed deer where its population is too large for the sustainability of the surrounding ecosystem) it will not even count as a negative moral factor at all. Again, neither individual creatures (human or otherwise) nor their states will be of intrinsic value, and their relative value will consist solely in their relative contribution to ecological stability. And since the present global human population is held to be a global disaster for the biotic community, it should be reduced (or so Callicott implies) to roughly twice that of bears.[44]

There is reason to be grateful to Rodman and Callicott for pointing out the fundamental divergences between the movement for more humane treatment of animals, with its emphasis on vegetarianism, whether as defended by Singer or (very differently) by Regan,[45] and the holistic land ethic of Aldo Leopold. This divergence has also been assessed from his own point of view in Singer's recent work.[46] Thus Singer is critical of environmentalists who support some forms of hunting; and, despite finding that environmentalists' campaigns to preserve rare species are often more effective in preventing, for example, whaling than campaigns against cruelty, maintains that rare nonsentient species should only be preserved where (as not always) the short-term or long-term interests of sentient animals are at stake, and also that even if whaling is carried on in a sustainable way, it is still objectionable because individual whales, 'sentient creatures with lives of their own to lead', would still be threatened.[47]

My disagreements with Singer over the extension of moral standing and intrinsic value will already be clear. Nor do I accept in full his case for vegetarianism, though I do accept his case against consuming the products of factory-farms and of other practices which cause significant animal suffering without sufficient reason. I am not convinced either that he has taken sufficient account of the need to limit some animal populations. But he is on entirely firm ground in stressing the evil of suffering, and the need to take strong measures to reduce it. Granted that the disruption of the biosphere would imperil the lives of all sentient creatures, we do not need for that reason (or any other) to treat its preservation as the sole ethical criterion, or to cease to regard suffering as evil in itself, or measures and attitudes aimed directly at its alleviation (attitudes such as sympathy, compassion, and respect for individuals who can suffer) as morally central. Further, if sentience and other capacities of individuals are morally significant (as has been maintained above) then it is morally imperative to extend moral consideration to nonhumans with such capacities — an instance this of the very method of reasoning at which Rodman protests. If, by contrast, the biosphere had moral standing and none of its individual members had such standing in their own right, matters would be different; but I have not discovered any arguments for holding this to be the case.

Callicott accuses Singer and others of a life-loathing philosophy, because of their opposition to avoidable pain and their concern to minimize such a natural and ecologically beneficent sensation. Singer probably understresses values beyond enjoyment, such as creativity, but, as Steinbock remarks, the ability to exercise such capacities is easily undermined by suffering.[48] Callicott also fears that his own position may appear to be gratuitous misanthropy.[49] Granted his own Leopoldian premise it is not gratuitous. But as this premise implies that human life, however worthwhile, is of no intrinsic value and has value only insofar as it preserves the biosphere, misanthropy is not an inappropriate description. There are ample grounds for preserving species and wilderness, based on the needs and the value of present and future creatures, and likewise for resisting 'the optimization of the biosphere' or the total use of the earth in the human interest:[50] but, although it is regrettable when some species are lost through wear and tear inflicted on the environment by humans, this alone in no way justifies holding that the lives of any of those humans are on balance an evil. Humans too have lives of their own to lead, with scope for valuable as well as pernicious trans- formations of the lands they have populated; and any criterion on which there are too many of them only begins to be plausible if it introduces something else of counterbalancing value. For some levels of population this can perhaps be done (see chapter 10), but the holists altogether fail to do it for any level.

Rodman for his part suspects that

the same principles are manifested in quite diverse forms — e.g. in damming a river and repressing an animal instinct (whether human or nonhuman), in clear-cutting a forest and bombing a city, in Dachau and a university research laboratory, in censoring an idea, liquidating a religious or racial group, and exterminating a species of flora or fauna.[51]

Like principles of oppression may be involved, and maybe all liberation movements are, as Rodman contends, natural allies (despite a clash alleged to exist by Francis and Norman between feminism and opposition to animals experiments).[52] But Rodman's examples cannot be regarded as comparable cases of oppression. Among interests there are priorities: I have tried above, in the modified version of Two-factor Egalitarianism which I have advanced, to delineate some which are rationally defensible.

NOTES

1   Arne Naess writes at p. 96 of 'The Shallow and the Deep, Long-Range Ecology Movement', *Inquiry,* 16, 1973, 95—100, of *'the equal right to live and blossom'* (his italics), and of biospherical egalitarianism.

2   'The Moral Basis of Vegetarianism', *Philosophy,* 53, 1978, 481—505, e.g. at p. 497.

3   Peter Singer, *Animal Liberation, A New Ethics for our Treatment of Animals,* London: Jonathan Cape, 1976, p. 9. The relevant chapter, entitled 'All Animals are Equal', is reprinted in Tom Regan and Peter Singer, *Animal Rights and Human Obligations,* Englewood Cliffs, NJ: Prentice-Hall, 1976.

4   Peter Singer, 'Utilitarianism and Vegetarianism', *Philosophy and Public Affairs*, 1980, 325—37, pp. 328f.

5   Thus John Rodman, 'The Liberation of Nature', *Inquiry,* 20, 1977, 83—145: similar views are present in Holmes Rolston III, 'Is There an Ecological Ethic?', *Ethics,* 85, 1974—75, 93—109; Kenneth Goodpaster, 'From Egoism to Environmentalism', in Goodpaster and Sayre (eds), *Ethics and Problems of the 21st Century,* 21—35; and in J. Baird Callicott, 'Animal Liberation: A Triangular Affair', *Environmental Ethics,* 2, 1980, 311—38.

6   Thus R. G. Frey, *Interests and Rights: The Case Against Animals,* Oxford: Clarendon Press, 1980.

7 *A System of Ethics,* trans. Norbert Gutermann, New Haven: Yale University Press, 1956, Part I, Section 2, chapter 7, 136—44; reprinted in Stanley and Roslind Godlovitch and John Harris (eds), *Animals, Men and Morals, An Enquiry into the Maltreatment of Non-humans,* New York: Taplinger Publishing Co., 1972, 149—55.

8 'Rights', *The Philosophical Quarterly,* 15, 1965, 115—27.

9 A transition is apparent in McCloskey's 'The Right to Life', *Mind,* 84, 1975, 403—25, where autonomy is required for the possession of rights. The newer position is more explicit in 'Moral Rights and Animals', *Inquiry,* 22, 1979, 23—54. For Feinberg's position see 'The Rights of Animals and Unborn Generations', in *Philosophy and Environmental Crisis,* 43—68, especially pp. 50f.

10 *Interests and Rights,* chapters II, V, VI and VIII. Frey's scepticism about natural rights is expressed in his Postscript, pp. 168—70.

11 'Animal Rights, Human Wrongs', *Environmental Ethics,* 2, 1980, 99—120; 'Utilitarianism, Vegetarianism and Animal Rights', *Philosophy and Public Affairs,* 9, 1979—80, 305—24. These papers develop the argument of his earlier paper, 'The Moral Basis of Vegetarianism', *Canadian Journal of Philosophy,* 5, 1975, 181—214.

12 'Death, Misfortune and Species Inequality', *Philosophy and Public Affairs,* 10, 1980—81, 47—64. (Cigman rejects belief in any non-human animals' right to life, but accepts that they have moral standing.)

13 'Not for Humans Only: The Place of Nonhumans in Environmental Issues', in Goodpaster and Sayre (eds), *Ethics and Problems of the 21st Century,* 191—206, at pp. 194f.

14 *Persons and Minds: The Prospects for Nonreductive Materialism,* Dordrecht, Boston and London: Reidel, 1977, chapters 8 and 9.

15 'The Moral Basis of Vegetarianism', p. 490.

16 Aubrey Townsend, 'Radical Vegetarians', *Australasian Journal of Philosophy,* 57, 1979, 85—93, p. 91.

17 'Supererogation and Double Standards', *Mind,* 88, 1979, 481—99, pp. 493f.

18 'Freedom, Autonomy and the Concept of a Person', *Proceedings of the Aristotelian Society,* 76, 1975—76, 109—30.

19 'Personal Freedom and Environmental Ethics: The Moral Inequality of Species', in Gray Dorsey (ed.), *Equality and Freedom,* Vol. II, New York: Oceana Publications and Leiden: A. W. Sijthoff, 1977, 401—24, especially at pp. 416—20.

20 'Killing Humans and Killing Animals', *Inquiry,* 22, 1979, 145—56.

21 'Not for Humans Only', p. 199.

22 Michael Lockwood, 'Killing and the Preference for Life', *Inquiry,* 22, 1979, 157—70, p. 168.

23 'Duty and the Beast', *Philosophy,* 53, 1978, 529—49, pp. 63ff.

24 'Interspecific Justice', *Inquiry,* 22, 1979, 55—79, pp. 63ff.

25 Ibid. p. 70. A similar point is made by L. W. Sumner, 'A Matter of Life and Death', *Noûs,* 10, 1976, 145—71, pp. 164f.

26 'Interspecific Justice', p. 64.
27 'Speciesism and the Idea of Equality', *Philosophy,* 53, 1978, 247—63, p. 254.
28 'The Moral Basis of Vegetarianism', p. 486.
29 *Animal Liberation,* p. 22. A similar view, couched in more speciesist terms, is expressed by Joel Feinberg at pp. 66f of 'Human Duties and Animal Rights', in Richard Knowles Morris and Michael W. Fox (eds), *On The Fifth Day, Animal Rights and Human Ethics,* Washington: Acropolis Books, 1978, 45—69.
30 'Duty and the Beast', p. 533.
31 *The Moral Status of Animals,* pp. 169—71.
32 'The Liberation of Nature', p. 94f.
33 'Eating Meat and Eating People', *Philosophy,* 53, 1978, 465—79, pp. 470f.
34 Cf. A. M. McIver, 'Ethics and the Beetle', *Analysis,* 8, 1948, 65—70.
35 VanDeVeer, 'Interspecific Justice', pp. 74f; Steinbock, 'Speciesism and the Idea of Equality', pp. 254f.
36 Leslie Pickering Francis and Richard Norman, 'Some Animals are More Equal than Others', *Philosophy,* 53, 1978, 507—27, p. 510.
37 'The Moral Basis of Vegetarianism', p. 503.
38 'Duty and the Beast', pp. 536f.
39 'Some Animals are More Equal than Others', pp. 518—27.
40 'The Moral Basis of Vegetarianism', p. 497.
41 'Interspecific Justice', p. 65 and p. 77, n. 15.
42 See n. 5 (above).
43 Rodman, 'The Liberation of Nature', p. 87. I defend this method in 'Methods of Ecological Ethics'.
44 Callicott, 'Animal Liberation', pp. 320, 332—3, 324—6.
45 Singer's and Regan's different bases for vegetarianism are explored in Regan's 'Utilitarianism, Vegetarianism and Animal Rights' (see n. 11 above), and Singer's 'Utilitarianism and Vegetarianism' (see n. 4 above).
46 In 'Not for Humans Only', especially at pp. 201—5.
47 Ibid. pp. 204f.
48 See n. 27 (above).
49 'Animal Liberation', p. 326.
50 See further Robin Attfield, 'Western Traditions and Environmental Ethics'.
51 'The Liberation of Nature', pp. 89f.
52 'Some Animals are More Equal than Others', p. 516.

10

Problems and Principles: Is a New Ethic Required?

In this chapter I shall briefly review the way the principles arrived at in the four preceding chapters bear on the problems of pollution, resources, population and preservation, and discuss their adequacy and the extent of such revisions as may be required to our moral traditions.

Pollution

Though I did not adopt the 'Polluters Stop' principle of Lippit and Hamada, a case was made out for the containment of pollution and the prevention of its escalation. The example given was the need to curtail the emission of waste heat; but there are many other cases where pollution can threaten the impoverishment or the actual poisoning of human and nonhuman life in the short term or the long term. In general I favour Kavka's Lockean standard by which each generation is required to leave equivalent opportunities to its successor; indeed even the technology the introduction of which Kavka urges to compensate succeeding generations for expended resources would need to be as free of pollution as possible, or it would fall foul of its own justification. I accepted Kavka's own qualification about the need for the present generation to invest in Third World development so that population levels can be stabilized and the Lockean standard become capable of fulfilment on the part of future generations; as the consequent activity would involve some pollution, it is all the more important to stress that pollutant processes which are unacceptable in developed countries should not be exported to the Third World.

I have also endorsed Hubbard's proposal for a consumption maximum for the use of nonrenewable resources, which would prevent exponential increases in pollution. The same qualification as above would apply again: the case for development in poor countries justifies a greater consumption than would otherwise be the fair share of the current generation. The consumption maximum is justified by the needs of future people, whether their existence is brought about by ourselves or otherwise. Already the principles adduced exceed those of the 'shallow ecology movement', but they stretch traditional morality only to the extent that it sometimes permits discounting the future. Yet concern for posterity is a keynote both of the Old Testament and of the Enlightment philosophers (see chapter 5). So there is no clear departure involved even in the principle also adopted that the generation of nuclear energy should not proceed until safe storage methods for the waste products have been discovered.

Where Passmore now finds Western traditions in need of supplementation is over pollution which damages or destroys natural beauty or nonhuman species.[1] In this area I have accepted, with Singer, the moral standing and significance of sentient nonhuman animals, and also, against Singer, the moral standing of nonsentient living creatures too. Human interests probably suffice to show that ecosystems such as the forests of Africa should not be imperilled by being sprayed with pesticides;[2] but human interests can also clash with those of wild (and of domesticated) living creatures, and even when it pays people to eradicate wild habitats there is still a moral case (and sometimes an overriding one) against doing so. The recognition of this would indeed stretch accepted practice, but it is in keeping with the teaching of the Bible and with the concern, expressed in the Stewardship tradition, for the care of the earth (see chapters 2 and 3). What would need to be revised would be the widespread presupposition that nonhumans have only instrumental value and that they are dispensable. In much current reflection, as when we accept our kinship with nonhumans, we reject this mechanistic view, and this rejection sometimes affects our practice; so the necessary revision is sufficiently familiar and acceptable to allow it to win acceptance.

Resources

There are problems here over the depletion of the stocks of non-renewable resources, over the imperilling of renewable resources, and over the gap between the availability of resources (of whatever sort) and expected levels of demand. These descriptions of the problem do not prejudge solutions. Thus, as Kenneth Sayre points out,[3] the energy problem may be solved either by increasing the rate of generation or by decreasing the level of consumption. The principles favoured above fall in fact somewhere in between.

Thus the use of non-renewable resources should be justly distributed between generations, depletions being counterbalanced by the devising of new techniques so that succeeding generations have opportunities matching those of their predecessors. This would require a consumption maximum, so pitched as to be more-or-less stable across the generations: expected levels of consumption in excess of the maximum would need to be curtailed in favour of simpler, less energy-intensive styles of life, though the use of renewable sources of energy would also have a major contribution to make. At the same time each generation would as far as possible be guaranteed a minimum of resources, including food (and to that end agricultural land and fisheries), energy (partly through the savings of earlier generations) and clean air and water. Once population levels have been stabilized, each generation should be provided for equally, and allow equal future provision by taking no more non-renewable resources than its share. If also each generation preserves vulnerable renewable resources (forests and natural cycles), the Lockean standard is observed by which each leaves enough and as good for its successor.

Forests too are resources in that they are usable by man, but they and other areas of wilderness are not just resources. There is a moral case, or so I have argued, against the felling of trees relating both to their intrinsic value and to their value to nonhuman animals. This case constrains the uninhibited use of what may otherwise fairly be construed as resources, and tells strongly against practices such as clear-cutting. It also requires sensitivity in the adoption of such otherwise ecologically sound principles as that of aiming at maximum sustainable yield, especially where the yield or harvest consists of sentient creatures.[4] Indeed some practices in which animals or plants are treated merely as resources are ruled out by Two-factor Egalitarianism as interpreted above, such as the hunting of whales, and indeed hunting in general, except where it is genuinely justified by necessity.

The main extension of our moral traditions called for in the area of resources, however, concerns the recognition of obligations to people of the distant future. Passmore is, I believe, mistaken to claim that utilitarianism (and cognate consequentialist theories) preclude such a recognition through their readiness to discount uncertain benefits.[5] Nor do we ordinarily assume that justice is only possible to those who, unlike future people, have bargaining power. So our traditions, including that of Stewardship, which involves handing over the earth in as good a state as we received it, provide for the recognition of these obligations much more than Passmore supposes. What is needed is an extension of sympathies to match our moral beliefs, on which time is as irrelevant as place. Education about how current actions and omissions can affect future people should help, as it can over effects on people who are geographically distant: ecological discoveries in the former case mirror the dawning realization in the latter that it is within our power to make a considerable difference for good or ill, and their dissemination could well, as education is beginning to do in the matter of world poverty, facilitate a change in attitudes.

Population

Though each worthwhile life is of value and there is nothing wrong with population growth as such, there is a great deal amiss when it takes place in a world where hundreds of millions of people already suffer the miseries of absolute poverty. The world population of humans is certain to grow in any case, even though the rate of growth is falling; and it is imperative that growth should cease at some sustainable level. Zero growth cannot and should not be introduced abruptly, but should be phased in. Only if population is stabilized can succeeding generations be provided for by constant rather than ever-increasing consumption: and accordingly the problems of pollution and resource depletion will *in the end* become unmanageable unless population growth is brought to a halt.

Some of the same considerations suggest that the lower the level at which stability is reached, the better. But I also concluded against the view that the level of the world population ought to be lower than at present, granted that it is possible to feed the current population and that every worthwhile life has its own intrinsic value. On the other hand if population eventually ceases to grow only when it has reached a level which generates too much pollution and exhausts remaining resources too rapidly, there would then be a case for a policy of gradual downward movement towards a level which can be sustained indefinitely without those who live being poisoned by pollution or impoverished through lack of resources.

That level, though not lower than the present one of 4,000 million, may well be less than the level at which population eventually ceases to grow.

The interests of nonhumans must also be taken into account in matters of population. At some very high levels of human population, planetary life-support systems could be fundamentally disrupted both for humans and for all other forms of life; if this were seriously in prospect, there would be conclusive moral reasons, despite what Stanley Benn seems to imply,[6] for calling a halt. (In fact this degree of disruption is threatened not so much by population growth as by the threat of nuclear war and nuclear accidents.) But there must also be somewhat lower levels of population than these which would be bound to threaten a great number of wild species and their habitats without the biosphere as a whole being ruined. (Such threats, e.g. to the Amazonian rain-forest, are already with us, but not as an inevitable outcome of current population levels.) The increased area which would need to be put under cultivation if population were, say, trebled could displace most of the larger nonhuman animals; and in addition it could easily fail to sustain its fertility, so that ever more desperate attempts at cultivating poorer and poorer land would have to be made, with yet worse ecological effects. So a stage could be reached where feeding an extra human involved accelerated ecological stress, including the loss not just of many existing nonhumans but also of all future ones of several kinds, through the extinction of their species. On the theory presented above, the interests of nonhumans count for enough to curtail the growth of the human population before that point is reached.

A more drastic conclusion would of course be reached on any theory of radical biotic egalitarianism[7] which counted as of equal significance not like capacities but animals, whatever their species, human or nonhuman. On such a theory there is no more value — even in general — in human than in nonhuman lives; so, granted the inherent value of diversity, and granted similar population densities for humans and nonhumans, we should halt population growth before any animal species became extinct. (Where lives are of equal value, diversity could serve as a tie-breaker.) Moreover, as the extinction of other species began long ago when the human population was much smaller and has become more frequent with the growth of human numbers, we should probably have to reduce the human population so as to avert the extinction of further species. I have however rejected such theories above. On the

modified form of Two-factor Egalitarianism accepted in chapter 9
no such conclusions follow, though nonhumans should not be killed
nor their species extinguished for the sake of peripheral human
interests. But the constraints upon the growth of the human
population added by this principle do not exceed those mentioned
in the last paragraph.

The principle does, however, in the form in which I have accepted
it, imply that it is wrong to perpetuate factory-farms by consuming
their products. Though I am not committed to vegetarianism, a
criticism could here be raised which is sometimes directed at
vegetarians.[8] For if the principle here commended were universally
adopted not only would many fewer animals be reared but also
vegetarian diets would become much more common, and food-
chains would become shorter and therewith more efficient. The
criticism which may therefore be raised is that this would lead to an
extra increase in the human population, with consequent ecological
damage. I reply as follows. First, the likelihood of the principle
being adopted widely enough for its adoption to have *these* effects is
slight. Second, the prospect of ecological damage would still
constitute a reason for restricting the human population, even if
food-chains allowed of an increase. Third, so would the misery for
humans which would result if population growth were not restricted.
Fourth, shorter and more efficient food-chains would make it
possible to feed adequately a much greater proportion of the actual
human population; and as long as population growth was
discouraged for the reasons just given, a very great deal of good
could thus be done without the evils supervening which are predicted
in the criticism. Indeed the possibility of feeding the earth's current
human population is a central reason for the widespread adoption
of a much more vegetarian diet.

Thus the principles adopted neither urge a drop in the world
human population nor allow of an exponential increase, but counsel
stabilization at a level which can be sustained indefinitely without
progressive ecological deterioration. This reinforces Kavka's point
that the current generation is justified in investing a share of
resources greater that the consumption maximum would otherwise
allow in the alleviation of poverty in the Third World, an effort
without which the rate of population growth is unlikely to decrease
sufficiently. This extra deployment of resources could lead to some
ecological stress in the short run, but must be endured if the
problem of population growth is to be reduced to manageable

proportions (and likewise the other ecological problems which it exacerbates).[9]

The moral innovations which Passmore now accepts in the matter of population are of two sorts. One is the need for people in largely non-Christian countries such as India to revise the tradition of 'early marriages and mandatory fruitfulness'.[10] This I do not dispute; but the revision is manifestly one which Indians have widely accepted, if not widely enough, and thus one which is clearly in keeping with some of the strands of morality as it is already understood in India, as Indian newspapers and my Indian relations attest. The other is the need to overcome objections, usually raised in the West, to publicity for contraceptives, and also to annul the injunction on males to procreate children. These changes too can be accommodated within existing moral traditions, Roman Catholic ones included. But, though Passmore is doubtless right in holding that not all males (or females) have an obligation to produce children, I have contended above, with Sikora and Anglin, that many people do have such an obligation; and thus I cannot support as extensive a revision as Passmore favours in this case. Rather people should be encouraged to have no more children than are required to replace themselves, because of the extra strains on resources, and in particular the extra impact on those in poor countries least able to buy food, resulting from each addition to the total population of the developed countries of the West. (In a world with severe undernourishment the Extra Person Obligation has its upper limits.)

With the population problem, as with the problem of resources, though there are large implications for both humans and nonhumans now alive, the main extension of our moral traditions which is required lies, in fact, in the matter of taking into account the interests of the people of the next several centuries hence.[11] In the matter of population the acceptance of this longer perspective has already become widespread, and not only in the West; but in areas of poverty, economic change is required before attention can be focused on the long-term future. Thus the alleviation of poverty remains the prerequisite for solutions to the population problem.

Preservation

Conservation is not only a matter of the husbanding of non-renewable resources and the protection of renewable ones, but extends also to the preservation of wild species and their habitats and of planetary life-support systems in general. As Passmore acknowledges, wanton destruction has long been condemned, and this condemnation can apply where natural organisms, species or their habitats are destroyed as much as over works of art.[12] Even when this recognition is not matched by an awareness of what it implies, i.e. the value of what ought to be saved from destruction, it allows the precarious position of wildlife and of wilderness to be seen as a problem.[13] Concern for animal welfare adds emphasis to this perception; and the scope of the problem is enlarged when it is realized that the habitats of all life on earth, humans included, are potentially at risk, and that life-support systems in general need to be preserved.

Long-term human interests are obviously at stake over life-support systems, including those relevant to agriculture and those which maintain the cleanness of air and water. The interests of present and future humans in medical and agricultural research, scientific investigation, recreation and the aesthetic appreciation of nature also constitute strong grounds for preserving most species and the terrains and ecosystems in which they participate. Nor should the symbolic significance of wild nature for our sanity and sense of perspective be overlooked. To these considerations Singer rightly adds the interests of nonhuman animals; like Goodpaster I believe that nonsentient creatures also have moral standing, since in most cases they too have interests. I have also pointed out that those future creatures which would otherwise realize their proper capacities but which we can blight or debar from existence must be taken into account, and that when this is done there is a much strengthened case for the preservation of even inelegant and unprofitable species.

The various interests just mentioned can, of course, conflict, and just as humans must eat to live, so must predation on the part of wild animals be allowed to continue if but the predators' interests are to count. In general, intervention with the natural order can often preserve or even enhance it, but the likely consequences (long-term ones included) must, as Byerly points out,[14] be taken fully into consideration. Positive action may however be necessary to preserve life-support systems: as just mentioned, the human population must not be allowed to reach a level which subverts them, and the same can be true with the populations of nonhuman species liable to ruin their own habitats. But except where this is true, or food is not to be had otherwise, the hunting and culling of wild animals is gratuitously cruel and to be condemned as such. In terms of Two-factor

Egalitarianism it involves the sacrifice of the animals' basic interests where no serious or basic interests of humans (or other species of greater psychological capacities than the hunted or culled animals) are at risk.

I have not adopted the view that what matters is the biosphere as a whole, or that its components matter only as they contribute to its stability: such a view involves a complete break with accepted ethical norms, and I do not see how to argue from them to it. Ecosystems should be preserved rather for the sake of the creatures which they support. Thus there is no decision to make between humans and the biosphere: the reason for preserving the latter lies in the interests of humans and of other creatures — and there could hardly be a stronger one.[15] The moral significance of individual nonsentient creatures is admittedly slight, but it is as well to be aware of it, especially where large numbers of present or future organisms are in question (as where a forest may be eradicated or a species eliminated).

Taking into account the interests of future people and of nonhuman living creatures in matters of preservation extends the range of obligations conventionally acknowledged. Thus the obligation to provide for future people (in the weak sense in which it was accepted in connection with Sterba's suggestions in chapter 7) probably involves preserving the greatest possible range of species; and the interests of future humans and nonhumans alike add strength to the need to institute a consumption maximum for every generation to abide by. Again, the interests of existing nonhuman animals in continuing to lead the kind of life to which they are adapted impose limitations on the conditions in which they may be reared or killed for food or for laboratory experiments, or exterminated as a by-product of modern agricultural or industrial techniques. All the more obviously all these interests reveal strong obligations not to overheat or poison the atmosphere or blight all future life with nuclear fallout.

Moral traditions

But all these recently mentioned obligations are recognizable extensions of acknowledged ones, either through a broader range of consequences being recognized or through interests analogous to already recognized ones being taken into account. They also accord with the tradition of Stewardship, and with its Old Testament origins in which wild creatures are regarded as valuable in their own right and subject to God's care. This tradition requires humans to care for the earth on which they live, and nothing more or less is involved in the extension of obligations delineated here.

Passmore now finds our attitudes to nature to stand badly in need of revision in matters of preservation.[16] This cannot be denied with any cogency. Like him, I do not reject cost/benefit analysis, but when most future costs and benefits are discounted and those of nonhumans disregarded, the exercise attracts an entirely specious authority. Worse still is the lust for short-term returns, common to East and West alike, with which, whether by companies, politicians or administrators, decisions are usually made, and the confidence in progress which seems to give assurance that all other considerations can look after themselves. Again, all unqualifiedly mechanistic and instrumental views of nature need to be overcome, as also does the view on which it is worthless until tamed and humanized by ourselves. But these metaphysical views can be countered from within existing bodies of accepted belief; thus neither of them sits easily with acceptance (on the basis of the theory of evolution) of our kinship with nonhuman animals, nor with the Stewardship interpretation of the Judaeo-Christian belief in man's dominion over nature. Similarly there already exist the moral resources to challenge and condemn the malpractices which lead to the despoliation of nature.

Here, as with other problems, education and the broadening of imagination both have a key role to play. So do pressure groups and political parties. But if these parts are to be played, a sound ethical theory is needed. This and the four previous chapters are a contribution towards presenting such an ethical theory and exhibiting its bearing on ecological matters; a theory which, as I argued in Part One, is implicit already in some of our more long-standing traditions, and in particular in the tradition of Stewardship.

NOTES

1   'Ecological Problems and Persuasion' in Gray Dorsey (ed.), *Equality and Freedom,* Vol. II, New York: Oceana Publications and Leiden: A. W. Sijthoff, 1977, 431—42, p. 438.
2   Several relevant articles appear in *Vole*, 4, (3), March 1981.
3   'Morality, Energy and the Environment', *Environmental Ethics,* 3, 1981, 5—18, p. 7.
4   Cf. Singer, 'Nor for Humans Only', in K. E. Goodpaster and K. M. Sayre (eds), *Ethics and Problems of the 21st Century,* pp. 201f.
5   'Ecological Problems and Persuasion', p. 439; *MRN*, pp. 84f. Passmore

has been criticized on this score in R. and V. Routley, 'Nuclear Energy and Obligations to the Future', *Inquiry*, 21, 1978, 133—79, and in chapter 6 above.

6   'Personal Freedom and Environmental Ethics: The Moral Inequality of Species', in Gray Dorsey (ed.), *Equality and Freedom*.

7   William T. Blackstone, 'The Search for an Environmental Ethic', in Tom Regan (ed.), *Matters of Life and Death*, Philadelphia: Temple University Press, 1980, 299—335, p. 303.

8   Callicott criticizes Singer on related grounds at 'Animal Liberation: A Triangular Affair', *Environmental Ethics*, 2, 1980, 311—38, p. 331.

9   It is notable that Dennis C. Pirages and Paul R. Ehrlich, despite Ehrlich's earlier views, now favour efforts directed at Third World development even at the expense of the West holding back over resource consumption, partly from the belief that it could assist the introduction of a steady-state world economy of the kind proposed by Herman Daly. See their *Ark II: Social Response to Environmental Imperatives*, San Francisco: W. H. Freeman, 1974, p. 243.

10 'Ecological Problems and Persuasion', p. 440.

11 Here at any rate I am in agreement with Robert Young, 'Population Policies, Coercion and Morality', in *Environmental Philosophy*, 356—75.

12 'Ecological Problems and Persuasion', p. 441; *MRN*, p. 124.

13 Thus the *World Conservation Strategy* (published in 1980 jointly by the International Union for Conservation of Nature and Natural Resources, the United Nations Environmental Programme and the World Wildlife Fund), though admirable in relating conservation to development, confines its arguments to ones based solely on human interests.

14 In 'Principles of Noninterference with Nature in Ecological Ethics', in *Ethics: Foundations, Problems and Applications, Proceedings of the Fifth International Wittgenstein Symposium*, Vienna: Verlag Hölder-Pichler-Tempsky, 1981, 318—20.

15 Cf. the case for conservation presented in W. H. Murdy, 'Anthropocentrism: A Modern Version', *Science*, 187, March 1975, 1168—72.

16 'Ecological Problems and Persuasion', p. 441.

A Review of Recent Literature

Ecological problems and social attitudes (chapters 1 and 5)

The reality of worldwide ecological problems is by now beyond dispute, with daily news reports of the greenhouse effect, holes in the ozone layer, radioactive emissions, acid rain, and polluted rivers, seas and oceans.

Some of the most striking disclosures since the first edition of this work was published have concerned the widespread pollution in Eastern Europe, and particularly in Poland, Czechoslovakia and East Germany. These disclosures cast further doubt on the theories that ascribe ecological problems to population growth, to affluence, or indeed to capitalism. Nor is it plausible that high technology is usually to blame (much of the emissions being from antiquated technology). Rapid industrialisation is, perhaps, more to the point, together with the attitudes of the erstwhile authorities. In the terms of this book, these attitudes had little to do with Christianity or Judaism, and rather more to do with belief in the inevitability of material progress. Yet, as is argued at pages 83f above, this is no reason to abandon all belief in progress or in the possibility of finding rational solutions to our problems. (Some of the diagnoses of the first edition will soon be available in USSR when Progress Publishers issue a translation of chapters 2, 5 and 10 above.)

About the possibility of collective, democratically controlled national and international action which would make selective use of science and technology to resolve or alleviate the problems, much can be learned from H. J. McCloskey, *Ecological Ethics and Politics*,[1] although, to say the least, very severe constraints on market economies would be required. On the nature of the problems themselves, however, McCloskey contributes most through his advocacy of clarity in the use of concepts such as 'resources' and 'overpopulation'; as Robert Elliot's critical notice in *Australasian Journal of Philosophy* points out,[2] his tendency to side with technological optimists, and thus to underestimate the extent of the problems, needs to be balanced, in matters of risk assessment, with the caution advocated by Robert E. Goodin in 'Ethical Principles for Environmental Protection'.[3] Some of the themes of an earlier version of Goodin's essay are discussed above in chapter 6. (Goodin's views are further developed in a work on ethical theory which is substantially in harmony with the present one, *Protecting the Vulnerable*.[4]) McCloskey's call for clarity about the concepts of 'resources' and 'overpopulation' is echoed by David Pepper in *The Roots of Modern Environmentalism*;[5] Pepper adds a sophisticated Marxist critique of environmentalism and of ecotopias, too relativist, perhaps, about values, but valuable itself for its critiques not only of ecocommunism and ecofascism but also of liberalism.

Different ethical perspectives, certainly, give rise to different perceptions of the nature of the problems, as is argued in chapter 1. Thus his more recent writings make it clear (despite the passage about him at page 3 above) that Arne Naess, the founder of the Deep Ecology movement, does regard the current global level of the human population as a threat to other species, and thus one of the causes of the problems. (See e.g. Principle 4 of the Basic Principles of the Deep Ecology Platform, set out at page 14 of 'The Deep Ecology Movement: Some Philosophical Aspects'.[6]) Some grounds for a different view are presented in chapter 7 above. If, as argued there, overpopulation is impending rather than actual, measures should certainly be considered to introduce population control, but not specifically to reduce the number of people to below current levels. Naess's ideas can be found more fully in his *Ecology, Community and Lifestyle*.[7]

Some reviewers regarded the discussion of the causal theories in chapter 1 as 'inconclusive', as no single theory was accepted without qualification (though some, such as Elliot, regarded this as a merit). Economic growth, for example, was regarded as no more than part of the explanation (p. 17); such explanations have to be supplemented, I maintain, by reference to attitudes. But the attitudes of Judaism and Christianity do not turn out to account for the problems (see chapters 2 to 4); the troublesome attitudes (as the more alert reviewers noticed) are rather found in belief in perennial material progress (p. 83), its rightness and its inevitability. To this I should wish to add the crucial role of the world system of economic relations and power relations, as depicted (for example) by Pepper and also in the Brundtland Report,

Our Common Future.[8] Such reports underline what several reviewers (and McCloskey too) have urged, the indispensable need for democratic national and international political solutions.

The Judaeo-Christian heritage and the stewardship tradition (chapters 2–4)

These issues have recently been tackled by the leading Protestant theologian, Jurgen Moltmann, in *God and Creation.*[9] According to Moltmann, what accounts for the rise of modern scientific and technological civilisation is not so much the biblical world view nor the economic, social and political circumstances of the early modern period, as the Renaissance belief in God's almighty power and the attempts of humanity (through the persons of Bacon and Descartes) to match it. Critics of the Judaeo-Christian tradition misunderstand the biblical passages about dominion, which concern rather 'the protective work of a gardener' than predatory exploitation, and which are not anthropocentric but theocentric. Humanity, even as the image of God, with a special position within creation, still remains 'a member of the community of creation' (p. 31), and, significantly, the God in whose image people are made is the creator and preserver of the world (p. 29). As Henry Vaughan, living in the seventeenth century, recognised (in a poem about Romans 8), the rest of creation awaits the manifestation of the sons of God no less than does humanity (p. 40). Clearly I have no quarrel with these interpretations, exaggerated as the role ascribed to Bacon and Descartes may be held to be.

Some parallel sentiments from an Orthodox standpoint are expressed by Paulos Gregorios in *The Human Presence.*[10] Gregorios points out that, for Maximus the Confessor, the 'decisively towering figure' of the Byzantine tradition (p. 73), man (*sic*) is a mediator between God and the cosmos. Gregorios stresses that, in place of a posture of domination, humanity needs a 'reverent-receptive' attitude to nature, responsive to its mystery; he finds examples of this attitude in thinkers of all 'climes and cultures' (p. 86), and not least in the Catholic poet Gerard Manley Hopkins. Without this attitude, 'replacing the concept of domination with the concept of stewardship will not get us very far' (p. 84); nevertheless the kind of mysticism which advocates a 'return to nature' is to be rejected, in favour of a posture which combines the attitudes of mastery and mystery (p. 87). While there may be doubts about the consistency of all this, it is not difficult to sympathise with much of Gregorios' overall position.

More recently the erstwhile muteness of the voice of the Catholic church on the deepening ecological crisis has been challenged by Sean McDonagh in *To Care for the Earth*.[11] McDonagh urges the need to move away from a theology concerned exclusively with human salvation to a theology of creation which would return to and develop 'the holistic creation theology of Paul, Benedict, Francis, Hildegarde of Bingen, Meister Eckhart and Thomas Aquinas' (p. 108), pressing into service the evolutionary insights of Pierre Teilhard de Chardin. Besides surveying the 'Bright and Dark Sides of the Christian Response' (commendably introducing into the literature therewith the celebration of the natural world of Hildegard of Bingen), McDonagh elicits celebrations of nature in Christian sacraments and also in non-Christian religions, and commends, as emanating from the proposed new theology, solutions including nuclear disarmament, the United Nations World Charter for Nature[12] and, in nonexploitative forms, birth control. Here, then, the religious seeds of an ecological ethic have been nourished (albeit in a rhetorical and semipopular form) along lines which many Catholics are increasingly prepared to take seriously.

Attitudes to nature in the Judaeo-Christian tradition are also surveyed by Arthur Peacocke and Peter Hodgson in chapter 7 of *Values, Conflict and the Environment*.[13] Peacocke and Hodgson claim that Christianity satisfies several of the criteria for a religious model that facilitates ecological decision making which are propounded by Don Marietta at page 154 of 'Religious Models and Ecological Decision-Making'.[14] In the following chapters the attitudes of Secular Humanism and of Environmentalism are depicted by me, and those of Marxism by Andrew Belsey. A secular version of the ethic of stewardship is presented by Robert Goodin at pp. 183ff of *Protecting the Vulnerable*.[15] Meanwhile an account of Christian history somewhat less sympathetic than mine is presented by Andrew Linzey in *Christianity and the Rights of Animals*;[16] Linzey also urges a recognition of animal rights on biblical grounds. Since then, the unfavourable attitude to wilderness and wild creatures often ascribed to early monasticism has been ably contested by Susan Power Bratton in 'The Original Desert Solitaire: Early Christian Monasticism and Wilderness', in *Environmental Ethics*.[17]

Since *The Ethics of Environmental Concern* appeared, the claims about Christian humanitarianism and the stewardship tradition (of chapter 3) have been substantially vindicated in the work of the historian Keith Thomas. Thomas' *Man and the Natural World: A History of the Modern Sensibility*,[18] as well as stressing the characteristic anthropocentrism of sixteenth-century English practice, takes to task John Passmore and Peter Singer for denying that Christians in the centuries prior to Montaigne ever regarded cruelty to animals as wrong in itself, and for suggesting that humanitarian attitudes were pioneered mainly by sceptics, being adopted by Christians only as an after-thought. Thomas' impressive array of evidence shows (among other things) that such judgements are to be found throughout the Christian centuries, and that there was a constant rationale underlying the preaching and (later) the pamphleteering against cruelty to animals from *Dives and Lazarus* (ca. 1400) right through to recent times. Similar points are in place in reply to Michael Zimmerman's article 'The Paradox of Naturalism' in *The Deep Ecologist;*[19] by contrast, Zimmerman's more recent work ('Quantum Theory, Intrinsic Value and Panentheism', in *Environmental Ethics*)[20] reflects a sympathetic appreciation of Christian panentheism. The debate about Christian attitudes to nature and the fitness of Christian theology to cope with environmental issues is continued in Eugene Hargrove's collection *Religion and Environmental Crisis.*[21]

Belief in humanity as the image of God (stressed, for example, by Moltmann) is, however, expressly rejected by James Rachels, who would doubtless also reject belief in the distinctive mediating role of humanity (stressed by Gregorios). In *Created from Animals* (subtitled 'The Moral Implications of Darwinism')[22] Rachels argues that Darwinism undermines both the design argument and the theistic belief in human distinctiveness; the speciesism of traditional morality lacks tenable foundations, and should be replaced by a more egalitarian ethic (as, in fact, McDonagh would agree: see p. 203). Rachels' ethical stance is to be applauded. But it is less clear that the design argument is overthrown by Darwinism; for an argument to the contrary see my earlier work *God and the Secular,* chapter 6.[23] Nor is it clear that the 'image of God' doctrine must be abandoned, in view of human moral capacities and responsibilities. (Extraterrestrials with like capacities and responsibilities, it should be granted, would fall under the same doctrine.)

Meanwhile supporters of the Deep Ecology movement, such as Warwick Fox (in *Approaching Deep Ecology: A Response to Richard Sylvan's Critique of Deep Ecology*),[24] have been contending that what is needed is identification with nature and the biosphere. Where identification simply involves concern for nature (etc.), this is an uncontroversial claim, though one which leaves issues of priorities unresolved. But if one of the more usual senses of 'identification' is intended, then, as Peter Reed has argued,[25] a sense of awe at nature's otherness could equally well foster appropriate actions and policies. Naess's reply[26] shows that awe and identification can be combined, but not that awe invariably involves identification, and could not have a role of its own.

Some shrewd criticisms of the kind of arguments deployed by Fox from the new physics in favour of an ethical paradigm shift are made by Eric Matthews in 'The Metaphysics of Environmentalism',[27] and deserve attention despite Matthews' anthropocentrism. My unpublished paper 'Sylvan, Fox and Deep Ecology: A View from the Continental Shelf'[28] includes a more explicit reply to Fox's metaphysics and his derogation of value-theory; at some points, I suggest, and despite certain misunderstandings, Richard Sylvan's 'Critique of Deep Ecology'[29] should be endorsed. (The 'Continental Shelf' paper may serve to amplify my response to Deep Ecology, with which some reviewers thought I took too short a way in chapters 8 and 9 above.)

Future generations (chapter 6)

Unlike Stephen Clark, who represents my normative theory as an Ideal Utilitarianism which turns on the maximisation of happiness,[30] Wayne Sumner's review argues that the ability to exercise essential capacities, central in the above account of intrinsic value, was in practice included under 'happiness' by classical utilitarians such as Mill, and could have been included by me.[31] If, however, it is agreed that the development of essential capacities is of intrinsic value, it seems better to make this explicit in a value-theory, rather than to rely on its tacit inclusion in happiness, an inclusion which is, to say the least, controversial. Sumner is, of course, a fellow supporter of the Total-View version of consequentialism; the relation of this position to moral rights is well discussed in his *The Moral Foundation of Rights*.[32]

Robert Elliot's critical notice[33] includes a defence of Rawlsian contractarianism involving a revised version of Rawls' original position. My difficulties with the revised original position, and with the principles which might emerge from it, have already been set out at page 10 of *A Theory of Value and Obligation,* to which interested readers may be referred. Meanwhile J. R. Cameron's revision of the Rawlsian original position in 'Do Future Generations Matter?'[34] is subject to the difficulties raised at pages 105f above. While no version of the Rawlsian scenario seems likely definitively to generate the key principles either of justice or of obligations towards future generations, the Rawlsian model continues to inspire valuable contributions to environmental philosophy, such as Robert L. Simon's essay 'Troubled Waters: Global Justice and Ocean Resources', in Tom Regan (ed.), *Earthbound*.[35] In the same collection the issues concerning future-oriented obligations are well surveyed by Annette Baier in 'For the Sake of Future Generations'.[36] I agree with Robert Goodin, however, (see *Protecting the*

Vulnerable, pp. 173–8) in preferring a consequentialist basis for these obligations to Baier's transgenerational contractarianism.[37]

Further light is shed on the nature and extent of people's responsibility with regard to further generations by Hans Jonas in his book *The Imperative of Responsibility.*[38] As his subtitle ('In Search of an Ethics for the Technological Age') suggests, Jonas holds that modern technology presents people now alive with unprecedented moral problems. While he is aware of the possibilities opened up by technology, his stress is on the dire threats which it poses, and on the apocalyptic choices thus generated, granted that the scope for the exercise of responsibility on the part of future people is never to be foreclosed (p. 107). By thus translating his own works *Das Prinzip Verantwortung* and *Macht oder Ohnmacht der Subjectivität,* Jonas has enriched Anglo-Saxon philosophy from an independent tradition; where necessary, readers can supply the refinements which a more analytic approach might call for. It is, however, a pity that such large parts of his grounds for better practice turn on human interests and on duties to humanity; the openness urged by Jonas to a nonanthropocentric axiology (p. 8) does not ultimately rescue him from anthropocentric tendencies. (I am grateful to Carl Talbot for access to a paper of his which alerted me to Jonas's work.)

The methodology of decision making as regards environmental and other issues with a bearing on future generations is discussed in *Values, Conflict and the Environment,*[39] where the method of Comprehensive Weighing is proposed and defended. The method incorporates a qualified use of discounting future costs and benefits, but only where some relevant factor such as opportunity costs or uncertainty is present; thus there is no radical disagreement here between that report and the current work. The application of Comprehensive Weighing would require considerable changes involving (in most countries) the restructuring of departments of government, and considerable reforms of the law and of education.

In some ways the practical counterpart of theories about responsibilities towards future generations is to be found in *Our Common Future,* with its advocacy of sustainable development and of a socially and environmentally sustainable world-system – which, to be sustainable, would have to be a just one. While principles of sustainability are discussed above in chapter 6, and the stabilising of the human population in chapter 7, the specifics of sustainability lie beyond the scope of this book. With very few reservations, however, I am glad to commend the analyses and the proposals of the World Commission on Environment and Development,[40] and to encourage readers to play what part they can to facilitate their implementation.

Multiplication and the value of life (chapter 7)

The philosophical reviewers of this chapter have not found much to add. Dieter Birnbacher (in *Allgemeine Zeitschrift für Philosophie*) is completely convinced by the case here presented for the Total-View version of consequentialism, and the advocacy of a sustainable population level which it yields;[41] Wayne Sumner, while endorsing both theory and conclusion, speaks of 'missteps', which, however, he does not identify, but finds the results 'quite impressive'.[42] Robert Elliot finds the discussion sensitive, but considers me too ready to 'find refuge in the claim that the allegedly unacceptable consequences of total utilitarianism would not arise in the actual world', pointing out that normative theories should apply to possible worlds also (p. 506).[43] But the text of pages 128f above discusses also the deliverances of the theory for ampler possible worlds, the only worlds for which a larger human population is indicated, and argues that this is an unobjectionable implication. In the actual world, now of 5,000 million people, the relief of absolute poverty takes obvious priority.

Meanwhile John Lemons, in *The Environmental Professional*,[44] complains at inadequate treatment of the relationship of population growth to environmental damage; but factors such as this do in fact modify the level of sustainable population commended at page 128. He also regrets the lack of coverage of population control programs, a topic explicitly disowned as beyond the scope of the book at page 136. Both these matters receive discussion in *A Theory of Value and Obligation* (172f) and in my essay 'Population Policies and the Value of People'.[45]

McCloskey[46] also defends the conclusions that there is no overpopulation problem at present, and that justice requires a redistribution which would enable all humans to be fed; while the benefits as well as the problems of the current human population, and the case for attaining a sustainable level, are well set out in *Our Common Future* (the Brundtland Report),[47] together with much wisdom about the value of population policies. Arne Naess's advocacy of a diminished population has been remarked in the first section of this chapter. A similar case is presented in greater detail, together with criticism of the implications of utilitarianism for population levels, in Richard Routley (now Sylvan), 'People vs the Land: The Ethics of the Population Case'.[48]

In 1984 the long-awaited, magisterial contribution of Derek Parfit to normative theory and related population issues appeared at last in *Reasons and Persons*.[49] As anticipated on the basis of his earlier work, Parfit supplied a defence (in Part Four) of the very Repugnant conclusion (Parfit's expression) which seems to invalidate Total-View consequentialism; Parfit's *tour de force* allowed me to return to the defence of the Total View in chapter 9 of *A Theory of Value and Obligation*, where population is presented as a test case of that theory, which (with the aid of one or two refinements concerning the concept of a worthwhile life) well survives the test.

The moral standing of nonhumans (chapter 8)

The conclusions of chapter 8 that nonsentient living creatures have moral standing, and that their flourishing is of intrinsic value, have come in for criticism from diverse directions; special attention is here paid to two in particular.

Gary E. Varner, in 'Biological Functions and Biological Interests',[50] endorses my rejection of Joel Feinberg's sentience-only account of interests, supplying an evolutionary account of the needs which belong distinctively to living creatures as opposed to human artifacts. This account may well help to dispel scepticism about the moral standing of nonsentient creatures, for which Varner goes on to argue. Varner, however, finds fault with my thought experiment concerning people's reactions to the last surviving sentient being who cuts down a tree. His first criticism applies only to an earlier version of this thought experiment, presented in 'The Good of Trees',[51] in which the tree is the last of its kind; he seems not to notice that in the version at pages 155f above it is claimed that the last human's deed would be regarded as wrong even if the tree is *not* the last of its kind. Varner's second criticism concerns the possibility that what gives the tree moral significance is its beauty rather than its interests. But the belief that beauty (as opposed to its appreciation) is of intrinsic value is countered above at pages 152f; and, of course, if that argument succeeds, then the tree's value, if related to its beauty, depends on its being the object of future appreciation, something which the thought experiment precisely precludes. So if, as I should claim, most people would still hold the act of the last sentient being to be wrong, this cannot be due to the tree's beauty. Thus if the arguments of chapter 8 which contest alternative explanations succeed, this pervasive judgement concerning the act's wrongness would have to be explained by the intrinsic value of the good of the tree itself.

Varner's main objection, however, concerns method. While 'widely shared intuitions . . . can serve as fixed points against which to check our moral theories', this applies to 'intuitions about "normal" cases', whereas in marginal cases (including the above thought experiment) 'a theorist should feel called upon to follow theory, rather than intuition'.[52] There are some misconceptions here. Varner glosses 'normal cases' as 'cases concerning human beings'; but if only these may be relied on, then far too many cases of pervasive judgements could be discounted or ignored in face of an adverse theory. (The relations of stable reflective judgements to theory are discussed further in my paper 'Methods of Ecological Ethics'.[53]) There again, at the stage in 'The Good of Trees' and in chapter 8 above where this thought experiment appears, theoretical grounds had already been adduced supporting the intrinsic value of the good of plants and also their moral standing; while these grounds (being ultimately analogical) were not claimed to be conclusive, they had already served to cast significant doubt upon the sentience-only position. Nor had I claimed that the thought experiment constitutes a conclusive argument in itself; my claim was rather that 'in this case intuitions confirm a theory which already has some independent support' (p. 155). (For Elliot's discussion of this same thought experiment, see pp. 506f of his review.)

Largely, however, belief in the moral standing of nonhumans must rest on arguments concerning needs which are recognised to be morally significant but which in no way depend on actual (or even hypothetical) preferences, or on sentience. Since such arguments move from the health or the harms of cases of recognised moral standing to other more controversial cases, they are inevitably analogical. Varner himself presents arguments of this kind, acknowledging that they are inconclusive; to my mind he accords too large a place within interests to interests related to preferences. Parallel arguments (which he does not remark) appear in 'The Good of Trees'[54] and above at page 153. Another writer who has deployed such arguments is Alan Holland, whose distinctive approach (which addresses the questions of harm and freedom alongside that of suffering) may be found in *The Biorevolution*.[55]

In another version the analogical argument appears together with the thought experiment argument at page 26 of *Values, Conflict and the Environment*.[56] Unfortunately the chapter which includes this passage never really replies to it, although various arguments for the sentience-only conclusion there adopted are supplied. My criticisms of this aspect of the report (and of its analysis of 'interests' in terms of informed preferences) are given, together with a defence of many of its other aspects, in an essay yet to be published.[57]

A different criticism of belief in the moral standing of nonsentient creatures has recently been made by Janna Thompson, who at the same time maintains that 'environmental ethics' in general, by which she means systems teaching that 'some entities in nature or in natural states of affairs are intrinsically valuable', fail the requirements of consistency, nonvacuity and of decidability (i.e. providing for clear-cut decisions).[58] In response to criteria of intrinsic value proposed by environmental ethicists and to applications of these criteria, Thompson poses a series of sceptical questions such as 'Why stop here?', seeking to show that no position which accords moral standing to creatures lacking subjectivity is tenable. While some of Thompson's criticisms correspond to my own criticisms of according value to nonsentient entities, and again of ethical holism, her targets include positions such as that defended in chapter 8 above, with its claim that things with a good of their own or interests of their own (i.e. nonderivative interests) have moral standing.

After citing Paul Taylor's defence of such a position (taken from p. 66 of his *Respect for Nature, A Theory of Environmental Ethics*,[59] Thompson proceeds to claim that the class of things with a good of their own includes organs and machines.[60] But the good of an organ is dependent on that of the organism to which it belongs, and of a machine on the interests of those who either invent, make, use or repair it, in a way which has no analogue where the good in question is the good of individual living creatures.

Indeed Thompson finds the need to eke out her sceptical case by asking why a thing's having a good of its own is relevant to the question of moral standing. Granted the similarities (in point of self-maintenance and integrity) between on the one hand crystals and rocks, which (strictly speaking) lack a good of their own, and on the other hand recognised bearers of moral standing such as sentient animals, it is inconsistent, she maintains, to ascribe moral standing to the latter and not to the former. But, quite apart from the question of the degree and quality of self-maintenance exhibited by crystals and by rocks, Kenneth Goodpaster's argument still stands: if a thing lacks a good of its own, there is no possibility of moral agents showing beneficence in its regard.[61] Indeed much the same could be said of the other attitudes appropriate to the bearers of moral standing.

While many of Thompson's particular criticisms of environmental ethics deserve sympathy, the impression comes across that the rigorous (and almost scathing) scrutiny of belief in the intrinsic value of natural entities or their states and conditions is not paralleled when positions ascribing intrinsic value to states of beings possessed of either sentience or subjectivity are under consideration. There again,

Thompson's own position is that the value of nonsentient creatures will be found to lie in their value for our lives, granted a suitably enhanced conception 'of what we are as individuals and of what a good life is';[62] while such a conception of the good life would involve recognition of nature's value, it is less plausible that in the absence of such a conception there would be no grounds other than instrumental ones for moral agents to respect or conserve nonsentient creatures. Yet in recognising the pivotal importance of the concept of intrinsic value, Thompson's critique represents an advance over approaches which would, if consistently pursued, undermine all reasons for all moral agents. (I have responded to one such critique in 'Deep Ecology and Intrinsic Value: A Reply to Andrew Dobson'.[63])

By way of response to the sturdy defence of anthropocentrism supplied by Bryan G. Norton in 'Conservation and Preservation: A Conceptual Rehabilitation',[64] it must suffice here to refer to the arguments of chapter 8 above. This is not said, however, to disparage arguments from human interests, which Norton ably deploys in his essay 'On the Inherent Danger of Undervaluing Species'.[65]

Inter-species morality: principles and priorities (chapter 9)

Ronald Preston's review in *Theology*[66] urges the according of priority to persons, as having a higher grade of being than other creatures, rather than heeding equal interests equally, as commended above. In practice, as I have maintained at pages 177f, such a policy may be justified in human society even in cases of severe subnormality, by reference to the interests of human third parties. To discriminate solely on the basis of personhood, however, would be close to speciesism in cases where greater interests are at stake for nonpersons. This is more clearly still a problem for the position of Holmes Rolston,[67] which recognises superiority in human beings as such. (See my review in *Environmental Ethics*.[68])

Not unrelatedly, some writers from one kind of stable (thus McCloskey)[69] continue to ascribe rights only to those animals possessed of moral autonomy (rights which can, however, be overridden by the welfare interests of other animals); alternatively rights are located in subjects-of-a-life, as by Tom Regan, whose earlier and ampler account of moral standing, depicted at page 146 above, seems to have been revised to cover just the bearers of points of view, and thus of subjectivity.[70] For Regan such rights can seldom be overridden, a grave source of problems this, as I have pointed out at page 168. Elliot[71] makes the related point against McCloskey that as long as animal rights can be overridden by other values, there need not be an irreconcilable opposition between animal welfarists and environmentalists (and thus there need not be fundamental problems for those sympathetic to both movements in parting company with McCloskey and recognising animal rights). Yet, while R. G. Frey (*Rights, Killing and Suffering*)[72] remains insufficiently sensitive to animal interests, his argument is to be applauded that little or nothing can be accomplished using the language of rights which cannot be accomplished in its absence.

Other philosophers suggest that, beyond locating the bearers of moral standing, philosophy cannot move further and produce well-grounded priorities among such bearers. This position appears in Lawrence E. Johnson's *A Morally Deep World*.[73] A reply could consist in my 'degrees-of-intrinsic-value' reply to John Benson (pp. 175f); indeed in the absence of a reply, environmental ethics would indeed fail one of Thompson's crucial tests, the requirement that decidability be provided for over a broad range of cases.

Priorities are also a problem for Paul Taylor. In *Respect for Nature,* Taylor advances five principles for the fair resolution of conflicts.[74] But, granted his biocentric egalitarianism, it is unclear how the principles are severally to be defended, or how conflicts between them are to be resolved by rational means. Some of the problems have been aired in my essay 'Biocentrism, Moral Standing and Moral Significance'.[75] Similar problems arise for the Deep Ecology Platform of Arne Naess, to the extent, that is, that the 'biospherical egalitarianism' of 'The Shallow and the Deep, Long-range Ecology Movement'[76] is to be taken seriously. (The Deep Ecology alternative, however, of abandoning value-theory, adopted by Warwick Fox and ascribed by him to Naess and to George Sessions,[77] seems to forego the possibility of supplying reasons for action altogether, and the possibility of conflict resolution therewith.) Without a principle requiring equal interests to be given equal consideration (and thus unequal interests unequal consideration) it is hard to see how reasonable resolutions of conflicts are to be possible.

To interpret this principle (taken from the works of Peter Singer), a qualified version of Donald VanDeVeer's Two-factor Egalitarianism is introduced above. Unlike some reviewers, Elliot recognises the qualifications, sees their force, and seems to endorse the principle which emerges, subject to his reservations about fundamental value-theory.[78] If, however, the interests of systems were somehow to be accorded intrinsic value, the possibility of any longer applying an 'equal interests' principle would be vanishingly small (and the prospects of complying with Thompson's decidability requirement vanishingly remote). But the case for recognising intrinsic value in systems is yet to be made out, at least to my satisfaction.

Similar principles for conflict resolution are presented in *Values, Conflict and the Environment*,[79] except that no morally relevant interests are recognised in nonsentient creatures, and that interests are expounded in terms of informed preferences. My response to these differences is to be found in a hitherto unpublished paper, 'Reasoning About the Environment'.[80] For most practical purposes, however, I am able to support the method of Comprehensive Weighing advanced in that report (see above), not just as being superior to cost-benefit analysis (including the variety upheld in David Pearce et al., *Blueprint for a Green Economy*)[81] or to the decision procedure proposed in Rolston's *Environmental Ethics*,[82] but as being well-grounded as to its theoretical content, immune from criticisms of cost-benefit analysis such as those of Mark Sagoff's monograph *The Economy of the Earth*,[83] and amenable to practical application.

Old principles, new politics (chapter 10)

The second edition (1980) of Passmore's *Man's Responsibility for Nature* includes his essay 'Attitudes to Nature',[84] which concludes by recognising the need for both 'a more realistic philosophy of nature' and for 'new attitudes to nature'.[85] In the light of this apparent shift from at least the tone of Passmore's first edition (1974) one of the aims of my final chapter was to gauge how far, in the light of the theories defended in the rest of this work, new moral attitudes or principles were required in the areas of pollution, resources, population and preservation. While I am yet to be persuaded that significantly new moral principles are required, this is because in my view the implementation of longstanding principles already requires some radical restructuring of society.

The point can be illustrated from more recent work. Thus on nuclear energy generation Daniel Shaw contributes to Nigel Dower's collection a hard-hitting article 'After Chernobyl: the Ethics of Risk-Taking',[86] which is very largely in keeping with the above principles and conclusions. And on most of the other practical issues discussed above, the World Commission on Environment and Development report *Our Common Future*[87] has valuable things to say, which would, however, involve the restructuring of international relations and of the international economic order.

McCloskey[88] is to be applauded for his arguments against totalitarian proposals for coping with the problems, and in favour of democratic solutions; there is no reason to trust despots, however ecologically benign their intentions. But whether the more regulated free-market system which he favours is equal to the problems is itself problematic. Murray Bookchin[89] is rightly scathing about ecophilosophers who ignore social problems and power relations; yet his own principles (and therewith his solutions) need revision in the light of the principles argued above.

Maybe a properly green solution requires (as Alan Carter has argued)[90] the bringing of production into decentralised, democratic control worldwide. As, however, such a solution may have to be long awaited, and much of value could be forfeited in the mean time, reflection and action at a more grass-roots level is both indispensable and, often, all that is possible. Actions which make lives more worthwhile cannot be valueless, even when their repercussions are less than cosmic; it may also be suggested (with Carter and with Keekok Lee)[91] that any such effort just might contribute to change which is both global and sustainable.

NOTES

1   H. J. McCloskey, *Ecological Ethics and Politics,* Totowa, NJ: Rowman and Littlefield, 1983.

2   Robert Elliot, Critical notice of *The Ethics of Environmental Concern, Australasian Journal of Philosophy,* 63, 1985, 499–505.

3   Robert Goodin, 'Ethical Principles for Environmental Protection', in Robert Elliot and Arran Gare (eds), *Environmental Philosophy,* St. Lucia: University of Queensland Press; Milton Keynes: Open University Press; University Park: Pennsylvania State University Press, 1983, 3–20.

4   Robert E. Goodin, *Protecting the Vulnerable,* Chicago: University of Chicago Press, 1985.

5   David Pepper, *The Roots of Modern Environmentalism,* London, Sydney, and Dover, NH: Croom Helm, 1984.

6   Arne Naess, 'The Deep Ecology Movement: Some Philosophical Aspects', *Philosophical Inquiry,* 8, 1986, 10–31.

7   Arne Naess, *Ecology, Community and Lifestyle,* trans. David Rothenberg, Cambridge: Cambridge University Press, 1989.

8   World Commission on Environment and Development, *Our Common Future,* Oxford: Oxford University Press, 1987.

9   Jurgen Moltmann, *God and Creation,* London: SCM Press, 1985.

10 Paulos Gregorios, *The Human Presence,* Geneva: World Council of Churches, 1978.

11 Sean McDonagh, *To Care for the Earth: A Call for a New Theology,* London: Geoffrey Chapman, 1986.

12 World Charter for Nature (annex to Resolution 37/7 of UN General Assembly, 1982), in United Nations, *Resolutions and Decisions Adopted by the General Assembly During Its 37th Session*, New York: United Nations, 1983.

13 Robin Attfield and Katharine Dell (eds), *Values, Conflict and the Environment*, Oxford: Ian Ramsey Centre, Oxford, and Centre for Applied Ethics, Cardiff, 1989.

14 Don Marietta, 'Religious Models and Decision-Making', *Zygon*, 12, 1977, 151–66.

15 Goodin, *Protecting the Vulnerable*.

16 Andrew Linzey, *Christianity and the Rights of Animals*, London: SPCK, 1987.

17 Susan Power Bratton, 'The Original Desert Solitaire: Early Christian Monasticism and Wilderness', *Environmental Ethics*, 10.1, 1988, 31–53.

18 Keith Thomas, *Man and the Natural World: A History of the Modern Sensibility*, New York: Pantheon, 1983.

19 Michael Zimmerman, 'The Paradox of Naturalism', *The Deep Ecologist*, 9, January 1984, pp. 9f.

20 Michael Zimmerman, 'Quantum Theory, Intrinsic Value and Panentheism', *Environmental Ethics*, 10.1, 1988, 3–30.

21 Eugene C. Hargrove (ed.), *Religion and Environmental Crisis*, Athens: University of Georgia Press, 1986.

22 James Rachels, *Created from Animals: The Moral Implications of Darwinism*, Oxford and New York: Oxford University Press, 1990.

23 Robin Attfield, *God and the Secular*, Cardiff: University College Cardiff Press, 1978, chapter 6.

24 Warwick Fox, *Approaching Deep Ecology: A Response to Richard Sylvan's Critique of Deep Ecology*, Hobart; University of Tasmania, 1986 (University of Tasmania Environmental Studies Occasional Paper 20).

25 Peter Reed, 'Man Apart: An Alternative to the Self-Realization Approach', *Environmental Ethics*, 11.1, 1989, 53–69.

26 Arne Naess, '*Man Apart* and Deep Ecology: A Reply to Reed', *Environmental Ethics*, 12.2, 1990, 185–92.

27 Eric Matthews, 'The Metaphysics of Environmentalism', in Nigel Dower (ed.), *Ethics and Environmental Responsibility*, Aldershot: Avebury, 1989, 38–56.

28 Robin Attfield, 'Sylvan, Fox and Deep Ecology: A View from the Continental Shelf' (unpublished paper).

29 Richard Sylvan, 'A Critique of Deep Ecology', Parts I, II, *Radical Philosophy*, 40, Summer 1985, 2–12; 41, Autumn 1985, 10–22.

30 Stephen Clark, Review of *The Ethics of Environmental Concern*, *Philosophical Books*, 26.3, 1985, 184–6.

31 L. W. Sumner, Review of *The Ethics of Environmental Concern*, *Environmental Ethics*, 8.1, 1986, 77–82, at p. 80.

32 L. W. Sumner, *The Moral Foundation of Rights*, Oxford: Oxford University Press, 1987.

33 Elliot, Critical notice of *The Ethics of Environmental Concern*.
34 J. R. Cameron, 'Do Future Generations Matter?', in Dower (ed.), *Ethics and Environmental Responsibility*, 57–78.
35 Robert L. Simon, 'Troubled Waters: Global Justice and Ocean Resources', in Tom Regan (ed.), *Earthbound: New Introductory Essays in Environmental Ethics*, Philadelphia: Temple University Press, 1984, 179–213.
36 Annette Baier, 'For the Sake of Future Generations', in *Earthbound: New Introductory Essays in Environmental Ethics*, 214–46.
37 Robert Goodin, *Protecting the Vulnerable*, pp. 173–8.
38 Hans Jonas, *The Imperative of Responsibility*, Chicago and London: University of Chicago Press, 1984.
39 See chapter 3 of Robin Attfield and Katharine Dell (eds), *Values, Conflict and the Environment*, Oxford: Ian Ramsey Centre, Oxford, and Centre for Applied Ethics, Cardiff, 1989.
40 For the details of *Our Common Future*, see note 8 above.
41 Dieter Birnbacher, Review of *The Ethics of Environmental Concern*, *Allgemeine Zeitschrift für Philosophie*, 11, 1986, 63 f.
42 Sumner, Review of *The Ethics of Environmental Concern*, p. 81.
43 Elliot, Critical notice of *The Ethics of Environmental Concern*, p. 506.
44 John Lemons, Review of *The Ethics of Environmental Concern*, *The Environmental Professional*, 6, 1984, 163–5.
45 'Population Policies and the Value of People', *Journal of Social Philosophy*, 14.4, 1983, 84–93; also in Yeager Hudson and Creighton Peden (eds), *Philosophical Essays on the Ideals of a Good Society*, Lewiston, NY: Edward Mellen Press, 1988, 191–201.
46 McCloskey, *Ecological Ethics and Politics*.
47 *Our Common Future*, chapter 4.
48 Richard Routley (now Sylvan), 'People vs the Land: The Ethics of the Population Case', in R. Birrell *et al.* (eds), *Populate and Perish*, Sydney: Fontana, 1984.
49 Derek Parfit, *Reasons and Persons*, Oxford: Oxford University Press, 1984.
50 Gary E. Varner, 'Biological Functions and Biological Interests', *Southern Journal of Philosophy*, 28.2, 1990, 251–70.
51 Robin Attfield, 'The Good of Trees', *Journal of Value Inquiry*, 15, 1981, 35–54.
52 Varner, 'Biological Functions and Biological Interests', p. 263.
53 Robin Attfield, 'Methods of Ecological Ethics', *Metaphilosophy*, 14, 1983, 195–208; republished with an updating postscript in Terrell Ward Bynum and William Vitek (eds), *Applying Philosophy*, Oxford and New York: Metaphilosophy Foundation, 1988, 176–90.
54 'The Good of Trees', p. 50.
55 Alan Holland, 'The Biotic Community: A Philosophical Critique of Genetic Engineering', in Peter Wheale and Ruth McNally (eds), *The Biorevolution*, London and Winchester, Mass.: Pluto Press, 1990, pp. 166–74.
56 For *Values, Conflict and the Environment*, see note 13 above.
57 Robin Attfield, 'Reasoning About the Environment' (unpublished essay).

58   Janna Thompson, 'A Refutation of Environmental Ethics', *Environmental Ethics,* 12.2, 1990, 147–60.

59   Paul Taylor, *Respect for Nature: A Theory of Environmental Ethics,* Princeton: Princeton University Press, 1986.

60   Thompson, 'A Refutation of Environmental Ethics', p. 153.

61   Kenneth Goodpaster, 'On Being Morally Considerable', *Journal of Philosophy,* 75, 1978, 308–25.

62   Thompson, 'A Refutation of Environmental Ethics', p. 160.

63   Robin Attfield, 'Deep Ecology and Intrinsic Value: A Reply to Andrew Dobson', *Cogito,* 4.1, 1990, 61–6.

64   Bryan G. Norton, 'Conservation and Preservation: A Conceptual Rehabilitation', *Environmental Ethics,* 8.3, 1986, 195–220.

65   Bryan G. Norton, 'On the Inherent Danger of Undervaluing Species', in Bryan G. Norton (ed.), *The Preservation of Species: The Value of Biological Diversity,* Princeton: Princeton University Press, 1986, 110–37.

66   Ronald Preston, Review of *The Ethics of Environmental Concern, Theology,* July 1984, 314–16.

67   Holmes Rolston, *Environmental Ethics: Duties to and Values in the Natural World,* Philadelphia: Temple University Press, 1988, chapter 2.

68   Robin Attfield, Review of Holmes Rolston, *Environmental Ethics: Duties to and Values in the Natural World, Environmental Ethics,* 11.4, 1989, 363–8.

69   McCloskey, *Ecological Ethics and Politics,* p. 66.

70   Tom Regan, *The Case for Animal Rights,* London: Routledge & Kegan Paul, 1983.

71   Elliot, Critical notice of *The Ethics of Environmental Concern,* p. 503.

72   R. G. Frey, *Rights, Killing and Suffering,* Oxford: Basil Blackwell, 1983.

73   Lawrence E. Johnson, *A Morally Deep World,* Canberra: Departments of Philosophy, Australian National University, 1987 (Preprint series in Environmental Philosophy, 17).

74   Taylor, *Respect for Nature,* pp. 263–307.

75   Robin Attfield, 'Biocentrism, Moral Standing and Moral Significance', *Philosophica,* 39, 1987, 47–58.

76   Arne Naess, 'The Shallow and the Deep, Long-range Ecology Movement', *Inquiry,* 16, 1973, 95–100.

77   Fox, *Approaching Deep Ecology.*

78   Elliot, Critical notice of *The Ethics of Environmental Concern,* p. 508.

79   For *Values, Conflict and the Environment,* see note 13 above.

80   Robin Attfield, 'Reasoning About the Environment' (unpublished paper).

81   David Pearce *et al., Blueprint for a Green Economy,* London: Earthscan Publications, 1989.

82   Rolston, *Environmental Ethics,* pp. 253–62.

83   Mark Sagoff, *The Economy of the Earth,* Cambridge: Cambridge University Press, 1988.

84   John Passmore, 'Attitudes to Nature', is included in the second edition of *MRN,* London: Duckworth, 1980 (207–18), and is also available in Royal

Institute of Philosophy (ed.), *Nature and Conduct,* London and Basing-stoke: Macmillan Press, 1975, 251–64.

85   *MRN,* 2nd edn, p. 218.

86   Daniel Shaw, 'After Chernobyl: the Ethics of Risk-Taking', in Dower (ed.), *Ethics and Environmental Responsibility,* pp. 110–31.

87   For *Our Common Future,* see note 8 above. (About nuclear energy generation, this report sits uncharacteristically on the fence.)

88   McCloskey, *Ecological Ethics and Politics.*

89   Murray Bookchin, *Towards an Ecological Society,* Montreal: Black Rose Books, 1980.

90   Alan Carter, 'Toward a Green Political Theory' (unpublished paper).

91   Keekok Lee, *Social Philosophy and Ecological Society,* London and New York: Routledge, 1989.

References

ARTICLES, ESSAYS AND REVIEWS

Anglin, William, 'The Repugnant Conclusion', *Canadian Journal of Philosophy*, 7, 1977, 745–54

Anglin, William, 'In Defense of the Potentiality Principle', in R. I. Sikora and Brian Barry (eds), *Obligations to Future Generations*, 31–7

Attfield, Robin, 'The Logical Status of Moral Utterances', *Journal of Critical Analysis*, 4 (2), 1972, 70–84

Attfield, Robin, 'On Being Human', *Inquiry*, 17, 1974, 175–92

Attfield, Robin, 'Toward a Defence of Teleology', *Ethics*, 85, 1975, 123–35

Attfield, Robin, 'Against Incomparabilism', *Philosophy*, 50, 1975, 230–4

Attfield, Robin, 'Racialism, Justice and Teleology', *Ethics*, 87, 1977, 186–8

Attfield, Robin, 'Supererogation and Double Standards', *Mind*, 88, 1979, 481–99

Attfield, Robin, 'How Not to be a Moral Relativist', *The Monist*, 62, 1979, 510–21

Attfield, Robin, Review of Renford Bambrough, *Moral Scepticism and Moral Knowledge*, *The Philosophical Quarterly*, 31, 1981, 177–8

Attfield, Robin, 'The Good of Trees', *Journal of Value Inquiry*, 15, 1981, 35–54

Attfield, Robin, 'Christian Attitudes to Nature', *Journal of the History of Ideas*, 44, 1983

Attfield, Robin, 'Western Traditions and Environmental Ethics', in Robert Elliot and Arran Gare (eds), *Environmental Philosophy: A Collection of Readings*

Attfield, Robin, 'Methods of Ecological Ethics', *Metaphilosophy*, 14, 1983, 195–208; republished with an updating postscript in Terrell Ward Bynum and William Vitek (eds), *Applying Philosophy*, 176–90

Attfield, Robin, 'Population Policies and the Value of People', *Journal of Social Philosophy*, 14.4, 1983, 84–93; also in Yeager Hudson and Creighton Peden (eds), *Philosophical Essays on the Ideals of a Good Society*, 191–201

Attfield, Robin, 'Biocentrism, Moral Standing and Moral Significance', *Philosophica*, 39, 1987, 47–58

Attfield, Robin, Review of Andrew Brennan, *Thinking About Nature: An Inves-*

tigation of Nature, Value and Ecology, Journal of Applied Philosophy, 6.2, 1989, 237–8

Attfield, Robin, Review of Holmes Rolston III, *Environmental Ethics: Duties to and Values in the Natural World, Environmental Ethics*, 11.4, 1989, 363–8

Attfield, Robin, 'Deep Ecology and Intrinsic Value: A Reply to Andrew Dobson', *Cogito*, 4.1, 1990, 61–6

Attfield, Robin, 'Sylvan, Fox and Deep Ecology: A View from the Continental Shelf' (unpublished paper)

Attfield, Robin, 'Reasoning About the Environment' (unpublished paper)

Attfield, Robin, 'The Comprehensive Ecology Movement', forthcoming in Edgar Morscher, Otto Neumaier and Peter Simons (eds), *Applied Ethics and Its Foundations*, 1992

Attfield, Robin, 'Preservation, Art and Natural Beauty' (unpublished paper)

Attfield, Robin, 'Has the History of Philosophy Ruined the Environment?', forthcoming in *Environmental Ethics*, 1991

Attfield, Robin, 'Attitudes to Wildlife in the History of Ideas', forthcoming in *Environmental History Review*, 1991

Auxter, Thomas, 'The Right not to be Eaten', *Inquiry*, 22, 1979, 221–30

Ayers, Michael, 'Mechanism, Superaddition and the Proof of God's Existence in Locke's *Essay*', *Philosophical Review*, 90, 1981, 210–51

Baier, Annette, 'The Rights of Past and Future Persons', in Ernest Partridge (ed.), *Responsibilities to Future Generations*, 171–83

Baier, Annette, 'For the Sake of Future Generations', in Tom Regan (ed.), *Earthbound: New Introductory Essays in Environmental Ethics*, 214–46

Baker, John Austin, 'Biblical Attitudes to Nature', in Hugh Montefiore (ed.), *Man and Nature*, 87–109

Barbour, Ian G., 'Attitudes Toward Nature and Technology', in Ian G. Barbour (ed.), *Earth Might Be Fair*, 146–68

Barr, James, 'Man and Nature: The Ecological Controversy in the Old Testament', *Bulletin of the John Rylands Library*, 55, 1972, 9–32

Barry, Brian, 'Justice Between Generations', in P. M. S. Hacker and J. Raz (eds), *Law, Morality and Society*, 268–84

Barry, Brian, 'Circumstances of Justice and Future Generations', in R. I. Sikora and Brian Barry (eds), *Obligations to Future Generations*, 204–48

Bayles, Michael, 'Harm to the Unconceived', *Philosophy and Public Affairs*, 5, 1975–76, 292–304

Bayles, Michael, 'Famine or Food: Sacrificing for Future or Present Generations', in Ernest Partridge (ed.), *Responsibilities to Future Generations*, 239–45

Benn, Stanley, 'Freedom, Autonomy and the Concept of a Person', *Proceedings of the Aristotelian Society*, 76, 1975–76, 109–30

Benn, Stanley, 'Personal Freedom and Environmental Ethics: the Moral Inequality of Species', in Gray Dorsey (ed.), *Equality and Freedom*, Vol. II, 401–24

Bennett, Jonathan, 'On Maximizing Happiness', in R. I. Sikora and Brian Barry (eds), *Obligations to Future Generations*, 61–73

Benson, John, 'Duty and the Beast', *Philosophy*, 53, 1978, 529–49

Bickham, Stephen, 'Future Generations and Contemporary Ethical Theory', *Journal of Value Inquiry,* 15, 1981, 169–77

Birnbacher, Dieter, Review of *The Ethics of Environmental Concern, Allgemeine Zeitschrift für Philosophie,* 11, 1986, 63 f.

Blackstone, William T., 'The Search for an Environmental Ethic', in Tom Regan (ed.), *Matters of Life and Death,* 299–335

Boulding, Kenneth, 'The Economics of the Coming Spaceship Earth', in John Barr (ed.), *The Environmental Handbook,* 77–82

Bratton, Susan Power, 'The Original Desert Solitaire: Early Christian Monasticism and Wilderness', *Environmental Ethics,* 10.1, 1988, 31–53

Breslaw, John, 'Economics and Ecosystems', in John Barr (ed.), *The Environmental Handbook,* 83–93

Brumbaugh, Robert S., 'Of Man, Animals and Morals: A Brief History', in Richard Knowles Morris and Michael W. Fox (eds), *On the Fifth Day, Animal Rights and Human Ethics,* 6–25

Burton, Robert G., 'A Philosopher Looks at the Population Bomb', in William T. Blackstone (ed.), *Philosophy and Environmental Crisis,* 105–16

Byerly, Henry, 'Principles of Noninterference with Nature in Ecological Ethics', in Edgar Morscher and Rudolf Stranzinger (eds), *Ethics: Foundations, Problems and Applications, Proceedings of the Fifth International Wittgenstein Symposium,* 318–20

Callahan, Daniel, 'What Obligations do we have to Future Generations?', *American Ecclesiastical Review,* 164, 1971, 265–80; reprinted in Ernest Partridge (ed.), *Responsibilities to Future Generations,* 73–85

Callicott, J. Baird, 'Elements of an Environmental Ethic: Moral Considerability and the Biotic Community', *Environmental Ethics,* 1, 1979, 71–81

Callicott, J. Baird, 'Animal Liberation: A Triangular Affair', *Environmental Ethics,* 2.1, 1980, 311–38; reprinted in J. Baird Callicott, *In Defense of the Land Ethic: Essays in Environmental Philosophy,* 15–38

Callicott, J. Baird, 'Non-anthropocentric Value Theory and Environmental Ethics', *American Philosophical Quarterly,* 21, 1984, 299–309

Callicott, J. Baird, 'Intrinsic Value, Quantum Theory and Environmental Ethics', *Environmental Ethics,* 7, 1985, 257–75

Callicott, J. Baird, 'On the Intrinsic Value of Nonhuman Species', in Bryan Norton (ed.), *The Preservation of Species,* 138–72

Callicott, J. Baird, 'The Conceptual Foundations of the Land Ethic', in J. Baird Callicott, *In Defense of the Land Ethic,* 101–14, and in J. Baird Callicott (ed.), *Companion to A Sand County Almanac: Interpretive and Critical Essays,* 186–217

Callicott, J. Baird, 'The Case Against Moral Pluralism', *Environmental Ethics,* 12.2, 1990, 99–124

Cameron, J. R., 'Do Future Generations Matter?', in Nigel Dower (ed.), *Ethics and Environmental Responsibility,* 57–78

Carter, Alan, 'Toward a Green Political Theory' (unpublished paper)

Cigman, Ruth, 'Death, Misfortune and Species Inequality', *Philosophy and Public Affairs,* 10, 1980–81, 47–64

Clark, Stephen, Review of K. E. Goodpaster and K. M. Sayre (eds), *Ethics and Problems of the 21st Century, Philosophical Books,* 21, 1980, 237–40

Clark, Stephen, Review of Robin Attfield, *The Ethics of Environmental Concern, Philosophical Books,* 26.3, 1985, 184–6

Coleman, William, 'Providence, Capitalism and Environmental Degradation', *Journal of the History of Ideas,* 37, 1976, 27–44

Craig, Leon H., 'Contra Contract: A Brief Against Rawls' Theory of Justice', *Canadian Journal of Political Science,* 8, 1975, 63–81

de George, Richard T., 'The Environment, Rights and Future Generations', in Ernest Partridge (ed.), *Responsibilities to Future Generations,* 157–65

Delattre, Edwin, 'Rights, Responsibilities and Future Persons', *Ethics,* 82, 1972, 254–8

Devine, Philip, 'The Moral Basis of Vegetarianism', *Philosophy,* 53, 1978, 481–505

Diamond, Cora, 'Eating Meat and Eating People', *Philosophy,* 53, 1978, 465–79

Dubos, René, 'Franciscan Conservation and Benedictine Stewardship', in David and Eileen Spring (eds), *Ecology and Religion in History,* 114–36

Elliot, Robert, 'Why Preserve Species?', in Don Mannison, Michael McRobbie and Richard Routley (eds), *Environmental Philosophy,* 8–29

Elliot, Robert, Critical notice of Robin Attfield, *The Ethics of Environmental Concern, Australasian Journal of Philosophy,* 63, 1985, 499–509

Elliot, Robert, 'Meta-Ethics and Environmental Ethics', *Metaphilosophy,* 16, 1985, 103–17

Feinberg, Joel, 'The Rights of Animals and Unborn Generations', in William T. Blackstone (ed.), *Philosophy and Environmental Crisis,* 43–68; also in Richard A. Wasserstrom (ed.), *Today's Moral Problems,* 581–601; and in Ernest Partridge (ed.), *Responsibilities to Future Generations,* 139–50

Feinberg, Joel, 'Human Duties and Animal Rights', in Richard Knowles Morris and Michael W. Fox (eds), *On the Fifth Day, Animal Rights and Human Ethics,* 45–69

Fiering, Norman S., 'Irresistible Compassion: An Aspect of Eighteenth Century Humanitarianism', *Journal of the History of Ideas,* 37, 1976, 195–218

Francis, Leslie Pickering and Norman, Richard, 'Some Animals are More Equal than Others', *Philosophy,* 53, 1978, 507–27

Frankena, William K., 'Ethics and the Environment', in K. E. Goodpaster and K. M. Sayre (eds), *Ethics and Problems of the 21st Century,* 3–20

Fyodorov, Yevgeny and Novik, Ilya, 'Ecological Aspects of Social Progress', in *Society and the Environment: a Soviet View* (ed. anon.), 37–55

Gerasimov, Innokenty, 'Man, Society and the Geographical Environment', in *Society and the Environment: a Soviet View* (ed. anon.), 25–36

Golding, Martin, 'Obligations to Future Generations', *The Monist,* 56, 1972, 85–99; also in Ernest Partridge (ed.), *Responsibilities to Future Generations,* 61–72

Golding, M. P. and Golding, N. H., 'Why Preserve Landmarks? A Preliminary Inquiry', in K. E. Goodpaster and K. M. Sayre (eds), *Ethics and Problems of the 21st Century*, 175–90

Goodin, Robert E., 'Ethical Principles for Environmental Protection', in Robert Elliot and Arran Gare, *Environmental Philosophy: A Collection of Readings*, 3–20; an abbreviated version of 'No Moral Nukes', *Ethics*, 90, 1980, 417–49

Goodman, David C., 'The Enlightenment: Deists and "Rationalists"', in David C. Goodman *et al., Scientific Progress and Religious Dissent*, 33–68

Goodman, David C., 'God and Nature in the Philosophy of Descartes', in David C. Goodman *et al., Towards a Mechanistic Philosophy*, 5–43

Goodpaster, Kenneth, 'On Being Morally Considerable', *Journal of Philosophy*, 75, 1978, 308–25

Goodpaster, Kenneth, 'From Egoism to Environmentalism', in K. E. Goodpaster and K. M. Sayre (eds), *Ethics and Problems of the 21st Century*, 21–35

Goodpaster, Kenneth, 'On Stopping at Everything: A Reply to W. M. Hunt', *Environmental Ethics*, 2, 1980, 281–4

Govier, Trudy, 'What Should We Do About Future People?', *American Philosophical Quarterly*, 16, 1979, 105–13

Gunn, Alastair, S., 'Why Should We Care about Rare Species?', *Environmental Ethics*, 2, 1980, 17–37

Gunter, Pete A. Y., 'The Big Thicket: A Case Study in Attitudes toward Environment', in William T. Blackstone (ed.), *Philosophy and Environmental Crisis*, 117–37

Hare, R. M., 'Abortion and the Golden Rule', *Philosophy and Public Affairs*, 4, 1974–75, 201–22

Hare, R. M., 'Survival of the Weakest', in Samuel Gorovitz *et al.* (eds), *Moral Problems in Medicine*, 364–9

Hargrove, Eugene C., 'The Role of Rules in Ethical Decision Making', *Inquiry*, 28, 1985, 3–42

Haworth, Lawrence, 'Rights, Wrongs and Animals', *Ethics*, 88, 1977–78, 95–105

Helton, David, 'Tsetse Fly and Ecology', *Vole*, 4 (3), March 1981, 16

Hesse, Mary, 'On the Alleged Incompatibility between Christianity and Science', in Hugh Montefiore (ed.), *Man and Nature*, 121–31

Hilton, R. H. and Sawyer, P. H., Review of Lynn White Jnr, *Medieval Technology and Social Change, Past and Present*, 24, 1963, 90–100

Holland, Alan, 'The Biotic Community: A Philosophical Critique of Genetic Engineering', in Peter Wheale and Ruth McNally (eds), *The Biorevolution*, 166–74

Hubbard, F. Patrick, 'Justice, Limits to Growth, and an Equilibrium State', *Philosophy and Public Affairs*, 7, 1977–78, 326–45

Hubin, D. Clayton, 'Justice and Future Generations', *Philosophy and Public Affairs*, 6, 1976–77, 70–83

Hunt, W. Murray, 'Are *Mere Things* Morally Considerable?', *Environmental Ethics*, 2, 1980, 59–65

Kavka, Gregory, 'The Futurity Problem', in R. I. Sikora and Brian Barry (eds), *Obligations to Future Generations*, 186–203; also in Ernest Partridge (ed.), *Responsibilities to Future Generations*, 109–22

Laslett, Peter, 'The Conversation Between the Generations', in Royal Institute of Philosophy (ed.), *The Proper Study*, 172–89

Lemons, John, Review of Robin Attfield, *The Ethics of Environmental Concern*, *The Environmental Professional*, 6, 1984, 163–5

Linear, Marcus, 'Zapping Africa's Flies', *Vole*, 4 (3), March 1981, 14–15

Lippit, Victor D. and Hamada, Koichi, 'Efficiency and Equity in Intergenerational Distribution', in Dennis Clark Pirages (ed.), *The Sustainable Society*, 285–99

Lockwood, Michael, 'Killing Humans and Killing Animals', *Inquiry*, 22, 1979, 157–70

Lovelock, J. and Epton, S., 'The Quest for Gaia', *The New Scientist*, 65, 1975, 304–9

McCabe, Herbert, 'The Immortality of the Soul', in Anthony Kenny (ed.), *Aquinas: A Collection of Critical Essays*, 297–306

McCloskey, H. J., 'Rights', *The Philosophical Quarterly*, 15, 1965, 115–27

McCloskey, H. J., 'The Right to Life', *Mind*, 84, 1975, 403–25

McCloskey, H. J., 'Moral Rights and Animals', *Inquiry*, 22, 1979, 23–54

McIver, A. M., 'Ethics and the Beetle', *Analysis*, 8, 1948, 65–70

Macklin, Ruth, 'Can Future Generations Correctly Be Said to Have Rights?', in Ernest Partridge (ed.), *Responsibilities to Future Generations*, 151–5

McMahan, Jefferson, 'Problems of Population Theory', *Ethics*, 92, 1981–82, 96–127

McRobie, George, 'The Inappropriate Pesticide', *Vole*, 4 (3), March 1981, 1

Marietta, Don, 'Religious Models and Decision-Making', *Zygon*, 12, 1977, 151–66

Matthews, Eric, 'The Metaphysics of Environmentalism', in Nigel Dower (ed.), *Ethics and Environmental Responsibility*, 38–56

Midgley, Mary, 'Duties Concerning Islands' in Robert Elliot and Arran Gare (eds), *Environmental Philosophy: A Collection of Readings*

Midgley, Mary, 'The Limits of Individualism', in Donald Ortner (ed.), *How Humans Adapt: A Biocultural Odyssey'*, 517–27. (This and the previous item also appear in Mary Midgley, *Evolution as a Religion*, as chapters 17 and 18 respectively.)

Moncrief, Lewis W., 'The Cultural Basis of our Environmental Crisis', *Science*, 170, 508–12; reprinted in David and Eileen Spring (eds), *Ecology and Religion in History*, 76–90

Murdy, W. H., 'Anthropocentrism: A Modern Version', *Science*, 187, March 1975, 1168–72

Naess, Arne, 'The Shallow and the Deep, Long-range Ecology Movement: A Summary', *Inquiry*, 16, 1973, 95–100

Naess, Arne, 'The Deep Ecology Movement: Some Philosophical Aspects', *Philosophical Inquiry,* 8, 1986, 10–31

Naess, Arne, 'Sustainable Development and the Deep Long-Range Ecology Movement', *The Trumpeter,* 5.4, 1988, 138–42

Naess, Arne, '*Man Apart* and Deep Ecology: A Reply to Reed', *Environmental Ethics,* 12.2, 1990, 185–92

Narveson, Jan, 'Utilitarianism and New Generations', *Mind,* 76, 1967, 62–72

Narveson, Jan, 'Moral Problems of Population', in Michael D. Bayles (ed.), *Ethics and Population,* 59–80

Narveson, Jan, 'Animal Rights', *Canadian Journal of Philosophy,* 7, 1977, 161–78

Narveson, Jan, 'Future People and Us', in R. I. Sikora and Brian Barry (eds), *Obligations to Future Generations,* 38–60

Nell, Onora, 'Lifeboat Earth', *Philosophy and Public Affairs,* 4, 1974–75, 273–92

New Internationalist, editorial, 79, September 1979

Norton, Bryan G., 'Conservation and Preservation: A Conceptual Rehabilitation', *Environmental Ethics,* 8.3, 1986, 195–220

Norton, Bryan G., 'On the Inherent Danger of Undervaluing Species', in Bryan G. Norton (ed.), *The Preservation of Species: The Value of Biological Diversity,* 110–37

O'Briant, Walter H., 'Man, Nature and the History of Philosophy', in William T. Blackstone (ed.), *Philosophy and Environmental Crisis,* 79–89

Oldak, Pavel, 'The Environment and Social Production', in *Society and the Environment: a Soviet View* (ed. anon.), 56–68

Parfit, Derek, 'Rights, Interests and Possible People', in Samuel Gorovitz *et al.* (eds), *Moral Problems in Medicine,* 369–75

Parfit, Derek, 'On Doing the Best for Our Children', in Michael D. Bayles (ed.), *Ethics and Population,* 100–15

Parfit, Derek, 'Innumerate Ethics', *Philosophy and Public Affairs,* 7, 1977–78, 285–301

Parfit, Derek, 'Energy Policy and the Further Future', in Douglas MacLean and Peter Brown (eds), *Energy and the Future*

Parfit, Derek, 'Overpopulation, Part One' (unpublished paper)

Parfit, Derek, 'Future Generations: Further Problems', *Philosophy and Public Affairs,* 11, 1981–2, 113–72

Passmore, John, 'Attitudes to Nature', in Royal Institute of Philosophy (ed.), *Nature and Conduct,* 251–64; also in the second edition of *Man's Responsibility for Nature,* [MRN], 207–18

Passmore, John, 'The Treatment of Animals', *Journal of the History of Ideas,* 36, 1975, 195–218

Passmore, John, 'Ecological Problems and Persuasion', in Gray Dorsey (ed.), *Equality and Freedom,* Vol. II, 431–42

Pletcher, Galen K., 'The Rights of Future Generations', in Ernest Partridge (ed.), *Responsibilities to Future Generations*, 167–70

Preston, Ronald, Review of Robin Attfield, *The Ethics of Environmental Concern, Theology*, July 1984, 314–16

Pritchard, Michael S. and Robison, Wade L., 'Justice and the Treatment of Animals: A Critique of Rawls', *Environmental Ethics*, 3, 1981, 55–61

Reed, Peter, 'Man Apart: An Alternative to the Self-Realization Approach', *Environmental Ethics*, 11.1, 1989, 53–69

Regan, Tom, 'The Moral Basis of Vegetarianism', *Canadian Journal of Philosophy*, 5, 1975, 181–214

Regan, Tom, 'Feinberg on What Sorts of Beings Can Have Rights', *Southern Journal of Philosophy*, 14, 1976, 485–98

Regan, Tom, 'Narveson on Egoism and the Rights of Animals', *Canadian Journal of Philosophy*, 7, 1977, 179–86

Regan, Tom, 'An Examination and Defense of One Argument Concerning Animal Rights', *Inquiry*, 22, 1979, 189–219

Regan, Tom, 'Animal Rights and Human Wrongs', *Environmental Ethics*, 2, 1980, 99–120

Regan, Tom, 'Utilitarianism, Vegetarianism and Animal Rights', *Philosophy and Public Affairs*, 9, 1979–80, 305–24

Regan, Tom, 'The Nature and Possibility of an Environmental Ethic', *Environmental Ethics*, 3, 1981, 16–31

Rodman, John, 'The Liberation of Nature', *Inquiry*, 20, 1977, 83–145

Rodman, John, 'Animal Justice: The Counter-revolution in Natural Right and Law', *Inquiry*, 22, 1979, 3–22

Rolston, Holmes, III, 'Is There an Ecological Ethic?', *Ethics*, 85, 1975, 93–109; also in Holmes Rolston III, *Philosophy Gone Wild: Essays in Environmental Ethics*, 11–29

Rolston, Holmes, III, 'Are Values in Nature Subjective or Objective?', in *Environmental Ethics*, 4, 1982, 125–51; also in Holmes Rolston III, *Philosophy Gone Wild: Essays in Environmental Ethics*, 91–117

Roupas, T. G., 'The Value of Life', *Philosophy and Public Affairs*, 7, 1977–78, 154–83

Routley, Richard, 'Is There a Need for a New, an Environmental Ethic?', *Proceedings of the XVth World Congress of Philosophy*, Varna, 1973, 205–10

Routley (now Sylvan), Richard, 'People vs the Land: The Ethics of the Population Case', in R. Birrell *et al.* (eds), *Populate and Perish*

Routley, Richard and Routley, Val, 'Nuclear Energy and Obligations to the Future', *Inquiry*, 21, 1978, 133–79

Routley, Richard and Routley, Val, 'Against the Inevitability of Human Chauvinism', in K. E. Goodpaster and K. M. Sayre (eds), *Ethics and Problems of the 21st Century*, 36–59

Routley, Val, Critical notice of John Passmore, *Man's Responsibility for Nature*, *Australasian Journal of Philosophy*, 53, 1975, 171–85

Routley, Val and Routley, Richard, 'Human Chauvinism and Environmental Ethics', in Don Mannison, Michael McRobbie and Richard Routley (eds), *Environmental Philosophy*, 96–189

Routley, Val and Routley, Richard, 'Social Theories, Self Management and Environmental Problems', in Don Mannison, Michael McRobbie and Richard Routley (eds), *Environmental Philosophy*, 217–332

Sagoff, Mark, 'On Preserving the Natural Environment', *Yale Law Journal*, 84, 1974, 205–67

Sayre, Kenneth, 'Morality, Energy and the Environment', *Environmental Ethics*, 3, 1981, 5–18

Schwartz, Thomas, 'Obligations to Posterity', in R. I. Sikora and Brian Barry (eds), *Obligations to Future Generations*, 3–13

Schwartz, Walter, 'Black Death from the East', *Weekend Guardian*, June 16–17 1990, pp. 4–6

Scott, Robert, Jnr, 'Environmental Ethics and Obligations to Future Generations', in R. I. Sikora and Brian Barry (eds), *Obligations to Future Generations*, 74–90

Semenov, Nicolai, 'Energetics for the Future', in *Society and the Environment: a Soviet View* (ed. anon.), 69–98

Shaw, Daniel, 'After Chernobyl: the Ethics of Risk-Taking', in Nigel Dower (ed.), *Ethics and Environmental Responsibility*, 110–31

Sher, George, 'Hare, Abortion and the Golden Rule', *Philosophy and Public Affairs*, 6, 1976–77, 185–90

Sikora, R. I., 'Utilitarianism: The Classical Principle and the Average Principle', *Canadian Journal of Philosophy*, 1975, 409–19

Sikora, R. I., 'Is it Wrong to Prevent the Existence of Future Generations?', in R. I. Sikora and Brian Barry (eds), *Obligations to Future Generations*, 112–66

Sikora, R. I., 'Utilitarianism and Future Generations', *Canadian Journal of Philosophy*, 9, 1979, 461–6

Sikora, R. I., 'Classical Utilitarianism and Parfit's Repugnant Conclusion: A Reply to McMahan', *Ethics*, 92, 1981–82, 128–33

Simon, Robert L., 'Troubled Waters: Global Justice and Ocean Resources', in Tom Regan (ed.), *Earthbound: New Introductory Essays in Environmental Ethics*, 179–213

Singer, Peter, 'Famine, Affluence and Morality', *Philosophy and Public Affairs*, 1, 1971–72, 229–43

Singer, Peter, 'A Utilitarian Population Principle', in Michael D. Bayles (ed.), *Ethics and Population*, 81–99

Singer, Peter, 'Reconsidering the Famine Relief Argument', in P. G. Brown and H. Shue (eds), *Food Policy*, 36–53

Singer, Peter, 'Killing Humans and Killing Animals', *Inquiry*, 22, 1979, 145–56

Singer, Peter, 'Not for Humans Only: The Place of Nonhumans in Environmental Issues', in K. E. Goodpaster and K. M. Sayre (eds), *Ethics and Problems of the 21st Century*, 191–206

Singer, Peter, 'Animals and the Value of Life', in Tom Regan (ed.), *Matters of Life and Death,* 218–59

Singer, Peter, 'Utilitarianism and Vegetarianism', *Philosophy and Public Affairs,* 9, 1979–80, 325–37

Sprigge, Timothy L. S., 'Professor Narveson's Utilitarianism', *Inquiry,* 11, 1968, 337–41

Stearns, J. Brenton, 'Ecology and the Indefinite Unborn', *The Monist,* 56, 1972, 612–25; reprinted in Richard A. Wasserstrom (ed.), *Today's Moral Problems,* 602–13

Steinbock, Bonnie, 'Speciesism and the Idea of Equality', *Philosophy,* 53, 1978, 247–63

Sterba, James P., 'Abortion, Distant Peoples and Future Generations', *Journal of Philosophy,* 77, 1980, 424–40

Sumner, L. W., 'A Matter of Life and Death', *Noûs,* 10, 1976, 145–71

Sumner, L. W., 'Classical Utilitarianism and the Population Optimum', in R. I. Sikora and Brian Barry (eds), *Obligations to Future Generations,* 91–111

Sumner, L. W., Review of Robin Attfield, *The Ethics of Environmental Concern, Environmental Ethics,* 8.1, 1986, 77–82

Surber, Jere Paul, 'Obligations to Future Generations: Explorations and Problemata', *Journal of Value Inquiry,* 11, 1977, 104–16

Sylvan (formerly Routley), Richard, 'A Critique of Deep Ecology', Parts I, II, *Radical Philosophy,* 40, Summer 1985, 2–12; 41, Autumn 1985, 10–22

Thompson, Janna, 'A Refutation of Environmental Ethics', *Environmental Ethics,* 12.2, 1990, 147–60

Townsend, Aubrey, 'Radical Vegetarians', *Australasian Journal of Philosophy,* 57, 1979, 85–93

Tribe, Laurence H., 'Ways not to Think about Plastic Trees', *Yale Law Journal,* 83, 1974, 1315–48

VanDeVeer, Donald, 'Interspecific Justice', *Inquiry,* 22, 1979, 55–79

Varner, Gary E., Review of Christopher D. Stone, *Earth and Other Ethics, Environmental Ethics,* 10, 1988, 259–65

Varner, Gary E., 'Biological Functions and Biological Interests', *Southern Journal of Philosophy,* 28.2, 1990, 251–70

Warren, Mary, 'Do Potential People Have Moral Rights?', in R. I. Sikora and Brian Barry (eds), *Obligations to Future Generations,* 14–30

Warren, Mary Anne, 'The Rights of the Non-human World', in Robert Elliot and Arran Gare (eds), *Environmental Philosophy: A Collection of Readings*

Welbourn, F. B., 'Man's Dominion', *Theology,* 78, 1975, 561–8

White, Lynn, Jnr, 'The Historical Roots of our Ecological Crisis', *Science,* 155 (37), 10 March 1967, 1203–7; reprinted in John Barr (ed.), *The Environmental Handbook,* 3–16

Williams, Mary B., 'Discounting Versus Maximum Sustainable Yield', in R. I. Sikora and Brian Barry (eds), *Obligations to Future Generations,* 169–85

'World Charter for Nature' (annex to Resolution 37/7 of UN General Assembly,

1982), in United Nations, *Resolutions and Decisions Adopted by the General Assembly During Its 37th Session*

Young, Robert, 'Population Policies, Coercion and Morality', in Don Mannison, Michael McRobbie and Richard Routley (eds), *Environmental Philosophy*, 356–75

Zimmerman, Michael E., 'The Paradox of Naturalism', *The Deep Ecologist*, 9, January 1984, 9–10

Zimmerman, Michael E. 'Quantum Theory, Intrinsic Value and Panentheism', *Environmental Ethics*, 10.1, 1988, 3–30

BOOKS

Aiken, William and La Follette, Hugh (eds), *World Hunger and Moral Obligation*, Englewood Cliffs, NJ: Prentice-Hall, 1977

Alexander, H. G. (ed.), *The Clarke—Leibniz Correspondence*, Manchester: Manchester University Press, 1956

Allchin, A. M., *Wholeness and Transfiguration Illustrated in the Lives of St Francis of Assisi and St Seraphim of Sarov*, Oxford: SLG Press, 1974

Aquinas, Thomas, *Summa Contra Gentiles*, trans. Anton Pegis *et al.* (5 Vols.), Garden City, NY: Image Books, 1955–57

Aquinas, Thomas, *Summa Theologiae* (60 Vols.), London: Eyre and Spottiswoode, and New York: McGraw-Hill, 1964

Aristotle, *De Anima*, trans. Kenelm Foster and Silvester Humphries, London: Routledge & Kegan Paul, 1951

Arseniev, Nicholas, *Mysticism and the Eastern Church* (1925), trans. Arthur Chambers, London and Oxford: Mowbray, 1979

Attfield, Robin, *God and The Secular: A Philosophical Assessment of Secular Reasoning from Bacon to Kant*, Cardiff: University College Cardiff Press, 1978

Attfield, Robin, *A Theory of Value and Obligation*, London, New York and Sydney: Croom Helm, 1987.

Attfield, Robin and Dell, Katharine (eds), *Values, Conflict and the Environment*, Oxford: Ian Ramsey Centre, Oxford, and Centre for Applied Ethics, Cardiff, 1989. (Copies of this report of the environmental ethics working party of the Ian Ramsey Centre are available from the Principal's Secretary, Westminster College, North Hinksey, Oxford, OX2 9AT.)

Bacon, Francis, *The New Organon*, ed. Fulton H. Anderson, Indianapolis and New York: Bobbs-Merrill, 1960

Bacon, Francis, *The Advancement of Learning and the New Atlantis*, ed. Arthur Johnston, Oxford: Clarendon Press, 1974

Baillie, John, *The Belief in Progress*, London, Glasgow and Toronto: Oxford University Press, 1950

Bambrough, Renford, *Moral Scepticism and Moral Knowledge*, London and Henley: Routledge & Kegan Paul, 1979

Baptist Hymn Book, The, London: Psalms and Hymns Trust, 1962

Barbour, Ian G., *Earth Might Be Fair,* Englewood Cliffs, NJ: Prentice-Hall, 1972

Barr, John (ed.), *The Environmental Handbook* (British Version), London: Ballantine and Friends of the Earth, 1971

Bayle, Pierre, *Historical and Critical Dictionary* (1697), trans. and ed. Richard H. Popkin, Indianapolis and New York: Bobbs-Merrill, 1965

Bayles, Michael D. (ed.), *Ethics and Population,* Cambridge, Mass.: Schenkman, 1976

Becker, Carl, *The Heavenly City of the Eighteenth-Century Philosophers,* New Haven and London: Yale University Press, 1932

Bieler, André, *La Pensée economique et sociale de Calvin,* Geneva: Georg, 1959

Birch, L. Charles, *Nature and God,* London: SCM Press, 1965

Birrell, R. *et al.* (eds), *Populate and Perish,* Sydney: Fontana, 1984

Black, John, *Man's Dominion,* Edinburgh: Edinburgh University Press, 1970

Blackstone, William T. (ed.), *Philosophy and Environmental Crisis,* Athens: University of Georgia Press, 1974

Bookchin, Murray, *Towards an Ecological Society,* Montreal: Black Rose Books, 1980

Boyle, Robert, *The Christian Virtuoso,* London, 1690

Brennan, Andrew, *Thinking About Nature: An Investigation of Nature, Value and Ecology,* Athens: University of Georgia Press, 1988

Brown, P. G. and Shue, H. (eds), *Food Policy,* New York: Free Press, 1977

Bury, J. B., *The Idea of Progress,* London: Macmillan Press, 1920

Bynum, Terrell Ward and Vitek, William (eds), *Applying Philosophy,* Oxford and New York: Metaphilosophy Foundation, 1988

Callicott, J. Baird (ed.), *Companion to A Sand County Almanac: Interpretive and Critical Essays,* Madison: University of Wisconsin Press, 1987

Callicott, J. Baird, *In Defense of the Land Ethic: Essays in Environmental Philosophy,* Albany: State University of New York Press, 1989

Calvin, Jean, *Commentaries on the First Book of Moses, called Genesis,* trans. John King (2 Vols.), London, 1847

Catherwood, Sir Frederick, *A Better Way, The Case for a Christian Social Order,* Leicester: Inter-Varsity Press, 1975

Christian Faith and Practice in the Experience of the Society of Friends, London: London Yearly Meeting of the Society of Friends, 1960

Clark, Stephen R. L., *The Moral Status of Animals,* Oxford: Clarendon Press, 1977

Clarke, Samuel, *Letter to Dodwell, Etc.* (1706) (6th edn) London, 1731

Cole, H. *et al., Thinking About the Future: A Critique of The Limits to Growth,* London: Chatto & Windus and Sussex University Press, 1973

Collins, F. Howard, *Epitome of the Synthetic Philosophy of Herbert Spencer,* London: Williams & Northgate, 1889

Commoner, Barry, *The Closing Circle,* London: Jonathan Cape, 1972

Cowper, William, *The Task,* Ilkley and London: Scolar Press, 1973

Cudworth, Ralph, *The True Intellectual System of the Universe* (2nd edn), London, 1743

Derr, Thomas Sieger, *Ecology and Human Liberation*, Geneva: WSCF Books, 1973

Descartes, René, *The Philosophical Works of Descartes*, trans. Elizabeth S. Haldane and G. R. T. Ross (2 Vols.), Cambridge: Cambridge University Press, 1967

Devall, Bill and Sessions, George, *Deep Ecology: Living As If Nature Mattered*, Salt Lake City: Gibbs M. Smith, 1985

Donaldson, Peter, *Worlds Apart*, London: BBC, 1971

Dorsey, Gray (ed.), *Equality and Freedom* (3 Vols.), New York: Oceana Publications, and Leiden: A. W. Sijthoff, 1977

Dower, Nigel (ed.), *Ethics and Environmental Responsibility*, Aldershot: Avebury, 1989

Ehrlich, Paul R., *The Population Bomb*, London: Pan Books/Ballantine, 1971

Ehrlich, Paul R. and Ehrlich, Anne H., *Population, Resources, Environment: Issues in Human Ecology*, San Francisco: W. H. Freeman, 2nd edn, 1972

Elliott, Robert and Gare, Arran (eds), *Environmental Philosophy*, St. Lucia: University of Queensland Press; Milton Keynes: Open University Press; University Park: Pennsylvania State University Press, 1983

Engels, F., *Dialectics of Nature*, New York: International Publishers, 1954

Engels, F., *Anti-Dühring*, Moscow, 1975

Fox, Warwick, *Approaching Deep Ecology: A Response to Richard Sylvan's Critique of Deep Ecology*, Hobart: University of Tasmania, 1986 (University of Tasmania Environmental Studies Occasional Paper 20)

Frey, R. G., *Interests and Rights: The Case Against Animals*, Oxford: Clarendon Press, 1980

Frey, R. G., *Rights, Killing and Suffering*, Oxford: Basil Blackwell, 1983

George, Susan, *How the Other Half Dies*, Harmondsworth: Penguin Books, 1976

Ginsberg, Morris, *The Idea of Progress: A Revaluation*, Westport, Conn.: Greenwood Press, 1953

Glacken, C. J., *Traces on the Rhodian Shore, Nature and Culture in Western Thought from Ancient Times to the End of the Eighteenth Century*, Berkeley, LA and London: University of California Press, 1967

Glover, Jonathan, *Causing Death and Saving Lives*, Harmondsworth: Penguin Books, 1977

Godlovitch, Stanley; Godlovitch, Roslind and Harris, John (eds), *Animals, Men and Morals, An Enquiry into the Maltreatment of Non-humans*, New York: Taplinger Publishing Co., 1972

Goodin, Robert, *Protecting the Vulnerable*, Chicago: University of Chicago Press, 1985

Goodman, David C. *et al.*, *Scientific Progress and Religious Dissent*, Milton Keynes: Open University Press, 1974

228 REFERENCES

Goodman, David C. *et al.*, *Towards a Mechanistic Philosophy*, Milton Keynes: Open University Press, 1974

Goodpaster, K. E. and Sayre, K. M. (eds), *Ethics and Problems of the 21st Century*, Notre Dame and London: Notre Dame University Press, 1979

Gorovitz, Samuel *et al.* (eds), *Moral Problems in Medicine*, Englewood Cliffs, NJ: Prentice-Hall, 1976

Gregorios, Paulos, *The Human Presence*, Geneva: World Council of Churches, 1978

Hacker, P. M. S. and Raz, J. (eds), *Law, Morality and Society*, Oxford: Clarendon Press, 1977

Hale, Sir Matthew, *The Primitive Origination of Mankind*, London, 1677

Hardin, Garrett, *The Limits of Altruism*, Bloomington: Indiana University Press, 1977

Hardin, Garrett and Baden, John (eds), *Managing the Commons*, San Francisco: W. H. Freeman, 1977

Hargrove, Eugene C. (ed.), *Religion and Environmental Crisis*, Athens: University of Georgia Press, 1986

Hargrove, Eugene C., *Foundations of Environmental Ethics*, Englewood Cliffs: Prentice Hall, 1989

Hart, Judith, *Aid and Liberation*, London: Gollancz, 1973

Heilbroner, Robert L., *An Inquiry into the Human Prospect*, London: Calder & Boyars, 1975

Hudson, Yeager and Peden, Creighton (eds), *Philosophical Essays on the Ideals of a Good Society*, Lewiston, NY: Edward Mellen Press, 1988

Hughes, J. Donald, *Ecology in Ancient Civilizations*, Albuquerque: University of New Mexico Press, 1975

Hume, C. W., *The Status of Animals in the Christian Religion*, London: Universities Federation for Animal Welfare, 1957

Hume, David, *The Philosophical Works*, ed. T. H. Green and T. H. Grose, London: Longmans, Green, 1974–75

Jaki, Stanley L., *Science and Creation*, Edinburgh: Scottish Academic Press, 1974

Johnson, Lawrence, *A Morally Deep World*, Canberra: Departments of Philosophy, Australian National University, 1987 (Preprint series in Environmental Philosophy, number 17)

Jonas, Hans, *The Imperative of Responsibility*, Chicago and London: University of Chicago Press, 1984

Kant, Immanuel, *Lectures on Ethics*, trans. Louis Infield, New York: Harper & Row, 1963

Karrer, Otto (ed.), *St Francis of Assisi, The Legends and the Lauds*, trans. N. Wydenbruck, London: Sheed & Ward, 1977

Kelly, J. N. D., *Early Christian Doctrines*, London: Adam & Charles Black, 4th edn, 1968

Kenny, Anthony (ed.), *Aquinas: A Collection of Critical Essays*, London: Macmillan Press, 1969

King-Farlow, John, *Self-Knowledge and Social Relations*, New York: Science History Publications, 1978

La Mettrie, J. Offray de, *Les Animaux plus que machines*, La Haye, 1751

Lecky, W. E. H., *History of European Morals from Augustus to Charlemagne* (2 Vols.) (1869), London: Longmans, Green, 1913

Lee, Keekok, *Social Philosophy and Ecological Scarcity*, London and New York: Routledge, 1989

Leopold, Aldo, *A Sand County Almanac and Sketches Here and There*, New York: Oxford University Press, 1949

Leopold, Aldo, *A Sand County Almanac with Other Essays on Conservation*, New York: Oxford University Press (2nd edn of the above), 1966

Linzey, Andrew, *Animal Rights: A Christian Assessment of Man's Treatment of Animals*, London: SCM Press, 1976

Linzey, Andrew, *Christianity and the Rights of Animals*, London: SPCK, 1987

Locke, John, *Works*, ed. T. Tegg *et al.* (10 Vols.), London, 1823

Lovejoy, A. O., *The Great Chain of Being*, Harvard: Harvard University Press, 1936

Lovelock, J. E., *Gaia, A New Look at Life on Earth*, Oxford: Oxford University Press, 1979

McCloskey, H. J., *Ecological Ethics and Politics*, Totowa, NJ: Rowman and Littlefield, 1983

McDonagh, Sean, *To Care for the Earth: A Call for a New Theology*, London: Geoffrey Chapman, 1986

MacLean, Douglas and Brown, Peter (eds), *Energy and the Future*, Totowa, NJ: Rowman and Littlefield, 1983

Mannison, Don; McRobbie, Michael and Routley, Richard (eds), *Environmental Philosophy*, Canberra: Australian National University, 1980

Margolis, Joseph, *Persons and Minds: The Prospects for Nonreductive Materialism*, Dordrecht, Boston and London: Reidel, 1977

Marx, Karl, *Selected Works* (2 Vols.), Moscow, 1949, and London, 1950

Marx, Karl, *Capital* (3 Vols.), ed. F. Engels, New York: International Publishers, 1967

Marx, Leo, *The Machine in the Garden: Technology and the Pastoral Ideal*, New York: Oxford University Press, 1964

Meadows, Donella H. et al., *The Limits to Growth*, a report for the Club of Rome's Project on the Predicament of Mankind (1972), London and Sydney: Pan Books, 1974

Mesarovic, Mihajlo D. and Pestel, Eduard, *Mankind at the Turning Point*, the second report to the Club of Rome, London: Hutchinson, 1975

Midgley, Mary, *Beast and Man: The Roots of Human Nature*, Hassocks: Harvester Press, 1979

Midgley, Mary, *Animals and Why They Matter*, Harmondsworth: Penguin, and Athens: University of Georgia Press, 1983

Midgley, Mary, *Evolution as a Religion*, London: Methuen, 1985

Milman, H. H., *The History of Christianity from the Birth of Christ to the Abolition of Paganism in the Roman Empire* (3 Vols.), London: John Murray, 1840

Mishan, Edward J., *The Costs of Economic Growth*, Harmondsworth: Penguin Books, 1969

Moltmann, Jurgen, *God and Creation*, London: SCM Press, 1985

Montefiore, Hugh (ed.), *Man and Nature*, London: Collins, 1975

Morris, Richard Knowles and Fox, Michael W. (eds), *On the Fifth Day, Animal Rights and Human Ethics*, Washington, DC: Acropolis Books, 1978

Morscher, Edgar and Stranzinger, Rudolf (eds), *Ethics: Foundations, Problems and Applications, Proceedings of the Fifth International Wittgenstein Symposium*, Vienna: Verlag Hölder-Pichler-Tempsky, 1981

Naess, Arne, *Ecology, Community and Lifestyle*, trans. David Rothenberg, Cambridge: Cambridge University Press, 1989

Narveson, Jan, *Morality and Utility*, Baltimore: John Hopkins Press, 1967

Nash, Roderick, *Wilderness and the American Mind*, New Haven: Yale University Press, 1967

Nelson, Leonard, *A System of Ethics*, trans. Norbert Guterman, New Haven: Yale University Press, 1956

Neuhaus, Richard, *In Defense of People, Ecology and the Seduction of Radicalism*, New York: Macmillan, and London: Collier-Macmillan, 1971

Nisbet, Robert, *The Social Philosophers*, London: Heinemann, 1974

Nisbet, Robert, *History of the Idea of Progress*, London: Heinemann, 1980

Norton, Bryan (ed.), *The Preservation of Species: The Value of Biological Diversity*, Princeton: Princeton University Press, 1986

Nozick, Robert, *Anarchy, State and Society*, Oxford: Blackwell, and New York: Basic Books, 1974

Ortner, Donald (ed.), *How Humans Adapt: A Biocultural Odyssey*, Washington, DC: Smithsonian Press, 1983

Parfit, Derek, *Reasons and Persons*, Oxford: Oxford University Press, 1984

Parsons, Howard L., *Marx and Engels on Ecology*, Westport, Conn., and London: Greenwood Press, 1977

Partridge, Ernest (ed.), *Responsibilities to Future Generations*, New York: Prometheus Books, 1981

Passmore, John, *The Perfectibility of Man [PM]*. London: Duckworth, 1970

Passmore, John, *Man's Responsibility for Nature [MRN]*, London: Duckworth, 1974; 2nd edn, 1980

Peacocke, A. R., *Creation and the World of Science*, Oxford: Oxford University Press, 1979

Pearce, David *et al.*, *Blueprint for a Green Economy*, London: Earthscan Publications, 1989

Pepper, David, *The Roots of Modern Environmentalism*, London, Sydney and Dover, NH: Croom Helm, 1984

Pirages, Dennis C. and Ehrlich, Paul R., *Ark II: Social Response to Environmental Imperatives*, San Francisco: W. H. Freeman, 1974

Pirages, Dennis Clark (ed.), *The Sustainable Society*, New York and London: Praeger Publishers, 1977

Price, Richard, *A Free Discussion of Materialism and Philosophical Necessity in a Correspondence between Dr Price and Dr Priestley, Etc.*, London, 1778

Price, Richard, *Sermons*, London, *c.* 1790

Priestley, Joseph, *An Essay on the First Principles of Government and on Political, Civil and Religious Liberty*, 2nd edn, London, 1771

Purver, Margery, *The Royal Society: Concept and Creation*, London: Routledge & Kegan Paul, 1967

Rachels, James, *Created from Animals*, Oxford and New York: Oxford University Press, 1990

Rawls, John, *A Theory of Justice*, London, Oxford and New York: Oxford University Press, 1972

Ray, John, *The Wisdom of God Manifested in the Works of Creation*, 11th edn, London, 1743

Regan, Tom (ed.), *Matters of Life and Death*, Philadelphia: Temple University Press, 1980

Regan, Tom, *The Case for Animal Rights*, London: Rutledge & Kegan Paul, 1983

Regan, Tom (ed.), *Earthbound: New Introductory Essays in Environmental Ethics*, Philadelphia: Temple University Press, 1984

Regan, Tom and Singer, Peter (eds), *Animal Rights and Human Obligations*, Englewood Cliffs, NJ: Prentice-Hall, 1976

Richardson, Alan (ed.), *A Theological Wordbook of the Bible*, London: SCM Press, 1957

Rivers, Patrick, *Living Better on Less*, London: Turnstone Books, 1977

Robinson, J. A. T., *The Body*, London: SCM Press, 1952

Rolston, Holmes, III, *Philosophy Gone Wild: Essays in Environmental Ethics*, Buffalo: Prometheus Books, 1986

Rolston, Holmes, III, *Environmental Ethics: Duties to and Values in the Natural World*, Philadelphia: Temple University Press, 1988

Routley, Richard and Routley, Val, *The Fight for the Forests*, Canberra: Australian National University Press, 1974

Royal Institute of Philosophy (ed.), *The Proper Study*, London and Basingstoke: Macmillan Press, 1971

Royal Institute of Philosophy (ed.), *Nature and Conduct*, London and Basingstoke: Macmillan Press, 1975

Sagoff, Mark, *The Economy of the Earth*, Cambridge: Cambridge University Press, 1988

Schmidt, Alfred, *The Concept of Nature in Marx*, New York: Humanities Press, 1972

Schweitzer, Albert, *Civilisation and Ethics*, trans. C. T. Campion, London: Adam & Charles Black, 3rd edn, 1946

Shrader-Frechette, K. S., *Nuclear Power and Public Policy*, Dordrecht, Boston and London: Reidel, 1980

Sikora, R. I. and Barry, Brian (eds), *Obligations to Future Generations*, Philadelphia: Temple University Press, 1978

Singer, Peter, *Animal Liberation, A New Ethic for Our Treatment of Animals*, London: Jonathan Cape, 1976

Singer, Peter, *Practical Ethics*, Cambridge: Cambridge University Press, 1979

Singer, Peter, *The Expanding Circle: Ethics and Sociobiology*, Oxford: Clarendon Press, 1981

Skolimowski, Henryk, *Eco-Philosophy*, Boston and London: Marion Boyars, 1981

Society and the Environment: a Soviet View, (ed. anon.), Moscow: Progress Publishers, 1977

Spinoza, Baruch, *Ethics*, trans. Andrew Boyle, London: Dent, Everyman's Library, 1910

Spring, David and Spring, Eileen (eds), *Ecology and Religion in History*, New York, Evanston, San Francisco and London: Harper & Row, 1974

Stone, Christopher, *Should Trees Have Standing?*, Los Altos, Cal.: William Kaufman, 1974

Stone, Christopher, *Earth and Other Ethics: The Case for Moral Pluralism*, New York: Harper & Row, 1988

Stone, Lawrence, *The Family, Sex and Marriage in England, 1500–1800*, London: Weidenfeld & Nicolson, 1977

Sumner, Wayne, *The Moral Foundation of Rights*, Oxford: Oxford University Press, 1987

Taylor, Paul, *Respect for Nature: A Theory of Environmental Ethics*, Princeton: Princeton University Press, 1986

Thomas, Keith, *Man and the Natural World: A History of the Modern Sensibility*, New York: Pantheon, 1983

Turner, E. S., *All Heaven in a Rage*, London: Michael Joseph, 1964

United Nations, *Resolutions and Decisions Adopted by the General Assembly During Its 37th Session*, New York: United Nations, 1983

Warnock, Geoffrey, *The Object of Morality*, New York: Methuen Press, 1971

Wasserstrom, Richard A. (ed.), *Today's Moral Problems* 2nd edn, New York: Macmillan Publishing Co., and London: Collier-Macmillan, 1979

Wenz, Peter, *Environmental Justice*, Albany: State University of New York Press, 1988

Westermann, Claus, *Creation*, London: SPCK, 1974

Wheale, Peter and McNally, Ruth (eds), *The Biorevolution*, London and Winchester, Mass.: Pluto Press, 1990

White, Lynn, Jnr, *Medieval Technology and Social Change*, Oxford: Clarendon Press, 1962

White, T. H. (trans. and ed.), *The Book of Beasts*, London: Jonathan Cape, 1954

Whitehead, A. N., *Science and the Modern World*, Cambridge: Cambridge University Press, 1926

Wiles, Maurice and Santer, Mark (eds), *Documents in Early Christian Thought*, Cambridge: Cambridge University Press, 1975

Williams, Bernard and Smart, J. J. C., *Utilitarianism, For and Against,* London
   and New York: Cambridge University Press, 1973
World Commission on Environment and Development, *Our Common Future,*
   Oxford and New York: Oxford University Press, 1987
World Conservation Strategy, (ed. anon.), New York: International Union for
   Conservation of Nature and Natural Resources, United Nations Environ-
   mental Programme and World Wildlife Fund, 1980

Index

Editors who are not referred to also as authors are omitted here, as are works whose titles are not presented in the main text. Bold type in subject entries indicates references of greatest importance.

PRAISE FOR THE BOOKS
OF GREGORY A. FREEMAN

The Gathering Wind

"An intense account of the last days and moments aboard the sailing ship *Bounty*. . . . Written almost minute by minute in places, Freeman's rendering of this horrific storm and the courage of the men and women aboard the *Bounty* and in the Coast Guard will place readers on edge until the last plane lands safely back at base . . . an incredible story of courage, endurance, and luck."
                                                                      —*Kirkus Reviews*

"Journalist and nonfiction author Gregory A. Freeman turns this story of folly and Coast Guard courage into a gripping thriller and object lesson. . . . *The Gathering Wind* reads as a detailed, incisive, and fair job of reporting. . . . The story is harrowing, gripping, and told with admirable clarity. . . . Take Dramamine and set sail with this chilling and cautionary tale."
                                                                      —New York Journal of Books

"Freeman is a fine nonfiction writer, with a sharp analytical eye, who always asks the important questions . . . an intelligent, even-keeled, and dramatic look at a much-publicized maritime disaster."
                                                                      —*Booklist*

The Forgotten 500

"Told in riveting detail for the first time, *The Forgotten 500* is a tale of unsung heroes who went above and beyond."
    —James Bradley, *New York Times* Bestselling Author of *Flags of Our Fathers*

continued . . .

ALSO BY GREGORY A. FREEMAN

The Last Mission of the Wham Bam Boys:
Courage, Tragedy, and Justice in World War II

Troubled Water: Race, Mutiny, and Bravery on the USS Kitty Hawk

Fixing Hell: An Army Psychologist Confronts Abu Ghraib
(with Col. [Ret.] Larry C. James, PhD)

The Forgotten 500: The Untold Story of the Men Who Risked All for
the Greatest Rescue Mission of World War II

Sailors to the End: The Deadly Fire on the USS Forrestal *and*
the Heroes Who Fought It

Lay This Body Down: The 1921 Murders of Eleven Plantation Slaves

THE GATHERING WIND

HURRICANE SANDY, THE SAILING SHIP *BOUNTY*, AND A COURAGEOUS RESCUE AT SEA

GREGORY A. FREEMAN

New American Library

NEW AMERICAN LIBRARY
Published by the Penguin Group
Penguin Group (USA) LLC, 375 Hudson Street,
New York, New York 10014

USA | Canada | UK | Ireland | Australia | New Zealand | India | South Africa | China
penguin.com
A Penguin Random House Company

Published by New American Library, a division of Penguin Group (USA) LLC. Previously published in a New American Library hardcover edition.

First New American Library Trade Paperback Printing, October 2014

REGISTERED TRADEMARK—MARCA REGISTRADA

NEW AMERICAN LIBRARY TRADE PAPERBACK ISBN: 978-0-451-46577-1

THE LIBRARY OF CONGRESS HAS CATALOGUED THE HARDCOVER EDITION OF THIS TITLE AS FOLLOWS:
Freeman, Gregory A.
Hurricane Sandy, the sailing ship *Bounty*, and a courageous rescue at sea/Gregory A. Freeman.
p. cm.
Includes bibliographical references.
ISBN 978-0-451-46576-4
1. Bounty (Ship: 1960) 2. Shipwrecks—Atlantic Ocean. 3. Search and rescue operations—
Atlantic Ocean. 4. United States. Coast Guard—Search and rescue operations—Atlantic Ocean.
5. Hurricane Sandy, 2012. I. Title.
G530.B687F74 2013
910.9163'48—dc23   2013025288

Printed in the United States of America
1   3   5   7   9   10   8   6   4   2

Set in Adobe Garamond
Designed by Patrice Sheridan

To Robin Walbridge and Claudene Christian

"We chase hurricanes."

—*BOUNTY* CAPTAIN ROBIN WALBRIDGE, AUGUST 2012

"According to Captain Robin Walbridge, *Bounty* has no boundaries. As her captain, he is well-known for his ability and desire to take *Bounty* to places that no ship has gone before."

—THE FIRST LINES OF WALBRIDGE'S BIOGRAPHY ON THE *BOUNTY*'S WEB SITE

CONTENTS

CONTENTS

CONTENTS

Principal Characters

(Ages at the time of the *Bounty*'s sinking)

BOUNTY

Robin Walbridge, 63, captain
Robert Hansen, 58, owner
John Svendsen, 41, chief mate
Matthew Sanders, 37, second mate
Daniel Cleveland, 25, third mate
Laura Groves, 28, bosun
Christopher Barksdale, 56, engineer
Adam Prokosh, 27, able seaman
Douglas Faunt, 66, deckhand and radio officer
Claudene Christian, 42, deckhand
Jessica Hewitt, 25, deckhand
John Jones, 29, deckhand
Drew Salapatek, 29, deckhand
Joshua Scornavacchi, 25, deckhand
Anna Sprague, 20, deckhand
Mark Warner, 33, deckhand
Jessica Black, 34, cook

COAST GUARD

Lt. Wes McIntosh, 33, pilot of the first Coast Guard plane on the scene

Lt. Mike Myers, 36, copilot of the first Coast Guard plane

Lt. Commander Peyton Russell, 39, pilot of the second Coast Guard plane to arrive

Lt. Aaron Cmiel, 28, copilot of the second Coast Guard plane

Lt. Commander Steve Cerveny, 43, pilot of the first Jayhawk helicopter

Lt. Jane Peña, 31, copilot of the first Jayhawk

Aviation Maintenance Technician 3rd Class Michael Lufkin, 25, flight mechanic on the Jayhawk piloted by Cerveny and Peña

Aviation Survival Technician 2nd Class Randy Haba, 33, rescue swimmer on Cerveny and Peña's Jayhawk

Lt. Steve Bonn, 44, pilot of the second Jayhawk helicopter rescuing survivors

Lt. Jenny Fields, 26, copilot of the second Jayhawk

Aviation Maintenance Technician 1st Class Neil Moulder, 38, flight mechanic on Bonn and Fields's Jayhawk

Aviation Survival Technician 3rd Class Daniel Todd, 27, rescue swimmer on Bonn and Fields's Jayhawk

Aviation Survival Technician 2nd Class Casey Hanchette, 29, rescue swimmer on the third Jayhawk, which recovered Christian

Aviation Maintenance Technician 1st Class Ryan Parker, 34, flight mechanic on the third Jayhawk, the one that recovered Christian

Commander Kevin Carroll, 41, U.S. Coast Guard lead investigator

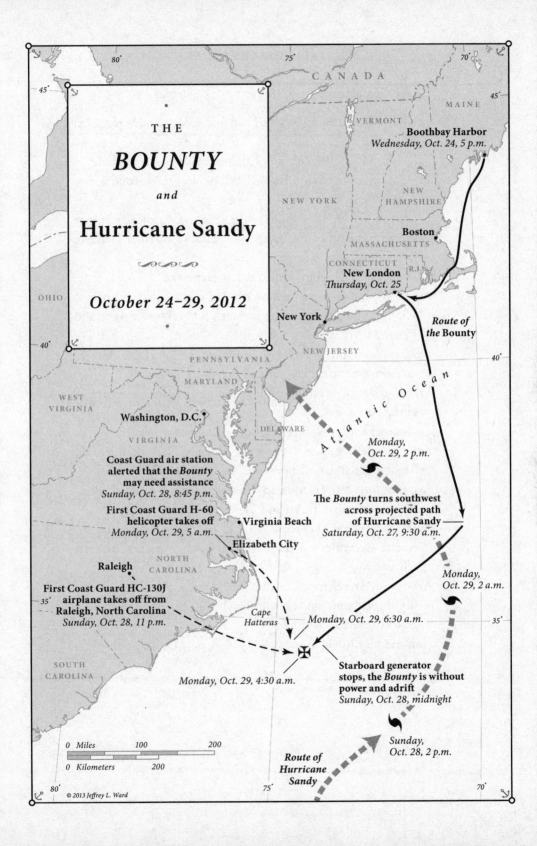

THE
BOUNTY
and
Hurricane Sandy

October 24–29, 2012

CANADA

MAINE

VERMONT

Boothbay Harbor
Wednesday, Oct. 24, 5 p.m.

NEW YORK

NEW
HAMPSHIRE

Boston
MASSACHUSETTS

CONNECTICUT
New London
Thursday, Oct. 25

R.I.

New York

*Route of
the Bounty*

OHIO

PENNSYLVANIA

NEW JERSEY

WEST
VIRGINIA

MARYLAND

DELAWARE

Atlantic Ocean

Washington, D.C.

VIRGINIA

**Coast Guard air station
alerted that the *Bounty*
may need assistance**
Sunday, Oct. 28, 8:45 p.m.

**First Coast Guard H-60
helicopter takes off**
Monday, Oct. 29, 5 a.m.

Virginia Beach

Elizabeth City

Raleigh

NORTH
CAROLINA

**First Coast Guard HC-130J
airplane takes off from
Raleigh, North Carolina**
Sunday, Oct. 28, 11 p.m.

*Cape
Hatteras*

SOUTH
CAROLINA

Monday, Oct. 29, 4:30 a.m.

*Monday,
Oct. 29, 2 p.m.*

**The *Bounty* turns southwest
across projected path
of Hurricane Sandy**
Saturday, Oct. 27, 9:30 a.m.

*Monday,
Oct. 29, 2 a.m.*

Monday, Oct. 29, 6:30 a.m.

**Starboard generator
stops, the *Bounty* is without
power and adrift**
Sunday, Oct. 28, midnight

*Sunday,
Oct. 28, 2 p.m.*

*Route of
Hurricane
Sandy*

0 Miles 100 200
0 Kilometers 200

© 2013 Jeffrey L. Ward

INTRODUCTION

IN OCTOBER 2012 a famed tall sailing ship and its crew were on a collision course with Superstorm Sandy, the largest hurricane ever recorded in the Atlantic Ocean, the storm that would go on to wreak devastation on the East Coast. In a remote Coast Guard station, brave men and women were about to be called to action. This is their story.

The accounts of individual crew members on the *Bounty* and of the Coast Guard rescuers are woven together from personal interviews with the author and their testimony at the U.S. Coast Guard hearings. All dialogue and internal thoughts portrayed in the story are based on what those people reported saying, hearing, or thinking at the time.

The precise sequence of some events in the last few days of the *Bounty*'s trip are difficult to know with certainty. All of the ship's written logs were lost in the sinking, and the memories of *Bounty* crew members differ on some details regarding the time line—especially on Saturday and Sunday, when the crisis escalated quickly. During their sworn testimony before the Coast Guard panel investigating the incident, many of the *Bounty* crew struggled to remember even what day certain events occurred; some were off by several days when relating known events. The author used his best judgment when testimony and other information conflicted.

A note regarding the name of the ship: The original ship was the

1

HMS *Bounty*, because it was a British navy vessel and the HMS designates His (or Her) Majesty's Ship. The ship that sank October 29, 2012, was an American-flagged civilian vessel and thus named *Bounty*, not HMS *Bounty*. But because it was a replica of the original ship and carried forth the history of that British vessel, it was commonly known as HMS *Bounty*.

CHAPTER 1

SURVIVORS

THIRD MATE DANIEL Cleveland was grateful to find a wooden grating from the *Bounty*'s deck, because he could hold on to that and use it to help him get away from the ship that he loved but that was now trying to kill him. The tall sailing ship, a romantic throwback to a bygone time and featured in big-screen pirate movies, was awash in the stormy sea off of North Carolina, a victim of hubris and Hurricane Sandy.

The ship was rhythmically rolling on its side at 4:30 a.m. on October 29, 2012, slamming its 115-foot mainmast and other rigging into the churning waters, where crew members were floating in their red survival suits, all of them desperately flailing and trying to swim away from the wreckage. With astonishing force the ship would right itself and then come slamming back down into the ocean, the masts and spars and all the miles of rigging slapping into the sea with the power of falling telephone poles. The rigging seemed to chase crew members as they tried to get away, the ropes and ropes and more ropes grabbing them and dragging them underwater. Everything seemed to be trying to kill Cleveland in different ways. As he tried to avoid the masts coming down on either side of him, lines were wrapping around him and pulling him beneath the surface. The wind and seas were forcing salt water down his throat with every breath. It seemed like it would never stop.

3

Cleveland managed to heave himself onto the floating grate so that his chest was resting on it; then he kicked his feet, directing the wooden grate away from the *Bounty* as he called out for his girlfriend, bosun Laura Groves. He had last seen her on the deck of the *Bounty* as they helped the other crew members prepare to abandon ship in an orderly fashion, and then . . . well, Cleveland wasn't sure yet what had happened. Suddenly they were all in the water and struggling for their lives.

"Laura! Laura! Where are you, Laura?" Cleveland shouted, his bearded face the only thing showing out of the neoprene survival outfit they called a Gumby suit. The hundred-mile-per-hour hurricane winds and the churning ocean made it hard to hear anything. "Laura! I'm over here! Laura!"

It was dark with just the moonlight, and the salt spray burned his eyes so much he had to resist the instinct to clamp them shut, willfully keeping them open to look for Laura. He could see other red Gumby suits in the water, but he couldn't tell which ones had people in them and which ones were empty. Was Laura in one of them? Was she okay? Had she been injured when the *Bounty* rolled? *God, where is she?* Cleveland thought as he floated along in the middle of a hurricane. *I have to find Laura.*

The wind-driven rain cut into his face like a thousand needles. The air was thick with sea spray, making every breath a combination of air and salt water. The waves were thrashing Cleveland, and it was all he could do to hang on to the wooden grating, but he kept yelling for the woman he loved. "Laura! Where are you?" It was like a dark dream, a nightmare, and all he could do was shout her name.

Finally—and at first he thought he was imagining it over the sounds of the wind and sea—he heard her calling back to him.

"Dan! I'm here!"

He couldn't believe it, but then he could see Laura nearby, bobbing up and down with the waves, nothing but her beautiful face showing in the red suit. It was a miracle that they would find each other in the ocean after being tossed off the *Bounty*. But they did. Cleveland kicked as hard as he could and steered his float closer to Laura, and soon she was able to grab on. It was joyful. They embraced clumsily in their Gumby suits.

As soon as they were together, Cleveland's mind reset and he was again a mariner with a job to do, getting right back to the task at hand. Both of them clinging to the wooden grate, they saw other red suits that seemed to be occupied. After a short while and some maneuvering of their improvised raft, they hooked up with engineer Chris Barksdale and deckhands Drew Salapatek and Jessica Hewitt. Like Cleveland and Groves, Salapatek and Hewitt were in a relationship, and they were grateful to finally find each other in the tempest. They had last seen each other on the sharply listing deck of the *Bounty*, huddled close and holding each other tightly, waiting for the order to abandon ship.

Soon able seaman Adam Prokosh, seriously injured even before the *Bounty* capsized, hooked onto the chain, glad to know that there were other survivors out there with him.

"We need to find to find a life raft," Cleveland shouted over the wind, swallowing a mouthful of salty water. "A life raft! We have to find one!"

Hewitt found Cleveland's voice to be calming after her own struggle to get away from the *Bounty*. The image of the *Bounty*'s masts and rigging coming down on chief mate John Svendsen was still vivid, and she wondered whether he'd survived. But Cleveland's firm, authoritative voice, without a hint of fear, and having her boyfriend nearby were bringing her peace again.

They floated in the rising and pounding seas for what seemed a long time, and then a white life raft canister, a bit larger than a beer keg but even more welcome, floated by. Nearly blind after losing his glasses, his eyes stinging from salt water, Barksdale nevertheless was able to grab a trailing lanyard and hold on to it, but Cleveland and Groves suggested they not inflate it right away. "It's charged, and we don't want it blowing up right on top of us!" Cleveland yelled. "Let it drift some and then open it!"

Barksdale held on to the line, known to sailors as a painter, and let it unspool from the canister until the barrel was far enough away and he felt some resistance, which meant the hundred-foot painter was all out. Then he, Cleveland, and Groves pulled with all their might, working hard in the Gumby suits and rolling seas to do what takes only a sharp tug in better conditions. The white canister exploded and the orange life raft inside instantly began to unfold, the compressed gas filling it and

creating a round refuge complete with a raised canopy in about thirty seconds.

The raft became their singular focus, the bright red-orange canopy standing out in the dark night. Letting go of the wooden grate, they formed a chain by hooking one person's feet under the armpits of the next person—a technique taught in water survival school. The *Bounty* survivors swam and thrashed their way closer to the raft, but it was taking forever. Sometimes they couldn't tell whether they were moving toward the raft or away from it. They tried to grasp the painter line but found that their big, thick Gumby fingers were almost useless on the thin rope. It was like trying pick up a piece of thread with puffy-fingered gloves.

When they reached the raft, it was maddeningly elusive even when it was right in front of their faces. The slick, wet rubber walls of the raft gave no handhold, and the lines draping off the perimeter—intended for people to grab onto—were as hard to grasp as the painter. The crew kept pawing at the lines as they were tossed violently in the rolling sea, trying to get a handhold to no avail, until Cleveland was desperate enough—and pissed off enough—to lunge at the raft and snatch one of the lines in his teeth. Pulling the line up and away from the raft, he got his fat neoprene fingers under the loop and held on to the raft.

"Bite it!" Cleveland shouted above the noise of the water and wind. "Use your teeth! Bite the line so you can grab it!"

Soon everyone was doing the same thing, lunging forward to grab lines in their mouths and then getting their hands on them.

Once they had hold of the raft, they thought the worst of their ordeal was over. All they had to do was climb in and they would have a safe refuge until the Coast Guard came. Cleveland and Groves stayed together as several of them moved toward the opening in the canopy that covered the entire raft like a tent, where a short rope ladder hung down into the water. Cleveland grabbed the top of the ladder and started moving her feet closer, kicking underwater to find the bottom rungs, but she made contact with nothing. After feeling around with one hand underwater, she realized that the ladder was ridiculously short, requiring her to pull one knee practically up under her chin to get her foot on the bottom

rung and give her leverage to hoist herself out of the water. With the bloated feet of her survival suit, each one holding a couple gallons of seawater, pulling one foot up that high was nearly impossible. But Groves kept trying. She managed to get a foot in the ladder, but then she didn't have the strength to hoist herself up, even with Cleveland and the others trying to push her.

"Go! Come on, Laura! You can do it!" her boyfriend shouted. It was exhausting, and all of them were already bone-tired when they hit the water. And it was *so* frustrating. She felt like crying. She just wanted to get out of the water and into the damn life raft. Why couldn't she get up in the raft? She was a strong woman. She should be able to do this. If she couldn't manage this, some of the others surely wouldn't be able.

She had to stop and rest, holding on to the raft as the waves surged and the winds of Hurricane Sandy blew. She lay there, holding her breath every time she could see a wave about to crash on her. They were all just holding on. The raft bounced around, slapping them in the heads and threatening to wrench itself away from them with sudden gusts of wind and surges of the sea, but the *Bounty* crew was determined to hold on. They bobbed in the ocean, trying to gain strength, and then someone else would try to get in the raft.

Groves knew from her safety training that the raft should have an inflated boarding ramp on the other side, opposite the ladder. It should be easier to use, but Groves looked at how far she would have to go around the raft and how many of the small handhold ropes she would have to grab onto as she made her way. There were at least twenty. She would have to bite each one, shove her gloved hand under it, move on to the next, bite it, and so on. She was so tired that she didn't think she could do it.

They rested and held on. Then there was another group effort, another frustrating attempt to do something that should be so simple, and another failure. They were all so demoralized, so dejected. *Why can't we do this?* Their only option was to hold on longer.

A man this time. Maybe he'd be strong enough to pull himself in— more upper-body strength. There were more struggles from the exhausted crew. Another failure.

Resting again in the water. Bobbing on the surface. Salt water in

their eyes, forced up their noses and down their throats by the never-ending waves. Clinging to the raft. Their arms becoming numb. Trying not to doze off. *I can't fall asleep. Can't let go.*

Cleveland had to try. They couldn't stay out there, and his innate leadership sense came to the fore. He had to get these people in the raft. He made his way to the ladder, holding on to the raft and the other Gumby suits to get there, and summoned all his strength to put his foot in the ladder rung and pull himself up. *Fuck!* he thought. *It's like I weigh five hundred pounds.*

Salapatek was trying to push him up, gaining no leverage in the water and not able to help much. The thirty-foot waves ripped Cleveland off the ladder just as he thought he might be moving up, making him grasp madly for the raft and the other survivors lest he be ripped away and on his own. After a long series of trial and error, Cleveland got his foot in the lowest rung of the ladder—a feat in itself—and hung on firmly. Then Salapatek put a knee on Cleveland's raised thigh and used that as a fulcrum to push against as he also grabbed the raft and pulled himself up. With other crew members pushing up against Salapatek as much as they could manage, he was lifted out of the water and flopped over the rim of the raft. Finally someone was inside. Cleveland knew that would make all the difference.

It had taken forty-five minutes to get the first person in the raft.

The effort had sapped the strength from Salapatek, Cleveland, and everyone else. They had to rest a few minutes before trying to get anyone else inside. Salapatek lay against the taut rubber of the raft, breathing heavily and coughing from the seawater he'd ingested, and the others bobbed in the water outside. Then Salapatek helped Cleveland get in, pulling him up as Cleveland pushed down on one leg against the ladder. The third mate flopped into the raft with a "Hell, yeah!" and clasped hands with Salapatek.

The two men helped Groves into the raft, pretty much just grabbing her arms and heaving her into it like a fish; then they did the same with everyone else until only Prokosh was left in the water. Prokosh was in a lot of pain from his cracked vertebrae, broken ribs, and other injuries, and he didn't relish the idea of being hauled in like that.

"Just let me stay here," he said. "I'll be okay. Just leave me here."

The others wouldn't leave him in the water. They soon managed to pull him inside, with Prokosh groaning and doing his best not to scream. He had thought the pain was bad while he was in the water, trying to get away from the *Bounty* and into the life raft, but once he was in and lying back, trying to catch his breath and calm down, he realized that the adrenaline must have been masking a lot of pain, because it was wearing off, and the pain was coming at him now like nothing he had ever experienced.

The *Bounty* crew members were exhausted and relieved, but they had no idea what had happened to the other people, their friends on the ship. There were only five of them in the raft. That left nine more crew members out there.

Cleveland and Groves looked out the entrance of the raft and saw their ship silhouetted against the light of the moon, looking both majestic and sad as it rocked back and forth in the heavy surf and wind, its masts and rigging rolling over into the water in rhythm with the waves. They realized that they were witnessing something rarely seen anymore, something that few people live to tell about. They were watching a tall sailing ship sink at sea. They were watching the last moments of the *Bounty*.

Chapter 2

TALL SHIPS

TALL SAILING SHIPS with soaring masts and billowing canvas filled the seas and harbors of the world until the mid-nineteenth century, when steam power overtook wind as the most efficient and fastest way to move goods and people across the oceans. Even then, ship captains and owners saw that there was no substitute for the seafaring skills learned by fearless young men and women who climbed more than a hundred feet up the rigging of a wooden mast, with its acres of canvas buffeted by the wind; their woodworking and mechanical knowledge; or their navigational skills honed by the challenge of keeping the wind at their backs and the sails full.

All these years later, when most sailing ships have become training vessels intended to keep old-world marine skills alive or used as movie props or tourist attractions, they still command attention and adoration from many. The sight of a tall sailing ship—a schooner, brigantine, brig, barque, or full-rigged ship—sailing into harbor instantly conjures romantic notions of a time when ships were more than a curiosity, a time when they represented the height of commercial transportation and man's willingness to challenge the seas in wooden-hulled boats, bringing only the captain's and crew's skills to bear against the might of the ocean.

Tall ships never disappeared entirely, but they were scarce for many

years and largely out of the public eye until the 1976 American bicentennial celebration, which pulled together an international fleet of tall-
masted sailing ships that paraded first in New York City on the Fourth
of July and then in Boston about a week later. The beautiful, majestic
ships docked and allowed the general public to board in both cities, and
the sight of them gathered together created unforgettable imagery for the
celebration. The experience reignited a love in Americans for tall ships
and a greater public interest in sailing on these throwbacks to centuries
past.

There are now more than 250 vessels registered worldwide as members of Tall Ships America, the professional body that organizes races and
other events as well as promoting safety standards and providing over-
sight for the many ships whose role is primarily sea training. Those ships,
the great majority of the tall ships around the world, take on groups of
young people eager to learn the traditional ways of sailing. They spend
months climbing the rigging to set sails, learning how to navigate by the
stars. Even a few months on a sailing ship in the middle of the ocean can
be a life-changing experience.

The U.S. Navy maintains a tall ship, the USS *Constitution*, a
204-foot-long, wooden-hulled, three-masted heavy frigate launched in
1797. Nicknamed "Old Ironsides" after defeating five British warships in
the War of 1812, the *Constitution* is still a fully commissioned Navy ship
and is used for sail training, education, and ceremonial duties. The U.S.
Coast Guard also has its own tall sailing ship, the USCGC *Eagle*, a 295-
foot barque launched in 1936 and used as a training cutter for future
Coast Guard officers. Cadets from the United States Coast Guard Academy and candidates from the Officer Candidate School train on the
Eagle each summer for periods ranging from a week to two months,
learning the fundamentals of sailing and seamanship. Unlike the *Bounty*,
the *Eagle* has a steel hull.

The *Bounty* was one of the best-known vessels in the tall ship community and always garnered attention when arriving in port, but the ship
and its crew were not typical. Unlike most other tall ships, the *Bounty*
did not operate as a sailing school for young people or take on paying
passengers of any type. It was not allowed to, because the ship did not

meet Coast Guard requirements for safety and seaworthiness. Instead, the *Bounty* was certified as a "moored attraction vessel," which meant it could receive visitors only when moored to a dock. At sea, only crew was allowed on board.

The *Bounty* was a 180-foot-long wooden-hulled ship, traditionally rigged with yardarms on all three masts. The mainmast was 115 feet high, and the ship used eighteen sails with ten thousand square feet of canvas. There were five miles of rigging on the ship. Weighing 412 tons, the *Bounty* displaced 558 tons of seawater. The top deck, also known as the weather deck, was configured similarly to most sailing ships, with the wheel toward the stern and a small enclosed compartment known as the navigation shack, or "nav shack," just forward of that to house the navigation and communication equipment. Two majestic lanterns perched on the corners of the stern. The deck immediately below had the berthing quarters and some workspaces; it was known as the "tween deck" because it was between the others. Below that, in the belly of the ship, were the engine room and bilge, the true bottom of the ship, where any incoming water accumulated. True to its origin, the ship carried four cannons capable of shooting four-pound balls, plus swivel guns. The *Bounty* was beautiful, an homage to a time past, and as authentically eighteenth-century as a ship could be in the twenty-first.

Built from scratch in 1960 at the Smith and Rhuland shipyard in Lunenburg, Nova Scotia, for the 1962 movie *Mutiny on the Bounty*, starring a young, rakish Marlon Brando as Lt. Fletcher Christian, the *Bounty* was a detailed reproduction of the original HMS *Bounty*, the British Royal Navy ship on which the real Christian led a legendary mutiny on April 28, 1789. The original HMS *Bounty* was a 250-ton armed cargo ship that left England in 1787 with a crew of forty-six under the command of Lt. William Bligh, headed for Tahiti and the West Indies.

The subsequent mutiny on the ship has prompted more than twenty-five hundred books, five feature films, and many television documentaries. The story of the mutiny has as many versions as vehicles for telling it, with some portraying Christian as the villain and some arguing that he did the right thing in seizing the ship from a misguided or incompetent Bligh. The original *Bounty* started out as a collier, or coal cargo ship,

built in 1784 and named *Bethia* after the designer's wife. Later bought by the Royal Navy and renamed *Bounty*, the ship came under the command of the thirty-two-year-old Bligh, who had made a name for himself as sailing master of the HMS *Resolution* during the final voyage of famed explorer James Cook. The Royal Navy had purchased the *Bounty* in order to conduct an agricultural experiment. The ship was to sail to Tahiti—known as Otaheite at the time—and procure breadfruit plants, then deliver them to the West Indies in hopes that they could become a cheap food source for slaves. As part of the mission, the captain's cabin was converted to a nursery for the plants, and Bligh was relegated to a small cabin next to the rest of the crew.

The original *Bounty* sailed for Tahiti on December 23, 1787, and after struggling with bad weather reached Tahiti on October 26, 1788. The crew proceeded with their mission and collected more than a thousand breadfruit plants, but then found that they would have to wait five months for them to mature enough that they could survive the ship transport. To that end, Bligh allowed the crew to move ashore and tend the plants. Over the next months, the tropical life of Tahiti agreed mightily with the English crew, and many of them formed relationships with the local women. The island life made the crew of the *Bounty* less willing to take instruction from Bligh, and resistant to any discipline he tried to instill, while the captain grew increasingly outraged at what he saw as laziness and disrespect. Christian, in particular, felt that he was being targeted by Bligh, possibly to make an example of the officer in hopes that the rest of the crew would be intimidated. As master's mate—the captain's right-hand man on a Royal Navy ship—Christian grew increasingly resentful of what he saw as intentional humiliation by Bligh in front of the crew and the local islanders. Bligh relied more and more on the use of flogging to punish crew members for real or imagined crimes, such as theft by the Tahitians, even though he had almost never flogged a crew member on the ten-month voyage to the island.

Tensions were high as the date of departure grew near, and the crew knew that not only were they leaving their island paradise, but they also were heading out for months of arduous and dangerous sailing. The

breadfruit finally ready for the voyage, Bligh, Christian, and their crew left Tahiti on April fifth. The conflicts continued between Bligh and Christian, and the crew was not doing well in their efforts to return to a life at sea. It was only twenty-three days into the voyage when Christian led a mutiny, he and some of the other crew barging into Bligh's cabin one night and seizing control. Christian was nearly out of his mind by that point, screaming to Bligh, "I am in hell! I am in hell!"

Eighteen of the crew joined Christian in the mutiny, twenty-two remained loyal to their captain, and two were neutral. No blood was shed, but the mutineers ordered Bligh into the ship's small boat along with four of his loyal crew. Another thirteen loyal crew joined them in the twenty-three-foot boat, choosing to take their chances at sea rather than be found on board a Royal Navy ship that had been the scene of mutiny. The captain and his fellow castoffs rowed their boat to the nearby island of Tofua, where they hoped to at least find food and water to add to the slim provisions provided by Christian. When they landed their boat, the local islanders stoned one of the crewmen to death. Bligh and his crew took their boat back to sea.

They spent forty-seven days in the open boat before arriving at Timor in the Dutch East Indies, a voyage that Bligh estimated as 3,618 nautical miles. Five crewmen died soon after landing. Bligh and his remaining crew returned to Britain in the coming months, and he reported the mutiny on March 15, 1790. It had been more than two years since he left on his voyage to Tahiti.

Christian and the other mutineers tried at first to settle on the nearby island of Tubuai, but found themselves unwanted by the locals, so they soon returned to Tahiti. Christian married the daughter of one of the local chiefs and, before leaving again, released sixteen crewmen. The remaining mutineers, along with six Tahitian men and eleven Tahitian women, then sailed the *Bounty* to the Pitcairn Islands, where they stripped the ship of everything useful before setting it on fire so that they could never leave.

On March 23, 1791, the Royal Navy ship *Pandora* arrived in Tahiti, looking for the *Bounty*'s mutinous crew. Fourteen were arrested quickly, and after searching nearby islands unsuccessfully for Christian and the

other mutineers, the *Pandora* set sail with the prisoners for Britain. But on August 29, 1791, the *Pandora* ran aground on the Great Barrier Reef and sank the next morning, killing thirty-one of its crew and four of the *Bounty* prisoners. The survivors eventually made it back to Britain, where the prisoners were put on trial and three men were hanged for their crimes.

Most of the *Bounty* crew on Pitcairn Island died there before long, including Christian. When the American seal-hunting ship *Topaz* arrived at the island in 1808, the one surviving mutineer told conflicting stories of how Christian and the others had died, but the stories all held the common thread of the English crew finding their tropical paradise spoiled by jealousy and infighting.

THE REPLICA OF the legendary HMS *Bounty* was the first ship to be built from the keel up for a motion picture, and was in fact a fully functional, authentic sailing ship—not just a superficial "movie prop," as critics would later call it. MGM was going all out on this production and wanted more than a facade on a barge or a boat that merely looked good from the right angle. The ship's design was based on the original plans of HMS *Bounty* from the British Admiralty Museum, but it was made a third larger than the original to accommodate the film crew, cameras, lighting, and other equipment.

The ship also was designed with high-capacity fuel tanks, because MGM needed to sail it from Nova Scotia to Tahiti, where the movie was to be filmed at the location of the actual mutiny, and they wanted to use the engines in addition to sail power for the extra speed. Producer Aaron Rosenberg had originally planned to shoot in sequence so that the earlier scenes on board the *Bounty* would be filmed under the gray skies of October before the rich color of the scenes shot in Tahiti. The *Bounty* was late in arriving from Nova Scotia, however, so director Carol Reed started shooting the island sequences first, or any footage that did not require the ship in the background. They still ran out of completed script pages before the *Bounty* arrived. Already the ship was making trouble.

The August 27, 1960, launching attracted more than twenty thou-

sand spectators in Nova Scotia. Once it arrived in Tahiti weeks later, the governor of Polynesia and island girls bearing leis welcomed the ship with a celebration reminiscent of how the original *Bounty* might have been greeted two hundred years earlier.

Filming commenced on the ship as soon as possible, but the crew encountered problems. Despite the *Bounty*'s being built oversize to accommodate the filming, technicians had difficulty finding places to hide and stay out of the shot. The ship also moved so much with each passing wave that the film crew was constantly seasick. Brando was obstinate and difficult to work with, using his star status to demand frequent script changes and new directors, while luxuriating in Tahiti and the attention of the local island women. The production dragged on for months past schedule, and when it came time for the climactic scene in which Christian's fellow crewmates burn the *Bounty* rather than complying with his demand to go back to England for trial, Brando said no. He had fallen in love with the beautiful ship and thought it would be a shame to burn it just for the sake of the movie. MGM explained that this was the plan all along; they had spent a huge sum to build this authentic-looking ship and it needed to burn to the waterline for the movie's dramatic ending.

Brando told them he wouldn't let it happen. If they burned the ship, he wouldn't finish the movie. It was a ridiculously brazen ultimatum, but he knew he held the cards in this situation. MGM relented and built a dummy ship to burn instead, and the *Bounty* lived on. After filming concluded, the *Bounty* later sailed back to the United States on a promotional tour of the West and East coasts, crossing the Atlantic before returning to New York for the film's premiere.

OVER DECADES OF seagoing and varying levels of care, the *Bounty* endured many rough years before 1986, when famed multimillionaire Ted Turner was surprised to find that he'd purchased the *Bounty* as part of the deal to acquire the MGM film library. He had no idea the ship was part of the package of classic movies—including the 1962 *Mutiny on the Bounty*—until he started getting bills for boat repair and maintenance. Being owned by an eccentric sailing enthusiast with lots of money was

beneficial to the *Bounty*, and Turner spent enough on the ship to keep it afloat. It was subsequently used in the 1990 movie *Treasure Island*, starring Charlton Heston, before Turner lost interest and donated it to the town of Fall River, Massachusetts, which planned to use it for school field trips and other paying passengers. But a hurdle that would prove ever challenging for the *Bounty* got in the way: The repairs and upgrades necessary to achieve the Coast Guard certification for paying passengers would be too costly. The *Bounty* was in rough shape, probably the worst condition ever for the ship. At that time a Coast Guard inspection found that the ship was taking on between twenty and forty gallons of water a minute. That's up to twenty-four hundred gallons an hour. A day's volume of that amount of water—more than fifty-seven thousand gallons—would easily fill a typical swimming pool.

Fall River put the *Bounty* up for sale at a price of $1.6 million and in 2000 found a buyer in Robert Hansen Jr., an avid sailor and founder of the Islandaire heating and air-conditioning company in Long Island, New York.

"She's a great boat with a lot of history, and thankfully we caught her before it was really too late," he told the *Times Record* newspaper in Brunswick, Maine. "That's what a little neglect does."

Hansen had big plans for the *Bounty*. "She's going to be available for corporate charters, and we're looking for corporate sponsors to defray the costs for the ship," he said. "The *Bounty* will fly the flags of its corporate backers, and also will be used for team-building and sail training." Hansen said his ultimate goal was to sail the *Bounty* back to Tahiti and the Pitcairn Islands, with himself and his family aboard.

"She's a movie star," Hansen told a reporter as he looked up at the *Bounty* dockside. "Even in her deplorable state, you can see she's spectacular."

Hansen was the third owner of the *Bounty* whom Capt. Robin Walbridge would work with. He was encouraged by the new owner's willingness to improve the ship, but he acknowledged to *The New York Times* that it would be a long haul to get the *Bounty* in fighting shape. "It will take forever," he said, but he added, "I've got the greatest job in the world. This is not about saving a ship; it's about saving the skills. It's important we keep

these skills alive so people remember how eighteenth-century square-riggers were sailed."

After Hansen signed the papers, in September 2001, the *Bounty* was taking on so much water that the Fall River Fire Department had to come to the rescue with its high-volume pumps to keep the ship from sinking at the dock.

Living out the old adage that a boat is a hole in the water you pour money into, Hansen subsequently invested substantial sums in repairing and improving the *Bounty*. He had the ship towed to the shipyard in Boothbay, Maine, for a yearlong overhaul that would include installing a completely new hull below the waterline. The Boothbay yard dates from the 1840s and is one of the few that still has artisans and engineers who know wooden-hulled sailing ships. Hansen paid $1.5 million for repairs in the first eighteen months he owned the *Bounty*, and he estimated the annual operating budget at $500,000. He has not disclosed how much he invested overall in the decade he owned the ship, but the positive effects could be seen by 2012.

IN RECENT YEARS, the *Bounty* had revived its image as a Hollywood star, known most commonly for being used to film the 2006 blockbuster *Pirates of the Caribbean: Dead Man's Chest*, starring Johnny Depp as Captain Jack Sparrow, and the 2007 follow-up movie. Contrary to popular belief, however, the *Bounty* did not have the starring role as the pirate ship *Black Pearl*. That ship was a filming rig built on a barge especially for the movies, and the *Bounty* actually appeared in the films as the *Edinburgh Trader*, seen in the background of several scenes. The public's misconception sometimes was allowed to go uncorrected, and people paid to go aboard "the ship from *Pirates of the Caribbean*." When the ship visited the United Kingdom in 2007, the UK *Daily Mail* trumpeted a story with the headline, "Boy, 12, exposes touring *Pirates of the Caribbean* ship as a fake." The boy was a big fan of the movies and, even before his mother paid 7.50 pounds for them to see the ship, he could see it was not the one that portrayed the *Black Pearl*. After some prodding, crew members on board sheepishly admitted he was right. The UK organizers

of the *Bounty* tour told the newspaper that they had been led to believe the *Bounty* had starred in the movie rather than playing a bit part, but the *Bounty*'s executive director at the time confirmed that was a common misconception. Leaving it uncorrected and even playing on that falsehood brought more visitors and more money to the *Bounty*, but perhaps that was in the pirate tradition. Jack Sparrow would have approved.

The ship also appeared in several other films, including *Yellow Beard* and *SpongeBob SquarePants, The Movie*. In 2006, city leaders in St. Petersburg, Florida, which leased dock space to the *Bounty* as a family-friendly tourist attraction, were shocked to find that the ship had been rented out for a porn movie shoot. With a reported budget of $1.1 million, *Pirates* was thought to be the most expensive pornographic movie made at the time. A hard-core movie that plays on the *Pirates of the Caribbean* theme and look, it went on to become one of the most successful porn movies ever. *The New York Times* cited the movie as "a relatively high-budget story of a group of ragtag sailors who go searching for a crew of evil pirates who have a plan for world domination. Also, many of the characters in the movie have sex with one another." Hansen's managers at the time claimed that they, too, were shocked to find that the movie was X-rated. They did have the foresight to ask that the *Bounty* and St. Petersburg not be thanked in the credits.

DESPITE THE LIVELY association with Hollywood and the romantic pirate life, those involved with sailing the *Bounty* knew that going to sea in a replica of an eighteenth-century wooden-hulled sailing ship is not to be taken lightly. Seafaring is a risky way of life even on a modern-day steel-hulled vessel with all of the latest safety advances, but sailing into the great blue on a fifty-two-year-old replica sailing ship greatly enhanced the challenge. Those in the tall ship community knew well the stories of the *Fantome*, the *Pride of Baltimore*, and countless other sailing ships that succumbed to the hazards of the sea.

The *Fantome* was one of the better-known tragedies, because it illustrated just how quickly a large sailing ship with a capable crew could still be outmatched by a storm at sea. A four-masted schooner 282 feet long,

128 feet high, and weighing 679 tons, the *Fantome* was considerably larger than the *Bounty*, and it had a steel hull. Built in 1927 for the Italian navy, it was then turned into a yacht by the Duke of Westminster, sold to Aristotle Onassis, and finally purchased by Windjammer in 1969 and used for cruises in the Caribbean. Beautiful and stately, it was the flagship of Windjammer's fleet of six.

The *Fantome* was a beloved member of the tall ship community, and its loss in 1998 struck hard. The ship had departed Honduras on October 24, 1988, for a six-day cruise at the same time Hurricane Mitch was building a thousand miles away in the Caribbean Sea. Capt. Guyan March, a boyish-looking thirty-two-year-old, had been on the *Fantome* for eleven years and seen it through storms at sea, but he still decided to head for the Bay Islands and linger there until the storm passed. But on October 25, it looked like Hurricane Mitch was changing course, and staying in the Bay Islands was no longer a good idea. March took the *Fantome* to Belize City and disembarked his passengers and some nonessential crew members; then he set a course northward in hopes of outrunning the storm. It soon became apparent, however, that the hurricane would hit the Yucatán Peninsula before the *Fantome* could get clear, and so March reversed his course to the south, trying to get away from the storm. He sought shelter on the southern side of Roatan, a small island, but by then Hurricane Mitch was a category-five storm, the worst and most powerful, and it was headed directly toward Roatan.

March hauled anchor again and tried to move east to the Caribbean, but Hurricane Mitch picked up speed and soon overtook the sailing ship. In one of its last radio contacts, when the *Fantome* was forty miles south of the hurricane's eye, the crew reported that the ship was fighting for its life in forty-foot seas and hundred-mile-per-hour winds. That was the last ever heard from the *Fantome*. Five days later, a helicopter crew found life rafts and vests from the ship, but nothing else. All thirty-one people on board were never seen again.

Another noteworthy loss was the *Pride of Baltimore*, a reproduction of a nineteenth-century Baltimore clipper topsail schooner, commissioned by the city of Baltimore and launched in 1977, soon after the bicentennial celebration engendered so much attention and admiration for

tall ships. At ninety feet long and seventy-nine feet high, the ship was quite a bit smaller than the *Bounty*, but struck an impressive pose on the sea with its huge sails totaling 9,327 square feet. The *Pride of Baltimore* was returning from a trip to the Caribbean on May 14, 1986, when it was hit by a squall about two hundred and fifty miles north of Puerto Rico, with winds of ninety-two miles per hour. The ship capsized and sank, killing the captain and three crew. Eight other crew members survived for more than four days in a partially inflated life raft before being rescued by a passing tanker.

The loss of a sail training vessel off the coast of Brazil on February 17, 2010, also was a wake-up call for members of the tall ship community. The *Concordia* was 188 feet long and 114 feet tall, with a steel hull. The ship was three hundred miles southeast of Rio de Janeiro in rough seas and high winds when it was suddenly knocked onto one side, heeling over completely within fifteen seconds. The ship sank twenty minutes later.

The capsizing was so fast that no radio distress call was made, but a distress radio beacon automatically activated when the vessel sank.

The sixty-four survivors—forty-eight students, eight teachers, and eight crew—spent nearly thirty hours in life rafts before rescue aircraft spotted them. After another eleven hours, everyone was saved.

Many people thought it was a miracle that no one died in the *Concordia* sinking. At the next annual meeting of Tall Ships America, captains, owners, and crew took notice. They could not have a disaster like that with one of their ships.

CHAPTER 3

FUTURE CAPTAINS OF AMERICA

THE MAKEUP OF the *Bounty* crew changed frequently, with the exception of the captain and a few hands who stayed on for years at a time. In the ship's final season, four of the sixteen crew had been on the *Bounty* for only a few months, and two—the engineer and the cook, two very important people on any ship—joined the crew just before it sailed into Hurricane Sandy. For both of them, their maiden voyage on the *Bounty* would be the ship's last.

The captain's right-hand man in the fall of 2012 was forty-one-year-old chief mate John Svendsen, who grew up in Nisswa, Minnesota, and joined the *Bounty* crew in February 2010. With a rugged, square-jawed face and long hair past his shoulders, he fit the bill of someone who had spent most of his adult life as a diving instructor and boat captain all over the world. More than anyone else on the boat, Svendsen had the ear of the captain, and worked directly with him in planning their voyages and commanding the crew. As a licensed captain, he also shared responsibility for complying with maritime law and practices. Svendsen communicates in an utterly calm, soft-spoken, almost Zen-like style that nonetheless commands respect. The *Bounty* was his third tall ship.

One of the bigger personalities on board the *Bounty* belonged to third mate Dan Cleveland, a twenty-five-year-old from St. Louis who

had worked on the *Bounty* for sixteen months. Tall, bearded, brash, and prone to swearing like the proverbial sailor, Cleveland was a strong leader and also a calming presence on the ship. With a confidence that came right to the edge of cockiness, Cleveland's deep voice always conveyed authority and a sense of order. He was not easily fazed by anything, and he wore that as a badge of pride. Cleveland was a real contrast to the more easygoing style of the *Bounty*'s captain, Robin Walbridge, and particularly to chief mate Svendsen's low-key demeanor. Thoroughly likable and engaging, fun to drink with, but serious about the art of sailing, Cleveland was exactly the kind of character you expected to find on a ship like the *Bounty*.

Cleveland learned everything he knew about sailing from Walbridge, having joined the *Bounty* crew in 2008. He had since earned a mariner's license and intended to make sailing his career. His adventure on the *Bounty* began with an impulsive decision to try a new pursuit. After working in landscaping and then holding an office job for a total of twenty-two days before it drove him mad, Cleveland was up for anything when he was walking on the pier in St. Petersburg, Florida, and saw the *Bounty*. There was a sign on the boat that said, CREW NEEDED. *Holy shit, I didn't even know they had these old boats anymore*, he thought.

Cleveland had no sailing experience but had always loved reading about nautical history, so he decided to give it a chance and was signed on as a deckhand. In his first year, he rode out a hurricane on the *Bounty*, studying his captain's every move as they charted a course behind the storm and off the coast of Central America.

He was in a relationship with twenty-eight-year-old bosun Laura Groves, who had been on the *Bounty* for three years. Her role as bosun meant she was responsible for supervising other crew members, assigning tasks, and pretty much ensuring that everything got done on the ship. Small in stature, with glasses and long dreadlocks, strong and confident in her sailing skills, the North Carolina native was an asset to the *Bounty* and a formidable match for Cleveland. Along with Hewitt and Salapatek, they were one of the acknowledged couples on the *Bounty*.

Romances were nothing new on the *Bounty*. After all, this was a vessel that existed to celebrate the romantic notion of young people sail-

23

ing a square-rigged ship to exotic places. How could they not fall in love? Walbridge tried to keep such relationships from getting out of hand and affecting the ship's operations, but for the most part he wouldn't interfere. He did cause a few hearts to jump one time when he called a meeting to discuss a serious problem about "reproduction" on the ship. The crew thought there must be some real juicy news about to be unveiled, but it turned out that Walbridge was concerned that there were now two bicycles on board and taking up too much space. "Let's keep it to one bike at a time, please," he said with a grin.

Though only twenty-five years old, Jessica Hewitt was one of the more qualified mariners on the *Bounty*. She was a 2009 graduate of the Maine Maritime Academy, followed by holding several crew positions on ships and captaining a supply boat. Hewitt held a maritime license and was working as deckhand on the *Bounty*, having joined the ship in August 2012. A surfer originally from San Bernardino, California, Hewitt has a bright, spunky personality that served her well on the *Bounty*. She found that Walbridge had his own ways of doing things on the *Bounty*, not necessarily the way she had been taught or how she had done them on other ships. But she took the job on the *Bounty* after meeting the crew the previous summer and getting a good sense of community from them. On some vessels knowledge is hoarded, because sharing can make a crew member's own position less secure, she knew. But the *Bounty*'s culture of sharing and teaching drew her in. Her relationship with twenty-nine-year-old deckhand Drew made days on the ship more than just a job. Salapatek was a bearded, long-haired sailor from Blue Island, Illinois, with a reputation for being gentle and quiet.

The second mate on the *Bounty*, thirty-seven-year-old Matt Sanders, was another graduate of the Maine Maritime Academy and had worked briefly on a schooner, but he had never worked on a wooden-hulled tall ship before. He joined the *Bounty* crew in March 2012. As second mate, part of his duties included assisting with navigation and weather forecasts.

Fifty-six-year-old Christopher Barksdale, from Nellysford, Virginia, joined the *Bounty* crew in September 2012 to serve as the ship's engineer. He did not hold an engineering degree or license, and he did not have any

merchant marine certification, but Barksdale had worked with engines, generators, and other systems for thirty years throughout a career in horticulture and as a handyman. Barksdale had met Chief Mate Svendsen at Palmyra Atoll in the Pacific when both worked on the research vessels there, with Barksdale maintaining mechanical systems for the Nature Conservancy. About a thousand miles south of Hawaii in the Line Islands of Micronesia, Palmyra Atoll is one of the most pristine marine conservancies in the world, making it a hot spot for researchers, the occasional private yacht visitors, and people like Svendsen and Barksdale looking to work in paradise for a while. Working on the *Bounty* would give Barksdale sea time that could help in his desire to get a marine engineer license or other certification for working on a ship.

Along with Barksdale, this would be the first trip on the *Bounty* for thirty-four-year-old Jessica Black. A graduate of the New England Culinary Institute, she had experience as a chef on private yachts and a research ship, but wanted the bigger adventure promised by the tall ship community. Her first trip on the *Bounty* also would be her first voyage on a tall ship.

The oldest crew member on the *Bounty* was sixty-six-year-old Douglas Faunt, whose title was able seaman, but who served as the ship's de facto electrician because he had retired from Cisco Systems, the IT corporation, which left him with expertise in communications and engineering. One of his first tasks upon joining the *Bounty* was to set up a ham radio system to augment the other communications and primarily to send e-mail. Tall, with gray, almost white hair and beard, Faunt usually wore a *Bounty* watch cap and looked every bit the seasoned sailor he was. He was volunteering on the *Bounty*, however, the only nonpaid crewman at the time. Before coming to the *Bounty*, he had been paid to work as a crew member on the tall ships *Europa* and *Endeavour*. Faunt had joined *Bounty* in May 2012, and he treasured being part of the sailing community. With a longtime interest in marine history and literature, he saw the *Bounty* as one of the most appealing ships for him to work on. Faunt particularly enjoyed how the ship welcomed visitors at every port, and he was always eager to conduct tours and teach people the rich history of the *Bounty* and sailing ships in general.

Twenty-seven-year-old Adam Prokosh had joined the *Bounty* crew eight months earlier, when the ship was in Puerto Rico, after serving on other tall ships for five years. Originally from Everett, Washington, and certified as an able seaman, Prokosh had sufficient experience to perform most duties on a tall ship, and aspired to captain his own vessel one day. His experience had also caused him to hesitate when first considering joining the *Bounty* crew. He was looking for work and responded to a help-wanted ad placed with the Tall Ships America organization. "I heard terrible things about the *Bounty*," he said later. "She had a really terrible reputation. The running joke was that everyone who sailed on the *Bounty* had a story about nearly dying on the *Bounty*. The *Bounty* is known for not being a boat to sail on if you want to protect your own safety and professionalism. It was called a death trap."

But when he talked to Walbridge, Svendsen, and the other *Bounty* crew, Prokosh got a different impression. He decided that the ship's reputation was outdated, if the truth ever was that bad. He looked at the type of mariners the *Bounty* was attracting and he respected them. People still spoke poorly of the *Bounty* in 2012, he recalls, but those same people would speak highly of the crew who sailed on the ship at that time. In his first interview for the job on the *Bounty*, Walbridge and Svendsen described how they were trying to build a familial structure of support, and help crew members learn skills they could take to the next level or the next ship.

One of the younger and newer crew members was twenty-five-year-old Joshua Scornavacchi, who had joined the *Bounty* in April at the start of the 2012 sailing season. A handsome young man whose cool glasses, carefully mussed hair, and hipster style might suggest a kid with few deep interests, Scornavacchi actually is quite spiritual and driven. He feels a connection to God through nature and particularly when he is on the sea, speaking with great affection about the beautiful mountains near his home in Mohnton, Pennsylvania, which has around three thousand residents. He had thought for many years that he wanted to sail around the world someday, and his first season on the *Bounty* was to be a step in that direction. As a certified master diver, Scornavacchi sometimes provided a valuable service to the *Bounty* by diving to inspect the hull and make

26

minor repairs while the ship was in the water, usually in response to evidence on the inside of the boat that a seam was leaking. First Scornavacchi hammered a piece of line into the leaking seam, followed by a clay sealer and then a copper patch hammered onto the hull to cover it. (The hull of the original HMS *Bounty* was sheathed entirely in copper, but that would have made it impossible for the replica's crew and the Coast Guard to inspect the wooden hull periodically for damage.) His diving skills also came in handy when lobster pots got tangled in the *Bounty*'s props. Scornavacchi brought a pet to sail with him on the *Bounty*—a betta fish he kept in his berthing area.

A new addition to the *Bounty* crew was forty-two-year-old Claudene Christian, a petite blonde with an outgoing, upbeat personality. Originally from Alaska and five feet, one inch tall, she was a former gymnast, a Miss Alaska National Teenager, and a cheerleader at the University of Southern California. She had always been motivated and aggressive in pursuing what she wanted, so it was no surprise when she launched a doll company inspired by the USC cheerleaders. The company was successful enough that Mattel sued her, saying she was infringing on their cheerleader Barbie doll. Christian lost and had to close her company, but she eventually succeeded in suing her own attorney for negligence and won more than a million dollars. The money funded a lifestyle of partying and questionable expenditures, and by 2006 Christian's parents were worried that her personality was more than just upbeat. Her father's therapist suggested that Christian might be bipolar. When her financial options dried up in California, she returned to live with her parents, who had since moved from Alaska to Vian, Oklahoma, near where her mother, Dina, grew up.

Christian's family believed Claudene was the great-great-great-great-great-granddaughter of the Fletcher Christian who led the famed mutiny on the *Bounty*, so Claudene felt drawn to the ship. After visiting another tall ship replica, the *Niña*, in port, she realized that it was possible to be hired on with no experience. She missed the sea and the sunny life of Southern California desperately, and she saw the *Bounty* as a chance to reclaim her life. She hoped that perhaps her business and marketing experience would be useful to the *Bounty* if it were to start taking school-

children and other passengers on board. When she showed up to join the *Bounty* crew in May 2012, she was pulling a rolling suitcase and carrying a guitar.

Christian volunteered on the *Bounty* for a while before being hired as a deckhand. Faunt recalls that she was sometimes slower to catch on, because she wasn't focused on the boat as much as the other new crew members. She was enjoying the experience and the people, he says, but sailing a tall ship didn't seem to be her passion. She was more focused on being part of the *Bounty* family and enjoying an adventure. The crew loved her spirit and how she always brightened up everyone around her. She was insanely curious, always wanting to know what was going on whether it was really her business or not, and no one could resist her charms. The crew quickly learned to use that to their advantage, sending Christian out on friendly reconnaissance missions if they wanted to know the latest scuttlebutt about the ship's operations or gossip about their friends. Christian seemed to come alive on the *Bounty*, with friends and family saying she was more like her old self, more like the vibrant girl they used to know and not the troubled woman of recent years.

The rest of the crew included twenty-nine-year-old deckhand John Jones, from St. Augustine, Florida. He joined the *Bounty* crew in May 2012, the first time he had ever worked on a tall ship. Anna Sprague's father, an avid sailor himself, launched his daughter on a pursuit of the same passion. The twenty-year-old with long blond hair joined the *Bounty* crew in May 2012, spontaneously asking for a job when she visited the *Bounty* as a tourist. She had majored in journalism at Auburn University in Alabama, where she also was a member of the sailing team. Thirty-three-year-old deckhand Mark Warner had joined the *Bounty* crew in May 2012 after working on three other tall ships.

ROBIN WALBRIDGE WAS more than the captain of the *Bounty*. With seventeen years at the helm, he had been with the *Bounty* longer than any crew member, longer than the owner, and longer even than a lot of the wood on the ship. The sixty-three-year-old Walbridge personified everything that the *Bounty* was in 2012—dedicated to the true spirit of sailing

and cutting a different course than even other tall ships and their captains. Unlike some of the other tall ship captains, for instance, Walbridge did not foster an old-world sailing appearance, with a bushy beard or a quirky nautical style of dress, or even the long-haired, free-spirit look of some of his younger crew. A Vermont native, he favored polo shirts, khakis, and golf caps, and he wore his wire-framed glasses with a neck chain that, along with his hearing aids, gave him the appearance of a kindly sailor more likely to take his grandkids out for a trip on the family boat than the leader of a tall sailing ship famous for its role in pirate movies. His sailing career began when he was eighteen years old and borrowed a sailboat one day, and in some ways never came back. He started working as a mechanic for houseboats at the Suwanee River in Florida and then moved to Massachusetts, where he trained Navy sailors to work on the service's tall ship, the USS *Constitution*. Before moving on to the *Bounty*, he piloted vessels in the Gulf of Mexico that worked with the oil rigs there, including evacuating workers before and during hurricanes.

An excellent photographer and master craftsman of furniture and kayaks, he wasn't keen on going to meetings of Tall Ships America and hobnobbing with captains and owners, but his crew found him approachable and always eager to teach. Asking a question of Walbridge was less likely to prompt an answer than a back-and-forth exchange about what the problem was, the different options, and what the sailor thought would be the right course of action. Walbridge almost always knew the right answer, of course, but he thought simply telling you was a waste of a good teaching opportunity. Crew members recalled that he would guide them to the way he wanted it done, but by the time they got there they felt like they had figured it out for themselves.

He often explained this teaching style by saying, "I assume you want my job, and that's great, because I want to go home one day." But they didn't really believe he ever wanted to leave the *Bounty*.

That hands-on, inclusive leadership style was one point that swayed Prokosh when he initially had reservations about the *Bounty*'s reputation. "I saw plenty of captains who would go to their cabins, make a decision, and then go tell the crew," Prokosh recalls. "Walbridge was different. He

always called us the 'future captains of America,' because he said we should be trying for our next position all the time."

Cleveland developed a deep respect and admiration for Walbridge, who passed on to the third mate his firm but calm style of leadership. He admired how the captain never gave any hint of being scared or nervous, even when there might be good reason to be, and he thought of Walbridge as a chess player always two steps ahead of everyone else.

Faunt, the oldest person on the *Bounty* and three years senior to Walbridge, loved his captain and wasn't afraid to say so. He was "someone to aspire to be like," Faunt says. Walbridge knew a great deal, thought logically, acted rationally and with reasons for what he did, Faunt says, and he was willing to teach anything he knew. Walbridge was willing to hear anything a crew member had to say, Faunt says, even if he went with his own decision in the end.

Not everyone revered Walbridge and his leadership style. Two former *Bounty* crew members, both now licensed maritime captains, told CNN in 2013 that they had bad experiences because Walbridge was a poor leader with no respect for protocol. They suggested that the praise of Walbridge's leadership style actually glossed over his tendency to skirt the rules of safe sailing and do things his own way. Sarah Nelson was a *Bounty* crew member for nine months in 2007, after friends in the sailing community tried to warn her away from the boat. She ended up quitting in the middle of a voyage, she says, because she got fed up with watching Walbridge take safety shortcuts and violate maritime law. Everything on the *Bounty* was about finding ways around the rules and standard procedures, she claims.

Samantha Dinsmore had similar memories of her time on the *Bounty*. Walbridge looked for easy solutions to potentially expensive problems like ship repairs, she said, and was "a brilliant chess master at finding ways to get around the rules."

Walbridge also may have been brilliant at staffing his boat with people who either admired his leadership style or did not know any better. Anyone looking for a different type of captain—and who had enough experience to choose where they worked—could apply on dozens of other ships. The crew he assembled in the fall of 2012 admired Wal-

bridge's leadership, though it was the only style many of them had ever seen on a sailing ship, because the *Bounty* and Walbridge were their only experience.

The ship's owner and the captain had talked often of wanting to sail the *Bounty* to Tahiti, re-creating the last port of call for the original HMS *Bounty* before the mutiny. Walbridge's big dream for the *Bounty* was to someday sail the Northwest Passage, a treacherous sea route through the Arctic Ocean along the North American coast that has lured sailors for centuries as a trade route and as a supreme test of a ship and crew. The legendary explorer Roald Amundsen first navigated the passage between 1903 and 1906 in a seventy-foot-by-twenty-foot sloop named *Gjøa*, with a crew of six, but transits thereafter were few. The heavy ice required a fortified ship or an icebreaker, often both, to get a ship through. Walbridge was intrigued by the news of warming seas beginning in 2007, however, which meant a passage might be possible for part of each year.

Sailing the *Bounty* through the Northwest Passage. What better way could Walbridge end his career? Svendsen, Cleveland, Groves, and several other crew members wanted to be right by his side.

CHAPTER 4

BLACK SHEEP

IN MANY WAYS the *Bounty* operated on the fringe of the tall ship community, enjoying an outsider status and a counterculture existence. The ship and its crew were known, affectionately by most, as the "black sheep" of the tall ship community. They were outliers, the renegades, the ones who didn't always follow the same rules as everyone else and didn't particularly care what anyone else thought of them. They were the pirate ship in the fleet of mostly slick, businesslike vessels. The crew did not have to worry about wearing uniforms authentic to the era represented by the ship, and they did not have to be "on" all the time because paying passengers were looking. With no passengers, they could be themselves, enjoy running the ship, and only when they were in port did they have to clean up a bit and put on big smiles for the tourists. This was their ship when they were at sea, and they liked it that way.

The *Bounty* stopped in about twenty-five ports on the Eastern Seaboard and Great Lakes area every summer, charging ten dollars a head or so to come aboard and experience a pirate ship. The ship also traveled to the West Coast occasionally and sometimes made a special trip to Europe. A season for the *Bounty* lasted eight to ten months, and the vessel would spend the winter months in a warm-climate port, often St.

Petersburg, Florida, but most recently Puerto Rico. Plans were to spend the 2013–2014 winter in Galveston, Texas.

The ship was always short on money, often using the day's receipts from tourists to buy groceries for that night's meals, and sometimes waiting to dock until the owner could wire money or pay off the ship's credit card. Money was never the goal for the crew, however, which was good, because they made as little as $100 a week gross. They were there for the adventure, and they got plenty of that. Cleveland fondly recalls the time the *Bounty* was waiting for its turn to pass through the Panama Canal and Walbridge forbade the crew from going ashore because the local village was too dangerous. After several idle days with the ship at anchor because the *Bounty* was a lower priority than the commercial shipping vessels going through the locks, one crew member couldn't stand it anymore. Sitting on the hot ship and staring at the bar just a quarter mile inland advertising cold, cold beer, the crew member broke and decided he had to head to shore in the *Bounty*'s rubber dinghy. Cleveland watched as he took the boat ashore, beached it, and made a beeline for the bar. After a short stay and a few beers, the young man decided to go for a stroll through the village, and before long realized that few people were on the street.

He soon came upon an old man sweeping the street and said hello. The old man would not look up at him, but was muttering something quietly. The *Bounty* crewman asked several times what he was saying, but didn't understand the old man's increasingly insistent "*¡Corre! ¡Corre!*" The villager was trying tell the half-drunk gringo to run. Run! It was just then that the crewman noticed a car had been following him, filled with young men armed with fearsome-looking guns.

Cleveland laughed hard as he watched his friend run full speed back to shore, dive into the dinghy, and motor back to the *Bounty* as fast as he could. Cleveland had his own adventures onshore, too, the most memorable having something to do with fighting Russian mobsters outside a bar in Ireland. He's not entirely clear on the details.

UNDER NORMAL OPERATIONS at sea or in port, *Bounty* crew members were assigned to four-hour watches or work parties. The number of people

assigned to each watch might vary depending on how many of the crew were aboard and what was going on with the ship, but typically a watch would include four people with different assignments. One person might be responsible for the helm, while others would be assigned to navigation or other needs. At least one person on each watch was responsible for conducting "boat checks," which involved patrolling through the entire ship to look for fire, water, or any other problems, and to log important information such as fuel levels for the engines and the status of the bilge in the engine room. The crew member conducting a boat check would gauge the level of the water in the bilge—the bottom of the boat, where all ships collect some amount of water seepage that must be pumped out—and operate the bilge pumps as necessary to clear it. A complete boat check typically took about half an hour. In any twenty-four-hour period, most deckhands stood watch twice and were on a work party once, meaning they worked twelve hours per day. There was always plenty of work to do on a sailing ship, everything from woodworking to mending sails, which sometimes was done in a "bitch and stitch" session, with a canvas sail spread out on the upper deck and several crew sitting around it.

BECAUSE OF ITS age, type of construction, and less than optimal maintenance over many years, the *Bounty* routinely took on more water than most ships, even most wooden-hulled tall sailing ships. It was often referred to as a "leaky" or "wet" ship in the sailing community, and years ago it had been known as "the Blue Sponge" when its hull was painted blue. Crew sometimes referred to the ship as the "Bondo *Bounty*" because of all the quick and dirty fixes on the hull.

Over the years, the leaking had been so bad that the *Bounty* sank in port on three separate occasions. With wooden-hulled vessels, some water leakage is normal, because it is impossible to seal the seams between the wooden planks perfectly and not have them loosen over time. As a vessel like the *Bounty* sails, the wooden planks "work"—the marine term for the wood twisting and moving as the ship is acted on by the forces of wind and water. The rougher the seas and winds, the more the ship works

34

and the more the seams open up. On a typical boat check, the 150-gallon-per-minute bilge pumps had to be run once or twice in a four-hour watch to clear out the accumulated water. Crew members were trained to operate the primary bilge pumps, but not the auxiliary hydraulic-powered pumps that would be used if the primary system could not clear the water.

Even those who admired both the *Bounty* and Walbridge acknowledged that the ship sometimes went its own way and didn't meet the standards of many other tall ships. Daniel Moreland, captain of the tall ship *Picton Castle*, called Walbridge a friend and enjoyed his visits to the *Bounty*, but he says the ship was "an outlier" among tall ships and had a rough reputation. "If people were out of work, the *Bounty* would get them through," he says, but it wasn't the vessel most tall ship mariners strove to work on.

Bert Rogers, the executive director of Tall Ships America, chooses his words carefully when talking about the *Bounty*, but he is emphatic in saying the ship was "not representative of how our fleet operates." Almost all other tall ships meet much higher requirements for safety and seaworthiness, he says. They are inspected as small passenger vessels or sailing school vessels.

"*Bounty* was an uninspected vessel. That meant she was inspected only insofar as required for her to be in port, open to the public as an attraction vessel," he told the author. "That is very limited. Beyond that she was an uninspected vessel, a moored attraction vessel. That has specific meaning within the Coast Guard regulations, and it means basically that when she sailed from port to port, she was doing so without any supervision."

Rogers noted that the *Bounty* was led by a licensed captain and chief mate, which assured some level of professionalism. He knew Walbridge and admired him as a captain, and he put stock in the fact that his crew respected him. Captaining a ship of any kind, and certainly a tall sailing ship, is a business in which you cannot fake your expertise, Rogers said. You won't get much opportunity to hide from your mistakes, and you won't get many second chances. If you're a poor captain, your crew will know it and soon everyone else will too. Walbridge's reputation as a mariner, and as the captain of the *Bounty*, was exemplary, Rogers said.

The ship itself was another matter. The *Bounty*'s status as a moored attraction vessel meant that potentially serious problems could go unnoticed or uncorrected for a long time, Rogers said.

"For an inspected vessel the regulatory supervision is much more focused, intense, frequent, and deeper," Rogers said. "And I think that that distinction is going to be meaningful in the final analysis of why she was lost."

SOME *BOUNTY* CREW, like Cleveland, enjoyed working on the ship precisely because it was old, underfunded, subject to minimal Coast Guard requirements, and barely getting along. That created challenges for the ship and crew, which was what some crew members wanted, rather than an easy sail on an up-to-date ship. They relished having to find ways to keep the *Bounty* afloat and to make do with what their counterparts of generations ago might have used, fashioning their own woodwork and riggings, finding a way to repair what others might replace. The *Bounty* was outfitted with the most necessary modern conveniences, of course, like radar and radios and safety gear, but to many of the crew the *Bounty*'s leaky hull and just-scraping-by existence lent more of an authentic feel to the tall ship experience. The crews on other, better-funded ships didn't get the same experience the *Bounty* crew got in solving problems, coming up with mechanical fixes on the fly, repairing wooden hulls. The *Bounty* crew knew that crews from other ships were jealous that the *Bounty* offered that experience.

That was one of the things that made the *Bounty* special to those who sailed it. It was really a "crew ship," a vessel that sailed as it might have a hundred years earlier, with no one but the crew out at sea and with no purpose other than to safely get the ship from one place to another. Though not allowed by its Coast Guard certification, the *Bounty* did take on children and corporate passengers over the years. One crew member told of a time years ago when the *Bounty* took a group of teenagers on board for a sail. Many of the kids spent the time at sea brushing their hair and painting their fingernails, acting as if they were there simply because they were forced to be. The crew did not miss them when they left.

The crew enjoyed being on their own because they were more than coworkers—they felt like a family. Together they worked long hours, under harsh and dangerous conditions, for little reward other than the experience of being at sea with one another. Being completely cut off from noncrew for days and weeks created quick and strong bonds.

All ship crews have a bond, and a lot of them will talk about being like a family, but other tall ship crews knew that the *Bounty* crew was close, and you didn't dare speak ill of one crew member without the others stepping up. They were known for their hospitality, being especially welcoming to other tall ship crews who wanted to see the famous pirate ship from the movies. Many tall sailing ships are strict about letting visitors on board, even sailors from other ships who could probably be trusted, but the *Bounty*'s gangplank was always open. If you came from another ship and yelled hello, some crew member was likely to greet you and tell you to make yourself at home. If they didn't have time to give you a tour, they'd at least point you in the right direction and tell you there was beer in the fridge.

The *Bounty* crew's existence on the fringe of the tall ship community did not mean, however, that they were cavalier about safety concerns. They were unorthodox with some approaches to safety and, according to some, took more risks than other crews. But they knew that sailing on any type of vessel could be dangerous, and sailing on a ship like the *Bounty* even more so. The crew drilled regularly for different types of emergencies, including fires, a man overboard, and the order to abandon ship.

With abandon-ship drills, Walbridge believed in training his crew for two different scenarios. The first was an all-out emergency in which, for instance, the *Bounty* had been run over by an oil tanker and was sinking fast. In that scenario, the abandon-ship drill is all about speed—donning immersion suits, grabbing the emergency transmitter beacons, and getting in the ship's two twenty-five-person life rafts as soon as possible. But Walbridge taught his crew that the more likely scenario for abandoning ship would be one in which the crew had more time for an orderly departure. They would know ahead of time that the ship was in distress and would have time to organize an abandon-ship under the best

possible conditions. That drill involved the same donning of immersion suits but then focused on gathering emergency gear, water and food, and important documents, and staging crew members for a safe, orderly exit from the ship to the life rafts.

Walbridge and his senior crew always urged crew members to work quickly so that they would be used to the pressure in a crisis. "Double-time! Double-time!" was heard often on the *Bounty*. The captain was particularly focused on certain safety issues, requiring extra steps such as the crew always clipping their harnesses onto the rig even when sailing in smooth seas and light winds. "That way you'll do it automatically later when it really counts," he told his crew.

The captain had a different approach to emergency response than most. On many ships, individual crew members are assigned certain tasks or stations during an emergency. On a Navy ship, for instance, sailors have assigned "general quarters" duties that they go to during an alarm no matter what they're doing or what shift they're working. But on the *Bounty*, Walbridge thought it better to have each watch assigned responsibility for a certain part of the emergency response. The type of emergency dictated the response, of course, but no matter the situation, the categories of work needed were divided in a general way. The first watch, for instance, might be responsible for lifesaving or firefighting—whatever the immediate emergency was—the second watch for continuing to sail the ship, and the third watch for communicating with other ships or the Coast Guard. It was an unorthodox method of assigning emergency duties, but Walbridge could be unorthodox sometimes, and some of the crew liked this approach better than the usual method.

One of Walbridge's greatest safety concerns was the possibility of someone falling overboard. A man overboard is serious for any vessel, but tall ships have the added liability of not being able to quickly backtrack to find the person in the water. Stopping, turning around, and heading back into the wind requires a great deal of time in a ship like the *Bounty*, and under some conditions can't be done at all. The *Bounty*'s rubber boat would be deployed in a man-overboard, and Groves and Cleveland had taken the boat out many times during drills. Simply deploying the boat took time, and then the crew still had to find the missing person, which

might be a major challenge in the dark and if the ship had sailed some distance away. All of that meant that a person in the water might be lost forever or dead by the time the *Bounty* crew arrived.

Walbridge addressed that worry with a bit of ingenuity. He devised a "man-overboard marker" that would serve a dual purpose. A simple device consisting of a waterproof five-gallon container with a strobe light attached, the marker was stowed on the rear of the ship so that when a man-overboard alarm was sounded, any crew member could quickly activate the strobe and toss the box overboard. That would ensure that the position of the missing person would be marked relatively close by, and the strobe could be used to home in on the position. In addition, the floating marker might give the person something to hang on to while awaiting rescue. Fortunately, the man-overboard marker had never been used.

The *Bounty*'s colorful history was both an asset and a curse. The ship's identity, its brand, depended on its being a bit of a renegade, operating outside the norm like the pirate ships it depicted in the movies. And without a doubt, it had earned that reputation for many years. But the *Bounty* in 2012 was not the same ship. Hansen's investments had begun turning the vessel around, and by some accounts, the *Bounty* was in the best shape it had seen in many years. That assessment is relative, of course, and the ship still was not up to the standards of most other tall ships, but it seemed the *Bounty* was on the upswing and could look forward to a better future.

CHAPTER 5

MORE THAN WORRIED

ON MONDAY, OCTOBER 22, 2012, the *Bounty* was tied to a dock at the shipyard in Boothbay, Maine, at the tail end of more than a month of intensive repairs and improvements while in dry dock. With the boat back in the water, the crew was watching the hull for leaks and found that the boat was drier than it'd been in a while. They worked to complete some of the planned tasks and were due to leave Boothbay in a few days.

Almost two thousand miles away, a low-pressure system was forming south of Jamaica, noticed by almost no one except the meteorologists at the National Oceanic and Atmospheric Administration (NOAA, pronounced like Noah), the government agency that tracks hurricanes and issues warnings to mariners and civil authorities. Late in the day on Monday, they classified the low-pressure system as a tropical storm and gave it the next name on the 2012 list: Sandy.

The storm moved slowly to the north.

THE *BOUNTY* HAD sailed to the Boothbay shipyard on September 17, 2012. For the month-plus that the *Bounty* was in dry dock, Walbridge and the ship's crew worked closely with Todd Kosakowski, lead shipwright and

project manager at the shipyard. In addition to having worked on wooden boats at the yard for more than six years, Kosakowski had spent two and a half years sailing on tall ships. He was skilled in the particular type of carpentry and other maintenance required for tall ships, particularly those with wooden hulls, and he had worked on the *Bounty* in 2006, when the ship was last in the yard for major work, and also in 2010, when it returned for less substantive repairs.

On this visit, Kosakowski was in charge of the *Bounty* project, and his first task was to pump the water out of the *Bounty* and haul the ship up onto the rails, where it would sit for work on the hull. Kosakowski's first impression of the *Bounty* was good. There wasn't a huge amount of water to remove, and when the ship came out Kosakowski thought its hull looked solid. Some maintenance was needed, but that was normal. The *Bounty* did not give the impression of a ship that was barely afloat, as it had in recent years. The seams looked tight and there was little weeping of water back out through the planks.

Five employees of the shipyard, including Kosakowski, worked on the *Bounty* along with the crew. Some of the more complicated repairs, requiring the skills of experienced carpenters or tradesmen, were performed by the shipyard employees, while other work that required less technical expertise was left to the *Bounty* crew. Part of Kosakowski's job was to oversee the woodworking that was needed, and Walbridge had phoned ahead of their arrival with a punch list of work to be done, so Kosakowski knew the captain wanted him to look at two spots on the ship that needed attention. There was one area on the port quarter where the wood seemed to be deteriorating, and another where the *Bounty* had rubbed against a dock during high winds.

The *Bounty* crew and shipyard workers had a substantial to-do list—mostly the *Bounty* crew, because, as usual, the ship tried to save as much money as possible by having its own crew do work that other ships might gladly hand over to the shipyard. Whether the *Bounty* crew was qualified to do all of this work would be debated later. Fuel tanks were to be moved forward from their current positions and crew quarters moved aft, which required a great deal of demolition and reworking, and two new nine-hundred-gallon water tanks were to be installed. In addition,

ballast—lead bars and loose pieces of lead—was to be repositioned to change the way the ship rode in the water. Hatches were moved, a new ladder installed. Chief Mate Svendsen was away, continuing his studies in Fort Lauderdale, Florida, to upgrade his mariner's license.

Aside from moving and installing the tanks, the most substantial work in the shipyard involved routine maintenance on the hull. This was performed entirely by the *Bounty* crew and represented some of the most true-to-the-era work they could do—one reason they did not mind the dirty, exhausting, backbreaking exertion of caulking seams on the wooden hull. This could be done only in the same way it was done hundreds of years ago—by hand—and with mostly the same materials and tools that the original HMS *Bounty* crew would have used. Though the planks on a wooden hull are placed as tightly together as possible, they are not watertight until each seam is sealed by packing in layers of cotton and oakum, a blend of hemp fibers coated with tar. The materials must be fitted into the seams just so and then hammered into place using a caulking iron with a thin blade and a heavy maul known as a beetle. The caulking materials have to be hammered in evenly and far enough to create a seal, but not so far that the cotton and oakum go through to the other side of the seam. Caulking the seams is an old-world art and requires a strong back. It must be performed regularly to reseal and tighten seams that have loosened through normal wear and tear.

Kosakowski was on-site most days supervising his own workers and observing the work of the *Bounty* crew. He was pleased to see that *Bounty* did not require tightening of more than five percent of the seams below the waterline and probably less than ten percent above. On this visit to Boothbay, Bosun Groves led the *Bounty* crew's caulking work, but Kosakowski saw different people under the boat every time he stopped by. His impression was that everyone on the crew was getting a hand at caulking, spelling one another on the arduous work and learning the specialized skill.

The main task for Kosakowski was to repair the two damaged areas that Walbridge reported—two planks of about twenty feet each, eight and a quarter inches wide and three inches thick, on either side of the

ship and above the waterline—so he inspected those soon after the ship was in dry dock. Kosakowski and his crew removed those planks and were surprised to see that the wood was showing "excessive signs of decay" for planks that had been installed only six and a half years earlier. Although he had been pleased by what he saw with the hull below the waterline, the *Bounty*'s planking above the waterline was in "rough shape" from excessive drying.

The planking was decayed from the interior of the vessel, reaching about two-thirds of the way through from the inside, with black cracks going cross-grained through the planking. If there hadn't been additional unrelated damage on the outside, the rot would not have been discovered. Even more disturbing was the damage evident on the frame underneath—one of the large structural members that make up the vessel's skeleton and actually hold the ship together. It was soft and damp, and it showed the same cross-grained cracks as the planking.

This represented a serious structural threat to the *Bounty*, and Kosakowski had to report the problem to the captain. Walbridge was not overly surprised to see rot in some of the planking, but he was "a little shocked," in Kosakowski's words, at the condition of the frame. The two men continued inspecting the nearby frames, and Walbridge's "shock turned to awe" once they saw signs of decay in some of the others.

Exploring further, Kosakowski found additional areas inside the ship that also displayed wood rot, including more frames that were soft and wet. He also found rotten and loose trunnels, essentially wooden pegs that are used to attach two pieces of wood together. The trunnel is sized to fit snugly, hammered in while wet, and then it expands as it dries. Once inserted, a trunnel is a tenacious fastener and should never come out. Kosakowski found one that he could just pull out because the surrounding wood was rotten.

The situation was clear to Kosakowski. What had started out as a routine dry-dock maintenance period for the *Bounty*, and a relatively short one as these things go, was turning into something much more. They were going to have to remove a substantial amount of planking to determine the extent of the rot, and from what he had seen so far he expected to find more. That would necessitate replacing much of the

planking and timbers in order to keep the *Bounty* seaworthy. He told Walbridge he needed to authorize the shipyard employees to start removing planks for a thorough assessment.

Right away, Walbridge said no. He didn't think the rot would be that extensive, and the investigation could wait until the next yard period. When Kosakowski pressed him to reconsider, Walbridge grew testy and told Kosakowski he didn't have any choice in the matter.

"We don't have the money or the time," Walbridge told Kosakowski.

The foreman let it go at first, seeing that Walbridge was not willing to debate the issue. But the problem still troubled Kosakowski as work continued on the *Bounty*, and he brought it up several more times with Walbridge. The conversations seemed to have some impact on the captain, because early one morning Walbridge met Kosakowski in the shipwright's office and said he had a plan for addressing the wood rot: They could apply a chemical to the rotting frame to halt the rot and harden the wood, but that was it for now. He was going to find and fix any other rotten wood the following year, when a full hull examination was due.

"I want this to stay between the two of us, but I've explained these problems to the owner. Todd, I want you to know that you don't need to be worried," Walbridge said. "I'm going to argue on the shipyard's behalf and tell Bob that the construction materials and everything that your yard did in the previous haul-out is not something to take to suit."

At first Kosakowski didn't follow. Argue on the shipyard's behalf? Then he understood. The wood in question had been installed at the Boothbay shipyard only six years earlier and was rotting far earlier than would be expected.

"Bob's first reaction was, 'Do we have a lawsuit against the shipyard for faulty material or faulty workmanship?'" Walbridge told him.

Kosakowski thanked Walbridge for being on his side, but two or three hours later, the conversation was nagging at him. Kosakowski approached Walbridge to clarify whether the HMS *Bounty* Organization, the company that owner Robert Hansen organized to run the ship's business side, was going to sue the shipyard. Kosakowski came away with the impression that Walbridge was urging the ship's owner not to go that route, but instead to divest himself of a ship that was only going to con-

tinue requiring more and more money. To Kosakowski's understanding, the rotting wood on the *Bounty* had been the final confirmation that Hansen's desire to sell the *Bounty*—not widely known at the time—was the right move.

That was when, according to Kosakowski, Walbridge made the statement that would later lend support to the notion that he and Hansen wanted to get the *Bounty* out of harm's way and south to where potential buyers could see the ship.

"I told Bob Hansen he should get rid of the ship as soon as possible," Walbridge said, according to Kosakowski.

IN THE END, only two planks were replaced: one starboard aft and the other port forward, both above the waterline. Many of the crew members were aware of the rotting wood, because they either saw it themselves during their work or they overheard Walbridge and others talking about it. Cleveland knew about the shipyard's concerns because Walbridge came aboard after one of the initial conversations with Kosakowski and he was angry. The captain seemed to agree that the rot on the frame was significant, and he was unhappy that it was decaying so soon. He and Cleveland discussed that the rot most likely was due to the *Bounty* taking on rainwater from leaks and openings in the upper deck, a problem that the crew had been trying to address for some time. Cleveland did not get the impression that the rotting frame caused Walbridge concern for the safety of the vessel, but the captain was nonetheless upset that the newest timbers were already damaged. The frame rot that Cleveland saw was in two areas, about three feet apart and the size of a softball and a golf ball. He considered it inconsequential on a vessel of that size.

Kosakowski came back from a couple days off work to find that the *Bounty* crew had given the rotten frame a fresh coat of white paint to make the problem go away.

FAUNT REJOINED THE *Bounty* on October 2 while it was in the shipyard at Boothbay, having taken some time off to fulfill another of his retirement

45

dreams—riding a motorcycle across India. He got right to work, finding that the demolition had been finished already on the tank-moving project and the new water tanks had been installed. The crew was still moving the fuel tanks into place. There was plenty of electrical work to do in relation to the reconfiguration, so Faunt stayed busy with that and other general grunt work. The amount of work and the pace worried the old man somewhat. With the crew putting in twelve-hour days, six days a week, he felt that they were trying to get too much done in too little time. The *Bounty* could extend its planned stay in Boothbay if necessary, but Faunt knew that Walbridge was determined to leave on schedule. Close in age, the two men were good friends, and Faunt often tagged along when Walbridge borrowed a pickup truck from the shipyard for a run to Home Depot. On one of those trips they discussed how much work still needed to be done in a short time, and Walbridge explained that they could not extend the shipyard time, because he had to get the *Bounty* to New London, Connecticut, by Thursday, October 25. The captain explained that they had to be there to conduct a day sail for the crew of the Navy submarine *Mississippi*, an excursion that *Bounty* owner Robert Hansen had arranged to thank the Navy for his recent tour of the submarine's base in Groton, next door to New London.

Faunt's understanding, based on his conversation with Walbridge, was that Hansen had made clear or at least "strongly suggested" that the *Bounty* not miss the date. Walbridge seemed to feel that, though the crew would have to work hard, the *Bounty* would be ready to sail for New London as planned on October 24.

THE NEW SHIP'S engineer, Christopher Barksdale, joined the *Bounty* during the last few days in dry dock. The previous engineer was no longer around, so Second Mate Matthew Sanders gave Barksdale a tour and explained the ship's systems. Barksdale's first impression was that he wanted to spend a week cleaning the engine room. The 375-horsepower John Deere engines looked old and well-worn, leaking both oil and fuel; plus the engine room was just a mess from the ongoing work. Barksdale looked for the maintenance records, but all he could find were daily

logbooks in which the information was spotty at best. The more detailed maintenance records were computerized, he was told, and Barksdale could not find out how to get access. He asked, but no one could find any records that indicated when required maintenance had last been done.

The *Bounty* splashed on Saturday, October 20, sliding back into the water and tying up alongside the shipyard. It stayed there for four days as work continued and the crew monitored the hull for leaks. The newly repaired hull was holding fairly tight, at least by the *Bounty*'s high tolerance for leaking. Svendsen arrived in Boothbay on October 20 and thought the *Bounty* was in much better condition than when he had last seen it. The ship's surveyor, David Wyman, assessed the repairs and told Svendsen that the *Bounty* was "in the best shape I've seen it." No one expressed any concern to Svendsen about the condition of the planking or the frames, or the shipyard's worries that there might be hidden damage.

EARLY ON WEDNESDAY, October 24, tropical storm Sandy was gaining strength and more attention from the scientists at NOAA. Early that day, the storm started forming a more structured body, with an eye developing in the middle of the swirling clouds. Sandy was moving steadily north.

At eleven a.m., the *Bounty*'s onboard weather systems received a bulletin from the National Hurricane Center:

BULLETIN

HURRICANE SANDY ADVISORY NUMBER 9

NWS NATIONAL HURRICANE CENTER MIAMI FL AL182012

1100 AM EDT WED OCT 24 2012

. . . SANDY REACHES HURRICANE STRENGTH . . .

. . . CONDITIONS DETERIORATING IN JAMAICA . . .

SUMMARY OF 1100 AM EDT . . . 1500 UTC . . . INFORMATION

LOCATION . . . 17.1N 76.7W

ABOUT 65 MI . . . 100 KM S OF KINGSTON JAMAICA

ABOUT 235 MI . . . 380 KM SSW OF GUANTANAMO CUBA

MAXIMUM SUSTAINED WINDS . . . 80 MPH . . . 130 KM/H

PRESENT MOVEMENT . . . NNE OR 15 DEGREES AT 13 MPH . . . 20 KM/H

MINIMUM CENTRAL PRESSURE . . . 973 MB . . . 28.73 INCHES

Sandy was now a hurricane and heading north. The *Bounty*'s plans called for it to leave Boothbay the same day and continue south.

There was no discussion among the crew about the storm, and most had no idea that a hurricane was moving in their direction. Many tropical storms and hurricanes form in the south Atlantic but peter out before making it to the United States coast or waterways, so at this point the storm would have been little more than a curiosity to most of the crew of the *Bounty*, but for Walbridge and his senior mates it was something to watch in the next few days.

Walbridge was ready to sail for New London on the twenty-fourth, but much of the work was still not done. Faunt was uneasy to see that temporary lights were still strung in some spaces because the electrical work had not been completed, and there were no lights at all in some berthing compartments.

Prokosh, one of the more experienced tall ship sailors but still relatively new to the *Bounty*, felt they were rushing out of Boothbay to stay on schedule for the *Bounty*'s arrival in New London and then St. Peters-

burg about two weeks later. Everything was done on the double. Pack and *go, go, go.*

Before they left, the yard foreman wanted a word with Walbridge. Kosakowski was still troubled by the rot that he had seen on the *Bounty*, and even more by the damage that he had not seen but very much suspected would have been found under the planking. If the rotting wood was as extensive as he thought, it could increase the risk of leakage from the twisting and torque that any wooden-hulled ship is subjected to. The torque exerted on the planks in stormy weather was exponentially worse than when the ship sailed in calm seas, and could cause the wood to shift enough that, no matter how tightly the seams were sealed in dry dock, gaps would open up and the ship would take on water. Some of this was expected and could be managed by the bilge pumps that expelled a normal amount of water leakage, but Kosakowski worried that the rotting wood would make the boards even less sturdy and allow more twisting and leakage. Another concern was that the *Bounty* had been in dry dock for more than a month, so the wood that normally stayed wet in the hull had dried out and might not have had time to soak and properly seal the seams.

Kosakowski pulled the captain aside and reiterated his concerns.

"The vessel might not be safe, because we haven't explored to determine the extent of the wood rot," Kosakowski told the captain. "I have to tell you that I don't think it's safe to leave without exploring the extent of the rot."

Walbridge assured him that he understood Kosakowski's concerns, and Kosakowski would recall later that the captain was "terrified" of what they had found. Nevertheless, Walbridge told him that he did not think the rot was extensive enough to require immediate work or any change in the *Bounty*'s plans. Kosakowski felt powerless to stop Walbridge, but he at least wanted to offer some words of advice.

"You have to pick and choose your weather. Don't use the vessel the same way you have in the last couple of years," he said, referring to the *Bounty*'s trip to England and sailing through storms.

Walbridge assured him they would be all right. Before long, Wal-

bridge and his crew were casting off lines and leaving Boothbay on a ship that Kosakowski was sure hid some dark and dangerous secrets.

ABOUT THE SAME time the *Bounty* was pulling out of Boothbay, NOAA's National Hurricane Center sent another update on Hurricane Sandy.

One of the most important services provided by the National Hurricane Center is the projection of where the storm is going to go and when, an analysis that is an art form based on a whole lot of science. No hurricane's path can ever be predicted with certainty, but the experts at NOAA massage a wealth of data and historical experience to come up with a prediction for where the storm will be over the next few days. That prediction is constantly updated with the addition of new data, and NOAA has a good track record of warning about a hurricane's eventual path. At five p.m. on Wednesday, the NOAA maps showed the hurricane hitting Jamaica, with a high confidence prediction that it would cross Cuba, then hit the Bahamas at two p.m. on Thursday, tack east slightly, and then move northward up the western Atlantic by two p.m. on Saturday. Beyond that, NOAA had less confidence in its predictions but tentatively projected that Sandy would continue northward off the East Coast and make landfall somewhere in the New Jersey or New England area.

The hurricane's path on the map took up the entire Eastern Seaboard.

CHAPTER 6

A NEW LIFE

AFTER A SHORT stop in New London, the *Bounty* crew knew that the next destination was St. Petersburg, Florida, where the famous ship had been a tourist attraction for years, and where Walbridge lived with his wife, Claudia McCann. The dock where it had been moored was about to be demolished, so the plan was for the *Bounty* to go down and have one last hurrah with the ship's fans in St. Petersburg.

Some crew had heard that the *Bounty* also was to be the centerpiece of a special charity event in St. Petersburg, but such events were frequent, and most crew did not know what made this one different. Walbridge was looking forward to the St. Petersburg stop because he thought a new relationship with the Ashley DeRamus Foundation could bring new attention and revenue for the *Bounty*. A private organization dedicated to raising awareness about Down syndrome, the foundation is named after an effervescent thirty-year-old woman with Down syndrome who had spent time on the *Bounty* recently. A petite, attractive young woman with a short blond haircut, DeRamus had medaled in swimming at the Special Olympics forty-three times, and now works as a teacher's assistant at a special-needs preschool in Birmingham, Alabama. She is an active role model for people with Down syndrome.

It all started in February 2012, when sixty-five-year-old Gary Kan-

negiesser, who had a two-year contract to be the *Bounty*'s official photographer, met Ashley DeRamus's mother, Connie, during the ship's winter stay in Puerto Rico. The DeRamus family soon toured the *Bounty* dockside, and Ashley fell in love with the ship. Walbridge had a soft spot for her and others with disabilities, so it wasn't long before they were talking about having DeRamus make a voyage with them and learn the art of tall ship sailing. DeRamus and her parents traveled on the *Bounty* in the summer of 2012, on its East Coast tour from St. Augustine, Florida, up through Maine and Nova Scotia. For three days DeRamus worked as a deckhand, standing watch and performing many of the same duties as the other crew, who all fell in love with the eternally upbeat young woman. Christian was especially close to her, and DeRamus considered her a mentor—even though Christian had just joined the crew herself— and sort of a surrogate mother when Connie couldn't make every leg of the journey. DeRamus was unable to perform some of the physical tasks because her hands are small, a common feature of people who have Down syndrome, and earlier surgeries on her ankles restricted her ability to climb. But she loved the sea and being part of the *Bounty* family, just like Christian.

Ashley's parents were impressed by the hardworking crew, who at first struck Connie DeRamus as a wild and woolly bunch of hippies on a boat. She soon found that they were a responsible, thoroughly respectable group despite the long beards, dreadlocks, tattoos, and piercings. The gentle Southern lady from Auburndale, Florida, still couldn't resist giving each of the female crew members a pretty Tahitian dress, though, just to feminize them a bit.

The potential partnership between the Ashley DeRamus Foundation and the *Bounty* seemed like a no-brainer. Both parties needed more attention from the public, the foundation so it could raise awareness about Down syndrome, and the *Bounty* so it could raise money and improve the ship. Walbridge and the DeRamus family, along with Kannegiesser, discussed the possibilities at great length and decided it could only be a winner for both of them. Walbridge got approval from the *Bounty* owner and plans moved forward, beginning with Ashley DeRamus setting up a table on the dock wherever the *Bounty* stopped, selling rubber bracelets

for her foundation. Kannegiesser sometimes helped out by dressing like Jack Sparrow, the Johnny Depp character from *Pirates of the Caribbean*. At the end of DeRamus's voyage, she and Christian cried when they had to say good-bye. But they had plans to see each other again when DeRamus returned to the *Bounty* with other special-needs visitors.

"Captain Walbridge had a real soft spot in his heart for kids and adults with special needs," Connie DeRamus told the author. "His plan was to convert the *Bounty* to a special-needs ship for a tour of the Great Lakes this summer [2013]. He was adding riggings that were smaller so that Down's people, who are smaller than your average person, could climb up to the crow's nest and the rigging. They would work on the ship two or three days, doing the same kind of duties that Ashley did, to develop some independence and responsibility."

Though there had been no contractual agreement between the *Bounty* and the foundation, plans were well under way to fulfill this vision. Just a few months after Ashley DeRamus sailed on the ship, the plan was for the *Bounty* to sail from New England to St. Petersburg and arrive the weekend of Friday, November 9. The Ashley DeRamus Foundation was promoting the weekend to several Down syndrome organizations, including the Down Syndrome Network of Tampa Bay, and encouraging families to come visit the *Bounty* that weekend for tours of the ship and day sails in which the special-needs visitors could get hands-on experience just as Ashley had. Interest was high.

About four hundred special-needs families were expected to attend over the weekend, Connie DeRamus told the author.

After the big kickoff weekend, the plan was for Ashley DeRamus and a few other special-needs visitors to sail on the *Bounty* to Galveston, Texas, and arrive by December 9, Ashley's thirtieth birthday. The *Bounty* would winter over in Galveston, as it had many times before, and Christian planned to stay aboard to help modify the ship so it could more easily accommodate special-needs visitors. The following summer season, in 2013, the Ashley DeRamus Foundation would sponsor special-needs children and adults to sail on the *Bounty*. In addition to what Connie DeRamus says would have been only a modest infusion of cash from the foundation itself, Kannegiesser was talking with potential corporate

sponsors, including a car manufacturer and a soft-drink company. The History Channel had expressed some interest in following the special-needs *Bounty* crew for a reality television show.

"Robin thought that it would give the *Bounty* a new purpose," Connie DeRamus says.

The *Bounty* would have had to improve its certification before being allowed to take paying passengers on board in this way, because its status as a moored attraction vessel clearly prohibited anyone but crew on the ship unless it was tied to a dock. DeRamus's previous trip on the *Bounty* required her to be a volunteer crew member, with the Coast Guard providing documents approving her voyage, to get around this prohibition. But the much grander plans for sponsored voyages and more special-needs visitors during transit would have stretched the Coast Guard prohibitions to the breaking point, so significant sums had to be found for upgrading the seaworthiness of the ship. And that was part of the plan. The increased attention, corporate donations, and other revenue would help make the *Bounty* a first-class sailing vessel and educational platform for people with special needs.

This first event in St. Petersburg would launch the *Bounty* on a second life—or third, fourth, or fifth, depending on how you measured. Some of the crew privately were concerned about this rebirth, because they did not have any training in working with special-needs visitors, and because—as much as they had fallen in love with Ashley—some of them didn't want the *Bounty* to become just another tall ship that took on schoolkids and passengers. They liked that the *Bounty* was a real working sailor's ship, just the ship and the crew out at sea. But Walbridge was excited about the plan, Connie DeRamus says, because he knew that the *Bounty* would continue to struggle for its survival from year to year if it did not find a new role to play. If this visit to St. Petersburg was a success, Walbridge, Hansen, and the crew could breathe easier, and maybe they could finally raise the standards on board. Maybe the *Bounty* could afford to fix its many problems, achieve a higher certification, be allowed to take on paying passengers, and no longer be known as the black sheep of the fleet.

But Walbridge, and perhaps Hansen, apparently felt that for any of

that to happen, the *Bounty* had to get to St. Petersburg on time. Kannegiesser exchanged e-mails with Walbridge as the *Bounty* was leaving Boothbay, and over the next day or so, both of them expressed excitement about the coming events.

There might have been another concern weighing heavily on Walbridge. He knew that his boss, Hansen, had decided he had spent enough time and money on the *Bounty*. Hansen was looking to sell the ship for $4.6 million. The *Bounty*'s promising future as a platform for people with disabilities—and the possibility of television exposure and marketing deals—might improve the chances of finding a buyer. But if the ship were left in port in New London and severely damaged by the storm, could that all change?

THE TRIP TO New London took about two hours, during which the *Bounty* encountered a squall and about half the crew got seasick, possibly because they had been working on land for so long.

Faunt completed much of the electrical work on the way to New London, getting the lights functional in most of the berthing areas so the crew would not have to keep sleeping on the tween deck and in the great cabin just to have some light at night. He also got the ship's general alarm functioning. The tank room lighting was still temporary, however. The new engineer, Barksdale, was not happy with how the engine room had been left after the work in Boothbay. The crew had cleaned before leaving Boothbay, but Barksdale could see that much of the ship was still a mess by his standards, with plenty of sawdust, wood chips, and other trash left in the nooks and crannies of the engine room and bilge. But the *Bounty* had left in a hurry, he thought, so maybe it couldn't be helped.

The transit to New London was the *Bounty*'s first sea trial after the shipyard period, and at one point Faunt was at the helm, controlling the big wooden wheel that steered the ship. He could see that the realignment of the ballast and the new tank configurations had the *Bounty* trimmed down so that it was sailing about five inches deeper on the stern. He expected that to result in more water aft on the boat, leaving the forward spaces drier than was typical before. Overall, he thought, the

Bounty was handling better than the last time he was on board, and Walbridge told him the same thing.

There was still a significant problem, however. On his boat-check rounds, which required checking the bilgewater levels and pumping out water as necessary, Faunt found that the bilge system was not performing well. With his engineering background, his experience on other sailing ships, and his hands-on work with the *Bounty*'s systems, Faunt was possibly the most qualified person on board to assess how well the bilge pumps were operating, and he was profoundly concerned. The main bilge pumps, which ran off power generated by the engines, were taking too long to get the water out of the boat while they were sailing in calm seas. The main problem seemed to be that the pumps could not stay primed; that is, they could not keep the system full of water instead of letting in air. While there is air in the pipes or the pump itself, the bilge system must work hard to first suck that air out and then start moving water, which is comparatively less taxing. Priming the pump, which means ridding the system of trapped air, is standard for any bilge pump, but the *Bounty*'s systems were struggling to do so over and over.

This doesn't feel right, Faunt thought. *Something is wrong here.*

Prokosh had the same misgivings on his boat checks, noticing that the pumps kept losing prime and that dewatering was taking twice as long as it had in his previous eight months on the ship. He had reported the slow pumping to Walbridge before they even left Boothbay, and the captain responded with, "I'll think about it." When the problem was no better on the way to New London, Prokosh reported his concern to the captain again and got the same reply.

Salapatek also was troubled by the bilge system on his boat-check rounds, so he took his concerns to Barksdale. The engineer wasn't familiar with the *Bounty*'s bilge systems and couldn't tell whether they were running normally or not, so he related the concerns to the captain, who went down to the engine room to see for himself. Walbridge worked the bilge system with Barksdale present and then declared the pumps were fine.

Faunt also reported his concerns about the bilge pumps to Svendsen, the chief mate and also the officer of the watch at the time, and to Walbridge directly. He did not bother discussing the problem with the engi-

neer because he knew Barksdale was not familiar with the *Bounty*'s bilge pumps. Svendsen and Walbridge seemed to take his concerns seriously, but they had no immediate solution to the problem. Faunt continued working with the bilge system and found that if he ran both bilge pumps simultaneously—not the usual procedure—the pumps would prime and then he could turn one off without losing prime on the other. It was a workaround, and that was nothing new on the *Bounty*. There was a backup bilge pump system also, operated hydraulically instead of electrically, but Faunt had seen that system in operation only twice during his time on the *Bounty*. He didn't want to have to depend on the hydraulic system.

Even with his workaround, the main bilge system pumps were never working to Faunt's satisfaction on the trip to New London.

AS SOON AS they arrived in New London on Wednesday afternoon, Cleveland and Groves took a train and a ferry to Long Island, New York, for a prearranged doctor visit for Groves. They spent the night there and would return to New London the next day.

AT ELEVEN P.M. Wednesday evening, the National Hurricane Center issued a new bulletin. The hurricane had crossed over Jamaica with winds of eighty miles per hour and was about to hit Cuba. Most important, Hurricane Sandy was growing in intensity:

BULLETIN

HURRICANE SANDY ADVISORY NUMBER 11

NWS NATIONAL HURRICANE CENTER MIAMI FL AL182012

1100 PM EDT WED OCT 24 2012

. . . EYE OF SANDY APPROACHING THE COAST OF SOUTHEASTERN CUBA . . .

... COULD BECOME A CATEGORY TWO HURRICANE BEFORE
LANDFALL . . .

SUMMARY OF 1100 PM EDT . . . 0300 UTC . . . INFORMATION

LOCATION . . . 19.4N 76.3W

ABOUT 85 MI . . . 135 KM SW OF GUANTANAMO CUBA

ABOUT 100 MI . . . 165 KM NNE OF KINGSTON JAMAICA

MAXIMUM SUSTAINED WINDS . . . 90 MPH . . . 150 KM/H

PRESENT MOVEMENT . . . N OR 10 DEGREES AT 13 MPH . . . 20
KM/H

MINIMUM CENTRAL PRESSURE . . . 954 MB . . . 28.17 INCHES

THURSDAY, OCTOBER 25, was Walbridge's sixty-third birthday. The *Bounty* crew started the day tired from their long days at the shipyard, the previous day's sail to New London, and the seasickness that some experienced on the way. There was much to do on Thursday, however, and the crew could not rest. They welcomed the crew members of the submarine USS *Mississippi*, taking them out on a sail around the harbor and showing the Navy sailors the ways of a traditional square-rigged sailing vessel. The *Bounty* crew enjoyed taking submariners out for a spin, but a day sail is hard work, with lots to do in running the ship and even more with supervising the visitors and letting them have a try at different tasks. Old enough to be grandfather to most of them, Faunt especially enjoyed having the Navy boys on the *Bounty*. He had been in the Navy years earlier,

and he relished telling the submarine's captain what to do when he was on the *Bounty*. Afterward, the *Bounty* crew visited the submarine for a tour—a visit that on most days would be a welcome treat, but by that point many of the crew, including Hewitt and Barksdale, were so tired they just wanted to have dinner and sleep. Most went and enjoyed the tour nonetheless; Barksdale skipped it.

It was during this visit on the submarine that many of the crew first heard about Hurricane Sandy. The Navy guys knew that the *Bounty* was scheduled to set sail soon, and several commented to the crew that they had to beat the big storm forming to the south. Most of the *Bounty* crew just laughed off the comments and joked that they might be in for a good ride.

Before saying good-bye to the Navy sailors, Walbridge remarked that he had now trained crew from both the oldest ship in the Navy, the tall ship USS *Constitution*, as well as the newest, the USS *Mississippi*.

When they returned to their ship, the *Bounty* crew still had plenty of work ahead of them to get the ship ready for sailing to the next destination.

Chapter 7

INNOCENCE

IN THE LATE afternoon, after the *Bounty* crew had returned from touring the submarine, Scornavacchi received a phone call from his mother back home in Pennsylvania. She had heard about a hurricane in the Atlantic and she was worried about the *Bounty*'s plans to sail to St. Petersburg. There was a big storm forming, she said. Plus, there was a nor'easter that was supposed to meet up with the hurricane and make it worse. Well landlocked in eastern Pennsylvania, even she knew that sounded ominous.

"You're not going to sail into that, are you?"

Scornavacchi assured his mom that they would be safe, that the captain wouldn't do anything to put them in danger, but he could tell that she was not relieved. She had never made this kind of call to him before. She was a mother, and all mothers worry, but this wasn't like her. She told her son that she'd had a terrible dream the night before, a nightmare about Joshua being caught in a storm at sea and . . . dying. He tried to explain that Walbridge was a good captain, an experienced mariner who knew what he was doing when it came to bad weather. But it stayed in his mind that perhaps they were facing a dangerous situation. Maybe they wouldn't sail as soon as everyone thought.

60

The National Hurricane Center was updating the storm's progress in real time on its Web site and issuing official bulletins as warranted, usually every two or three hours. The bulletin issued at two p.m. Thursday, before the crew returned from the submarine, showed that Sandy was still strong. By the time it hit Cuba earlier that day, Hurricane Sandy skipped past category two and was upgraded to category three: 96- to 110-mile-per-hour winds, and a nine- to twelve-foot storm surge. Thursday afternoon it was in the Bahamas north of Cuba and still producing winds of 105 miles per hour:

BULLETIN

HURRICANE SANDY INTERMEDIATE ADVISORY NUMBER 13A

NWS NATIONAL HURRICANE CENTER MIAMI FL AL182012

200 PM EDT THU OCT 25 2012

. . . CENTER OF SANDY MOVING BETWEEN LONG ISLAND AND GREAT EXUMA . . .

SUMMARY OF 200 PM EDT . . . 1800 UTC . . . INFORMATION

LOCATION . . . 23.5N 75.4W

ABOUT 25 MI . . . 40 KM E OF GREAT EXUMA ISLAND

ABOUT 125 MI . . . 200 KM SE OF ELEUTHERA

MAXIMUM SUSTAINED WINDS . . . 105 MPH . . . 165 KM/H

PRESENT MOVEMENT . . . N OR 5 DEGREES AT 20 MPH . . . 32
KM/H

MINIMUM CENTRAL PRESSURE . . . 963 MB . . . 28.44 INCHES

The officers on the ship were checking the weather forecasts and knew about the approaching hurricane. Groves was somewhat concerned about the weather forecasts, and she discussed the situation with Cleveland. Together, they took their concerns to Svendsen. The chief mate knew that Groves and Cleveland were experienced and not easily spooked, so he seriously considered what they said. Svendsen had been following the weather himself since first hearing about a storm named Sandy on October 23, two days earlier, and he had misgivings also. His girlfriend had called him earlier in the day to ask whether they were still planning to leave for Florida.

When he realized that the captain was planning to go ahead and sail that night, he was more concerned. The ship would sail south by southeast as Hurricane Sandy moved northward, Walbridge explained, and then the captain would see where the storm went and decide the rest of their path then.

Svendsen was troubled enough to ask the captain to step off the boat for a private conversation. They left the *Bounty* and stood on the pier to talk. Svendsen brought up the possibility of staying in New London or finding another, safer port.

"There are people concerned about the hurricane, and I want to discuss options for what we're going to do to accommodate the weather," he told Walbridge. "No matter what course we plot, we're going to encounter winds that are thirty-five to sixty knots. That's almost hurricane-strength winds. I think we should look at options available for us and what the best plan is."

Walbridge said no, that he appreciated the input but he was confident the *Bounty* could depart for St. Petersburg as scheduled. They had to sail, because "A ship is safer at sea."

He did say, however, that he would address the crew about their concerns. Svendsen had little choice but to accept Walbridge's answer.

Walbridge exchanged e-mails with the Ashley DeRamus Foundation, he and Kannegiesser remaining upbeat, and expressing how excited they both were about starting their new adventure. The growing storm was not discussed; Kannegiesser was only vaguely aware of a storm in the Atlantic, and Walbridge did not volunteer any information about how it could affect their big kickoff weekend in two weeks—about the time it would take to get to St. Petersburg if the *Bounty* left right away, on schedule.

About four p.m. the crew gathered at the capstan, a mechanical piece on the rear of the deck that stands a few feet tall and is used to wind rigging or anchor lines, and traditionally a common spot for crew meetings on any sailing ship. They were there on a beautiful fall day to hear the captain talk about a coming storm.

"I know some of you have gotten phone messages and text messages from your family and friends concerning Sandy, the hurricane that is out there," Walbridge said. For some crew members, including Faunt, this was the first news that the weather was anything to be worried about. Many of them had heard talk of a storm forming, but they did not realize it was anything serious until the captain brought it up. "If you feel you wish to get off the ship, you can do so and I won't hold it against you."

Walbridge explained that because of the approaching storm he wanted to depart within two hours. He told them in a general way that Sandy was building in the Atlantic and would flow northward along the Gulf Stream, making landfall somewhere in New England. He said nothing about the growing intensity of the storm or anything that would indicate this hurricane was unusual in any way. The *Bounty* would go to the east well before the hurricane moved that far north, he told his crew, gaining plenty of sea room. The ship should be able to go all the way out to the east, wait for Sandy to turn inland to the west, and then the *Bounty* could cut back in toward its next destination in Florida, Faunt recalls the captain saying. "A ship is safer at sea," Walbridge explained to his crew, repeating what he had told Svendsen. He emphasized that the *Bounty* was not going to set forth on a straight line to St. Petersburg, because if Sandy turned west earlier than predicted, the ship could be trapped between land and a quickly closing hurricane—an extreme version of what is known to sailors as a "lee shore" situation. Cleveland

knew how bad that would be. A lee shore is one in which the winds, in this case hurricane winds, are blowing toward the shore rather than away from it. That can be dangerous to any vessel that is drifting or underpowered, because the wind can cause it to run aground. Sailboats and square-rigged ships like the *Bounty* are especially vulnerable to lee shores. The plan to go east and wait for Sandy to make her turn inland would avoid that risk, Walbridge explained.

Cleveland responded well to Walbridge's explanation, and he had complete confidence in his captain. He knew that before coming to the *Bounty*, Walbridge had piloted boats that evacuated workers from oil rig platforms in the ocean as hurricanes approached, and Cleveland already had ridden out a hurricane with him.

For some of the crew this was the first they had heard of Hurricane Sandy, so all they had to go on was what Walbridge told them. Prokosh, for instance, had not seen a newspaper, watched television, or been online in days. Hewitt's cell phone had rung about noon on Thursday, and it was her mother. "Are you guys still going out even though there's a hurricane?" she asked. With all the work regarding the day sail, Hewitt didn't have a lot of time to talk with her mom, and she easily dismissed the call. *She's a mom,* Hewitt thought. *She's a worrier.* After hearing Walbridge's plans, she thought the hurricane couldn't be that bad if he was willing to take the *Bounty* into it.

Barksdale had not previously heard of the storm, and at first he didn't have any idea what Walbridge was talking about. When the captain said they would sail into a hurricane, Barksdale briefly thought about raising his hand to leave. But he didn't.

Faunt thought most of the crew was concerned, even if they weren't willing to speak up. Everyone looked worried, he thought, but no one was willing to say good-bye to the rest of the crew.

The plan made sense to those few crew members who had any knowledge of how to navigate around severe weather, and the rest of the crew took Walbridge's calmness as an indication that he knew what he was doing. They had supreme, unwavering confidence in Walbridge. Even if he had told them directly and explicitly that he planned to take a south-

westerly course, cutting across the path of the hurricane and trying to outrun it, many said later they still would have trusted him. They might have been worried, but they would have chalked that up to their own inexperience and lack of balls.

The crew would remember the meeting as a proactive outreach from the captain, offering them a chance to leave when he was not obligated to do so, but what Walbridge left out was more noteworthy. Some of the crew noticed that Walbridge did not solicit input from them about whether to sail from New London or what the other options might be. He just told them the *Bounty* was sailing soon with plans to outmaneuver a hurricane, and they could stay or go. For many ship captains, this would not be remarkable. It was the way most of them ran their boats; the captain made decisions and informed the crew. But Walbridge was renowned for his different style. His crew admired the way he involved them in decision making, encouraging suggestions or at least questions from even the most inexperienced deckhands. That was the Walbridge way of leadership, a Socratic method of guiding his crew to making the right decision rather than simply telling them what to do. But not today. He did not lay out the scenario and encourage discussion of the options for sailing, staying, or moving to a safer port. He did not seek opinions on the decision he had already made. Why not? It was out of character for Walbridge. Perhaps he did not want to hear what the crew would have said, did not want any encouragement for anyone to second-guess his decision.

The captain did not discuss what other tall ships, or modern vessels, were doing in response to the storm forecast. Walbridge also made no mention of the Ashley DeRamus Foundation, or why it was so important to get to St. Petersburg on time. The impression left with his crew was that the *Bounty* was simply sailing as scheduled despite the hurricane, with no special deadline that might affect his judgment, with no notion that Walbridge was putting them at risk for what he thought was a good reason.

Perhaps most important, Walbridge said little about the severity of Hurricane Sandy or the specifics of its expected path. He had access to

the most sophisticated weather information and storm plots, but Walbridge glossed over just how dangerous the voyage might be.

The *Bounty* did not lack for sophistication in its ability to receive weather forecasts and follow the projected path of Hurricane Sandy. The ship was equipped with a Rose Point software system that helped plot waypoints and navigation, a WeatherFax system that received free radio broadcast satellite weather facsimile (WEFAX) images and text weather data, radar, e-mail communications, as well as multiple paper charts and books. WeatherFax was particularly useful, because it gave the crew both surface analysis and upper-atmosphere analyses, printing out maps that look something like what local television meteorologists show on the evening news, except they are black-and-white and much more detailed. The maps show the latest data for wind speed, direction, jet stream, wave height, and the location of gales and hurricanes. The ship was able to receive frequent updates from the National Hurricane Center, including the projections of the storm's path.

In addition to the brief bulletins about the hurricane, the National Hurricane Center issues lengthy "discussions" that are filled with deep, detailed data as well as the meteorologists' reasoning for their predictions about the storm. The discussion posted at five p.m. on Thursday explained that Sandy was expected to weaken slightly but then regain strength:

SATELLITE IMAGERY SHOWS THAT THE CENTER OF SANDY MADE LANDFALL OVER SOUTHEASTERN JAMAICA AROUND 1900 UTC. THERE HAS BEEN LITTLE DEGRADATION TO THE SATELLITE PRESENTATION SINCE LANDFALL . . . AND THE INITIAL INTENSITY IS MAINTAINED AT 70 KT FOR THIS ADVISORY. THE CENTRAL PRESSURE OF 970 MB IS SUPPORTED BY A RECENT OBSERVATION OF 972 MB AT KINGSTON WITH 38 KT OF WIND. ASIDE FROM LAND INTERACTION . . . CONDITIONS APPEAR FAVORABLE FOR SANDY TO AT LEAST MAINTAIN INTENSITY UNTIL IT MOVES ACROSS EASTERN CUBA . . . WHERE SOME WEAKENING IS EXPECTED. THE HURRICANE AND GLOBAL MODELS SHOW THE CYCLONE INTENSIFYING OVER THE BAHAMAS AS IT INTERACTS WITH AN

UPPER-LEVEL TROUGH . . . AND THE OFFICIAL FORECAST SHOWS
SANDY REGAINING HURRICANE INTENSITY BY 36 HOURS. AFTER
THAT TIME . . . ONLY A LITTLE WEAKENING IS EXPECTED AS
SANDY IS MAINTAINED AS A STRONG CYCLONE WITH AT LEAST
SOME CONTRIBUTION FROM BAROCLINIC PROCESSES THROUGH
DAY 5.

The discussion also included a "forty-eight-hour outlook":

LOCATED NEAR LATITUDE 25.3 NORTH . . . LONGITUDE 76.1
WEST. SANDY IS MOVING TOWARD THE NORTH-NORTHWEST NEAR
13 MPH. A TURN TOWARD THE NORTHWEST AND A DECREASE IN
FORWARD SPEED ARE EXPECTED TONIGHT AND FRIDAY . . . FOL-
LOWED BY A TURN BACK TOWARD THE NORTH AND NORTHEAST
FRIDAY NIGHT AND SATURDAY. ON THE FORECAST TRACK . . . THE
CENTER OF SANDY WILL CONTINUE MOVING NEAR OR OVER THE
NORTHWESTERN BAHAMAS TONIGHT AND FRIDAY.

PERHAPS MOST IMPORTANT, Walbridge had access to the hurricane path
projections from NOAA, and by this time on Thursday evening the picture was quite clear. NOAA's "cone" showing the expected path of Hurricane Sandy had the storm southeast of Cape Hatteras, North Carolina,
by two p.m. on Sunday, then turning westward and making landfall on
Monday or Tuesday as far south as Cape Hatteras, or farther north into
Virginia, Maryland, Delaware, New York, New Jersey, Connecticut, and
Maine. The projection past two p.m. on Sunday was less certain, but still
there was no doubt that NOAA expected the storm to turn west sometime on Sunday afternoon or evening.

The bulletins issued at eight p.m. Thursday indicated Sandy's winds
were still at a hundred miles per hour. At eleven p.m., the bulletin noted
that the eye of the hurricane was passing Eleuthera Island in the northwestern Bahamas, with ninety-mile-per-hour winds.

Hurricane-force winds extended outward from the storm up to thirty-five miles from the center, and tropical storm–force winds reached as far as 230 miles out. Sandy was now a category-two hurricane.

THOUGH NO ONE was willing to challenge the captain at the capstan, several members of the crew talked privately afterward and expressed their concern or at least their curiosity about the potential danger. For many, like Scornavacchi and some of the other less seasoned crew, they simply did not know whether to be concerned or not. At face value, sailing into a hurricane sounded risky, and the captain's blunt offer to let anyone off the ship seemed to reinforce that idea. But at the same time, sailing on a ship like the *Bounty* always involved some danger, and they had great confidence in Walbridge, who did not seem scared at all. The less experienced crew turned to those who had been through rough seas and even hurricanes with the *Bounty*, like Cleveland and Svendsen. Those more experienced sailors reassured them that the captain was right: They would be safer at sea, and it was entirely possible for the *Bounty* to maneuver around the storm in such a way as to avoid the worst of Sandy. This hurricane was not classified as especially powerful, they told the crew, which helped reassure Scornavacchi and others. Some of them, Prokosh included, even felt excited by the prospect of finally testing their skills in some rough weather after seeing nothing but fairly smooth sailing and dry-dock time for months.

Besides, this would not be the first big storm for the *Bounty*. Many of the crew had heard the story of how the ship had run into a big storm in the fall of 1998 en route from Massachusetts to St. Petersburg. After the ship took on on water, the *Bounty* crew had to be rescued by a Coast Guard helicopter, two cutters, a tugboat, and two Navy vessels. The resulting Coast Guard investigation attributed the incident to Walbridge's misjudging the severity of the water leaking. Then in 2002 a storm caught the *Bounty* in the Gulf of Mexico, and the crew dropped anchor in an attempt to stop the ship from being blown onto shore or into oil rigs. The ship kept drifting and the captain had to order the anchor chain cut. The most recent big storm for the *Bounty* was in 2010 near Puerto

Rico, where the newly joined Cleveland rode out a storm big enough to destroy sails, a mast, and one generator.

Barksdale, the engineer, was still concerned about sailing into a hurricane, especially since he had virtually no experience on the *Bounty* or any tall ship. But even after only thirty days with the *Bounty* crew, he felt an obligation to them, especially his good friend Svendsen, who had gotten him the job. Others felt that same sense of obligation. Black, the cook, couldn't leave the crew without someone to feed them. Christian decided to stay for similar reasons. She didn't want to leave this family she had joined, and she trusted that the captain and the more experienced crew were making the right decisions.

The older, more experienced Faunt was concerned that the crew was too tired to set sail, especially into rough weather. He expressed his concerns to Walbridge, but the captain said it wouldn't be a problem. He had made the same voyage with only six crew in the past, he told Faunt. The *Bounty* was due in St. Petersburg on November 9, and at the *Bounty*'s top speed of five knots or six miles per hour under full sail, it would be a fourteen-day voyage from New London even before accounting for any delays due to the weather. That meant the *Bounty* needed to leave port tonight, Walbridge explained. Delaying the departure so the crew could rest would mean waiting until Saturday—not the next day, Friday— because Walbridge adhered to the old sailors' superstition that you should never leave port on a Friday. (Such superstitions are especially common on tall ships, where tradition is prized. Walbridge also insisted that pots and pans hanging in the galley be positioned so that they could catch the prevailing wind.) If they didn't set sail tonight, Walbridge explained, they'd lose almost two days of travel time.

The *Bounty* was about to set sail with a weary crew, rotten timbers, and malfunctioning bilge pumps—and it was going to try to outrun a hurricane. It was going to try what the *Fantome*, a much larger, more powerful, better-maintained ship, had failed to do, and thirty-one people died for that effort. Even without having all the pertinent information available to them, and no matter how much they tried to assure themselves that everything would be all right, some of the *Bounty* crew could not shake their worries. Scornavacchi texted several family members and

close friends to tell them that the *Bounty* was about to start moving south to St. Petersburg. He had one request for all of them: Pray for us.

He talked to his mother again before the ship set sail. She was terribly worried the *Bounty* was headed for disaster. Scornavacchi was too old for her to tell him to get off the ship and come home, but she could remind him how much he was loved, how important he was to her and the rest of his family. "Promise me," she said. "Promise me you won't die out there." He promised.

Hewitt was also having misgivings about the trip, but the feelings surprised and confused her. Logically, she told herself that she trusted Walbridge's experience and judgment, and she saw no reason they could not weather this storm at sea. But at the same time she felt a need to say good-bye to some important people in her life. She was never one for making a big deal out of good-byes, especially since she came and went on ships all the time, but something about this departure felt different. She contacted a few relatives and friends to say she was going, and she was taken aback by their responses. She texted the father of her boyfriend and crewmate Drew Salapatek, who was a big fan of the *Bounty* even before his son joined the crew, and his response was dead serious: "We'll be praying for you."

Wow, that's heavy, she thought.

Christian and Hewitt were pals on the boat, and Christian was following the weather closely, talking to Warner a lot about the predictions for the hurricane. She came to Hewitt that evening and said, "Jess, you won't believe it. This thing is huge!" She was carrying a printout of a weather map showing Hurricane Sandy's current size and position. "You know how Florida is, like, this big?" she said, gesturing with her hands. "Well, the hurricane is *this* big!"

"No way," Hewitt replied, taking the map to look for herself. After seeing it with her own eyes, she said, "We're going to have go all the way out to England to avoid this."

At that moment, Christian's parents were driving from their home in Vian, Oklahoma, to pick up their daughter. She had confided in Hewitt before arriving in New London that some of her family members were having a difficult time and she needed to be home, and Hewitt did not

press for more information. As much as she hated to leave the *Bounty*, Christian had told Hewitt, she was going to depart the ship in New London.

Christian never told anyone on the ship why she decided to sail with the *Bounty* on Thursday evening instead of meeting her parents the next day as planned. Perhaps she had perceived the conference with Walbridge as a challenge, a test of her mettle, and she feared going home now would look as if she were abandoning her oceangoing family just as they needed all hands on deck. The most anyone ever asked her about it was that evening after the meeting, when Hewitt said, "So, are you going to stay or are you going to go?"

"I'm staying," Christian said. "I want to see this through."

Christian may have been sure about her decision, but she was worried. She had called her parents already to tell them she was staying aboard, but she called again before the ship left port. "We're heading out and I just wanted to tell you and Dad that I love you," her mother recounted later to the Canadian Broadcasting Corporation. Her mother asked Christian why she was saying that.

"Just in case something happens."

Then she e-mailed her friend Rex Halbeisen. She was "very concerned for their safety and was 'praying to God that going to sea was the right decision,'" Halbeisen told the *Los Angeles Times*.

"You know me, I am not a mechanical person but the generators and engines on this ship are not the most reliable. . . . They are always stewing over them. I would hate to be out to sea in a storm [and] the engines just quit or we have no power."

———

CHRISTIAN HAD JOINED the *Bounty* in May 2012, and one of her five months on board had been spent in dry dock. She had never been through any rough weather on the ship. The engineer too had never been to sea on a sailing ship, much less on the *Bounty*. One of the most capable

and dedicated-to-the-sea sailors on board was the young, brash, bearded Cleveland, but his five years' experience on tall ships had been spent on the *Bounty* and under Walbridge's guidance. In addition to Christian, the other inarguably green sailors on the ship were Scornavacchi, Sprague, Barksdale, and Black. That was five of the fourteen crew members.

Ten of the crew had been on the *Bounty* for less than eight months. Nine, including the third mate, had never been on any other tall ship. The second mate had one summer's experience as an intern and no other tall ship familiarity. The average tall ship experience for the deckhands was one year, and their average time on the *Bounty* was six months.

They were going to face a hurricane in a ship with many problems. This was not a fair fight.

CHAPTER 8

SUPERSTORM

THE *BOUNTY* SET sail from New London soon after sunset on Thursday, October 25. The crew was tired and no one thought they were ready for the journey. Hewitt was normally diligent about preparing properly before casting off the lines, but she felt that for this trip they had time only to toss items on board and go.

It was a beautiful, calm evening and they sailed easily through the night, but the talk among the crew was almost entirely about the coming weather. The sailors who had experience in rough conditions, like Cleveland, were not looking forward to the next few days, even if they weren't frightened by the prospect of the hurricane. Everything could turn out in the best way possible, but Cleveland knew they still were going to be wet, miserable, and tired until they got past this storm. Groves was nervous about sailing into a hurricane, but Cleveland assured her they could trust Walbridge's decision.

The next morning the crew awoke to a gorgeous day with no hint of the hurricane closing the distance between them. The captain called an all-hands meeting at 12:45 p.m. and reiterated his plans for avoiding Hurricane Sandy. "I want to make tracks," Walbridge said. "I want to get as far southeast as possible, as quickly as possible." To that end, Walbridge explained that the *Bounty* would use both its engines on this trip,

rather than depending only on sail power, the way it typically traveled at sea.

He also discussed the weather and gestured to the clear blue skies with just a few wispy white clouds, asking the crew whether they could tell foul weather was imminent.

"Two hundred years ago, sailors wouldn't even know there was a hurricane coming," Scornavacchi heard him say. "But because we have GPS and radar and these other capabilities, we can track where the storm is, know where it's going. It makes it very different for us."

Right after that meeting, at 12:54 p.m., Walbridge sent an e-mail to owner Hansen and the manager of the HMS *Bounty* Organization:

"Sandy looks like a mean one. Right now we are on a converging course. I am actually headed to the dangerous side of it. Hoping like a deer if I aim at it, it won't be there when I get there. . . ."

Walbridge continued by elaborating on his plans:

"We are headed S x E waiting to see what the storm wants to do. I am guessing it wants to come ashore in NJ/NYC. We are running trying to stay on the east side of it. Bad side of it until we get some sea room. If we guess wrong we can run towards Newfoundland. If it turns and wants to tangle with us that means it is pretty far offshore and we can turn and go down the west side of it. I need to be sure it is well offshore before we can take advantage of the good weather for us. Right now I do not want to get between a hurricane and a hard spot. If you can send us updated track info (where it is projected to go) that would be great. We know where it is; I have to guess (along with the weatherman) where it is going."

MUCH OF THE crew time on Friday and into Saturday was spent getting the *Bounty* ready for rough weather. The main task was "sea stowing" the

boat, which meant securing everything that could move when the ship hit high seas and high winds. The *Bounty* would be rolling and heaving in the extreme, and everything had to be tied down—from the sails themselves to the tiniest things in the crew's cabins. Anything that could hurt you when it came flying across the deck—a cannon, for instance— was a major concern, but even small items could be a hazard underfoot. Something as simple as a loose sock from someone's bunk could be problematic during a hurricane, because if water enters the ship that sock will get tossed around and make its way down to the bilge pumps and clog the intakes. So every single thing was lashed down securely with heavy line or twine, a job that took a great deal of time on a ship the size of the *Bounty*. Scornavacchi stowed his pet fish in the safest way he could come up with: He put the betta in an empty peanut-butter jar filled with water, screwed the lid on, and hung it from the ceiling in his berthing compartment with a string long enough to let it swing freely with the boat but not bump into anything that would break it. The fish was in for a wild ride, but it should survive, he thought.

The crew also set up jack lines in some areas of the ship—ropes strung from one end to the other of a cabin or open space to give an extra handhold when the ship rolled. One of the first priorities was the galley to help Black feed the crew without being tossed around too badly. In her first two days at sea with the *Bounty*, from Boothbay and then from New London, Black had quickly ingratiated herself with the crew by providing more creative and tastier meals than what they were used to while at sea. They did their best to make sure she could keep feeding them well.

Groves and other crew members lowered and securely stowed some sails, and she double-checked the safety nets that would help keep sailors from falling into the sea if a wave or winds shoved them off. Walbridge declared the next day, Saturday, a "ship Sunday," which meant there were no standing work parties and people could get some much-needed rest once they completed sea stowing. Cleveland and Groves rigged their hammock to share, which they knew from experience would be a better rest when the boat was really moving.

Barksdale couldn't rest even when the *Bounty* was sailing in calm weather, still many miles from anything pushed ahead by Hurricane

Sandy. The *Bounty*'s hard-earned reputation as a wooden jalopy was already testing his engineering skills on Friday and Saturday. One of the crew noticed during a boat check that the port engine generator was moving around a lot, bouncing crazily on its mounts and making an increasing racket, so the crew shut it down and notified the engineer. The *Bounty* had two generators connected independently to the port and starboard engines. Mounted a few feet above the water to keep them dry even if the ship took on water, each generator drew power from the engine on that side of the boat. The engine, which drove the propeller on that side, had to be working if the generator was to run. The electricity from one generator was sufficient for the *Bounty*'s needs, so the engineer typically ran only one at a time.

Barksdale checked the port generator and found that some of the bolts had backed out of the mounts, probably just the result of vibration over time, so they switched to the starboard generator while he let the bouncy one cool down enough to work on it. He got the port generator back in order again, but it wasn't long before Barksdale discovered that another problem, though seemingly small, would prove significant over time.

While in Boothbay, the *Bounty* LLC office was responsible for ordering and arranging delivery of some supplies for the ship. Barksdale conducted an inventory of supplies for the engine room and found that the office had mistakenly purchased the wrong size fuel filters for the *Bounty*'s generators. Instead of twenty-micron fuel filters, Barksdale had two-micron filters. They still fit on the generators and worked, but they worked too well. Filtering at two microns instead of twenty meant that the filters clogged much faster than intended, and each clogged filter had to be replaced to keep the generator working. Barksdale discovered the problem as soon as the ship left Boothbay, and Walbridge called ahead to New London for the correct filters. But once they arrived, the filters delivered to the dock were twenty-micron filters of a different type, sized to fit the main engines and not the generators. With the fast exit from New London, there had been no time to get the correct filters.

Barksdale was vigilant about checking the fuel filters, especially since

he figured there must be contaminants in the fuel due to the new fuel tank installed in Boothbay. The fuel from the old tank had been transferred to the new one, and any contaminants that had settled in the old tank were probably now well mixed into the fuel. About every day or day and a half, Barksdale planned, he would shut down the generator that was running and switch to the other one so he could replace the fuel filter with a fresh one. It was much more maintenance than normally required for the generators, but there was no choice when using the more efficient filters. If they clogged, the generators would stop running.

The *Bounty* was making good time, at least by the standards of an old wooden ship with underpowered engines. With both mainsails full of wind and both engines running about as fast as anyone dared to push them, the *Bounty* was on its way.

At 10:21 p.m., Walbridge e-mailed Hansen again:

"We are still heading towards the storm and waiting for it to make up its mind as to where it wants to go. I am hoping it heads a little further out to sea so we can sneak down the west side of it. Otherwise we will be heading to Newfoundland."

At eleven p.m. on Friday, the National Hurricane Center issued another bulletin:

BULLETIN

HURRICANE SANDY ADVISORY NUMBER 19

NWS NATIONAL HURRICANE CENTER MIAMI FL AL182012

1100 PM EDT FRI OCT 26 2012

. . . SANDY REMAINS A HURRICANE AS IT MOVES SLOWLY NORTH-WARD AWAY FROM THE BAHAMAS . . .

SUMMARY OF 1100 PM EDT . . . 0300 UTC . . . INFORMATION

LOCATION . . . 27.7N 77.1W

ABOUT 90 MI . . . 145 KM N OF GREAT ABACO ISLAND

ABOUT 395 MI . . . 630 KM SSE OF CHARLESTON SOUTH CARO-
LINA

MAXIMUM SUSTAINED WINDS . . . 75 MPH . . . 120 KM/H

PRESENT MOVEMENT . . . N OR 10 DEGREES AT 7 MPH . . . 11
KM/H

MINIMUM CENTRAL PRESSURE . . . 969 MB . . . 28.61 INCHES

ONE OF THE lead scientists providing input for those bulletins, discussion posts, marine advisories, and other information available to the *Bounty* was Joseph Sienkiewicz, chief of the Ocean Applications Branch at the NOAA Ocean Prediction Center in Washington, D.C. A merchant mariner in an earlier career who spent five years piloting tugboats in New York and sailing on other ships, Sienkiewicz had been in his share of high seas and winds. His passion for understanding ocean storms and improving the ability to forecast them was driven by the loss of his mentor at the State University of New York Maritime College, Robert Gove. By October 1980, Sienkiewicz had returned to graduate school and was pursuing a career in ocean weather forecasting. Gove was working as third mate on the cargo ship SS *Poet*, which set out on October 24 from Delaware with a load of corn bound for Port Said, Egypt. Gove was the last person on the ship to speak with anyone on land, contacting his wife by ship-to-shore radio before the vessel got out of range. He told her nothing about the storm they were headed into off the coast of Virginia. Nine days later,

when no one had heard from the ship, the owners reported it missing. But an extensive search by the Coast Guard turned up nothing—not even one life jacket or one bit of debris. The Coast Guard's investigation concluded that the *Poet* had encountered storm winds of sixty knots and waves of thirty feet, causing some type of catastrophic damage to the big cargo ship that led it to sink so suddenly that no one had time to send off a distress message. All thirty-four crewmen, including Sienkiewicz's good friend and mentor, went down with the ship.

Sienkiewicz had no idea that the *Poet* was going down as he monitored that storm in the Atlantic. When he realized that Gove had died in a storm that did not appear to forecasters as especially severe, the loss prompted Sienkiewicz to search for ways to improve weather forecasting over the ocean. He knew how unpredictable ocean storms can be, and how complex they all are.

Sienkiewicz had just returned to the States from a trip to India on October 21 and saw Sandy developing in the Caribbean. He kept an eye on it along with scores of other meteorologists and oceanic experts. In all, about two hundred government scientists were busy collecting and analyzing data.

On Friday, October 26, Sandy was in some ways a typical hurricane, and not an especially powerful one. All hurricanes are powerful and dangerous, of course, but Sandy was not yet building strength in a way that suggested she might become like Hurricane Katrina, which reached a Category 5 level—with winds of 175 miles per hour or more—for an eighteen-hour period in 2005. Katrina had become a Category 3 storm, with winds of more than 111 miles per hour, by the time she came ashore and devastated New Orleans, along with much more of the Gulf Coast.

But Sandy had other things going for her. The intensity of the hurricane might have been ordinary, but other factors were coming together to make Hurricane Sandy a far more dangerous storm than indicated by her fluctuating Category 1 or Category 2 rating, which denote winds of between seventy-four and 110 miles per hour. The Saffir-Simpson Hurricane Wind Scale determines the 1 to 5 ratings based only on a hurricane's sustained wind speed, certainly a key determinant of the storm's force and potential for damage, but not the only factor.

Working mostly from his home so he could focus intently on the data, away from the fray of hurricane response at NOAA headquarters, Sienkiewicz could see even from the early stages that Hurricane Sandy was not evolving or tracking in usual ways. This was not the typical tropical storm that would track to the northeast and never pose any serious threat to the United States. From the start, Sandy looked like a storm that would cause trouble.

The key to understanding Sandy, Sienkiewicz explained, is that there was more than just the hurricane itself at work. As he studied the data, Sienkiewicz realized that a high-pressure system over the mid-Atlantic was migrating southwestward, restricting the storm from being able to escape out to the northeast, away from land. An elongated region of low pressure also was digging into the Eastern United States, which helped envelop the circulation of Sandy. Instead of the hurricane tracking to the east or northeast, the storm was going to arch back toward the coast.

The effect was that of a run-of-the-mill hurricane surrounded by a separate storm. The other storm, which was large and powerful in its own right, encircled Sandy, embraced it, and made the hurricane the center of a much larger weather system that spanned hundreds of miles, practically filling the western Atlantic Ocean on satellite weather maps. At one point, the area including tropical storm–force winds, known as the wind field, reached a thousand miles across.

The encirclement by the other storm gave Sandy staying power. Tropical storms are full of thunderstorms, and for a tropical storm to survive, those thunderstorms need to be as clustered and vertical as possible rather than spread out. The vertical thunderstorms concentrate the release of heat, and that is what lowers the pressure and gives the tropical storm its power. Sandy had those vertical thunderstorms, but with any hurricane the question is always how long they would last. The wind speeds increase significantly with height, and so a hurricane risks losing its cohesiveness as the vertical thunderstorms tilt, and can be torn apart. But the larger storm wrapped around Sandy, providing a stable environment for the core hurricane and allowing the thunderstorms to continue releasing heat, lowering pressure, and keeping Sandy alive at its core.

This hurricane-within-a-storm was so wide-ranging—flinging pow-

erful and varied weather off its rotating arms even hundreds of miles from the eye of the hurricane—that it prompted NOAA to issue a first-ever warning of its type: The forecasters accurately warned that Hurricane Sandy would cause blizzard conditions in the Appalachians, bringing several feet of snow much earlier than normal. That was the first blizzard warning ever issued in conjunction with a hurricane public advisory.

"Hurricane Sandy became the inner core of a much larger storm," Sienkiewicz says. "I've seen that happen far out at sea, but not impacting the U.S. coastline. And I haven't seen it happen with that scale and that intensity."

This wasn't just a hurricane. It was a superstorm.

CHAPTER 9

A WESTERLY TURN

ON SATURDAY MORNING Walbridge brought printouts from the Weather-Fax system to the nav shack and discussed the projections with Svendsen, the mate on watch. They discussed wind speed and direction, barometric pressure, sea states, all that could be derived from the maps and data transmitted to the *Bounty*. The printouts were posted in the nav shack. The eight a.m. bulletin from the National Hurricane Center was not encouraging:

BULLETIN

HURRICANE SANDY INTERMEDIATE ADVISORY NUMBER 20A

NWS NATIONAL HURRICANE CENTER MIAMI FL AL182012

800 AM EDT SAT OCT 27 2012

. . . AIR FORCE AIRCRAFT FINDS HURRICANE-FORCE WINDS
AGAIN . . .

ON SATURDAY MORNING, the NOAA projection maps showed Sandy east of Florida at five a.m., and the expected path had been updated so that the high-confidence cone went as far as two a.m. on Wednesday, when the storm was expected to be far inland in Pennsylvania. More important for the *Bounty*, the projected path before that showed the hurricane well out at sea off of North Carolina until two a.m. Monday, when it was expected to take a hard westerly turn and head for a direct hit on New York and New Jersey.

Svendsen listened as Walbridge insisted that they could turn west, because the National Hurricane Center was wrong. The hurricane was going to take the Gulf Stream and move farther north than the experts were saying, Walbridge explained, so a turn to the west would put the *Bounty* on the southwest side of the storm, the best position for a ship to be in. The counterclockwise rotation of the hurricane would put wind at the *Bounty*'s back, allowing it to scoot south as Sandy moved north and then west. It was a bold move, but certainly not the first for Walbridge or the *Bounty*. Svendsen told Walbridge he was concerned about the decision, but if they were going to do it, they should try to get south as fast as possible.

The *Bounty* was about three hundred miles east of Virginia Beach, Virginia, on Saturday about 9:30 a.m. when Walbridge ordered the course change. Superstorm Sandy was about six hundred miles away.

This moment was pivotal. The *Bounty* had turned westward, directly across the projected path of Hurricane Sandy.

In doing so, Walbridge not only put the *Bounty* in the path of the hurricane, but also risked getting caught in the "lee shore" situation he told the crew he would avoid, the one in which Sandy's winds could push the ship toward land and run it aground.

In retrospect, this call would be questioned even more than Walbridge's decision to leave New London. Why, with the projected path of Hurricane Sandy clear to him, would the captain decide to cut in front of it? Svendsen had questioned the westerly turn when he heard Walbridge was planning the move, but the captain explained that he knew better than the experts at NOAA.

Scornavacchi heard that they were turning west because the storm was turning east. He and most of the crew had no idea that the *Bounty* was cutting right across the projected path of Hurricane Sandy.

An hour and a half later, at eleven a.m., the hurricane bulletin still warned of danger:

BULLETIN

HURRICANE SANDY ADVISORY NUMBER 21

NWS NATIONAL HURRICANE CENTER MIAMI FL AL182012

1100 AM EDT SAT OCT 27 2012

. . . SANDY SLOWLY MOVING AWAY FROM THE BAHAMAS AND FLORIDA . . .

. . . TROPICAL-STORM-F6ORCE WINDS ARE ALREADY NEAR THE COAST OF NORTH CAROLINA . . .

SUMMARY OF 1100 AM EDT . . . 1500 UTC . . . INFORMATION

———————————————

LOCATION . . . 29.0N 76.0W

ABOUT 190 MI . . . 310 KM NNE OF GREAT ABACO ISLAND

ABOUT 355 MI . . . 570 KM SE OF CHARLESTON SOUTH CAROLINA

MAXIMUM SUSTAINED WINDS . . . 75 MPH . . . 120 KM/H

PRESENT MOVEMENT . . . NNE OR 30 DEGREES AT 9 MPH . . . 15 KM/H

MINIMUM CENTRAL PRESSURE . . . 958 MB . . . 28.29 INCHES

The projected path of Hurricane Sandy, the cone that the *Bounty* was sailing into, had not changed.

BARKSDALE HAD BEEN seasick since Friday and was no better on Saturday. Being in the engine room with its noise and hundred-degree temperatures was nearly unbearable at times, so he made frequent trips to the weather deck for fresh air. It was on one of these visits that a big wave rolled the *Bounty*, and he was suddenly tossed across the deck. He smashed his hand, breaking no bones but leaving several fingers unusable from severe bruising or tendon damage. He was in bad shape and getting worse at an alarming rate.

Early Saturday the seas were up to between eight and twelve feet, and the winds were at twenty-five knots. The ship was moving fast through the water, and Cleveland noted that he had never seen the *Bounty*'s engines pushed so hard. If they weren't at maximum output, they must be close, he thought. He also noticed that the generator was spitting out some unusual blue smoke he had never seen before.

On Saturday, Barksdale became concerned about the rising water in the bilge. Seawater seeped down the walls of the ship, apparently from leaks in the hull. He notified Svendsen, who told him to report the problem to Walbridge. "That's something the captain is going to want to see for himself," Svendsen said. Barksdale followed orders, and Walbridge went to the engine room for a look, but left without saying much at all to Barksdale. The engineer's impression was that the captain was concerned.

Faunt, however, continued to worry about the bilge pumps, which were still giving him fits during his boat checks. He kept Walbridge aware of the unchanged status, and the captain went to see the situation for himself—again—on Saturday afternoon. He agreed with Faunt that they weren't operating properly—speaking more freely and honestly with his old friend than he had with the new engineer—but he did not see the difficulty as reason to alter his plans for getting around Hurricane Sandy. The ship sailed on as the bilge pumps sputtered inconsistently and the bilgewater sloshed back and forth under Faunt's feet.

Scornavacchi was pumping the bilges every hour when he was on watch, and was having difficulty keeping the pumps primed. On his watch, Prokosh found that he could get the pumps to run about four minutes out of every fifteen. "I felt like I was fighting for seconds here and seconds there," he recalls.

Some of the crew stopped by the galley once in a while to check the latest weather maps that Walbridge and Svendsen posted. The maps displayed Hurricane Sandy and the *Bounty*'s most recent position, and it looked like a classic face-off. Each time a new map was posted, the ship and the storm inched closer. Prokosh was in the nav shack at one point on Saturday and took a look at the Automatic Identification System (AIS), a radar that shows signals from the transponders on ships, painting a picture of all the vessels within hundreds of miles. Normally the AIS had blips all over the screen, showing commercial ships, private yachts, Navy ships, and any other vessels. On Saturday, the screen was blank. At first Prokosh wondered whether the AIS was malfunctioning. Then he realized they were the only ship in a large swath of the Atlantic. It sent a chill down his spine.

It looks really lonely out there, he thought. *No one else went to sea.*

Prokosh kept the AIS information to himself. He had been on board the tall ship *Liberty Clipper* during Hurricane Irene in August 2011, just over a year earlier. That experience had shown Prokosh the power of a hurricane, but the *Liberty Clipper* had stayed docked in a Boston harbor and ridden out the storm with minimal damage. If the decision had been his—and he did want to captain a tall ship one day—Prokosh would have kept the *Bounty* in port. Prokosh knew that the *Bounty*, making six or seven knots tops, could not outrun a hurricane with seventy-five- or hundred-mile-per-hour winds. But they were committed now. They were going head-to-head with Sandy.

The barometer was dropping steadily as the *Bounty* closed the distance from Hurricane Sandy. As Saturday wore on, conditions on the ship were getting much worse for the crew. The seas and wind rose steadily until Cleveland estimated they were being tossed around in thirty-foot seas and ninety-knot winds. Walbridge e-mailed an update to

the HMS *Bounty* Organization office at his scheduled check-in time, 7:30 p.m. The *Bounty* was "trying to go fast and squeeze by the storm and land as fast as we can," he said.

The ship was rolling hard and constantly, the wood twisting so much that it created a terrible racket. Some crew members started to wonder whether anything was wrong, but most put it out of their minds and focused on their work. Christian, however, always knew what was going on throughout the ship—her curiosity showing a practical use—and was aware of the problem with the bilge pumps. She also was concerned about sailing into the hurricane. On Saturday evening she conducted boat checks and made her way to the engine room to talk with Faunt, whom she knew to be very approachable. In the stifling heat of the engine room, the white-bearded, bespectacled Faunt was wearing just shorts and a T-shirt.

"I'm seeing things that make me uncomfortable," she told Faunt. "I'm telling people about problems and they're ignoring me. It's because I'm a small woman here and these guys don't want to listen to me."

Faunt tried to comfort Christian and reassure her that people weren't ignoring her, but rather the crew already knew about the concerns she was raising.

"We're doing the best we can under the circumstances," he told her. She seemed less upset and offered to keep watch over the bilge pumps, which were running at the moment, while Faunt went up top for some fresh air.

Later that evening, Faunt spotted Christian sitting alone on the top deck, looking aft out into the increasingly rough waters, the wind blowing her blond hair. She was smiling.

She's enjoying what she's doing, he thought.

The ship's wooden planks continued to noisily work and twist under terrific strain, and Faunt had a difficult time trying to sleep Saturday night despite all his experience in a similar environment. Or perhaps it was his worries that kept him awake. Barksdale was also restless on the noisy ship, though that wasn't unusual—he often couldn't sleep at sea even under peaceful conditions. During Hurricane Sandy, even wearing

sound-dampening headphones from the engine room, Barksdale had no hope of sleeping.

It sounds like a couple of thousand pieces of wood rubbing up against one another, he thought.

AT ELEVEN P.M. on Saturday, the National Hurricane Center's bulletin made clear that the East Coast of the United States was no place to be:

> . . . SANDY CONTINUING NORTHEASTWARD PARALLEL TO THE
> COAST OF THE SOUTHEASTERN UNITED STATES . . .

> . . . STRONG WINDS AND SIGNIFICANT STORM SURGE ARE EX-
> PECTED IN THE MID-ATLANTIC STATES AND SOUTHERN NEW EN-
> GLAND . . .

The discussion posted at the same time addressed the expected movement of the hurricane:

> SANDY IS EXPECTED TO MOVE GENERALLY NORTHEASTWARD
> FOR THE NEXT 24 HOURS OR SO . . . STEERED BY A DEEP-LAYER
> TROUGH MOVING INTO THE EASTERN UNITED STATES. AFTER
> THAT . . . A DEVELOPING MID/UPPER-LEVEL RIDGE OVER NORTH-
> EASTERN CANADA AND INTERACTION WITH THE U.S. TROUGH
> SHOULD CAUSE THE CYCLONE TO TURN TOWARD THE NORTH . . .
> NORTHWEST . . . AND EVENTUALLY WEST-NORTHWEST. THIS MO-
> TION SHOULD BRING THE CENTER INLAND OVER THE MID-
> ATLANTIC REGION BETWEEN 48–72 HOURS. AFTER
> LANDFALL . . . SANDY IS EXPECTED TO MERGE WITH THE U.S.
> TROUGH TO FORM A LARGE DEEP-LAYER LOW PRESSURE
> AREA . . . WITH THE RESULTING SYSTEM MOVING NORTHWARD
> AND NORTHEASTWARD AFTER 72 HOURS. AS NOTED IN THE PRE-
> VIOUS ADVISORY . . . IT IS STILL TOO SOON TO FOCUS ON THE
> EXACT TRACK . . . BOTH BECAUSE OF FORECAST UNCERTAINTY

AND BECAUSE THE IMPACTS ARE GOING TO COVER SUCH A
LARGE AREA AWAY FROM THE CENTER.

———————

HEWITT WENT TO bed late in the evening on Saturday, staying up later than she should have because the new cook had made a really good curry for dinner and she didn't want to miss it. Scheduled to take the midnight watch, she woke a few minutes before and went to meet the others. She found Sanders, who would be leading the watch, at the capstan, ready to brief Hewitt and the others.

"The situation in the engine room is really serious," he told them. "Someone's going to have to stay down in the engine room and pump the bilge all the time."

Hewitt could tell from Sanders's tone that this was more than *Bounty*'s usual leakiness. He was clearly concerned, and this was the first clue for Hewitt that anything was seriously wrong on the boat. At one point Groves went below to assist with pumping the bilges and was surprised to see the captain already there helping out. His presence in the engine room told her that they didn't have enough manpower to run the bilges as much as they needed.

THE BILGE PUMPS were running constantly as Saturday night turned into Sunday morning—or more accurately, the crew was attempting to run them constantly. The pumps were still losing prime repeatedly and not keeping up with the incoming water.

At eight a.m. on Sunday, the National Hurricane Center's bulletin placed the eye of Hurricane Sandy about 260 miles southeast of Cape Hatteras, North Carolina.

. . . SANDY EXPECTED TO BRING LIFE-THREATENING STORM
SURGE FLOODING TO THE MID-ATLANTIC COAST . . . INCLUDING

LONG ISLAND SOUND AND NEW YORK HARBOR . . . WINDS EX-
PECTED TO BE NEAR HURRICANE FORCE AT LANDFALL . . .

At that hour, the *Bounty* was on a collision course with what the
media were now calling Superstorm Sandy.

AS THE *BOUNTY* continued sailing southwest on Sunday, the ship encountered the Gulf Stream, the powerful ocean current that flows northward
along the East Coast. The ship pushed against the current with the help
of winds from the counterclockwise rotation of Sandy. Contrasting
winds and seas work a sailing ship hard, putting more stress on the
seams that keep out seawater. When Hewitt returned to her bunk after
working the midnight-to-four-a.m. shift—during which she had seen
the rising water in the engine room and been stymied by the cantanker-
ous bilge pumps—she found that bilgewater rolling up the interior of
the hull as the ship rocked had made its way to her bunk. The filthy
water drenched everything in the crew's berthing areas and made it
difficult for Hewitt to rest.

When she got up and went to the galley for some breakfast, she could
hardly eat a bowl of cereal because the ship was rocking so much, requiring her to hold on to something as the bowl slid across the table. She
realized she'd never been on a ship moving that much.

When Groves awoke on Sunday morning she attended a mates'
meeting and learned that the *Bounty* had changed course the previous
day, making the move to the southwest. She was not concerned by the
strategy, because she understood that Walbridge was trying to get below
the hurricane before it moved farther west. Sandy's projected path was
posted in the nav shack, so she and the others could see that they were
crossing it, but Groves and others trusted that this was a judicious move
by the captain.

This certainly was the worst weather that some of the *Bounty* crew
had seen, but it wasn't yet the worst that Cleveland, Groves, Svendsen,
and Walbridge had been through. The winds and sea were so rough that
two people were required to man the helm, the additional manpower

necessary just to move the wheel that controlled the rudder. It was exciting in a "scared shitless" kind of way, as Groves describes it. They knew they were in a serious, potentially life-threatening situation, but as mariners they had a peculiar disconnect from the emotional parts of their brains. Their bodies certainly knew something crazy was going on, because they were flooded with adrenaline, which kept them superalert, oriented, and driven to action. They also simply didn't have the time to stop and think about how scary their predicament was, which worked to their advantage.

Still, the worry crept in. Faunt had spent most of the eight-a.m.-to-noon watch in the engine room, constantly pumping water out of the ship, or trying to. He was there because he knew the system far better than the engineer, and because he was one of the few people who could stand to be in the noisy, uncomfortable engine room for such a long stretch.

At noon on Sunday, Svendsen was exhausted and went to his berth to take a nap, knowing he would need all his strength later on. Cleveland relieved him and took responsibility for the watch. Sleep came quickly. Svendsen knew that the *Bounty* was in a tough situation but was still holding her own. Both electric bilge pumps were running continuously, struggling to keep up with the incoming water, which was up to about two and a half feet in the engine room, filling the keelson—the space between the very bottom of the hull and the flooring in the engine room.

There was work to be done everywhere on the ship, because the rough transit was tearing everything apart. Groves spent a half hour lashing a large piece of metal, left over from the old fuel tank that had been removed, so that it wouldn't be tossed around and hurt someone or damage the ship. As soon as she finished that, she helped repair a table in the galley that had been ripped off its hinges by people holding on to it as the ship rolled.

Crew continued working in the engine room, struggling to keep the bilge pumps functioning, but the water level just kept creeping up and up. Cleveland and Groves inspected the entire ship and found more leaky seams. In most cases they couldn't see the water seeping in because of the

internal planking, but they could hear it. They would stand quietly and listen, and sure enough, the sound of water trickling down into the ship was unmistakable.

Periodically, the shrill blast of the water alarm sounded on the tween deck, rattling everyone's nerves until someone rushed down to shut it off. The alarm had never been heard on the *Bounty* since it was installed in 2011, even with the ship's wet lifestyle, but now it was sounding over and over. Situated on the keelson, it was meant to signal a true emergency on the ship, a water level so high that immediate action was needed, but that water level was quickly becoming the norm on this voyage. Finally Faunt disconnected the alarm. They knew how high the water was, he thought. No need to listen to that thing all the time.

A POST ON the *Bounty*'s Facebook page Sunday quoted Walbridge as saying the ship would avoid the storm by going east. "So far, so good!" it said. But then another post said, "*Bounty* has now positioned herself to pass on the west side of Hurricane Sandy." To many, the significance of that comment might go unnoticed. But to anyone watching the projected path of the storm, it was a disturbingly calm, if not strangely upbeat statement.

In his last post on the Facebook page, Walbridge expressed his first note of concern to the public. "I think we are going to be into this for several days. We are just going to keep trying to go fast and squeeze by the storm and land as fast as we can." The message suggested that, whatever Walbridge had been thinking when he turned into the path of the storm, his plan wasn't working out as he had hoped. Those watching the drama unfold through the occasional Facebook posts on their computers began questioning Walbridge's judgment. The HMS *Bounty* Organization's Facebook page administrator came to his defense.

"Rest assured that the *Bounty* is safe and in very capable hands," the administrator wrote. "*Bounty*'s current voyage is a calculated decision . . . NOT AT ALL . . . irresponsible or with a lack of foresight as some have

suggested. The fact of the matter is . . . A SHIP IS SAFER AT SEA THAN IN PORT!"

Christian texted her mother again, not knowing it would be the last. "And just be sure that I am ok and HAPPY TO BE HERE on *Bounty* doing what I love . . . And if do go down with the ship & the worst happens . . . Just know that I AM TRULY GENUINELY HAPPY!! And I am doing what I love! I love you . . ."

Despite the worsening conditions and an overall sense of worry among many crew members, some thought they were doing fine in relation to Hurricane Sandy. Cleveland and Groves, for instance, still thought Walbridge's plan was panning out. They were about even with the storm's eye, just to the west, and the *Bounty* was flying. They were doing eleven knots under no sails, so they were confident they were going to skirt by Sandy and be on to their destination in fine time.

THE *BOUNTY* THRIVED on an old-school romanticism—sails full of wind, the crew climbing the rigging to perch high off the deck, risking life and limb the way generations of mariners had before them. Up top was where the glory could be found, the captain facing the wind and a brave sailor manning the wheel while others climbed and hoisted lines, not to mention the occasional fight with pirates and the sounding of cannon fire. That was the classic image, but the real life of many ships is found belowdecks, and is much more mundane. The *Bounty* crew was learning that on this voyage there would be no glory up top, just a desperate struggle in the bowels of the ship to keep it alive.

It was a group effort, with nearly everyone spending time in the engine room either trying to get the systems back online or helping keep the bilge strainers clear. Barksdale was so sick and injured that he could spend only about ten or fifteen minutes at a time in the sweltering space before having to go topside for some air. Walbridge was down in the room frequently, lending his expertise to the engines and generators. Everything seemed to be happening at once, and nothing was getting better. The water was rising and the bilge pumps wouldn't stay primed.

The strainers kept getting clogged with wood chips and other debris, strangling the bilge pumps when the crew did manage to get them working for a few minutes.

On Sunday, Groves noticed that while she was used to seeing the water in the engine room empty in about two minutes, the pumps were now taking much longer. Part of that, she realized, was because the ship was rolling so hard that water sloshed away from the bilge intakes. Still, she had been on the *Bounty* in twenty-five-foot seas before and never seen this kind of problem with the bilge pumps.

Walbridge had already ordered the crew to activate the hydraulically powered backup bilge pumps to augment the struggling main pumps. As they tried to use the backup pumps, one permanently fixed to the bilge manifold and the other portable, the crew found that the fittings where a hose would be attached had corroded and would have to be cleaned first. As they worked, everyone had to stay alert for the movement of the ship and be ready to brace and watch for floorboards that were floating and being tossed around by the bilgewater. The boards could pin a crew member's leg against the equipment if they weren't careful.

It was a hundred degrees in the engine room, noisy, and everyone was soaking wet, yet Groves took notice of how some crew members still found it all exciting. They had never experienced severe weather like this and were big eyed, like they still thought it was all an adventure.

For two days now the *Bounty* crew had been struggling to keep the bilge pumps primed, and no one could figure out exactly why they kept losing suction. They knew the problem wasn't as simple as clogged intake strainers, because they had been able to keep them clear before things got really rough and the water rose higher. But now, with the high water and the trash being sloshed around the ship and into the bilge, the clogged strainers were just making the bilge problem worse. Using their headlamps to see when the generator took a rest, Scornavacchi and Prokosh, frequently joined by other crew, ran their hands along the perforated strainers at the bilge intakes to pull away any clogs.

It was time for Barksdale to change the fuel filter on the port generator, so he switched it off and turned on the starboard generator, then went topside while he allowed the port generator to cool before working

on it. While he was away from the engine room, he sensed that the port engine had stopped. He returned quickly and someone reported to him that the port day-tank sight tube had been broken. The day tank was the fuel supply for the engine and generator on that side of the ship, and the sight tube was a glass tube that ran vertically on one side of the tank. Protected partially by a metal frame around it, the fuel inside the day tank ran through the glass tube, and as the level in the tube fell, the crew could tell how much fuel was left in the tank. Somehow and sometime—nobody would ever figure it out or confess—the glass tube was broken and the diesel fuel poured out of the tank while no one was looking. The idea of the sight tube being broken was not far-fetched in these conditions, with people and everything else being thrown around the ship in heavy seas, but the real crime was its not being discovered right away. Most of the fuel had apparently leaked out of the tank, though it was hard to tell with so much filthy water in the engine room. Barksdale had filled the day tank that morning with about 250 gallons of diesel, more than enough for the day even with the ship's engines running hard, but now the tank was empty. The engine could have been stopped safely, the valves on the sight glass tube closed, and the tank refilled before restarting the engine. But no one had noticed the accident in time, and as the fuel ran out of the day tank, the port engine ran dry and stopped working.

Faunt was away from the engine room when he felt the change under his feet as the port engine died. He started toward the engine room, moving quickly for his age. Along the way he asked why the engine had stopped and someone explained the sight tube issue. He picked up his pace, knowing how hard it is to restart a diesel engine after it runs dry. Once he got there, he worked with Barksdale and the others to restart the port engine, but without luck. The *Bounty* was now down to one engine and one generator.

The seas by this point were thirty feet high and the winds at ninety knots.

As water sloshed around the engine room and onto the raised starboard generator, the engine was running rough, faltering and surging like an old man falling asleep and then suddenly waking up again. The lights

dimmed and flashed in response, each flicker telling the crew that the *Bounty*'s second generator was fighting its own battle, and losing. Barksdale surmised that, in addition to the seawater threatening the starboard generator, it probably was struggling with contaminated fuel from the switch to the new fuel tanks. The generator was barely hanging on.

Hewitt was struggling with the bilge pumps at one point, trying to get the system pumping water for more than a few seconds at a time, when she asked Barksdale for help. She watched as he manipulated a valve that had nothing to do with the bilge system and realized that he didn't know the bilge pumps even as well as she did. She decided to wait until Sanders could help her.

The crew members were getting fatigued, even with all the adrenaline of being in a hurricane and trying to save the ship. The adventure was turning into something real for those who had relished the chance to see the *Bounty* in severe weather, and the crew was moving more slowly now, with less excitement and more dogged determination.

CLEVELAND AND GROVES were eating a simple meal in the galley Sunday afternoon about two p.m. when they heard Prokosh shout that the forecourse was blowing out. Knowing this would be a difficult problem in a storm, Cleveland and Groves both called out, "All hands on deck! All hands on deck!" Available crew rushed up to the top deck and found that the lowest and biggest sail on the most forward mast of the ship had been ripped in half by the battering winds. The forecourse was one of the *Bounty*'s two storm sails, made of a heavy-duty material and the lowest to the deck, used to give some direction and control to the ship even when the mainsails were down. It was typically the only sail left up during a storm, and Sandy's winds were proving too much for it.

Cleveland stepped out on deck, immediately beaten by sixty-knot winds and raindrops that felt like needles flying through the air, and saw that one portion of the forecourse was flapping wildly. The brand-new, super-heavy-duty, industrial-stitched Dacron was bubbled out in the wind, but a gash in the sail was rapidly opening wider, responding with equal violence to every gust and threatening to tear itself apart. Cleve-

land was soon joined by Walbridge, who assessed the situation and took command.

"I want my strongest men up there!" the captain shouted.

Salapatek, Prokosh, Scornavacchi, and Groves climbed the mast to try to secure the loose sail as Cleveland stood by with a life ring, standard procedure in case anyone fell off the rigging and into the water. As Hewitt watched the petite, dreadlocked Laura Groves work in the driving rain, she smiled to herself. Walbridge had called for his strongest men, and there was the five-foot-four-inch Groves climbing up without hesitation. Claudene Christian also emerged on deck carrying a life ring, ready to assist. Hewitt recognized her, even in her foul-weather gear, from the distinctive way she bobbed her head as she moved along, as if she were listening to some tune and didn't have a care in the world. Hewitt turned to the captain and jokingly said, "Hey, what about sending Claudene?" Everyone loved Christian, but knew that she was too small and inexperienced for a job like this. Hewitt expected the captain to laugh with her, but Walbridge turned and replied, "Actually, she's done very well."

The four crew members fought the wind and rain as they tried to bring the sail back under control, eventually managing to bring the canvas in and secure it tightly to the spar. Every movement was a battle in the high winds, but after a half hour they were successful in tying the forecourse down and setting the headsail, forward of the mast, to take its place.

As the ship lurched from side to side with the waves, crew all over the *Bounty* struggled to hold on. The decks were angled over to starboard and everything was wet. Simply staying upright, or anything close to it, was a real challenge. On Sunday afternoon Barksdale was on the top deck, trying to beat down his seasickness, when he stopped in the great cabin where the captain was working and Hewitt was curled up trying to rest. Barksdale looked up just as a big wave slammed into the *Bounty*, forcing it to suddenly roll to port. The engineer managed to hold on to something, but before he knew what was happening, the captain was thrown across the room and slammed into the sturdy wooden map table, his back making contact with the edge loudly enough to wake Hewitt up. A jolt

of pain shot through him as he doubled over, reaching for anything to hold on to as he fell to his knees.

Barksdale staggered over, concerned that Walbridge must be seriously injured after such an impact. He helped pull the captain to his feet and asked what else he could do.

"I'll be fine," Walbridge said with a wince. "I'm going to be really sore, but I'll be okay."

Barksdale didn't believe it.

CHAPTER 10

DANGER TOMORROW

CHIEF MATE SVENDSEN awoke from his nap about four p.m. Sunday afternoon, and Third Mate Cleveland immediately presented him with a damage report from his latest boat check. Svendsen realized that things had gone to hell while he slept.

"Small electrical fire on the light switch to the oven in the galley, suppressed by turning the breaker off . . . Sight tube broken on port day tank, tank at least partially drained . . . Port main engine and port generator not running . . . Starboard generator failing and causing lights to flicker . . . Captain fell and sustained potentially serious back injury, limited mobility . . ."

The broken sight tube on the day tank was a particular concern. The *Bounty* typically used about ten to twenty gallons an hour to power the engines and generators, and no one seemed sure how much fuel had been lost. The lights on board were indeed flickering, he could see, and that usually meant that the generator was starving for fuel. But was the day tank empty or were the too-efficient fuel filters on the generators clogged? Cleveland told him that Sanders, Barksdale, and Jones were working in the engine room—with water up to their knees—but not making much progress with getting the systems back up. Svendsen went to find Cleveland and Walbridge to talk about the state of the boat. They needed to

start making plans for getting the hydraulic pumps working and trying to figure out how to get the port generator running.

As he left his bunk, Svendsen could tell that the storm had intensified since he went to sleep. Sandy was about 270 miles east-southeast of Cape Hatteras, North Carolina, but the *Bounty* kept cutting the distance, moving in closer to the worst part of the hurricane. The ship was rolling hard with the twenty-five- to thirty-foot waves, and the wind was howling even louder and faster than before. The ship was wet all over, inside and out, rain making its way through every hatch and dripping off of every crew member who stumbled from one area to the next. The ever-present smell of salt air now mixed with that of wet clothes, wood that was intended to remain dry, and whatever mix of oil, fuel, spilled food, and vomit might be covering a crew member's foul-weather gear. Svendsen found Walbridge in the great cabin and could see right away that his captain was hurt. Walbridge moved with difficulty, hunched over much of the time, obviously in pain. Svendsen could see where the map table was loose from its floor anchors, suggesting the captain must have hit it pretty hard.

Walbridge filled Svendsen in on what he knew of the action down in the engine room, including the frequent oil-filter changes, the constant pumping of the bilge, difficulties in maintaining a prime on the pumps, and the fact that crew members were frequently clearing the strainers.

The stress took its toll. Sailing in the seas off of North Carolina was proving too hard for the *Bounty*. "I believe we're losing the battle with the bilgewater," the captain told Cleveland about four p.m. on Sunday, as they conferred about what to do next. Walbridge ordered the crew to heave to, a nautical term that involves putting the wind a couple degrees off to the left or right of the ship, either from the front or the rear. The rudder is turned over so that you're heading into the wind, and the sails are set so that they are one aback, with one stalled and not driving the vessel forward, but another filled and trying to move the ship. A ship that is hove to is essentially parked in the water and wind, not going anywhere and minimizing the vessel's reaction to strong wind and seas. The *Bounty* might heave to for swim calls, for instance, when the crew wanted the ship to stay in one place without dropping anchor, or in rough seas when

the crew was too tired or too busy to run the boat and just wanted to wait out the storm.

In this situation, heaving to offered another benefit: Heaving to causes the ship to roll over toward one side, and Walbridge ordered the *Bounty* hove to so that the water sloshed to the starboard side of the bilges, where the hydraulic bilge pump was still working but struggling to stay primed as the boat moved from side to side. Every time the wind and wave action caused the *Bounty* to roll to port, the water would move that way and cause the starboard bilge pump to suck air and lose prime. By heaving to, Walbridge could help keep the water on the starboard side of the ship and improve the dewatering. The ship still rocked, especially when a particularly big wave slammed into it, but Walbridge was doing his best to keep the water in the bilge to one side.

After the heave-to order, Cleveland went down to the engine room to assess the situation and was shocked at what he saw. It was the most water he had ever seen in the *Bounty*. He could see water entering the hull through a few short lengths of seam on the port side of the engine room, above the waterline. Every time the ship rolled and the sea hit that side, Cleveland could hear the *sssssst* of water being forced through the seams. But there was no catastrophic failure in the hull, no gaping holes or planks that had sprung loose. The seawater coming in was not good, but Cleveland did not believe the amount was sufficient to explain the problem with dewatering. The bilge pumps should be able to handle that amount of water, he thought.

The crew continued struggling in the engine room with the incoming water and the failing systems, but by nearly six p.m. most were able to gather for a simple dinner of macaroni and peas. It was the best that cook Black could come up with in these conditions, and it went down well. With the ship hove to, the wheel was lashed in place, so no one had to stand out in the weather and steer.

Prokosh and Hewitt were in the nav shack, making lame jokes to help each other through. At the same time, they saw the forecourse blowing out and Prokosh started yelling for help.

The crew members came running again, but this time they faced an impossible task. Cleveland surmised that there must have been at least a

tiny area where the lashing wasn't tight enough. Wind is like water, he knew, and would always find its way into any area that was not sufficiently braced against it.

The wind was so strong now that Scornavacchi did not even have to hold on to the rigging. The immense pressure of the gusts pinned him up against it so hard that he had to use all his effort to move in any direction. He inched his way out to the billowing sail, but then he couldn't raise his arms to stuff the violently flapping canvas down and secure it. There wasn't enough space for more than one man to work on the loose sail at the same time.

After half an hour it was clear to Cleveland and Groves that the effort was futile.

Fuck it, Cleveland thought. *We'll buy a new sail.*

As they called the crew back belowdecks, Cleveland looked to the rear of the ship and saw a new problem with the spanker gaff, a sail on the most rearward mast, or mizzenmast, that is positioned in line with the ship, as opposed to perpendicular like the big driving sails. The spanker serves almost as a rudder for the ship, helping drive it left or right instead of forward. The sail had been brailed in like all the others, of course, but the spar—the wooden beam holding the sail aloft—had broken and was flying around in the wind. Cleveland couldn't tell for sure why it had broken, but it wasn't hard to guess.

It was just tired. It said, "Screw this shit; I'm outta here," Cleveland thought. *There's all kinds of wind up there and that spar just said to hell with it.*

The broken spar was a problem not only because it was near radio antennas at the *Bounty*'s stern, but if it broke free and went flying across the deck, the splintered wooden beam would present a danger to the crew. Cleveland called the hands from the forecourse to help with the spar, everyone forced to make their way to the stern on their hands and knees. With ninety-knot winds, piercing rain, and the boat listing at close to forty-five degrees, walking upright was not an option.

Cleveland's crew finally reached the spanker gaff and tried to seize control of the wildly flying spar. Scornavacchi grabbed the broken piece, but his weight was not enough to stop it, and the spar jerked him off his

feet in a sudden game of crack the whip. Prokosh jumped to grab onto Scornavacchi, but even two men weren't enough to stop the mad rigging. Finally four people caught hold with all their strength, and managed to pull the spar down and secure it. The spar couldn't be fixed under such conditions, but at least for now it wouldn't cause more damage as it swung in the wind.

Once they were belowdecks again, Cleveland and Groves exchanged looks, the rain dripping off his beard and her dreadlocks. The couple didn't have to articulate much. They just knew things had changed. The *Bounty* was in serious trouble, worse than they had ever seen, and both were in leadership positions. Their focus was now on leading this crew through a serious situation. They saw Svendsen soon after, and he asked what it had been like out on the deck.

"Well, I was slightly out of my comfort zone," Groves replied. Coming from an experienced sailor not known for complaining, the comment's meaning was clear to Svendsen.

Groves went below to her bunk to try to rest, but soon she was startled by the sudden enormously loud slap of a wave against the stern of the *Bounty*. Almost immediately, she heard water coming into the ship. She hopped out of her hammock and raced up to the top deck to find Cleveland, who was on watch.

"We just took a wave from behind and some water came in through the great cabin windows," he shouted over the wind. Groves returned to her bunk, but found it impossible to sleep with all the noise and rocking of the ship.

Prokosh was in the engine room, attempting to clear the bilge pump strainers. Standing in filthy water, the strongly built young man would bend down far enough to reach the strainers while trying to keep his head above the rising water level as he dumped handfuls of debris into a trash bag. Suddenly Prokosh had an idea and ran out of the engine room, making his way to the galley.

He found Black trying to stay on her feet and keep pans of boiling water on the stove while the ship rolled and heaved. Her long black hair soaked from occasional time out on deck, she was working as hard as anyone else on the ship, and she knew that keeping the crew fed was

crucial if they were going to save the *Bounty*. Her meals wouldn't be anything special in these conditions, but she had to at least give them pasta or beans or whatever she could manage. When Prokosh came in, he quickly asked Black whether she had any spaghetti strainers. She handed one over and Prokosh raced back down to the engine room, where he used the colander to hold the debris he scraped off the bilge intakes. That method worked far better than the plastic trash bag, which became unwieldy as it filled with water.

Scornavacchi stopped by the engine room and saw that the water had risen since he left. Seawater continued to seep in, but was pumped out only sporadically. The room was crowded, with Walbridge, Prokosh, Barksdale, and Sanders all working on the port generator, trying to get it running again. Periodically sparks would fly and the terrifying hum of electrical shorts would fill the room, making everyone wonder whether they were about to be electrocuted. Every time the ship rolled to starboard, Scornavacchi could see water running down the interior walls from the room's ceiling. The more the ship rolled, the more water seeped in each time. The starboard generator was running, but sputtering and stalling often, causing the lights to dim and then go out until it could be restarted. The white-bearded Faunt soon joined them and tried to work on both generators.

Scornavacchi asked what he could do to help. Prokosh showed him how he was trying to keep the bilge intakes clear, and though the room was so full of people that it was hard to move around, Scornavacchi squeezed in and got to work. Prokosh gave him the colander and said he was going to the galley to get another one.

Making his way back toward the galley, Prokosh was crossing the tween deck when the ship rolled sharply and he went flying. He landed hard on the bulkhead and knew right away that he was injured. At first the pain was so intense it seemed to be everywhere, but as he lay crumpled on the tween deck he started isolating exactly where it was coming from. His back and chest were both searing with a hot pain, and his shoulder throbbed. Prokosh would find out later that he had a fractured vertebra, three broken ribs, a separated shoulder, and head trauma. He lay on the wet deck in extreme pain, unable to move and disoriented. He

didn't know how long he had been there when he realized two pretty women—a blonde and one with jet-black hair—were trying to help him. Black, the cook, had heard him hit the bulkhead and came from the galley to help, and Christian was passing through when she saw Prokosh lying in a heap. Christian ran to get Svendsen, who checked Prokosh for any signs of paralysis, asking him to move his arms and legs. When he didn't seem to show signs of a spinal injury, they gently moved him onto a thin twin-size mattress retrieved from one of the bunks and laid on the tween deck near where Prokosh fell. There was little more they could do for him.

Around the same time that evening, Barksdale was thrown across the engine room by a sudden and violent roll. The engineer, still terribly seasick and dehydrated, at first thought he had broken his leg, but the injury turned out to be only a severe bruise. He also sustained a severe cut on his arm. The blood dripped into the several feet of water in the engine room and disappeared.

As everyone on the *Bounty* realized the seriousness of their plight, the normal watch rotation ended. No longer would crew members be relieved to rest in groups while others took responsibility for running the ship. This was an all-hands operation from now on, but still, no one was thinking the ship was really in crisis. After all, this was the *Bounty*. Problems that might bring other sailing ship crews to tears were normal for the *Bounty*. Taking on water was routine. Water came in, and you pumped water out. Systems failed and you fixed them. Storms came and you rode them out.

And yet, even on the *Bounty*, this was not normal. The bilgewater was approaching the tween deck, higher than anything Cleveland had seen in five years on the boat. He and Groves knew that the situation was getting bad, but they reacted with orderly preparations. As water rose to the second level of the ship, Groves, in charge of the bosun's shop, ordered other crew to gather important gear from the shop that might be needed later. They collected essential tools, including hammers, nails, screws, duct tape, batteries for the drills, and other items, anything they might need later when they were repairing the ship after getting through the hurricane. Scornavacchi assisted, going to the berthing cabins below

to grab flashlights and batteries. The headlamps and flashlights many of the crew were using were now growing dim. Once they took everything they could from the bosun's locker and moved buckets of paint and other items that might end up in the bilge, Groves declared the shop off-limits because the rising water made it too dangerous.

After assisting Prokosh when he fell, Jessica Black continued doing her best to help keep her crew fortified as they worked. Few had time to stop by the galley for food, so Black roamed the *Bounty*—often on her hands and knees as she struggled with the rolling ship—handing out bottled water, bananas, oranges, sandwiches, cold hot dogs, and other snacks.

Svendsen was concerned. Running through the situation in his mind, he routed out different paths this story could take if things improved in the engine room or if they worsened, and he assessed which outcome was more likely. Svendsen realized the *Bounty* was in distress. This was no longer just a rough voyage that they would all recount later with a laugh. This was a potential disaster.

Approaching six p.m., the captain and chief mate were in the nav shack assessing their situation. With both of them holding on to the nav shack's counters and fittings as the ship rolled, Svendsen had to speak loudly over the sound of the storm outside. He was concerned not just about the *Bounty*'s predicament, but also Walbridge's insistence that the ship would endure. His long hair dripping water on the maps in front of them, Svendsen explained to the captain that, from what he had learned in recent coursework to improve his mariner's license, the prudent move at this point would be to contact the Coast Guard. The course instructor had emphasized that it was best to contact the Coast Guard early, when you knew you were in trouble but before your ship was in a true emergency. "Don't be reluctant to send a pan-pan," the instructor had said, referring to the international code word for a vessel in distress but not yet in immediate need of rescue. It was much better to pan-pan instead of waiting till you had no choice but to call Mayday. That way the Coast Guard could begin monitoring your situation and be ready if the worst happened, but they also might be able to provide assistance that kept you from getting to that point.

"We should contact the Coast Guard now," Svendsen told Walbridge in the calm but intensely serious tone the crew associated with him. "We shouldn't wait until things get worse. Let's apprise them of what's happening with our office, and that way we can make informed decisions with all of us involved."

Walbridge said no, he didn't want to contact the Coast Guard yet. The best thing to do, he told Svendsen, was to focus on getting the generators running and improving the bilge pumping. Despite having admitted to Cleveland earlier that they were losing the battle in the engine room, Walbridge would not yet admit defeat to his chief mate.

The captain had made his decision, but Svendsen was not comfortable with it. He left the great cabin to go to check on the engine room. He spent about an hour helping and assessing the situation before deciding he had to go back up top and speak with the captain again.

At about six p.m. on Sunday, Svendsen returned to the captain and reiterated his advice to call the Coast Guard. This time he made his case more forcefully. The ship was taking on water at an alarming rate, he told Walbridge, and he did not have confidence that the bilge systems could keep up, or that the generator situation could be improved. Walbridge thought it over and agreed that the intervening time had changed his mind. No captain is eager to admit that his ship is in distress, that it could go under if things don't improve, but the time had come to make that call. Walbridge told Svendsen to contact both the Coast Guard and owner Bob Hansen.

Walbridge also ordered the crew to activate one of the ship's distress beacons. Known to mariners as EPIRBs, pronounced *ee-perbs*, the devices are designed to send a signal to a satellite that then relays the information to rescue organizations. Many will start signaling for help automatically when submerged, but they can be activated manually as well. By the ship's activating the EPIRB, rescuers could get a fix on the *Bounty*'s location.

With Faunt lending his expertise, Svendsen and Walbridge tried the marine radio with no luck, and the ham radio that Faunt had built for the ship. None of the hardwired radios would work when the generator went out, so it was a frustrating up-and-down, wait-and-try-again pat-

tern as the power cut in and out. Eventually they found that the ham radio was working, but only for sending e-mails, not voice calls. Walbridge focused on that while Svendsen tried the satellite phone.

Svendsen took the handheld satellite phone up to the top deck, into the hurricane winds and the piercing rain. The phone wouldn't transmit or receive well belowdecks. He first tried to contact Hansen, then Tracie Simonin, offshore operations director for the HMS *Bounty* Organization in Setauket, New York, the company that Hansen formed to manage the ship. Then he attempted to communicate with the Coast Guard, using two phone numbers he found in books on the ship. He could hardly hear above the shriek of the wind, and the phone's connections were sporadic in the midst of the storm. Svendsen struggled to hear anything coming from the other end, shouting into the receiver if he thought someone was on the line. He couldn't tell whether he was getting voice mail or a live person. After several tries to the different people he was trying to contact, he thought he was getting the best response from Hansen. It was still difficult to communicate, and Svendsen couldn't really make out the words the owner was saying, but Hansen seemed to be on the other end of the line and acknowledging that Svendsen wanted to contact the Coast Guard. Svendsen kept shouting the coordinates of the ship over and over, hoping that Hansen was getting the lat-long clearly enough to relay it to the Coast Guard.

"Thirty-three degrees, fifty-four north; seventy-three degrees, fifty west. Thirty-three degrees, fifty-four north; seventy-three degrees, fifty west . . ."

Next Svendsen called a number he had for Commander Michael Turdo, the executive officer of the *Eagle*, the Coast Guard's own tall sailing ship. In the tall ship community, the *Eagle* and her Coast Guard crew are highly respected, and Svendsen knew Turdo personally. He was hoping to make contact and get some advice from a Coast Guard leader who also was extremely skilled with sailing ships. Unfortunately he could only leave a voice mail for Turdo.

"This is John Svendsen, chief mate of HMS *Bounty*," he yelled into the satellite phone, not in a panic but trying to be heard over the storm and the iffy connection. "*Bounty* is in distress! I repeat, *Bounty* is in dis-

tress! Our position is thirty-three degrees, fifty-four north; seventy-three degrees, fifty west."

Svendsen went back inside the great cabin and told Walbridge he thought he had gotten his message through to Hansen, but he wasn't sure whether the Coast Guard or anyone else heard him. Walbridge took a turn with the satellite phone and went out on deck to try calling the Coast Guard again. When he returned, he reported a similar experience but thought the Coast Guard had heard him.

In fact, none of the efforts to communicate directly with the Coast Guard were successful, but Svendsen was correct in thinking that Hansen had heard him. Hansen contacted Simonin at the *Bounty* office and told her to contact the Coast Guard and alert them to the *Bounty*'s situation. The ship was not sinking and they didn't need rescue, he emphasized, but they did want the Coast Guard to know what was going on. Soon after she talked with Hansen, Simonin received an e-mail from Walbridge with the same information:

"We are taking on water. Will probably need assistance in the morning. Sat phone is not working very good. We have activated the EPIRB. We are not in danger tonight, but if conditions don't improve on the boat we will be in danger tomorrow. We can only run the generator for a short time. I just found out the fuel oil filters you got were the wrong filters. Let me know when you have contacted the USCG so we can shut the EPIRB off. The boat is doing great but we can't dewater."

Simonin picked up the phone and called the Coast Guard.

CHAPTER 11

GRAVEYARD OF THE ATLANTIC

SIMONIN'S PHONE CALL first went to a district office of the Coast Guard—the sector that oversees operations for several bases and coordinates communication and planning. Officers there took the information and relayed it to Coast Guard Air Station Elizabeth City in North Carolina at 8:45 p.m. on the evening of Sunday, October 28:

> "OWNER OF VSL [vessel] RPTS HE RCVD E-MAIL FM VSL BOUNTY REPORTING: NO DANGER TONIGHT. VSL ON GENERATOR POWER THROUGH MORNING. NOT ABLE TO DEWATER ATT [at this time]. IF SITUATION WORSENS THEY COULD BE IN POSSIBLE DANGER. SHOULD BE OK THROUGH TOMORROW. VSL REPORTED TO BE IN SEAWORTHY CONDITION ATT. IF WX [weather] CONDITIONS DO NOT SUBSIDE VSL BOUNTY WILL NEED ASSISTANCE TOMORROW."

Located in the far east flatlands of North Carolina on the Pasquotank River, the air station was built in 1940 on the old Hollowell Plantation near the small town of Elizabeth City. The area to the west of the station is still full of cotton fields and other farms, the white fluff of raw cotton drifting alongside the roadside, and twiglike plants

still standing in the fields with bits of the South's history clinging tenaciously after the machinery comes through for the harvest.

On this night, the air station was being pummeled by the advance winds and rain of Hurricane Sandy. Only the most necessary personnel remained on duty, and the whole community was bracing for the coming storm.

Situated about a hundred miles north of Cape Hatteras, the air station can assist with search and rescue (SAR) cases throughout most of the Atlantic Ocean. The cape is a bend in Hatteras Island in the Outer Banks, the two-hundred-mile-long string of thin barrier islands that make up most of the North Carolina coastline. Known as a tourist destination and the site of the Wright Brothers' first heavier-than-air flight, Cape Hatteras is a treacherous but heavily traveled area for ships in the Atlantic.

The air station's close proximity to Cape Hatteras is no accident. The waters off the cape can be particularly dangerous because of the area's unique weather and geography. The two great basins of the East Coast meet there, and two major Atlantic currents—the southerly flowing coldwater Labrador Current and the northerly flowing warm-water Florida Current, more commonly known as the Gulf Stream—collide off of Cape Hatteras. While this creates great conditions for surfing, it also makes for turbulent waters and a large expanse of shallow sandbars. The cape also is struck by frequent storms and many of the hurricanes that move up the East Coast. With every storm, old sandbars shift and new ones form, which means captains can't always trust their maps to help them avoid hazards.

The danger does not cause captains to steer wide of Cape Hatteras, however. The fast currents tempt mariners to come in close to the shoals, because their ships can pick up speed, risking the shallow, rough water and frequent storms for a shorter journey. The gamble does not always pay off, and the many shipwrecks over the years prompted the area off the cape to be called the "Graveyard of the Atlantic." The risks also made the area a popular hunting ground for pirates, who took advantage of trade ships' difficulty in maneuvering and easily attacked those that ran

aground. Lighthearted tributes to the pirate culture are still popular along the beaches of North Carolina.

Since 1995, the air station has averaged 360 search and rescue missions each year. In the last sixty years the air station has launched more than twenty thousand missions and aided more than ten thousand people.

In the operations center, a small room filled with computers and radios that is one of the most secure areas at the air station, the *Bounty* information was received by a Coast Guard officer at the console where distress calls arrive in a number of ways. Boats fairly close to shore will be able to reach the Coast Guard station through normal radio contact, but Mayday calls from those farther out reach the "ops center" through more sophisticated satellite communications, EPIRB signals, and increasingly by e-mail. Once the message is received, the officer evaluates the need for assistance and, if necessary, scrambles an HC-130J airplane or an HH-60 Jayhawk helicopter. During the day, the ops officer may set off the "whoopee" siren that sounds throughout the air station, signaling everyone from maintenance technicians to pilots that they should be on alert for an immediate assignment, which would be transmitted through individual pagers to the specific crew and support techs that are needed. At night, the ops officer will skip the whoopee siren so as not to wake up other personnel who are on duty but sleeping.

In this case, the ops officer assessed what was known of the *Bounty* situation and determined that while there was no need for immediate rescue, there certainly was reason to be worried. He had been watching hurricane updates on the big flat-screen television in the room and knew from the other weather data he was getting firsthand from the Coast Guard and NOAA that the *Bounty*'s state was likely to worsen. He was surprised to hear that any ship was in that location, much less a wooden sailing vessel, but he also knew there could be many explanations for how it got there. The Coast Guard had been flying warning missions across the near Atlantic for the past couple of days, sending radio calls from HC-130Js that a hurricane was approaching, urging all mariners to find safety. But sometimes people didn't get the message. Or they didn't listen.

The first priority, at least while the crew reported that they were still keeping the ship afloat, was to ensure that the Coast Guard could main-

tain communication with the *Bounty*. The district office had suggested sending an HC-130J plane out as a communications platform, and the ops officer agreed. The big plane would not be able to pluck people off the ship or out of the water, but it could pick up radio communications and relay them back to the air station. The HC-130J crew also could drop emergency equipment to the *Bounty*, such as water pumps, life rafts, locator beacons, survival suits, and other supplies, all deployed by parachute.

Coast Guard Air Station Elizabeth has five HC-130J Hercules aircraft, similar to the C-130 Hercules transport plane used by many branches of the military, but customized for Coast Guard search and rescue missions. Often called Hercs, the Coast Guard planes are equipped with extremely effective radio and navigation packages. Aircrews consist of two pilots, a flight engineer, navigator, radio operator, and dropmaster. The HC-130Js are often tasked with escorting helicopter crews offshore on long-range missions, ensuring they reach their destination successfully and return home safely. They have also been known to deploy Navy SEALs and Air Force parajumpers by parachute when helicopters and other resources were unable to reach individuals in distress.

White with a black nose and the Coast Guard's orange and blue stripes, the plane itself is huge, with a wingspan of more than 132 feet and a length of just under 98 feet—wider than it is long. With a minimum crew of three but typically seven, the Herc has four turboprop engines and can fly at 350 knots (402 miles per hour), with a maximum range of 5,500 nautical miles and a maximum time aloft of twenty-one hours. Far more technically advanced than the typical cargo plane it might resemble, the Coast Guard HC-130J has five multifunction liquid-crystal display screens, a digital moving map, and heads-up displays, known as HUDs, that allow both the pilot and copilot to monitor critical data while looking straight ahead out the cockpit windows. The plane may be a workhorse designed for practicality rather than comfort or style, but it has all the latest technology that a crew could want.

Once an HC-130J crew is needed, the ops officer normally would set off the pagers of the crew on duty at the air station, who might be working on other duties or resting in the small, dormlike ready rooms in the

hangar building. But in this case, the ready crews weren't in Elizabeth City; nor was their plane. They were in Raleigh, North Carolina, about 160 miles farther inland.

Thirty-three-year-old Lt. Wes McIntosh was the commander for an HC-130J crew that evening. With nine years' experience flying the E-6 airborne command post and communications plane, McIntosh had been a T-34 flight instructor for the Navy before joining the Coast Guard. He had been flying the HC-130J for three years out of Elizabeth City, and on this night the copilot on his crew was thirty-six-year-old Lt. Mike Myers, an army medevac pilot who transitioned to the Coast Guard first as a helicopter pilot doing drug interdiction work on the West Coast before becoming a platform engineering officer for the Herc. Though he had extensive flight experience, including two combat tours overseas, Myers was a relative newcomer to the HC-130J and fixed-wing aircraft in general. The first time he ever flew an airplane, as opposed to a helicopter, was when he piloted an HC-130J at Elizabeth City in mid-September, only a month and a half earlier, making him one of the greenest copilots at the air station. McIntosh had confidence in him nonetheless, and the two men got along well in the cockpit and out. They epitomized much of what one sees in Coast Guard personnel—a couple of good-looking young guys, accomplished way beyond their years, ever professional but fun at the same time, not afraid to break into some harmless ribbing and braggadocio while getting the job done. Myers jokingly referred to McIntosh and himself as the "dynamic duo."

McIntosh and Myers, along with the other five crew members on the team, were told to reposition the aircraft to Raleigh on Saturday, October 27, because of the approaching hurricane. Although the plane is built to withstand some abuse in the air, taking off and landing can be dicey in strong crosswinds due to the enormous wingspan and how the broad, tall tail of the plane can act like a sail. Elizabeth City was already getting twenty-five knots of wind—almost thirty miles per hour—blowing perpendicular to the long runway needed for the HC-130Js, so taking off would push the safety parameters of the plane. The winds were sure to pick up later, making a takeoff truly dangerous. They'd do it if lives were at stake, but it was better to move the planes inland.

McIntosh had been on mile nine of a ten-mile run when he got a phone call telling him the ready Herc, the plane that was kept ready to go with minimal preparation, and his next-in-line plane both needed to be repositioned. He conferred with the other crew about where it would be best to take the planes, and both teams decided to fly to the Raleigh-Durham International Airport, where a longer runway would make it possible for them to take off and land safely. Raleigh's location farther inland might also mean the airport there would get less of a blast from the approaching hurricane.

On Saturday, the two crews repositioned the planes to the Raleigh airport, which was already starting to see flight delays and cancellations. The crews parked their planes at the airport and made their way to the Courtyard by Marriott hotel less than a mile away, settling in for what might be a stay of several days if the planes couldn't be moved back to Elizabeth City soon. Throughout Saturday evening and most of Sunday, the crew members made frequent phone calls to their families in Elizabeth City, ensuring they were safe and ready for the storm. They also hung out in one another's rooms, alternating between watching the Weather Channel and Sunday football games. The first ready crew's duty time expired at eight a.m. on Sunday, making McIntosh and his men the ready crew from that point. It was quiet, but the crew suspected they would get called up eventually.

"As big as this storm is, I think we'll go," Myers told his pilot. "There are trends to these things, and there's always somebody who gets caught, and doesn't take heed of the warnings."

McIntosh didn't disagree. They might get called up for a rescue on Monday, he thought, or maybe just for a poststorm damage assessment. Flying then might still be rough, but at least it would be better than flying straight into a hurricane. He hoped any actual rescues would be in the inland waterways and handled by the helicopters, because a rescue at sea in this weather would be tough.

That evening, the pilots convened to talk about whether they should reposition themselves to Wilmington, North Carolina, about 130 miles south of Raleigh, and right on the coastline. The winds were picking up, and it looked like Monday might be too harsh for them even this far

inland; Wilmington was below the center of the storm now, so it wasn't getting the worst of the weather anymore. They decided to wait until Monday morning, and if conditions looked bad, they would get the planes on down to Wilmington. McIntosh returned to his room and was trying to relax, watching some football on television, when his cell phone rang about 9:30 p.m.

It was Lt. Todd Farrell, the operations duty officer, or ODO, at the air station. The ODO pretty much runs the place during his or her shift.

"We got a SAR case for you," Farrell said. "It's a hundred-and-eighty-foot ship called the HMS *Bounty*. The sector has gotten word that an e-mail was sent to the ship's owner saying they had some generator problems and were taking on water. The ship's owner couldn't get any more communication with them, so they called our sector, who called us to see if we could serve as a communications platform for them. We're going to get you guys to take on this thing."

"Roger that," McIntosh replied. After taking some more information from Farrell, he ended the call and texted the other six members of his crew, instructing them to meet immediately for a SAR. One crew member had the group's van waiting at the front entrance, and everyone jumped in quickly for the short ride to the airport. In the van, McIntosh's phone rang again. It was Farrell telling him to continue to the airport but not to take off yet. Senior leaders from the district at the air station were still conferring on whether it was a good idea to send the plane up in this weather.

McIntosh was familiar with the risk assessment that the Coast Guard had to carry out for any SAR mission. Anytime someone is in distress, the rescue crews naturally want to rush out and save them. But the Coast Guard and their flight crews have to carefully assess each mission to determine whether the need for assistance is great enough, and the likelihood of success is high enough, to justify the risk to the crew and the aircraft. There was no sense in sending the personnel out on a suicide mission, and the equipment had to be valued as well. If they sent an HC-130J out on a mission where it was lost, that was a valuable resource that wouldn't be available for the next rescue mission. The entire Coast Guard has only six of these planes, all in Elizabeth City, and one is always in a

"hard down" status for maintenance that can last months. Coast Guard crews are more than willing to risk their lives to save others, but at the same time it is not done cavalierly. That's one reason it typically takes an hour to get a Herc into the air and a half hour to get a Jayhawk up, even though at least one aircraft and crew of each type are always on standby. A fast response is a top priority when lives are at stake, of course, but Coast Guard planes and helicopters can't deploy like fire trucks, rolling out within seconds of an alarm. On any mission, critical planning and assessment must be done, and it can't be done until the situation is known. It was clear that the higher-ups doubted whether the pros outweighed the cons on this mission.

As the seven crew members discussed what kind of tall ship this was, McIntosh remembered that Farrell had said there was a Web site they could go to. One of the crew pulled up the site of the HMS *Bounty* Organization on his phone and read aloud some of the information about how the ship had been in movies. Myers sent his wife a text message saying, "Looks like we're going to fly into the eye of the storm. I love you." He got the reply right away: "I love you too. Take care of yourself." The ride was short, however, and once they arrived at the plane everyone got busy.

When they got on board the plane they had access to the radar and could see why their bosses were hesitating about giving them the go signal. Farrell had given McIntosh the latitude and longitude of the *Bounty*'s last known location and they looked it up on the ship's radar. Damn if it wasn't right there in the worst part of the radar sweep, right where one of the big bands of wind, rain, and turbulence was looking really ugly. McIntosh had to think seriously about flying into the winds of a hurricane, even though he knew the plane was capable. The plane is made for severe weather, and the "Hurricane Hunters" at Air Force Reserve's 53rd Weather Reconnaissance Squadron in Biloxi, Mississippi, regularly fly a similar version of the C-130 into hurricanes. It can be done, but it's still not something you do without the potential for real gain from doing so, McIntosh knew. And at this point, no one was saying that the *Bounty* was in need of rescue.

The crew continued their preflight preparations, with Myers and

McIntosh especially interested in the radar and the weather advisories. They conferred with others back at the air station and determined that just to the southwest of the *Bounty* there was a strong line of thunderstorms, but just south of that the skies were relatively clear. Not clear, but relatively clear. There were still strong winds, but McIntosh and the others at the air station felt that the Herc could go out to that position and that would be close enough to get radio communication with the ship on channel sixteen, the international distress frequency. The plan was to set up an orbit there to establish communication with the *Bounty* and relay information back to the air station, optimizing the rescue response if needed. If the *Bounty* recovered, the Coast Guard plane would monitor it until it was clear of the storm and headed toward port.

"That's our plan. We won't go bombing into the worst of the storm unless something changes and gets worse," McIntosh told his crew.

Myers and McIntosh discussed one known problem with this HC-130J. The Herc is equipped with a deicing system for the propellers, but on this particular plane the system did not always work properly. It was being addressed by the maintenance crew, but on any complex airplane it is not unusual for some system or device to be nonfunctional or at least unreliable. If the system is not critical and there is a way to work without it, the problem does not ground the plane. In this case, they knew they could not count on the prop deicing, so McIntosh and Myers filed a flight plan that called for them to fly in a narrow band between seven and nine thousand feet, where the weather conditions most likely would not cause icing. The fact that they even had to worry about icing in a hurricane struck them as a little strange, but the weather folks were telling them this was just another oddity of Hurricane Sandy.

Myers wondered what he was getting himself into. With fewer than sixty hours of flight time in this plane, he was about to go into a hurricane that was being called Superstorm Sandy, Frankenstorm, and the Storm of the Century. But he had confidence in the plane, McIntosh, and the rest of the crew.

As they taxied out at eleven p.m. and requested permission to take off, the two pilots noticed that the air traffic controller had an unusual tone in his voice. Controllers typically are busy managing multiple

flights, so they converse in a style that is clipped and efficient. On this stormy night when aircraft were being grounded, the controller knew the Coast Guard plane was not embarking on a routine flight.

"You guys going out to Sandy?" he asked.

"Well, yes, that's affirmative," Myers replied with a bit of a chuckle. "Yes, we are."

There was a long pause before the controller replied.

"Well . . . good luck."

CHAPTER 12

KIND OF SURREAL

BACK AT THE air station, other crews were following the *Bounty*'s developments. Right about the same time McIntosh and Myers were taking off, Walbridge managed to get an e-mail through to the Coast Guard with an update:

> "We are 34-07 N x 074-08 W, course 130 speed 2.6 kts, 17 people on board. I do not know how long I will be able to receive e-mail. My first guess was that we had until morning before have to abandon; seeing the water rise I am not sure we have that long. We have two inflatable rafts. We have activated our EPIRB. Robin HMS Bounty."

Walbridge's report put the *Bounty* about a hundred miles southeast of Cape Hatteras. He mistakenly told the Coast Guard there were seventeen people on board rather than the actual sixteen, an error that would be passed along as the rescue unfolded.

There was other confusion. Only minutes after that message, at 11:07 p.m., the Coast Guard e-mailed the *Bounty* with an urgent appeal for clarification on the ship's situation:

> USCG request you send e-mail reply . . . USCG received report from

owner that VSL Bounty is not in distress . . . Reply as soon as possible
with an update of your situation.

The updates from the ship were watched closely at Elizabeth City,
but the news that an HC-130J was going up from Raleigh was considered
especially significant, because it meant two things: One, the *Bounty*'s
situation was serious enough to warrant sending out a communications
platform in this mess of a storm, and two, the Coast Guard leaders
thought the rescue craft and crews could handle it.

Lt. Jane Peña was one of those crew members. As a Jayhawk helicopter copilot, she could be called upon if the *Bounty*'s situation worsened.
At thirty-one years old, Peña was, like Myers, one of the pilots with the
least experience at the air station. She had received a degree in history,
with a minor in German language and literature, before marrying her
husband, a prior Marine who entered the Coast Guard two months after
their wedding. Peña spent two years as a Coast Guard spouse before
joining, partly because she had always wanted to fly.

Peña's crew had come on duty at 7:45 a.m. that Sunday morning,
thirteen hours before the *Bounty*'s trouble call was received. Now she and
the rest of her team paid close attention as others discussed whether to
send the Herc out, what they knew of the *Bounty*'s situation, and options
like dropping a portable water pump onto the struggling ship. While the
decisions were being made, Peña and a couple of colleagues looked up the
Bounty on the Internet to see what kind of ship they were dealing with.
She was shocked to realize that a tall sailing ship was out in this weather.
With her history degree, she was familiar with the story of the original
HMS *Bounty* and the mutiny, but she had not heard about this replica—
and some of the first references she found online disparagingly described
it as only a movie prop rather than a functional vessel.

Her Jayhawk pilot, forty-three-year-old Lt. Cdr. Steve Cerveny, was
also senior duty officer at the station that evening. He would be staying
up late to get McIntosh's HC-130J out and then monitoring the situation, but he ordered his crew to get some rest.

"You'd better go get some sleep, because we're probably going to get
called out on this later," he told Peña. She and the rest of her crew went

to bed in the on-duty quarters adjacent to the Jayhawk hangar, trying to maximize their readiness for whatever time they might be called to fly into a hurricane.

Another crew watching the action was led by thirty-nine-year-old Lt. Cdr. Peyton Russell, a Herc pilot who had flown helicopters in the Army for seven years before he was lured to the Coast Guard by his younger brother, who had gone to the Coast Guard Academy right after high school. Russell was stationed in Germany at the time, working in a hangar that had survived World War II and still had bullet holes from enemy strafing. When he took a break and visited his brother's Coast Guard station in Miami, Florida, Russell couldn't believe the difference. His kid brother was working in a gleaming, modern airplane hangar so clean that Russell wouldn't have hesitated to eat off the floor. Like many others who transition from other armed services to the Coast Guard, he realized the Coast Guard offered certain lifestyle benefits that the Army couldn't, such as stability in assignments and no risk of being deployed overseas. For many in the Coast Guard, those benefits make it possible to have a normal family life. Russell also was impressed by the professionalism and skills of the Coast Guard aviators, so as soon as he was eligible he applied for a transfer. He was at Disney World with his family when his brother called with the news that he was the Coast Guard's newest aviator.

After spending a few years piloting Jayhawks in drug interdiction, Russell transitioned to the Herc. Similar to the experience of Myers, the first fixed-wing airplane Russell ever flew was the massive C-130. He skipped flying the little T-34s in Navy flight school or working his way up from other small planes. So on October 28, Russell was the pilot of one of the Hercs still in the hangar at Elizabeth City, known to the crews as E-city. He and his crew were standing duty at the air station while the two Hercs were in Raleigh, but they had resigned themselves to the fact that they were third-string, with little chance of going out anytime soon. They had been told to be at the ready, but that the two planes in Raleigh were primary because the weather was considerably better there. The winds at the air station, Russell knew, were right on the edge of the safe parameters for a Herc to take off. Having Russell's plane and crew ready even though takeoff conditions were bad and the other two planes were

available was typical of how the Coast Guard layers its resources and response readiness. There was always a chance that one of the planes in Raleigh could break down, or there could be two SARs simultaneously.

Russell had been in the duty office when the *Bounty*'s call was relayed, and like others, he was surprised to hear that a ship was in the middle of this storm, and what ship it was.

"You mean HMS *Bounty*? Like in the book?" he asked in his animated, enthusiastic way of talking. People call their boats all kinds of weird names, he thought, so he was hesitant to think it was *that Bounty*. Someone said, "Yeah, I think so," and soon someone else came into the room with a printout from a computer search. It was from the HMS *Bounty* Organization's Web page, showing the last posted positions of the ship.

"Yeah, that's a tall ship!" Russell said, surprised at the thought of such a vessel in a hurricane. "That is *the* HMS *Bounty* from the movies. That's kind of surreal."

As they pondered the situation and monitored some of the discussions, Russell and his crew heard the whoopee siren go off throughout the base around ten p.m. He was surprised to hear the siren notifying everyone to be on the alert for a SAR callout. *Whoa . . . third string is going?* he thought. He went to talk with Cerveny and the others planning the response, and it wasn't long before Russell's crew was told to stand down, that the Coast Guard was going to send the McIntosh crew from Raleigh instead. But still, Russell knew the situation at sea was serious, and he knew from experience that things could change quickly in a SAR case. As he was watching the Weather Channel, he kept thinking about the last reported position of the *Bounty*.

They're where? he kept thinking to himself. *They're ninety miles off Cape Hatteras, and that's where the eye of this hurricane is. There's no way that this is it, that we're not going to have to do more.*

He gathered his six other crew members and briefed them on the situation and the plans so far.

"Okay, no more video games, no more TV. Go to bed now," he told them. "I don't think this is over. Our services are going to be required at some point."

———————

THE FLIGHT OUT to a SAR is usually the easiest part. The crew is rested, the weather typically is calm, and it's a relaxed ride to where the real work begins. Crew members can use the time to brief themselves on the situation, study radar patterns, and plan what actions they'll take on-site in a fairly relaxed setting while the plane's autopilot guides them to their destination.

Not on this flight for McIntosh, Myers, and their crew. Everyone had anticipated that at some point they would be in for a rough ride, but almost as soon as the Herc got airborne from Raleigh, the entire crew knew this would be even worse than they feared. The big plane was pummeled by rain and wind right away, making for a violent chop that caused the aircraft to ride like an old pickup truck bumping over a country road. Once it started, the severe turbulence never subsided, and only worsened as they got farther into the flight. Herc crews are no strangers to being thrown around the plane a bit, but this was different. It wasn't long before McIntosh and Myers felt decidedly uncomfortable in their well-worn sheepskin-lined seats in the cockpit, and they knew what that meant for the guys in the back of the plane. Every bit of turbulence they felt in the cockpit would be about three times worse in the back.

McIntosh was busy troubleshooting the radar, which had given off warning bells as soon as they took off, signaling that it wasn't working properly. He knew that on this plane the radar warning bell sometimes sounded a false alarm, so he was trying to figure out whether the system really was down or not. McIntosh tried setting the radar to a mode in which it painted the ground surprisingly well, providing an accurate rendering of the coastline and ground structures below and ahead. As the Herc flew near New Bern, North Carolina, and toward Morehead City, McIntosh watched for the distinctive coastline that would appear in that area. He knew they were getting close, but the image never materialized on the radar.

"I'm not getting a coastline at all," he told Myers. "Basically, our radar is totally not working."

McIntosh thought about what that meant for their mission. The ra-

dar maps they checked on the ground before leaving showed some nasty-looking patches of red, yellow, green, and everything else out there where they were going, and now they were going to have to fly into it without the benefit of onboard radar that could help them navigate around the worst of the storm. At least they had a full moon. Even in the heavy rain, a full moon gave them some light and some sense of what was ahead of them. They donned their night-vision goggles, known as NVGs, which look sort of like high-tech binoculars attached to the front of their flight helmets and suspended in front of their eyes. The goggles greatly intensify even the smallest available light and provide the wearer with a view that can look like the equivalent of green-tinted daylight. Even when there is very little light, such as at sea when the skies are overcast and there is no moon, the NVGs can help crew members see weather formations and objects in the water. On this moonlit night, the NVGs were a godsend after the radar went out. McIntosh and Myers could look out the cockpit windows and see cloud formations ahead, enabling them to at least steer clear of the very worst pockets of turbulence.

"Big one up ahead, don't want to fly through that one," Myers called out in the dark cockpit.

"I agree," McIntosh replied. "Come right."

They flew like that for about an hour.

CHAPTER 13

DON'T LOSE ME

SINCE FIRST LEARNING of the *Bounty*'s distress, the Coast Guard had considered all options for sending help. Soon after notifying Myers and McIntosh that they would be flying into the hurricane, the sector commanders turned to the Navy, known as the blue force, to see whether any ships were in the area to assist. The response: "No blue forces in the vicinity of HMS *Bounty*." Next the Coast Guard checked for any civilian ships that might help. Using its radar and other technology to sweep the Atlantic for any other vessels in the area, the Coast Guard found that the seas were a lonely place that night. The nearest vessel was the *Torm Rosetta*, a six-hundred-foot-long oil tanker from Denmark, which was about thirty-five miles away from the *Bounty*. The Coast Guard began calling for the *Torm Rosetta* on the radio.

At the same time, it issued an Urgent Marine Information Broadcast to anyone who could hear, alerting mariners to the *Bounty*'s distress and location. "Mariners transiting through this area are requested to check their electronic equipment and keep a sharp lookout for signs of distress." It was mostly a formality and an attempt to cover all the bases. The Coast Guard knew no one else was out in this area, so close to Hurricane Sandy.

After calling out to the *Torm Rosetta* for forty minutes and getting no response, the Coast Guard got in touch with the ship's owner. In the

e-mail relayed to the Coast Guard, the owner made it clear that the big oil tanker was fighting its own battle with the hurricane:

"Master of the *Torm Rosetta* said they are in really bad weather and are unable to assist at this time. They are in ballast, making 5–7 knots heading east. They are pitching 25 degrees, and they need to get out of the weather."

At 11:24 p.m. Sunday night, the Coast Guard received an e-mail from Simonin at the *Bounty* LLC office, relaying a message from Walbridge:

"This is the latest e-mail I received from the boat: 'Do they know we are in trouble? I am probably going to lose power shortly.' Not sure what to do next. Has the ship sent you anything?"

Walbridge's question suggested that the *Bounty* was not receiving all of the e-mails sent by the Coast Guard or the ship's office. At 11:47 p.m. Sunday, the office relayed another message from Walbridge that the *Bounty* had activated its second EPIRB. The Coast Guard started picking up the signal seven minutes later.

The Coast Guard radioed to Myers and McIntosh with an update: "*Bounty*'s situation is worsening. They are losing power and may abandon ship."

AT ALMOST MIDNIGHT the water finally overtook the *Bounty*'s starboard generator and it stopped. Crew members noticed the sudden quiet on the boat, the only sounds the hurricane winds outside and the wrenching timbers of the hull. There was nothing to be done. Both engines and both generators were down and the *Bounty* was adrift, at the mercy of Hurricane Sandy. No engines, no electricity, nothing left to do but hold on.

Hewitt had been dozing off in the nav shack when Svendsen and Walbridge made their distress calls, and when she woke up she realized she couldn't hear the generator. She found Salapatek in the engine room and asked him what was going on. He started running down all the problems on the ship, and Hewitt couldn't believe everything had gotten so much worse in the short time she was asleep. She was sure her boyfriend was joking.

"You're just jerking my chain, right?"

"No, Jess, this is for real," he told her, looking her firmly in the eyes. "Don't lose me if the ship goes down."

Svendsen told Groves to get motion-sickness medicine from the forward heads and give it to all crew members. She went around the ship distributing the pills to everyone, whether they were admitting to seasickness or not. She and the other experienced mariners on the *Bounty* knew that seasickness was more than just a nuisance. It could be debilitating, especially over long periods, sapping even the strongest crew members of the strength needed to survive in a bad situation. Many sailors were reluctant to admit to being seasick, Groves knew, because they saw it as a sign of weakness. Barksdale was already viciously seasick but complied with the order and choked the pills down. They came right back up. Groves urged Walbridge to take the motion-sickness pills, too, but he refused.

Cleveland went up on deck to check the wind speed again. Standing in the blowing wind, rain pelting his face and jacket, he held up the anemometer and watched the cups rotate in a blur. When he checked the reading, it said ninety knots, just under 104 miles per hour. And the anemometer was broken.

The winds were even higher on the *Bounty* than they were in the middle of the hurricane. A NOAA Hurricane Hunter airplane had recently flown through the storm and found that, unlike most hurricanes, the highest winds were not to be found in the eye of the storm. There was a pocket of much higher winds, at least sixty knots, or sixty-nine miles per hour, and gusting to much higher about a hundred miles southwest of the storm's center. Right about where the *Bounty* was.

By midnight, it was obvious to everyone on board that the ship was in distress, and though no one was yet willing to say it aloud, many of the crew were wondering whether the *Bounty* could get through this hurricane. An adventure was turning into a crisis.

CHAPTER 14

BLACK VELVET CURTAINS

AS THE BIG Herc flew through the increasingly rough air toward the last known position of the *Bounty*, the hour of constant, violent turbulence was starting to rattle the seven crew members. These were guys who didn't get airsick easily, but they all felt it coming on, that queasy feeling in the stomach that told them sooner or later things would get ugly in this plane. McIntosh still hadn't decided whether to continue on to the location of the *Bounty* or just get close enough to make radio contact and assess the ship's situation. It was possible that they might make contact and find out that the ship was faring better, in which case the HC-130J would turn around and head home rather than continuing into the hurricane.

Approaching the coordinates near midnight, McIntosh tuned the radio to channel sixteen, the international channel for emergencies, and tried raising the *Bounty*. He wasn't too hopeful about reaching them this soon. "HMS *Bounty*, this is Coast Guard C-130 on channel sixteen."

McIntosh was surprised when Svendsen replied, coming in plainly. "Hey, Coast Guard C-130, this is HMS *Bounty*. Loud and clear." There was a controlled sense of elation in his voice. Svendsen was happy to hear that the cavalry was coming, and so was Walbridge.

"HMS *Bounty*, this is Coast Guard C-130. What is your position? How many people are on board, and what is the nature of your emergency?"

Svendsen reported the ship's coordinates off of Cape Hatteras, which McIntosh and Myers saw were pretty close to the last known position they had been given. That meant they were nearly there already and wouldn't have to spend time changing course. There were sixteen people on board, Svendsen reported.

"We currently have no generators, no engines, and the radio is operating on battery power only. We have just a limited time left on the radio, Coast Guard," Svendsen continued, shouting into the mic. He managed to retain his calm demeanor even as he yelled about such serious matters. "We have about six feet of water and we are taking on water at a rate of about one foot per hour."

McIntosh and Myers exchanged glances. This was worse than what they had last heard about the ship. Clearly the situation had deteriorated in the time it took them to reach the site. Whereas the *Bounty* previously had been a ship in distress, it now was essentially helpless in the water, at the mercy of the storm. The ship couldn't maneuver and they might lose radio communication at any time. Once that happened, the Coast Guard would have no way of knowing whether the crew was abandoning ship or otherwise getting into worse trouble. The pilots understood that the situation was dire.

Svendsen and Walbridge were reassured by the clear radio communication with the HC-130J. For the time being the *Bounty* could be watched over closely by the airplane above, and it was still able to send and receive e-mail. Just before one a.m., the Coast Guard e-mailed the *Bounty* after trying to find one of its own cutters that might be able to come to the ship's aid:

Closest surface asset is 10–12 hours away from your position. USCG can coordinate a planned evacuation of your vessel in the morning. Planning for this evacuation needs to start soon if this is your intent. If situation worsens and you are starting evacuation of vessel, energize another EPIRB and contact USCG. If EPIRB is energized, USCG will

take that to mean evacuation of the vessel has started and will respond appropriately.

The *Bounty* responded at 1:12 a.m.:

If closest vessel is eight hours away, crew would be able to be saved, but vessel would be lost. Vessel has 6 feet of water on deck and is taking 2 feet per hour.

That information was passed on to McIntosh. One of his first concerns was the *Bounty*'s lack of generators. Being adrift with no engines was bad enough, but no generators meant no pumps to dewater the ship. Svendsen's report, along with the e-mail update, illustrated just how quickly seawater was taking over the ship.

McIntosh and Myers also discussed how, if the *Bounty* were without power, the position the crew gave may have been their last-known position and not current. The Coast Guard team couldn't know until they reached the coordinates how close the *Bounty* really was, and both the pilot and copilot were hoping it was pretty damn close. Given the hurricane conditions at sea level and where the Herc was, and the lack of radar for picking out a vessel below, it would be a real challenge to just fly around and try to find even a ship of that size.

McIntosh verbalized what Myers was already thinking: that if there still had been any doubt about whether the *Bounty*'s situation justified the risk to them and their crew, that doubt was gone. Myers quickly concurred. The other five crew members had been privy to all the chatter before the mission and during the fly-out about relative risk and gain, but as they listened to the radio exchanges on their headsets it was clear to all aboard now that the sixteen lives on the *Bounty* were in great jeopardy and would need rescue.

"Okay, we'll be going on into the coordinates," McIntosh said into his mic. He heard a chorus of six men replying with a terse "Roger that."

The dropmasters in the rear of the plane—Joshua Vargo and Joshua Adams—immediately began readying a portable water pump for a parachute drop to the *Bounty*. They didn't have to be told; they could infer

from the radio communications that a drop might be in order. Portable water pumps have saved many a ship from being lost at sea, and dropping one to the *Bounty* seemed like the next logical step.

Boxed in a bright orange floating aluminum crate, a dewatering pump is similar to the gasoline-powered "trash pump" that the *Bounty* crew had on board. The latest models used by the Coast Guard are made by Ohler and are about the size of a large microwave oven, with a lawn mower–size four-horsepower gasoline engine. The newest models are optimized for easy use in an emergency, with simple on-and-off hose connections and a prewound starter cable. The crate includes a gallon of gasoline, a fifteen-foot intake hose and a twenty-foot discharge hose, and an instruction card. With the rear ramp opened, a Herc crew can push the crate out the back of the airplane and it will float down on parachutes to be recovered by the crew of the ship in distress. The pilots of the Herc aim for a spot upstream of the vessel so that it will land near the ship and then float closer. Long trail lines are deployed from the crate when it parachutes down, ideally drifting out on either side of the target ship and making it possible for the crew to grab the lines and haul the crate on board. Once they have the dewatering pump, the ship's crew attaches the hoses, fills the fuel tank, starts the engine with a rope pull just like a lawn mower, and pumps a lever a few times to prime the pump. The rest is simple—intake hose where you have water, output hose over the side of the ship. The pump will get rid of about 150 gallons per minute, nine thousand gallons per hour. For many vessels, that 150 gallons per minute has made the difference between sinking and staying afloat. Even if the boat eventually sinks, a Coast Guard pump can slow the sinking enough to make a rescue of the individuals possible, or safer than it might otherwise be.

McIntosh's immediate concern was getting closer to the *Bounty*. And that meant flying directly into a wall of water and wind.

Big dark clouds off to their left blocked the view of the area where the ship was supposed to be, and the heavy rain made visibility low even closer to the plane. However, the clouds in the immediate area were not very convective, meaning they were not the tall, vertically moving clouds that signify instability in the atmosphere and a real mess for airplanes

and ships. They were mostly low-level clouds topping out at seven thousand feet or so, rather than the thunderstorms that can reach fifty thousand feet. Normally no good can come from flying into those thunderstorms. The clouds in the immediate area were more straight-line winds rather than the severe updrafts and downdrafts found in a thunderstorm, and which can throw an airplane out of the sky. It was a bumpy ride for sure, but doable.

Getting to the *Bounty* meant flying into what looked like black velvet curtains hanging from the sky. The crew was going from stormy weather that would make most civilian pilots piss themselves, and into something that looked almost impenetrable—a dark wall that would prompt an almost reflexive turn of the airplane's yoke in another direction. The tall thunderstorm on the edge of Hurricane Sandy was like a column of black water and wind, distinct from the rest of the chaos around them. Any pilot with a lick of sense and not wearing a Coast Guard uniform would find somewhere else to go, but McIntosh warned his crew to stay buckled in tight, and Myers set the autopilot to start turning toward the dark storm clouds, descending. The plane was flying into the wind at first; then almost immediately, as the aircraft hit the black wall of the storm, the wind shifted and hit the plane broadside like a slap across the face. Ninety-knot winds battered the plane from the left, trying to push the Herc out of its flight path. The engines roared as the autopilot fought to keep the plane in the air, Myers monitoring it closely and ready to take over if necessary. The whole ship shook and vibrated, the sound of wrenching metal echoing throughout the cabin. Myers and McIntosh knew exactly when they were breaching the wall of the storm, but they were still shocked by the sudden cacophony of rain hitting the plane's skin, reminding them both of the sound of an automated car wash, maybe times a thousand, or the most torrential downpour on the interstate at high speed. The pilots wore noise-canceling headphones, but they weren't up to this task. The windscreen was awash with the driven rain, coating the glass as if they were underwater. Myers could tell the autopilot was struggling to stay within the parameters he had set, trying to maintain a somewhat level flight as the storm tossed the Herc up and down violently.

God bless you, Lockheed, he thought, referring to the plane's maker. *You're flying this thing now.*

McIntosh looked out his side window at the Herc's big wing and was amazed to see it flexing up and down about five feet in each direction— way, way more than normal. He said nothing about it to Myers, whose attention was fixed on the autopilot. His copilot was still too green to be notified that the Herc's wings were flapping up and down like an albatross's, McIntosh thought. He'd do better not knowing that till later.

It was about that time that Myers told his pilot that the autopilot was overwhelmed and couldn't handle these conditions.

"Well, just hand-fly it then," McIntosh said dryly.

"Roger," Myers said, but he was sarcastically thinking, *Oh, great, I get to hand-fly this thing through a hurricane.*

McIntosh's order showed he had confidence in his relatively inexperienced copilot to fly the Herc manually into a hurricane, with no autopilot and no radar, just flying the behemoth of a plane the same as a civilian pilot would fly his Cessna on a clear Sunday afternoon. But it also meant Myers was going to be taking the physical brunt of this mission, at least for a while. Flying by hand for a long time can be a physical challenge even in good conditions, and in this kind of weather it meant fighting the controls constantly, wrestling to keep the plane in the air and on its flight path. He knew it would be exhausting. Myers's stress level surged, the knot he already had in his stomach starting to grow and expand outward.

Myers took the controls as the ride got rougher and rougher, the Herc continuing down to a thousand feet so they could get a visual on the *Bounty* and position the craft for a water pump drop. The plane was tossed around so viciously that calling it turbulence didn't even seem adequate anymore. With the winds constantly shifting and swirling, the HC-130J was jumping up and down over and over, suddenly rising two hundred feet in just a second or two and then slamming back down two hundred feet just as quickly. Myers was intently focused as he tried to keep the plane on something resembling the glide path they wanted, staring at the HUD screen while his mind raced with constant calculations of airspeed, altitude, and attitude. At one point the aircraft's exte-

rior lights were bouncing off the clouds and illuminating the rain droplets enough to produce a disorienting and distracting *Star Trek* warp-speed effect as they whizzed by, so Myers shut off all the exterior lights.

McIntosh was hoping the plane would pop out below the storm at a thousand feet, and then they could decide how to proceed with helping the *Bounty*. At this point McIntosh and Myers assumed that the *Bounty* would still make it out of the hurricane and safely to port. The question was what they could do to really help the *Bounty*. The Herc arrived at the one thousand feet mark, and both men expected there to be a noticeable change in the winds and rain. But there wasn't. The plane was still in a fierce driving rain, with visibility so low that they couldn't even see the ocean below. They proceeded on to the coordinates where the ship should be, but as they flew over they saw nothing at all. No ship, no ocean, just rain and blackness.

"Okay, obviously a thousand feet isn't going to do it," McIntosh said. "Let's go down to five hundred feet."

They circled back toward the target coordinates again as Myers took the plane down to five hundred feet, the knot in his stomach growing ever bigger as he thought about how the Herc was being tossed up and down two hundred feet at a time, not leaving a lot of wiggle room if a particularly strong downdraft shoved the plane toward the sea. At five hundred feet, they could finally see the ocean. It didn't look like anywhere a ship should be. The moonlight couldn't penetrate the heavy clouds, so it was pitch-black at the surface. With their NVGs, McIntosh and Myers could see the waves swelling to twenty or thirty feet, looking huge and scary even from five hundred feet above. As each wave swelled, the hurricane winds blew the top off and created a spray that skittered across the water like dry snow blowing across a street. They were astonished at how the waves were coming from every direction all at once. There was no pattern, no way to anticipate where the next swell would rise or what direction it would go. The water churned violently, and McIntosh thought it looked angry. Not in a poetic or dramatic way, but just . . . angry.

The visibility in front of the plane was still terrible, maybe an eighth of a mile but probably even less. The contrast was almost mesmerizing to

Myers and McIntosh. They looked out the front of the cockpit and saw almost nothing but rain hitting the windscreen, but then they looked down and saw whitecaps and waves roiling just below. For Myers, the two images painted a picture of what it must be like on the *Bounty* at the moment, tossed by a merciless sea while also facing the fury of the wind and rain.

The mission system operators in the back of the plane were checking their radar for any sign of the ship, since the cockpit radar wasn't working, but they couldn't get any useful data, because the high waves were creating radar returns that practically filled the screen. If the *Bounty* was there, it wouldn't stand out among the huge swells. Myers and McIntosh set the plane on an orbit around the last-known coordinates of the ship, circling around in what they called a racetrack pattern as they and the crew in the back of the Herc watched out their windows for any sign of the helpless vessel. Myers switched on the exterior lights, including the landing lights, so that they would be as visible as possible if the *Bounty* crew was trying to spot them.

The plane had made a few laps around the orbit when McIntosh glimpsed something.

"One o'clock, front right side, light in the water," he called to his crew.

Myers looked to that spot and saw it also. Through their NVGs it appeared as if someone on the *Bounty* were shining a spotlight directly at them, though in fact it probably was a much smaller light that happened to break through the wind and spray enough to be amplified by the goggles. Myers turned the plane toward the light and flew over that position. They could still see the light as they drew closer, but when they were almost directly overhead Myers saw something else from his position in the right seat.

"There it is," Myers said.

"How's it look?" McIntosh asked as they passed over and beyond the *Bounty*.

"It looks like a big pirate ship in the middle of a hurricane."

CHAPTER 15

WE'RE STILL HERE

MYERS PULLED THE Herc back around to orbit in closer to the ship, still buffeted and bounced by the winds, especially when making each turn across or into the hurricane's gales. As they came back around, McIntosh got a good look at the *Bounty*, and it registered as one of the oddest sights he had ever seen in his career. He knew the ship was 180 feet long, but when the waves pounded it, McIntosh thought it looked like a toy pirate ship in a bathtub. Waves broadsided the ship over and over as it listed forty-five degrees to the right, riding up and down on the swells. To McIntosh and Myers, the *Bounty*'s situation looked dire. Yet the crew had not yet declared any intent to abandon ship or a desire to be rescued. Watching from above in the green tint from their NVGs, the Herc crew thought the scene looked downright eerie—a wooden ship from days gone by listing in the darkness, whitecaps in contrast with the black water swelling around.

They had found the ship within seven miles of its last-known position, and both cockpit crewmen were relieved. If they had not spotted the light so soon, their next step would have been to broaden the search area and start a slow, deliberate visual hunt in the areas where they expected the ship to have gone. Conditions for a visual search were so bad that they knew the effort most likely would not have succeeded, espe-

cially since they found the *Bounty* in a direction away from where they would have expected.

McIntosh radioed the *Bounty*, where Svendsen, Walbridge, and some other crew had seen the Herc fly over. The roar of that huge plane going overhead was a huge relief to them, assurance that the Coast Guard knew where they were in this vast blackness of the Atlantic. Cleveland, Groves, and several other crew members stepped out onto the weather deck when they heard the plane coming around. They couldn't help waving their arms joyously when they saw the Herc cut through the dark clouds and rain.

"HMS *Bounty*, this is Coast Guard C-130 on channel sixteen. We have a visual on your location."

"Coast Guard, this is *Bounty*. We can see the airplane," Svendsen replied.

McIntosh reported the ship's location back to the air station, where other crews and Coast Guard leaders were monitoring the radio traffic and plotting the positions on a map, while passing information up to the sector level. Now that they knew where the ship was and that it was in serious distress, the Coast Guard had to decide what to do. Sector leaders were urging the Herc crew to drop a dewatering pump to the *Bounty*, but McIntosh wasn't sure that was the right move. The HC-130J and HH-60 crews practice dropping the pumps and other gear all the time, but those drops are performed in the Albemarle Sound near the air station, usually during daylight on a calm day. Perfect conditions for a safe, accurate drop. But this was not.

Dropping pumps or other supplies from a Herc is not done lightly. Rather than the pilots flying over, eyeballing the target, and deciding when to throw things out of the plane, the drops are performed with parameters predetermined in a precise, scientific way. Herc crews must factor in a number of conditions in the air and on the sea, and then the tables will tell how to fly the plane in a specific way—the right approach angle, airspeed, and moment to drop.

McIntosh knew this was not at all like an easy training day. They couldn't hold their altitude to within two hundred feet of what they wanted, so they'd never be able to drop from the prescribed two hundred

feet without risk of wind shear slamming the Herc into the ocean. Plus, the *Bounty*'s masts reached up 115 feet from the deck, and even though the ship was listing, it could roll back up at any moment and reduce the margin of error even more. If they were going to drop a dewatering pump, McIntosh realized, they'd have to do it from five hundred feet. There are no charts for dropping at that level, so there would be a whole lot of guesstimating involved. In addition, the winds at the ocean surface were about sixty knots, almost seventy miles per hour, which is never expected for a pump drop. The bottom line, McIntosh realized, was that the Coast Guard didn't have any procedures for a Herc dropping supplies in the middle of a hurricane. At night and in bad weather? Sure. But this was so much more.

Without their radar, McIntosh and Myers had to visually reacquire the *Bounty* every time they came back around in the orbit, and that was sometimes a struggle even when they knew where the ship was. To drop the pump from five hundred feet, they would have to see the ship from much farther out than they were able to in this weather—which was usually about two miles out. To make things even more difficult, the HUD cursor, a tool on the instrument display that they normally used to help mark the location of the ship, was acting up. The marked position of the ship kept creeping off the edge of the screens. McIntosh had to make a command decision. Could they drop this pump or not?

He thought through how the drop might go. If they executed a perfect drop in hurricane conditions and without radar or the HUD cursor, the *Bounty* crew would have to go out on deck and retrieve the seventy-five-pound crate from the water as waves crashed over the ship. People could easily get swept overboard. That risk would be especially high if the Herc dropped the pump too far out and it could not be retrieved fairly easily. The *Bounty* crew would see that orange crate coming down like a gift from heaven and they would be convinced it would save them. They might do anything to get to the pump.

And even if they did manage to retrieve the pump, McIntosh thought, would it really make a difference? With a ship that big and holding that much water, and still taking on water at a fast rate, a pump probably wasn't going to change the situation significantly, he thought.

And what if the drop did not go well? There was a risk of dropping the pump onto the deck or hull of this wooden ship, creating a big hole that would take on even more water.

It was a tough call, and Myers took note as McIntosh thought aloud about which way to go. Most of his experience had been in helicopters, where he reached the people in need, hovered, and lowered supplies directly to them. But now, flying a Herc plane, Myers was taking in the lesson as McIntosh made his decision. Myers had assumed they would drop the pump, but as he listened to McIntosh talk through the scenario, he realized that they might have to protect the *Bounty* by limiting what they provided to the ship.

"We can't drop the pump," McIntosh finally decided. "Hopefully they can weather the storm until daylight, and the worst of the storm will pass by then. After daylight the conditions will be better for a drop if they still need it. Let's hold on to the pump, monitor the situation, and relay every bit of information we can to the sector."

"Roger that," Myers replied.

McIntosh relayed his decision to the Coast Guard sector, which replied by asking him whether it would make a difference to send a Jayhawk HH-60 helicopter to winch down two dewatering pumps, known as P100s, making a more precise delivery than the Herc could manage. The helicopter couldn't come until the weather got better, but maybe the *Bounty* could still be saved. McIntosh relayed the question to Svendsen at about 2:15 a.m.

"If we get you two P100s, could you save the ship?" he asked. As they waited for a reply, they could hear Svendsen saying he had to ask the captain. This was the first indication to the Herc crew that they hadn't been talking to the captain already, but they didn't know about Walbridge's injury.

Svendsen kept the mic keyed as he talked to Walbridge in the background. The Herc crew heard Walbridge say, "Yes, two P100s would be great, but two P250s would be even better!" Walbridge was referring to larger pumps, and the answer made Myers chuckle. Levity in the face of danger can be a sign of professionalism, he thought, and he realized Walbridge was maintaining his role as captain and leader even in the

worst of times. He imagined the comment must have amused Svendsen and anyone else within earshot, boosting their spirits to know the captain still had some spark.

The Herc continued to circle the *Bounty*, staying in contact with Svendsen on the radio, performing its mission as a communications platform. The Coast Guard pilots didn't know Svendsen's name or what position he held on the boat, but they were both impressed by his professionalism and his calm, levelheaded demeanor with every contact. Knowing how rough it was in the air, and how terrible conditions looked down on the water, they wouldn't have held it against Svendsen if he had been harried and overwrought with emotion. But he wasn't.

McIntosh and Myers talked with Svendsen frequently, checking for any change in the status of the boat and offering the *Bounty* crew some personal contact and reassurance. Myers was learning that while rescue helicopters can swoop in, grab people, and get out, a fixed-wing airplane can still help by providing a comforting presence, offering hope to people in distress. Every time a *Bounty* crew member looked up and saw the Herc flying close by, flashing its landing lights in a signal of solidarity, the exhausted and frightened crew members were assured that they were not alone. The Coast Guard was there, watching over them, and they wouldn't leave them in this crisis. The Herc crew was flying through their own crisis of sorts, trying to keep their airplane safe in a hurricane while being thrown around, and the crew members were increasingly airsick, details the *Bounty* crew didn't know but could easily guess. They looked up from the deck of their own ship, heaving and rolling in an ugly sea, and they could imagine the Coast Guard crew wasn't having an easy time of it either. It made them appreciate the Herc crew even more every time they saw those flashing lights.

"*Bounty*, we know right where you are and we're not going anywhere," Myers told Svendsen, knowing that hope was a critical need for those in a survival scenario. They had to keep spirits up on the *Bounty* as much as possible so the boat's crew could remain effective in their efforts to save the ship and themselves.

As time wore on, McIntosh talked to the Coast Guard sector about possibly sending a ship to help the *Bounty*, but officials said that no one else could come. On the Herc's operational radar, McIntosh and Myers

could see a line of a dozen large commercial ships hundreds of miles away, struggling with their own conditions even though they were far outside the edges of Sandy, but they could offer no assistance. They also could see the *Torm Rosetta*, the big Danish tanker the Coast Guard had queried about assisting, heading away from the storm as quickly as it could.

The Herc and the *Bounty* would be alone together for a long time, just the two crews and their vessels out in the Atlantic, fighting Sandy. But the Coast Guard crew didn't relay that information to the *Bounty*. Telling them what *wasn't* possible, what *couldn't* be done for them, could only be detrimental. Instead they passed on only what was beneficial to the *Bounty* crew to know, or at least strictly factual information. They didn't want to create false hope, but they were especially careful not to dash whatever hopes the *Bounty* crew had left.

The Herc crew had already been in contact with the *Bounty* for about an hour, and over the next hour, McIntosh and Myers both started feeling a kindred bond with Svendsen, and through him the rest of the crew. They kept the content of their transmissions strictly professional, but their emotions were rising with each exchange. "Will you be able to make port after the worst of the storm passes?" "Is the water getting higher?" "How are you guys doing now?"

The more McIntosh and Myers heard Svendsen's voice, the more they could feel how real this situation was, that this wasn't just an exercise and it wasn't a routine assistance call. HC-130J crews typically do not spend that much time communicating with people in distress, more often delivering supplies, relaying some communications, and then heading home as the Jayhawks come in for the glory of pulling grateful people out of the water. This case was different, and they felt it—deeply and in a way they didn't have to verbalize. Even the Jayhawk crews don't usually have time to feel any real kinship with the people they rescue. In Myers's time as an army helicopter pilot, he had performed many rescues in which he would turn around to see happy people in the cabin, patting one another on the back and giving a big thumbs-up to Myers and the other pilot. Smiles all around, and then he landed and never saw them again. He was taken a little off guard when he realized how much he was starting to bond with the *Bounty* crew.

But they were all professionals, and together the Herc crew and Svendsen kept one another on point. They were preparing for the worst—the *Bounty* crew going into the water—though that was not inevitable yet. Radio communications continued as they approached the second hour, McIntosh and Myers steadily talking through possible scenarios with an equally calm Svendsen, all three of them realizing where the facts were leading them: The *Bounty* would not survive. In that case, the next-best scenario would be a controlled abandon-ship in which the crew had enough warning to put on their immersion suits, prepare emergency supplies, launch the life rafts, and leave the ship in a planned and deliberate way. Svendsen relayed Walbridge's assessment that he thought the *Bounty* was stable enough to survive until dawn, at which point they could decide whether to abandon ship.

As the emotional bond grew, McIntosh and Myers were frustrated that they couldn't give the *Bounty* crew a firm endgame solution by telling them that a ship would arrive at a certain time or that the helicopters were on their way, but heavy winds and churning seas prevented such rescue attempts. All they could do was stay in contact to assure the *Bounty* crew that they were not alone. They tried not to chatter too much, because the *Bounty* needed to preserve the radio's battery life, and they knew everyone on the ship was busy.

"Coast Guard C-130 to *Bounty*. We're still here," Myers would call to Svendsen if too many minutes had passed. More than once it took Svendsen a while to reply, but he would acknowledge the call.

"*Bounty* to Coast Guard. We read you. Thank you."

CHAPTER 16

FIGHTING FOR DAWN

AROUND TWO A.M. on Monday, after the Herc had been on the scene for close to two hours, the Coast Guard sector asked McIntosh for an updated operational risk management score, known as the ORM. This score is based on the aircraft commander's assessment of the Coast Guard craft and crew's situation, everything from mechanical difficulties to how tired people were, essentially asking how well the rescuers could carry on with the mission. McIntosh talked to his entire crew on the Herc's comm system.

"Hey, how's everyone feeling?" he asked.

McIntosh waited for replies and got nothing but silence. He knew what that meant. Silence means crew members are in bad shape, either unwilling or unable to speak up about it. Airsickness was hitting everyone pretty hard, so the pilot decided to climb to seven thousand feet, where they would be above the worst of the storm and able to fly in smoother air. They orbited at that level for a while to give the crew a break, and the altitude also enabled them to communicate a bit more clearly with shore bases.

Periodically the Herc dipped back down to take a look at the *Bounty* and check in on the radio. The news was never good. Six feet of water had become ten feet of water.

"How many feet remain until you're awash?" Myers asked Svendsen. After a long pause, Svendsen replied. "Two feet until we're awash."

The pause spoke volumes to McIntosh and Myers. Their communication each way with the *Bounty* had been completely professional, neither side speaking a word about the frustration or despair they felt. They hid those emotions behind crisp, curt statements of fact. But one thing that never lied was the pause. The delay in responding meant the person was thinking of how to respond professionally, trying to contain his emotion before speaking. They always did in the end, but the pause told the whole story.

McIntosh and Myers understood that the seawater was overtaking the ship. Two feet to go didn't mean that the water level was that close to the top deck, but rather that the ship had two feet to go until it was hopelessly flooded and unstable. Add to that the forty-five-degree list, and they figured the ship must be taking on water at an astounding rate, because the portion of the hull intended to be above water, and the seams not reinforced to avoid leakage, were well underwater. As McIntosh communicated with the Coast Guard sector, he found out that they were planning to send Jayhawk helicopters out to the *Bounty* at dawn to lower dewatering pumps so that the ship could remove enough water to limp to port. McIntosh acknowledged the transmission, but he was thinking, *Yeah, that's not gonna happen.*

ABOUT THREE A.M. on Monday, the *Bounty* was in a full-fledged fight with Sandy. They were head-to-head—a 180-foot ship built for a movie versus one of the most fearsome hurricanes in recent history—and somebody was going to lose.

The crew remained on the very wet but not-yet-flooded tween deck, except for Svendsen and Walbridge, who were in the nav shack so they could monitor radio communications and keep an eye on the rigging, poking their heads out once in a while to assess any new damage. At one point they saw that the inflatable dinghy had come loose from its lashings forward and was flopping around in the wind, so Cleveland went up on deck with Scornavacchi and Salapatek to tie it down again. Sprague

came up also, but stayed in the nav shack to watch and go for help if someone didn't make it back.

The young Scornavacchi made his way along the port side while Cleveland and Salapatek inched up the starboard side. The three young men were bent forward against the wind, holding on to the railings and anything else they could grab, timing each movement so that they had something to hold on to when the ship rolled, then letting go and moving a bit farther. Slowly they made their way to the stern, where the rubber raft was on the verge of being ripped off the ship. The rain stung any exposed skin as they manhandled the raft back down and tied it again. Scornavacchi kept his face down as much as he could, trying to hold the raft and tie the lines without looking, because the rain hurt so much when it was driven into his open eyes.

There was no longer any doubt that the *Bounty* was fighting for her life. Both engines were down, the generators were out of commission, the primary bilge pumps had long ceased working, and the hydraulic pumps were dead. Water had drowned out every system beyond any hope of repair, making it unsafe for the crew. There was some concern that the water could be electrically charged from the generators and battery storage, posing an electrocution risk. As the water continued to climb, it would next reach the tween deck and eventually make those spaces unusable.

Dewatering the ship was the top priority, and with engineering abandoned, the "trash pump" was their last option—and it wasn't much of an option. A portable, gas-powered device, the pump was meant only to augment dewatering efforts rather than take on the whole fight. Even in the best of circumstances it wouldn't be able to pump enough water to save the *Bounty*, but it might be able to slow the rising water enough to give the ship some more time. Every extra minute was going to matter, because sinking at night in the worst of the storm would be a lot different from delaying that moment to daylight and less extreme weather. But the damn thing wouldn't work.

Cleveland, Groves, Barksdale, and others struggled endlessly with the portable pump, every effort made exponentially harder in the rolling seas, high winds, and blowing rain. At one point they lost the pump's gas

tank cap, and Groves spent considerable time looking for it so the fuel wouldn't be ruined by water getting in the tank. She finally found it sloshing around in someone's berthing quarters belowdecks. At first they couldn't get the gasoline engine to start, pulling the starter cord over and over again, getting nothing but a sputter and a cough. When they finally got the engine running, the pump would not prime and start moving water. Scornavacchi took a five-gallon bucket and went below to where the water was rising and filled the bucket, then went back to pour the water into the pump's intake hose in an effort to prime the pump. He did that a few times but it didn't seem to help. They thought maybe there was a problem with the intake hose that came with the pump, so they attached one of the *Bounty*'s fire hoses instead. No use. Maybe the gasoline had gone bad, so they obtained fresh fuel and tried that. Nothing. Finally, as a last desperate measure, they pulled out the owner's manual and read through it as the hurricane howled around them. Crew members tried over and over as hours wore on, but they could never get the pump to do more than run a few minutes and cough out a few cups of water.

If the crew was going to abandon ship in the middle of a hurricane, it would be vital to stay in communication with the rescuers and be able to transmit their exact location. Despite all the technological assets of the Coast Guard, Cleveland and Groves knew that finding a ship—not to mention a far smaller life raft or a single person—in the ocean during a storm was no easy task. One EPIRB was already pinging their location, so they obtained the other two to be sure they would have them handy if, or when, the crew left the ship. Conferring with Svendsen and Walbridge, they activated one of the EPIRBs, making two that were now sending signals. After the Coast Guard got a fix on the two distress signals, Myers told Svendsen they could turn one of the two transmitting EPIRBs off and reactivate it only if they abandoned ship.

After securing the two distress beacons, Cleveland and Groves were making their way through the tween deck when they saw Adam Prokosh lying on the mattress placed on the deck. He was obviously in pain. Scornavacchi came by about the same time and saw his friend lying there, but thought maybe he was just tired. Cleveland and Groves asked what happened and found out about Prokosh's back injury. They realized

he was hurt even worse than Walbridge, who was still managing to stay upright and move around with great difficulty.

IN THE EARLY morning on Monday, everyone involved could deduce that the *Bounty* was not going to make it. No ships could come to the rescue, the Herc couldn't drop pumps, and the Coast Guard helicopters couldn't launch yet because of the weather. The *Bounty* would have to be abandoned, and the only question was when.

Svendsen suggested to McIntosh that they start thinking about an eight a.m. target for entering the life rafts.

McIntosh radioed the Coast Guard sector with the update on the plans to abandon ship. They figured that by 7:30 a.m. on Monday, the worst part of Sandy would be past the *Bounty* and they could send the Jayhawks out to pick up the crew. If the crew was able to abandon ship in an orderly fashion, boarding the life rafts under the watchful eyes of the Herc if the Jayhawks hadn't arrived yet, then the rescue should be fairly straightforward. The planners at the Coast Guard station radioed back to Myers and McIntosh:

"We concur with them going forward with 0800 abandon ship. We need to let them know that we're going to move ahead with 0800 abandon ship. If they're comfortable with that, we want them to start making preparations for that eventuality and let them know another C-130 will come out and establish communications with them and two HH-60s will come after that."

So it was happening. McIntosh passed the information on to Svendsen, who agreed this was the best plan. Everyone was feeling confident at this point that the *Bounty* story might end reasonably well.

Scornavacchi thought about the oddity of being on a tall sailing ship—on the *Bounty*, no less—in a hurricane, with the ship about to sink. *Everyone is so calm*, he thought. *This is surreal.*

McINTOSH AND MYERS realized that they weren't trying to save the ship anymore. They were trying to save lives. Myers's experience in helicopter

rescues told him that the Coast Guard needed to send two helicopters, not one—sixteen people couldn't be rescued by one Jayhawk.

The two pilots watched their own fuel consumption carefully, constantly calculating how soon they would reach "bingo fuel," the point at which they had just enough to make it back to base. Because they would be flying against the wind on the way back, a two-hour trip instead of the half hour on the way out, they would need much more fuel on the return. McIntosh requested a phone patch directly to the Elizabeth City air station, bypassing the higher-ups at the Coast Guard sector, and it was Lt. Jane Peña who answered the phone. Her SAR pager had gone off about two a.m. on Monday, when the officers at the air station realized a Jayhawk crew might be needed soon. She and her pilot, Lt. Cdr. Steve Cerveny, had monitored the radio traffic closely and knew the *Bounty* crew was planning an orderly abandon-ship after dawn. At that point the Coast Guard probably would send another crew, because her team's watch would end at eight a.m.

McIntosh knew Peña, and was comfortable enough to tell her the straight truth. He wanted to make clear to her what he was seeing and hearing directly from the *Bounty* crew, just in case any information had been lost or misconstrued after being relayed through sector.

"Hey, there's going to be sixteen people in the water here shortly, just so you know what's going on out here," he told her. "We know the weather's bad, but we definitely need another C-130 to relieve us out here, because we're going to hit our bingo fuel before too long. If there's any way possible, we need helicopters here. *Two* helicopters."

Peña thanked McIntosh for the update, and he was satisfied that the air station was on the same page and realized they would soon be pulling people out of the water, even though the information from sector suggested the *Bounty* might make it till dawn.

Peña spread the word about McIntosh's report. This rescue was going to happen sooner than they thought.

CHAPTER 17

A LAST LESSON

EVER PROFESSIONAL AND organized, Svendsen briefed the Herc pilots on their plans for abandoning ship. They would enter two life rafts and carry three EPIRBs, with one activated in each raft. They also planned to carry four handheld radios, but they weren't sure whether they would work once they got wet. McIntosh and Myers were impressed that the *Bounty* crew had such a clear and orderly plan for abandoning the ship.

When she could, Groves stopped by where Prokosh was lying on the tween deck to update him on what was going on. Used to being one of the strong young men on board, Prokosh felt helpless lying where he had fallen, watching his crewmates rush around with great purpose. Drenched and dripping, Groves leaned over him to explain how the bosun's shop had been evacuated and the Coast Guard had been called, and told him of the plans to abandon ship at dawn. Christian stayed with him much of the time, the slight blond rookie finding that her best role in the crisis was talking with him and doing anything she could to make him more comfortable. When the water began rising on the starboard side where he lay, Christian became scared that they would drown if they stayed there, so she helped Prokosh crawl to the other side of the ship. The movement was excruciating. Prokosh could feel one specific part of his back that did not want to support any weight at all, and he winced every

time the vertebrae grated together. When he got to the port side, he collapsed and just remained motionless, totally spent.

Walbridge also was moving slowly and with great pain in his back and one leg, staying in the nav shack with Svendsen to monitor the storm and the ship's condition, and to try communicating with Simonin, Hansen, and his wife. He was wet, like everyone else, and his glasses were twisted from his fall and sat crooked on his face. As the *Bounty*'s future became clearer, as he realized that the ship he loved so dearly would not survive this storm, Walbridge must have realized that he still had a duty to his crew beyond helping them survive. He must have realized that he still owed his future captains of America one last teachable moment. Walbridge had spent most of his life helping younger people learn the craft of tall ship sailing, always eager to teach them the important lessons they could learn nowhere else, to guide his protégés to finding the answers themselves rather than just telling them what they needed to know.

The captain called muster in the nav shack, and everyone who wasn't injured or involved in a vital operation, like trying to get the gas-powered water pump working, gathered there. All were wet and exhausted, and they knew that they would soon have to leave their ship. They were going to lose the *Bounty*. It was still a few hours to dawn, and the howl of the storm, the creaking of wooden beams wrenching and twisting, was all they heard in the nav shack as Walbridge prepared to speak. His pain was obvious, and Groves could tell that Walbridge was worried.

The captain looked them over silently. After a long pause, he began by updating the crew on their communications with the Coast Guard and the plans to abandon ship after sunrise. Saying those words aloud seemed difficult for him. Because he believed strongly in visualizing different outcomes and preparing for them, Walbridge talked to his crew about what would happen as they abandoned ship, how it was important to stay together and get into the rafts safely. He worried that a crew member might fall into the ocean while trying to descend from the ship to an inflated life raft alongside, so he suggested the crew wear their climbing harnesses—the ones they used when working up on the rigging—over their immersion suits. That way they could secure a rope

to each person as they descended to the life rafts. If they went in the water, they also might be able to clip their harnesses and stay together.

"Water bottles. Don't forget to take your own water bottle with you. . . .

"Make sure there's an EPIRB activated in each life raft. . . .

"Stay together. . . ."

But then Walbridge got to what was really on his mind. He must have understood that his decision to set sail from New London was a mistake. And Walbridge always taught his crew to learn from their mistakes. This was to be his last teachable moment for the crew of the *Bounty*.

"I'd like everyone to brainstorm where we went wrong," he said, his voice strained from the pain, physical and otherwise. To Groves, the look on her captain's face and the tone in his voice told her that he knew they had failed. Walbridge knew that the *Bounty* would not survive this voyage, but more so, he thought he had failed his crew. The defeated look on Walbridge's face, the way he seemed to be blaming himself, saddened Groves.

"How did we get here?" Walbridge asked loudly, looking around the nav shack, still in command of his ship. "What went wrong?"

The crew listened intently, all eyes on Walbridge, but no one offered any answer, any criticism. They stood there, water flowing from their foul-weather gear, long hair, beards, and dreadlocks soaked with seawater and rain, some struggling to keep their eyes open despite the enormity of the moment, others struggling not to cry as they felt Walbridge's pain.

"At what point did we lose control?" Walbridge looked from one crew member to the next, making eye contact, a captain with a purpose.

They knew the captain wasn't asking because he couldn't figure it out himself. His tone wasn't angry or desperate. This was how he taught his crew: by asking them to think. He wanted his crew to come to their own conclusions as to why the *Bounty* was about to sink to the bottom of the ocean. He knew, but he wanted them to get there on their own. To learn.

There was only silence as Walbridge looked around the room. His crew watched him intently, but some had trouble meeting his gaze. They knew what Walbridge was saying to them.

"Learn from this," Walbridge said more quietly.

After a long pause, Walbridge told the crew that they had done all

they could, and everyone who wasn't working on the gasoline-powered pump or preparing to abandon ship should sleep. He looked weary in a way the crew hadn't seen before.

"Get some rest while you can," he said. "You're going to need it in a couple of hours."

THE CREW DISPERSED and set about performing the tasks needed to abandon ship. They had practiced this scenario before, the situation in which they had hours to prepare for leaving the ship rather than hastily escaping. Several crew members began organizing ditch kits, accumulations of various supplies they might need after leaving the *Bounty*. Groves supervised the operation to gather all the supplies, aided by Scornavacchi, Jones, Christian, Black, Hewitt, and Sprague. They went to the crew quarters and gathered their own personal belongings in dry bags and also took the dry bags from the other crew's quarters, trying to spot anything of personal or monetary value. As they could take a break from other tasks, the remaining crew went to their own quarters and grabbed their most important possessions—pictures, mementos, valuables, anything they could stuff in a dry bag or shove inside their clothes. Hewitt passed by the injured Prokosh at one point and he asked her to grab some cash from under his mattress, his favorite peacoat, and his mariner's license, "Because that thing is a bitch to replace."

Christian helped her friend Groves tear off a strip of the baby blanket she had carried with her since childhood. Groves stuffed it into her foul-weather gear so she would still have a piece of it, at least. The oldest crew member, the white-bearded Faunt, also grabbed his teddy bear named Mush—and his rescue knife.

Scornavacchi cut down the peanut-butter jar holding his pet fish and put the jar inside a dry bag with other belongings. On the way back from his berth he passed the captain's quarters and noticed that the door was open, which was unusual. He looked in and saw Walbridge sitting on the edge of his bunk, staring at a picture of his wife.

When he passed by again a little later, Walbridge and the photo were gone.

All of the dry bags and other gear were gathered on the tween deck, where the crew was organizing the abandon-ship. All of the ship's logs, the crew's mariner licenses, passports, cell phones, and cash were secured in a dry bag. Other bags contained items like extra flares, batteries for headlamps, and any other useful thing they could think of. Groves had people packing shrink-wrapped bottles of water in heavy-duty garbage bags, and tying them together with rope. Then they attached extra life jackets to the bundles to help keep them afloat and visible. All the remaining life jackets were tied together in one large bundle to serve as an orange floating beacon. So far, the abandon-ship preparations were going just as they had planned and practiced many times. Once dawn broke and they could get off the ship safely, they would have all the necessary supplies, valuables, and documents tethered to their life rafts.

And still the water rose. Walbridge and Svendsen realized they might not be able to wait until dawn to abandon ship. The outlook for the *Bounty* was worsening at an astounding pace. The captain and chief mate tried to determine how long they could stall, and they agreed that if the water rose to the flooring of the tween deck, the level just below the top deck, that would be their cue to abandon ship. Both hoped that wouldn't happen until dawn, but neither thought the *Bounty* would make it that long.

In the early morning, the crew gathered on the tween deck, waiting to see what would happen next. With the generators out, their only light came from the headlamps and flashlights used by some of the crew. They sat in the dark, everyone soaking wet, some talking, some in their own worlds. Everyone was so tired. They waited, rolling with the ship, listening to Hurricane Sandy roar outside. At one point Scornavacchi got up and found a guitar in the crew quarters and took it to Christian. "Let's have one more song," he told her. But they ran out of time.

Around three thirty a.m., Walbridge ordered the crew to put on their survival suits.

Cleveland protested that it wasn't safe to put on the immersion suits belowdecks because they could trap you if the ship capsized, the buoyancy making it difficult for a person to swim underwater and escape. Svendsen said he understood that was the protocol, but that it was too

dangerous to have everyone on the top deck. The two men argued for a minute and Svendsen won.

Called Gumby suits because they make the wearer resemble the 1960s-era flexible toy that probably few on the *Bounty* had ever seen, the immersion suits zip up the front to cover the wearer from head to toe, exposing only the face. Generously sized to fit over a person's normal clothing and shoes, so no time is lost in donning it in an emergency, the immersion suits on the *Bounty* came in a small size packaged in red storage bags, a medium or "normal" size packed in orange bags, and in green bags with extra-large suits. Because the *Bounty* sometimes carried more than the sixteen crew on this voyage, the ship had many extra immersion suits in the medium size. Only a few small sizes were available, and everyone on board knew that Christian and a couple of the other women needed them.

Made of buoyant neoprene in a highly visible reddish-orange color, the immersion suits are capable of keeping a person on the surface of the water and insulated from the cold for a substantial period of time. No additional life jacket is needed with the suit. The *Bounty*, like most other vessels with Coast Guard certification, regularly trained crew members on how to don the immersion suits. In the advanced survival training that some of the more experienced *Bounty* crew had undergone, they practiced putting on the suits and jumping into the water feet-first, which was supposed to force the air up and out of the suit through the hood. That provided a snug fit and didn't allow more than a moderate amount of water in. Some water was expected and actually helped insulate the wearer.

The *Bounty* carried more than thirty immersion suits and more than a hundred life jackets.

Hewitt and Christian helped each other get their Gumby suits on, joking as they pulled the bulky suits from their storage shelves. "Remember which number suit you have so you can put it back in the right place later," Hewitt said. They both chuckled at the absurdity.

For some crew members, donning their immersion suits was the breaking point. They had held it together this far, focused on the work to be done and still holding out hope that this whole trip would turn out

to be just a crazy experience with a happy ending. When they pulled on those ungainly, oversize neoprene suits, it was like the final sign that this was real, that they were really about to leave the *Bounty* in a hurricane. One crew member was in a near panic, suddenly emotional and scared. Others were keeping it together, but this was frightening now, and no one could be blamed for showing it. Svendsen and Walbridge came below to put their suits on, and the captain needed a lot of help to get into his. Prokosh managed to don his by himself, though with great difficulty and pain. Some of the senior crew, including Groves, Cleveland, Svendsen, and Walbridge, put their suits on only halfway, leaving their arms out so they could still work. Many of the crew put their climbing harnesses on over the immersion suits, hoping they would provide an extra measure of safety for clipping onto lines and one another. Mark Warner used multi-tool pliers to help people cinch their climbing harnesses tight over the Gumby suits, and Svendsen was checking each person's suit to make sure they were on properly. With only a few small-size immersion suits on board and several women needing them, Scornavacchi ended up in a suit that felt massive on him. He put his climbing harness on over it and attached a plastic bag with a small survival kit he'd made for himself containing water and a few other items he thought he might need. For Barksdale, this was the first time he had ever put on an immersion suit. His safety orientation upon joining the *Bounty* in Boothbay did not include learning about the suits or trying one on.

After they had their suits on, Svendsen and Walbridge went back up to the nav shack along with Groves and Cleveland. The rest of the crew formed a fire line to transfer all the emergency gear up to the weather deck, and at one point Hewitt grew frustrated that they weren't moving the supplies quickly enough. But then she looked and saw that at the end of the line the crew was taking the time to stack the gear neatly. She was impressed.

Shit's going down, but people are still being professional and really levelheaded, Hewitt thought.

As the crew was transferring the ditch kits and gear, Walbridge sent another e-mail to the Coast Guard at 3:41 a.m. His assessment was oddly—or admirably—optimistic, as if he were holding on to the idea that he could still save the ship:

"We have lost all dewatering abilities. Estimate 6 to 10 hours left. When we lose all power we lose e-mail—there should be an EPIRB going off—water is taking on fast—we are in distress—ship is fine, we can't dewater—need pumps."

With the gear moved, the crew members sat down on the tween deck in the dark, watching the water rise in the light cast by the headlamps that several people wore. Most tried to rest. Hewitt was desperately sleepy, but she couldn't doze off. She also didn't like being belowdecks in her Gumby suit, because it went against her safety training. So she went up on the top deck to help with the portable water pump, where she saw Walbridge out in the weather, and her first thought was, *Oh, his hearing aids. I bet those aren't waterproof.*

Cleveland was watching the water level from the door of the nav shack, and it wasn't long before he turned to the captain and told him the water was overcoming the tween deck. Walbridge acknowledged Cleveland and ordered everyone to the top deck, where they first gathered in the nav shack with Walbridge, Svendsen, Groves, and Cleveland.

The crew members crawled, crouched, and staggered their way through the rising water from the tween deck to the top deck. Everything was so slow. The crew had to be methodical with every handhold, every release, to move forward without being thrown around the deck. When Prokosh emerged from the tween deck, clutching a life jacket, he was fighting the pain as much as he was the ship and the hurricane.

"Adam Prokosh coming on deck!" he shouted. "I'm injured and I can't help anyone, but I'm here!"

The *Bounty* was listing at forty-five degrees at this point, making the deck a steep, wet, slippery obstacle course. As each person came to the door of the nav shack, Svendsen, Groves, and Cleveland checked his or her immersion suit, harness, and any other gear. Svendsen kept a head count so he would know when everyone was accounted for. Once they got the okay, each person crawled or walked in a deep crouch along the port side to the rear of the ship. Faunt, Salapatek, Prokosh, and Jessica Hewitt were among the first to make their way out on deck. A wave washed over the deck and ripped the life jacket out of Prokosh's arms, but

another jacket came floating by seconds later and he grabbed it. When Christian came to the door, Cleveland checked her suit and saw that she had donned it properly. Taking Christian's hand from Groves, Cleveland gave her instructions before sending her out to the stern.

"Stay low! Go from me to the fife rail around the mast!" he called to Christian, shouting through the storm noise and the hood over her head. "Use any objects on the deck to keep from sliding down the boat. Grab the hand of the person next to you when you get there and stand by!"

Christian may not have heard any of the instructions. Cleveland and Groves directed their crewmates out onto the stormy deck mostly with hand motions, because they couldn't be heard over the wind and the sea, especially when people had their immersion suit hoods up and covering their ears. Some made their way far aft and others stopped closer to the midway point on the deck where the emergency supplies had been placed. Some of the crew, including Christian, clipped their climbing harnesses onto the jack lines that had been strung down the length of the ship for security when the ship was rolling. Some of the more experienced crew members knew that could be risky if the ship suddenly rolled over, because it would be difficult to unlatch from the jack line once you were being tossed around or dragged underwater. In the howling winds and spraying seas, that caution was not passed along.

Even wearing the climbing harnesses over their immersion suits was unorthodox and potentially risky, because, unlike the slick immersion suits, harnesses or the water bottles and other gear some crew attached could snag rigging lines or other debris. Many of the crew also put life jackets on over their immersion suits and climbing harnesses, which was cumbersome and also not in accordance with any survival training. While certainly providing even more buoyancy, the effect also was to make a smooth, already sufficiently buoyant immersion suit subject to entanglement by ropes and other debris.

Making their way across the deck and pausing to determine their next move, Christian and Scornavacchi ended up next to each other, lying flat on the deck with their feet jammed onto the fife rail surrounding the ship's mainmast to keep from sliding down the angled deck. With only their faces visible in the red Gumby suits, everyone looked the same as

they huddled together, heads down in defense against the driving rain and wind. As they were settling into their spots, Scornavacchi looked over at Christian next to him, wet wisps of her blond hair peeking out from her hood. She smiled sweetly at him and hunkered down tight against the deck with a look of determination. He didn't think she looked scared at all. Then she moved on toward amidships, where the emergency supplies were gathered.

Hewitt ended up near the helm, on the wooden storm grating, with her boyfriend, Salapatek, next to her. They clipped their harnesses together so they wouldn't be separated and just held on to each other, waiting for dawn. Prokosh was braced at the stern, pain nearly overpowering him now. Like most of the crew, Faunt had been awake for twenty-four hours. He was one of several who actually fell asleep as they braced themselves on a forty-five-degree sloping, heaving wet deck in the middle of a hurricane, knowing they were about to abandon ship. Hewitt heard Groves shout out to everyone, "The Coast Guard will be here in three hours!" and then she fell asleep.

It was about 4:20 a.m. on Monday.

With everyone accounted for on deck, Cleveland was at the stern preparing rope to assist in getting the crew safely into the life rafts. He also tied extra hundred-foot lines to each of the two life raft canisters, making them easier to find and grab in the water. Svendsen was back with the captain in the nav shack. The chief mate was about to radio the Coast Guard Herc with an update when he felt the boat pitching forward. Standing there with his Gumby suit open to the waist, Svendsen saw that the foredeck was awash and realized the boat was sinking by the nose. They didn't have any more time.

"Robin, I think we should abandon ship," Svendsen said to the captain.

"No, no, I think we have more time," Walbridge replied.

Svendsen was getting more and more concerned. He watched another big wave wash over the forward part of the ship, submerging a large part of the bow.

"I think it's time for us to abandon ship," he said again to the captain, this time with more urgency in his voice.

Still the captain resisted giving up his ship. "We have more time," he said. "We can wait."

Svendsen knew they couldn't. "Robin, we have to abandon ship now!" he said for the third time, and he purposefully made a dramatic gesture of starting to put his left arm in his immersion suit to don it completely. Walbridge got the message and acquiesced.

"Okay, I trust you," he said. "We should abandon ship."

At 4:30 a.m., Svendsen pulled on his immersion suit the rest of the way and was about to leave the nav shack to convey the order to the crew. The life rafts would launch and everyone would board them to wait until rescue was possible at daybreak. They might lose the *Bounty*, but the crew would survive.

Before crawling out on deck, Svendsen first wanted to notify the Coast Guard that they were abandoning ship immediately. He picked up the mic. Less than a minute had passed since Walbridge ordered the abandon-ship. Just as he was about to call the Coast Guard, the *Bounty* suddenly heaved out of the water, rolling to the right and forward.

"She's going under!" someone shouted.

Faunt awoke to the urgent cry and opened his eyes just in time to see himself being thrown up and into the sea with the rest of the crew. Hewitt woke to Salapatek shaking her and screaming, "Wake up! Jess, we have to go! It's going!"

Svendsen managed to get out a last radio call to the Coast Guard before he and Walbridge escaped the nav shack.

CHAPTER 18

WE SEE YOU

THE HERC WAS not in visual contact with the *Bounty* when the tall ship keeled over, so McIntosh and Myers were surprised by the sudden call on the radio. Even before they realized what Svendsen was saying they knew that this was not the clear, calm, precise communication they had come to know from the chief mate.

"We're abandoning ship! We're abandoning ship!" Svendsen yelled into the radio. No formalities, no calm demeanor. Clearly, the *Bounty* was going down unexpectedly.

"Acknowledged, you are abandoning ship," McIntosh replied. He waited for a response. "Acknowledged, *Bounty*, understand you are abandoning ship. What are your plans?" he tried again.

Nothing.

"Coast Guard C-130 to *Bounty*. Understand you are abandoning ship. What is your status? *Bounty*, what are your plans?"

Silence.

No one on the plane spoke for a moment, and then McIntosh said, "Okay, let's reconfigure for a modified ASRK drop." But he didn't need to tell his crew; the panicked abandon-ship call told all of them what they needed to do.

Everyone on the Herc realized that the *Bounty* crew would soon be

161

in the water, if they weren't already. What had sounded like a remarkably orderly plan to abandon ship had suddenly turned into an all-out emergency. The Herc was about five miles out in the racetrack pattern, heading away from the *Bounty*, when they heard the call. Myers needed no invitation to point the nose of the Herc back around to the *Bounty* and descend, as McIntosh relayed the information to sector. The crew in the back of the plane also responded before they heard McIntosh, unbuckling from their harnesses to start readying for the deployment of an aerial sea rescue kit, known as an ASRK-24. The kit contains three life rafts and parcels of survival gear, including flares, strobes, sea dye markers, food, and water. Myers was on the radio immediately to convey the news to the Coast Guard sector: "We have received abandon-ship call from the vessel *Bounty*. We are in descent at this time to try to get on scene and visually acquire the target again and ascertain their status."

As Myers maneuvered the Herc for the kit drop, McIntosh got another phone patch directly to Peña at the air station. Peña and Cerveny's crew—twenty-five-year-old flight mechanic Michael Lufkin and thirty-three-year-old rescue swimmer Randy Haba—were about to go back to bed because either they would fly at dawn or another crew would step up as their watch ended. When Peña picked up the phone, she knew immediately from McIntosh's voice that everything had changed.

"This is McIntosh. They are abandoning ship *now*! They are going into the water! The *Bounty* is abandoning ship *now*!"

Peña quickly confirmed the coordinates and turned to alert the rest of the air station's personnel. "Hey, everybody, that was McIntosh. The *Bounty* is abandoning ship. It's happening now."

Her pilot looked at her calmly and ordered, "Go get dressed. Let's go."

A Herc would be needed on scene for quite a while still, and the first was about to head back to refuel. Pilot Peyton Russell, twenty-eight-year-old copilot Lt. Aaron Cmiel, and the rest of their HC-130J crew were quickly rousted from their bunks.

"Let's go, let's go!" they heard. "You've got seventeen people in the water."

Russell, who had been in a deep sleep before he was awakened, propped himself up in bed and just said, "What?" He was having trouble

understanding from a dead sleep how the situation had changed so drastically. And weren't they third-string? What was going on?

"Just go," the other voice said. "The one Herc is running out of gas, and they're going to have to leave soon. And the other crew in Raleigh will take too long. By the time we wake them up, get them out of the hotel and in the air, it'll be two hours getting them on scene. Just go!"

About then they heard their SAR pagers go off. "One-hundred-and-eighty-foot sailing vessel, ninety miles east of Cape Hatteras, possible PIW [person in water]."

Russell and his crew bounded out of bed and raced to the Herc that was already being readied. One of the two dropmasters was twenty-nine-year-old Jonathan Sageser, who got to work preparing the back of the Herc, working on the information that there could be up to seventeen people in the water. He and his fellow crew pulled extra SAR gear from another Herc onto their plane so they'd be ready to drop up to six eight-person life rafts and other survival gear. With all the prep and planning that had been done while they slept, Russell's crew was able to get airborne in twenty minutes. Cmiel was the second-least-experienced copilot in the Herc fleet, behind Myers, with fewer than a hundred hours' experience.

AS McINTOSH RELAYED the situation to Peña, the dropmasters in the Herc moved the dewatering pump off the ramp at the back of the plane, holding on to whatever they could as the aircraft bounced through hurricane gusts and Myers struggled to provide some semblance of steady flight. Once the pump was out of the way, they had to manhandle the ASRK into position, the crew bouncing off the fuselage, the floor, and the ceiling the whole time. The dropmasters opened the ramp at the rear of the plane, the floor dropping down and exposing the crew to the weather outside. The rear crew secured themselves with "gunner's belts," heavy rigging belts that tied them to the inside of the plane and kept them from being swept out. Once the ramp was open, the howling wind was incredible, creating an otherworldly effect with the blue interior lighting of the Herc's cargo hold. The crew members there had no idea how the plane

was oriented or what maneuvers the pilots were about to make, so they couldn't brace themselves in anticipation and were left to react to each lurch and heave of the aircraft. Already airsick before they had to leap up and prepare the ASRK drop, the crew in the back of the Herc became more and more ill as they went about their tasks. Not a single complaint was heard.

McIntosh and Myers had to assume sixteen basketballs were in the water, a Coast Guard reference to how difficult it is to spot a human being bobbing in the ocean.

"HMS *Bounty*, this is Coast Guard C-130. How do you hear? What is your status?" McIntosh called out every few minutes. There was no response.

McIntosh realized he was not likely to get any answer. He could only hope the *Bounty* crew was still receiving his calls.

"HMS *Bounty*, this is Coast Guard C-130. We are preparing to drop life rafts to you."

About ten minutes after the ship rolled over, the Herc came in low, right over the last position of the *Bounty*. In the plane's rear, a green "go" light illuminated at the ramp, signaling the dropmasters to shove the ASRK into the night. Other types of midair deployments use a drogue chute to pull the package out, or more accurately, to hold the pallet steady and let the Herc fly out from underneath it. But the ASRK is dropped perpendicular to the wind and free-falls without parachutes to give it the most accurate landing. The dropmasters gave it a good push and off it went.

As the ASRK went down, McIntosh and Myers got a good look at the *Bounty* after it had keeled over and thrown everyone into the water. If the scene had looked eerie as the ship struggled to stay afloat, the sight before them now in their NVGs was downright scary. In the roiling waters they could spot two life rafts, debris floating on the surface, and a few strobe lights. It reminded Myers of the scene of a commercial airline crash—bits of debris everywhere, pieces of a vessel that looked oddly askew, colors here and there that made him wonder about people in the water. *That's not right*, he thought. *A ship shouldn't be lying on her side like that.* And then suddenly it was all gone again as the Herc flew on.

The ASRK deployed into the *Bounty*'s debris field, the three life rafts

opening automatically when they hit the water and all of the gear spreading out in a one-thousand-foot line designed to optimize the chances of people in the water finding the attached grab lines. Myers pulled the Herc up from the dangerously low altitude and circled around again as McIntosh told the crew in the back to prepare for dropping a self-locating datum marker buoy, known as an SLDMB, a device that floats but has little above-water surface area to be carried by the wind. About three feet long and with red fins in the shape of a cross, the SLDMB is equipped with a global positioning satellite (GPS) sensor, and is designed to be simply thrown out the back of an aircraft. The SLDMB moves more with the water than with the wind, which means it travels in a manner similar to people or objects in the water. Jayhawk helicopters and other Hercs can home in on the SLDMB as the location of debris and survivors, even as it drifts in the ocean currents.

The crew in the back of the Herc was so sick at this point that it truly was all they could do to struggle to the front of the cargo area, grab the SLDMB, and make their way back to the open ramp. Several of the crew had thrown up on the ramp, unable to wait until they could grab an airsickness bag, so the metal grooved ramp was slick with their vomit. One dropmaster clipped the gunner's belt on again, nauseated beyond anything he had experienced before, and waited at the ramp for the green light from the cockpit before tossing the buoy out.

AFTER DROPPING THE SLDMB, the Herc crew kept circling, searching for any signs of survivors or life rafts in the dark water, dangerously close to their bingo fuel. They soon got word that Elizabeth City was launching Jayhawk HH-60 helicopters, which could fly now that Sandy was moving northward and the weather was easing up a bit, and that another HC-130J was on its way to relieve the McIntosh and Myers crew.

They watched their fuel level as they waited for relief. But they weren't eager to leave. Every few minutes, McIntosh sent a radio call into the ether, just hoping the *Bounty* could hear.

"HMS *Bounty*, this is Coast Guard C-130. Rescue helicopters are on the way. I repeat, rescue helicopters are on the way."

Nothing but silence. It pained both Myers and McIntosh to hear nothing, to know that Svendsen—though they never knew his name—was not responding with his crisp, professional words. They could only wonder what was happening below, and their minds reeled with the images.

"HMS *Bounty*, this is Coast Guard C-130. Rescue helicopters are coming. Rescue helicopters are on the way. Rescue is on the way. Rescue is on the way. Rescue is on the way."

They hoped that the *Bounty* crew could hear them and just could not respond. The Herc hummed along, the engines roaring and pulsing, rain shattering on the windscreen as the two pilots looked forward, hidden in their own worlds behind their helmets and NVGs, both thinking the same worried thoughts.

"HMS *Bounty*, rescue is on the way; rescue is on the way," McIntosh called out in clipped, terse words. "HMS *Bounty*, rescue is on the way; rescue is on the way."

McINTOSH AND MYERS stayed on scene as long as they could, finally hitting bingo fuel. McIntosh called back for the dropmasters to close the ramp at the rear of the plane. The physical action of closing the ramp is minimal, basically hitting a switch, but requires a sequence of call-and-response between the cockpit and the rear of the plane. As McIntosh called out from the checklist, there was a long delay as he waited for a response. Finally another crew member came on the comm and told him the dropmaster was too busy puking to reply. After more long delays, Hector Rios, the flight mechanic positioned behind the pilots, offered that he could close the ramp from his position, an option McIntosh had never utilized.

"Yeah . . . if you could do that . . . that would be great," someone in the back replied.

The dropmasters were lying on the deck, bruised from being tossed around for hours, sick beyond belief, and all they could do was crawl away from the ramp enough to let it close. Still, not a single man complained or said he couldn't do his job. As Rios closed the ramp from his

position, McIntosh realized his dropmasters were in a truly serious condition if they couldn't manage hitting a switch no matter how much they tried.

The big Herc circled the *Bounty*'s debris field a few more times before heading home, flashing its lights every time it went over and sending out constant radio calls.

"*Bounty*, we see you; we see you. HMS *Bounty*, this is Coast Guard C-130; we are still here. Repeat, we are still here. We see you; we see you. Rescue is on the way. We see you; we see you. Rescue is on the way."

CHAPTER 19

I PROMISED

SCORNAVACCHI HAD CLOSED his eyes for just a second, probably about to doze off as he waited on the deck for the abandon-ship order, when the *Bounty* suddenly went up and over. It all happened so quickly, but in his mind, it was slow enough for him to see every detail in front of him.

His crewmates around him were flying through the air or sliding quickly down the deck, some immediately caught in the rigging, struggling like ungainly red bugs trapped in a terrible spiderweb. Because Scornavacchi had been bracing his feet on the fife rail that ran around the mast, he ended up standing on top of it as the *Bounty* rolled over onto her side. He was able to stand there long enough to think about what he should do next. Knowing he should get away from the ship as fast as possible, Scornavacchi jumped into the water near several other people who were already floating, waving their arms and legs clumsily in what he assumed to be an effort to get away.

Once he was in the churning water, the waves still swelling high and hard, Scornavacchi was barely able to poke his head to the surface for a breath when he felt the *Bounty* trying to suck him and the other crew closer. Every time the ship heaved up on a roll out of the water, there was a pulling sensation, as if they were being dragged back and under the ship; then it threatened to crush them as it rolled back down again.

Everywhere in the water was a hazard: something as simple as a half-inch-thick nylon line that could get stuck in your climbing harness, wrapped around the water bottle clipped to your belt, and suddenly pull you to your death underneath the *Bounty*. Everything about the *Bounty* was a potential killer to the crew now. They were nearly helpless in their Gumby suits, floating, but unable to move with any efficiency or purpose in the heaving seas and hurricane winds. None had landed far from the *Bounty*, which was now in its own death throes. The water and wind had taken over the *Bounty*, but it was struggling to stay afloat as Sandy rolled it back and forth, the ship's 115-foot mast and other rigging slamming down into the sea with each roll back to starboard. Every time the ship turned back their way, the crew could see the huge timbers of the masts and spars coming down toward them. And they could do little but pray that they missed.

Scornavacchi fought to get a breath, having just barely broken the surface and still trying to find a way to breathe with the waves and rain forcing water down his throat. His face was angled away from the ship, and as he turned to look back he could see debris being sucked under the hull with each rocking motion. He reached out to anything floating nearby, and there was plenty, trying to hang on to something that might keep him from being pulled back to the *Bounty*, but he couldn't keep a grip on anything with his big Gumby fingers. He felt himself being sucked back by the ship and pushed by the wave action, and then before he could enjoy one good gulp of air, he was suddenly dragged underwater by a loose line that became entangled in the plastic-bag survival kit attached to his climbing harness. The *Bounty* rolled again and held him there for a long time, the buoyant suit wanting to pull him to the surface but the tangled line remaining taut as he struggled to loosen it. The suction of the line pulling down on his body and the suit pulling up ripped the work boots off his feet, where they settled in the bottom of his oversize immersion suit.

As an experienced diver, Scornavacchi knew how to control himself underwater and manage his breathing, but this was different. He wasn't breathing at all, because he'd never gotten a breath of air after being thrown from the ship and instead had swallowed a good amount of water

before being dragged under. He worked to free himself from the rigging line, but he quickly felt himself losing muscle control. His body was getting no oxygen, and so his arms and legs just stopped taking commands. He was pushing on the line that trapped him, fighting for a bit of slack to free himself, and his arms wouldn't work anymore. With great clarity, Scornavacchi realized he was going to die. He wasn't sad for himself, but for his mother and younger brother. He was really upset with himself.

I promised them I wasn't going to die, he thought. *I promised them.*

Scornavacchi floated there underwater, where it was surprisingly calm, Hurricane Sandy and assorted hell taking place on the surface above him, and he was beginning to feel a remorseful peace when suddenly something told him it was not his time yet. At that instant the plastic bag on his harness broke away and Scornavacchi shot to the surface. He opened his mouth and took a deep, rasping breath, sucking in as much seawater and rain as air. But he was breathing again, however poorly.

Coughing and gasping for more air, he looked out in the moonlit night and saw the startling silhouette of the *Bounty*, the masts and yards swinging up and down with the rolling ocean, ten miles of rigging line now loose and wrapping the ship in all directions. He had no idea whether anyone else was alive. There was so much debris in the ocean now, empty life jackets and immersion suits, things he couldn't identify, all of it being thrown violently by the sea. It was chaotic, but Scornavacchi thought he could see one of the piles of emergency gear with extra life jackets attached floating nearby. He swam on his back to the pile and then tried to climb on top of it, hoping to use it like a raft, but every time he tried to hoist himself up, a wave would knock him off again. He stayed close to the pile but realized that it was still too close to the *Bounty*. He was trying to decide whether to let go of it and swim farther out when Jessica Black's face popped out of the waves next to him. The cook on her maiden voyage with the *Bounty*, her first voyage on any tall ship, grabbed onto the ditch kit pile with Scornavacchi and looked to him for advice.

"What do I do?" she shouted over the hurricane.

Scornavacchi told her to hang on to the floating pile and made sure

she was securely attached to a life jacket that would help her stay afloat even if she lost the rest of the gear. They stayed like that for a short while—they couldn't tell how long—but they were drifting closer to the *Bounty* the whole time. The wind and waves were pushing them back to their ship, which was still rolling violently, the masts angrily slapping the water every few minutes and then rising up again. They were watching the ship get closer and closer, trying to decide what to do, when suddenly they were too close. The *Bounty*'s huge mainmast slammed down right on their makeshift raft and destroyed it with a terrifying bang, like a tree falling, and just missed Scornavacchi and Black. The hammering of the mast tore apart all the life jackets and survival gear, tossing the two crew members into the air as the package exploded and parts became entangled in the rising mast.

Scornavacchi and Black were split up again, and Scornavacchi was in another fight to get away from the *Bounty*. Not only were the masts going to kill him if they came down on him again, but the sea around the *Bounty* was a nightmare of rope, wood, trash, everything that had ever been on the ship. Every bit of it promised to drag him under and take his breath, to make him break that promise to his mother and little brother. One line wrapped around his leg and pulled him below the water, but he managed to get free and surface again. He swam hard to get away as the *Bounty* rose up and prepared to slam the masts and rigging down on top of him once more, making it close to the stern of the ship before it rolled back. The mizzenmast at the rear of the ship slammed down right next to him, and compared to everything else around him, it looked like a relatively safe place to be. Scornavacchi climbed onto the mizzenmast, intending to work his way out to the top end and farther away from the ship. As he straddled the thick wooden beam, he hoped maybe the *Bounty* would stay still for a while, just take a rest on its side and let him stay without trying to kill him again.

It didn't. The *Bounty* awakened as before, the mizzenmast rising out of the water and drawing an arc through the howling wind and rain as Scornavacchi clung to it. He tried to grab onto anything that would keep him from being thrown off the mast and down to the deck when the ship righted itself, but there was nothing on this part except slick, round wood

that he couldn't grasp with his gloved hands. He held on as tightly as he could with his arms and legs, but as the ship rolled and the mast arced up five degrees, ten degrees, twenty and thirty degrees, Scornavacchi realized he was in trouble. If he lost his grip and fell to the deck, he'd be seriously injured, if not killed outright. And if he were injured, he'd never get away from the *Bounty*. He felt his grip slipping.

"Jump!"

Scornavacchi heard it as clear as day, even through the hurricane, but he couldn't see anyone around him.

"Jump!"

And he did. Scornavacchi leaped off the mizzenmast just in time to land in the water instead of on the deck, even missing all the debris rolling in the sea. When he surfaced, he could see the white barrel of an uninflated life raft in the whitecaps in the distance. He swam toward it as hard as he could, still thinking he might be the only survivor, or maybe he and Black. When he got there, he found John Jones trying to inflate the raft, which requires pulling a lanyard that sets off an automatic device. In the rough seas, exhausted, fumbling through Gumby suit gloves, this seemingly simple operation was difficult. As the two men were trying to inflate the raft, Black popped up alongside them, and just as quickly, it seemed, she was gone again.

They were still trying to inflate the life raft when an already inflated raft floated right by, so they pushed the closed raft away and went to the open one. When they got there, they found Mark Warner and Anna Sprague already clinging to it, trying to get inside. Jones and Scornavacchi joined them, but even with all four working together it took a long time to get the first person in the raft. The rolling and heaving seas, the wind, their utter exhaustion from their ordeal so far, and the extremely cumbersome immersion suits made it nearly impossible to just hoist one person up and into the open door of the enclosed raft. Their suits were heavy with seawater—far more than was intended—making it nearly impossible to lift their legs out of the water and into the raft. Scornavacchi's boots still free-floated in the feet of his oversize immersion suit, making his legs even heavier and more cumbersome.

Finally all four people were in the raft. Scornavacchi had swallowed

a lot of water and whatever else was in the ocean, so he was immediately suffering stomach pains as they fell back into the raft.

AFTER GETTING THE last frantic call off to the Coast Guard, Svendsen held on in the nav shack as the *Bounty* rolled over, eventually managing to pull himself out and jump forward, bouncing around on the deck and in the water that was overcoming it. As he did, he caught a last glimpse of Walbridge making his way toward the stern. Svendsen grasped for anything he could hold on to, but the ship was going over. He decided to make his way out on the mizzenmast, which was almost horizontal by that point but still looked like the best path away from the ship. He inched his way out on the mast as far as he could, the rain hitting his face so hard he could barely see the waves coming closer and closer underneath him, and the ship dipped farther down.

He jumped, or mostly fell, off the mast and struggled in the water like everyone else, flailing in his immersion suit to swim away from the ship that he loved. Cleveland and Groves were doing the same. Everyone was.

STRUGGLING IN THE water, the hulk of the *Bounty* threatening her as it had Scornavacchi and others, Hewitt vowed she would never again wear a climbing harness over her immersion suit. *What a bad idea*, she thought. The harness and the survival gear she had attached had become tangled in lines and debris so much that she feared she was going to die. She had clipped her harness to her boyfriend Salapatek's harness as they waited on the deck, not wanting to be separated from each other if they went into the water. Now his harness was empty and hanging off hers, creating even more of a magnet for debris and lines, and making her wonder what had happened to Drew.

In the midst of her own struggle, she saw Chief Mate Svendsen nearby, also trying to get away from the ship. She screamed as she saw a spar slam down on Svendsen, and she turned away, afraid to look anymore.

PROKOSH HAD STAYED with the *Bounty* as long as he could when it reared up out the water, hoping it would settle back down, but then he felt in his gut that there was no chance.

This is where I get off, he thought, as he jumped into the water and tried to avoid the rigging. He felt like a fishing bobber, bouncing up and down with little control, and soon he was struck on the head by a large piece of wooden grating that fell from the stern. He was left dazed as all the pain and fear merged together into one horrible feeling, but he also was highly motivated to get away from the *Bounty*. When he opened his eyes after being hit, he saw the main top yard—the big horizontal cross-beam on the mainmast—above him. It looked so far up in the air, but damn, it was coming right for him. He thrashed as much as he could, trying to get away, but with little effect, and the yard slammed down on him. In the fast-moving chaos, he couldn't tell how much of the yard made contact with him, because he already hurt so badly in so many places, but he held on to the life jacket he was using as a float and kicked hard.

After a while—minutes, hours, he couldn't tell anymore—he found a clutch of survivors. Chris Barksdale, Dan Cleveland, Laura Groves, Jessica Hewitt, and Drew Salapatek had found one another and were forming a chain by hooking one person's feet under the armpits of the next person. Prokosh joined in.

They found a life raft canister, inflated it, and then undertook the unbelievably difficult challenge of getting inside. After forty-five minutes, everyone was in the life raft.

FAUNT STRUGGLED IN the water like everyone else, dodging a broken spar that looked like a jagged wooden spear, fighting to clear himself from the rigging. He found a life ring at one point that at first seemed like a god-send, something to grab onto and stay afloat, but he had the presence of mind to see that it seemed to be moving in a way that suggested it was not free-floating. If it had a line that was still attached to the boat, it could suck him under. He decided to forgo the life ring and kicked away as hard as he could, and after some time he saw an inflated life raft. He

made his way toward it and managed to grab one of the ropes on the outside, but the sea and wind were throwing the raft around so violently that it was as if Faunt were trying to stay on a bucking horse. He refused to loosen his grip on the line no matter how much the raft tried to throw him, and with one mighty buck Faunt felt his shoulder dislocate. He still held on, despite the intense pain.

Still clinging to the raft, Faunt saw cook Jessica Black pop up next to him, and her face in the red immersion suit was a huge relief to him. He realized then that he was not alone, which he had very much feared up to that point. As he and Black held on to the raft, they then realized that there were people inside already.

Once Faunt and Black were inside, the *Bounty* crew peered outside to see whether they could make out any other survivors. They couldn't see anyone else in the water, but they did see another inflated life raft. They called out, trying to get the attention of the other raft, but they quickly realized that was futile. No one would hear them over the storm, and the raft was quickly being blown away. They lay back in their Gumby suits, so fatigued they were barely able to move, a faint battery-operated light illuminating them from the raft's ceiling.

The survivors caught glimpses of all their dry bags floating by, filled with survival items, cash, cell phones, passports, ship's logs, everything valuable. The bags would never be seen again.

The mood in both life rafts was somber at first, everyone still in a daze from being thrown off the *Bounty* and making it to the rafts, and those in each raft wondered whether they were the only survivors. After a few minutes, they realized that they were going to survive and the mood became more joyous. In the raft with Cleveland and Groves, the crew members went through the emergency supplies and found there was no bailer, so they drank the water from a bottle Cleveland had attached to his harness and used it to bail out the foot of water in the raft. The task was done mostly just to keep busy, and Cleveland started nudging people who wanted to doze off. Cleveland wanted to get the water out of his Gumby feet, remembering how problematic that weight had been when they tried to enter the raft, so he started rocking onto his back and throwing his heavy feet into the air as high as he could, letting the accu-

mulated water fall down his legs and out his face mask. He did that over and over until he was too tired to continue.

Even though hypothermia didn't seem to be a big risk, it seemed better to keep everyone awake. They started singing sea shanties as they bounced around with each wave. Just as they started to relax a bit, a huge breaker would smash into the raft and remind them that they were in a life raft in a hurricane.

Once in a while they could hear the deep rumble of a Coast Guard HC-130J overhead. It was a sweet sound.

CHAPTER 20

OFF THE RADAR

BACK IN E-CITY, Peña, Cerveny, Lufkin, and Haba quickly donned their dry suits and other gear. They made their way to the HH-60 Jayhawk that had been readied by the mechanics, and the pilots immediately started their preflight checklists. A medium-range recovery helicopter, the Jayhawk is outfitted with the most comprehensive all-weather electronics package available, plus an array of equipment that increases the crew's ability to detect persons and vessels in the water, including forward-looking infrared radar (FLIR), direction-finding (DF) radio equipment, and the same NVGs that McIntosh and Myers were using. White with the Coast Guard's orange striping forward and rear, the craft is sixty-five feet long and seventeen feet tall. With two General Electric gas turbine engines, the Jayhawk can hit 170 knots and stay aloft for more than six hours in some scenarios—but it is often restricted to shorter flight times because of the weight it carries, weather conditions, and other factors that affect fuel consumption. The helicopter has a working distance of three hundred nautical miles from land, giving it access to the most common offshore emergencies. Jayhawk crews typically zip out to the scene and either lower a dewatering pump from its cable winch or pick up a survivor or two, then quickly head back. Because the HH-60s also are used to chase down drug runners from

some bases, the Coast Guard Jayhawks are modified with an airborne "use of force" package—including weapons for firing warning and disabling shots, and armor to protect the aircrew from small-arms fire.

Cerveny and Peña had been watching the weather carefully, so they knew what they were getting into. The eye of Hurricane Sandy was moving northward and taking the most severe weather with it, but this flight out would still not be easy. In darkness, with nasty weather all around, they decided to fly instrument flight rules, known as IFR, directly from Elizabeth City to Cape Hatteras at an altitude of three thousand feet. Going IFR meant they would fly the aircraft by referring primarily to instruments in the cockpit without visual reference to the ground. That flight path would keep them clear of most commercial airways, though on this night no one else was in the sky but the Coast Guard.

Cerveny was at the controls when the Jayhawk lifted off in the wind and rain before five a.m.—oh-dark-thirty, as military folks like to say—taking extra care to gain sufficient altitude before turning into the desired flight path. They were using all the automation available in the Jayhawk—autopilot, altitude hold, all the radar options, everything—because it was pitch-black outside the cockpit. They could not depend on the view for anything. Even when they put their NVGs on after takeoff, the goggles offered no help, because the helicopter was in the thick clouds and rain, with not a speck of light to be found.

Peña immediately focused on the craft's fuel consumption, always the critical determinant of how long they could stay in the air. They had a fifty-knot tailwind on the way out, helping them travel at about 170 knots without using much fuel. But, of course, that same wind would be hindering them on the way back, forcing the Jayhawk to push through molasses, slowing them down to a veritable crawl while also burning fuel at a rate far higher than normal. Peña had to calculate these effects, adjusting and readjusting to the conditions frequently, figuring in the effect of time on scene, the fuel consumption while hovering to hoist in heavy winds, and the added weight of survivors. There was a science to this, but also a fair bit of guesstimation. Whatever the precise figure for bingo fuel would be, it was looking clear to Peña that they wouldn't be able to stay on scene long at all.

The *Bounty*, pictured in 2011, one week out of San Juan, Puerto Rico, and on the way to Plymouth, England. The ship was a replica of the original British naval vessel HMS *Bounty*, the subject of the famous 1789 mutiny. The modern ship was built for the 1962 movie *Mutiny on the Bounty*, starring Marlon Brando. CAROLYN (CAZ) LUDTKE.

Robin Walbridge, captain of the *Bounty,* performs some carpentry work on the ship in 2011. He spent seventeen years as captain of the *Bounty.* CAROLYN (CAZ) LUDTKE.

Captain Walbridge (*right*) and other *Bounty* crew work to repair a broken main course yard. The timber snapped when a sudden gust of wind hit the ship during a man-overboard drill off the coast of Puerto Rico in 2011. CAROLYN (CAZ) LUDTKE.

Chief Mate John Svendsen at the helm of the *Bounty* in 2010. Second in command of the ship, Svendsen was respected for his calm, confident style of leadership. Carolyn (Caz) Ludtke. Used with permission. All rights reserved.

Bosun Laura Groves, with crew member Chris Mallon, works on rigging in 2010, while in transit from New Brunswick to Boothbay, Maine, for a haul out. CAROLYN (CAZ) LUDTKE. USED WITH PERMISSION. ALL RIGHTS RESERVED.

Third Mate Dan Cleveland performs maintenance on rigging in 2011. The white canister behind him is one of the *Bounty*'s two inflatable life rafts. Cleveland was a natural leader among the crew. Carolyn (Caz) Ludtke. Used with permission. All rights reserved.

Deckhand Claudene Christian in August 2012. Descended from the Fletcher Christian who led the mutiny on the original HMS *Bounty*, she was inexperienced on tall ships but eager to be part of the *Bounty* family.
The Associated Press

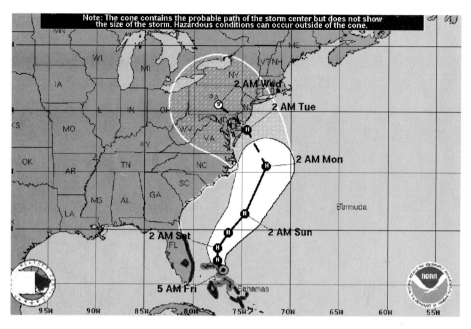

The National Hurricane Center's projected track of Hurricane Sandy on Friday, October 26, 2012, at eight a.m. Eastern. This information was available to the *Bounty* crew and updated several times per day, along with other weather data. NOAA

Hurricane Sandy covers most of the Eastern Seaboard on Sunday, October 28, 2012, at nine-oh-two a.m. Eastern. One of the unusual features of the hurricane was how much of the Atlantic it affected, with winds covering an area eleven hundred miles across. NOAA

The *Bounty* partly upright but awash in the seas of Hurricane Sandy. COAST GUARD

The *Bounty* lies on her starboard side before sinking completely off the coast of North Carolina. The wreckage lies more than two and a half miles deep in the area known as the Graveyard of the Atlantic. COAST GUARD

An HC-130J airplane and an H-60 helicopter from the Coast Guard station at Elizabeth City, North Carolina, like those used in the rescue of the *Bounty*. COAST GUARD

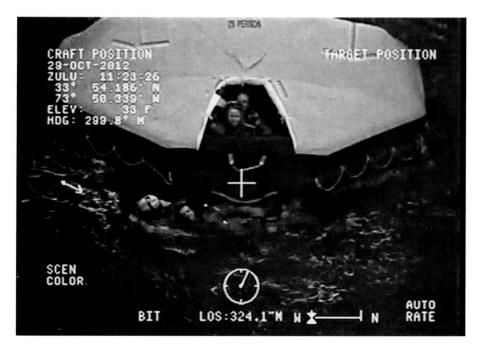

Bounty crew member Adam Prokosh in the water outside one of the life rafts, with Coast Guard rescue swimmer Dan Todd about to help him be lifted into the helicopter. Others are waiting in the raft. COAST GUARD

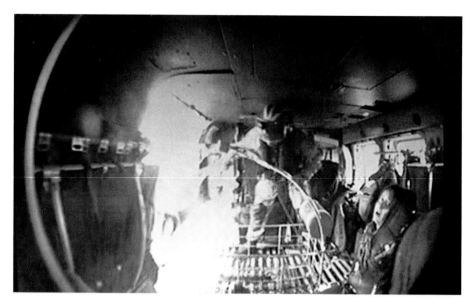

Bounty survivor Laura Groves immediately after being lifted into the Coast Guard helicopter. Flight mechanic Neil Moulder is readying the basket for the next rescue. COAST GUARD VIDEO/AUTHOR PHOTO

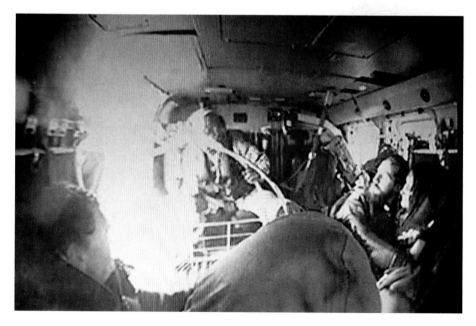

Daniel Cleveland and Laura Groves embrace as survivors begin to pile up in the Coast Guard helicopter. Chris Barksdale is to the left and Jessica Hewitt's head is in front of the camera. The helicopter would soon hold nine *Bounty* survivors. COAST GUARD VIDEO/AUTHOR PHOTO

HC-130J crew members participating in the *Bounty* rescue: (*back row, left to right*) Jonathan Sageser, Corey Lupton, Aaron Cmiel, David Dull, Michael Canham, Lee Christensen, Peyton Russell; (*front row*) Michael Meyers, Hector Rios, Joshua Vargo, Eric Laster, Wes McIntosh, Jesse Embert, Joshua Adams. COAST GUARD

H-60 crew members participating in the *Bounty* rescue: (*back row, left to right*) Randy
Haba, Dan Todd, Steve Bonn, Ryan Parker, Michael Lufkin; (*front row*) Casey
Hanchette, Neil Moulder, Steve Cerveny, Jane Peña, Jenny Fields. Coast Guard

Coast Guard Commander Kevin Carroll, who led the Coast Guard hearings on the sinking of the *Bounty*. The Coast Guard hearings lasted ten days and were intended to find the reason for the loss of two crew members and the *Bounty*. Unfolding much like a tense trial, the hearings revealed important information and raised questions about decisions leading to the loss of the ship. *The Virginian-Pilot*, Norfolk, Virginia, pool photo

Chief Mate John Svendsen at the Coast Guard hearings on the sinking of the *Bounty*. Svendsen was the senior surviving crew member of the *Bounty*; he defended the actions of his captain while also explaining that he sometimes disagreed with his decisions. *THE VIRGINIAN-PILOT*, NORFOLK, VIRGINIA, POOL PHOTO

Third Mate Dan Cleveland consults exhibits during the *Bounty* hearings. Like all of the *Bounty* crew who testified, Cleveland was steadfast in defending his captain's character and skills as a mariner. *The Virginian-Pilot*, Norfolk, Virginia, pool photo

Bosun Laura Groves is sworn in to testify at the Coast Guard hearings. Along with her boyfriend, Dan Cleveland, Groves was instrumental in leading the *Bounty* crew during the crisis. THE VIRGINIAN-PILOT, NORFOLK, VIRGINIA, POOL PHOTO

Engineer Chris Barksdale at the Coast Guard hearings on the sinking of the *Bounty*. THE VIRGINIAN-PILOT, VIRGINIA, POOL PHOTO

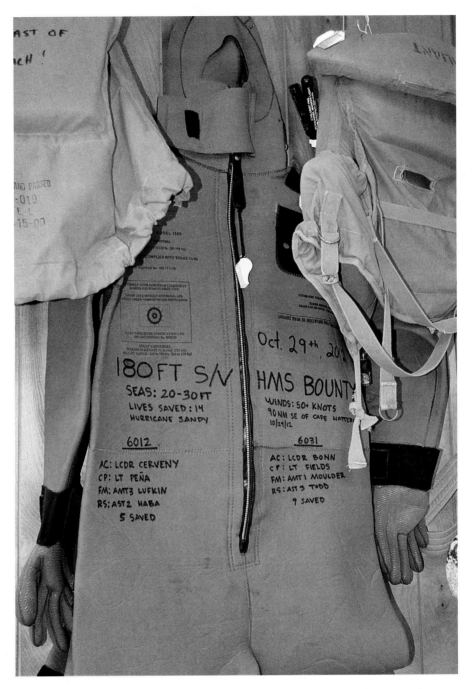

A "Gumby" survival suit worn by one of the *Bounty* survivors now hangs in the rescue swimmers' work area at the Coast Guard station in Elizabeth City, North Carolina. The Coast Guard considers the *Bounty* rescue one of the most challenging and significant in its history. COURTESY OF THE AUTHOR

As Peña continued working toward the bingo number, the Jayhawk was passing over Cape Hatteras. She heard air traffic control pass them off to the next sector. "Coast Guard HH-60, Cherry Point approach. Passing you off to Giant Killer. Good luck."

Peña tried making contact with Giant Killer, the military air traffic control that would have the best chance of monitoring their flight over the ocean. In those conditions, the Jayhawk made only sporadic contact and then Peña let it go. That was not unusual for the Jayhawks anyway, because they typically flew too low to talk with Giant Killer. Peña called back to Cherry Point and told the controller the Jayhawk crew wanted to stay with them until the helicopter was off the radar, and the controller was happy to oblige.

They continued to fly through the blackness, turbulence steadily increasing as they went farther from shore. Cerveny started descending and they got below the clouds at about seven hundred feet, but the crew couldn't see the water until they hit an altitude of three hundred feet. They could see the wave action below, and weren't too concerned. The waves seemed to be five to eight feet high, with the wind still steady at fifty knots. They had little visibility, however, even with their NVGs.

After a while they heard the radio again.

"Coast Guard HH-60, Cherry Point approach. Okay, that's it, guys. You're off the radar. See you when you get back."

Peña acknowledged with a crisp, "Roger that, Cherry Point." About that same time, she noticed a change in the helicopter's Digimap, which provides a map of the surface below, sort of a much more sophisticated version of the GPS map unit in a car. The Digimap showed blue for water, but once the helicopter was far out to sea, the screen just went black. *Whoa*, Peña thought to herself. *We're off the radar and off the map. It's just us, flying into a hurricane.*

The idea sent a little shiver through Peña, but also a sense of excitement. She still thought of herself as a newbie in this business, and here she was copiloting an HH-60 into one of the biggest, funkiest hurricanes anyone had seen in a long time. Like many of the *Bounty* crew when told of Walbridge's plan to sail, Peña thought, *A little scary, but that's an experience you can't pass up.* And like the *Bounty* crew, she trusted her captain

and the rest of her crew, all more experienced than herself. That was the only reason she could be there with confidence.

AHEAD OF THE Jayhawk, the second HC-130J was already well into its trip to relieve the McIntosh and Myers crew. The seven men on this Herc were enjoying the ride every bit as much as the first crew. Their journey started off with similar concerns about faulty deicing on the propellers—Russell thought it really weird to have icing in a hurricane—so the pilots took the plane to three thousand feet to stay below any possible icing conditions. That proved beneficial to the Jayhawk crew, because the Herc could feed back info about what the helicopters were likely to encounter. A little sporty sometimes, Russell told Peña, but not all that bad.

In the back, dropmaster Sageser might have had a different assessment. He and the other crew were prepping their SAR gear as the plane flew toward the scene, and at one point he was struggling to get a toss-over radio ready for deployment. The radio is in a sort of can and the crew needs to test it and make sure it's set to channel sixteen before throwing it out. That's usually a pretty simple task, but Sageser was doing everything he could to hold on to the can as he stood on the angled ramp at the back of the plane, jostled by hurricane turbulence. He and the other crew finally sat on the deck and braced themselves against the other strapped-down SAR gear as they tried to set the radio.

BY ABOUT 5:45 a.m. the sun was just starting to rise as McIntosh and Myers turned their plane for the trip back to Raleigh, the weather improving by the minute as the worst of Hurricane Sandy continued north. But the sea still churned violently, and, unable to make out individuals in the water, they had no way of knowing of the life-and-death struggles going on beneath them.

They made contact with the Herc coming in to relieve them and briefed the fresh crew on what to expect when they reached the site of the sinking. Soon they also heard radio chatter from the inbound Jayhawk

helicopters and relayed the exact location of the ship and the debris field, explaining that the ASRK rafts were in the water along with those from the *Bounty*. The Coast Guard sector had relayed most of what had been reported to them, but these inbound crews were men and women whom McIntosh and Myers worked with every day, and they wanted to personally brief them. The two pilots also were worried about the people they had watched over for so many hours, and they wanted to be sure their colleagues knew everything as they handed over responsibility. "You're going to see the boat, which is still visible in the water. A couple miles east you're going to see a life raft, and then farther east of that are going to be a couple more life rafts," McIntosh told them. He also told the incoming crews to look for ASRK strobe lights on the three rafts.

Coming on scene, Russell was painting a mental image of what McIntosh had described and planning how they would set up an orbit. He began descending through the clouds, and the turbulence really picked up considerably, throwing the plane up and down in the sky just as it had done with the first Herc. Russell's plane didn't seem to like the turbulence at all, and the autopilot gave up, which caused the human pilot to groan with displeasure. He didn't know it at the time, but he was following the same scenario as McIntosh and Myers, not looking forward at all to the prospect of hand-flying the plane for several more hours in this kind of slop. Russell tried pulling back up into smoother air to troubleshoot the autopilot, but it didn't help. He called to McIntosh, asking for any ideas from his avionics guy, but nobody had a solution.

"All right," Russell said with a sigh as he started descending again. "It's going to be a long day."

At about seven hundred feet the Herc emerged from the clouds. They were still using their NVGs, but a small bit of sunlight was making its way through the cloud cover to the water. Russell and Cmiel scanned the sea for the debris field and lifeboats, but everything looked so odd in the green tint and the rough, choppy water. Russell thought he saw something, but he couldn't make sense of it.

"Why are there telephone poles out here in the middle of the ocean?" he said, thinking aloud. He was looking at three poles sticking out above

the water. *Are those telephone lines on the poles? Is this some kind of shipping debris? Shoals? What the heck is that?*

Cmiel replied, "I think that's the *Bounty*."

IN THE BACK of the Herc, dropmaster Sageser, who had years of experience on rescue helicopters, was realizing this was by far his most dramatic rescue. He was astounded by what he saw below him through his NVGs. The ocean was like nothing he had seen before. Waves raced from every direction, violently tossing up thirty-foot walls of seawater. Like several other crew members that morning, one of the first ways he thought to describe it was "angry."

He also wondered why there was a boat out in this weather. But then he dismissed that thought, reminding himself that he didn't get to make that call about right and wrong. *In any case, I don't know if anybody can survive out there in those crazy seas*, he thought.

AS McINTOSH AND Myers headed toward Raleigh, they hoped they wouldn't encounter icing, and wondered whether Raleigh was still an option, because they knew the crosswinds were picking up there. Little conversation was made on the two-hour flight back. The entire crew was near the point of exhaustion from being up all night, extremely airsick, and fighting the turbulence as they carried out their tasks. McIntosh and Myers in particular were mentally drained as well from talking with Svendsen for hours and then suddenly losing contact. They didn't know whether the crew was alive or dead, in the water or in the rafts. Though other help was on the way, none of the crew liked the idea of flying away and not knowing. The mood on the plane was somber.

CHAPTER 21

EERIE

RUSSELL AND CMIEL turned their Herc around to come back over the *Bounty* again, searching the debris field. They could see three life rafts from the first Herc's ASRK drop, with strobe lights. Coast Guard crew members in the back of the plane were using the FLIR camera to look down and spotted two more life rafts with no strobes. The canopies on the rafts obscured any heat signatures, so even with the FLIR the Herc crew couldn't tell which, if any, were occupied. Russell pointed the Herc's landing lights straight down so they would not overwhelm their NVGs. As the lights hit the water, Russell suddenly felt a knot in the pit of his stomach.

There was reflective tape everywhere. *Everywhere.* All over the place. Gumby suits and life jackets no matter where he looked.

My God, how many people are in the water? They said seventeen. This looks like a cruise ship went down. This is bad.

Russell worried that the Coast Guard response was not enough. If there were this many people in the water, it would take forever for the Jayhawks to pull them out. He knew from his experience in helicopter rescues that it would be very time-consuming to go to one Gumby suit, pull that person up, go to the next, pull that person up, and so on. Figuring in the long, fuel-sucking ride back in that headwind, a Jayhawk would be able to get only a few before heading back.

He also was taken aback by the sea conditions. The surface was so windy that the tops of the waves were sheared off and white spray was dancing across the churning water. The wind was out of the west, but the current was out of the east, so they canceled each other out to some extent in terms of movement on the surface. Russell realized this actually was beneficial, because, given the hour or two since the rafts went into the water, he would have expected them to drift far from the original site. But the current was pulling everything back toward the boat even as the wind tried to blow it away, keeping the lifeboats and debris field relatively well contained. Another one of Hurricane Sandy's odd characteristics was working in their favor this time.

His task at hand, however, was to start plotting the scene so the Jayhawks could get to work as fast as possible when they arrived. Russell and Cmiel started building "tac plots," short for tactical, which were essentially grids on their computer screens that showed where everything was—the ship, the debris field, lifeboats, and anything else worth noting. Like McIntosh and Myers before them, they also programmed a calculated air release point, known as a CARP, that created the pattern the Herc would fly around the debris field. If the autopilot had been working, it could have flown the CARP while the pilots did other things. With the system down, Russell and Cmiel would hand-fly the CARP. As they were doing that, Russell kept noticing a faint light that was not near the strong strobes of the Coast Guard life rafts. Sageser saw it, too. The light registered in his NVGs, but he couldn't make out what it might be. It was definitely a light, not something reflective.

"What is that?" Russell said aloud several times. Cmiel saw it but also had no clue what it might be.

As they circled, Sandy's winds kept throwing the Herc up and down. As with the previous Herc, the crew in the back was jostled around much more than the pilots. In the cockpit, the plane's automatic warning systems were confused by the frequent and sudden drops in altitude. Hardwired to alert the pilots to a sudden change in altitude of more than two hundred feet up or down, a computerized voice that the crews call Ann constantly called out warnings. *Constantly.*

"Altitude, altitude," Ann said over and over again, in a pleasant, calm

voice that nevertheless was louder than most of the other cockpit messages. "Altitude, altitude." It was like having your mother-in-law in the backseat repeatedly warning you about something you already knew. Ann kept saying those words to them for hours. Sageser and the others heard it too, over and over.

Russell finally got so tired of hearing the warnings that he turned the system off and told the flight mechanic sitting behind him to just call out "good" or "bad" when the altitude changed. "Good" meant a sudden bump up, and "bad" meant they were suddenly being shoved down to the sea and Russell would adjust accordingly.

At one point, Russell needed to go relieve himself. There is a lavatory in the back of the airplane, on the right side near the ramp. It's basic, of course, and not even fully enclosed, a dry toilet up on an elevated platform and behind a waist-high door. Russell unbuckled from his seat in the cockpit and struggled to get back to the head, the turbulence throwing him up and down as he tried to walk, grabbing onto anything as he slowly made progress. He managed to get back there to do his business, but as he sat on the toilet he took note of how hard it was for the crew in the back, looking out the windows for any sign of survivors as they held on to the fuselage. *My God, the noise!* It was so much worse than when he was sitting in the cockpit with his noise-canceling headphones. He could hear the aluminum frame of the plane twisting this way and that, the wind wrestling its way through the propellers. It sounded ugly, just . . . wrong somehow.

He sat there holding on for dear life.

Damn, I'm gonna be thrown right off this toilet! he thought.

He couldn't believe what he was seeing as he sat there trying to finish and get on with life. Damn if it didn't look like the front and tail of the airplane were twisted, some kind of weird torque as it flew through a hurricane, not lined up like you would expect. *This isn't right. What the hell do these guys go through back here?*

Russell climbed down from the head but he could barely return to the cockpit. Every step was like trying to move through some sort of zero-gravity chamber. He finally arrived and vowed he would stay there for the duration. When he finally sat down and buckled in, he was far, far more airsick than when he got up.

I will piss my pants before I go back and do that again, he thought. *I was only back there for three minutes, but that was three minutes too much.*

SVENDSEN WAS ALONE in the water, seeing none of the other survivors around him, when he looked up soon after entering the water and saw the Coast Guard plane circling overhead. He knew he should stay underneath that plane if at all possible, so he kicked and swam in that direction. After swimming for two hours, his body aching and his throat on fire from the salt water he was swallowing, he came across a miracle in the water. It was Walbridge's man-overboard beacon. He grabbed onto it and activated the strobe light.

As the Herc flew around the *Bounty* survivors, Svendsen clung tenaciously to the improvised man-overboard box, the cumbersome gloves of the immersion suit making it difficult for him to get a firm grip. He did his best to bear-hug the floating box as the waves pounded him, every movement of the ocean seeming a purposeful effort to wrest him away from this box, this wonderful box. Svendsen was in terrible pain but he couldn't tell from exactly what. He just knew something on him was broken, something was hurt, but he was still alive. He was starting to wonder just how long he could hold on. Like everyone else from the ship, he was physically exhausted. The adrenaline from trying to stay alive was the only thing keeping him going at that point, but he had enough presence of mind to wonder how long it would last. This box, this last gift from the captain he loved, was keeping him alive, and he wasn't going to let go of it.

Looking up through the salty spray and the driving rain, Svendsen took solace in the lights of the HC-130J circling above. The Coasties were still there. They were still watching over them. He had no way of knowing that it was a different plane and crew now, but the circling lights and the roar of the plane's engines as it passed overhead provided a reassurance that could make all the difference in the world. He just had to hang on long enough to be rescued—all of the crew, not just him. They weren't out there alone. *The Coast Guard is here; rescue is coming.*

As he clung to the box and watched the lights of the Herc going

around, coming back again, and going around, Svendsen's mind focused on one thought. He kicked the heavy, water-filled legs of his Gumby suit over and over again. Whatever strength he had left went into kicking those legs, pushing himself forward.

I want to be in that circle, he thought. *God, just keep me in that circle.*

THE LIGHTS FROM Russell's circling Herc were the first visual cue to Cerveny and Peña that their helicopter had reached its target. They radioed the plane to acknowledge that they were on-site, and Russell briefed them on what the Herc crew knew so far.

Russell gave them the coordinates of the mystery light and told the Jayhawk crew that should be their first priority.

"There's something here that's different from everything else. I think this is worth looking at," Russell told Peña and Cerveny.

The Herc crew watched as the Jayhawk went directly to that position and lowered into a sixty-foot hover over Chief Mate John Svendsen. Svendsen waved one arm as wildly as he could manage in the Gumby suit. All seven men on the Herc listened closely. What they heard made them smile.

"Coast Guard Jayhawk Sixty-twelve. PIW. Preparing to hoist."

Chapter 22

WHERE'S EVERYBODY ELSE?

APPROACHING THE END of their mission, McIntosh and Myers heard that the Jayhawk was about to rescue a survivor, and that buoyed the spirits of the Herc crew. A sigh of relief went through the plane, and a lot of gloved thumbs went up. They would have been even happier to know that the first person pulled out of the water was the one they had been talking to all night, the one with whom they had bonded so closely.

When McIntosh and Myers finally landed their aircraft in Raleigh, in much worse conditions than when they'd departed, the crew refueled the Herc and prepared it for the next call-out. With the plane all set, the weary crew walked into the fixed base operator, known as the FBO, which is sort of like a service station for aircraft. As McIntosh and Myers stepped through the door in their Coast Guard jumpsuits, looking and smelling exactly like they'd been up all night in hellish conditions, several civilians in the FBO looked them over. The pilots watched the men's faces as they connected the dots.

"Wait a minute . . . Were you . . . Were you out with the *Bounty*?" one man asked.

"Yeah, how do you know?" Myers replied.

The other guy pointed to a television and said, "Look!"

The pilots and several of their crew sat down in the FBO and for the

188

next hour watched the recovery of the *Bounty* crew with the rest of the world.

CERVENY AND PEÑA hovered nearby over Svendsen as the crew went through its rescue checklist, preparing to pull the chief mate out of the water. They avoided hovering too close to him until time for the hoist, because the prop was enough to blow an already weakened survivor off whatever he was holding on to—and what was that thing anyway?—and underwater. In the back, the crew was moving fast. Cerveny had informed his crew on the way out to the site that there would be seventeen people in the water, maybe each one a separate rescue, and so they had to be ready to work fast before bingo fuel. Swimmer Randy Haba switched his NVGs for a face mask and snorkel, then put on his fins. Flight mechanic Michael Lufkin was ready to lower him down with the winch. Tall and with a chiseled jawline, Haba looked like a G.I. Joe action figure in his rescue gear. He was known around E-city for being extraordinarily stoic and matter-of-fact about the lifesaving business, considering something like the *Bounty* rescue just another day at the office. Those who worked with "the Robot" knew he was actually a lot of fun when you were having a beer after work. Haba grew up in Colorado and admired one of his high school teachers who was a smoke jumper, the über-firefighter who parachutes into forest fires. That led Haba to an interest in a SAR career, which led him to the Coast Guard. At thirty-three years old, he already had fourteen years' experience jumping out of helicopters to save people in the water. Lufkin, however, had been certified for less than a year and had been out only a few times on actual rescues. The flight mechanic directs nearly everything during hoist operations, actually controlling the winch himself and instructing the pilots—who can't see what's happening directly below the craft—to move this way and that, sometimes as little as a few feet.

Because time was critical and they could see that Svendsen was conscious, Lufkin and Haba decided to do a direct hoist—instead of Haba jumping from the helicopter or being lowered partway and then jumping, he would remain on the winch line and be lowered directly to the

189

PIW. The method can carry risks when the winds and waves are high, because the swimmer could be thrown into debris or the survivor. But it's the fastest option, so Haba was winched straight down toward Svendsen, who held on to his buoy with one hand as he reached out to the approaching swimmer with the other. As he got to within about thirty feet of the water, Haba signaled for Lufkin to stop the descent. When doing a direct hoist in relatively calm waters, the Jayhawk tries to put the swimmer close to the survivor, compensating for the wave action to make the contact as gentle as possible. This wasn't relatively calm water, however. It was Hurricane Sandy. Haba decided to change plans and released himself from the hoist line, dropping thirty feet into the churning sea. When he came up, he was about thirty or forty feet from Svendsen. After giving a thumbs-up to Lufkin to signal that he had entered the water safely, he applied all his considerable swimming power to closing the distance. Every time he would make it ten or twenty feet, another big swell would knock him farther back. On the third attempt he got close enough to grab Svendsen's outstretched hand and they both hugged the Walbridge buoy.

"Hi, I'm here to help!" Haba yelled over the sound of the ocean, the wind, and the Jayhawk. Svendsen nodded that he understood. "How are you doing? Are you hurt? Do you have any back issues?" Haba asked. His first concern was determining whether Svendsen might have a back injury or other problem that would necessitate a different type of hoist than what he was planning. Svendsen shook his head no and Haba was satisfied that he could handle a direct hoist.

Haba put his "quick strop" sling over Svendsen's head and helped pull the survivor's arms through so that the webbing was under the arms. Pushing the slide buckle forward to snug it up against Svendsen's Gumby suit and attaching the stainless-steel clip on the other end to his own swimmer's harness, Haba signaled to Lufkin that he was ready to be hoisted by pointing his index finger straight up and making a circling motion. Haba and Svendsen were swiftly lifted out of the water and to the cabin door, where Lufkin helped wrestle them inside. Haba disconnected from the winch line and removed the quick strop from Svendsen; then he evaluated him for injuries. Haba could see that Svendsen had

trauma to the face and possibly a broken wrist. As Lufkin and Haba helped Svendsen out of his water-filled immersion suit so he could start warming up, the swimmer asked him whether he had been with anyone or seen anyone nearby. "No, I was by myself," Svendsen said. "I think the other people made it into the rafts."

Haba passed that information on to Cerveny and Peña. It was still dark outside, so Peña's attention was drawn to another strobe light at her eleven o'clock position. Cerveny took the Jayhawk over to check and it turned out to be the *Bounty* itself. As they got close they could see the masts sticking out of the water as the ship listed to starboard. They still couldn't tell for sure what the light was coming from, but it appeared to be attached to a spare survival suit or raft that had become tangled in the rigging. Cerveny and Peña circled the *Bounty* three times, looking carefully to be sure the light wasn't coming from an individual trapped in the rigging.

When they decided it wasn't, they continued searching the area, looking for people in the water. The sun was up enough now that the Jayhawk crew could flip their NVGs up, but the winds were just as ferocious in the daylight. Cerveny was flying the helicopter and had to be particularly careful about turns that had the winds hitting the craft broadside, throwing a lot of air through the tail rotor and threatening a loss of power. After about an hour of finding nothing, they contacted Russell and Cmiel for directions to the life rafts, which had all stayed fairly close together. Continuing to circle above, Russell and Cmiel kept trying to make sense of what they saw below them. With the sun up and the clouds beginning to break, they could see much more of the debris field and start to identify objects better. There were yellow Coast Guard life rafts bobbing in the waves, and the two reddish-orange life rafts from the *Bounty*, which were much larger. They still couldn't tell whether the life rafts had anyone in them. If they did, those people were getting tossed around pretty badly in the wind and waves.

They were down lower now, about eight hundred feet, and that made the ride even more turbulent than before. The ramp was lowered in the back, and Sageser was sitting on it, secure in his gunner's belt as he kept an eagle eye out for PIWs. There was so much debris, but they threw a

191

salt water–activated flare every time they thought there might be a PIW. That created a target that the Herc and Jayhawk crews could go back and take a closer look at. Sageser couldn't believe how much he was seeing—debris, immersion suits, life jackets, all sorts of things.

"Mark, mark, mark, flare away," he called over and over again. But the winds were so intense that sometimes the crew couldn't find the flare when they circled back again. They had been thrown off course so much, and some of the flares had drifted far enough, that they were impossible to locate.

In the cockpit, the pilot was starting to get frustrated that they hadn't seen any more survivors.

They said seventeen, Russell thought. *We got one. Where's everybody else?*

THE HERC CREW provided the coordinates to Cerveny and Peña, who soon found the rafts. But like the Herc crew, they couldn't tell right away whether any were occupied. The first and second, dropped by the Coast Guard Herc, appeared to be empty. No one showed themselves as the Jayhawk hovered close. As they hovered near the third one, the entry flap popped open and someone waved up at the helicopter.

"We have survivors in the raft. The raft is occupied. Prepare to hoist," Peña said, as Lufkin was already helping Haba rig for a harness delivery, in which he would be winched partially down to water level and then disconnect. The hover altitude for a hoist rescue is usually handled mostly by the avionics on board, which can be set to hold the craft thirty feet or whatever distance is optimal over the water's surface. Cerveny could see that wasn't going to happen. The computer couldn't get a good read off the massively undulating ocean below, so he would have to hand-fly the hover. "All right, we're going to hoist from where we are now," Cerveny told his crew. "It might be twenty feet and it might be sixty feet, depending on what the water's doing, but let's start."

Haba dropped about thirty feet into the water again and swam toward the raft. The survivors helped pull him inside, where he found seven people—Sanders, Faunt, Jones, Scornavacchi, Sprague, Warner, and

Black. He went through the regular meet-and-greet routine, doing a visual assessment of what sort of victims he was working with, and asking whether anyone had any serious injuries. The *Bounty* crew all seemed to be in shock, sitting wide-eyed and quiet, just nodding their heads yes or no in response to Haba's questions. They were excited to see him, intently focusing on his every word, but it was clear to Haba that these folks had been through a lot. Haba explained the basics of what would happen, that the helicopter would lower a basket, and each person would climb out of the raft, into the water with Haba, and be hoisted up one at a time. "If we can't take you all right now, don't worry!" Haba shouted to the group. "There are other helicopters on the way!"

Haba had to figure out whom to take first, and his eyes settled on a man who seemed to be the oldest in the group, sitting hunched over in the middle of the raft with his white beard visible in the hood of his suit. He seemed less alert and interactive than the other crew sitting around the perimeter, so Haba went over to Faunt and said, "Okay, you're going." He helped Faunt crawl over toward the raft opening. Haba jumped out of the raft first and helped pull Faunt out after him. Keeping a tight grip on Faunt's immersion suit, Haba pulled him along as he swam toward the basket that Lufkin was already lowering, swimming directly into the swells as he was taught in swimmer school so he could duck under them instead of being tossed around. Once they got to the wire basket, Haba helped Faunt climb inside and take a sitting position, holding on to the sides. As soon as he could see Faunt was securely inside, Haba gave the hoist signal to Lufkin and the basket rose. Standing in the open cabin door, one hand on the winch line, and using all his strength to push it this way and that in response to the winds blowing the basket, Lufkin brought the survivor up. He pulled the basket into the cabin just long enough to help Faunt get out and then maneuvered it back out the cabin door, beginning its descent. Faunt dragged himself over to where Svendsen was waiting, and both men were glad to see each other.

Meanwhile, Haba was swimming with all his might to get back to the raft, pull the next person out and into the water, and swim them both to the basket. Each trip to get someone into the basket took about fifteen minutes, sometimes shortened when Lufkin would provide a "hover

taxi" service by lowering the winch line to Haba, who would clip on and be lifted up, then deposited close to the raft. On the second or third delivery to the basket, a cresting wave smacked Haba in the face so hard that it knocked off his mask and snorkel. Even as he was being battered by the ocean, he had a moment to be angry about it. That was his favorite mask, the one he had used for fourteen years, since first joining the Coast Guard. He'd never see it again.

Haba was helping the next person out of the raft, sitting on the edge, when suddenly a wave crashed on top of it, slamming tons of water down on the canopy. The force of the crash and the volume of the water knocked Haba off and shot him a dozen feet away. Regaining his senses, he fought his way back to the raft again. *Okay, that's a wake-up call*, he thought. *Things are getting serious out here.*

Things were pretty serious up in the 6012 Jayhawk cockpit, too. Cerveny was working hard to keep the craft in a steady hover despite the strong winds, responding to Lufkin's directions for altitude and directional changes, while Peña was in the left seat acting as the "safety pilot," meaning she did everything else but fly the helicopter. She took care of navigation, talking on the radio, and calculating fuel consumption. Every time the fuel in the main tanks dipped below 3,200 pounds, she transferred more from the auxiliary fuel pods outside the cabin. She also had to monitor the wave action. She kept an eye on the waves so she could call out warnings for an especially big one, but Peña was finding that almost impossible in these seas. The waves were huge, nothing smaller than ten feet and most around thirty feet, but there was no pattern. She thought it was like looking down into a washing machine and trying to tell someone which way the water would go next.

Chapter 23

RESCUES

HAVING ARRIVED ABOUT twenty minutes after Cerveny and Peña's helicopter, the 6031 Jayhawk piloted by forty-four-year-old Lt. Steve Bonn and twenty-six-year-old copilot Lt. Jenny Fields was still preparing to take on its first survivor. Bonn was no stranger to this kind of high-stakes drama. He started out flying similar HH-60 helicopters in the Army and had spent time flying for the Coast Guard in Alaska between tours of duty at E-city. Alaska was where he gained real experience in extreme sea rescues, most notably the Coast Guard rescue of the fishing factory ship *Alaska Ranger*. That ship sank in 2008 in the legendary Bering Sea, where conditions can rival that of any hurricane. After the forty-seven crew members abandoned ship in the middle of the night, many forced to jump into the frigid waters and unable to get to a lifeboat, forty-two were rescued by Bonn in his Jayhawk, a Coast Guard HH-65 Dolphin helicopter, and a sister ship of the *Alaska Ranger*. The Coast Guard calls it the largest cold-water rescue in its history. With twenty-one years' experience flying and twelve in the Coast Guard, Bonn was one of the most seasoned and skilled pilots around.

On the flight out to the *Bounty* scene, Bonn used the time to discuss different scenarios with the crew, how they would proceed if individuals were in the water, if they were all in rafts, if someone was still on the ship.

He reviewed who had been to the Coast Guard's Advanced Helicopter Rescue School, which trains crew members how to work in high seas, as opposed to the relatively calm waters in which most SAR cases occur. He was relieved to hear that along with himself, thirty-eight-year-old flight mechanic Neil Moulder and twenty-seven-year-old swimmer Daniel Todd also had been.

Fields had been flying for only about a year, so Bonn gave her a quick lesson on rescuing in high seas and winds. Although Bonn would fly the helicopter during the rescue, he also told his green copilot not to be shy about taking the controls when necessary. "This helicopter is going to bounce up and down a lot more than you've ever seen before," he told her. Jayhawk crews normally fly with the "two-challenge rule," which means that if one of the pilots notes a problem, such as deviating from the set altitude, he or she is to notify the pilot in control of the craft once, and then a second time if the issue is not addressed. After the second time, the pilot is authorized to take the controls and fix the problem.

"We're going to fly this mission under a 'no-challenge' rule," Bonn explained. "Since things are moving around so much, we're down so low over the water, and the waves are so big, you don't have to give any warning. If you see something, feel free to grab whatever and correct it. Then we'll talk about it."

The flight out to the scene had been in the dark, as rough a ride as the other aircraft had experienced, but Moulder and Todd didn't know how bad it really was until they heard the pilots say they were taking off their NVGs and turning on the searchlight to get a look at the conditions.

"Oh, crap . . ." was all they heard next from one of the pilots. That was not reassuring. Todd was already feeling a bit seasick.

Once they were on scene, they confirmed that the 6012 Jayhawk was still working with the first occupied raft. The Herc directed Bonn's Jayhawk to another raft about a mile away that might be occupied. They headed in that direction and could see the little orange speck of a raft canopy peeking out from behind cresting waves and then disappearing again. Bonn set up a hover on the second raft, the hurricane constantly trying to push the helicopter downwind. In the raft, Cleveland, Groves,

and the other four heard the Jayhawk hovering and a couple of them opened a flap in the canopy, waving up to their rescuers. After waiting in the life raft for several hours, they were excited.

Great, Cleveland thought. *Now we can stop thinking about trying to survive out here and start thinking about things like hot coffee.*

Moulder decided that he would send the swimmer down in a sling, which is wrapped around and under his arms, but not directly connected to him. When he's ready, the swimmer puts his arms up and slips out of the sling. Moulder knew it was the best method for heavy seas because the swimmer could watch the waves and slip out easily at just the right time.

As Todd was swimming toward the raft, Bonn and Fields surveyed the water nearby to make sure there were no individual PIWs. They didn't see any, so the crew proceeded with preparing for basket recoveries. Moulder realized—or hoped, at least—that he was going to have a crowded house. As Todd was fighting the waves to get to the raft, Moulder was figuring out where to put everybody. His first thought was to fold up the seats on the side of the cabin to make more room.

"What do you guys think? Should I just move up the troop seats and stick 'em on the floor?" Moulder asked Bonn and Fields.

"Yeah, if that'll make it easier," Bonn replied.

"Roger, I believe it will," Moulder replied with a grunt as he moved around the cabin to make more room. "STAN Team wouldn't like it," he said, referring to a Coast Guard standardization team that evaluates crews on their procedures. "But you know what? They're not here."

Having first served in the navy, Moulder had fifteen years' service in the Coast Guard. He was experienced, and his colleagues respected him as a highly skilled flight mechanic who taught others this all-important SAR position. They also knew that, as nice as he could be, he had a low tolerance for bullshit. The media frenzy after the *Bounty* sinking would test him mightily in that area. Moulder was like many flight mechanics on HH-60s: stronger and tougher than they looked. Controlling the winch on a Jayhawk involves a lot more than just pushing a button. The flight mechanic has to guide the cable line, pushing and pulling against incredibly strong winds, so that the swimmer, survivor, basket, or what-

ever is on the end of that line doesn't swing wildly out of control. The rescue basket and a survivor easily can weigh three hundred pounds, and even though the winch does the heavy lifting, it is up to the flight mechanic to keep that load from swinging wildly in the Jayhawk's own prop wash and whatever other winds are on the surface. A swinging person or package can come to a bad end, and in the worst cases can bring down the helicopter. Even once the survivor is at the cabin door, the flight mechanic still has to manhandle the person and the rescue basket inside. It is a surprisingly physical job, and Moulder's body showed the effects of more than sixteen hundred hours in the back of a Jayhawk. He knew that, like all HH-60 flight mechanics, his body would wear out long before he was ready to give up the job.

Those who knew him could always tell when it was Moulder in the cabin door during a rescue, despite the helmet and other gear that could make the crew members indistinguishable from a distance. They could tell because Moulder had a distinctive way of bracing his left foot against the edge of the cabin door, a move that wasn't really necessary when he was secured to the cabin with a gunner's belt so he couldn't fall out. But this was a man who made a living hanging out the open door of a helicopter—and he had a terrific fear of heights.

Bonn was flying the helicopter, holding it as steady as he could and responding to Moulder's instructions for moving this way and that way, five feet here and ten there, as the raft drifted in the water and the Jayhawk was pushed around in the air. The pilot had warned Moulder on the flight out that in this weather, he wouldn't be able to make the fine adjustments that are possible in most SAR cases. Remembering his experience with the *Alaska Ranger*, Bonn told Moulder he'd do his best, but if he was asked to move left, it was probably going to be a jerk to the left instead of a smooth and easy slide.

Todd muscled his way through the swells—bodysurfing on the way down each wave as it passed under him—and reached the life raft, the *Bounty* crew trying to help as he climbed aboard and flopped inside.

"Hi, my name is Dan and I heard you guys needed a ride," he said, pulling his mask and snorkel off. The swimmers' casual, utterly calm greetings don't come just from their personalities, though they are a laid-

back bunch. It's a purposeful strategy to reassure people in distress that help is there and the rescuers are totally relaxed and confident about their ability to handle the situation. Like Haba in the other raft, Todd assessed everyone to see whether anyone was hurt or would need special assistance. He found six survivors, all in pretty good shape except for Prokosh, who seemed to have a back injury. Todd decided to take him first. The others— Hewitt, Groves, Barksdale, Cleveland, and Salapatek—would wait.

"I'll take you one at a time," Todd told the survivors. "Once we're out, I'll swim you over, get you in the basket, and then we'll get you inside the helicopter. You just have to relax and listen to my instructions. There's going to be a *lot* of wind and spray."

As they waited for Todd's status report, Bonn and Fields watched an exceptionally big wave build behind the raft, coming right toward it. Bonn cringed as it came closer, the wave looking gigantic even in this sea of huge waves. The wave crashed right on top of the life raft, slamming down on the canopy with thousands of pounds of force. Inside the raft, Todd and the *Bounty* crew were slammed hard against the inflated floor and edges of the raft, needing a few breaths to get their orientation again and realize they hadn't capsized.

Bonn and Fields were relieved when their swimmer indicated he had six people in pretty good shape, so they could stick with the plan for basket rescues.

The Jayhawk crew watched as Todd jumped back into the water and Prokosh slid out next. Bonn worked to keep the helicopter positioned downwind of the raft, so that the winds on the surface would help blow away the hurricane-strength rotor wash as they also pushed the swimmer and survivor toward the hovering Jayhawk. When all that worked well, the helicopter could stay in pretty much the same position relative to the raft—far enough away that the rotor wash didn't upset the life raft—and the people needing a hoist would end up underneath. The problem, in this case, was that the winds were so high that they caught the life raft canopy like a sail and pushed it downwind far more than they pushed Todd and Prokosh.

That left the swimmer and survivor in exactly the wrong position, still very close to the raft as Bonn maneuvered away from it. Knowing

they had limited fuel and multiple survivors, Bonn decided they had no choice but to move in close to the raft and put the basket down. The rotor wash hit the life raft hard and Todd helped Prokosh get inside the basket as quickly as possible. Like everyone else in their Gumby suits, Prokosh couldn't move well, and his back injury slowed him down further. Once he was inside the basket, Todd gave the signal for Moulder to hoist. Prokosh was up at the cabin door in seconds, leaving the rescue swimmer in the water. Moulder manhandled the basket inside and started motioning for Prokosh to get out.

"Get out! Get out so I can get your friends!" Moulder yelled at him.

Prokosh moved as quickly as he could, but not fast enough for Moulder, who kept motioning and yelling for him to hurry. Prokosh winced as he had to grasp the rails of the basket and heave himself out, pretty much falling onto the cabin floor. Moulder would say later that he felt bad about the moment, because he had no idea at the time that Prokosh was injured. But time was everything here if they were going to get all these people before bingo.

As Prokosh slid himself over into a front left corner of the cabin behind Fields, with Moulder gesturing the whole time for him to go farther, *farther!* up against the wall, Fields reached back from her left seat position and handed him a snack bar. The very grateful, very hungry Prokosh struggled to open it with his Gumby hands, finally tearing the wrapper off with his teeth and chomping down.

Down below, Todd was having the damnedest time trying to get back to the raft for the next survivor. The waves were tossing him around like a cork, under the water and on top of it, flipping him upside down as he swam hard. He was ingesting a lot of seawater and periodically throwing up. Bonn and Moulder realized he needed a hover taxi like Haba had used, so they moved in close to let Todd hook on and they flew him close to the raft, where he disconnected and went for the next survivor, Jessica Hewitt. Soon Moulder was pulling her into the cabin, wrestling the winch line with his left foot firmly braced, and urging her to move far back into the cabin with Prokosh. She pushed up against the front cabin wall behind Bonn, the furry fringe of her parka hood sticking out from her immersion suit.

CHAPTER 24

WE'RE MISSING THREE

THE CRAZY AIR was still throwing the Herc around violently, and one of the mission system operators sitting behind the pilots was so ill he couldn't continue his work. As he sat sideways, staring at a computer screen, not getting to see the horizon or anything outside that might help, the airsickness was hitting him hard, and Russell could understand why. The operator went to sit and puke in the back of the plane, which left the youngest person in the entire crew at the computer panels trying to work the radar, operate a video camera, and conduct radio communications on his own. And he was pretty sick, too.

Russell had started to feel better once the sun came up and he could take off the heavy NVGs, which seemed to exacerbate airsickness because of the green tint and unnatural vision. But he was realizing that his crew was in bad shape. He'd seen them get sick before, but this was not the typical "puke and rally" situation where a person got sick, felt better, and carried on. The dropmasters in the back of the plane were "actively airsick," Russell's polite term for a whole lot of vomiting going on. It wasn't always pretty, but puking doesn't stop the Coast Guard.

Russell's crew stayed on-site as the Jayhawks pulled the survivors out of the water, trying to keep count as the helicopters reported the number

rescued. It sounded like they were still missing two or three. They surveyed the scene over and over again as they flew overhead, looking through the tons of wood, debris of every type, immersion suits, life jackets, an overturned inflatable boat, and who knows what else. They were looking for something the size of a basketball from five hundred feet up, going 190 knots on the upwind leg of the racetrack and ninety knots on the downwind side, and being knocked from side to side in the turns. All the time each crew member was saying to himself, *Is that a person, or is that not a person? Does that suit have a face or just a black hole? What about that one lying facedown?*

Sageser had been sitting on the ramp, doing a visual search for three hours, and in addition to the airsickness, his back was killing him. Around 11:30 a.m., he heard sector say that his crew was being relieved and they could button up for the ride home. Sageser crawled off the ramp and closed it up, and then he realized that the airsickness was hitting him much harder. Sitting on the ramp, bouncing up and down steadily with the plane and able to see the horizon had helped him keep the nausea to a minimum. But now that he was on his feet with the ramp closed, the waves of sickness just kept coming through his gut.

After hand-flying the Herc for four hours, Russell also was running low on energy.

"Aaron, here, knock yourself out, dude," he told his copilot. "I'm spent."

Cmiel took over hand-flying the plane as they got word that the crew number was sixteen, not seventeen, but there were still people missing. After a while the Coast Guard sector asked the Herc to drop another SLDMB, the buoy that helps them track the movement of the debris field, because the one dropped by the first crew wasn't sending any signals. *Oh, man*, Sageser thought, *I have to open the ramp again.*

Just as with the first Herc crew, such a simple operation became an ordeal with the extreme airsickness. Sageser told Michael Canham, the other dropmaster, that he wasn't up to it.

"I'm sick. I'll help you drop that SLDMB; I'll get out there on the ramp and drop it, but I can't operate the controls," he told his crew.

"Opening the door and all that . . . nah, I can't do it. I'll get my gunner's belt on and I'll be on the ramp, and we'll be safe about this. We'll get the job done, but you're going to have to make the calls. You're going to have to operate the controls, because I just can't do it."

Canham somehow retained a chipper attitude. "Sure, no problem. I'll do it."

Sageser and Russell went through the deployment checklist, one of the first steps of which is safety equipment. Russell was waiting for the "check" reply from Sageser and it didn't come. That was because Canham had noticed that Sageser didn't have his gunner's belt on—he could easily be thrown out into the sea once the ramp was open. Canham motioned to Sageser that he needed his belt.

"Hold on . . ." Sageser said, and then vomited into an airsickness bag. Once he finished, he started putting on his safety belt. "Hold on again." Sageser retched some more, producing little but still heaving with gusto. He finally clipped the belt on.

"Okay, are you good?" Canham called.

"Yeah, I'm okay. No, hold on. . . ." And Sageser puked again. He tied up the bag and stowed it nearby.

The mic was hot, so Russell could hear everything as Sageser retched and heaved. Then he came back online.

"Okay, Sageser's done puking. Continue checklist."

THE COCKPIT CREWS of the two Jayhawks coordinated their work as they hovered over the two rafts. "Six-zero-one-two, six-zero-three-one," Peña called from 6012, and copilot Fields answered her from 6031, telling her to go ahead. "Hey, we've got the raft over here and we've got six in here. So quick head count, that's everybody, right?"

Bonn replied from the 6031 Jayhawk, "That's negative. We're looking for a total one-seven people," he said. The correct number of *Bounty* crew had not yet been clarified to all the rescuers.

Peña did the math quietly but it was picked up on her hot mic. ". . . six, seven, eight . . . Shoot, we're missing three."

"What are you looking for?" Cerveny asked.

"If we've got six, they've got six more in the raft, with two on board, six and six is twelve; it's fourteen. We're missing three."

"Yep," Cerveny replied. "Keep your eyes peeled for anybody floating around. If we see somebody actually in the water, we'll break off and go pick them up."

Cerveny and Peña's Jayhawk had just taken on its third survivor from the raft when Peña told Cerveny the aircraft was at the bingo fuel number they had predetermined. "Give it another hundred pounds," the pilot said. "That'll give enough time to get one more." They did get one more, and after four of the seven raft occupants had been hoisted up, Peña finally figured out what that odd noise was in the back when a new survivor came on board. They were cheering each time they saw another face.

Haba was riding the hover taxi back for the fifth survivor from this raft, when Lufkin suddenly winched him back up to the Jayhawk. As Lufkin pulled Haba back into the cabin, he said, "We're bingo. We have to go." Knowing there were three people left in the raft, Haba offered to go back down and stay with them until they could be rescued. Cerveny said no, that it wasn't necessary because they had plenty of rescuers on scene by that point. The other Jayhawk would remain behind, and the Herc was still up there, so Cerveny and Peña's HH-60 was returning with five survivors. His ocean work done, Haba got to his next duties. Coast Guard rescue swimmers are fully trained emergency medical technicians, so once they pull someone out of the water, their next task is to provide medical care. He and Lufkin helped the *Bounty* crew out of their immersion suits, gave them blankets, and cranked up the heater to full blast. Haba checked everyone for any serious problems and found nothing emergent. The Jayhawk had gone out without the water bottles it usually provided to survivors, so Haba grabbed his own and took a sip, then passed it around. More than being thirsty, a lot of the survivors just wanted to wash out the salt water, which nearly everyone had involuntarily swallowed in large gulps. The *Bounty* crew was excited at first, everyone talking with one another and comparing notes on what had happened, but they settled

down quickly as the loud helicopter bumped and bounced through its two-hour trip back to E-city. They were beyond fatigued and some were quite seasick, especially Svendsen, who retched and heaved for much of the return trip because of the seawater he had ingested. It was a long ride back for everyone, as the cabin deck was covered in vomit and everything that came out of the immersion suits when they were removed.

CHAPTER 25

WE CAN'T LEAVE

WATCHING FROM ABOVE, Russell was impressed by what he saw of the helicopter rescues. He had seen plenty of Coast Guard rescues before, plenty of instances in which his colleagues put their lives on the line to save others, but the scene in front of him made him swell with pride and admiration for the people with whom he worked. Those were still some damn ugly seas below, even after the worst of this storm had passed, and he admired his friends who were willing to jump in voluntarily to save people who had been thrown into it involuntarily.

Once the second SLDMB was dropped, the Herc was relieved and a third was on its way.

"RTB," Russell called to his crew. They were returning to base.

Thank God, Sageser thought as he curled up on the deck of the cargo area, still hoping his insides would stop churning. *Let's just get back to land.*

MEANWHILE, THE 6031 Jayhawk was still on scene, plucking people out of the first raft it went to. The life raft grew less and less stable every time someone left. With two survivors in their waterlogged immersion suits gone, the raft was about four hundred pounds lighter now. While the

Jayhawk crew was hoisting Hewitt up and the helicopter was turned away to maneuver back to a safer position, the rotor wash hit the raft hard about the same time as a big wave. The raft flipped upside down and stayed that way.

Inside the raft, the four survivors were struggling in the dark, flopping around like dying fish in their immersion suits, desperately trying to figure out which way was up. Cleveland didn't dare open his mouth, but he was swearing up a storm in his head.

Seriously? Seriously? he thought as he struggled underwater. *I was just about to be rescued and now I'm going to drown in this fucking rubber suit? With a Coast Guard helicopter right there?*

As Bonn turned the helicopter back toward the life raft, the Jayhawk crew winced as they saw the raft upside down. Bonn imagined what it must be like in there, seawater flooding into the canopy. He knew the survivors were exhausted, maybe injured.

This is bad, Bonn thought. *I can't imagine those people are able to help themselves now.*

Bonn saw that the swimmer noticed the problem, Todd's reaction reminding him of the way a sea otter pops his head up and fixates on something in the distance. When his face came up, it was clear to Bonn that the swimmer was on it. He started kicking furiously, and after diving down a few feet he was able to grab the line to the raft's sea anchor, a sort of parachute in the water that helps stabilize the raft.

Underwater, Todd was struck by how calm and clear the water was. Chaos was roaring overhead, but just a few feet under he was gently rocking in the current and could see for thirty yards in the crystal blue water. It also was much warmer down there than up in the blowing wind. For just a few seconds, Todd marveled at the peace below the storm. Then he grabbed the line and kicked hard with his fins to advance toward the raft.

At the same time, the four survivors found themselves sitting on the canopy roof now with the life raft upside down. There was a big pocket of air, but they didn't know how long the raft would hold steady that way. They talked about just jumping out of the raft into the water. They all agreed that was a good idea, but then Cleveland thought maybe they

should discuss it, maybe stay in the raft. But the next thing he knew, people were diving out.

Fuck it, Cleveland thought. *Let's go.*

The Jayhawk crew couldn't see the people exiting the raft. They watched and imagined Todd was going to have to enter the upturned raft and drag people out as fast as he could, but suddenly Bonn and Fields saw a red immersion suit hood pop out of the water with a face in it. Then another. A third. And after what seemed like a long time, the fourth one appeared.

Groves, Salapatek, Barksdale, and Cleveland were able to grab the ropes on the side of the raft and wait there. The Jayhawk crew was relieved to see they had all gotten out safely, and now Bonn realized that, ironically, things would move more quickly at this point.

Groves was next, falling out of the basket and moving toward the left cabin wall, looking toward Prokosh with her mouth agape and an expression that seemed to say, *Oh, my God!* She could hardly move from exhaustion, and Prokosh had to help pull her in closer. Then came Barksdale, looking relieved to be in the helicopter and moving forward up against the right side of the cabin. Then Salapatek.

Cleveland was the last one left outside the raft. He realized that this was the only time he had been alone through the whole ordeal. As he watched Salapatek ride the basket up, the swimmer some distance away, Cleveland felt a mixture of anxiety and peace as he was there in the ocean by himself. But when he was finally ascending toward the Jayhawk, his personality was back to full strength and he could not contain his joy. Sitting in the basket after Moulder pulled him in, Cleveland was giving the "hang loose" sign with index and pinkie fingers, yelling victoriously until Moulder gave him a shove and told him to get out of the damn basket. Cleveland fell out and into his girlfriend Groves's arms, both embracing each other awkwardly in their Gumby suits as Cleveland looked at Prokosh and yelled, "Fuck!" out of sheer excitement and relief. He and Prokosh grasped hands and then Cleveland squeezed in tight with Groves, his arms around her.

Barksdale was helping Hewitt get out of her immersion suit, which prompted others to start removing theirs, but Moulder yelled and mo-

tioned for them to stop. He had a helicopter chock-full of people and still more to come, and he had to think about the possibility of the Jayhawk going down. If they crashed, the crew's immersion suits might be the only thing that saved them—again.

After pulling six people from one raft, the rescuers were about to move on to the second and get the three people whom 6012 had to leave behind. They first had to retrieve swimmer Todd, who was still in the water after sending Cleveland up in the basket. Before leaving the upside-down raft, Todd used his knife to slash it several times, making big long cuts to ensure it would sink. Otherwise it could create false alarms for the Coast Guard and other ships. After pushing the basket back toward Cleveland, who held it out of the way as he lay on top of Groves, Moulder braced himself in the cabin and helped Bonn maneuver the hook close to the swimmer.

"Back ten, easy left, left five, and swimmer's at your three o'clock, right, forward right, *right!*" Moulder called out as Bonn fought the winds to make the adjustments. "Right ten, hold. Hold," Moulder said. "Trying to take a load." Todd had secured the harness at the end of the hook, and Moulder was ready to winch him up. "We have a load." Todd zipped out of the water quickly but was hit by a cresting wave, and then the wind swung him wildly on the ascent. Moulder, left leg braced in his trademark position, wrestled to steady the hoist line. "I feel so bad. I'm jerking him around in the water," Moulder said, breathing heavily from the exertion.

Moulder pulled Todd into the already crowded cabin as Bonn moved forward to the other raft. On the way, Fields conferred with Russell's Herc about an immersion suit that the plane crew thought might be a person in the water. The Herc was trying to track it, but the visual was difficult at the Herc's speed. Russell was about to go back around and drop a second flare on it for the Jayhawk. Fields was doing the math again and figured they could account for fifteen *Bounty* crew if that was indeed a PIW.

"If you fly left about maybe a half of a mile, three-quarters of a mile, object in the water right at your nine o'clock," Russell told them.

"All right, we're looking," Fields replied, as Bonn moved the helicop-

ter to the left. They reached the red immersion suit quickly, but just as quickly they could tell it was empty. Bonn moved on to the second raft. He found the waves and wind abusing this raft in the same way. Facing the same challenges of how to position the ship in the strong winds and heavy seas while trying to keep the rotor wash from the raft, Bonn was focused on the craft's position relative to the survivors when he suddenly felt his copilot take control of the collective, the control that moves the helicopter up and down. She quickly adjusted the Jayhawk's altitude as she called out, "I'm pulling up!" Bonn felt the helicopter rise quickly.

"Hey, there was a big wave coming from the left side over here and it looked like it was going to hit the helicopter," Fields explained.

Todd managed to get Sprague out of the raft and into the basket. She was wearing ski goggles to ward off the salt water and wind, and Cleveland let out a hearty cheer on her arrival. She fell out of the basket and into Cleveland's arms.

So far, so good. Bonn was maneuvering back for the second hoist, giving Todd a hover taxi, and Moulder was doing his best to keep the swimmer from swinging wildly. Moulder was wedged into the doorframe, right hand on the hoist controls and left hand wrestling mightily with the cable as he tried to keep Todd from being hammered by the waves, when he felt a pop in his left shoulder. Almost at the same time, he overextended his left elbow. The pain was excruciating—Moulder figured he must have dislocated his shoulder—but he held on to the cable until he got Todd safely in the water. Then he turned to the seat he occupied in the rear of the cabin, next to the door, and rammed his shoulder into the seat frame as hard as he could to reset the joint. He felt the arm pop back into place and felt better instantly.

Down below, the same factors came together and flipped this raft, too.

Bonn maneuvered the Jayhawk around to minimize the rotor wash as Todd swam toward the upside-down raft. The Jayhawk crew thought they could not possibly be lucky twice with these flipped rafts. Surely this time someone was going to be trapped underwater and struggling inside the raft. But as he moved into a position where he could see inside the flap of the life raft, Bonn was surprised to spot two young men—Jones and Warner—sitting calmly, legs crossed, waiting for the swimmer.

Bonn looked away for a moment as they prepared for the next hoist, and when he looked back the raft was flipped right side up. He wondered whether it was the wind and waves again, or if the intrepid survivors had performed a hamster-wheel move inside the raft to right it.

Jones and Warner were hoisted up into the cabin and greeted warmly; then they climbed onto the pile of people in Gumby suits, now stacked three deep. There were now nine *Bounty* survivors in the Jayhawk.

Bonn and Fields checked the head counts and realized they were still missing two, not three, because the *Bounty* crew had corrected the total number on the ship to sixteen. The Jayhawk crew wanted to stay and search for them, but they were hitting their bingo fuel mark. Rather than just heading straight back to E-city, however, Bonn flew a wide arc around the debris field so they could at least make a quick look. They saw nothing and headed back to base.

Bonn was tired from hours of stressful flying, so he handed the controls over to Fields and let her take the crew home. The adrenaline was wearing off for everyone, both the *Bounty* and Jayhawk crews, and they all were tired and quiet. The *Bounty* crew talked among themselves a bit, straining to be heard over the helicopter noise, and compared notes on who saw whom in the two rafts. Soon they realized two people were still in the water.

"We can't leave! They're still out there!" one of the young male survivors screamed at Moulder and Todd. The Coast Guard crew had no idea who this survivor was, but he was passionate about not leaving his crewmates. "We have to go back! There are still two people out there!"

Moulder explained that they had no choice, because they were low on fuel, but that another Jayhawk was on the way to search for the remaining survivors. The explanation didn't sink in with the overwrought, exhausted survivor, and he continued pleading for the Jayhawk to turn around. No matter how much Moulder tried to explain, he couldn't calm the man down.

Moulder called up to Bonn with an idea. "We've got a survivor back here who's really upset that we're leaving without the other two people," he said. "I keep telling him there's another HH-60 on the way but it's not helping. He's still really emotional. Is there any way we can get close

211

enough to the incoming HH-60 to let him see it? So he'll know we're not leaving them behind?"

It was an unusual request, but Bonn didn't see any reason they couldn't do that. He contacted the incoming HH-60 and told them the plan, and as the two helicopters converged Fields moved their craft over until they were within about a mile of each other. The two Jayhawks slowed down for a moment and Moulder helped the *Bounty* crewman to a sitting position, where he could look out the window on the cabin door. Moulder pointed at the identical Jayhawk going in the other direction.

"See? They're almost there already!" he shouted over the noise.

The young man looked out the window, with tears in his eyes, at the Jayhawk racing out to find Robin and Claudene. He looked back at Moulder with appreciation, nodded that he understood, and fell back into the heap of immersion suits with his fellow survivors, finally able to relax.

CHAPTER 26

A LONG RIDE

IRONICALLY, THE TWO-HOUR ride back to land was the most physically uncomfortable part of the entire experience for many of the *Bounty* crew. They were packed in tight—"I just stack 'em like cordwood," explained Flight Mechanic Moulder, whose all-time record is seventeen people crammed in a Jayhawk during Hurricane Katrina—and they were still in their immersion suits filled with cold water, piss, and worse. The heavy water made even shifting weight or moving off someone's sore legs a chore, and the helicopter constantly vibrated and bounced up and down. The cacophony from the helicopter rotors and engines meant that talking to one another required shouting directly into someone's ear.

Groves was unnerved by the flight, the extreme turbulence making her wonder whether they were going to make it back in one piece. What a crappy outcome that would be, she thought, to survive a ship sinking in a hurricane only to die in a helicopter crash. Wedged in close with Groves, Cleveland was having similar thoughts as he watched the Coast Guard crew's faces during some of the worst turbulence. He could see they were talking with one another on their headsets, but he couldn't hear anything over the noise of the helicopter. Their faces told him plenty, however, and he didn't like what he saw. Every time one of the rescuers

looked concerned, Cleveland's mind would flash with scenarios: *Fuck, what's wrong? Do we have enough fuel? Is there an engine problem?*

But the adrenaline was wearing off. Several of the *Bounty* crew fell asleep.

RUSSELL AND CMIEL'S Herc would stay on scene for eight hours, overseeing the continuing search for the missing crew members. The airsickness never got better and the entire crew was physically drained by the time they headed back to base. On the two-hour return flight, Russell climbed up into some smooth air and everyone was quiet, just trying to recover from the experience. As they flew along in silence, suddenly the cockpit rang out with a huge bang. Cmiel and Russell both jumped, startled and confused.

"My window is broken," Cmiel said dryly.

"Really?" Russell replied, thinking this was one of the strangest missions he'd ever been on. But sure enough, he could see that the windscreen panel in front of Cmiel was shattered. It didn't take long to realize that it must have been because the windscreen deicing system, which heats the window internally, had malfunctioned. They were forced to descend and lower the pressure differential in the airplane, and as they did so, they encountered icing.

"Perfect," Russell said quietly and with heavy sarcasm. "That just makes this even better."

Because the prop deicing wasn't working, Russell had to descend even lower, to three thousand feet and right back into the vomit zone. It was a long ride home.

CHAPTER 27

HOPE

AS THE JAYHAWKS approached the Coast Guard air station at E-city, the *Bounty*'s Facebook page was updated with the good news: "THE CREW IS SAFE."

The helicopters landed as close as possible to the hangar and adjacent administration building instead of farther out on the tarmac as they usually would. The first Jayhawk arrived with Chief Mate John Svendsen, Second Mate Matt Sanders, cook Jessica Black, deckhand Joshua Scornavacchi, and deckhand Douglas Faunt. Svendsen was taken to Albemarle Hospital in Elizabeth City to be treated for injuries to his head, neck, face, abdomen, chest, and leg, a dislocated shoulder, and an inflamed esophagus from swallowing so much seawater.

On the second arrival, the noise in the cabin meant the rescuers had no way to tell the nine survivors that the helicopter was about to land, and none of the *Bounty* crew knew that a helicopter would come in gradually to land like an airplane, most of them expecting it to hover and then settle straight down. So when they looked out the windows and saw treetops and streets, Cleveland and a few others wondered whether they were crashing. But then the craft jolted to a stop and Moulder slid the cabin door open.

They were greeted by fire department and ambulance personnel,

along with other Coast Guard members, who helped the traumatized *Bounty* crew off the helicopters. They stepped out into a windy rain, still wearing their immersion suits. By now they were freezing cold. Many could barely move without help, because the boots of the suits were full of water, making them balloon out, and the weight was difficult to swing with each step. For some of the worst cases of Gumby foot, Coast Guard personnel used knives to cut holes in the feet of the suits and let the water drain. The emergency personnel helped them to a door leading to a large training room with a podium up front, a screen for presentations, and dozens of rows of blue chairs. They slumped in the chairs while medical personnel gave them a quick evaluation and provided bottles of water. The *Bounty* crew was thoroughly impressed by the professionalism and caring attitudes of the Coast Guard personnel. For every survivor, there were about three people tending to his or her needs.

As the second group came into the room, cheers and hugs erupted as *Bounty* crew members reunited. In the Jayhawks the crew had tried to piece together who was safe and who might still be missing, but it was confusing, because one of the helicopters had taken people from both rafts. Nobody could be entirely sure of the head count until they were all together. Svendsen had been taken to the hospital, as had Prokosh. As they talked, it became clear to all of them at once: They realized there were only fourteen.

"Robin and Claudene . . ." several people said at once.

WHEN RUSSELL'S HERC arrived at E-city, the crew was spent. They had nothing left, physically or emotionally. They had gotten no more than six hours of sleep before being called up, and then they were on point all day. Stress and extreme airsickness left everyone feeling like they just wanted to go home, fall into their own beds, and sleep for a long time. But as the plane taxied up, maintenance control called Russell and told him to keep his crew on the plane.

Oh, crap, we're in trouble, he thought. *What did I do?*

But then Chief Petty Officer John Fultz came on board and asked to speak to the entire crew back in the cargo hold. "There're fourteen people

in the large training room who would like to say thanks. Would you guys mind?"

Russell and the other men felt awkward. Fixed-wing guys never saw the survivors. They had no idea what they would say.

"What do you want us to do?" Russell asked. "Go inside and say, 'Hey, good job surviving'?"

"No, just go in there and shake their hands," Fultz said.

Russell told his crew that if they wanted to go inside and greet the survivors, great. But if they didn't, he understood. They still had work to do to put the plane away. The crew as a whole decided they would go see the *Bounty* survivors.

THE THIRD JAYHAWK continued on after its close flyby of the craft carrying nine survivors, the strong tailwind helping it quickly reach the scene of the shipwreck. That helicopter was already searching the miles of sea around the *Bounty* when the fourth Jayhawk arrived about noon, after an hour of flying. In the rear, twenty-nine-year-old swimmer Casey Hanchette and thirty-four-year-old flight mechanic Ryan Parker knew that they were searching for two crew members still missing more than seven hours after the ship went down. Hanchette grew up in Southern California and loved surfing, so he was drawn to a job where he could jump in the ocean and save people. He had been in the Coast Guard for eight years.

As they approached the area of the sinking, they listened to the radio communication between their pilot and copilot and the other crews already on scene. The crews of the HC-130J and the other Jayhawk were telling Hanchette and Parker's crew not to bother going all the way into where the *Bounty* could still be seen floundering on the surface, the rough seas continuing to batter the ship. The first instinct of anyone on a SAR mission is to go to the site of the accident and search outward from there, but the newly arriving crew was to start searching a specific sector some distance away, in the direction that the debris was drifting. Before they had taken off, Parker had spoken with a swimmer from one of the earlier crews, who told him, "Do not waste your time going to look at the boat.

You don't have that much time out there, and with that headwind it takes you two hours to get back. Start hitting the debris field as soon as you get there. But just be aware, there are a *lot* of Gumby suits out there."

Hanchette and Parker were hopeful that they could find Christian and Walbridge. They knew the crew had donned survival suits, and the Atlantic wasn't cold enough to cause hypothermia too quickly. Hanchette thought that if he were out there in the dry suit he wore, he could easily survive the water temperature for a full day. They were trying to be optimistic, but they knew that the chances of finding the missing crew members were slim. Fourteen people were rescued because they were located immediately after the ship capsized, and because they were able to stay relatively close to the ship and one another. The only thing working in the rescuers' favor was a by-product of Hurricane Sandy's conflicting winds and currents, which was keeping the *Bounty*'s debris field tighter than most and only seven miles from the *Bounty*'s last-known position. Hours after the ship went down, the debris field was about four miles long. In winds of fifty to sixty knots, that's nothing.

With each passing hour, the Coast Guard rescuers knew, the likelihood of finding a single person floating in the Atlantic grew more challenging. But still they tried. Just as they had been warned, debris was spread all over, and a disconcerting number of survival suits were floating in the water. Seeing that many suits was not typical on a sea rescue, and it proved to be frustrating and concerning for the crew of the Jayhawk; normally an immersion suit signaled success because there was someone in it. That wasn't the case here.

The pilot and copilot scanned the debris as they flew about fifty knots—fifty-eight miles per hour—and as low as they dared over the swelling sea. Parker was in his seat next to the open door of the cabin, and Hanchette was on his left, peering out a window that provided a much narrower view because it looked over the fuel pods on the port side of the helicopter. All four crew members struggled to determine quickly whether a red survival suit was just empty or if it might contain a person. Some were clearly empty from the way they were folded or tangled up, but others were lying flat on the water like a person would. Some empty suits even seemed to wave at the helicopter when the rotor wash or the

storm winds blew the hands up in the air. Flying by quickly and some-times getting only a glimpse of the red suit between wave swells, they all worried that they might make the wrong call on a suit and accidentally bypass one of the survivors. At first, the crew was calling out suits on the radio every time they saw one. "There's a suit. There's a suit. There's a suit." Soon the pilot came on and said, "Hey, guys, these suits are every-where. We can't check 'em all out. Let's focus on the ones we think might have somebody." Everyone was feeling a knot in their stomachs about just letting a suit go by, but time was limited.

The weather was much clearer by this time, but the wind and sea were still rough. The helicopter was being thrown around during the search pattern, the pilot fighting the controls when making a turn across the wind, which would slam the broad side of the craft and shove it side-ways. When the crew saw a suit that looked promising, they would take the helicopter down for a closer look. Each inspection yielded an empty suit at first, but then after only about twenty minutes of searching, Parker saw another that got his attention. He couldn't be sure, but he told the crew they had to go back and look at that one. He just had a feeling that he didn't want to pass this one.

"Man, I saw a Gumby suit all laid out," he said into his microphone. "It was pretty flat, but I'd hate to pass it by thinking it was empty. Let's check it out."

As the Jayhawk turned back and settled down lower over the red suit lying facedown, Parker and Hanchette were both looking out the cabin door, searching for any sign that it was occupied. The suit was completely open, the arms and legs spread-eagled, but so were a lot of the empty suits. The hurricane-strength rotor wash from the Jayhawk was kicking up sea spray and pushing the debris around, and as the crew stared at the suit they suddenly saw the hood fly backward. In that instant they saw the blond hair of Claudene Christian.

Hanchette immediately put on his swim fins, and Parker rigged the sling to lower him on the winch. The swimmer was out the door in less than thirty seconds and dropped from the sling about twenty yards from Christian, swimming hard through the rolling surf to get to her. Watching from the cabin door, Parker was hopeful. Even though she

wasn't moving, he knew that could be the result of hypothermia or shock.

Hanchette reached her quickly and knew right away that she was unconscious. Turning her over and wrapping the sling around and under her arms, he clipped it to the rig on his chest and signaled Parker that he was ready for the hoist. The Jayhawk already was maneuvering in closer, and Parker soon had the winch line close enough for Hanchette to grab and clip on. Within seconds the two were pulled into the helicopter cabin, Hanchette hugging Christian's limp body tightly, with his arms and legs wrapped around her. They released Christian from the sling and laid her on the cabin floor, noticing that she had no apparent injuries other than a superficial cut on the tip of her nose. She still had her water bottle clipped to her climbing belt. Less than five minutes had passed since they saw her blond hair in the water.

Hanchette got to work checking for vital signs and could not find a pulse. Christian also was not breathing, and with no apparent trauma the rescuers had to assume she had drowned. Parker assisted him in taking off her immersion suit while telling the pilot and copilot that the victim was unresponsive. The pilot replied that they would proceed directly to Albemarle Hospital in Elizabeth City. Hanchette and Parker felt the Jayhawk's engines surge and the nose tip down as the pilots stepped on the gas.

Hanchette proceeded to perform cardiopulmonary resuscitation on Christian, doing chest compressions and providing air through a squeeze bag. Parker assisted by doing compressions when Hanchette paused to check for improvement, and when he applied the leads for the portable defibrillator on board. If they could get some sign of life, enough of a signal from her heart that she might possibly be revived, the automatic defibrillator would deliver an electric shock. But it never came.

They were experienced enough in lifesaving that both men in the helicopter cabin knew there was very little chance of Christian coming back. CPR works in only a small fraction of cases when applied right after a person's heart stops, and they could see that their work was almost certainly futile. But there was hope, however small, and Hanchette would not stop. *This woman has a family somewhere*, he thought, *and they would want me to keep trying.* As the Jayhawk flew into the headwind as fast as

it could go, Hanchette was intently focused on performing chest compressions and providing air to Christian. For two hours he fought for her life, spelled frequently by Parker. Two hours of nonstop effort. When the helicopter finally arrived at the hospital, both men were soaked with perspiration, the sweat pouring from their faces, strong men at the edge of collapse. But it wasn't until he had transferred Christian to the hospital's care and conveyed all the necessary information that Hanchette allowed himself to rest. He and Parker both still hoped for a miracle.

Attempts to revive Christian continued at the hospital, including rewarming her and continuing CPR, but to no avail. At seven p.m., more than fourteen hours after the *Bounty* capsized, the woman who loved the sea was gone.

CHAPTER 28

I'M SO SORRY

THE SEARCH FOR Walbridge continued. The *Bounty* crew and the Coast Guard rescuers still held hope that he would be found alive. If he had only gotten separated from the others and was not seriously injured, he might still make it. The immersion suits were designed to keep people alive for 120 hours even in much colder seas than the warm western Atlantic waters, so it was too early to give up. They just had to keep looking.

After all fourteen survivors were gathered in the training room, the Coast Guard members took them to the showers used by on-duty personnel and helped them get out of the Gumby suits and their wet clothing underneath. The suits were foul inside, as many crew members had involuntarily relieved themselves during their ordeal.

Blue Coast Guard jumpsuits were handed out, and Bosun Laura Groves ended up with one of the biggest, which was several sizes too large for her. Cleveland politely declined the pink socks with the grippy footing on the bottom, deciding he'd rather go barefoot than look that ridiculous. When the newly clean crew gathered in the training room again, the Coast Guard gave them box lunches, coffee, and blankets, and individual Coast Guard personnel lent them cell phones they could use to call home.

Soon the crew from Russell's Herc stepped inside to say hello. It was the first time the HC-130J crew had met survivors after a rescue; they

were used to not making personal contact with the people whose lives they helped save, and even the Jayhawk crews usually didn't see the people they rescued after landing. Coast Guard leaders knew this was a particularly harrowing and noteworthy rescue, however, and the *Bounty* crew wanted to express their gratitude.

The Herc crew filed down the line of *Bounty* personnel, shaking each survivor's hand. They felt awkward, knowing that this was not yet a completely successful mission. Two people were still missing, and it was hard to look the *Bounty* crew in the eyes knowing that they were wondering where their friends were.

Russell felt like he didn't deserve the thanks from the *Bounty* crew. He imagined they must be thinking, *Hey, you're the search and rescue asset. Why didn't you find the other two people?* They weren't thinking that, of course, and were most gracious in thanking the Herc crew for all they had done. Still, Russell's mind was thinking this whole situation was weird, that he and his men hadn't pulled anybody out of the water. They made things a little easier on the Jayhawk crews, he thought, but these folks were thanking the wrong people. It would be weeks before he could really appreciate that moment, looking back on it as a truly meaningful part of his career.

A similar scene unfolded when Russell and Cmiel's Herc returned. The crew was asked to go see the *Bounty* survivors, and as sick and tired as they were, they agreed. It was awkward again, but Sageser will always remember Faunt asking whether theirs was the HC-130J circling overhead as they were rescued. Sageser said it was.

"That was the greatest sound in the world, just knowing you guys were there," Faunt told him. "Hearing that C-130, I knew we were going to be rescued."

The comment really hit home with Sageser. He realized then that he wouldn't remember this mission for his own ordeal, his own discomfort and fears, but rather what his work meant to other people who didn't know from one moment to the next whether they would live.

Cleveland drank what seemed like gallons of coffee, and though he had stopped smoking sometime earlier, he accepted when a Coast Guard man walked in the room and asked whether anybody needed a smoke.

The Coast Guard member had driven to a convenience store near base and bought several packs of cigarettes, knowing that if anyone in this group smoked, they'd need one now. Several of the survivors, including a couple who didn't even smoke, raised their hands and then went outside to stand in the cold wind, rain swirling around and Cleveland in bare feet, for a well-deserved cigarette break. It was comforting, but Cleveland didn't pick up the habit again.

The Coast Guard reps informed the *Bounty* that they had already contacted many of their family members to let them know they were safe. As soon as they felt up to it, many of the crew used the cell phones provided them to call home. Cleveland stepped outside the training room and into a large, brightly lit HC-130J hangar for a little privacy. The Coast Guard had not been able to reach his mother, so Cleveland's voice on the other end of the line was the first time she knew her only child had survived.

Cleveland had been stoic and strong through the last several days, never showing fear or panic and trying to lead other crew members through their crisis with a show of confidence. But when he heard his mother's voice on the phone, her fear and relief, Cleveland broke down and sobbed uncontrollably.

"I'm sorry, Mom," he cried. "I'm so sorry."

BY EIGHT A.M. on Monday, the eye of Hurricane Sandy was 265 miles southeast of Atlantic City, New Jersey, and accelerating. Winds were at eighty-five miles per hour and the storm was projected to continue on a northwesterly course and make landfall in New Jersey about two a.m. Tuesday. The outer edges of the storm were already battering communities north of North Carolina to Massachusetts.

New York and New Jersey were evacuating some communities and preparing for a direct hit by Superstorm Sandy, and both were operating under a state of emergency. Even with the storm still well out at sea, New York City was beginning to experience severe flooding from the storm surge, with subways and tunnels flooding.

GROVES CALLED HER parents and found out they were already driving from their home in western North Carolina, having set out toward Elizabeth City before they even knew whether their daughter was alive. Because they lived relatively close to the far-flung Coast Guard station, they would be the first relatives to arrive. They completed the eight-hour drive that Monday afternoon and had an emotional reunion with their daughter.

The survivors waited at the Coast Guard station all day, talking and wondering what they would do from there. The American Red Cross was arranging hotel rooms for them and also provided each survivor with $200 to buy clothes and other necessities. Late in the afternoon, the *Bounty* crew decided to make a trip to Walmart. Cleveland and Groves drove there with her parents, while the rest of the crew went in taxis.

Cleveland and Groves arrived first but didn't know whether the others were there yet. Cleveland was barefoot in his blue jumpsuit, with a seven-inch beard, and Groves was waddling along in her oversize suit and pink socks, her long dreadlocks still wet. They hadn't slept in more than twenty-four hours, and so in every way they were quite a sight. The elderly greeter at the entrance saw them approaching and had no idea what to make of them. They might have escaped from jail, for all he knew. The look on his face amused Cleveland, and his personality rose to the occasion. He strode right up and, motioning to himself and Groves, said, "Hey, you seen a bunch of other people who look like this in here yet?" The greeter quietly said no and stared as they walked on past.

As they shopped for clothing, Faunt received a phone call from the Coast Guard. Another person had been found. With his phone, he spread the word to the other crew throughout the store, but the Coast Guard had not said who it was. Their surreal shopping trip continued, most of them in a daze, at least on the inside, even if it didn't show outwardly.

Cleveland was looking at a dress shirt he thought he could tolerate wearing, with Groves next to him and her parents nearby, when the cell phone in his jumpsuit rang. It was Faunt with another update.

"It was Claudene," he said, "and she didn't make it."

Cleveland was stunned. He turned to Groves. "Claudene didn't make it." Groves broke down and embraced her father, who did his best

to console her. Cleveland stood for a moment, his mind seemingly unable to process what he had heard. He had just been told that Claudene was dead. How could that be? He'd seen her smiling and laughing just hours earlier.

With Groves in the care of her parents, Cleveland busied himself with his next task. He had to buy some shoes. This was his way of dealing with difficult emotions: by getting to work. He walked over to the shoe department and found Salapatek and Hewitt already there. As gently as he could manage, but in his straightforward way, Cleveland told them that Claudene was gone. The young Hewitt was immediately stricken with grief and nearly collapsed into her boyfriend's arms. After sobbing for a while, she left to find the others, leaving Cleveland and Salapatek standing there in the shoe department of a Walmart in eastern North Carolina.

They didn't say much. Cleveland tried to focus on the task at hand, but without much success.

How am I supposed to pick out shoes? Cleveland thought to himself. *We just lost a good friend. Claudene was a great person.*

The two young men stood there together for what seemed like a long time, staring at the sneakers and work boots but not really seeing them.

CHAPTER 29

BLUE RIBBON AND A REEF KNOT

NEWS OF THE *Bounty*'s sinking had become public early on the morning of Monday, October 29, even before the surviving crew members were back on land. By nine a.m. Eastern, the story was part of the lead hurricane coverage by anchor Carol Costello on CNN. She began the morning's top news with the hurricane that was "within hours expected to explode into this superstorm. Most of us have never seen anything like it in our lifetime. It's already huge, with tropical storm–force winds spanning a width of nearly a thousand miles." Seconds later she moved on to "a drama unfolding out at sea. A rescue is under way for the crew of the HMS *Bounty*, the ship built for the Hollywood movie *Mutiny on the Bounty*. Unbelievable."

That was the word that set the tone for news coverage, and the public's reaction, in the days and weeks that followed: unbelievable. A tall sailing ship was in Hurricane Sandy and—perhaps not so surprisingly—sank. The full force of Hurricane Sandy had not been felt yet on the East Coast, but already the size and scope of the storm were common knowledge. As questions came quickly and people mourned the loss of a great romantic sailing ship, while praying for the safe rescue of the two missing crew, social media took the lead with instant tributes and criticism. The fact that the ship was the *Bounty,* rather than some other tall sailing ship

227

with less name recognition, engendered even more interest. The loss of any ship, or even any tall sailing ship, would have been tragic news, but this was one ship that the media and the public could instantly identify: the replica ship built for *Mutiny on the Bounty*, the one that was in *Pirates of the Caribbean* with Johnny Depp, the one that had been such a popular "pirate ship" attraction at stops around the world. Former crew, relatives of crew, and hundreds of others who felt some kinship with the *Bounty* went straight to the HMS *Bounty* Organization's official Facebook page to express their concern, wish those in peril well, and begin the long, difficult search for answers. For weeks after the tragedy, the Facebook page remained alive and open to anyone who wished to post their comments. The comments posted by the HMS *Bounty* Organization during the crisis remained, providing a ghostly time line of a ship sailing into disaster. The emphatic comments from the Facebook page's administrator, apparently relayed after talking with Walbridge, looked sadly hubristic after the fact: "*Bounty*'s current voyage is a calculated decision . . . NOT AT ALL . . . irresponsible or with a lack of foresight as some have suggested. The fact of the matter is . . . A SHIP IS SAFER AT SEA THAN IN PORT!" But on that Monday it was apparent that the *Bounty* wasn't, and would never be seen in port again. The posts were difficult to read if you had a loved one on the ship and already knew how the story ended.

Criticism came amid the outpourings of grief and well-wishing, at first gently and with a questioning tone that would become familiar whenever the *Bounty* was discussed in any venue. Why? Why was the ship at sea in the hurricane? If Walbridge was right about its being safer at sea, what went wrong? As more time passed, the criticism became more direct. On other Internet sites, there was little pretense of being polite in the face of the human loss. Experts in sailing, and those who fancied themselves experts, piled on the *Bounty* and Walbridge with little pity.

The Web site Sailinganarchy.com even started an "Official Trash the *Bounty* Thread" in its forums for members who wanted to criticize the decisions that led to the ship's sinking, and the *Bounty* in general. The harsh Monday-morning quarterbacking was rebuffed in kind by those who

thought the ship's captain should be given the benefit of the doubt. It produced a spirited debate, with hundreds of posts. A typical comment: "Trying to thread the needle of the Gulf Stream and the Hatteras Shoals in a HURRICANE 1,000 MILES WIDE takes either balls of titanium or brains made of Swiss cheese. You decide."

Joseph Sienkiewicz, chief of the Ocean Applications Branch at the NOAA Ocean Prediction Center and instrumental in tracking Sandy, told the author, "I was surprised to hear that there was a traditional sailing vessel in that area, with the threat coming northward. Pretty much any vessel, even a large container ship, shouldn't be in that storm. This is one category of ship that shouldn't be there, but pretty much anybody else, too."

In retrospect, the analysts at NOAA and the National Hurricane Center were accurate with their predictions of the storm's path and behavior, Sienkiewicz says. Early analysis clued them in to the unique nature of the superstorm, and a retroactive review of the storm's actual experience matched closely with what the experts warned would happen.

Even as the search for Walbridge continued, news reports began to convey the doubts of some of the crew who had contacted friends and family as they were sailing into the storm. Claudene Christian's e-mails to her friend Halbeisen quickly became a media sensation, evidence supposedly that she and other crew members were never confident of sailing into the storm, that Walbridge or someone else had led them to the slaughter. The media treatment of the tragedy was textbook journalism: Find a likable victim and portray her as an innocent lamb lost to the misdeeds of others and forces so great as to mystify. In this case, the victim was perfect for the American media—an attractive white woman with blond hair and a beautiful smile who was enamored with the romantic life at sea. She had little experience and depended on others to protect her—an innocent girl who wanted only to sail on the famous ship, the stories consistently said. She was instantly dubbed the "former USC song girl"—cheerleaders at USC are called song girls—by reporters, and coverage often showed pictures of her in her college days dressed in her USC song girl uniform, giving people the impression that she was much younger than her forty-two years. She became the sympathetic face

of the *Bounty* tragedy, and, some crew would complain bitterly, Walbridge became the scoundrel. Or the scapegoat.

FOUR DAYS HAD passed since the fifteen crew members of *Bounty* were recovered by the Coast Guard, and with each passing day the chances of finding Walbridge decreased. The crew, and Walbridge's wife, knew that survival in the Atlantic depended on a quick rescue. Even though cold temperatures were not a threat, a man alone in the open sea with no raft, no drinking water, and no other supplies could not survive for days. His immersion suit should have kept him afloat, if it wasn't tangled in ropes, if it wasn't torn, if . . . But even if he stayed afloat, his chances were slim. With the captain's age, his injury during the last day, and the real possibility that he had been hit by rigging or dragged underwater, those waiting for the news of his safe return knew that it likely would not come.

On November 1, the Coast Guard announced that it was calling off the search for Walbridge. Four days of around-the-clock efforts with a Coast Guard cutter, a buoy tender, and several aircraft—covering twelve thousand square nautical miles—had yielded no sighting of the captain of the *Bounty*. Thermal imagery showed no indication that he had gone down with the ship—deciding to "fucking *Titanic* it," as Cleveland says in his unique way. The Coast Guard flew over the *Bounty* many times during the rescues, when the ship was still at the surface, and the FLIR devices that can detect the residual heat signature of a body revealed nothing. Though no one had seen Walbridge after the last sighting on the top deck just before the ship capsized, Cleveland says his captain would never have decided to go belowdecks and ride the ship down to the bottom. He would have wanted to help his crew survive after leaving the ship, Cleveland says. And more important, he would never have left his wife.

"He loved his wife. I used to accidentally hear him on the phone once in a while talking to her, and it was really sweet," Cleveland told the author. "It was almost like a slightly different tone in his voice anytime he would be chatting with her."

Though no one was truly surprised, the finality of the Coast Guard

announcement hit the *Bounty* crew hard. They were staying at a house rented for them by ship owner Robert Hansen—they thought of it as a "McMansion"—each of them trying to avoid the many interview requests from reporters and seeking a way to deal with their own trauma. They were being portrayed as the plucky crew who had survived a dramatic shipwreck, with Walbridge and Christian, of course, receiving most of the public's sympathy. The surviving crew were the lucky ones, as most people saw it, but outsiders had no idea of the emotional devastation they were dealing with in that rented house. They had survived, but just barely, and the sheer terror many of them experienced in those last hours on the ship and in the water would stay with them. Some second-guessed themselves and wondered whether they could have performed better in the ship's last days and hours, inevitably asking themselves—as most survivors of a tragedy do—why they had lived and others had died. These were emotions and questions that would not quickly fade.

THE *BOUNTY* CREW was still struggling with their emotions when they agreed to do a group interview on ABC's *Good Morning America* less than a week after the sinking, and almost immediately after hearing that Walbridge could not be found. Reporters and producers had been trying to get interviews with the crew from the start, contacting individual crew members, their families, and anyone associated with the ship or the HMS *Bounty* Organization to try to persuade them. To ease the pressure, and because they thought Walbridge and Christian deserved to be remembered, the crew decided they would give one group interview and be done with it. The experience would not be a positive one.

The survivors were taken to a local television studio, where, as Cleveland would recall later, they were held for hours before beginning the interview. As time wore on, the crew members became more anxious and irritated, bristling at what some thought to be a brusque and uncaring attitude from the producer, who was going to reap professional kudos for the exclusive. The crew was hungry, not yet recovered physically from the ordeal, and more fragile than any of them would admit, yet they were kept waiting as the producer made more demands and the crew resisted

with increasing intensity. Several times the crew members discussed whether they should just walk out, but they decided to go through with it in the end.

The interview aired on *Good Morning America* on November 6, 2012, with the network touting its exclusive as the "survivors speak for the first time." Reporter Matt Gutman hosted the interview with the crew members sitting together, none of them looking pleased to be there. Rather than a focused narrative about their experience, the edited videotape was a series of short statements from crew members. The first comment was, "But I wasn't scared," from Scornavacchi, followed later by, "Like a washing machine in an earthquake, while going down giant slides," from Groves, delivered just like that, in staccato sound bites between the reporter's comments. Most of the piece proceeded in the same fashion, telling the story of the *Bounty*'s loss in video snippets using file footage of the *Bounty* and scenes from the Coast Guard rescue. The much-hyped exclusive interview by ABC yielded little more than pictures of the crew sitting together, spliced together with other videotape and voice-overs by the reporter. The five-minute segment showed six crew members speaking a total of 338 words.

Throughout the interview and the negotiations preceding it, the crew was frustrated by the line of questioning. They wanted to take the opportunity to remember Walbridge and Christian, but it was clear to them that the ABC team wanted to focus only on getting dramatic sound bites about the ship going down. In the videotape that aired, Cleveland refuses to look up most of the time and told the author that at one point he was staring at an electrical connection for the camera and sound equipment. He looked up at Salapatek and back down at the connection, implying that he could unplug the whole thing before anyone could stop him. Salapatek subtly shook his head no.

The interview did include Svendsen explaining how he owed his life to the improvised beacon that Walbridge had devised for a man overboard, and which Svendsen was clinging to when the Coast Guard found him. "I give my life to Robin, and to his ingenuity, and to his leadership that I am here today," Svendsen said. Others praised Christian and said she was having the time of her life on the *Bounty*. Several spoke of how

they would miss Walbridge and Christian, and how they would always remember them. Scornavacchi spoke movingly of how coming so close to death yourself changes you, as did Faunt, who said, "I'll never have another bad day in my life."

Cleveland and others were left frustrated nonetheless, knowing that they had tried hard to focus the interview on Walbridge and Christian but feeling that they were overshadowed by the need for drama. Walbridge's widow was just off camera, however, and Cleveland is at least happy that she heard the crew speak so well of her husband.

A PRIVATE MEMORIAL was held for Walbridge in St. Petersburg, Florida. As the time of the memorial approached, Third Mate Dan Cleveland recalled an old mariner's tradition of painting a blue line around the hull of a ship to signify that its captain had died. Before the surviving crew gathered to go to the memorial, Cleveland and others bought enough blue ribbon for each of them to fashion an armband in respect for their lost captain. They made sure to tie the armbands with a nice, secure reef knot, a staple for any sailor.

ON DECEMBER 1, another memorial was held for Walbridge and Christian at the Marine Museum at Fall River, Massachusetts, which the *Bounty* called home from 1993 to 2001. Surviving crew members, past crew, friends, and family packed the museum to say good-bye. Many in attendance wore crew sweatshirts, rubber boots, and caps with the *Bounty* logo. Others dressed in the formal uniforms of bygone navies, and there were dress uniforms from the Coast Guard.

Those attending the memorial knew the *Bounty* like no others could. They could look at one another and know that they had all learned from Walbridge, had shared the same fears and joy when climbing the rigging to set sails, felt the pride of being on the ship everyone wanted to see in port, that they too had experienced the long, hard days at sea and the indescribable peacefulness of nights on deck watch. They knew one another, and they knew the *Bounty.*

Many people at the memorial spoke of their memories of Walbridge. Shelly McCann, his stepdaughter, recalled him as "the most gentle, caring soul" she had ever met. "One poet said it best: 'He loved the sea, he loved his ship, and he loved us.'" She went on to recall that she had learned so much about her stepfather from those who expressed their love for him after the sinking, citing his penchant for silly phrases like, "Wakey, wakey, little snakey," and, "Uppy, uppy, little guppies." Those phrases prompted chuckles of fond remembrance.

Christian was remembered by L. Jaye Bell, a journalist who had sailed on the *Bounty* earlier in the year and come to know her as a free spirit. "Claudene was in her element on the *Bounty*," he said. "She loved the waters, the ocean. She enjoyed being part of something big."

The *Bounty* itself was remembered also. After services in the museum, the mourners walked through a softly falling snow behind a marching band from the Colonial Navy of Massachusetts, headed to the battleship USS *Massachusetts*, docked nearby. It was the same battleship that Hewitt had visited as a child, when she was "innocent . . . to the risks of going to sea," she told the author. They gathered on the teak deck of the huge ship's bow to drop three wreaths into Mount Hope Bay. Ashley DeRamus led the Pledge of Allegiance. Following a song and a prayer, longtime friend of the *Bounty* Joe Perreira spoke in a booming voice. "I will tell you every ship at sea, most especially a sailing ship, is a living and breathing entity . . ." he said. "Three souls were lost that day. The captain, Claudene, and the *Bounty* herself."

Three wreaths slowly drifted off.

Chapter 30

INVESTIGATION

ONE HUNDRED AND six days after the *Bounty* sank in the Atlantic, the U.S. Coast Guard convened its hearings on the tragedy in Portsmouth, Virginia, in the Hampton Roads area that is home to the Norfolk Naval Shipyard, which builds and overhauls Navy ships. Situated on the Elizabeth River across from the city of Norfolk, Portsmouth has a history and current community centered almost entirely on shipbuilding and repair. The site was chosen because it is the headquarters of the Coast Guard's Atlantic Area, which covers the Eastern United States, the Atlantic Ocean, and the Gulf of Mexico, but a hotel overlooking a busy shipyard and a harbor with centuries of marine history proved to be a fitting place to delve into the most troubling questions about why the *Bounty* went down and, more important, why two people lost their lives.

The hearings were convened on February 12, 2013, by lead investigator Coast Guard commander Kevin M. Carroll, the chief of inspections and investigations for the Coast Guard Fifth District. Looking fit and more youthful than his forty-one years, Carroll immediately set the tone for the next eight days of hearings. "This investigation is meant to determine the cause of the casualty, and the responsibility therefore to the fullest extent possible, and to obtain information for the purpose of preventing or reducing the effects of similar casualties in the future,"

Carroll stated. "This investigation is also intended to determine whether there is any evidence that any incompetence, misconduct, or willful violation of the law on the part of any licensed officer, pilot, seaman, employee, owner, or agent of such owner of any vessel involved, any officer of the Coast Guard, or other employee of the United States, or any person caused or contributed to the cause of this casualty. . . ." With a no-nonsense demeanor and a military bearing that suggested this was a man who probably slept at attention, Carroll explained that witnesses would testify under oath and be subject to penalties for perjury. From the first moment of the hearing to the end, Carroll conducted the hearings with the utmost professionalism and demanded the same of everyone else involved. At times he would seem almost protective of the *Bounty* crew when they were testifying, conveying a respect for their seamanship and not allowing them to be badgered unreasonably.

Along with Carroll's fellow Coast Guard investigators and a Coast Guard attorney, the panel was joined by Captain Rob Jones, senior marine accident investigator for the National Transportation Safety Board (NTSB), which was conducting its own investigation and would produce a separate report on the incident. Jones, a former tanker captain, joined the Coast Guard hearing to minimize the duplication of effort during the investigations.

Sitting in front of the panel at separate tables were the "parties in interest," the term used by the Coast Guard to denote those people or entities who would either be the primary focus of the investigation or who might offer key information to the investigators, along with any party that might have an interest in questioning the witnesses and therefore draw out more useful information. In this case, the parties of interest were *Bounty* chief mate John Svendsen, the highest-ranking officer to survive the ship's sinking, since Captain Walbridge was lost at sea; the HMS *Bounty* Organization, LLC, which operated the ship for owner Robert Hansen; and the parents of Claudene Christian. Her mother is also named Claudene but goes by Dina. Her father, a retired firefighter, is named Harry but goes by Rex.

The Christians had driven for nearly a week from their home in Vian, Oklahoma, to be in the front row every day, directly behind the attorneys

representing them and their daughter. On her pinkie finger, Dina wore the opal birthstone ring they had given Claudene, and which she was wearing when she died. Looking at times fragile, devastated, and furious as they listened to the testimony, the Christians were there because they wanted justice for their daughter and believed with an absolute certainty that her death at sea was no act of God, no unfortunate accident, but rather the direct and predictable result of wrongdoing by the people Claudene trusted. Throughout the hearings they were visibly upset by testimony in which crew members claimed that everyone on board the *Bounty* was calm and upbeat, even joking, during the worst of the crisis. They had been told otherwise in personal conversations with crew members, Dina Christian told the author, and they were especially troubled by testimony juxtaposing the other crew's good outcome with images of what Claudene must have gone through. As Third Mate Cleveland explained first the ordeal of being in the water and trying to get into a raft, then told the Coast Guard panel that the people in his life raft were in good cheer, singing sea shanties and joking as they waited for a helicopter rescue, Claudene's mother sobbed into her hands. Her father was red faced and crying.

In the weeks after the sinking, the Christians made their feelings clear to many of the crew members who initially sought to convey their condolences, and they told more than one that they intended to sue the HMS *Bounty* Organization, Hansen, and possibly others. The crew, already circling the wagons in those early days to protect the captain they loved and respected, was dismayed by the Christians' fury and intent to seek punishment. They distanced themselves from the Christians, because though they felt the loss of Claudene acutely themselves and had great sympathy for the grieving parents, they could not support legal action that they would consider an insult to Walbridge's memory and threaten the already precarious financial future of Walbridge's widow. As the following days of testimony would show, to the consternation and bewilderment of some on the panel and many observers, the crew's dedication to Walbridge knew no bounds, even after their near-death experience under his command.

"If I had died out there, my parents wouldn't have sued," Cleveland told the author. "I know that for a fact."

Groves agreed, saying, "There's no way mine would sue either. They know I'm doing what I love."

The difference may be, as the testimony in the hearings showed, that Cleveland and Groves were dedicated mariners, experienced and trained. Their parents likely know of their son's and daughter's devotion to the craft and way of life on a tall ship, whereas the Christians knew that their Claudene was excited about the adventure, eager to be part of the *Bounty* family, but she did not have years of experience and training. She was troubled in some ways, looking for a life she could embrace. She was not like Cleveland and Groves and several other *Bounty* crew members in that respect, and she depended on the crew to guide her—and to protect her. This betrayal of a naive and vulnerable woman, as the Christians see it, was at the heart of their barely contained rage against the HMS *Bounty* Organization, owner Hansen, and some crew members in particular. Svendsen, as the number two in command, was at the top of their list, and he knew it.

Aware of the Christians' focus on him and many of the crew members' descriptions of the Christians as irrationally "out for blood" anywhere they could get it, Svendsen approached Carroll before the hearings convened and expressed concern about his personal safety. As a result, Carroll arranged to have armed Portsmouth police present during the hearings. Each morning, Svendsen made a point of saying hello to the officer assigned that day and thanking him or her for being there.

THE FIRST DAY'S testimony was preceded by a surprise announcement from Commander Carroll. Robert Hansen, the owner of the *Bounty*, had been subpoenaed like the rest of those on the witness list but he would not be testifying. Hansen had sent word to Carroll though his attorneys that he was invoking his Fifth Amendment right against self-incrimination. The news sent a murmur through the reporters, interested parties, and others in the room, because everyone knew the key question that the Coast Guard panel would have asked Hansen: Did you contact Captain Walbridge before he left New London and pressure him to sail into the hurricane?

With Hansen refusing to answer that or any other questions, the Coast Guard investigators and everyone else would be left to speculate. Fair or not, many observers in the room immediately concluded that Hansen's refusal to testify conveyed the answers to those questions. After all, the only other person who could conclusively say whether Hansen contacted Walbridge was Walbridge himself, and he was gone.

Refusing to testify did not keep Hansen away, however. He sat in the first row, behind the attorneys representing the HMS *Bounty* Organization, and frequently consulted with and provided direction to them during the hearings. He did not give the appearance of a man worried for his future, as he enjoyed a pocketful of candy most days during the hearings, partial to Swedish gummy fish, and joked with the *Bounty* attorneys. In a few instances during breaks in the proceedings, Hansen's jocular mood spilled over into inappropriateness, considering the focus of the hearings and the presence of mourning parents just fifteen feet away. During one break, he joked with the *Bounty* team about how one of the Christian attorneys had protested a statement, laughing and gesturing theatrically about how he expected the opposing attorney to jump up and shout, "I object!"

The hearings began with Carroll questioning Svendsen about what happened in the last days before the ship's sinking. Dressed casually but neatly, with his long blond hair and a light beard, Svendsen looked as if he were ready to step aboard a ship and get right to work. His demeanor was calm, focused, and professional in the extreme. Soft-spoken but used to leading a crew through difficult sailing, Svendsen took seriously his task of representing Walbridge and the *Bounty*. Svendsen at one point had considered going to law school, and his performance in the hearing suggested he would have handled himself well in court. He was not represented by an attorney, even though the Coast Guard could revoke or limit the maritime licenses of himself and other officers on the ship if the panel concluded that they were at fault.

Much of the questioning, in fact, would obliquely suggest that there could have—or should have—been another mutiny on the *Bounty* if the officers thought Walbridge was leading them into disaster.

After preliminary testimony establishing facts about the *Bounty*'s

construction, Carroll addressed one of the most sensational issues. In an interview in the summer of 2012 for a Maine public-access TV show, Walbridge claimed he chased hurricanes and downplayed the danger of bad weather. After the sinking, the comments seemed prophetic and telling.

When asked whether he had ever run into rough weather with the *Bounty*, Walbridge replied, "Have we run into stormy seas? We chase hurricanes." Comparing a hurricane to an amusement park ride, he said, "You get a good ride out of it," and, "There is no such thing as bad weather, only different kinds of weather." He went on to explain: "You try to get up as close to the eye of it as you can and you stay down in the southeast quadrant, and when it stops, you stop." Walbridge also offered that the *Bounty*'s engine is "probably way underpowered for this size of boat. . . . We sail as much as we can. We just use the engines to get in and out of tight harbors."

Was Walbridge just playfully boasting for the benefit of the interviewer? Did he choose unfortunate wording to describe a legitimate strategy for stormy seas?

Carroll asked Svendsen, who had been on the ship for three years, whether the comment about chasing hurricanes was consistent with what he knew of Walbridge. Svendsen said yes, because he knew Walbridge's philosophy on hurricanes to be that you get on the southeast side of the storm in order to get favorable winds and because it was the safest and most navigable position for the ship. He described being on the *Bounty* in 2010 when the ship was sailing from Boothbay to Puerto Rico and encountered a storm, and Carroll asked him whether Walbridge intentionally put the *Bounty* in close proximity to the storm.

"I never witnessed Robin seeking out a storm," Svendsen said. "If there was a storm, he would put the ship in the safest position in the storm."

Third Mate Dan Cleveland and Able Seaman Douglas Faunt agreed, both saying that Walbridge's words were misconstrued in hindsight. Faunt added that he thought Walbridge was relaxed and having a bit of fun with the interviewer, who conducted the entire interview in a light-hearted way. (The NTSB investigator, Jones, later told the author that

any talk about the "safest" side of a hurricane was nonsense. One side might be slightly less dangerous for a ship, he said, but any side of a hurricane is still far from safe.)

The parties in interest were allowed to question each witness, and it soon became apparent that the attorneys representing the Christians were trying to extract information that would be of use in their lawsuits, and the HMS *Bounty* Organization was trying to get information that would help in its defense. Witnesses were asked repeatedly about the condition of the bilge pumps, the generators, and the caulking on the hull. They were grilled over the details of when systems on the ship began to fail and why the ship ended up in the path of a hurricane.

As the HMS *Bounty* Organization was questioning Svendsen about how the crew prepared for sailing toward a hurricane, seeking to show that Walbridge led a crew diligent in taking extra safety measures, such as tying down even the smallest items that might be thrown about the ship in a storm, the normally controlled Carroll interrupted in exasperation.

"Why would you *be* on a vessel heading into a hurricane?" Carroll asked with incredulity. Peering over his eyeglasses at Svendsen, he compared the talk of extensive preparations to what one might do on land when there is no choice but to face the oncoming storm. But you don't have to sail your ship into a hurricane, he said. Carroll seemed to imply that all the testimony about how much the *Bounty* crew had done before sailing into Hurricane Sandy actually underscored the foolishness of the decision, rather than showing how responsible Walbridge and his crew were.

When Third Mate Cleveland testified, he insisted that Walbridge's decision to leave New London could be justified. He, Groves, and others on the *Bounty* discussed at the time that there might be other options, he said, but he would not criticize Walbridge's decision even in hindsight. If the *Bounty* had stayed in port at New London, the senior crew and probably others would have stayed on board to care for the ship, he said. "So you can't say the crew would have been any safer," he added.

"But if you get into trouble, you can jump to the pier," Carroll replied, peering at Cleveland over his glasses.

"Have you ever been on a pier in a hurricane?" Cleveland retorted with a bit too much attitude, considering whom he was talking to.

"Yes," Carroll said, never taking his gaze off the witness.

"You don't want to be on a pier in a hurricane," Cleveland said.

"No," Carroll agreed. "You don't want to be anywhere near a hurricane."

Under questioning, Svendsen admitted that he had tried to talk Walbridge into staying in New London or seeking another port, but he ultimately deferred to the captain's greater experience. At one point, an attorney for the Christians asked Svendsen whether he could have called the HMS *Bounty* Organization office for help when he disagreed with the captain's judgment—which would have amounted to a modern-day mutiny on the *Bounty*—but Svendsen deflected the question by saying that Walbridge was in communication with the office.

TESTIMONY ALSO FOCUSED on the *Bounty*'s certification as a "moored attraction vessel." The intricacies of certification for various types of vessels were discussed at length, but the pertinent issue was that the *Bounty*'s certification allowed her to take visitors on board only while tied up at a dock—tourists and locals who wanted to take a look at the ship famous for its role in big-screen movies. *Bounty* could not have paying guests while at sea, unlike many other tall sailing ships that routinely took on students and others for day sails or weeks of sail training, all for pay. In order for *Bounty* to charge people for sail training or even as mere passengers while at sea, the ship would have had to achieve a higher level of certification that came with far more extensive inspections and safety requirements that the ship could not meet without costly modifications. Achieving that higher certification had been a goal for the *Bounty* for years but had always been out of reach because of the structural changes that would have been necessary, according to the testimony of several crew members and a representative of the HMS *Bounty* Organization. The *Bounty*'s certification as a moored attraction vessel was unknown to the public and would have been meaningless to them anyway, but for people within the tall ship community, the meaning was clear: This was

a ship that could be trusted to have people walk on board and take a look around while at the dock, but no authority was making any promises about its being safe and seaworthy.

The ship's status as a moored attraction vessel also played into discussions about whether the crew was truly employees or, as the Christians' attorney suggested in his line of questioning, their pay was a pittance intended as a technicality to overcome the fact that they were, in effect, paying with their own labor for the privilege of learning to sail. The Christians' attorney elicited from Tracie Simonin, previously the personal assistant to owner Robert Hansen and then the offshore operations director for the HMS *Bounty* Organization, that Claudene Christian was paid $100 a week gross. The impression left after his questioning was that she, and probably the other crew, were not working on the *Bounty* for the money, but were in effect paying their own way through daily labor. Even the one volunteer on the *Bounty*'s final voyage, Douglas Faunt, was required to work just as much and just as hard as any paid crew, Simonin testified. Claudene Christian worked as much when she was an unpaid volunteer as after she became paid crew, Simonin said. The implication was that the *Bounty* could have been violating the limits of its certification by having people "pay" for passage on the ship through their own labor. A stretch perhaps, but the HMS *Bounty* Organization countered by asking Simonin whether Claudene Christian ever cashed any of her paychecks, and the answer was no. The attorney asked Simonin whether she ever tried to persuade Claudene Christian to cash the checks accumulated over four months of employment, but Carroll cut him off and said the question was irrelevant. Apparently the HMS *Bounty* Organization was heading toward an effort to show that Claudene Christian loved the *Bounty* so much that she never bothered to cash the paltry paychecks, but the question came off as amazingly insensitive, since the answer could have been that she never got a chance to. The checks were mailed to her parents' home.

The *Bounty*'s status as a lesser vessel in the tall ship fleet was confirmed by Bert Rogers, executive director of Tall Ships America (TSA), the Newport, Rhode Island, organization that acts as the professional group for the country's tall sailing ships, organizes sailing events and

festivals, and promotes best practices for the fleet. The group has 170 vessel members in the United States, and almost all hold a higher certification than the *Bounty* did, Rogers testified. Trying to put a better spin on the *Bounty* story than when he earlier told the author emphatically that "the *Bounty* was not representative of how our fleet operates," Rogers explained that the *Bounty* was an active participant in TSA and "as a moored attraction vessel was very successful." The group often made the *Bounty* a headline attraction when promoting its events, because the public loved coming to see the pirate ship from the movies. The ship never achieved higher certification because that is difficult for a foreign-built hull, and the cost of retrofitting such an old ship to modern standards would be greater than the *Bounty* could ever earn back, he said.

"The vessel had a long history and there were different perceptions," Rogers said. "It almost didn't survive at one point but it was on the upswing, with the owner investing money to bring it up to standards. We felt our job was to cheerlead and encourage. But we knew this job was not done."

Rogers said he would have recommended the *Bounty* to crew looking for work, but he would have warned them about the ship's uninspected status. An experienced captain himself, Rogers was asked what he would have done in Walbridge's place.

"I would not have sailed," he said, explaining that he would have found an alternate harbor or stayed in New London.

The Christians' attorney asked Rogers how many TSA ships had been on the East Coast at the time of Hurricane Sandy. About fifty, Rogers answered. And besides *Bounty*, how many had left port?

None.

CHAPTER 31

REVELATIONS

ON EACH DAY of the hearings, Carroll held a moment of silence for those lost on the *Bounty*.

About ten a.m. each morning, a Coast Guard Jayhawk helicopter just like the one used to rescue the *Bounty* crew made a routine low-level flight across the harbor just outside the hotel and on down the Elizabeth River. So close to the hearing room that the thumping noise of the rotor blades could drown out the testimony for a moment, each day's passing seemed like an honorary flyby that was hardly noticed by most in the room.

THE *BOUNTY*'S TIME in dry dock at Boothbay, Maine, days before sailing into Hurricane Sandy, became a primary focus of the investigation and led to some of the most startling testimony. Lead shipwright and project manager Tom Kosakowski, the clean-cut, fresh-faced young man who supervised the shipyard's work on the *Bounty*, had six and a half years of experience doing woodwork on wooden ships and had sailed on wooden- and steel-hulled tall ships for the past ten years. He testified about the condition of the ship when it arrived and was pulled out of the water for maintenance and repairs. The hull looked to be in excellent shape, he said, with few "weeping" seams where water already in the boat leaks

back out when the ship is on land. Weeping seams indicate leaks where the boat takes on water, but Kosakowski's first impression of the *Bounty*'s hull was that it was "very tight." He went on to describe how he saw Bosun Laura Groves lead the team that was caulking the seams needing repair, which he estimated to be only about five percent of those below the waterline and ten percent above the waterline.

Excessive leaks in the hull seams would have been dangerous in heavy seas, and though the Christians' attorneys would dig more and insinuate that the caulking at Boothbay by the *Bounty* crew might have been substandard, Kosakowski made clear that he saw no concern there. He did have grave concerns about something else, though. In a shock to most people following the *Bounty* story up to that point, Kosakowski told the Coast Guard panel of how he had spotted rotten wood on the ship and worried that more might be hidden behind the outside planks. But Walbridge would not approve opening the ship up to see how bad it was, he testified.

Walbridge had been aware that two planks on either side of the ship and above the waterline needed to be replaced, but that was not unusual maintenance for a ship of this type. Kosakowski and his crew removed those planks and determined that the wood was showing "excessive signs of decay" for planks that had been installed only six and a half years earlier, he testified.

Kosakowski went on to describe in detail his conversations with Walbridge about the findings and the need to search for more rotten wood under the planking, and how the captain had flatly refused.

Kosakowski noted that the crew also knew of the discovery. "It was right at a gangway, so most of the crew saw what we were looking at and were part of pieces of our conversation," he said.

Carroll asked whether the decay would have been visible from within the ship and Kosakowski explained that it would not, because the *Bounty* had an inner planking, sort of the inside wall, that covered structural frames and outer planking. Fuel and water tanks, machinery, and other apparatuses also obscured the few places where the frames or outer planking might have been visible, he said.

Carroll asked how rotten wood is typically dealt with in a wooden-hulled vessel. Kosakowski replied that the "the only way to deal with it

is to remove it and replace what is rotten." He'd recommended to Walbridge that the shipyard staff examine the rest of the boat to see how far the degradation extended and to dig out the severest sections of the rot, replacing it with new white oak planking and frame pieces.

"Did you make recommendations to Walbridge or anyone else on board this vessel to remove more planks and see how far this goes?" Carroll asked.

"I believe I did and it was very quickly shot down by the captain," Kosakowski answered. Did Walbridge give a reason? "That it would have involved a significant amount of time and money, and both were not budgeted."

The commander asked what would be the risk of not removing more planks to see how extensive the rot was in the ship.

"The risk of not investigating further is being ignorant of something that is widespread throughout the boat," Kosakowski said. He also noted that rotted frames would allow the boat to "work" more than normal at sea, meaning the wooden members would flex and separate excessively, potentially opening seams enough to let in water. There was a chance that the rotten wood could allow a plank on the exterior of the hull to "spring," that is, to break away completely and open a large hole in the ship, he said.

Coast Guard inspectors had visited the shipyard to inspect other maintenance work done on the *Bounty* during the haul-out, primarily the movement of fuel and water tanks to new locations in the ship, so Carroll asked whether Kosakowski had mentioned the wood rot to them. When Kosakowski said no, Carroll wanted to know why not.

"I believe the owner's representative is kind of the extent of my debt," Kosakowski said. "That's who I answer to, the owner's representative and my boss." He informed his boss at the shipyard, Kosakowski said, and he was shocked that the *Bounty* had so much rot in wood that the Boothbay shipyard had installed during the *Bounty*'s 2006 yard period. Kosakowski did allow that, in hindsight, he should have alerted the Coast Guard.

Walbridge and Kosakowski agreed to treat some of the rotten wood found on the framing inside the ship with a chemical application that can stop the rotting process, though Kosakowski told the panel that such treatments are an imperfect solution, because the chemical often does not penetrate far enough to reach all the rot.

"The plan was to treat them [the rotten areas exposed inside the ship] in some way. I missed about a day and a half of work and when I came back they had painted with what I believed to be just regular white enamel paint over the framing, to receive the new planks," Kosakowski said.

"The white paint was put over the rotted frames?" Carroll asked.

"Yes, by the *Bounty* crew," the shipwright said.

"Was that good? Was that bad?" Carroll asked.

"I would say that it probably did not have an impact on what was in the frame."

As Kosakowski described in detail the visible rot and Walbridge's declining to explore how far it went, Dina Christian was visibly upset and being consoled by her husband and their attorneys. The shipwright explained how he and his team did the work that Walbridge wanted, which amounted to putting new wood on top of what everyone knew to be frames that were rotten to some extent, but no one knew how far the rot went. Though he was critical of Walbridge's actions regarding the rotten wood, Kosakowski told Carroll that he was comfortable with the repairs done at the shipyard—a seeming contradiction that Carroll had trouble understanding.

"Say that again? The repair that was done, you were comfortable with the repair?" Carroll asked. "You were comfortable with taking a new plank and putting it onto a frame that has decay and had been painted with just paint?"

"That's correct," Kosakowski said. Saying otherwise, of course, would have left him and the shipyard that employs him potentially liable if their work were determined to be a cause of the sinking. "Given what we were allowed to do, [the repairs] wouldn't have been a first choice by any means, but I thought they were more than adequate."

Kosakowski went on to recall that he emphasized to Walbridge that it was unsafe to take the *Bounty* to sea without removing more planks to explore the extent of the wood rot, and that Walbridge shut him down with assurances that he knew the rot was not so bad, and besides, he had neither the time nor the money to address it then. The testimony was damning and had everyone at the hearings on the edge of their seats.

No one else was present for the conversation, the shipwright stated, a fact that would lead Svendsen to prod him later about the discussion in

which his captain was said to be terrified. Did he ever think to talk with Walbridge and the shipyard owner together? No. Did he ever have a conference call with Walbridge and Hansen? No. With Kosakowski already seeming to cover for himself and the shipyard by saying he was satisfied with the work they did but still extremely concerned for the ship's welfare, some crew members were speculating that the whole conversation never happened.

Kosakowski's testimony that Walbridge was "terrified" by the rotting wood gained considerable attention at the hearing, but *Bounty* crew members later disputed that assessment in their testimony. "Terrified" is a word they could not imagine applying to Walbridge, especially when simply standing in a shipyard and talking about a rather common problem among wooden vessels, several crew testified. Cleveland and Groves told the author that Walbridge wasn't terrified, but he was "pissed off" that such new wood was rotting.

Was Kosakowski making up the whole thing to cover for the shipyard letting the *Bounty* sail with rotten frames—wood that the shipyard had installed itself and that was rotting far earlier than would be expected? But on the other hand, would the rotten frames have even become known after the sinking if Kosakowski hadn't brought it up with Coast Guard investigators? If he and the shipyard were worried about culpability—worried enough to commit perjury—why not let the issue die quietly instead of volunteering it to the panel?

There was little doubt, however, that the *Bounty* did have extensive rotten wood in October 2012. Kosakowski presented the Coast Guard panel with numerous photographs and even the box of pieces of the rotten wood that were removed from the ship. In addition to typical wet and soft rot, Kosakowski also found areas of a more unusual dry rot that left the wood looking charred and blackened. After going through all the photographs and discussing them, Carroll asked whether Kosakowski was surprised that it took twenty-six photographs to document only the damage that was visible without more exploration. He said he was not. He kept the samples, he said, because it "struck me as important material."

"Were you worried about covering your butt a little bit?" Carroll asked him directly.

"I don't remember thinking that," he replied.

Chapter 32

NEVER CROSS THE T

THE NEXT WITNESS was Joe Jakamovicz, a genial white-haired man who knows the art of boat working intimately and enjoys educating everyone else about it. He worked at the Boothbay shipyard the last time *Bounty* came in for maintenance but is now semiretired. He recalled that when the boat arrived in winter 2006, Walbridge told him the ship was so leaky that he was pumping thirty thousand gallons an hour.

"I was flabbergasted," he said. "This guy must be crazy."

But when the *Bounty* was hauled out of the water and drained, Jakamovicz was astounded at the amount of water pouring out and knew that Walbridge's estimate was on target. He also saw that the bottom was all wormy, riddled with holes. Robert Hansen was present and authorized extensive repairs. Hansen had the wormy wood saved and made into gift clocks for many of the *Bounty* crew and other friends. Jakamovicz still has his.

Hansen ended up spending about $250,000 to repair planking and frames in 2006, Jakamovicz testified. He also worked on the *Bounty* in 2010, when he saw that the keel still had an eight-inch "hog"—a gap that develops in the middle of the keel, pulling away from the hull—he had spotted in 2006. The hog was still there in 2012 when he helped haul the boat out of the water, he said. Hogs are a natural development

for old wooden boats, but if not fixed they can weaken the vessel, he explained.

"A hog means a vessel is getting tired. It warns you to be careful about what you do with the vessel," he said. "When you take a boat with a tired backbone to sea, it's going to work more. And when it works more, you take on more water."

When shown the pictures of wood rot that Kosakowski took, Jakamovicz said the rot was concerning, he said, but not the worst he's seen. While he praised Kosakowski's abilities, Jakamovicz pointed out that he has forty years' experience to Kosakowski's five or six. "This is the worst *he's* seen, but I've seen worse," he said.

Still, Jakamovicz acknowledged that Kosakowski was right to be concerned and that Jakamovicz had not personally inspected or helped repair the *Bounty* in 2012. From what he saw in his work to haul the ship out for maintenance, Jakamovicz said, he thought "in calm and reasonable conditions the vessel would not have a problem."

Later in his testimony, NTSB investigator Rob Jones asked Jakamovicz whether that meant he thought it was safe for the *Bounty* to proceed in the condition he had seen in October 2012, without even knowing of the rot depicted in the photographs.

"Oh, I had no idea it was going to go into a hurricane," he replied.

Jakamovicz also confirmed that if there was any question about hidden rot, "you gotta take the plank off." But he also supported Kosakowski's story when he explained there had been times when a Coast Guard inspector came by and told him to remove planks and inspect for rot.

"I said, 'You're talking to the wrong guy,'" he recalled. "'Talk to the owner or the owner's representative, and if they say do it, I know I'll get paid.'"

Jakamovicz related that he had talked to Walbridge extensively about the need to better ventilate the boat, because allowing humid air, such as that found in Florida and other common stops for the *Bounty*, contributed to the dry, charred-looking rot that Kosakowski had seen inside the ship. He said he never saw any efforts to provide better ventilation.

Walbridge told him in 2012 that his current crew was the best he'd ever had, Jakamovicz said. Was the boat well maintained? Jones asked.

"They were doing the best they could," he said.

Jakamovicz was asked about his reaction when learning that *Bounty* was in Hurricane Sandy.

"Oh, my God. I would keep track of the *Bounty* through the years. On that Friday, I looked at the Web site and saw it was in New London. I thought, 'Oh good, they'll stay in New London or close off the coast.' When I saw it on Monday, I was flabbergasted. No idea why they would do that."

After his testimony, Jakamovicz told the author that he hopes the *Bounty* tragedy does not prompt the government to overregulate and make it impossible to sail tall ships in an authentic manner.

"But the owners and captains also have a responsibility not to needlessly endanger their ships and crew, and put rescuers in danger," he said.

DAVID WYMAN, THE surveyor hired by the HMS *Bounty* Organization over the years to inspect the ship, document its condition, and make recommendations for improvement, testified that he thought the wood rot depicted in the photos was "relatively minor." His testimony was undercut, however, when Carroll asked him whether his most recent survey of the ship in 2012 was completed. No, Wyman explained, he started it but did not get to complete the survey. The documentation provided to the panel was only his informal notes from the partial survey, not a final report.

Are you in the habit of sending your informal notes to clients before completing a final report? No, of course not, Wyman said. "Then why does the notation on the notes say '*Bounty* LLC' at the bottom?" Carroll demanded. Wyman was flustered and couldn't explain why, finally saying maybe he did give the notes to Hansen. That agitated Hansen and his attorney, both of them leaping out of their chairs to talk to the HMS *Bounty* Organization lawyers at the table in front of them.

"Sit down!" Carroll barked at them. He continued grilling Wyman and then handed the questioning over to attorney Jacob Shisha, representing the Christians. Shisha asked whether Wyman had spoken about his testimony with Hansen or the HMS *Bounty* Organization before the

hearings. When Wyman said yes, he had had a conference call with them in the past week, the normally calm and cool Carroll looked as if he might explode.

"As a witness in a Coast Guard hearing, you had a conference call with the attorneys for a party in interest?" he asked, the anger and incredulity hidden not at all.

"They called me and wanted to talk, yes," Wyman said.

A red-faced Carroll immediately ended the hearings for the day and stormed out a side door.

OTHER ISSUES CAME to the fore during testimony, with the Christians' attorneys at times going on a fishing expedition to inquire about anything that might conceivably have contributed to the sinking of the ship. Some of the inquiries obviously were pertinent, however, and of interest to the Coast Guard panel. There was considerable curiosity about the specifics of how the ship's hull was caulked by the *Bounty* crew in Boothbay, including exactly what method was used and what products were used to seal the seams. Testimony from several witnesses established that a window glazing and sealant sold under the brand name DAP 33, commonly available in retail stores, was used to seal the seams below the waterline after the cotton and oakum were hammered in. Kosakowski noted that the shipyard does not use DAP 33 because it does not consider the product appropriate for underwater use, even though it can cost one-tenth that of seam compounds specifically made for boat hulls.

The shift in ballast during the 2012 dry-dock work also became an issue. Testimony from *Bounty* crew indicated that they moved approximately five thousand pounds of lead ballast farther aft, but that apparently was in violation of the "stability letter" issued by the Coast Guard in 2012. The stability letter was a routine directive issued by the Coast Guard after an inspection, stating that the vessel is "stable" as currently configured but prohibiting the addition or removal of ballast, or any other changes that might affect the vessel's weight or stability, unless the Coast Guard is notified so it can inspect the ship's stability again. The ballast shift in the 2012 dry-dock period was not reported to the Coast

Guard. The testimony also indicated that the ballast—mostly lead bars weighing about thirty-five pounds each, but also some loose pieces of lead scrap—was not secured to keep it from moving when the ship rolled. The movement of the water and fuel tanks also affected the ship's stability and was not reported.

The attorneys for the Christian family suggested that the relocation of the fuel tanks and ballast caused additional, and previously unseen, stresses on the *Bounty*'s hull, which was exacerbated by the unsecured ballast shifting and possibly slamming against the planks as the ship rolled in heavy seas.

The bilge pumps and the rate of water intake for the *Bounty* were another line of inquiry. The *Bounty* had long been known as a leaky ship, but the Coast Guard panel and the attorneys wanted know just how leaky it was in October 2012, and how well the bilge pumps were working. Svendsen testified that it was normal, under typical sailing conditions, for the *Bounty* to run its bilge pumps every two to four hours to empty water from the ship. Normal for the *Bounty*, maybe, but not for other sailing ships, witnesses said.

"In my experience in sailing ships, daily bilge pumping is normal, but every two to four hours is excessive," Kosakowski said.

The bilge pumps were running nonstop by October 28, but still weren't able to keep up with the water coming in, according to several witnesses. A great many questions were aimed at trying to determine why the primary bilge pumps, and then the auxiliary hydraulic pumps, could not keep the ship free of water, but no conclusion was reached during the hearing. It was clear, however, that Walbridge and other crew members knew that the bilge pumps were not working properly when the ship sailed from New London.

The backup gas-powered pump, known as the trash pump because it is designed to move some solid material along with the water, also received considerable attention. It was the pump of last resort, similar to the emergency dewatering pumps that the Coast Guard drops to ships in distress, and it had been run only one time. The previous year, when the *Bounty* sailed to Ireland, authorities there inspected the ship and wanted to see the crew test the pump. It worked fine then, but afterward Wal-

bridge ordered that it be sealed in a plastic container and not used except in an emergency. Walbridge preferred not to overtax equipment with periodic testing or unnecessary usage. When engineer Chis Barksdale first came aboard, Walbridge told him his practice was not to alternate the two generators, putting equal stress and run time on them as was common practice for ships, but to use the port generator almost exclusively.

And what about the ship's engineer? Chris Barksdale had been recommended by Svendsen and had some prior experience working with small boats, but when the *Bounty* hit the hurricane, crew members testified, he was largely out of commission with seasickness. In the hours when the *Bounty*'s fate would be determined by whether the crew could get the bilge pumps and generators working properly, the engineer was mostly out of the picture, spending a good deal of his time on the weather deck throwing up. Other crew members were left to struggle with the machinery below, to no avail. In eight hours in the engine room, Sanders said he saw Barksdale come and go a few times but spend no significant time working on the machinery there. Furthermore, Barksdale was not a licensed engineer, a point NTSB investigator Jones seemed to find an important failing.

With multiple stories of crew falling asleep in the most harrowing conditions before the *Bounty* went down, the panel also addressed whether the *Bounty* crew was fatigued before they even set sail into Hurricane Sandy. They had sailed from Boothbay to New London, worked hard to provide a day sail for the Navy sailors and then toured their submarine, and then they left port that same night to go to sea and try to avoid a hurricane. Why not get some rest and set sail the next day? Because Walbridge would never set sail on a Friday, Faunt explained. It was an old sailor's superstition and Walbridge took it seriously. They had to either leave Thursday evening or wait until Saturday, which Walbridge thought would put them behind schedule for St. Petersburg and make the hurricane more difficult to outrun.

The investigators also were keenly interested in the meeting Walbridge held with the crew before leaving New London, the one in which he said they were going to sea near a hurricane and any crew members

could leave without it being held against them. Crew had uniformly cited that meeting as evidence that Walbridge was being honest and reasonable with them, letting them make their own decision. The Coast Guard panel and NTSB investigator, not to mention the Christians' attorneys, did not view the meeting in the same way. Perhaps because they are older and have more life experience than much of the *Bounty* crew, they questioned the witnesses regarding whether Walbridge was truly asking for informed consent or was only giving them half of the story and allowing them to fall back on youthful enthusiasm, naïveté, loyalty to one another, and peer pressure. Crew members' memories differed on exactly what Walbridge told them about the scope of Hurricane Sandy, but most made clear that Walbridge did not tell them all that was known about the storm on the day he held that meeting. Several crew members testified that they were excited to go into some rough weather with the *Bounty*.

Testimony from crew members and HMS *Bounty* Organization administrator Tracie Simonin established that if any crew members had chosen to leave that day, they would have had to pay their own way home, as was customary anytime someone left the ship. Third mate Cleveland did point out that the crew had a fund, accumulated from tip jars when tourists came on board, that could have been used to pay for someone's departure from the ship.

Perhaps the most maddening question for the Coast Guard panel— even more than the decision to go to sea from New London—was Walbridge's turn to the southwest, directly across the path of Hurricane Sandy. Carroll and the attorneys questioned Svendsen and other crew members about how well they were tracking the storm's projected path, and all agreed that Walbridge and his senior crew were staying on top of the latest forecasts. They knew where the storm was projected to go. They knew it would turn west toward the New England coast. The *Bounty*'s plan, Walbridge had told his crew, was to go southeast, wait for the storm to make its move to the east or west, and then go on the other side of it. When they were at sea, Walbridge knew without a doubt that Hurricane Sandy was projected to turn west.

But on October 27, when the ship was north of the storm, Walbridge

altered his course to go southwest, cutting across the projected path of Hurricane Sandy. Why in the world would he do that? Kosakowski had already warned him to take it easy on the ship, not to sail in rough weather. That was akin to a car mechanic saying, "You have bald tires and bad brakes, but if you insist you can't afford to fix it, at least drive carefully on the way home." One investigator later told the author that deciding to turn west into the storm's path was like trying to outrun a train at a rail crossing, but instead of a sports car you're driving an old bus that sputters and breaks down all the time.

Svendsen testified that despite the wealth of data fed to Walbridge from meteorology services and the HMS *Bounty* Organization—which had never seen fit to send storm data directly to Walbridge before—the captain disagreed with their forecasts and thought the hurricane would follow the jet stream and not hit landfall as far south as predicted, giving him more time to slip to the southwest before Sandy made its move west. Svendsen said he knew the turn would put the ship in the path of the hurricane but trusted Walbridge's judgment.

Walbridge's desire to get to the southwest could be supported to a limited extent by long-held seafaring strategy. *The American Practical Navigator*, a book first published in 1802 by the early American mathematician Nathaniel Bowditch, and updated extensively to reflect modern technology, is still considered the bible of navigation. It teaches that in the northern hemisphere a vessel is safer on the western side of a storm's track. Moving to the southwest was a by-the-book maneuver in that sense.

"The safest procedure with respect to tropical cyclones is to avoid them," the guide states. "If action is taken sufficiently early, this is simply a matter of setting a course that will take the vessel well to one side of the probable track of the storm, and then continuing to plot the positions of the storm center as given in the weather bulletins, revising the course as needed."

If the ship is found to be within the storm area, the proper action to take depends in part upon its position relative to the storm center and its direction of travel, the guide says.

"The part to the left of the storm track is called the less dangerous

semicircle, or navigable semicircle. In this part, the wind is decreased by the forward motion of the storm, and the wind blows vessels away from the storm track (in the forward part)," it explains. "Because of the greater wind speed in the dangerous semicircle [to the right of the storm track], the seas are higher than in the less dangerous semicircle."

So heading for the less dangerous semicircle was not a crazy idea. But Carroll and Jones (not to mention scores of would-be sailing experts) implied that Walbridge made a fatal error by gambling that he could carry out that maneuver in a very troubled ship before Sandy caught up with him. In addition, the Bowditch tome does not instruct captains to take sailing vessels directly across the *path* of a tropical storm, with relatively little sea room to maneuver between land and storm; it advises that the western quadrant of a storm is the best place to be, but it does not condone the notion of trying to outrun it in order to get there—especially when the ship can continue out to sea or otherwise away from the storm.

In addition, NOAA's Hurricane Center explicitly warns mariners to "Never Cross the T":

"Never plan to cross the track (cross the 'T') of a hurricane," NOAA states in many publications and on its Web site, along with other specific, detailed advice to mariners on navigating near hurricanes. "Done out of respect for the negative effects that heavy weather places on vessel speed/handling, sudden accelerations in hurricane motion can ultimately place a vessel in conditions not originally expected, thereby resulting in disaster. Adjustments to course & speed in order to remain clear of the danger area in a hurricane are the most prudent navigation decisions a mariner can make in these instances."

NOAA's position on Walbridge's move could not be clearer. The hurricane experts do not merely advise against crossing the hurricane's projected path and leave the final decision to the captain. They say "never."

The reasoning behind the move was not explained to the crew at the time. Deckhand Joshua Scornavacchi testified that he heard the storm had turned east, so they were going west. But even if Walbridge had told him before leaving New London that they were going to cut into the storm's path, Scornavacchi says he probably would have stayed. "I really like being there. I like the people and would trust that they could handle

it," he said. "Knowing that we were going to cut in front of the storm would have made me question it, but I probably would have stayed. You know, loyalty to the crew."

Deckhand Jessica Hewitt made a similar statement, saying a plan to turn west would have given her pause, reminding her of the *Fantome* disaster, but "maybe he was trying to get us closer to land." She explained that maybe some of the information available at the time should have set off red flags for her, but, "I trust the people I work for. I guess you would call it oblivious innocence."

That unrelenting trust and admiration for Walbridge were noteworthy throughout the proceedings. Every single crew member, and nearly every other witness—including those who disagreed with Walbridge's judgment in some key areas—had only high praise for the man as a captain and a leader. He was experienced, levelheaded, and extremely wise in the ways of the sea, according to everyone who testified that they knew him. Even those few who did not praise him did not have anything bad to say about him as a mariner.

The endless praise for Walbridge, even after witnesses had established a litany of what seemed to be poor decisions in his last days, was becoming an issue in itself. In breaks during the hearings, attorneys, reporters, and others in the hearings were heard expressing wonder at how the crew could be so unceasingly complimentary of a captain who had sailed them into a hurricane and lost the ship, his own life, and the life of a crew member.

Wearing a yellow sweater over a black dress, the perky but teary Hewitt had been testifying for more than an hour and the clock was moving past six p.m. Everyone in the hearings seemed to be getting tired and perhaps a bit testy, but Ralph J. Mellusi, one of the attorneys for the Christians, wanted to finally address the consistent and unmitigated praise of Walbridge from every single crew member who testified.

"This captain was intimately familiar with his vessel, had been aboard many years," Mellusi began in his methodic, carefully measured way of speaking. "Makes a decision to go to sea, with a group of young people, puts them in harm's way. The vessel proves to be totally unsuitable for the weather conditions that they encounter, pumping is not working, water is coming on at an excessive rate . . ." Carroll interrupted

him to urge that Mellusi ask a question, but the attorney replied he was getting to it. "Generators are failing, the vessel is . . ."

The HMS *Bounty* Organization attorneys objected at that point and Carroll agreed. When Mellusi tried to respond, Carroll shut him down with a sharp, "Don't argue!" and instructed the attorney to ask a question rather than making a statement. Mellusi, not one to back down easily, continued.

"The vessel sinks, he loses his life, Claudene loses hers, and here in this proceeding, crew member after crew member heaps praises on him. Why is that?" After more hectoring from Carroll about whether that was an appropriate question for Hewitt to answer, Mellusi continued with his thought. "Was he *that* charismatic that people cannot criticize him?"

Hewitt asked, "What's your question? Just what I think of him?"

"No criticism of him from the crew, in spite of a voyage that ended horrendously," Mellusi said. In the overlap with Carroll telling her she didn't have to answer, Hewitt laughed slightly and answered, "That's awesome."

Carroll had reached his limit with the attorney and told him he was finished. Hewitt was dismissed and, as she left the witness table and headed toward the rear of the room, Dina Christian caught her eye. Dina was unhappy with Hewitt's testimony, growing increasingly angry as she listened, because she thought Hewitt had changed her story about Claudene's last moments—especially whether Claudene was clipped onto the jack line when Hewitt last saw her. An earlier statement to the investigators indicated Hewitt had last seen Claudene clipped in, which would have been disastrous as the ship rolled over, because she would find it nearly impossible to unclip from the line as she was dragged underwater. But in testifying before the panel, in tears, Hewitt said she could not remember whether Claudene was still clipped to the line when the ship rolled. "I wish I did remember," she said, her voice trembling.

As Hewitt walked past, Dina held her hand up to show her Claudene's ring, in a gesture meant to convey that Dina knew Hewitt had changed her story. Hewitt, misinterpreting the gesture as a wave for her to come over, went to Dina. She bent down and hugged the grieving mother, saying, "I'm glad you got the ring." In her anger, Dina was repulsed by

the hug and with fury in her eyes said to Hewitt, "How could you leave her there?" Hewitt quickly pulled away and hurried out of the room, sobbing. Dina turned in her seat to follow her all the way out, her eyes red with a look of barely contained rage.

Out of the meeting room, Hewitt met up with several other *Bounty* crew members and past crew. Some had not seen one another in weeks or months, and there was considerable crying, hugging, and praise for Hewitt's steadfast refusal to criticize Walbridge.

Her "That's awesome" comment was repeated many times, with approval.

CHAPTER 33

RECKLESSLY CAVALIER

A KEY QUESTION left for the Coast Guard investigation—and in the mind of the public—was whether Walbridge's decisions to go to sea during Hurricane Sandy and to turn directly into her path might have been made by another captain in a similar position. Even if they seemed to be mistakes in hindsight, might the captain of another tall sailing ship have made the same decisions for some reason?

Testimony provided by experienced captains of two other sailing ships answered those questions with alarming clarity. Consulting the captains of sailing ships similar to *Bounty*, rather than just any maritime expert, was important because tall sailing ships hold a certain mystery even to those experienced in more conventional ships. The decisions made by Walbridge might have seemed obviously in error to those with no experience on the sea or even those who sail other types of vessels, but was there some secret known to tall ship captains that could explain his decisions?

Apparently not. The Coast Guard panel first called on Daniel Moreland, captain of the *Picton Castle*, a three-masted barque 170 feet long and a hundred feet high, with a steel hull. The *Picton Castle* was in its home port of Nova Scotia—about sixteen hundred miles north of New London, Connecticut—in October, with the crew planning to leave Oc-

tober 19 for Bermuda. But Moreland and his colleagues were studying the weather reports and watching one hot spot in the south Atlantic that eventually turned into Hurricane Sandy, so they delayed their departure. As the hot spot grew into a larger storm, Moreland had to tell his crew they wouldn't be going anywhere for a while. Testifying by phone while his ship was in Tahiti, the site of the mutiny on the original *Bounty*, Moreland explained his decision.

"We're not going to go to sea and try dodging that hurricane," he recalled telling the crew. "It's very broad. It fills the whole Atlantic."

With twenty years sailing tall ships, Moreland was equally qualified and experienced as Walbridge, if not more. Carroll asked Moreland whether he agreed with Walbridge's statement that "a ship is safer at sea" than in port during a hurricane.

"No, I do not," Moreland said, explaining that the "safer at sea" theory is a holdover from two hundred years ago, when ships did not have many options for safe ports during a storm. Unlike past years, many ports today are positioned so that they can offer protection from much of the wind and sea surges of a hurricane, he explained, and there were plenty of options in the New London area for moving the *Bounty* to relative safety. He could have taken the ship to Mystic Seaport, Connecticut, or New Bedford, Massachusetts, Moreland said, but "in all likelihood" the *Bounty* would have been fine staying in New London.

Even if the ship is damaged in the port, that's better than being damaged at sea, he said. The Navy sometimes takes its ships to sea during a hurricane, he noted, but they are entirely different from the *Bounty*. Their ships are steel hulled, fast and maneuverable, and their mission is to remain combat ready at all times. In other words, he said, Navy ships can outrun a hurricane, and they have good reason to be out there. The *Bounty* couldn't and didn't.

Walbridge was a friend of about ten years, and Moreland said he respected his experience and skills as a mariner. That was why he reacted the way he did when he heard on October 26 or 27 that the *Bounty* was at sea in Hurricane Sandy.

"I was very surprised, even shocked," he said. "I can't imagine for the

life of me there would be any reason to head out under those forecasted conditions. If I had been aware of his plans, I would have called him and harangued him, said, 'What are you thinking?'"

Moreland had been aboard *Bounty* many times and knew her to be "extremely well built." His most recent visits left him impressed with the crew. The *Bounty*'s going down in a hurricane was not because of the type of ship she was, he told the Coast Guard panel. It was because she went into an enormously dangerous hurricane for no good reason. When asked about the specific track of Hurricane Sandy and *Bounty*'s path, Moreland responded that the hurricane was so big that the predicted path of the storm was almost irrelevant.

"Just being in the Atlantic was a bad idea," he said.

When an attorney representing the HMS *Bounty* Organization questioned Moreland and pressed him to admit that he didn't know Walbridge's thought process, he ended up with an even more enthusiastic criticism from Moreland.

"You don't know what Walbridge was thinking, do you?" the attorney asked.

The satellite phone crackled as Moreland shouted his response. "I don't know *what* he was thinking! I can't *begin to imagine* what he was thinking!"

Moreland went on to answer questions about the *Bounty* captain's judgment in proceeding toward Hurricane Sandy when his ship's systems were not functioning correctly. What if the bilge systems were not working properly, but he still went into a hurricane? "It would be unconscionable on a good day," Moreland said. What if the gasoline-powered pump had never been used? "We have an emergency gas pump on board and we use it for fire drills and we test it every few weeks. All this machinery works better if you actually work it. It's not right to not check your gear."

And what about the caulking job performed by the crew of the *Bounty* while in dry dock in Boothbay, Maine? Moreland explained that he had no knowledge of the caulking done at that time, but he was quite experienced in caulking procedures. The job is a hard one, he said, and he'd rather shoot himself before being a professional caulker. Alluding to

the fact that the *Bounty*'s caulking was performed largely by Bosun Laura Groves and other women on board, Mellusi, the attorney representing the Christians, asked whether it took a certain amount of upper-body strength to caulk properly.

"For a ship of the type and scale of the *Bounty*, the answer is yes. This is a big, heavy job for quarterbacks and fullbacks," Moreland replied. "It's a brutal thing, and at the end of the day your arms ache and your shoulders ache, and you're tired."

At one point in his testimony, Carroll asked Moreland whether he had ever received input from "management" regarding when to put to sea or how to plan a voyage. Unfortunately the captain did not understand the question, apparently because the satellite connection was imperfect, and he answered regarding whether other crew on the ship had input. Carroll just let it go and moved on.

CAPTAIN JAN MILES of the *Pride of Baltimore II*, a wooden-hulled topsail schooner 157 feet long and 107 feet tall, testified that he also was stunned to learn that Walbridge had set sail. Miles's ship rode out Hurricane Sandy docked in Baltimore. His ship was launched in 1988, the replacement for the original *Pride of Baltimore* that had sunk sank two years earlier in a storm, with the loss of the captain and three crew.

"I drew a blank. I couldn't understand it. I basically drew a blank," he said when asked what he thought on learning the *Bounty* was at sea. Given the accurate forecasts for the massive hurricane, "I was rather stunned at the idea she was out there," Miles said. "It's one of those questions that has no answer."

Miles told the Coast Guard panel that one of his goals is to expose his ship to the least amount of heavy weather possible. He said he had "no interest, no desire, no plan" to take the *Pride of Baltimore II* out with the storm bearing down.

Miles referred in his testimony to an open letter he wrote to Walbridge a month after learning that his friend and fellow captain had been lost at sea and the search for him was called off. He posted the letter on Facebook and did not try to temper his anger in writing to the ghost of

Walbridge. Miles stated publicly what many in the sailing community were saying privately:

"It has been a month now since the USCG stopped looking for you. Claudene is dead and *Bounty*, like you, is lost at sea as a result of your decision to sail directly toward Hurricane Sandy. . . . Why did you throw all caution away by navigating for a close pass of Hurricane Sandy? I was so surprised to discover that *Bounty* was at sea near Cape Hatteras and close to Hurricane Sandy Sunday night, October 28! That decision of yours was reckless in the extreme!

"The outcome of your action makes you the only captain of the current crop of long-experienced American maritime licensed sailing vessel masters actually willing to voyage anywhere near a hurricane! Did you not remember the fate of the *Fantome*? Like *Bounty* she was a slow, less-than-ten-knot-capable vessel under engine power. Not fast enough to run out of range of the reach of Hurricane Mitch. Additionally the master of *Fantome* had too much confidence in hurricane forecasting accuracy. Mitch made an unexpected left turn after consistent movement westward before slowing down to near stopped about the time *Fantome* made her run eastward from Belize trying to escape Mitch. A stationary hurricane is nearly impossible to predict future motion. To the best of anyone's knowledge [*Fantome* was lost with all hands.] Mitch ran right over her. You, on the other hand, maneuvered directly toward a very accurately forecast and steadily moving Hurricane Sandy with a slow-moving vessel of wood construction. *Fantome* was of metal. Also, *Bounty* is quite a bit smaller than *Fantome*. Still you aimed all but directly at Sandy. That was reckless, my friend! Was it wise or prudent to set off into the teeth of Sandy in *Bounty*? Did it make any sense at all? Virtually all of your professional friends and colleagues back here do not think so, not at all.

"You told everyone you were going east around Sandy. But you did not even try to do so. Your track line indicates unequivocally a trail all but directly toward Sandy. When I heard east around was the

strategy I immediately wondered about it. I am not the only one to know that *Bounty* is not highly powered with her engines. . . .

"An even more distressing puzzle is brought forth by *Bounty*'s steady movement directly at Sandy after you had abandoned your original notion of going east around. Friday October 26 forecasting confirmed an even higher confidence Hurricane Sandy would turn left after some more time going north. But *Bounty* continued straight southward! Why did you not turn for New York Harbor? . . . If *Bounty* were in the Inner Harbor of Baltimore by early Sunday she would have been sheltered from wind by all of those tall city buildings that ring the north side of the Inner Harbor. There would have been no sea action. Harbor water levels did indeed increase above normal, but only by 3–4 feet. *Bounty* would not have floated over any dock. Even if she had, the damage would unlikely be the loss of the ship and certainly not the loss of any life!

"So what was it you were thinking by not diverting toward shelter once you knew about the confirmed forecasting that not only continued to indicate Sandy going ashore in New Jersey but also Sandy would likely be the largest hurricane in some time? No slow boat was going to be speedy enough to get out of Sandy's long reach from where *Bounty* was on Friday. . . . Why did you persist in steering *Bounty* directly toward Sandy? Was it confidence in her physical strength after all of the rebuilding over the last several years? If that was the case, that is recklessly cavalier to the extreme! Not even the big powerful tug-and-barge combinations that regularly ply the East Coast were fooling around with facing Sandy! But you were. I find myself wondering again . . . what were you thinking?

"On top of this, you told folks during the southbound journey directly toward Sandy that it was safer to be at sea. Hmmm . . . an interesting and vague notion, that. It is true the U.S. Navy in Norfolk goes to sea ahead of an approaching hurricane. But they are high-endurance (high-speed) ships with mariners trained and contracted to go in the way of danger, not young keen professionals and volunteers on a harbor attractions vessel! . . .

"Yeah, you were a reckless man, Robin. I would not have con-

tinued to proceed as you did. Frankly, I do not know anyone with a lot of experience in large, slow (still faster than *Bounty*), strong, steel motor vessels like the powerful tug-and-barge combinations we see plying the East Coast [who] would have considered heading toward a hurricane like you did with Sandy . . . not only forecast as going ashore rather than turning toward sea . . . but also described as a "storm of the century." Those tug-and-barge operators would seek shelter inshore or not proceed to sea at all. I also do not know any sailing vessel masters that would head toward a hurricane as you did with hopes of negotiating a pass like two vessels meeting head-on. . . . I cannot imagine there was any reason existing that would force *Bounty* to directly approach a hurricane. Loss of *Bounty* is so permanent. No more voyages after losing the ship . . . don't you know!

"But the loss of life is the most tragic. You not only lost your own, you lost that of Claudene's. Hell, man, the *Bounty* can be replaced. But why ever risk loss when it is so much more important not to risk a crew member's life? Having *Bounty* remain in port, or seek port when it became evident Sandy was not going to turn eastward as most often hurricanes do, might have meant damage to *Bounty*, but unlikely any loss of life. If you found no dock willing to accommodate *Bounty* up the Delaware or in the Chesapeake Bay, put her in the mud and hang on. Doing that would mean no reason to fear sinking completely below water. Even if she were to roll on her side while aground she would not have sunk below the surface. Maybe she would have become a total loss, but the crew could remain sheltered in her hull, assuming there was no safe way to get off of her and ashore before high winds arrived. Putting *Bounty* aground for the winds of Sandy because of no dock option would have been a bold decision! . . .

"Robin, for all of the experience you have, it was recklessly poor judgment to have done anything but find a heavy-weather berth for your ship, rather than instead intentionally navigate directly toward Sandy with no thought given to deviate if the original plan of yours was not panning out. . . .

"While there are many memories I have of conversing with you

about things marine affecting what we do as masters of sailing vessels, we never discussed the topic of delivering on schedule as promised and the problems of failure to arrive as promised. This is coming oh so very much too late, but I feel compelled to share that during my many years as master of vessels, there has never been any pressure put on me to make sure promises of arrival were kept. What I was told is that safety was most important. Safety of the ship was desired. But safety of the crew was most essential. As a result I have been master aboard when I have had to inform the company the intended arrival would not occur as scheduled due to weather. Sometimes the weather concern involved a hurricane. Sometimes the concern was a cold front and resultant headwinds or a typical midlatitude low passing by. The decision we were going to be tardy to the destination port had to do with risk of damage to the ship. Preventing ship damage most often meant there would be little to no additional risk of injury to the crew and in the case of an inspected vessel also the passengers. Yep, unlike *Bounty*, most of the sail training vessels in America are certified and inspected for underway activities; several in the American fleet are certified for ocean service. Those that are wood built are pretty strong. Yet they avoid hurricanes. Being tardy always meant there would be another opportunity in the future. With *Bounty* now gone, with you and Claudene as well, there is no future to share with Claudene, with you, with *Bounty*, for all of us . . . for everyone.

"If confidence was the basis in your decisions, no ship is invulnerable. And in a career at sea one cannot avoid every gale or nasty storm—but you set out with the *Bounty* with whatever her strengths and weaknesses into the biggest one some of us have ever seen dominating the Western North Atlantic. Many stronger, faster ships than *Bounty* chose to stay in port for this one. What was your need?

"Well, my very recklessly cavalier friend, I cannot say I told you so. But I sure can say I am surprised! Not Robin! This stunt is so amateurish as to be off the scale! But stunning surprise of surprises! It is Robin! Heading directly at a hurricane in a small, slow boat. Instead of running and hiding . . . or not venturing out at all. You have provided everyone with a great deal of hurt and sadness and

consternation as well as a firestorm of gossip nearly full of blame and foolishness directed at the whole of our sailing community.

"That is an inestimably be-damned legacy, my friend."

AMID ALL THE condemnation of Walbridge's decisions, Miles had addressed what many thought to be the only explanation for why he would be so reckless: He said, "There has never been any pressure put on me to make sure promises of arrival were kept." Only two people could say with any certainty whether such pressure was exerted on the captain of the *Bounty*.

Alas, Walbridge did not survive to say whether he felt pressure to make the promised arrival date for the rebirth of the *Bounty* and to protect a ship the owner wanted to sell, or whether he put that pressure on himself. And Hansen pled the Fifth.

EPILOGUE

SUPERSTORM SANDY BECAME the deadliest and most destructive hurricane of 2012, killing at least 285 people in seven countries and causing damage estimated at $75 billion, making it the second-costliest hurricane in U.S. history. Only Hurricane Katrina in 2005 caused more damage. When it was off the East Coast, Hurricane Sandy was the largest Atlantic hurricane ever recorded, with winds covering an area eleven hundred miles across. Twenty-four states were affected, with New York and New Jersey the hardest hit. In New Jersey, more than two million households lost power, and 346,000 homes were destroyed. Thirty-seven people were killed in the state, and Governor Chris Christie called the damage "almost incalculable . . . probably going to be the worst we've ever seen." New York City was hit hard by the storm surge on Monday, October 29, the day the *Bounty* sank, with flooding subway tunnels, streets, and buildings. Tunnels into the city were closed for two days, as was the New York Stock Exchange. Homes and businesses were destroyed, and fifty-three people died in New York. The name Sandy was retired because of the storm's impact, never to be used for another hurricane.

The *Bounty* rests in the Graveyard of the Atlantic, approximately thirteen thousand feet deep—more than two and a half miles—far too deep for divers to visit the shipwreck. The *Titanic*, by comparison, was found by unmanned exploration vehicles at a depth of about 12,600 feet.

The exact coordinates of the shipwreck are not known, because the *Bounty* could have drifted laterally for some distance as it sank from the last-known position on the surface.

Cleveland and Groves are still dating and sailing together on another ship, the *Sørlandet* from Norway, a three-masted ship like the *Bounty*, and the oldest fully rigged ship in the world still in operation. Soon after surviving the *Bounty* tragedy, they both got blue ribbons tattooed around their upper arms in tribute to their beloved captain. Groves also has another special tattoo on her left upper arm and shoulder to remember Claudene Christian. It depicts Christian as a mermaid, blowing wind into the sails of the *Bounty*, which she holds in the palm of her hand. Groves speaks highly of Christian, and the loss of her friend affected her deeply.

Other crew members also found new ships and returned to the sea, while some needed more time to deal with the physical and emotional injuries from their experience on the *Bounty*. Hewitt, for instance, had to take time off to recover from the mental distress and the loss of two people she held dear. Asked in the Coast Guard hearings whether she had looked at the projected path of Hurricane Sandy on Saturday, when the *Bounty* turned westward across the storm's path, Hewitt began to cry—not for the first time during her testimony—and said she had not been able to look at the path of the storm since her ordeal. She and Salapatek ended their relationship in the months after the *Bounty* sank, primarily because they had to heal in their own ways and Salapatek needed to be with his family. They are still close.

Joshua Scornavacchi, the deckhand who heard God tell him to jump from the mast as he was trying to escape the *Bounty*, wears a small wooden pulley block around his neck as a reminder of the ship's rigging.

Walbridge's widow believes her husband went down with his ship, not on purpose but most likely trying to help Claudene Christian escape.

The captain is greatly admired by those who knew him. Cleveland remembers Walbridge as the most influential person in his adult life, the person he learned the most from aside from his parents. Cleveland grew up on the *Bounty*, he says, becoming a man and a responsible adult, learning what he was capable of and determining his life's purpose. He

wants to make sure Walbridge's dedication to the craft and traditions of sailing live on. "He deserves that." Hewitt, Svendsen, and other crew members passionately agree.

Wyman, the architect who had such a long association with the *Bounty* and was a close friend of Walbridge's, told Cleveland about having a dream that the captain escaped the sinking of the *Bounty* by taking the dinghy—the small rubber boat used for man-overboard rescues or getting to shore when the ship is at anchor—from the ship and taking it ashore somewhere, heaven maybe. The idea makes Cleveland laugh, because Walbridge thought the boat was just a nuisance, a pain to store on deck and deploy. Cleveland loves the irony that the captain hated the dinghy but had to take it for his final voyage. A skilled amateur painter, Cleveland created a depiction of the dream that he sees as a tribute to the man he admired so much.

The *Bounty* crew remains steadfast in their defense of Walbridge, still refusing to criticize the decisions that led to the sinking. Cleveland's attitude is typical: He explains that, if Walbridge were alive today and proposed sailing into another hurricane or storm, Cleveland would go with him, because the outcome of the *Bounty*'s last voyage was not inevitable. The loss of the ship and two lives was the result of a series of problems, he says, and that sequence of events does not have to repeat itself. If just a few things had turned out differently, the *Bounty* would have made it through Hurricane Sandy, he insists. In the weeks after the sinking, Groves was visiting friends in Miami when she encountered a young man who, upon learning that she and her friends were part of the tall ship community, started talking smack about the *Bounty* and Walbridge, and making fun of a sailor who had recently fallen from the rigging on another ship. Groves made sure to rip off his bike helmet before decisively beating him down. "I'm glad Dan wasn't there. He would have killed him," Groves says.

Ashley DeRamus and her family were heartbroken to hear of the *Bounty*'s loss, and particularly the deaths of Christian and Walbridge. They remember Christian as an especially warm, loving person, and Walbridge as a complete professional whose heart seemed to melt around Ashley. In the months after the *Bounty* sank, the captains of six other tall

ships invited Ashley to sail with them on the Great Lakes for the reenactment of the War of 1812, the event to which Walbridge intended to sail the *Bounty* with Ashley.

An immersion suit worn by one of the *Bounty* survivors hangs on the wall in the swimmer's workshop at the Coast Guard base in Elizabeth City, North Carolina, the feet sliced open to release trapped water. With the particulars of the *Bounty* rescue written on the suit, it is a point of pride for the rescue crews, hanging alongside life preservers and other items that denote dozens of noteworthy rescues from recent years. The crews involved in the rescue, and particularly the swimmers, are remarkably modest about their accomplishments. Pilots Wes McIntosh and Mike Myers remember the *Bounty* as an especially moving event for them because of the time they spent bonding with Svendsen on the radio. "There's never a time I close my eyes and think of the crew of the *Bounty* and think anything but highly about them," Myers told the author. "I think they did a remarkable job, posturing themselves for it to turn out as well as it did, going back as far as their training."

Dropmaster Jonathan Sageser, on the second Herc sent to help the *Bounty*, says every mission from now on will be compared to the *Bounty*. Bad weather? Airsick? Logistical challenges? All measured now by the yardstick of the *Bounty*. *How does it compare to the* Bounty? *Was it worse than the* Bounty? The magnitude of the weather is what people can't understand, he says. He can talk of thirty-foot waves and sea spray obscuring everything, but it is hard to understand unless you were looking down at that water, he says. Flight mechanic Neil Moulder agrees, saying the hoist cam video from his Jayhawk—used in television reports after the rescue—doesn't do justice to what the seas were really like. The reality was far worse than it looks on the video, he says. In his fifteen years of rescuing people, Moulder has never met one of them afterward, including the *Bounty* survivors. If he ever gets the chance, he says he wants to apologize to Adam Prokosh for yelling at him to get out of his basket faster when he had a back injury.

Herc pilot Peyton Russell and flight mechanic Michael Lufkin from the Jayhawk piloted by Cerveny and Peña were invited to the annual meeting of Tall Ships America in February 2013, just three months after

the *Bounty* tragedy. They were honored to be feted by the tall ship community and to receive an award on behalf of the Coast Guard, but Russell was most moved by meeting the four members of the *Bounty* crew who attended—Chief Mate John Svendsen, Bosun Laura Groves, Third Mate Dan Cleveland, and cook Jessica Black. At the awards dinner, he and Lufkin were seated at a table with all four of them. No one had warned them that they would be seated with the survivors, and as they were fixed-wing crew who normally do not interact with survivors or receive much of the public glory, the evening was memorable. "I'm going to retire from the military in three years, and I would say that the pinnacle of my search and rescue career will not be the scary stuff. It will be that dinner," Russell told the author. "Talking to that person and knowing that that young girl is someday going to have kids and we, as an organization, had a small part in her being here, to someday have kids."

After the *Bounty* rescue, a Coast Guard admiral visited E-city and asked Russell whether he would do it all over again. "Absolutely not, would I ever, *ever* volunteer to do something like that," he replied. "But of course, if I was on duty, if my number was up, I'd go out there again." He heard snide comments from other pilots that he had gotten lucky with the big, glamorous assignment, but he told them that anytime he's on duty, they're welcome to come take his place. SAR isn't fun, he told them. It means people are dying or dead already, or at least people are suffering. SAR is their duty, Russell says, but he'd much rather be on a training mission. SAR is not glamorous, it's not glorious, and it's always a sad, potentially tragic situation, he says.

Swimmer Casey Hanchette and Flight Mechanic Ryan Parker say the memory of Claudene Christian stays with them, and they deeply regret not being able to save her. They both hope that bringing her home at least provided some small measure of solace to her family.

Dina Christian filed a lawsuit against owner Robert Hansen and the HMS *Bounty* Organization in May 2013, seeking $90 million—$40 million for predeath conscious pain and suffering and $50 million in punitive damages. Calling the tragedy "the greatest mismatch between a 'vessel' and a peril of the sea that would ever occur or could ever be imagined," the lawsuit alleges that Walbridge negligently and recklessly sailed

into danger knowing the ship was in poor condition, the crew was un-qualified, and that he was violating common rules of marine safety—all with Hansen's knowledge.

The Christians struggle daily with the loss of Claudene, and they don't expect to ever get over losing her. They find the slightest comfort in Claudene's favorite teddy bear from her childhood, Duffordson. Claudene had collected many stuffed animals, but Duffordson was her favorite and the one chosen to accompany her to college at USC. It wasn't long, how-ever, before Claudene brought Duffordson home to stay with her parents, explaining that because USC plays the University of California Golden Bears in football, anything resembling a bear on the USC campus was subject to theft and abuse. "You can't imagine what the boys would do to a teddy bear like Duffordson," she told them. So Duffordson stayed home and was still there when Claudene set sail on the *Bounty*, because she also worried that the ship might be too dangerous for him. After Claudene's death, Dina and Rex gave Duffordson a more prominent role in their lives, keeping him close at all times. He went to the Coast Guard hearings with them and stayed in the hotel room, and at home he spends his days sunning in a window, where they can see him often.

At night, Duffordson beds down between Dina and Rex. Occasion-ally, Rex will talk with Duffordson before going to sleep. It makes Dina smile.

"I don't say so to him, but I know he's talking to Claudene," she says.

ACKNOWLEDGMENTS

DOCUMENTING THE STORY of the *Bounty* was an honor, and as with most endeavors there are many people who deserve recognition and thanks. First I thank my dear wife, Caroline, and my son, Nicholas, for their support. I wish to acknowledge Peter James Morrow, a fan of my earlier work who recognized before I did that the story of the *Bounty* was well suited for my style. Thank you, Peter, for not letting this one slip by me.

Special thanks, and more, go to Dan Cleveland and Laura Groves for sharing their stories with me, a complete stranger asking them to trust that I would do right by them and the people they loved. Though parts of the *Bounty* story are difficult to reconcile, I have the utmost admiration for Dan's and Laura's professionalism as mariners, their work in the *Bounty*'s darkest hours, and their loyalty to their captain. I also wish to thank the other crew members who spoke with me, including Jessica Hewitt, Jessica Black, Joshua Scornavacchi, and John Svendsen. I also thank Dina Christian for sharing her memories of Claudene. I wish them all the best.

I thank former *Bounty* crew member Caz Ludtke for providing photos from her time on the ship. Bert Rogers was helpful in introducing a nonsailor to the tall ship sailing community, and I thank you. I also extend a special thank-you to my friend and "senior intern" Michael Barrett for his research assistance. Your contribution was significant and I appreciate it.

ACKNOWLEDGMENTS

This book would not have been complete without the cooperation and substantial assistance of the United States Coast Guard. All of the Coast Guard personnel who participated in the *Bounty* rescue were consummate professionals, and I thank each of you for sharing your stories with me. In addition, I wish to single out Lt. Jon McCormick and Lt. Jane Peña, who were exceptionally helpful in facilitating access to the crew at Elizabeth City and providing additional information. I thank Capt. Joseph P. Kelly, commander of Air Station Elizabeth City, for welcoming me to his base and providing complete support.

The Coast Guard hearings on the *Bounty* tragedy were a study in how to conduct such a proceeding with the utmost dignity and clarity. I thank Cmdr. Kevin Carroll for his support of public access to the hearings, and Lt. Mike Patterson for assistance provided during and after the hearings.

Thank you, Brent Howard and the rest of the team at Penguin Group, for the excellent work on this book. And I thank my agent, Mel Berger of William Morris Endeavor, for helping make all of this happen.

GAF

NOTES

Chapter 2

p. 11: "Unlike the *Bounty*, the *Eagle* has a steel hull." Interestingly, the U.S. military does have wooden-hulled ships. Some U.S. Navy minesweepers are constructed with wooden hulls as a defense against the type of mines that are designed to latch onto ship hulls with magnets. The 225-foot USS *Guardian*, a minesweeper ship that struck a coral reef in the Philippines in 2012, had a hull of oak, Douglas fir, and Alaska cedar. The ship was stuck there for three months before the Navy cut it apart to avoid further damaging the reef.

p. 12: "a 'moored attraction vessel,' which meant it could receive visitors only when moored to a dock": The U.S. Coast Guard Inspection and Certification Procedures for Moored Attraction Vessels are found in the U.S. Coast Guard Marine Safety Manual, Vol. II: Section B: Chapter 4.

p. 15: "so that the earlier scenes on board the *Bounty* would be filmed under the gray skies of October before the rich color of the scenes shot in Tahiti." *Behind the Camera on Mutiny on the Bounty*. TCM.com, July 16, 2013.

p. 17: "That's what a little neglect does." "Careening the *Bounty*." *Times Record*, Brunswick, Maine, September 7, 2001. Accessed online.

p. 17: "and also will be used for team-building and sail training." Ibid.

p. 17: "Even in her deplorable state, you can see she's spectacular." "Long Island Has Its Own Tall Ship Again." *The New York Times*, August 4, 2002. Accessed online.

p. 18: "so people remember how eighteenth-century square-riggers were sailed." Ibid.

p. 18: "Hansen paid $1.5 million for repairs in the first eighteen months he owned the *Bounty*, and he estimated the annual operating budget at $500,000." Ibid.

p. 18: "He has not disclosed how much he invested overall in the decade he owned

the ship. . . .": Hansen declined in-person and telephone requests to be interviewed for this book.

p. 21: "The loss of a sail training vessel off the coast of Brazil . . .": "Poor training standards to blame in SV *Concordia* sinking." *National Post*, September 29, 2011, Ontario, Canada. Accessed online.

Chapter 3

p. 27: "Christian lost and had to close her company, but she eventually succeeded in suing her own attorney for negligence and won more than a million dollars" White, Matt. "The USC Song Girl and the Sea." *Los Angeles Magazine*, February 11, 2013. Accessed online.

p. 27: "Her father's therapist suggested that Christian might be bipolar." Ibid.

p. 30 : "Two former *Bounty* crew members, now licensed maritime captains, told CNN in 2013 they had bad experiences because Walbridge was a poor leader with no respect for protocol." Patterson, Thom. *Life & Death on the Bounty*. CNN.com, March 30, 2013. Accessed online.

Chapter 4

p. 35: "but it wasn't the vessel most tall ship mariners strove to work on": Testimony of Daniel Moreland, United States Coast Guard Hearings on the Sinking of Tall Ship *Bounty*. February 20, 2013, Portsmouth, Virginia.

Chapter 6

p.: 55: "the *Bounty* had to get to St. Petersburg on time." Connie DeRamus, mother of Ashley, confirmed to the author that no one associated with the foundation urged Hansen or Walbridge to make the planned date for the event in St. Petersburg. Everyone associated with the foundation was as surprised as everyone else to hear that the *Bounty* was in Hurricane Sandy and trying to get to St. Petersburg, she says.

p. 55: "The trip to New London took about two hours, during which the *Bounty* encountered a squall and about half the crew got seasick . . ." Deckhand Joshua Scornavacchi testified at the Coast Guard hearings that half the crew was seasick on this trip to New London, but no one else mentioned it. Other crew mentioned in their testimony, and in conversations with the author, that mariners typically try to hide their seasickness as long as possible, because they do not want to be seen as weak or complaining. Ships' officers, on the other hand, try to spot the symptoms in their crew, because they know how dangerous seasickness can be to the crew's performance, leaving a person dehydrated and severely fatigued, especially if it goes on for days and in harsh conditions. The early onset of seasickness in the week before the *Bounty* sank became yet another challenge in the crew's struggle to save the ship.

Chapter 7

p. 71: "'We're heading out and I just wanted to tell you and Dad that I love you,'" her mother recounted later to the Canadian Broadcasting Corporation." "1 Dead, Captain Missing After 14 Saved as *Bounty* Sinks." *USA Today*, October 29, 2012. Accessed online.

p. 71: "They are always stewing over them. I would hate to be out to sea in a storm [and] the engines just quit or we have no power." "HMS Bounty: Woman Killed in Tall Ship's Sinking Loved the Sea." *Los Angeles Times*, October 30, 2012. Accessed online.

Chapter 8

p. 78: "the cargo ship S.S. *Poet*, which set out on October 24 from Delaware with a load of corn bound for Port Said, Egypt": U.S. Coast Guard. Marine Casualty Report, SS *Poet:* Disappearance in the Atlantic Ocean after Departure from Cape Henlopen, Delaware, on 24 October 1980 with Loss of Life. Marine Board of Investigation Report and Commandant's Action, Report No. USCG 16732/11486, 1982.

Chapter 9

p. 93: "And I am doing what I love! I love you . . .": "Hurricane Sandy Rescue: HMS Bounty Survivors Speak." *Good Morning America*, ABC, November 6, 2012.

Chapter 10

p. 106: "so Black roamed the ship—often on her hands and knees as she struggled with the rolling ship—handing out bottled water, bananas, cold hot dogs, and other snacks": Cleveland and Groves were particularly complimentary about Black's performance in the crisis, considering that it was her first time with the crew and her first voyage on a tall ship. Cleveland said she was "a real fucking trouper."

Chapter 15

p. 141: "The Coast Guard pilots didn't know Svendsen's name or what position he held on the ship . . ." The pilots never knew whom they had been talking to until the author told them. In the moment, they were not especially concerned with anyone's title or name, and they usually assume they are talking to the captain.

Chapter 17

p. 156: "One crew member was in a near panic, suddenly emotional and scared." The author is aware of which crew member panicked at this moment but

NOTES

chooses not to identify that person. The reaction is entirely understandable considering the circumstances, and singling out the crew member by name would serve no purpose. When Bosun Laura Groves testified in the Coast Guard hearings, she resisted naming this person in a public forum, and Commander Carroll agreed to the unusual move of allowing her to write the name on a piece of paper to submit to the panel. Others simply denied that anyone lost their composure.

p. 158: "Some of the crew, including Christian, clipped their climbing harnesses onto the jack lines that had been strung down the length of the ship for security when the ship was rolling." Whether Christian was clipped onto the jack line at the moment the *Bounty* capsized is unknown, and it is a major point of contention for her parents, who say she should have been warned not to do so. Testimony at the Coast Guard hearings indicated that some people did clip into the line for stability, at least briefly, and crew members testified that they saw Christian clipped in at some point. If she was clipped on when the boat suddenly capsized, it is feasible that she struggled to release herself and was trapped underwater for some time. She was not found attached to the jack line, but it may have broken or come free at some point after it was too late.

Chapter 19

p. 172: "Jump!": Scornavacchi testified at the Coast Guard hearings that it was a male's voice and that he heard it very clearly even though no other survivors were nearby, and certainly not close enough for him to hear through all the noise of the storm. He asked the other survivors after their rescue and no one remembered seeing him on the mast or yelling for him to jump. For the very spiritual Scornavacchi, the explanation is obvious.

Chapter 25

p. 209: "Otherwise it could create false alarms for the Coast Guard and other ships": When the swimmer doesn't have the time to sink the raft, they can stay afloat for quite a while, and many from the Atlantic end up somewhere on the English coast. When they remain adrift, the Coast Guard puts out a notice to mariners so they do not prompt false rescue attempts.

p. 211: "'We can't leave! They're still out there!' one of the young male survivors screamed at Moulder and Todd." Moulder and Bonn described this scene in detail to the author but did not know which of the survivors was upset. No introductions were made in the heat of the moment, and all Moulder could see was a somewhat young-looking, scruffy or bearded male face in the immersion suit. None of the survivors testified to this exchange in the Coast Guard hearings or mentioned it elsewhere in the public, but the author's

experience with the survivors indicates that they are fiercely protective of any information that may be seen as embarrassing to another crew member, such as a person becoming emotional.

Chapter 28

p. 223: "It would be weeks before he could really appreciate that moment, looking back on it as a truly meaningful part of his career." Russell recalls in that in the ensuing media frenzy, the fixed-wing aircraft crews were often over-looked or their roles minimized. A Coast Guard public affairs officer, not one stationed at Elizabeth City, once remarked to him that he heard the Jayhawk crews were the first on the scene. "Well, you heard wrong," Russell told him tersely. "There was a C-130 there all night long and then a second one before the Jayhawks ever showed up. They showed up *after* the C-130s told them where to go." The public affairs officer replied that "if it wasn't on video, then it didn't happen." The Jayhawks had onboard video cameras that captured dramatic footage of the rescues, unlike the workhorse HC-130Js that got the job done but didn't record it on tape. "Well, I have seven people who would like to argue that point with you," Russell replied, "but we won't. You go with that story."

Chapter 29

p. 228: "For weeks after the tragedy, the Facebook page remained alive and open to anyone who wished to post their comments": At the Tall Ships America annual conference held in February 2013, many of the educational sessions for ship owners, captains, and crew obliquely addressed the *Bounty* disaster. Not wanting to discuss the *Bounty* loss outright until the official investigations were complete, the presenters nonetheless touched on some important lessons. One of the primary lessons was that the public relations and media management could have been much better. In particular, presenters said, the HMS *Bounty* Organization should have closed the Facebook page immediately or at least censored some of the criticism.

p. 233: "an old mariner's tradition of painting a blue line around the hull of a ship to signify that its captain had died": Cleveland, Dan; interview.

p. 233: "Many in attendance wore crew sweatshirts, rubber boots, and caps with the *Bounty* logo": Grady, Mary. "Saying Good-bye to *Bounty*." *Rhode Island Monthly*, Dec. 3, 2012, accessed online. Most of the description of the memorial scene comes from this source.

p. 234: "Shelly McCann, his stepdaughter, recalled Walbridge as 'the most gentle, caring soul' she had ever met": "Marine Museum Hosts Memorial for *Bounty*, Crew Lost on Ship." *The Herald News*, Dec. 2, 2012, Fall River, MA. Accessed online.

Chapter 30

p. 235: "Carroll immediately set the tone for the next eight days of hearings." For the sake of clarity, the testimony from the hearings is not conveyed in a strictly chronological manner. Questioning often jumped around from one subject to another and then back again, even with the same witness, so some comments—while verbatim and conveyed in context—are consolidated to make the content clear.

Chapter 32

p. 253: "A red-faced Carroll immediately ended the hearings for the day and stormed out a side door." Carroll's reaction left the impression that Wyman had acted improperly, and it is true that many other witnesses, including the *Bounty* crew, were asked not to discuss the issue with anyone before the hearings. The next morning, however, Carroll began the day by reading a statement saying his reaction was not meant to convey that Wyman had violated any specific law or instruction. Rather, Carroll said he was simply trying to elicit information through an aggressive line of questioning.

p. 257: "teaches that in the northern hemisphere a vessel is safer on the western side of a storm's track": Bowditch, Nathaniel. *The American Practical Navigator: An Epitome of Navigation,* Bethesda, MD: National Imagery and Mapping Agency, 2002, pp. 514–15.

p. 258: "NOAA's Hurricane Center explicitly warns mariners to 'Never Cross the T.'": National Hurricane Center. Marine Safety. http://www.nhc.noaa.gov/prepare/marine.php.

p. 260: "in a gesture meant to convey that Dina knew Hewitt had changed her story": The author witnessed this exchange and the reactions of Hewitt and Dina Christian. Later that day, Dina Christian explained what was said in the conversation to Bill McKelway, a reporter for the *Richmond Times-Dispatch* newspaper, who conveyed the information to the author.

Epilogue

p. 271: "The *Bounty* rests in the Graveyard of the Atlantic, approximately thirteen thousand feet deep . . .": Rear Admiral Steven Ratti, commander of the Coast Guard's Fifth District. Statement to the media. November 2, 2012.

p. 272: "Walbridge's widow believes her husband went down with his ship . . .": Couwels, John; Patterson, Thom. "Widow Tells of HMS *Bounty*'s Last Moments." CNN.com. February 12, 2013. Claudia McCann did not respond to the author's request for an interview.

p. 276: "Claudene's favorite teddy bear from her childhood, Duffordson": Christian, Claudene (Dina); interview.

BIBLIOGRAPHY

Interviews and Correspondence with Author

Black, Jessica

Christian, Claudene (Dina)

Cleveland, Daniel

DeRamus, Connie

Groves, Laura

Hewitt, Jessica

Jakamovicz, Joe

Jones, Rob

Sienkiewicz, Joseph

Books

Alexander, Caroline. *The* Bounty: *The True Story of the Mutiny on the* Bounty. New York: Penguin Books, 2003.

Bligh, William. *The* Bounty *Mutiny: Captain William Bligh's Firsthand Account of the Last Voyage of HMS* Bounty. St. Petersburg, FL: Red and Black Publishers, 2008.

Bowditch, Nathaniel. *The American Practical Navigator: An Epitome of Navigation.* Bethesda, MD: National Imagery and Mapping Agency, 2002.

Carrier, Jim. *The Ship and the Storm: Hurricane Mitch and the Loss of the* Fantome. San Diego: Harvest Books/Harcourt, 2001.

Parrot, Daniel S. *Tall Ships Down: The Last Voyages of the* Pamir, Albatross, Marques, Pride of Baltimore, *and* Maria Asumpta. Camden, MA: International Marine/McGraw-Hill, 2003.

Sail Tall Ships! Newport, RI: Tall Ships America, 2012.

Thompson, Kalee. *Deadliest Sea: The Untold Story Behind the Greatest Rescue in Coast Guard History.* New York: William Morrow, 2010.

Wilber, C. Keith. *Tall Ships of the World: An Illustrated Encyclopedia.* Old Saybrook, CT: Globe Pequot Press, 1986.

Documents

Blake, Eric S., and Christopher W. Landsea. NOAA Technical Memorandum NWS NHC-6: The Deadliest, Costliest, and Most Intense United States Cyclones from 1851 to 2010 (and Other Frequently Requested Hurricane Facts.) Miami, FL: National Hurricane Center, 2011.

Christian v. HMS Bounty *Organization and Robert E. Hansen.* United States District Court, Eastern District of New York, May 6, 2013.

FNL Emergency Response Plan Version 6-24-2012. Erie, PA: Flagship Niagara League, 2012.

U.S. Coast Guard. Marine Casualty Report, SS *Poet*: Disappearance in the Atlantic Ocean After Departure from Cape Henlopen, Delaware, on 24 October 1980 with Loss of Life. Marine Board of Investigation Report and Commandant's Action, Report No. USCG 16732/11486, 1982.

Hearings and Meetings Attended by Author

United States Coast Guard Hearings on the Sinking of Tall Ship *Bounty.* February 12–21, 2013, Portsmouth, VA.

40th Annual Conference on Sail Training and Tall Ships. February 4–6, 2013, Erie, PA.

Periodicals and Online Resources

"1 Dead, Captain Missing After 14 Saved as *Bounty* Sinks." *USA Today*, October 29, 2012. Accessed online.

"A Night to See the Stars Actually Wearing Clothes." *The New York Times*, January 10, 2006. Accessed online.

"Behind the Camera on *Mutiny on the Bounty*." TCM.com, July 16, 2013.

"Boy, 12, Exposes Touring *Pirates of the Caribbean* Ship as a Fake." *Mail Online*, August 30, 2007. Accessed online.

"*Bounty* Victim Was Mutineer's Relative." *The Chronicle Herald*, October 29, 2012, Halifax, Nova Scotia. Accessed online.

"*Bounty*'s Final Hours: A 'Haze of War.'" Soundingsonline.com. February 28, 2013.

"*Bounty*'s Ill-fated Trip in Face of Hurricane Scrutinized." Hamptonroads.com. November 11, 2012.

"Careening the *Bounty*." *Times Record*, September 7, 2001, Brunswick, ME. Accessed online.

"Close Ties Between Coast Guard, HMS *Bounty*." Military.com. October 31, 2012.

Couwels, John, and Thom Patterson. "Widow Tells of HMS *Bounty*'s Last Moments." CNN.com. February 12, 2013.

Grady, Mary. "Saying Goodbye to *Bounty*." *Rhode Island Monthly*, Dec. 3, 2012, Providence, RI. Accessed online.

HMS *Bounty*. Facebook.com. October 22–November 14, 2012.

"HMS *Bounty*: A Tall Ship's Final Hours in Hurricane-Ravaged Seas." *Washington Post*, October 29, 2012. Accessed online.

"HMS *Bounty* Sinking to Be Investigated; Victim Was 'Very Concerned.'" *Los Angeles Times*, November 2, 2012. Accessed online.

"HMS *Bounty*: Woman Killed in Tall Ship's Sinking Loved the Sea." *Los Angeles Times*, October 30, 2012. Accessed online.

Hujer, M., and S. Shafy. "A Legendary Ship's Final Hours Battling Sandy." *Der Spiegel*, Dec. 2, 2012, Hamburg, Germany. Accessed online.

Hurricane Sandy Advisory Archive. National Weather Service. www.nhc.noaa.gov/archive/2012/SANDY.shtml.

"Hurricane Sandy Rescue: HMS *Bounty* Survivors Speak." *Good Morning America*, ABC, November 6, 2012.

"Long Island Has Its Own Tall Ship Again." *The New York Times*, August 4, 2002. Accessed online.

"Marine Museum Hosts Memorial for *Bounty*, Crew Lost on Ship." *Herald News*, Dec. 2, 2012, Fall River, MA. Accessed online.

Miles, Kathryn. "Sunk: The Incredible Truth About a Ship That Never Should Have Sailed." Outsideonline.com. February 11, 2013.

National Hurricane Center. Marine Safety. http://www.nhc.noaa.gov/prepare/marine.php.

Patterson, Thom. "Life & Death on the *Bounty*." CNN.com, March 30, 2013.

"Poor Training Standards to Blame in SV *Concordia* Sinking. *National Post*, September 29, 2011, Ontario, Canada. Accessed online.

"Porn Film Duplicity Puts City on Guard." *Tampa Bay Times*, January 20, 2006, Tampa, FL. Accessed online.

"Robin Walbridge [obituary]." *Tampa Bay Times*, November 6, 2012. Accessed online.

Rubin Daniel. "Remembering Those Who Vanished with the S.S. *Poet*." Philly.com. October 11, 2010.

"The Story Behind the HMS *Bounty*, Sunk by Sandy off N.C. Coast." *Christian Science Monitor*, October 29, 2012, Boston, MA. Accessed online.

"The 1980 Disappearance of the SS *Poet*." Baltimoresun.com. March 4, 2006.

Thompson, Kalee. "Disaster on the *Bounty*." *Popular Mechanics* 190, no. 2 (New York): 45–48, 110.

White, Matt. "The USC Song Girl and the Sea." *Los Angeles Magazine*, February 11, 2013. Accessed online.

"*USS* Mississippi on the *Bounty*." *The Day*, October 25, 2012. Accessed online.

Video

Cabin Video During Rescue of *Bounty* Survivors, HH-60 6012. Elizabeth City, NC: U.S. Coast Guard, October 29, 2012.

Cabin Video During Rescue of *Bounty* Survivors, HH-60 6031. Elizabeth City, NC: U.S. Coast Guard, October 29, 2012.

Winch Video During Rescue of *Bounty* Survivors, HH-60 6012. Elizabeth City, NC: U.S. Coast Guard, October 29, 2012.

Winch Video During Rescue of *Bounty* Survivors, HH-60 6031. Elizabeth City, NC: U.S. Coast Guard, October 29, 2012.

"Interview with HMS *Bounty* Captain." *Soundings* magazine: http://www.youtube.com/watch?v=53HBSgGEMP4.

Mutiny on the Bounty. Metro-Goldwyn-Mayer, 1962.

Pirates. Digital Playground, Van Nuys, CA, 2005.

Gregory A. Freeman is an award-winning writer and a leader in the field of narrative nonfiction. Known for books that make a true story read like a gripping, fast-paced novel, his previous works include *The Forgotten 500*, *Sailors to the End*, *Troubled Water*, and *The Last Mission of the Wham Bam Boys*. He lives in the Atlanta area.

CONNECT ONLINE

gregoryafreeman.com